Save the

TRIUMPH BONNEVILLE!

The inside story of the Meriden Workers' Co-op

Save the
TRIUMPH BONNEVILLE!
The inside story of the Meriden Workers' Co-op

Foreword by TONY BENN

VELOCE PUBLISHING
THE PUBLISHER OF FINE AUTOMOTIVE BOOKS

CONTENTS

DEDICATION

It would be wrong not to recognise that once established, Triumph's continued existence as a workers' co-operative was due to the extraordinary partnership between its very special friends and the inspirational workforce. Amongst many of these special friends, seven individuals, all giants in their chosen profession, made a fundamental contribution. To these people I dedicate this book.

Jack Jones MBE, visionary leader of the Transport and General Workers' Union and magnanimous supporter of all 8 trade unions involved at the Triumph Co-op.

Tony Benn, a true-conviction politician, who not only believed in British workers, but as a Minister invested in them.

Geoffrey Robinson MP, a very gifted commercial negotiator who could always secure a deal.

Paul Morton BSc(Eng), DSc(Eng), FREng, CEng, FIMechE, FRSA, brilliant engineer whose gift provided the future to which the Co-op aspired.

Peter Johnson, senior partner at Price Waterhouse who first recognised that the Co-op had the commercial basis upon which to build a viable Triumph future.

Terry Pitt, senior advisor to the West Midlands County Council on Economic Development, who appreciated the efforts made by the Co-op and had the courage to try and help save it.

Peter Davis, Triumph's Company Solicitor, whose advice and support remained ever constant.

The other participant in this extraordinary partnership was, of course, the Triumph Co-op workforce; a workforce that in many respects was like a very large family that possessed the ability to disagree passionately one minute, and then totally unite moments later when its company was once again under threat! It was this immense strength of purpose that regularly enabled the workforce to achieve the impossible, throughout all 8 years of the Co-op's existence. If commitment and sacrifice had a monetary value then I'm sure the members of the Triumph Co-operative would all have been millionaires.

The author wishes to acknowledge the help received from friends (unfortunately there isn't space here to mention them all) who contributed generously to the writing of this book.

I must also pay a massive tribute to the support and encouragement of my family – Sharon, Paul, and particularly my wife of 40 years, Chris, who deciphered my kitchen table scribble, allowing the real story of the Meriden Co-op to be told. They were always there for me, as I am sure all the other families were for the rest of the workforce; without this level of support none of us would have been able to pursue a viable future for Triumph, and this story might never have been told.

John Rosamond

Publisher's note:
To ensure the most accurate account possible of the Meriden Co-op story, much of the research for this book involved substantial use of primary sources – minutes of meetings, letters, etc. – which have often been incorporated in the text ad verbatim in the interests of authenticity.

Subsequently, the narrative frequently moves from first person to third person. For the sake of clarity, readers should therefore note that, throughout the book, 'the Chairman,' John Rosamond' and 'I' all refer to the author.

FOREWORD BY TONY BENN

MERIDEN — THE STORY OF CO-OPERATIVE ENTERPRISE

This book, which tells the story of the Meriden Motorcycle Co-operative, is one of the most important and relevant histories of British industry that I have ever read, and the reason is that it was written by somebody who was involved on the picket lines with workers determined to keep the plant open to the end, over ten years later.

My involvement was a brief one, from my appointment as Secretary of State for Industry in the Labour Government that followed the defeat of Ted Heath in 1974, up until my removal in June 1975 by Harold Wilson.

I noted in my diary the day I was appointed that the future of Meriden was at the top of my agenda and I was determined to support it as strongly as I could.

The Co-operative had begun earlier, when Geoffrey Robinson, then Chief Executive of Jaguar, later MP for Coventry North West, working with the shop stewards and Les Huckfield MP were trying to safeguard the motorbike industry which was threatened with closure.

I sought an early meeting with the stewards and Geoffrey and received strong support from Jack Jones, then General Secretary of the Transport and General Workers' Union, and raised the question of Meriden with my officials who were universally hostile to the idea of co-operatives. So indeed were Harold Lever who was in my department and Joel Barnett, representing the Treasury view, which was always hostile to funding industry in contrast to the generous bailouts available to the banks at the time of writing.

I came to the conclusion that they believed that capitalism depended upon two disciplines to survive: one was the right to sack workers who caused trouble to their management and the other was the value of bankruptcy as a way of disciplining failed enterprises.

For those who took that view, any encouragement for shop stewards or co-operatives provided a new lease of life for manufacturing industry which did not depend upon private ownership.

This is why a book written by John Rosamond, who was deeply involved with the shop stewards throughout the whole story, is so appropriate because it sees this whole problem from the perspective of those who made the bikes and not those who owned the factories.

Shop stewards are usually presented in the media as negative and destructive, and what emerges from this story is that they were passionately committed to the engineering product they were making and well-skilled in seeking the investment needed to make them succeed. They are the heroes of this book.

In 1970 Britain had the biggest motorbike industry in the world – bigger than Japan, the US and Germany. But successive governments let it go, along with shipbuilding, computing and many other engineering industries. Today we don't even make railway trains, which Britain invented.

For me, the whole Meriden story was an education in the meaning of common ownership, and all the credit goes to the shop stewards and those who worked with them.

My instinct was to support them and I am proud that I was able to do so, even though it was during a very brief period as Secretary of State. Looking at the crisis we face I am utterly convinced that we would be foolish not to defend and expand our manufacturing industry rather than just fund the banks with their big bonuses.

Visiting the plant and experiencing the excitement and innovation there was a real inspiration that can only come from industrial democracy, and offers us lessons for today.

That is why this is such an important book, and I strongly recommend anyone interested in the future of Britain to read it carefully.

Tony Benn

(Courtesy Mirrorpix)

PROLOGUE

The first post of 2007 contained a surprise for me!

Dear Sir,
I hope that my letter finds you in good health and may I take this opportunity to wish you a happy new year.
I hope that I am writing to the Mr John A Rosamond who was from the world famous Triumph Motorcycle factory at Meriden and subsequent venture at Hinckley. If I have contacted you in error, please discard this letter. May I advise you that I located your address through the electoral roll for the Mr J A Rosamond whose name appears as a Director on Meriden headed notepaper.
I am a barrister in private practice by profession, but for a long time have been a keen motorcyclist riding Triumph machines made during your time at Meriden. I ride a TR65 Thunderbird, a TSX and a TR7T Tiger Trail, all of which give me great satisfaction whether I am riding for work or pleasure. I am grateful for your persevering with Meriden for as long as you did to manufacture the motorcycles that myself and others still derive much joy from. I confess that I share the same birthday (though not the year!) as Edward Turner and was born and bred in Solihull before my family moved to London after Meriden's closure.
It would be my great pleasure if you could find the time either to share a correspondence with me or indeed for me to meet you either in London or in the West Midlands. If the former, may I invite you that day to see the London Motorcycle Museum, the Ace Café and Reg Allen, a former Triumph dealership that keeps our bikes running as good as new!
Of course if you do not wish to be disturbed then please do drop me a line to say, I shall not be in the least offended but hope you can accept my grateful thanks for keeping 'the legend' alive for as long as you did. Thank you for your time in reading this letter.
Yours faithfully,

Intrigued, I replied, and further correspondence took place over the following weeks, leading to a meeting in London. In the morning we met 'in chambers' at Lincoln's Inn, followed in the afternoon by nostalgic memory-provoking visits to the London Motorcycle Museum, Reg Allen, Harwoods Motorcycles, and the Ace Café.

The absolute dearth of information written by anyone who had lived the real story meant everyone wanted to talk about the Meriden Co-op. At the end of the long but very enjoyable day in London, decades after my time at Meriden and the new Triumph company both at Exhall and Hinckley, I was convinced that the inside story of the Co-op must now be told.

The story that follows by the welder (John Rosamond) who became the Co-op Chairman of the Board of Directors, provides a detailed account based on the facts as I saw them at the time; an account of how the people at the Meriden factory fought courageously against all the odds to preserve the legend of which they were so deservedly a part.

Many other United Kingdom companies were destroyed in 1973 when, due to a global oil crisis, crude oil prices that had averaged $20 a barrel for 50 years increased by 150 per cent. This initially caused a period of raging 'double digit' inflation, during which the Government capped pay increases and provided zero support for industry, resulting in massive industrial unrest. Unemployment rose to levels not previously seen since the depression of the 1930s. It should be remembered that these traumatic events in the history of UK industry took place while the 'windfall' benefit of North Sea oil contributed billions of pounds to the National Exchequer ...

Clockwise from above: John Rosamond (left) with Gary and Bill Crosby (right) at the London Motorcycle Museum; Erum Waheed and the author visit Harwoods Motorcycles; the author's visit to the Ace Café caused so much interest he was invited to Triumph Day later in the summer. (Courtesy Erum Waheed's archive)

1

BAPTISM OF FIRE

he world-famous motorcycle manufacturer Triumph Engineering, located at Meriden, near Coventry in the West Midlands, exhibited all the trappings of a very successful and profitable business. A subsidiary of the large BSA Group, it still retained all its own Triumph trademark identity, and was reported to contribute over half a million pounds' profit each year to the Group's results. As such, in 1970 the Triumph factory provided an excellent prospect for employment when my full-time trade union official, Mr Andy Smart, contacted me to see if I was interested in a production welding job. Triumph's wage rates for production welders during the late 1960s and early '70s were always in the top three for large factories in Coventry and District. Whilst high wages were paid, it was generally recognised that day or night shift working at Triumph on individual piecework meant everyone earned their money. Triumph Engineering had a closed-shop agreement with the Birmingham and Midland Sheet Metal Workers' Union; there were seven other staff and shop floor trade unions at the company. When Triumph needed to recruit production welders it approached the Sheet Metal Workers' Union in the full knowledge that only suitable candidates would be sent along for a trade test and interview; this was a partnership of convenience that had stood the test of time.

I was twenty-five years of age, a qualified production MIG welder, married with a young family and a house mortgage, seeking the security of employment in a high earnings factory; Triumph provided that opportunity. Accordingly, I was very pleased that following my introduction to Triumph by the trade union, I was successful with my welding trade test and interview. It was explained at interview that the company was expanding its MIG welding capacity in preparation for production of the new all-welded Bonneville and Trophy P39 frame; the new frame was being introduced for the high volume 1971 Bonneville and Trophy 650cc twins, production of which was about to start. As instructed in my letter of appointment, I reported for work at the factory in mid-November 1970. The Meriden shadow factory had been built in 1942 on a 22 acre greenfield site north west of Coventry, to rehouse motorcycle production after the previous Priory Street Coventry factory was destroyed by the German Luftwaffe, in the Blitz of 1940. On my first day at Triumph I expected to be confronted with mass production individual piecework. I was certainly in for a shock – there was no work to do, and I was shown into an almost silent factory. The welding section charge hand explained that there was a major problem with the new P39 frame and it had not yet been released for production. The BSA Group had set up a divisional Research and Development Centre at Umberslade Hall, Hockley Heath, Birmingham.

The famous Triumph factory at Meriden. (Courtesy John Hallard's archive)

The new all-welded Bonneville and Trophy P39 frame. (Brochure picture)

This R&D centre undertook the majority of new projects for all Group subsidiaries, including Triumph, and the new all-welded mild steel frame for the big twins, Triumph's volume sellers, was its first serious motorcycle involvement; it was now nearly three months late for production.

Without the release of the new frame design drawings, everything was held up. In an effort to try and counter this production disaster, the Meriden factory had been pre-building for stock Daytona 500 models that did not use the new frame. However, a complete year's projected requirement of this model had now been stockpiled. In addition, 3-cylinder Tridents had also continued to be built, but market demand for triples was much less than for the big twins. Engines for Bonneville and Trophy models had also continued to be built as per the scheduled build programme, and were now stockpiled all over the factory awaiting motorcycle assembly as soon as the new P39 frames became available – so all was not totally lost!

Once Umberslade released the new frame design drawings the welding jigs and fixtures required for production could be rapidly completed.

One young welder who had worked at Triumph for two years told me that to maintain morale during the past three months, inter-section crib, domino and chess tournaments had been organised to prevent boredom. Management had taken the view that it was not the men's fault they had no work and everyone had been paid 'average' earnings and were very happy! Well, perhaps not everyone. A welder with fifteen years service who overheard his young colleague's comments explained that this production delay was unprecedented, and that the company must be losing an absolute fortune, going on to say that happiness and security at Triumph was only guaranteed when high-targeted production and sales levels were achieved. The past 3 months should have been spent building and shipping 1971 Bonneville and Trophy models for Triumph's major, very seasonal American market. All late arriving 1971 models that were not available for sale in America before next May would remain in stock to be heavily discounted the following spring.

The recruits were then shown the new welding section where the P39 frame would be produced. The section was laid out logically on a flow line basis, with high volume in mind. Day and night shift working was planned, with thirty welders on days and thirty on nights, with the appropriate number of frame builders and machinists to support the required production. Whilst we were looking at the new section, one of the first frame assembly jigs arrived. I was amazed. It was certainly impressive; I'd never before seen a welding jig with ground finishes and painted a beautiful shade of royal blue. Whilst I was admiring it the charge hand told me there were to be two further back up duplicates of every jig and fixture. The Group must have spent an absolute fortune.

The Wavis frame driller machines were also being installed. Once a frame had been completely welded it was clamped into one of the 2 duplicate frame drillers that would then precisely ream the existing pilot holes. By so doing, the exact dimensions of every important hole on the frame was guaranteed. Finally, the steering head tube was bored at each end for the bearings and the frame was finished. The swing arm assembly was just as precisely made so that every new 1971 Bonneville and Trophy rolling chassis was identical, guaranteeing Triumph's excellent road handling qualities.

My first day as a welder at Triumph soon came to an end and I hadn't even struck an arc! With the expected high volume piecework I had thought I would go home physically tired, but I didn't. I was, however, mentally exhausted wondering exactly what I had got myself involved in.

My second day started much the same as the first, with one exception: any previous thoughts about a secure job and working environment had now completely disappeared. Confronted with chaos and the thought of having to try and retrieve 3 months lost production

500cc Daytonas and Tiger 100s were pre-built for stock, as they did not use the new P39 frame. (Brochure picture)

3-cylinder 750cc Tridents also continued to be built, as, like the 500cc models, they did not use the P39 frame.
(Courtesy James Crosby photography, London Motorcycle Museum)

with a totally unknown new frame assembly certainly made me very apprehensive about the future. It was clear from the comments of other new welding recruits that my feelings were much the same as theirs. However, with the new recruits and the Triumph old hands seeing the P39 frame for the first time, we were certainly all in it together to make what we could of the situation. With a number of production jigs and fixtures arriving in the area where I was to work, a start was made.

The major new design feature of the all-welded mild steel frame for the 1971 Bonneville and Trophy models was the integral engine oil tank. The large 'backbone' main tube of the P39 frame was to contain the engine oil. Accordingly, it was vital that all welding on the oil tank was of a pressure vessel standard, guaranteeing no oil leaks. I was to work at the beginning of the welding flow line, the seat loop to main tube oil tank assembly. This assembly also contained the centre swing arm pivot tube and various brackets. The steering head tube had already been welded to the main tube as a sub-assembly. Our first pre-production build was a disaster; when tested with compressed air in a large water tank, the main tube oil tank leaked like a sieve. Not a good sign when only recently a cartoon had appeared in a motorcycle monthly suggesting that Triumph had by now employed the famous oil well firefighter Red Adair to try and stop the engine oil leaks! Luckily, one of the large influx of welders from all over Coventry and District had MIG welding experience on pressure vessels. Triumph's welding equipment was suitably adapted to enable the 'spray transfer' MIG welding technique to be used. This required very high welding amperages, a reduced filler wire diameter and a change from pure CO_2 shielding gas to an argon and CO_2 mix. Once the new process was perfected there were very few oil tank leaks to repair.

With thousands of stockpiled 1971 Bonneville and Trophy engines all over the factory awaiting the new frame, and with the frame section now fully equipped, there was massive pressure to complete the first-off pre-production build, prior to mass production getting under way. The first-off pre-production frame assemblies were checked practically in the Triumph way: the installation of a Bonneville engine. When the engine was found to be too big, a full dimensional check by the Inspection Department was called for. Every P39 frame dimension was checked against the Umberslade design drawing and found to be correct – astonishingly not only was the new 1971 frame design release 3 months late, the engines for which it was designed would not fit into it!

To try and correct this situation the Meriden engineering staff had to modify the cylinder head rocker boxes, cylinder head studs, and associated bolts. Following these modifications the engines could be installed without the rocker boxes, which were then fitted once the engine was in the frame. This was not the only problem with the new frame; as designed, it increased the motorcycle seat height by 3in (75mm) making it difficult to touch the ground safely if you were not at least 6ft (1.83 metres) tall. (There were three attempts at frame modifications during the 1971 model year to try and reduce the seat height to that of the previous successful Bonneville and Trophy models.) Subsequent negative press comments about the seat height confirmed that all riders of Triumph's new big twins needed to be tall. There were also positive comments made about the 1971 Bonneville and Trophy models, which were said to have excellent road handling characteristics and be very comfortable to ride.

Whilst these production problems were being experienced at Triumph Meriden, management tried to bolster sagging morale by reminding everyone how well the 1971 Bonneville and Trophy models had been received at the London launch in the Royal Lancaster Hotel. On 25th November 1970, only two weeks after I started at Triumph, all employees were asked to attend a mass meeting of the workforce in the works canteen. The meeting would be addressed by the BSA Group Managing Director. We all thought we were going to receive a further morale boosting vote of thanks for our efforts to try and retrieve the production chaos of the previous months; nothing could have been further from the truth! The meeting was called to order and told that any thoughts we may have had of a wage increase that year would have to be justified with extra productivity, and if this was not forthcoming the Meriden factory would be closed! Not surprisingly the meeting broke up in complete disarray. None of the company's trade union stewards or conveners had attended the mass meeting; given prior notice of exactly what was to be said, they had decided to boycott the meeting in protest. This mass meeting and the events that followed were to create further deep-rooted and ongoing distrust of the BSA Board of Directors and its motives towards Triumph at Meriden.

To say my first two weeks of employment at Triumph Engineering had been different was certainly an understatement. When I reflected on what had happened, the only conclusion I could reach was that the BSA Directors were so far out of touch with what was actually taking place at Meriden they had come to totally the wrong conclusion. They obviously believed that because of the disastrous delay of the new 1971 frame design release from Umberslade Hall, the workforce at Meriden was going to exploit the situation and blackmail the company for more money, and only then would it be prepared to retrieve the three months lost production! The real position was totally the opposite; the majority of the Triumph employees had worked for the company for many years and fully recognised that the only way out of the P39 fiasco was hard graft, not – as the BSA Board seemed to be attempting – blaming the Meriden workforce for a problem that was certainly not of its making.

It was generally accepted that Triumph paid well because of high productivity levels – certainly much higher productivity was achieved at Meriden than at the BSA Small Heath factory. The high Triumph productivity levels were guaranteed by the individual piecework payment structure that over the years had achieved proven results.

When a new production job was introduced, such as the all-welded P39 frame, each operation to be undertaken on the frame section (as with other sections) had to be allocated a value based upon the time it took to complete.

Accordingly, each of the three types of frame section employees working on the new frame (welders, frame builders and machinists) would establish by practice, prior to a time and motion study, the time it took to complete their particular operation. This time was divided into the hourly rate of pay being earned, thus an approximate piecework price was established in the individual production worker's mind. The frame assembly jigs and fixtures were installed in identical pairs. Whilst the welder was welding the components in one, the frame builder was loading or unloading the other; in so doing the welder and builder were able to work continuously. Once the production employees became proficient through practice, one of the company's rate fixers would complete a study by observing each production operation, whilst timing it with a stopwatch. Based upon this study, he would suggest a piecework price that should apply. The rate fixer had usually got a time and price in his mind based upon similar jobs already in production, so his study was only a matter of confirmation. If mutual agreement could not be reached, another employee (having gained proficiency on the operation) would undertake the time and motion study for comparison. Usually agreement was reached very quickly as the company needed to balance the flow of components against the production levels of the line. Any operation without an agreed time/price in the flow line would delay the whole line. Until all the individual jobs had agreed prices on them, the piecework flow line payment system could not be adopted and average earnings were paid; this inevitably meant fewer components were produced.

I had now been employed at Triumph for five weeks and everyone was getting in the

Christmas spirit. However, 1970 had been a memorable year for Triumph employees for all the wrong reasons. I would certainly never forget my initial period of employment with the company, but at last most of the production problems had been sorted, and 1971 model Bonneville and Trophy motorcycles with the new frame were now coming off the end of the assembly tracks, albeit months late!

There's nothing like a holiday to give lots of time for quiet reflection; Triumph's Christmas and New Year break provided just that for me! The increased wage levels I enjoyed during my first five weeks ensured my family and I had a very enjoyable festive time. In the quieter holiday moments, I was able to try to make some sense of exactly what was happening at my new workplace. It was obvious almost from day one how much the labour force identified with 'its' Triumph motorcycle, and the concern it had regarding the new 1971 models – models that for the first time had been created away from the Meriden factory at the BSA Group Divisional Research and Development Establishment, Umberslade Hall, Hockley Heath, Birmingham. There appeared to be a complete lack of confidence in this R&D outfit, summed up well by the workforce's often disparaging references to "that lot at Slumberglade."

It was common knowledge in the factory that, although most of Meriden's senior design staff had now been transferred to Umberslade Hall, Bert Hopwood and Doug Hele (two highly respected senior Meriden engineers) had refused to transfer, staying instead at Meriden and concentrating on the racing triples. All Meriden's design and development work on the Triumph big twins had been stopped, awaiting the new 1971 models from Umberslade Hall. Hopwood and Hele had over the years led the design and development team responsible for many of the new features so well received by Triumph motorcycle enthusiasts all over the world. Very few of Meriden's workforces had ever seen the prototype 1971 Bonneville and Trophy models prior to their production, having to rely on snippets of grapevine information from transferred ex-Meriden design and development staff.

Communication by this route was obviously unlikely to be of a reassuring nature, as bad news always seems to travel fastest! The revelations that the new Umberslade P39 frame's three month delay was caused by the need to modify 1200 design drawings had gone round the Meriden factory like wildfire, which only added to the general feeling of concern, especially by long service Triumph employees who knew exactly how important the 1971 Bonneville and Trophy models were to the company's future. The big twins with the new frame would have to be high-volume sellers in America if past financial success was to be maintained.

When the fears about Umberslade Hall's involvement were totally justified, it was obvious to all at Triumph Meriden that an uncertain future lay ahead. However if this was supposed to persuade the Meriden factory employees to just roll over and give up, it had totally the opposite effect. Their true British bulldog-like spirit was summed up in the statement, "the Germans failed to destroy Triumph in the 1940s, that lot at Slumberglade won't succeed in the 1970s!"

The battle for Triumph would start in the new year!

2

BATTLE FOR TRIUMPH

The festivities over, Triumph production restarted early in January 1971 – shift working was now a reality. My first stint on the rota was a month on days; this was only possible because there were enough new recruits who preferred to work regular nights enabling the majority to avoid the dreaded 'fortnight about' shift working pattern. I always found night shift work a most alien practice; the only thing that made it bearable was the extra premium in my wage packet!

Pressure in those first weeks of the new year for increased production was intense, as the new employees like myself came to terms with the Triumph working culture, in particular the fact that any previous work experience we had from elsewhere was now completely redundant. At Triumph we were all told that there is "the right way, the wrong way, and the Triumph way!" Over the years the factory had proved that the Triumph way was the best, so that's what happened there.

A significant part of 'the Triumph way' was a keen sense of humour and fair play; during the coming months this was to play a major part in the Meriden workforce's ability to fight for its motorcycles. Also, families were very well represented throughout the Meriden factory. The welding department was a good example; the foreman's son was a welder, the welding charge hand's son-in-law a welder, the frame builder's charge hand had a wife working in the assembly area, and the charge hand machinist's wife worked in the machine shop. Accordingly, anything that threatened Triumph's future, such as the P39 frame chaos, threatened the entire way of life for these families.

The Triumph factory was fully unionised, but equally as important to employees was the aforementioned very strong family involvement. In fact, when I joined the company the welding section had very informal union representation, choosing not to be part of the overall factory union activity. The seven other trade unions in the company had a joint shop stewards' committee, with regular meetings to discuss matters of mutual interest. Although the Sheet Metal Workers' Union had chosen not to be part of this body, in the event of any disputes the sheet metal workers always made sure not to aggravate the situation! When new recruits like me arrived at Triumph, the Sheet Metal Workers' Union's lack of representation was a concern, without even a shop steward (known on the welding section as the 'shop stupid'). There was a feeling that a shop steward was not necessary, as different individuals would take it in turn to attend meetings with the company. However, I did note that at our first welding section union meeting, a number of the older welders who had been with Triumph many years did raise this as a point of concern. The P39 frame fiasco and the BSA Board hostility had focused attention on the possible threat to ongoing employment at Triumph. Accordingly, an election for shop steward and shop Chairman was organised.

Edgar Thorpe, who had extensive experience elsewhere in this role before he recently joined Triumph, was elected shop steward, and I was persuaded to take on the job of shop Chairman (perhaps because I always had plenty to say about having a shop steward to formally represent us, in what could be a difficult time). At least we now had a formal union structure; this was subsequently accredited by the trade union full-time official and Triumph.

Edgar Thorpe was an excellent trade unionist from whom I learned a tremendous amount about procedure. I lost count of the number of times we were representing one of our members who was being disciplined for some insignificant breach of the rules, finding after investigation with the personnel officer (no 'human resources' in those days, only human beings) that the matter was totally incorrect and unsubstantiated! Edgar was a very calm, laid-back, middle-aged individual that on the odd occasion when discussions became heated would jump up out of his chair and thump the table; this was usually accompanied by his top set of dentures flying out of his mouth – miraculously though, he always managed to catch them! This direct action seemed to win the argument, the point having been well made!

The change to formal shop representation was well timed, as what appeared to be a campaign of trade union bashing was starting to take place in the media. The Edward Heath Conservative Government of the day was having great difficulty with the British economy due to high rates of inflation. One of their proposed strategies to try and control this was to cap pay rises, which was incensing the trade union movement, whose members were being faced with higher prices without the possibility of negotiating increased wages. The Heath Government focused its attention on the large powerful unions like the National Union of Mineworkers, whose officials were making forceful speeches to its members against wage capping, and threatening industrial action. The reason that this situation is important to note regarding Triumph is that a considerable number of employees from the Meriden factory lived in mining communities in the Coventry and Nuneaton areas. Accordingly, they were very aware of the strength of feeling in the National Union of Mineworkers, and the strong representation their union was providing for its members. Similar uncertain circumstances now existed at Triumph, so full factory unionisation was felt to be essential. In discussions with the welders during half hour lunch breaks, it was very evident that so far as pay was concerned, everyone was happy. On the odd occasion there had been disputes over recent years at Triumph, it had always been settled very quickly, no one being prepared to lose too much money by being out on strike.

The pressure for more and more production was now moving towards unlimited overtime, as all welding sets were fully manned. However, unless a balanced number of welding section employees were prepared to work the overtime, the flow line production system just became inefficient. Accordingly, the sections' response to management's request for more overtime from welders, frame builders and machinists had to be a united one or it would not work. Thankfully it was, and soon 30 per cent above the planned level of output was regularly being achieved by the day and night shifts. The overtime working soon spread downstream of the welding section, quickly making considerable inroads into the stockpiles of Bonneville and Trophy engines and the company's ability to ship finished motorcycles to the United States of America.

The increased income that we received due to the regular overtime working helped with the inflationary pressure on prices. However, long service employees were regularly commenting to the younger welders like myself, "don't start living on the overtime, it won't last forever!"

Out of the blue came the first inter-union dispute after a brief time at Triumph for me. One of the young welders made the mistake of taking a light bulb out of the next welding booth in order to replace the blown bulb in his booth. He was seen doing this by one of the company's electricians and they all walked out on strike. The company could not carry on production without electrician cover, so the whole factory was immediately laid off. As luck would have it, it was only one hour before the end of the day shift, and the night shift electricians reported for work that evening as normal. An apology was offered to the electrician's convener John Grattan, and no other welder ever made that mistake again! It was very important for the welders to maintain a good working relationship with the electricians; they maintained the welding sets we used for our job. When an electrical breakdown occurred, welders received one third less wages for the period of the breakdown, so if you upset the electricians you felt it in your pocket!

Communications to shop floor workers at Meriden from the parent BSA Group had been poor over many years, I learnt. On the odd occasion it had taken place it had apparently been in the form of meetings with graphs, wall charts, and critical path analysis (or as it was known at Triumph, 'typical crap analysis') presentations. Such communications were totally mistrusted and seen as a complete waste of time by the majority.

All through my employment at Triumph Meriden, no matter how bleak developments seemed at the time, I was always inspired – as were the majority – when coming to work on a Monday and seeing the notice boards providing details of the latest production race victories achieved by the all-conquering factory Triumph and BSA 750cc triples. Communication regarding these fantastic achievements were always first rate, and I am sure the pride they brought to the workforce helped maintain the manufacturing quality of Triumph motorcycles being produced in these very troubled times. The best quality motorcycles from Triumph were always produced, it was said, when morale was high. This was because so much of the quality control on manufacturing operations was entirely in the hands of the individual undertaking it!

Percy Tait (recognised as Mr Triumph because of his many race victories on Triumph motorcycles all over the world) was one of the fantastic, highly talented, race winning works

Percy Tait winning the 1969 Thruxton 500 on a works triple.
(Courtesy John Nelson's archive)

triple riders. The larger-than-life stories that were often told around the factory about Percy Tait and the latest practical jokes he had supposedly played on some unsuspecting victim (usually his long suffering colleagues in the experimental department) were the source of everyone's amusement, and each time they were told they became more and more elaborate!

One particular story went as follows: after the latest triple race win, Percy had returned with the race bikes to the Meriden factory, only to be repeatedly asked by a new young apprentice to take him for a ride on the pillion of one of the Triumph mileage-development bikes. Initially he had refused, but when the young lad persisted he agreed to take him for a brief ride down to the village of Meriden and back during the lunch break. Both suitably attired in the correct safety gear, Percy took the young apprentice for his ride.

At the top of the hill down into Meriden village is a small offset traffic island that is negotiated in an almost straight line as you approach to go down the hill. On the return journey back to the factory, the offset traffic island forms a sharp chicane that has to be negotiated slowly. Percy's joke was said to be that he waited till there was no oncoming traffic, and then he came up Meriden hill to the traffic island, flat out. The unsuspecting youth knew that Percy would have to slow down to negotiate the traffic island chicane, but Percy didn't slow down – at the last possible moment he drifted the motorcycle to the wrong side of the road and negotiated the island on the straight line side, flat out! Percy pulled back into the factory and the young apprentice dismounted, shaking and as white as a sheet!

Another humorous story about Percy Tait, told by one of the long-service welders, was that when Percy was doing development testing on the Triumph Tina Scooter he had played one too many practical jokes on his fellow testers, so they decided to get their own back. Percy set off on the Tina Scooter, but with two big twins following – each of the bikes were 'two up' so their riders could safely execute the plan! Percy was going along the Meriden straight mile at about 35mph (50kph) when the two bikes accelerated up and drew level on either side of the Tina, at which point the two pillion passengers reached out and took hold of Percy's arms. The two bikes accelerated hard, taking Percy with them! On release it took all of Percy's fantastic riding skills to stay with the notoriously poor handling Scooter.

My first two fortnights of working the night shift passed uneventfully, other than the fact I was working on a completely different welding job on the section – cradle tube assemblies. This made a refreshing change once I became familiar with it.

What was clear from my night shifts was that the level of supervision was minimal, leaving great scope for activities other than work! As with most other large West Midlands factories of the day, there was an 'alternative economy' in operation where almost anything could be purchased at very competitive prices. What supervision there was seemed to turn a blind eye to these activities so long as the required production levels were achieved, which they always were. Whilst everyone else seemed to be happy with this arrangement, there was a progress chaser nicknamed 'the weasel' who in order to curry favour with the night shift superintendent had been telling tales about the extracurricular activities. This resulted in several individuals being disciplined, including the night shift supervision. A few weeks after this had happened the weasel came into work in a beautiful new full-length sheepskin overcoat. He left his new overcoat in his locker for the night, returning to collect it half an hour before the end of the shift the following morning, at which time he found his coat was missing. After a thorough search he found his coat – it had gone through the black enamel paint vat onto the conveyor and then through the stoving oven; it was now bright gloss black and stiff as a board!

The weasel took his coat to the superintendent, who immediately called a mass meeting of all the night shift employees, before they left for home! The superintendent asked them if

The Tina scooter photographed on the Meriden factory lawn. (Courtesy John Nelson's archive)

anyone knew who was responsible for this act of vandalism against a fellow worker. Initially there was complete silence then a loud anonymous voice from the back of the meeting shouted "the only thing that's wrong with this action is that the weasel wasn't wearing it at the time!" The meeting broke up in uproar; not only had night shift 'natural justice' been done, more importantly it had been seen to be done. The company replaced the sheepskin overcoat and the weasel told no more tales!

By May 1971, rumours were circulating the factory (subsequently confirmed by management) that having arrived too late for the spring selling season, 11,000 Triumph and BSA 1971 models were left in stock in the USA. These would now have to be stored and heavily discounted the following year. At the end of July 1971 the BSA Group Board made the first of a number of financial statements, each one worse than the previous, and confirming the losses that had been made in the current trading period. The Meriden workforce's fears had been confirmed. The BSA Group was now in dire straits; all our efforts to try and catch up had managed to pull back only some of the three months late production and shipments to the USA of 1971 models. BSA Group shares fell from 71 to 37 pence. The Triumph workforce's total lack of confidence in the BSA Group management and Board of Directors had now been confirmed. The BSA Board announced its intention to reduce the workforces at Small Heath, Umberslade Hall and Meriden. Shortly after, in August 1971, the 1972 Bonneville and Trophy models were introduced, with confirmation that the P39 frame seat height would be reduced to that of previous acceptable models.

An extraordinary general meeting of the BSA Group took place in November 1971, this following a further press disclosure that another £3m had been lost with an additional £1m being required for Group reorganisation. Lord Shawcross became the interim Chairman of the BSA Board – Eric Turner, the previous Chairman, stood down, but still remained on the Board.

Lord Shawcross contacted Her Majesty's Government at this time, advising it of the very serious financial situation the motorcycle division of the BSA Group was in and asking about the possibility of financial support. Mr Brian Eustace was appointed as the new Chief Executive, and it was further announced that the overall trading loss of the BSA motorcycle division was over £5m. BSA shares fell to an all time low of seven and a half pence, and share trading on the stock exchange was suspended. Eric Turner's last act before standing down as Board Chairman was to start implementing the Coopers Management Consultants' plan to restructure the motorcycle division. This involved closing the BSA factory at Small Heath with the loss of 3000 jobs, and concentrating motorcycle production at the Meriden Triumph factory, which was considered to be a smaller self-contained unit with lower overheads.

Whilst all this was going on, press speculation was rife as to what the final outcome would be. Morale in the Meriden factory was at rock bottom, and overtime had long since ended as the production of 1972 model motorcycles for export to the USA went ahead. None of the Meriden factory management knew what was happening so far as future plans were concerned. However, that was not surprising – the BSA Group had always passed over what they considered to be the 'home spun' Triumph Meriden management personnel when it came to recruiting for more senior roles within the organisation, always preferring to recruit individuals with non-motorcycling backgrounds, for what was seen as 'consumer durable' manufacturing and marketing. The consequences of this shortsighted bad management practice at the highest level within the BSA Group was now there for all to see!

In desperation, BSA – who previously had never missed a chance to put down the motorcycle-orientated Triumph Meriden management – appointed Bert Hopwood to the main Board of Directors in December 1971. At last there was a highly rated motorcycle engineer in a position of influence at Board level; perhaps everyone at Meriden hoped he would not be too late to save Triumph! Bert Hopwood was well known to the long service employees at Meriden, with a reputation for plain speaking, but at the end of any argument with him a sound way forward had always been found.

In January 1972, we heard that Umberslade Hall had closed with the loss of 300 jobs, although some key engineers would move back to Meriden. Eric Turner, when he was Chairman of the BSA Board, set up the Umberslade Hall research and development centre. Three and a half years had been spent designing the P39 frame for the big twin motorcycles at Triumph and BSA. The frame's three months late arrival for production with serious design faults contributed to the root cause of the BSA Group financial collapse!

In March 1972, another of the design projects undertaken by BSA under Eric Turner's stewardship – the disastrous Ariel 3 tricycle – came to an end, costing the Group an estimated £2m.

The pressure of the factory rumours and constant press speculation about what was going to happen to Triumph at Meriden were having a tremendous effect, especially on the younger employees with large financial and family commitments. One such young welder, married with a family and mortgage, felt the pressure more than most. His marriage was on the verge of collapse and his wife had run off, leaving him with the young children, who were about to be taken into care by Social Services. He already worked regular night shifts as he needed the extra premium. He finally broke down one night, turning up for a shift the worse for drink – his welding colleagues, knowing of his difficult personal problems, put him to bed under a welding bench that was not being used, to sleep it off. The young welder's work for the night was divided amongst the rest of the welders, so no production was lost and supervision was none the wiser! An indication of the sort of camaraderie that existed at the time amongst welders. This was to happen on a

Left to right – Bert Hopwood, Malcolm Uphill and Doug Hele at Malcolm's presentation for a 100mph Isle of Man lap. (Courtesy John Nelson's archive)

number of occasions before a reconciliation took place and family stability was restored. There were no easy employment options if you were a production welder in the 1970s. If you did not work, you did not get paid – simple as that!

Rumours were circulating the Meriden factory suggesting that Bert Hopwood, who had recently been appointed to the BSA Board, would shortly address a mass meeting of the Meriden workforce regarding the future of the company. Some of the long service employees who knew Bert Hopwood well had been speaking to him, trying to persuade him to address a meeting of the total workforce, and he was considering it. Bert Hopwood was well known for his plain speaking and strong views about the militant trade unions at Meriden. I was sure this would be a meeting not to be missed, especially when I heard that many shop floor employees were preparing questions to be put to Bert.

The notorious Ariel 3. (Brochure picture)

Mass meeting questions for Bert Hopwood:
It must have been known that the P39 Umberslade frame had problems before it was left to Triumph Meriden to sort out – why was this done?

Your Triumph Trident design was ready for production in 1964/5 – why was it delayed until 1968 only months before the very successful Honda 4 introduction, thus losing 3-4 years in the marketplace without competition?

Your brilliant racing triples developed by Doug Hele and his small team are winning everything in 750 production racing, whilst the factory is trying to sell a model range mostly based upon the ageing twin cylinder designs – why are we not selling motorcycles based upon the triples?

Why was £2m squandered on the Aerial 3 tricycle when Meriden's machine shop is desperate for new machine tools, some of which were rescued in 1940 when the old Priory Street factory was bombed?

The marketplace is crying out for highly profitable Triumph spare parts, many of which are in daily production – why don't we supply the market? We are leaving it open for pirate spare parts suppliers.

1973 model year 750cc T140V Bonneville with front disc brake and five-speed gearbox. (Brochure picture)

Unfortunately, the meeting never took place; further rumours in the factory suggested that the BSA Chief Executive had vetoed the possibility.

August 1972 brought the introduction of the new 1973 model year production. The main change to the Bonneville and Trophy models was a front disc brake and a progressive increase of engine capacity, up to 750cc. This, we were told, was a vital requirement for the US market, making the twin cylinder models more competitive and enabling the company and dealers to charge a higher price. It was also formally announced that the P39 frame now provided a motorcycle with a 31in (787mm) seat height.

The popular dual purpose 490cc TR5 was replaced for 1973 by the TR5T Trophy Trail or Adventurer; this involved the Meriden welding section in the production of the new P51 frames for this model. Like the P39, this new P51 frame also doubled up as the oil tank. However, unlike the P39 frame, the frame for the Trophy Trail was very similar to those produced before for single cylinder models (albeit not at Meriden). Also unlike the P39, proven jigs and fixtures and production techniques were available from day one. Group management had learnt the lessons of the P39 fiasco!

Introduced for 1973, the TR5T Adventurer. (Brochure picture)

The X75 Hurricane custom styling for the American market, by Craig Vetter.
(Courtesy James Crosby photography, London Motorcycle Museum)

The frame section became involved at this time in a late modification to the BSA Small Heath-produced frames for the X75 Hurricane, now to be assembled at Meriden. This eye catching custom-styled model had been created by Craig Vetter for the American market. Triumph X75 Hurricanes used the sloped BSA Rocket 3 variant of the T150 Trident engine.

Also at this time, we heard that a Government response to Lord Shawcross' request for financial help had been received. It was not prepared to help the existing BSA Group, but was prepared to help in the formation of a new company. The BSA Board of Directors was unable to challenge this decision because the Group was at the absolute limit of the £10m overdraft facilities, and the bank had threatened that unless Government support was forthcoming a receiver would be appointed!

On 14th March 1973, the Industry Secretary Christopher Chataway announced in the House of Commons that the Government was supporting a plan to save the British Motorcycle industry by forming a new company from the two existing major motorcycle groups, Norton Villiers and BSA/Triumph. It was to be known as Norton Villiers Triumph (NVT), and the Department of Trade and Industry would be providing up to £5m of support aid. Part of this deal was the acquisition of the profitable BSA non-motorcycling companies at a knock down price by Manganese

**Dennis Poore – Chairman of the new company Norton Villiers Triumph (NVT).
(Courtesy John Nelson's archive)**

Bronze, whose Chairman, Dennis Poore, would also become the Chairman of NVT. In return, BSA received Norton Villiers. We all felt a lot happier at the Meriden factory with what looked like a new beginning without the BSA Group millstone round our necks. Dennis Poore was said to have already succeeded in turning round the ailing Norton Villiers factory at Wolverhampton, making it into a profitable organisation. All in all, things now looked more hopeful, although this had already come at a cost with the voluntary redundancy of 300 employees at Meriden, and the planned closure of the BSA motorcycle factory at Small Heath, Birmingham.

We found out much later that with the help of the British Government, Dennis Poore, it would seem, had pulled off an excellent deal for Manganese Bronze in 'getting rid of' what would turn out to be the financially ailing Norton Villiers company, and acquiring cheaply the non-motorcycle profitable BSA Group subsidiary companies.

The improved Triumph factory morale created the atmosphere for the settlement of a wages dispute at Meriden that was taking place just before the annual summer holiday. When we returned after the break, the first job for the new NVT management was to resolve this. As soon as that was achieved, a request was made for discussions regarding Triumph Meriden's future within the new NVT organisation. This meeting of the trade union full-time officials, stewards, conveners and factory supervision was scheduled for noon on 14th September 1973 in the work's canteen. Mr Dennis Poore would address those present.

As we walked to the meeting we noticed that copies of the mid-day edition of the local *Coventry Evening Telegraph* were being sold at the factory gate. This was unusual, so one of the stewards went and purchased a copy. There in the late news was a headline:

"Triumph Meriden factory to be closed on 1st February 1974 with the loss of 1700 jobs."

The *Coventry Evening Telegraph*'s shocking news spread around the Meriden factory like wild fire as we gathered in the work's canteen. Dennis Poore stated that "there would be an orderly three stage closure of the Triumph Meriden factory during which 7500 motorcycles should be produced." Also included in his 5 minute address were a few brief conditions that would apply. As he paused for breath the sheet metal workers' full-time union official, Mr Andy Smart, jumped to his feet and said "In all my years in the trade union movement, I've never heard such a callous statement! Can I ask you a question?"

Stuttering very nervously, he replied "I've got a train to London to catch from Coventry station at 12.30," and left the meeting in uproar!

A two-page company statement headed "Closure at Meriden – Basic Plan" was then made available to those attending the meeting, and is reproduced here:

It is proposed to maintain full production at Meriden until November 30th and every effort will be made by the management to maintain normal working throughout the factory and to ensure that supplies of material are available.

During this time it is planned to negotiate all the details of the closure and this will allow full consideration to be given to all the problems that emerge.

The management's initial plan is based on:
The work force being reduced by one third on November 30th.
The work force being reduced by a further third on January 1st.
The final closure taking place on February 1st.

It should be possible to produce at least 7500 motorcycles between now and February 1st, and the plan is that production should carry on at the rate of 700 motorcycles per week up to November 30th. Material is being procured on a basis of a production of a minimum of 6600 motorcycles of which 2200 will be Tridents and the balance will be 750cc twin cylinder machines. It will be the aim of the management to complete the production of the Trident as quickly as possible and then transfer future production of this motorcycle to Small Heath. During this time there is no doubt that the company will be incurring very heavy losses, but the final date of February 1st has been chosen to enable the factory to be closed in an orderly manner.

The management realise that it is difficult to expect enthusiastic co-operation during this period but hope that everything will be done to minimise the losses that are occurring. If the financial losses in the next month are greater than have been estimated, and this will certainly happen if the output falls below 600 motorcycles per week, the date of the closure will have to be reviewed and may be brought forward.

On redundancy terms, these will be similar to those which applied to the Small Heath factory in 1971 and this means that in addition to the basic redundancy payments required by the law, each employee will receive a further day's wages for every year of unbroken service and one-quarter of one day's wages for each additional or part of three months service. This additional payment will only be paid to those employees who leave at the date agreed with the management.

It is important to recognise that the production plan will only be achieved by maintaining a balanced labour force during the run-down period. It is anticipated that many employees will apply for early redundancy and the only way of maintaining the required balance of labour will be by greater mobility between jobs than is normal. Here again it must be emphasised that increased financial losses due to failure to achieve the production plan could affect the closure date.

Should any employee wish to work at Small Heath their application for work, under the terms and conditions applying at Small Heath will be given every consideration and they will be offered jobs as soon as they become available.

As those attending the 15 minute meeting with Dennis Poore left the work's canteen, dazed workers stopped us and asked what was happening. By now most of them knew, but were seeking a glimmer of hope. All we could do was refer them to a mass meeting of the whole Triumph workforce in the large factory car park that would be addressed by the full-time trade union officials. It would start as soon as a makeshift platform and public address system was ready so that all 1700 employees could hear exactly what was being said.

The announcement by Dennis Poore had been totally unexpected and contrary to the previous BSA Board's planned reorganisation of the motorcycle division in line with the Coopers Management Consultants' plan. As far as Triumph Meriden employees had known, the 'reorganisation plan' to be implemented would involve closing BSA with the loss of 3000 jobs, with all future motorcycle production to be concentrated at the Triumph factory at Meriden. Out of the 3000 planned BSA redundancies at Small Heath, 2000 had already happened, confirming the Coopers reorganisation was already under way.

Clearly the Government proposal to support the British motorcycle industry under the NVT banner was to be based upon a new plan!

We didn't know at the time but we later discovered there had been a second group of management consultants commissioned by the BSA Group Board. Their report completely contradicted the earlier Coopers report, and favoured concentrating all production at the BSA Small Heath factory. Dennis Poore was to later confirm this in the press, stating that he never considered the Meriden factory as a viable option; it simply was not large enough to house all the planned NVT manufacturing activities.

So there we have it, the Triumph Meriden union representation and management supervision had been caught completely off guard. When all 1700 employees assembled in the work's car park, the trade union full-time officials took it in turn to address the mass meeting. Their individual messages were the same – none of them had ever experienced before what had happened today at Triumph and they intended to mobilize the whole of the trade union and labour movement to oppose this alleged act of blatant asset stripping. Immediate steps would be taken with local MPs to establish exactly what the Tory Government had intended when it announced in Parliament, "investment to save the British motorcycle industry." Finally it was stated that senior management had left the factory and the main gates had been chained behind them. A 24 hour picket would begin immediately and remain until the battle for Triumph Meriden had been won!

Dennis Poore had had the advantage of surprise on his side, especially as most of the Triumph workforce saw NVT with him at the helm leading them out of the BSA Group wilderness, to a brighter future. Dennis Poore's brief and callous 5 minute statement at noon on 14th September 1973 attacked the Triumph Meriden 'family' and its way of life. The consequences of this would be felt for some time to come.

3

FACTORY OCCUPATION

D ennis Poore's factory closure declaration on 14th September 1973 was seen by the Triumph family as an attack on its motorcycle and way of life. The employees' reaction was therefore very predictable: total opposition to NVT and its leader Dennis Poore's proposals. Initially, the workforce continued to work normally, though this was soon to change. The factory occupation required a bargaining position – it was 'what we have we hold'. Everything within Triumph Meriden was secured by a 24 hour, seven day a week security picket, whose role it was to prevent anything moving.

The pickets' placards outside the factory proclaiming the occupation force's intentions said it all! (Courtesy Mick Duckworth's archive)

A picture of picket leader Dennis Crowder-Johnson (right) taken in happier times, with Grand Prix road racer Phil Read on a 750cc Bonneville. (Courtesy Mirrorpix)

Following the symbolic chaining of the factory gates directly after Poore's statement, the organisation of the occupation fell to John Grattan. His Scottish heritage, which had previously established him as one of the most militant of all of Triumph's trade union conveners, was ideally suited for the new job in hand, and he set about his task with military gusto. Each picket shift was to be of 6 hours' duration, with shifts identified by a letter of the alphabet and the picket shift rota organised in alphabetical order. If you were unsure of when your turn on picket duty was, you simply phoned the factory and confirmed the letter of the current picket. Volunteers from the 1700 workforce manned the picket shifts, which were organised on a sectional/family basis. I was on D-shift – the frame section – whose picket leader was Edgar Thorpe, the sheet metal workers' convener. I acted as Edgar's deputy in his absence.

Temporary lean-to shelters were erected at the main Triumph factory gate and also at the number two works gate, 200 yards down the road. It was from the number two works that finished motorcycles and spare parts were packed and shipped. The gate lean-to shelters were heated in the traditional picketing method with open fire braziers, fuel for which was donated by local coal tradesmen or miners who lived in the same communities as many of the Triumph workforce. A Triumph factory closure 'fighting fund' was established using the many cash donations being received from all over the world – the general public was horrified at the callous action taken by Dennis Poore and NVT. Additional fund-raising social events were also organised, the appropriate anthem for which became the hit tune of the day, *Part of the Union* by The Strawbs.

When we arrived for each picket shift we signed in with the picket leader who provided petrol expenses (4 pickets to a car). No one was receiving wages now; everyone was unemployed and signing on the dole. The shift leader also allocated individuals duties. Each picket shift was divided into five groups; 1 and 2 groups manned the two factory gates, 3 and 4 patrolled inside the factory buildings or the factory perimeter, and group 5 was on rest in the canteen. The picket groups rotated their duties during the 6 hour shift, keeping everyone alert and preventing boredom.

Dennis Crowder-Johnson, Triumph's brilliant statesman-like leader, made official contact with the local police as soon as the factory gates were chained. He provided them with assurances on the legitimacy of the official trade union action. This responsible approach was very quickly reinforced when the pickets caught people breaking into the factory to steal Trident T150 engines. The thieves were taking six units on a trolley across the main factory car park to a waiting van. Thus an excellent relationship was established with the local police, who then regularly called in at the factory day and night to have a tea break with the pickets and make sure all was secure! Halfway through each 6 hour picket shift, a hot meal (usually eggs, sausage and mash) was provided from the factory canteen by volunteer wives or women pickets. These meals were particularly welcome during the long, cold winter months. When the mains services were disconnected, arrangements were made to use the electric, gas and water following reconnection, paid for by the occupants.

The first two weeks of picketing passed uneventfully. As a relatively new Triumph employee, I started to understand exactly what employment at the factory meant to long-service workers and their families. I was to spend many hours with such individuals whilst on picket duty, when they liked nothing better than to reminisce about their past experiences; good or bad, it all poured out!

Patrolling the silent, freezing cold factory machine shop in total darkness aided only by torchlight was a very eerie experience. Row upon row of very old worn out machines, some rescued in 1940 from the old bombed Priory Street factory in Coventry, yet the Triumph craftsmen still managed to turn out a fantastic motorcycle. On one occasion I misdirected the beam of my torch, illuminating the face of my fellow patrolling picket – tears were streaming down his face as he peered into the darkness where he had spent a large part of his working life. When we returned from our patrol he recalled how much money had been squandered by bad management, money that could so easily have been reinvested in more efficient production equipment. I will always remember his comment that "much was said about Triumph's militant trade unions and their restrictive shop floor practices, yet there was nothing more inefficient and restrictive than having to work on worn out machine tools."

The Transport and General Workers' Union (T&G), with 1200 members out of the total of the 1700 Triumph workforce, continued to take the lead role in the occupation. Bill Lapworth, the union district official, and local Nuneaton MP Leslie Huckfield, in conjunction with Dennis Crowder-Johnson, started to explore the possibility of establishing Triumph Meriden as a Workers' Co-operative (Co-op). They were supported in these exploratory discussions by Jack Jones, the T&G General Secretary, and his deputy, Harry Urwin. The other seven Triumph trade unions were not particularly interested in the Co-op proposal, believing in a more traditional trade union opposition to a factory closure. However, they did not oppose the Co-op idea in principle, and left the T&G to explore the possibility.

Meanwhile, Dennis Poore, reeling under the weight of the very negative press he and NVT were receiving over their decision to close the Triumph factory, made some conciliatory comments in the media along the lines of "if the Triumph workers can come up with the money to purchase the Meriden factory at a fair price, NVT will certainly consider it."

Whilst Dennis Poore was exhibiting a more caring face, his managers behind the scenes

Bill Lapworth – District organiser of the Transport and General Workers' Union at Coventry. (Courtesy Mirrorpix)

Leslie Huckfield MP for Nuneaton. As well as being a sharp dresser, he was very supportive of the efforts to save Triumph Meriden. (Courtesy Mirrorpix)

were certainly not. They were warning concerned US Triumph motorcycle dealers not to visit the factory at Meriden, because the pickets were "hard line, left wing communists" who would stone them on sight! Luckily one such dealer who had known the Meriden workforce for many years ignored Poore's NVT managers and told the pickets what was being said.

In the middle of October 1973, Leslie Huckfield and Bill Lapworth paid a visit to Triumph's major market – the United States of America – in order to enlist vital dealer support for the proposed new Triumph Workers' Co-operative. They received a very positive reaction from the dealers, who, like the Meriden workforce, had also suffered badly at the hands of the BSA Group management. This was in total contrast to the many happy years of dealing with the previous independent Triumph Engineering Company. Bob Myers, the US Triumph dealer's organisation representative, became a very strong supporter of the proposed new Co-op, visiting England on several occasions to express the US dealers' support! As there was no positive progress with

**Jack Jones, General Secretary of the Transport and General Workers' Union.
(Courtesy Mirrorpix)**

negotiations, Poore declared that the Triumph Engineering factory at Meriden would officially close on 10th November 1973, at which time redundancy payments would be made to the workers.

Leslie Huckfield MP, as part of his discussions on the possibility of a Co-op, published in the House of Commons a sheet entitled *Triumph at Meriden – The Facts*. It is reproduced here:

TRIUMPH AT MERIDEN – THE FACTS
BSA, TRIUMPH AND MR DENNIS POORE
The name and reputation of Triumph at Meriden has been built up over the years, based on the famous Triumph twin design and the excellent handling characteristics of the bike. It is not a mass-produced machine, but precision built by a labour-force of skilled craftsmen, many of whom have been at the plant for up to 30 years.

Until 1968 the BSA Group, of which the Triumph plant at Meriden was a successful part, made a good profit. Triumph was making more than 1000 bikes a week, some 70 per cent of which were

Production started again briefly when it looked like a deal could be done with Poore and NVT in October 1973, but the possibility soon faded. (Courtesy *Coventry Evening Telegraph*/Mirrorpix)

exported to the United States. In 1961, Triumph at Meriden had been fully absorbed by the larger but ailing Birmingham group, in an endeavour to resurrect the motor cycling prowess of the Small Heath plant. After 1970 BSA/Triumph made losses despite the profitable plant at Meriden. In October 1971, Lord Shawcross, a former Solicitor General and now a prominent city financier agreed, though he said reluctantly, to chair the company.

3000 men lost their jobs at the Small Heath plant and following the recommendation of Cooper Brothers, the independent consultants, production and assets were concentrated at Meriden.

Still the group's fortunes did not improve and by late summer 1972 they were reported to be in discussion with Harley Davidson and also with Dennis Poore, Chairman of Norton Villiers. There was talk too of British Government money being available to help get the industry on its feet.

By spring 1973 the company's position had deteriorated so much that there was discussion on whether its quotation on the London Stock Exchange should be suspended. Amid wild speculation and rumours of 'insider trading' the beginning of March saw a run on shares. The Government had to step in and on Monday 19th March Mr Christopher Chataway, Minister for Industrial Development, announced to the House of Commons a proposal for a new Norton Villiers Triumph company under Mr Poore involving £4.8m ($11.5m) of British Government money. Through Dennis Poore's holding company, Maganese Bronze Holdings, there was a further £4.8m, £1.3m ($3.12m) of which was to be in the form of convertible preference shares, but £3.5m ($8.4m) in cash for Poore's acquisition of the BSA non-motorcycle and most profitable interests (sintered components, the guns divisions and car bodies, which included London taxicabs).

Though Mr Chataway made his House of Commons statement on 19th March and at that time met two deputations of shop stewards led by Mr Huckfield who stressed they wanted to know the plant's future, it was not until September that the picture became clearer. During this period Leslie Huckfield impressed on Mr Chataway in Parliamentary Questions, and in writing, the great uncertainties of the Meriden workforce and the need for some positive statement to be made by Mr Poore. Mr Chataway even wrote to Mr Poore to this effect.

When nothing had been heard at the end of the summer, Mr Huckfield met Mr Poore privately and again pointed out the need for consultation. It was not until the Friday morning of 14th September that Mr Poore suddenly visited the plant. He announced abruptly that all manufacturing there would cease before 1st February 1974, and then left hurriedly.

As a result of his sudden announcement, further press statements had to be issued in Britain and America, stressing that Triumph was not ceasing production altogether.

At the beginning of October Mr Poore announced that layoffs were to start immediately. Because they were determined that bikes should continue to be made, especially to fulfil vital American export orders, the workers staged a 'work-in' and carried on production. This they have continued, even working without pay or insurance cover – which had been withdrawn from them.

A WORKERS' CO-OPERATIVE

Leslie Huckfield MP and Bill Lapworth, South Midlands Divisional Organiser of the Transport and General Workers' Union, with the unanimous support of the workforce, put forward a plan for purchasing and operating the plant as a 'Workers' Co-operative. Both before he left for the United States on 15th October to talk to dealers about this, and as a result of further discussion since his return, Mr Huckfield and Mr Poore had found a formula for a return to normal working at the plant, based on continuing production till July 1974, with a target of 750 bikes per week. Though the workforce fully understands the importance of servicing American dealers for the vital buying season at the beginning of 1974, on each occasion the local management at Meriden has insisted upon the introduction of further conditions not agreed between Mr Huckfield and Mr Poore.

THE FACTS ABOUT MERIDEN

Mr Huckfield insists that the agreement between Mr Poore and himself still stands and he hopes that local management will not delay in implementing this initiative to get things moving.

STRIKES – It is not true that Meriden is always on strike. Not only has the workforce accepted a reduction in its rate of pay for 'waiting time', but has recently been working without pay and insurance cover.

OUTPUT – It is the workforce who has been insisting, through Mr Huckfield and union representatives, on a guarantee of the plant's output. Management has been reluctant owing to "continued supply difficulties." The workforce is tired of getting the blame for lost production and delays which are not its fault. In his original closure statement Mr Poore made it clear that he was not blaming the Meriden workforce. Mr Poore's own plan for the relocation of production in Small Heath will involve substantial gaps in production when the market will not be supplied.

MERIDEN VERSUS SMALL HEATH

When both plants were producing, productivity at Meriden was much higher than Small Heath, and the local Coventry tradition of skilled engineering still predominates. Mr Poore himself has said in

Geoffrey Robinson seen here having resigned from Jaguar Cars and become MP for Coventry North West. (Courtesy Mirrorpix)

discussion with Mr Huckfield and Mr Lapworth that overall productivity is more important than rates of pay, and has quoted his own problems in getting an adequate production and labour force in Wolverhampton because the Government's policies do not permit him to pay those more.

LESLIE HUCKFIELD MP
HOUSE OF COMMONS
30th October 1973

Whilst all the preparatory work on the possible Co-op was taking place, there was of course always the possibility of the factory blockade being forcibly broken by strong-arm eviction. To counter this threat, John Grattan was once again brought into play. He formulated an emergency call-out plan to strengthen the factory occupation picket if required. In the event that bailiff action began to evict the factory pickets by force, reinforcements could be at the factory within 15 minutes. Extensive detailed lists of individual picket's telephone numbers were compiled, and then subdivided many times like a family tree. Five initial telephone calls from the factory very quickly multiplied, enabling over 500 individuals to be contacted. All these pickets were within 15 minutes journey time from the factory and could be quickly summoned to stiffen its defence. The existence of this 'reinforcements plan' became known, and perhaps contributed as a deterrent; no such threat of eviction ever took place until the spring of 1974.

Leslie Huckfield, Bill Lapworth and Dennis Crowder-Johnson now had what appeared to be a workable Co-op proposal; however, it still lacked credible commercial input to guarantee it would stand up to close Government scrutiny. This problem was encapsulated in a report back to the pickets as follows: "there is one door we can only knock on; we need someone who can knock at the door and be invited in."

That person the planning team chose to approach was Geoffrey Robinson. Geoffrey, with socialist (albeit unorthodox) ideas, had quite recently become the Chief Executive at the Coventry Jaguar Cars factories. As such he was known to Bill Lapworth, who had a large T&G membership employed there. An indication of Geoffrey Robinson's different approach is apparent from his first meeting with the Jaguar factory's full-time union officials, which as the story goes took place one Saturday afternoon. Most Coventry trade union full-time officials were not known for taking part in Saturday afternoon meetings. However, the new Chairman of Jaguar Cars was a very important employment provider, and had invited them to meet him for the first time at the Post House Hotel where he was staying. On arrival Geoffrey welcomed them, and told them to relax, take their suit jackets off and sit down, which they did in front of a large screen television, expecting a corporate video presentation on Jaguar. They were in for a surprise. The purpose of this initial meeting was to have a quiet social drink whilst watching the England football match that was on that afternoon. Geoffrey is said to have commented "I think watching it will be a good way for us to spend a little time getting to know each other, before our meetings at the factory looking after our mutual interests, a bright future for Jaguar Cars and the workers who produce them"!

The draft proposal for the Triumph Co-op was taken to Geoffrey Robinson for his commercial comments on the likelihood of it being acceptable to the Government's Department of Trade and Industry. Geoffrey studied the proposal in his own time over the weekend and redrafted it, particularly in three areas – management of the Co-op, marketing of the Co-op's motorcycles, and new model design and development. Geoffrey felt that these key areas were generally seen as very weak at the old BSA organisation, and the reason the Government supported the formation of NVT over BSA. Therefore, to try and convince Civil Servants and Government that a Co-op with no proven record could be successful and worthy of their financial support without addressing these shortcomings would be impossible. Geoffrey Robinson redrafted the Co-op proposal with the new venture being only a manufacturing organisation selling its motorcycles (the existing big twin cylinder designs currently in production at Meriden until the occupation) to NVT. It would market them in the short-term and also be responsible for new designs. In essence, negotiations with the Government would be to secure a loan large enough to purchase the Meriden factory site, manufacturing rights and equipment to restart production so that the Triumph factory at Meriden could reopen as a Workers' Co-op. The attraction to Dennis Poore would be that there was a chance to secure the sale of the Meriden factory to the Co-op and liberate the stockpiles of pre-closure motorcycles, thus bringing valuable cashflow that was desperately required by NVT.

Geoffrey Robinson's new draft of the Co-op plan, when discussed with the trade union conveners, was not very well received as they knew their membership's expectations were to get rid of Dennis Poore and NVT. It was felt that having established the new Triumph Workers' Co-op, Dennis Poore and NVT would try and strangle it at birth! However, when Geoffrey Robinson expressed his honest belief that it was only with this more commercially realistic proposal or something similar, that the Meriden workforces' concerns were withdrawn allowing negotiations to continue.

Negotiations with NVT were extremely protracted and at times very acrimonious, feelings running high on both sides. Dennis Poore maintained his public stance that he would do a deal, if a satisfactory proposal could be achieved that did not negatively affect the profitability of NVT. On one particular occasion that became well known in the folklore about the Triumph occupation, John Grattan was with the other seven union conveners at a meeting in Central London with Dennis Poore and his Executive Managers. The meeting had convened on the top floor of a six storey office block. The NVT and trade union representatives gathered around a large boardroom-type table occupying all the seats. Geoff Fawn (Chief Negotiating Director of NVT) arrived late for the meeting, entered, and on seeing there were no seats left, supposedly said in a loud voice "Where shall I sit?" Quick as a flash, John Grattan replied "On the window sill outside," causing roars of laughter; the office being six floors up. This set the uncompromising tone for the rest of the meeting, but did change a little from the dictatorial approach some of the NVT managers had been taking at previous meetings!

At the beginning of 1974, the Conservative Government, led by Edward Heath, introduced a three-day working week. All commercial users of electricity could only do so for three pre-arranged days each week, consuming electricity for a maximum of six hours on each of those days. This action was undertaken to try and combat a long-standing industrial work-to-rule by the National Union of Mineworkers that had caused stockpiles of coal to become depleted. There was also an oil crisis on the world markets, which contributed to driving the price of coal higher. The Government's three-day week was to try and preserve what coal stocks there were, negotiations with the miner's union having failed. Manufacturing industry in general, including NVT, was now in great difficulty.

Edward Heath called an election, basically looking for the country's support and a positive answer to his question "Who rules the country, the Government or the miners?" Edward Heath received his answer, but not the one he hoped for! The Conservatives lost the election and the Labour Party came to power in February 1974, with Harold Wilson as Prime Minister of a minority Labour Government. He appointed Tony Benn as his Industry Secretary at the Department of Trade and Industry (DTI). Tony Benn was a well-known Workers' Co-operative supporter, so the Triumph conveners requested an early meeting with him, at which he agreed to appoint consultants to aid the preparation of the Triumph Meriden proposals for a Co-op. Also at this meeting, the conveners were to show Tony Benn a press statement they had prepared to try and prevent their eviction from the Meriden factory by NVT, before he'd had time to consider the Co-op proposals. To help delay NVT's legal action, Tony Benn added to the Triumph convener's statement that "the Minister intended to give full consideration to the proposal, once it was finalised."

Tony Benn, MP and Industry Secretary in the Labour Government. (Courtesy Mirrorpix)

The new factory occupants set up a showroom display in the dispatch area behind the security gatehouse. (Author's archive)

In return Tony Benn asked the conveners to consider releasing some of the equipment desperately needed by NVT at Small Heath; this would enable them to start manufacture of the three cylinder Triumph Tridents. He also felt this would demonstrate an act of good faith on their part. As an act of solidarity, Tony Benn and his wife were to join the Meriden factory picket the next time they were in the Midlands, and assure them he would do all he could to help find a viable plan for the future (he joined the factory picket anonymously on three further occasions during the months of occupation).

In March 1974, NVT began legal proceedings, issuing a writ in order to gain access to the Triumph factory at Meriden to recover its contents. This stimulated further urgent action by Tony Benn, once again persuading the pickets to release more of the vital items needed at Small Heath for the production of the Triumph three cylinder Tridents and some further sales of stockpiled Bonnevilles. By so doing Tony Benn assured the pickets he felt he would gain the vital time he needed. Hugh Palin, NVT's Marketing Director, was given the job by Dennis Poore of day-to-day negotiations at the factory with the Meriden pickets. He paid £3 to the fighting fund for each Bonneville loaded on the lorry bound for NVT.

Tony Benn held a 19th June meeting at the House of Commons between NVT and the union

Tony and Caroline Benn with Bill Lapworth (right) and Dennis Crowder-Johnson (left) admire a Bonneville during the HMG agreement pickets' factory celebrations. (Courtesy *Coventry Evening Telegraph*/Mirrorpix)

conveners from both Meriden and Small Heath. He gave verbal reassurances to the Small Heath conveners that the Government support of the Co-op at Triumph would not negatively affect Small Heath. In July 1974, Benn announced in the House of Commons that the Government would loan £4.2m plus provide a £750,000 grant to the Triumph Co-op at Meriden. As this amount was under £5m there was no requirement for a full House of Commons debate. This was considered important because of the recent history of the motorcycle industry and the minority Labour Government; a full Commons debate would have been unlikely to support it. Most of the money would go to NVT for the purchase of the Meriden factory, manufacturing rights and plant and machinery for the production of big twin cylinder Triumphs plus work in progress.

Just prior to this agreement being reached, I was forced to leave the Meriden factory picket; a county court judgement for non-payment of my mortgage arrears was being threatened. Like many of the other young pickets I faced a terrible dilemma: take one of the many jobs on offer and pay my mortgage arrears, or continue the picket and lose the family home. The most difficult decision of my life was made and I started another job in Nuneaton. I still supported the picket shifts but from this point, as with many others, it had to be only in the evenings and at weekends. Before starting my new job I reached an understanding with the frame section D-shift picket that as soon as the Co-operative commenced production, I would be one of the first invited to return.

It was very strange working for another company after all that we had gone through at Triumph, however, I certainly fell on my feet. When I arrived they were in trouble with a welding contract they had undertaken on a fixed-price contract basis, the more they produced the more money they lost! I had the ideal experience for this job and immediately saw a solution. We needed to change the welding process; this involved converting their welding equipment. Once this had been done I was able to turn the loss maker into a big profit earner, my credibility with the company was sky high and I was made a very welcome new member of staff!

Picketing at Triumph whenever I could kept me in touch with developments, and was appreciated by the other pickets, who by this time were becoming thin on the ground. Following the elation of Tony Benn's announcement of the Government loan agreement, the final negotiations with NVT that were required to complete the deal and reopen the factory had not gone smoothly.

In October 1974 there was another Government parliamentary election. Labour won again, with a small majority of three. Tony Benn was retained as Industry Secretary at the Department of Trade and Industry. The Industry Secretary contacted the Small Heath conveners and asked them to withdraw the objections they still had regarding the Government loan to the Triumph Meriden Co-op. The BSA conveners are said to have forcefully replied that the Small Heath employees were insisting on more than a Tony Benn verbal assurance regarding their future. He offered to speak to a mass meeting of the Small Heath employees; this was arranged for 8th November 1974. When he arrived, he was greeted by a very hostile welcome. If ever it was needed, the meeting confirmed for Benn the bitterness felt by BSA workers at Small Heath regarding what they believed to be the Government's preferential treatment of Triumph Meriden.

Afterwards Benn was interviewed by the press. It was put to him that the meeting had been very hostile, and he agreed, feeling that the hostility was understandable and due to the workforce's vivid memories of past bad management practices. Profits had been squandered not reinvested, and there remained a desperate need for investment in new plant and machinery. Benn further commented that if British workers were provided with the tools that bring security, they would do the job, they are the best in the world – the contradictions of the present situation now had to be reconciled by talking to both the Small Heath and Meriden stewards regarding everyone's long-term interests. Finally, he was asked about Dennis Poore's latest NVT Government loan application to fund a three-factory British motorcycle industry. As yet, the Minister stated, he had not seen the full details. However, any further funding would have to be justified to and agreed upon by the Cabinet and the House of Commons. This at a time when urgent progress needed to be made, and presently there was not much goodwill about!

Due to lack of progress with the detailed financial negotiations with NVT, on 9th November 1974 the pickets at Triumph renewed the full Meriden factory blockade.

In December 1974, NVT announced that the Government needed to provide it with £12-£15m of loan finance in order to sustain what was now being proposed, a three-factory British motorcycle industry. If this was not forthcoming from the Government, the Meriden pickets must vacate the factory to allow NVT to realise its valuable assets – it was now entirely up to Mr Benn to decide what happened next, said NVT. Tony Benn held high-powered negotiations in Downing Street between several senior Cabinet members and Jack Jones, the T&G General Secretary, and a deal was finally done on 6th March 1975. The Triumph factory at Meriden was refinanced by a Labour Government loan of £4.2m plus a grant of £750,000, and would re-open as a Tony Benn Worker's Co-operative. The news was greeted by tremendous celebrations on the picket line; after 18 months the Triumph factory occupation would finally be over. The loan to the Triumph Co-op (the new company initially to be known as Synova Motors) was needed to purchase from NVT the Meriden factory site, plant, machinery, and manufacturing rights to produce the Triumph large capacity twin cylinder motorcycles, at a price of £3.9m. A two year sales and worldwide distribution contract was also agreed with NVT, for it to market through its dealer networks 1500 right foot gear change models (many of which were already complete and still in the factory), plus 48,000 left foot gear change motorcycles required to meet new USA legislation for the 1976 selling season.

The left foot gear change and right foot brake design changes to meet the new US legislation had been completed by the pickets during the eighteen month factory occupation; Chuck Knight undertook exhaustive testing in the factory car park, with road-going insurance unavailable until the legal formation of the Co-op. Chuck said to Robert Taylor in the *New Society* article 'Patriots of Meriden' (08.08.75): "I believe in this place, it's my whole livelihood … We don't just make bikes here, we ride them as well." When challenged by another journalist who said the occupying pickets would be "starved out of the Meriden factory," Chuck simply replied "we'll eat grass before giving up on Triumph!"

Geoffrey Robinson, the socialist with a brilliant commercial brain and staying power of a marathon runner, had led the negotiating team to a deal that most said would be impossible. Geoffrey took the original conception of a Workers' Co-operative – thinking of Leslie Huckfield MP, Bill Lapworth the T&G Union official, and the Triumph worker's leader Dennis Crowder-Johnson – and turned it into commercial reality, worthy of Government support.

Everyone involved accepted that the deal had many weaknesses, but it was the best that could be

Don Yielding moves the first Co-op-produced T140V (right foot gear change) Bonneville off the assembly track on 10th March 1975. (Courtesy *Coventry Evening Telegraph*/Mirrorpix)

(From the right) Dennis Crowder-Johnson, John Grattan, Ron Atkinson and Tony Bennett present Tony Benn with a Co-op 'thank you' placard on 21st May 1975. (Courtesy *Coventry Evening Telegraph*/Mirrorpix)

Conversion of Triumph's best-selling twins to left foot gear change/ right foot braking was achieved during the factory occupation. (Author's archive)

Chuck Knight, the Co-op's chief road tester, was restricted to car park testing to develop the left-foot gear change, right-foot brake. (Courtesy Mrs Pat Knight)

achieved at the time. We had won one battle, but the Co-op leadership accepted there would be more to come before Triumph Meriden could be sure of long-term viability. NVT still continued to pursue Government for extra finance, convinced that in the new circumstances of the three-factory British Motorcycle industry (i.e. Meriden, Small Heath and Wolverhampton) it would require an extra £12-15m. Although the Government showed no interest in providing this extra money to NVT, it seemed that problems NVT had been having with export credit finance facilities had eased.

In May 1975 there was a Government ministerial reshuffle, and Tony Benn was replaced as Industry Secretary by Eric Varley. This caused further delays in the outstanding detailed negotiations with NVT. Dennis Poore told the new Minister that he urgently needed £30m to £40m to run NVT in the new three factory situation.

In May 1975 I received the phone call I'd been waiting for from the Co-op – an invitation to rejoin Triumph. I gave notice to my Nuneaton 'temporary' employer, having thoroughly enjoyed my time with them and paid off my mortgage arrears. The company owner took the time to try to persuade me to stay, knowing through the massive publicity there had been about the Triumph Co-op that I, like all other skilled employees choosing to return, would be experiencing a drop in earnings of 30 per cent. He had great difficulty understanding why I was going back; we agreed to differ, shook hands, and I thought that would be the last I'd see of him.

At the end of the week, having served my notice and said my goodbyes to my colleagues, I was washing my hands before leaving for home when the company owner came to say a final goodbye. He had one last attempt to persuade me to stay, but accepted defeat and said "Well you had better make the most of these hand washing facilities – next week you will be washing your hands in a bucket."

He received the obvious reply "My bucket," and with that I left normal employment to become a member of the Triumph Co-op.

4

GLAD TO BE BACK

My return on 12th May 1975 to employment at Triumph (now known as Synova Motors, trading as Meriden Motorcycles Co-operative) was a mixture of emotions; on the one hand, after what had happened it was where I had chosen to be, and on the other hand, there was sadness at the recent death of my good friend and colleague Edgar Thorpe following a short illness. He did an excellent job as shop steward/convener for all the Sheet Metal Workers' Union members. I will always remember him for his fantastic sense of humour, usually in the most difficult of circumstances.

I reported to the security office at the main Co-op factory gate and reintroduced myself. I was collected by Edgar Thorpe's replacement, Ron Briggs, the Sheet Metal Workers' Union Co-op Board Director. Ron Briggs was the son of Ron Snr, the Triumph Engineering Company's frame section foreman. He took me to the time clock where I had to register my presence for work each day. I clocked in; other individuals were doing the same. One man who I immediately recognised as a picket from the factory occupation acknowledged my "hello, how are you?" with a curt reply of "new starters that side" – not the sort of welcome I had been expecting! My Director took me to the welding section, and explained that the majority of long service individuals who had completed the 18 month picket would have preferred that those who didn't were not invited back! Ron went on to explain that when the welding section told the Personnel Department it wanted to invite me back, initially the answer was "No!" The welders had to really insist before it was finally agreed. It seems that, unknowingly, I nearly caused the first dispute at the Co-op! Ron Briggs advised me to "keep my head down and mouth shut, they'll soon get over it." This was certainly not what I had expected on my first day back, and memories of my previous first day at Triumph Engineering almost five years earlier came flooding back – déjà vu or what?

One of the more enlightened long service welders, who picketed for the full 18 months of factory occupation, told me that what seemed to have been totally forgotten when Co-op recruitment was being considered, was that there were a number of key individuals (maybe two or three on each section) without whose knowledge and experience the 'worn out' Triumph factory would not function. Regardless of whether or not these individuals picketed for the full 18 months of the occupation, their total commitment to the Co-op was vital if success was to be achieved.

Most of these key individuals were amongst the first to return to the Co-op, and did so accepting the lower pay rates. However, what they did not expect was to be treated as second class citizens by the pickets who had completed the full 18 months' occupation.

This loss of the respect that they had earned and previously enjoyed over their many years at Triumph Engineering was the catalyst that meant their morale was soon rock bottom, leaving them questioning why they had decided to return. More generally, low morale at Triumph had always in the past been recognised as the reason for poor quality.

The pickets who had completed the 18 months factory occupation were known as founder members, and many had a very negative attitude to 'new starters' who had not. This was said to be due to broken promises they believed were made to them by the leadership during the protracted negotiations. When the occupation force numbers were falling, it was claimed that the leadership had implied that those pickets who continued to support would be compensated when the Co-op opened, with jobs for life or the opportunity to work part time on reaching normal retirement age. Those pickets nearing the age of retirement, and there were now quite a few, chose to take these alleged comments from the leadership as firm promises.

This belief that promises had not been honoured led to such comments to 'new starters' like me as "you wouldn't have a job if it wasn't for the pickets." What some elderly pickets seemed to ignore was that the workers who had returned to Triumph had usually left much better paid jobs; this was their commitment to the Co-op. They also returned believing all members of the Co-op would be equal, only to find that some picket members were more equal than others! A very vocal elite had been created.

During the final months of picketing the welding section had been relocated, and was now a lot more compact and efficient. All the knowledge we had amassed about producing the P39 frame had been utilised in the new frame section layout. This allowed efficiency improvements of 30 per cent to be achieved; exactly what the Co-op was all about. The new layout was also safer than before; shielding gas for the welding operations was now plumbed in via a piped supply from a large bulk container outside the building. I was asked to undertake the same day shift welding operation I performed at the old Triumph Engineering Company – at last it felt like I was coming home! The productivity improvements we were introducing would enable the production target of 300 frame assemblies a week to be achieved without the need for night shift working. The second shift was then available should demand really take off. Supervision was very thin on the ground, with just one organiser replacing the previous foreman and three charge hands! Organiser Billy Earl told me the Co-op thinking regarding the need for less supervision: "As everyone receives the same weekly wage and we all know exactly what production is required, all we need to do is get on with it." My organiser provided me with a statement of certain terms and conditions of employment:

SYNOVA MOTORS LIMITED trading as MERIDEN MOTORCYCLE CO-OPERATIVE
This statement of certain terms and conditions of your employment is being given to you to comply with the provisions of an Act of Parliament – The Contracts of Employment Act 1972 as amended by the Industrial Relations Act.

Details of your salary, which is paid weekly on Thursday of each week, are recorded in the Personnel Department and can be seen upon request.

Your normal hours of work are 40 hours. The starting and finishing times are on record and available for reference in the Personnel Department. Any future mutually agreed change in normal hours will be posted on the notice boards. On arriving for work you are required to clock in morning and afternoon. In the event of agreed overtime being worked you are required to clock off at the end of each extended shift.

Overtime payments may not be made without the approval of the Secretary of State for Industry.

The terms and conditions relating to:
(a) Holidays and holiday pay.
(b) Incapacity for work due to sickness or injury.
(c) Grievance procedure.
(d) Disciplinary procedures are on record and may be seen in the Personnel Department.
You must be a member of an appropriate trade union. The appropriate unions are specified and may be seen in the Personnel Department.
Your employment may be terminated either by you or the Co-operative giving to the other one week's notice to that effect, or by the Co-operative paying to you any salary entitlement that may be due to you under the Contracts of Employment Act 1972, as amended.
The Personnel Department will keep, in accordance with the terms of the Act, up to date copies of the relevant documents and a copy of the Act which may be seen upon request.
Insofar as any terms in this statement may conflict or be inconsistent with the Co-operative rules, the terms of this statement shall prevail.

Billy Earl told me a little about the Co-op structure. There were three company shares held in trust by the Co-op Trustees on behalf of the Beneficiaries (the owners of the company). The Beneficiaries were the 140 founder members who completed the 18-month occupation of the old Triumph factory; any other individual joining the company would have to complete 12 months' service before becoming a Beneficiary part owner. Each of the eight Co-op trade unions elected a Director to the Supervisory Board, which made the Co-op policy, and we were to be kept up to date on progress at a weekly Saturday morning mass meeting attended by the employees. Dennis Crowder-Johnson from the T&G Union was the Chairman of the Supervisory Board.

I was immediately struck by the level of informality and the general belief that a complex engineering business like Triumph could be co-ordinated with a weekly get-together of all personnel. There was no doubting Billy Earl's sincerity, and our charismatic leader Dennis Crowder-Johnson obviously had a clear vision on how the Co-op would function. In these circumstances, my Director's advice to "keep my head down and mouth shut" seemed a great idea for a 'new starter' at the Co-op, so that's what I did.

Starting with me on the Co-op frame section was Jim Dowling, a machinist. He had been recommended for employment at the Co-op by his good Labour Party friend Billy Earl. Jim was a member of the AEUW trade union, and was previously employed at the nearby Coventry Ryton Chrysler car plant. Like myself and many others, he was a skilled man who had accepted the lower pay structure of the Co-op, believing the Co-op offered the opportunity to establish a company without the normal industrial conflicts that blighted UK manufacturing industry. I was impressed by Jim Dowling's level of commitment to make the Co-op work. If all the other hundreds of new recruits were like-minded, we certainly had a great chance of making the Co-op a success.

The Co-op's personnel recruitment strategy was to continue the successful Triumph Engineering Company practice of employing relatives or close friends of existing employees. By so doing, it was hoped to secure the same level of commitment to Triumph. Whilst initially this was successful, because of the numbers to be recruited and the range of skills required there were now problems. Not every husband could secure a job for his wife or every wife a job for her husband. This resulted in disappointments and some accusations of favouritism, which affected morale. My and Jim Dowling's wives were not interested in employment at the Co-op, so it did not affect us personally, although it did some of our colleagues. Jim always had plenty to say at the Saturday mass meetings – I would have been proud to make many of his comments regarding where improvements could be achieved myself, but my mouth remained firmly shut.

On the 8th July 1975 we were informed that Geoffrey Robinson had succeeded in recruiting Mr David Jones as Managing Director of the Co-op. It was also announced that Brenda Price, a

Miss Brenda Price, the Triumph Co-op's link with all things commercial, becomes Company Secretary. (Courtesy John Nelson's archive)

longstanding Commercial Executive at Triumph, had been appointed Company Secretary. Both these individuals would attend Supervisory Board meetings. It was also confirmed that on the 19th April, Bill Lapworth, the T&G District Trade Union Official and one of the original negotiating team that established the Co-op, had resigned as an advisor to the Board.

There were major production problems at this time. The labour force of 400 needed to achieve a production target of 230 motorcycles each week for a financial break even. The Co-op was falling well short because of the production 'lead times' required for the introduction of the 1976 model design changes; the US legislation-driven shift to left-foot gear changing and right-foot braking. The new MD would immediately concentrate his efforts upon trying to resolve these problems. The first Sheet Metal Workers' Union Director, Ron Briggs, resigned for personal reasons in mid-August 1975.

Whilst the Triumph Co-op had been trying to recruit employees and establish volume production, NVT – to whom our total motorcycle production was sold – had been falling apart. Eric Varley, the Government Industry Secretary who replaced Tony Benn, announced in the House of Commons that NVT now had 13,000 unsold motorcycles in stock around the world, and had no chance of selling them. Dennis Poore claimed this was not true, and that they were all sold. Eric Varley also stated that NVT's £4m export credit guarantee finance was to be withdrawn, and its application for £30m to £40m extra finance to fund a three-factory British Motorcycle industry refused. Dennis Poore publicly stated that the Government had done more damage to the British motorcycle industry than the might of the Japanese, and it would inevitably lead to redundancies and factory closures. However, it was not unreasonable to suspect that Dennis Poore wasn't at all surprised when his application to HMG for £30-40m was turned down. On the two previous occasions (NVT 1973 Conservatives, and Co-op 1975 Labour), HMG investment in the motorcycle industry had been deliberately kept below the £5m level that the Department of Industry Minister could personally agree without argument, because it was felt that a debate in the House of Commons would not support more.

On 11th August 1975, NVT's Wolverhampton factory was put into receivership and the workers began a sit-in. Receivers were also appointed at Small Heath and closure followed very quickly. As preferential creditors, the Government recovered its £4m export credit guarantee finance. All of this disastrous NVT activity had a dramatic impact on its ability to honour the product sale agreement with the Co-op, and protracted negotiations began on two fronts, the aims being:

• To achieve a higher ex-works price for Bonneville models to enable HMG interest on the £4.2m loan to be paid.

• NVT and the Co-op concurring that in the new circumstances an alternative to the product sale agreement is required.

About this time we heard that Geoffrey Robinson had resigned as Chief Executive of Jaguar Cars, being unable to agree with the Ryder Plan to amalgamate Austin, Morris, Rover, Triumph and Jaguar into the BLMC group.

The Sheet Metal Workers' Union elected Mike O'Brien as its new Advisory Board Director. Before this could happen, however, legal advice had to be sought from the Company Solicitor regarding whether a non-Beneficiary founder member (i.e. an employee with less than twelve months' service) could become a Director. This legal point cleared, he joined the Board on 4th September 1975.

With the problems of the product sale agreement, many recalled their worries during the factory occupation that NVT's continued involvement could result in the Co-op being strangled at birth. Whilst this had not yet happened, and NVT's predicament seemed partly due to Government action, it was indeed resulting in what now looked like a lingering death for the Co-op. Geoffrey Robinson stated that if he had believed at the time that the Government would not support the British motorcycle industry, he would not have embarked on this route. Accordingly it was decided to reconvene the original negotiating team that was responsible for the product sale agreement.

Bill Lapworth declined involvement, as he said that he did not participate in these negotiations. The reassembled team was, therefore, Geoffrey Robinson, Denis Crowder-Johnson and Peter Davis (Company Solicitor). A further Board Director's involvement was required, and unsurprisingly, John Grattan was nominated to join the team. It was felt that John Grattan's steel-like qualities, so evident during the formation of the Co-op, would be an advantage in what were once again going to be very difficult negotiations with NVT and HMG. Inevitably, these talks would involve compromise on some of the principles held so dearly at the Co-op. However, it would be an absolute disaster if all of the new, hard-won Co-op practices were lost, causing a return to all that was bad in 'normal' manufacturing industry.

Geoffrey Robinson was officially appointed Financial and Commercial Advisor to the Co-op Board of Directors to negotiate with NVT, Government and other third parties, and report to the Board for approval on the course of action to be pursued.

On 12th September, David Jones MD stated that the Co-op required an improved organisation structure and controls throughout the factory. On the welding section we were told that the MD felt rules and regulations were vital, and those individuals responsible for organisation needed proper authority to carry out their duties. Action also needed to be taken to reduce the excessive absenteeism. All genuine Co-op members recognised the desperate need for the changes David Jones was requesting. We on the welding section, with only a few employees compared to the likes of the machine shop and assembly tracks, had our own problem individuals, and could fully appreciate exactly what it must have been like in those areas where large numbers were employed.

The leadership of the Co-op did not seem to have anticipated that when you recruit hundreds of people, there will always be a number who want to exploit every opportunity for their own benefit. Such individuals were attracted to working regular nights at the previous company, Triumph Engineering, because of the lack of supervision and discipline, which had the obvious consequences. This same behaviour was now drastically affecting Co-op production levels and quality standards, and to correct these problems increased supervision and disciplinary procedures would have to be introduced. The difficulty at this late stage was that such measures had to be 'negotiated in', when they should have existed from day one. As genuine non-founder members of the Co-op had been made to feel like second class citizens, without the normal disciplinary protection of a shop steward, an independent appeals committee was created to fulfil this role, with Jim Dowling one of those elected to the body. With morale rapidly getting worse, attendance at the weekly Saturday mass meetings steadily declined to about 100. Unfortunately, the 100 who regularly attended were those who totally believed in the Co-op already, and didn't need convincing of its potential by Dennis Crowder-Johnson's inspirational speeches. Eventually the mass meetings stopped, and the hard-core believers in the Co-op like Jim Dowling, Billy Earl and I continued our discussions in private.

The leadership that planned the Co-op's operation unfortunately lacked an input of good old fashioned production realism to balance its idealism. This lack of forethought was now causing the Co-op to flounder – the road to bankruptcy is paved with good intentions! As the Co-op's financial situation worsened, MD David Jones developed a plan for survival, which was discussed with the membership on the sections. Organisers were to have section 'leading hands', and at last it seemed disciplinary procedures would be implemented. It was not going to be a very happy 1975 Christmas for the majority; the only ones who were satisfied with their experience of the Co-op so far were those who had been abusing it!

Back to work following the festive holidays, January 1976 passed quickly. On 6th February 1976, we learned that the MD David Jones had resigned. The job had not turned out the way he hoped and he felt he could not contribute anymore to the Co-op. Geoffrey Robinson secured the services of three top GKN engineers for a period of three months by way of secondment. Under the leadership of Mr Alistair Brown, they would try and help solve some of the manufacturing problems the Co-op was experiencing. We were told that alternative Co-op income from new products was being investigated. These new projects were the assembly of a 125cc Moto Guzzi motorcycle, the assembly of a Steyr-Daimler Puch moped, and an exercise jogger. CKD assembly of the Moto Guzzi Co-Uno project was nearest to production. We were also said to be investigating possible further involvement with NVT; an initial prototype was produced using an NVT-provided T160 Trident engine fitted into a P39 frame utilising Bonneville cycle parts. To NVT's amazement, this prototype exercise was completed over a weekend by a small Co-op team led by Jim Barclay.

As an alternative product to Triumph models a batch of Moto Guzzi Co-Uno bikes were produced. (Courtesy Erum Waheed's archive)

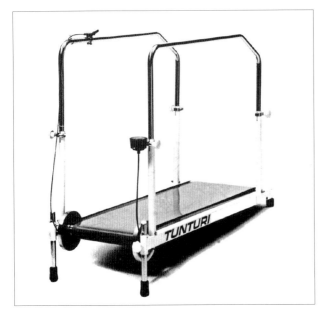

A further alternative product was the Puch Tunturi Jogger. (Courtesy John Nelson's archive)

The prototype Trident T160 engine in Bonneville P39 frame and cycle parts is about to be road tested by Chuck Knight prior to NVT's arrival. (Courtesy Mrs Pat Knight)

NVT came to inspect the prototype at 9.00am on Monday morning, expecting a mock up. Chuck Knight, the Co-op's chief tester, was just returning to the factory having completed the first fifty test miles. The Co-op's interest was in a possible triple T180 Superbike to be produced by us at a much higher ex-works price.

The sudden death of local Coventry MP Maurice Edelman created an opportunity for Geoffrey Robinson to pursue his parliamentary ambitions as a Labour Party MP, in what had to be the most appropriate constituency for him in the country. Coventry North West was where both Jaguar factories were located, employing sixteen thousand people. Geoffrey had been a very popular Jaguar boss – many of the luxury car maker's employees lived in this Coventry

Following a long hard weekend, R&D team members John Hallard (left) and the author pose with the triple hybrid Note the 007 'secret service' trade plate. (Courtesy Mrs Pat Knight)

The Meriden triple hybrid now belongs to the National Motorcycle Museum. (Courtesy Mick Duckworth's archive)

The Co-op's interest in the triple hybrid was down to the possibility of a 900cc superbike. A modified P39 frame was produced here with a T180 engine installed. (Courtesy James Crosby photography, London Motorcycle Museum)

constituency, and had been deeply saddened when in 1975 he resigned over the Ryder Plan. Accordingly, it was not surprising that Geoffrey Robinson was considered by the Labour Party to be an excellent candidate for this vital by-election. Victory was essential for the Labour Government because its small majority, obtained in October 1974, had by this time dwindled to one, and that was Coventry North West. Geoffrey Robinson's hoped-for win would therefore maintain a slim but workable majority in the House of Commons. On 4th March 1976 Geoffrey duly obliged, retaining the seat for Labour with a majority of 3694. This was an exceptional result considering the country's dissatisfaction with the Labour Government at that time. A large number of the Triumph Co-op's membership were now also Geoffrey's constituents. Once Labour's majority had been retained it was believed that Harold Wilson felt he could resign as Prime Minister without it appearing he was going because of the parliamentary situation. He was replaced as Prime Minister by Jim Callaghan.

Later in March 1976 there was a pay rise for everyone at the Co-op. This was an attempt to retain disillusioned, key-skilled employees, for whom there were now many vacancies in local industry. Key individuals who returned to Triumph looking for something better in their employment by way of the Co-op were now thinking it was a mistake, and were seriously considering returning to more secure, higher paid, normal employment.

On 10th March 1976, GKN's Mr Alistair Brown provided a summary of its engineers' findings at the Co-op:

"The Co-op should for the foreseeable future concentrate on production of the Bonneville. There's a need for a formal management structure, and it's necessary to pay key people plus organisers more than the single standard rate of pay."

Alistair Brown further indicated that he was circulating for discussion an organisational chart with existing 'personalities' identified upon it. It was suggested on the chart that the Electricians' Union (the ETU) Director, John Grattan, should run production, but the machine shop organisers and leading hands felt this was inappropriate because of his lack of engineering experience, and two of the organisers resigned.

Absenteeism, late starting, and early finishing times were continuing to have a big effect on production, especially in the machine shop where 'fixed' time cycles, once lost, could not be retrieved. Accordingly, John Grattan and Johnny Williams were undertaking an investigation for consideration by the Board. This was seen as a spying mission, and lowered morale even further. By the end of March, rumours were circulating that the Directors had been told by the Company Secretary that continuing shortfalls on target production effectively meant every motorcycle sold to NVT effectively had £80 under the saddle!

Alistair Brown's seconded GKN team had been making a valid contribution to resolving the production problems. It advised in April that most workers were now making a fair effort, and the Co-op would achieve the required 350 motorcycles a week production target in the near future. It was now vital to put a plan to the Government for future support. He also stated that GKN's three-month secondment was nearing an end, and it would be important for the Co-op to recruit suitably qualified engineers to carry on the work that had been started.

Another rumour that circulated the factory in late May indicated that, due to a slight improvement in production, there was now only £70 under the saddle of each bike leaving the factory for NVT. Seat locks were still to be improved!

The workforce was notified that the Co-op's first Annual General Meeting of Beneficiaries would be held at 2.30pm on Friday 9th July 1976. The initial purpose of the meeting was to elect the Beneficiaries Committee of eleven, their job to direct the trustee shareholders on how to vote in the event that the required majorities were not achieved at the Annual General Meeting of the company. This was in accordance with the Co-op trust deed. The Advisory Board agreed that all employees, regardless of whether they qualified as Beneficiaries (i.e. had completed 12 months' service), could attend the AGM. However, Dennis Crowder-Johnson had asked the Directors to consider if the Co-op should continue to receive Director nominations from each of the eight trade unions, or whether this should now be changed to any eight from the total membership. Shop floor soundings confirmed that the established Co-op practice for electing Directors, one from each of the eight trade unions, should continue.

Mike O'Brien, the Sheet Metal Workers' Director, had confided in me and others that he was feeling the strain. The almost constant pressure at every Board meeting he had attended over the past ten months regarding negotiations to improve ex-works motorcycle sale prices, or find an alternative to the NVT product sale agreement, had been stressful. The movement towards recognising management with a pay differential had focused the welders and other skilled members' minds on pursuing a similar approach. It was clear in the Sheet Metal Workers' Union section discussions that there was a majority that felt the Director who was now to be elected should be raising this issue for further Board discussion. During these section discussions I decided that I had kept my mouth shut and head down long enough. I offered my services as Sheet Metal Workers' Director, and was duly elected. It was now time for me to open my mouth where perhaps I could do some good.

At the end of May, copies of Geoffrey Robinson's *Co-op report and projections to Her Majesty's Government* were considered by the Board, the contents of which were based upon his and GKN's findings, the aim being to negotiate a secure and viable future for the Co-op, with it in control of its own sales and marketing organisation. With the financial position worsening by the day, there was an urgent need to proceed with the application to HMG. The report was presented by Geoffrey Robinson for discussion at a fully attended (current/previous Advisors and Directors) Board meeting on 18th June 1976.

The Co-op detailed report and projection to HMG was in four parts:

1. A review of the Co-op's first year of operation, 6th March 1975 to 31st March 1976.
2. Profit & loss and cashflow projections for 1976/77, assuming no new products.
3. Proposal for introducing a face-lifted Bonneville and a 900cc superbike (T180).
4. Assuming (iii) profit & loss and cashflow projections for 1977/78 on an ongoing basis.

Geoffrey Robinson had advised the Directors that with GKN's involvement now ended, the Co-op would need to be managed correctly to achieve the projections contained in the report.

The Beneficiaries' Annual General Meeting (AGM) took place on 5th July, followed by the AGM of the Co-op (Synova Motors Limited) on 9th July 1976. The Co-op AGM began with the Chairman, Dennis Crowder-Johnson, welcoming the two new union nominated Directors, Bill Farndon and John Rosamond – Bill from the AEUW and me from the Sheet Metal Workers', both skilled trade unions. The business of the AGM was then duly performed by the Trustees discharging their duties. The annual report and accounts for the previous thirteen month period ending 31st March 1976 were agreed and adopted – they indicated a loss of £1m. The nominated Directors were formally appointed, the remuneration of the auditors was agreed, and finally a special resolution was passed: the Co-op trading name of Synova Motors Limited was to be changed to Meriden Motorcycles Limited. The earlier intention to have the word Co-operative in the company's name had not proved possible for legal reasons.

Back at work on the frame section the following Monday, my mind wandered, thinking about the worsening financial position of the Co-op and the negotiations now taking place with HMG and NVT to try and improve our situation. Unfortunately, as with all Co-op negotiations, they would be protracted.

One of the first Board meetings I attended in July 1976 had been called for the Directors to receive legal advice regarding the Co-op continuing to trade. The Company Solicitor, Peter Davis, had been asked to meet with the Directors because of the worsening financial position. He was to advise that under section 332 of the Companies Act 1948, concerning Directors' personal liabilities in the event of fraudulent trading, Directors must satisfy themselves that they are continuing to trade because they believe the financial situation they are currently experiencing will improve. By so doing, the Directors are continuing to trade in the best interests of the creditors. The latest Geoffrey Robinson report and projections for HMG would enable the Directors, following discussion, to decide that they are behaving correctly. This was becoming an extremely bad habit of mine at Triumph – every new experience is a dramatic one!

The Board decided later in July that without an official waiver or deferral by HMG, the £4.2m loan interest of £128,589 due on 21st July 1976 would be paid on the due date. A volunteer team of Co-op members agreed to work over the annual two weeks summer holiday, shipping eighty four motorcycles and improving the financial situation following the HMG interest payment.

Bob Myers, the USA Triumph dealers' spokesman and a good friend of the Co-op, contacted the Chairman during the summer holiday to advise him of quality problems being experienced by dealers. Bob was invited to visit the factory to talk directly to the individual members responsible, and the Co-op offered to cover the cost of this important visit. An additional problem the Co-op was experiencing with the NVT product sale agreement was no feedback from the marketplace. Subsequently checking with NVT revealed numerous letters of complaint regarding quality issues. Copies of these letters were placed on the factory notice boards for the membership to see, and had a dramatic effect, highlighting where quality problems had been purely due to lack of care. The other quality problems were the ones the GKN production engineers had been working on, and underlined the vital need for this production engineering

Here in happier times, Bill Lapworth talks to US dealers leader Bob Myers at Free State Cycle. (Courtesy Mrs Pat Knight)

initiative to be kept going by the Co-op's own recruits. NVT subsequently pushed the Co-op for an increase in its warranty guarantee allowance because of these quality issues.

The media coverage of the Co-op was more apparent to me when I became a Director. The Co-operative approach to business certainly seemed to polarise public opinion, either totally in favour or totally against. The scrutiny made it feel like working in a goldfish bowl. I felt I had to complain to the Co-op Chairman about being informed of company developments through the press, whilst at the same time receiving legal advice from the Company Solicitor regarding my possible personal liabilities as a Director in continuing to trade.

Lack of motorcycle dispatches during August was due to NVT still trying to finalise with HMG an export credit guarantee pre-shipment pool; when resolved, dispatches began again. The Chairman stressed to meetings of the membership that the immediate Co-op priorities now

Chairman Dennis Crowder-Johnson (left) and Chuck Knight are the other two Co-op representatives visiting Bob Myers at Free State Cycle. (Courtesy Mrs Pat Knight)

were for 350 good quality Bonnevilles to be produced every week. Other top priorities included the introduction of cost savings, and the setting up of a production engineering department to implement the identified engineering changes, now that GKN was coming to the end of its very helpful secondment.

As a Director, I became more exposed to the other production areas of the Co-op and the problems they were experiencing. I soon realised how very lucky I was in the frame section where we had (with only a few exceptions) an excellent team. However, it was always when something different was needed like the alternative product prototypes (the P39 Trident, the Steyr-Daimler Puch moped, and the exercise jogger) that the long-service key skilled members still on some of the sections proved their commitment to the Co-op was still there, if the Directors could only find a catalyst to rekindle their previous enthusiasm. Much of this alternative product prototype work was completed unpaid and out of normal production time, to avoid missing the 350 a week motorcycle build target.

At the end of August 1976, the Co-op had the opportunity to assess buyer reaction by exhibiting an updated premium Bonneville on the Lucas stand at the Earls Court Motorcycle Show. This unofficial exhibit was prohibited under the product sale agreement with NVT, who immediately threatened legal action if it was not removed. The premium model Bonneville was well received on press day, the only exception being the revolutionary (at the time) three-spoke alloy wheels. This Triumph Co-op bike made most of the trade magazines, confirming that in the UK at least, there was a market for an improved superbike Triumph twin at a higher sales price.

On 9th September 1976, the Company Secretary Brenda Price advised that she had become an unpaid Non-Executive Director of P S Motors. The owner of the new company was a Mr Reinhardt, who had been the Triumph distributor in Denmark for many years. He had now purchased from the receiver of NVT Manufacturing Limited the number two Triumph Engineering factory at Meriden (located 200 yards down the road from the Co-op) and the old pattern Triumph spare parts stored inside. P S Motors had been set up to dispose of the 'old pattern' spare parts stock. As P S Motors was only going to sell old pattern Triumph spare parts, Brenda believed her involvement would not be a conflict of interest with her Company Secretary duties at Meriden Motorcycles, the Co-op only producing and selling 'current' Triumph Motorcycle spare parts. Knowing the fundamental part Brenda Price had played in the formation of the Co-op, was now playing in its survival, and would play once the current negotiations were successful and long-term viability pursued, her new circumstances were accepted by the Board.

In response to correspondence from HMG, we would once again have to consider our personal legal position regarding the question of the Companies Act clause 332. This would have to be considered on a number of occasions over the coming months. Geoffrey Robinson's advice was that the Co-op should continue to trade pending a decision by HMG on the waiver of the interest payment, which was due to be paid on 31st December 1976. The negotiating strategy was as follows:

• Renegotiate with HMG the structuring of the capital to reduce or eliminate the interest payment.

• Acquire the marketing rights from NVT, which would involve renegotiating the acquisition of the stocks and product liability insurance and setting up a selling organisation.

• Plan the year 1977/78 with Bonneville production only.

• Pursue new projects for manufacture at Meriden and continue negotiations with Moto Guzzi, Ducati and Steyr-Daimler Puch.

On 27th September, it was reported that the Chairman and Geoffrey Robinson had met the HMG minister Mr Alan Williams and his officials, who were advised that a new Co-op ex-works price to NVT of £650 had been established for the next 3000 motorcycles. This provided continuity of production up to 31st December, but to continue to trade the Co-op still needed the HMG interest waived. On that basis, the Co-op had three months to achieve the three following key elements for future viability:

• Establish proposed new distribution outlets for direct worldwide sales from January 1977 onwards.

• Negotiate terms for the acquisition of selling rights from NVT.

• Establish alternative new products to be produced at the Meriden Co-op from 1978 onwards.

A factory doctor was appointed on an annual retainer plus call-out fee, to assist the Co-op when personnel medicals were required. The on-site surgery was being upgraded, so no-one was

(Left to right) Jim Barclay, Bob Haines and Chuck Knight admire the Premium Bonneville, to be unofficially exhibited at Earls Court. (Courtesy Mrs Pat Knight)

really surprised regarding this issue. Around this time, rumours started to circulate about one of the Directors misusing the Triumph emergency ambulance to look after his horses – remnants of straw bales had been found inside! This was an opportunity for the Triumph's wicked factory sense of humour to play its part. In mid-October there was an overnight snowfall that had made it difficult for members to travel to work, and it was the main topic of conversation that morning; however this was soon to change.

Word circulated the factory that an elderly 'picket' who worked in the machine shop had suffered a serious heart attack. He had been rushed on a stretcher to the works ambulance, which was found to be full of bales of hay, which had to be unloaded before the ambulance could set off for the Coventry and Warwickshire Hospital Accident and Emergency department seven miles away. Lights flashing and siren sounding, the ambulance had finally set off, only to run out of petrol before exiting the factory gates. An emergency 999 telephone call then had to be made for a replacement ambulance, though unfortunately, all of the delays resulted in the man's death before the back-up ambulance's arrival.

Within minutes of this rumour starting, 700 individuals were discussing and protesting about what appeared to be a very sad state of affairs at the Co-op; there was absolute outrage. It was, of course, all a complete fabrication based on what could happen if the Co-op's emergency ambulance continued to be used as a horsebox. The desired effect had been achieved; pre-occupation Triumph humour had returned with a vengeance!

On 11th October, Mr Farndon presented a written statement signed by 96 skilled Co-op members, seeking to determine future policy on the introduction of differential wage rates. I had previously raised this matter, as key-skilled individuals were leaving for higher wages elsewhere. The skilled members' statement would be circulated, enabling consideration of the implications of this possible change to the Co-op.

Verbal approval had now been given by HMG for overtime working at the Co-op. Discussion regarding the waiver of interest and capital reconstruction would be delayed until the Boston Consulting Group had completed a report on the future viability of the Co-op. The negotiating team had expressed a wish to be involved in setting the consultancy group's terms of reference. The Minister of State had recommended Mr Phil Love for the vacant Co-op Chief Executive's job. Mr Love, prior to his retirement two years earlier, was Managing Director and Chairman of Glacier Metals. He also came highly recommended by Sir Wilfred Brown, a colleague of Harry Urwin (Deputy General Secretary of the T&G) on the Industrial Advisory Board. Love indicated that his views were in harmony with those of the Co-op, and, having considered the Co-op's present trading situation and what was being asked of him, he was prepared – for a period of one year – to accept the position of Chief Executive. He was subsequently appointed on 25th October 1976.

Phil Love started at the Co-op on 1st November 1976, immediately getting involved in ex-work price negotiations with Dennis Poore at NVT. By December, a complete breakdown in talks had occurred, and, at the request of the Directors, Geoffrey Robinson became involved again. Robinson soon advised that in view of the present impasse, the only options now available were that the Co-op purchases the marketing rights from NVT, or NVT purchases the Co-op! NVT indicated that it was not interested in purchasing the Co-op. Dennis Poore agreed to withdraw from the agreement he thought he had reached with Phil Love in principle, which on detailed examination was found to be unacceptable. Negotiations to sell the marketing rights to the Co-op then began in earnest. By 8th December the Co-op was experiencing a critical cashflow situation, and once again we were considering our legal position regarding continued trading on behalf of the creditors. NVT was informed of the critical financial position of the Co-op, and a final formal offer of £500,000 subject to contract was made to Dennis Poore, dependent on HMG providing sufficient loan capital to complete the transaction. On 9th December 1976, the NVT Board accepted in principle the Co-op's offer of £500,000 for the Triumph marketing rights and associated assets. With the principles of the deal with NVT agreed, it was then a matter of reaching agreement with HMG to finance the purchase and restructure the original £4.2m loan capital, enabling the Co-op to continue trading. These negotiations would take time to conclude, so production levels needed to be cut back in the New Year.

The plan put to HMG was based upon new marketplace soundings for distribution, and a sale of envisaged production levels of 14,500 motorcycles a year. Initial indications coming from the Boston Consultancy Group, who had taken into account the build up of motorcycle market stocks during the protracted negotiations with NVT, suggested production levels of 11,000/12,000 a year would be more realistic. In this situation, production levels at the factory would have to be about 270 a week – a 23 per cent reduction on the original planned levels. This cutback equated to 160 redundancies, or a 4-day week, or further alternative product work; not pleasant prospects for the Co-op to consider over the festive break.

On 5th January 1977, we were advised that HMG had refused to provide the additional £500,000 finance to fund the Co-op's purchase of the NVT marketing rights and assets. However, it was prepared to provide the Co-op with time to consider other options by agreeing to defer the £207,636 interest payment that had been due on 31st December 1976.

On 14th January it was reported that an intervention by Jack Jones, General Secretary of the T&G, had succeeded in persuading HMG to ask Harold Lever (Chancellor of the Duchy of Lancaster) to further consider the Co-op's submission for finance to purchase the NVT marketing assets. Once again, the T&G and Jack Jones had come to the rescue of the Co-op. Harold Lever asked Geoffrey Robinson to resubmit a modified plan for consideration accompanied by his personal commitment that with the changes now being proposed, there would be a good chance of Co-op success. Geoffrey Robinson agreed, providing that certain conditions were met by HMG, NVT and the Co-op; these were outlined in a letter to Harold Lever dated 13th January 1977:

As far as Government support is concerned the following is required:

i) The purchase of NVT's selling rights will be carried out in a way that does not add to Meriden's current level of indebtedness to HMG.

ii) The Government will waive interest on its existing debenture for the whole of 1977 and 1978.

iii) The Government will subordinate its security on Meriden assets.

iv) The Government will make available to Meriden a further £200,000 interest free loan.

v) The Government will arrange to switch the entire ECGD export finance facility of £6m to Meriden in such a way as to enable the Co-op to re-purchase all motorcycles already sold to NVT at a price agreed between NVT and the Co-op, which price shall not represent more than the updated cost of these machines to NVT.

vi) The Government will agree to consider on a commercial basis any future proposition put forward by Meriden.

vii) The Government will grant Meriden flexibility to establish a two tier wage structure for employees at the Co-op as part of its Phase II agreement, which will be operative from 1st March 1977, to appoint management on terms of its own discretion and to arrange working hours for all employees without reference to the Department of Industry.

As far as NVT is concerned the following is required:

i) That the £500,000 paid by HMG (via the Co-op) to NVT for the selling rights will be returned to HMG in partial redemption of HMG's preference share holding in NVT. The terms of this transaction will be negotiated between NVT and HMG and will be on the basis that there will be no loss to HMG on a reasonable commercial assessment of the value of the number of preference shares so redeemed.

ii) NVT will make available to the Co-op a two year interest free loan of £300,000. Dennis Poore has clearly privately indicated to me his willingness to do this.

iii) NVT will sell back to the Co-op those motorcycles in its ownership at their updated cost to NVT as already indicated in point (v) above.

iv) NVT will use its best endeavour to encourage its USA selling operation to work on the present basis for Meriden.

As far as the Co-op is concerned the following will be required:

Mr Dennis Crowder-Johnson will continue as Chairman of the Policy Board, subject to re-election, for a period of at least two years.

A reconstitution of the Policy Board to include at least two Non-Executive Directors (initially myself and Mr Jim Houlston – Managing Director of HPL Consultants Limited) and a Managing Director to be appointed who will be responsible for execution of the policy and objectives of the Policy Board.

A formally constituted Management Board, headed by the Managing Director, will be established to carry out the objectives of the Policy Board. The Management Board will be constituted as follows:

Formally Constituted Management Board
Managing Director – TBA
Company Secretary and Finance Director – Miss B Price
Supply Director – Mr B Baldwin
Sales Director – TBA
Engineering Director – TBA

The Board of Directors indicated that it would like to discuss Geoffrey Robinson's proposals with him, and a meeting was scheduled for Sunday 16th January, which ultimately endorsed the revised Co-op proposals that had succeeded in persuading HMG to subordinate the loan, defer interest and also possibly buy out NVT. However, HMG had made its agreement conditional on production being cut to reduce stocks in line with those figures provided by the Boston Consultancy Group. This was the reason for the factory having to close for February 1977 and the lower production rate of 250 motorcycles per week in the revised plan projections.

Geoffrey Robinson spoke on 22nd January of the possibility that Sir Arnold Weinstock, Chairman of GEC, was considering providing the required Co-op management by way of secondment, and might also be getting financially involved. It was only with the promise of GEC participation that HMG was prepared to reconsider the Co-op proposals. The Co-op Chairman was invited to attend a meeting with Alan Williams, the Industry Minister, on 24th January at which he felt he would probably be asked to indicate that the Co-op would accept management and all the conditions in the revised proposals of 13th January. Subsequently, it was unanimously agreed that the Chairman could provide that commitment to the Minister in line with the revised proposals submitted to Harold Lever on 13th January 1977. On 25th January, the Chairman reported on the previous day's meeting with the Minister; John Grattan and Geoffrey Robinson had also been in attendance. The Minister had indicated what the Government may be prepared to do subject to Cabinet approval, namely:

• Subordinate its security on all the assets to all other creditors.
• Capitalise all interest payments due from the Co-op for a period of two years.

• Make available by way of a grant the necessary finance to acquire the selling rights and related assets from NVT.

• Switch the £6m ECGD facility presently held by NVT.

It was understood that GEC's provision of assistance would be:

• It would immediately purchase from the Co-op 2000 bikes at an ex-works price of £500 each.

• It would retain a handling charge of £15 on each bike sold, but apart from the handling charge it would pay back to the Co-op the entire surplus between the £500 ex-works price and the actual price at which they resold the bikes.

• It would provide, free of charge and on an interim basis, a Managing Director and Sales Director, and help to establish as soon as possible a management team along the lines set out in the Co-op's submission to the Department of Trade. Whilst establishing this, it would bridge the gap with supporting management personnel as required and as agreed between itself and the Co-op.

• It would make available, free of charge, research and development support to help resolve current problems on the Bonneville motorcycle, in particular those relating to vibration and oil leaks.

The Chairman further reported that he had drawn the Minister's attention to the fact that the offer did not fully meet the assistance requested by the Co-op in the following four areas:

1) The Government offer did not provide for the extra £500,000 working capital.

2) The terms under which GEC would purchase the 2000 bikes provided a less immediately beneficial cashflow to the Co-op than if the bikes were shipped against ECGD guarantee – but admittedly, there were other off-setting benefits in the GEC proposals.

3) The Government proposals did not provide cash to meet the excess costs of the stock repurchased from NVT over the ECGD guarantee used by NVT for its initial shipment.

4) The immediate effect of the above three factors would be to make the current cash situation very tight.

Following discussion, it was agreed that provided Geoffrey Robinson could secure the bank overdraft facility of £500,000 he was actively pursuing, the best course of action to take in the interests of the Co-op Beneficiaries, trade creditors and the Government was to proceed with the acquisition of the selling rights and assets in accordance with the Government and GEC proposals. Agreement to the Government proposals had to be given by Cabinet, and it was expected that a reply would be received later that week.

The implications of the new Co-op proposal were considered. With great reluctance, production had to cease for the month of February, and thereafter be reduced to 250 motorcycles a week. To achieve this, it would be necessary to reduce the number of members by 160. A mass meeting of the whole workforce would need to take place as early as possible that week.

5

FACING UP TO COMMERCIAL REALITY

The Co-op Chairman, Dennis Crowder-Johnson, had held a mass meeting of the membership on 6th January 1977 to report on the critical state of negotiations with HMG, who had refused the Co-op's request for further loan capital to purchase the Triumph sales and marketing rights from NVT. However, HMG had provided a glimmer of hope at that time, agreeing to the Co-op's request to defer the £207,636 interest that should have been paid on 31st December 1976.

This decision had provided the Co-op Directors and their advisors with a little time to consider possible alternative proposals. Unfortunately, news of the HMG decision had been leaked to *The Financial Times* and a story appeared in the following day's edition. The Chairman had asked for and received the mass meeting's endorsement that the Directors should explore all avenues left open to the Co-op, and report further once a plan of action had been determined. The Meriden Co-op was not going to fold without a fight.

Once again, the T&G and its leadership had not been found lacking, coming to the aid of the Co-op in its hour of need. Jack Jones' crucial intervention with Government, via Harold Lever, secured the start of support for a Stage 2 Meriden Co-op. This would not have happened if it was not for Geoffrey Robinson's brilliant and tenacious leadership of the Co-op negotiating team. The provision by GEC's Chairman, Sir Arnold Weinstock, of £1m liquidity capital for 2000 stockpiled motorcycles, and by way of secondment some of his top GEC management, were further vital elements of the revived Co-op proposals.

However, the overall plan upon which HMG's further support now totally depended was the reduction of Triumph motorcycle stocks, and a cutback of factory production capability from 350 to 250 motorcycles each week. The suggested way of achieving the production capacity cut was by redundancy. Initially, the Co-op Directors were stunned by the clinical commercial simplicity of the proposed action; lay the factory off for the month of February, make 160 members redundant and restart production again on 1st March 1977, now manned to produce just 250 motorcycles a week.

In discussions with the Department of Employment, the trade union full-time officials and over several more Advisory Board meetings, it was clear that there was major opposition to 160 redundant members paying with their jobs for the benefit of a Stage 2 Meriden Co-op. Accordingly, a more palatable way of achieving the cuts to motorcycle stocks was agreed. The factory would be laid off for three weeks, starting 7th February. Motorcycle production would recommence on 1st March working a four-day week, and in addition every effort would be made to start production of the planned alternative products. Although by so doing it was accepted that this was less commercially satisfactory, a four-day week working would share equally amongst the membership the level of individual economic pain.

Whilst this was the overall plan, the Chairman had indicated there would be a need for key members to work and be paid normally from the second week of the February layoff, and also to continue to work normal hours during the short-time working period, if the Co-op was still to function.

When addressing the membership on 31st January 1977, the Chairman would bring them right up to date, with full details of the resubmitted HMG proposals and their implications regarding the motorcycle stock reduction, factory layoff and short-time working as an alternative to redundancies, and also the vital need of key individuals continuing to work whilst this was happening.

PROPOSED MOTORCYCLE STOCK REDUCTION PROGRAMME
Stop materials intake during February.
Lay off the workforce for three weeks commencing 7th February, except for key people who would be required to:
• Carry out conversions to the stocks of finished motorcycles.
• Balance finished component stocks.
• Build up spare part stocks.
• Assemble the Moto Guzzi motorcycles.
• Assemble Steyr Daimler Puch joggers.
• Assemble Steyr Daimler Puch maxi mopeds.
Operate a 4-day working week from March onwards with no redundancies – this situation to be reviewed monthly.
Suspend for a period staff status terms.

The Chairman indicated to the mass meeting that following discussion, he would be asking the members for their endorsement of the motorcycle stock reduction programme, upon which rested the HMG funding proposals for Stage 2 of the Co-op. This endorsement was subsequently received.

The seconded GEC management team attended its first Co-op meeting on 14th February. Mr W Morgan (Deputy Managing Director GEC Limited) was the most senior individual. He indicated that it was GEC's intention to provide advice, not make decisions for the Co-op; there was no limit to the seconded management support. All concerned were prepared to help in any way possible.

The initial GEC team would be Mr M Craddock (General Management), Mr J Lightfoot (Production Engineering), Mr B Reilly (Sales) and Mr P Morton (Design Engineering vibration expert) – not present on this occasion.

Mr Craddock presented an initial overview of the Co-op situation with charts showing projected sales, production and market stocks for 1977. These projected sales indicated present losses of £47 per bike in the UK and £91 in the USA, although these were based on a 5-day week with production increasing to 300 motorcycles a week, and no spare parts margin had been included. Mr Craddock went on to say that in view of these facts, he felt it essential that material and labour savings were made. He was advised by Derrick Hudson, responsible for personnel, that the uncertainty regarding the Co-op's future had already reduced the membership from

700 to 670 without resorting to redundancy; this trend would probably continue. It was hoped to retain the key members, however, as without their contribution the Co-op would not function. Mr Craddock envisaged the cash inflow from GEC to re-finance stockpiled motorcycles would be £1/2m in February and £1/2m in March, reducing as bikes were financed against the proposed ECGD facility, then building up once again with the £1m GEC funding from July onwards.

John Grattan commented that he did not want anyone in the seconded management team to be under any illusion that the Co-op membership would ever be a 'tame' workforce!

By the middle of February 1977, the draft agreement covering sales of motorcycles to GEC had been drawn up and implemented, and by the end of February, Geoffrey Robinson was able to advise that the difficult and protracted detailed negotiations to purchase the Triumph marketing rights from NVT had now reached a heads of terms agreement acceptable to the Co-op.

In preparation of implementing the Co-op's own marketing activities, there was now urgent action required to set up distribution companies in the USA and Australia. Miss Brenda Price, the Co-op's Company Secretary, would undertake setting up the USA company and running it for the initial three months of operation. Lord Stokes (Geoffrey Robinson's old boss at British Leyland) had agreed to help with the vital formation of the Co-op's new distribution activities. Initially he would be aiding Brenda Price in the USA. Mr Len Hamilton, who was the previous Australian Triumph factory representative up to 1973, was prepared to undertake the required setup work.

Although a great deal of progress had been made, it was felt that to go ahead as planned with the March resumption of factory production even on a 4-day working basis, without first establishing overseas distribution, would quickly result in a critical cashflow situation prejudicing the ongoing operation of the Co-op. Accordingly, it was reluctantly decided to continue the factory layoff until negotiations had at least finalised the agreements to sell motorcycles in the UK, Canada, Europe and Australia.

A mass meeting would now take place at 8.00am on Monday 28th February, when the membership would be brought up to date by Geoffrey Robinson and the Co-op Chairman on the need to continue the factory layoff to conclude the negotiations.

Sufficient progress with the negotiations enabled factory production to restart on Wednesday 23rd March at the rate of 250 motorcycles per week. Demand in the marketplace for motorcycles and spare parts allowed 5-day working, with selective overtime to soon be considered. The majority of the members (including myself) had been 'laid off' for seven weeks, so it would be nice to return to the day job for which I was paid – and there was even a 5 per cent pay increase to look forward to. The GEC seconded management expressed concerns regarding a basic rate increase, feeling a productivity based scheme would be more appropriate. However, it was decided to go ahead immediately with the basic rate increase in an effort to retain the key members that were continuing to leave.

Given the possibility of at last reaching the calmer waters of a refinanced Stage 2 Meriden Co-op, I was able to reflect on the fifty Board meetings I had attended over the eight months since I became a Director. My predecessor had warned me of the stressful nature of the job, but I don't think any amount of forewarning could have prepared me or any other new Directors for what they would face! There were very few Board meetings during my period of involvement when we were not considering either a critical financial problem or a breakdown of negotiations, or both, which as a direct result could lead to personal liabilities. At least I could escape from time to time, and bury myself in my day job. When my colleagues saw me deep in thought, they always raised my spirits with a dose of Triumph humour. One particular comment

**Production of the super light, high performance Strongbow grass track
Bonneville sponsored by Bulmers provided a welcome distraction.
(Courtesy James Crosby photography, London Motorcycle Museum)**

I remember well was "Don't worry about it, in years to come you will see this experience as character building!"

Factory security at this time was considered inadequate, and I was asked to take on the responsibility of improving it, and reporting progress as this was achieved. Mr Craddock suggested that a book on factory security be procured, and he would also provide an introduction to one of GEC's senior security officers.

Mr W H Farndon, the AEUW Trade Union Director, resigned in mid April; he was to go into hospital for an operation and would require several months to recover. Mr J F Williams was elected as the new AEUW Director on 15th April 1977. John Williams had previously undertaken this role prior to Mr Farndon.

On 29th April it was agreed that a detailed memorandum signed by the Chairman would be distributed to all Co-op members at 8.00am that day, prior to a 9.00am mass meeting. This would provide details of the completed negotiations, prior to the Directors signing the various legal agreements. By adopting this procedure it would enable the membership's approval and authorisation of the Director's action to be secured. The mass meeting would be taken by the Co-op Chairman; Geoffrey Robinson would be present should the membership wish to ask him any questions on the deal.

MEMORANDUM TO ALL MEMBERS OF MERIDEN MOTORCYCLE CO-OPERATIVE
The purpose of this letter is to inform all members of the Co-op that the negotiations have now been completed for the Co-op to acquire the selling rights for Triumph motorcycles from NVT. The new arrangements which have been negotiated with the various parties and which have made the acquisition possible are set out below. They are recommended by the Board for acceptance by the members of the Co-op. The terms are as follows:

i) The Government has waived interest for two years on its loan of £4.2m.

ii) The Government has removed its security on the Co-op's assets.

iii) The Government has made a grant to the Co-op of £0.5m for the purchase of the selling rights, spare parts and certain other assets.

iv) The Export Credit Guarantee of £6m has been switched from NVT to the Co-op.

v) The Co-op's bank, the National Westminster, has agreed to extend an overdraft facility of up to £0.5m. In exchange for this the bank has assumed the prior charge on the Co-op's assets previously held by the Government.

vi) The General Electric Company has agreed to provide £1m working capital for three years. This will be done by GEC purchasing up to 2000 bikes at £500 per bike. As these bikes are sold (at the full price of course) GEC will withhold a £15 handling charge per bike. There will be no interest payable on the GEC money and the scheme, even taking account of the handling charge, is an extremely advantageous arrangement from the Co-op's point of view, meaning an effective rate of interest of only 3 to 4 per cent.

vii) The Co-op will pay no royalty payments to the receiver and/or liquidator until January 1979. These could have amounted to approximately £70,000 in that period. Instead NVT will make arrangements for payment up to December 1978. Thereafter the Co-op will negotiate its own arrangements with the receiver and liquidator.

viii) The Co-op will acquire at no cost NVT's spare parts stock for Bonneville and Trident machines. The Co-op will also receive the special tooling for the Trident.

ix) There will be no manufacture by NVT or a subsidiary company of NVT of Triumph spares for Bonneville or Trident machines unless we do not want to manufacture any specific Trident parts.

x) The Co-op will acquire on completion NVT's worldwide stocks of Triumph Bonneville motorcycles (expected to be about 3000 in all) at their ECGD financed cost with a further payment towards NVT costs of only £10,000. This sum to be paid out of the sale of Trident parts.

It has been a long, nerve-racking and complicated negotiation. It has involved using lawyers in the USA and Australia as well as in the UK. It has involved us in all sorts of different problems; getting the agreement of the Treasury, Department of Industry, the Department of Trade, the ECGD, the GEC, the National Westminster Bank, the liquidator and receiver of the old NVT manufacturing companies, not to mention getting a deal with NVT. There's no need to say what a hell of a task that is. It has also involved setting up new companies owned by the Co-op in the USA and in Australia. All in all it has taken four months to do. But the Board firmly believes that it was worth fighting the Government's refusal to back us last December, even though it has meant hardship and uncertainty for everyone. The original Government decision was a Cabinet one which we were told was "not negotiable." But with the backing of Harold Lever, Jack Jones and Geoffrey Robinson we decided to fight it nonetheless.

We knew it was going to be a tough time and we knew it could only be done if those of us at the factory had the courage to stick out a layoff and if those negotiating for us had the nerve to go to the brink in the negotiations with the Government and with NVT.

Because we held together and gave that support we have pulled it off. Sales are going well. It is now up to us. Lord Stokes and Brenda Price, who will be for a transitional period of 2-3 months in charge of our American selling operation, will be leaving for the United States over the weekend to organise the American market, which is the top priority. Thereafter Lord Stokes will be heading a sales drive in other overseas markets.

This is a comprehensive package that, whilst not getting everything we might have wanted, particularly in respect of products liability insurance cover which it is becoming increasingly difficult for all motorcycle manufacturing companies to obtain for those of their machines sold in the United States market, the Board nonetheless considers gives the Co-op a sporting chance to prove its competitiveness and viability. And it is on this basis that it is recommended for approval to the members of the Co-op. If approval is given the Board will sign all relevant documents this Friday, 26th April, 1977.

Dennis Crowder-Johnson (Chairman)

The mass meeting of the membership gave their approval of the outcome of the negotiations and authorised the Directors to sign the various legal agreements on their behalf.

On 6th May, the Chairman invited GEC's senior seconded manager, Mr W Morgan, to put forward his views with regard to the current operation of the Meriden Co-op and the involvement of his team. The other GEC managers present would also advise of their initial findings!

Mr Morgan said that at the outset of GEC's involvement with Meriden, they had discussed the situation as far as they saw it and outlined what they then felt needed to be done. Decisions were taken on the areas requiring assistance and certain projects had been implemented in those areas under the guidance of GEC personnel. Congratulations were offered on the completion of the NVT agreement. The business was now launched and we should look at the situation as it presents itself today.

Mr Morgan advised that "we now have a business which is no longer a manufacturing unit doing sub-contract work for someone else, it is therefore important to realise that you are very directly responsible not only for the products but also for the 700 people in this plant, and those people employed in companies abroad, and this is a vastly different situation from that which existed previously. You will very quickly realise that business is a 24 hours a day operation and problems will be presented to you at all times and they have to be solved. Your commitment therefore must be total, in order to operate the business on a sound commercial basis. It is obvious that expertise is in extremely short supply at Meriden, but as far as one can, one learns what has to be done and the role of the GEC team in this respect is to assist and advise."

He then stressed that "the GEC people had become fundamentally interested in the Co-op, and having recognised the dedication of the 700 people involved, felt sure that with constant effort, their desire to re-build the British Motorcycle industry could be fulfilled. Meanwhile in a Co-op where everyone must be treated as equal, it is imperative that you have very clearly uppermost in your minds the well being of both the business and the workforce. I am just as keen as you are to make the Co-op successful, but you must take a tremendous involvement in this."

Mr Morgan was followed by Mr Morton's overview of the engineering development work required.

Mr Morton explained that he had separated the development required into two problem areas, defined by warranty claims that attacked the Co-op's economy. These faults had been statistically summarised in order to establish a clear picture of the situation. It looked like the Co-op was going to lose £8000 to £9000 on imminent warranty claims, many of which could have been avoided by improved quality control or with the aid of simple good housekeeping techniques. Importantly, though, this indicated that it was not just about making costly engineering development changes. In addition to this, the two main areas indicated by the warranty claims that needed investigation were engine improvement and engine vibration.

a) Engine improvement

Cooling system

Oil holes in connecting rods

Redesign of piston

Redesign of cylinder block

Ignition settings

Increased oil flow

b) Engine vibration (possibilities being pursued)

Engine isolation – Mr Phil Love (Consultant)

180 degree crankshaft

Contra rotating balance shafts

In summarising the engineering development work that the GEC team had started, Mr Morton stressed that the Co-op's current minimal approach to engineering would have to change. Mr Jim Barclay had to date almost singlehandedly held the Co-op design, development and production engineering effort together – a fantastic achievement. However, just considering the engineering development now required, the current four-man team needed to be doubled. Paul Morton, assisted by Keith Fentone, subsequently made a speedy breakthrough with piston redesign work, solving a major area of customer warranty complaints. In addition to the attack on warranty claim costs, work needed to be urgently started to meet the future lower exhaust emission levels dictated by legislation, without which the Co-op would no longer be able to sell in the vitally important USA market.

Mr Lightfoot and Mr Chaplin then outlined the GEC production engineering effort that had taken place since their involvement, much of which followed on directly from Mr Morton's earlier development comments.

Many of the problems found were self inflicted; there was a failure to maintain proper quality control standards both on components made at the Co-op and goods bought in finished. Not many suppliers were supplying to the dimensions specified on the engineering drawings, and it was a well known fact that 'suppliers would supply rubbish as long as you paid for it!' Many of the engine castings machined in the factory did not have flat joint faces, challenging the belief widely held at the Co-op that oil leaks were a result of vibration. Mr Chaplin believed it had now been confirmed that by improving the families of tools with which the Co-op manufactured components in four priority areas – crankshaft, cylinder head, gearbox and crank cases – major engineering improvements would be achieved. It was all about setting design standards, and by basic inspection, maintaining them.

Similarly, it was also believed that the variations in levels of engine vibration were due to variations in manufacturing dimensional standards. To achieve the desired improvements the Co-op needed to be spending £4000 to £5000 per month on new manufacturing tooling. By so doing, we would guarantee repeatability and would attack many of the warranty engineering problems.

The seconded GEC team had provided a frank, warts and all report of its initial assessment of the Co-op's engineering production methods and practices, including bought-out component parts. Based upon these findings, it had set objectives to make an immediate positive impact at the Co-op; and had certainly achieved that! To me as a self-declared pragmatic realist, GEC's comments were more severe than I had expected, based upon my own experience and conclusions since I rejoined Triumph. A Meriden Co-op factory using obsolete and worn out machine tools, with the vitally important key workers' morale rock bottom, was bound to create an end product of a lower quality standard than what GEC was used to achieving.

The Co-op's more idealistic members present to hear the GEC comments must have felt devastated, and if this was representative of what 'professional managers' running the Co-op would be like, then their worst fears were vindicated.

It soon became very obvious to me that GEC's strategy was to fulfil its management secondment role with total commitment, until the Co-op's own recruited managers could take over the job it had started. On a number of occasions, Mr Craddock reminded the Directors of this commitment.

Dennis Crowder-Johnson thanked the GEC team for an interesting and informative discussion, and said that the manufacturing difficulties reported by the team all came back to one thing: organisation. He was now sure that everyone recognised the many responsibilities that had to be faced, and agreed that these must be integrated and an organisation structure established.

In June 1977, the membership was advised by way of a USA marketing report from Lord Stokes (placed on works notice boards) of the encouraging situation in the American market. This showed anticipated sales of $600,000 worth of spare parts that year, and $1,000,000 worth of spares and 12,000 motorcycles the next year; very positive information that had a dramatic impact on morale and production levels. On the frame section we were producing frames for a USA spare parts stocking shipment, although prior to this positive report, we were already aware that with the 1977 USA spring selling season over, and 1000 1977 models still in US warehouses, no further motorcycle shipments other than the proposed Silver Jubilee models could be scheduled until the 1978 model production started. Investigations were also under way to establish if some of the US 1977 models could be sold in other markets, as an alternative to heavily discounting their eventual sale in the spring of 1978. Fifty of these stock motorcycles were stripped for sale as spare parts, the availability of which in America was now at critical levels awaiting shipment from the Meriden factory. Mr Brian Reilly (GEC Sales Executive) attended his second meeting on 9th July and presented the finalised proposals on his Silver Jubilee model project.

Mr Brian Reilly reminded that the objective of the commemorative Silver Jubilee model was to rework and convert stockpiled motorcycles into what was planned to be the most attractive and desirable product available during Her Majesty Queen Elizabeth II silver jubilee celebrations. The brilliant Co-op paint shop's staff had brought its vast, unique hand-finishing expertise to bear, in producing a very distinctive and attractive limited edition motorcycle; extra chromium plating glitter crowned the effect. It was believed this model would appreciate in value in years to come. Everyone Reilly had approached in marketing and media circles was extremely excited to be involved, and accordingly was charging only a fraction of their normal fees. It was planned that there would be full page trade press coverage in *Motorcycle, Motor Cycle News, Bike, Which Bike* and *Two Wheeler Dealer*. There would also be half page adverts in the *Sunday Mirror* and *Sunday People*. The *Daily Mirror* had agreed, in view of the planned press coverage, to run a Spot the Ball competition, and the BBC Television programme *Tomorrow's World* was going to raffle a Silver Jubilee bike at the Earls Court Motorcycle Show. The programme's presenter, Raymond Baxter, had agreed to be the personality involved on the basis of the proceeds going to the Royal National Lifeboat Institute charity. A dealer meeting launch would be held at the Meriden factory on Wednesday 10th August 1977, with a press conference the following day. The Co-op membership would be involved prior to the dealer and media promotions, seeing a complete run-through of the planned events, including the television advertisement, and hearing the radio advertisements the dealers could personalise to promote their own dealership locations. In addition, all sales literature would be available for examination.

Mr Reilly and his small team, which included the Co-op's Roger Bryant and Doug Cashmore (UK sales representatives), were congratulated. A very impressive Silver Jubilee project had been created. Initial concerns regarding the promotional expenditure being excessive had now diminished, as the cost had been incorporated into each Silver Jubilee model at £30 per bike, and hopefully would guarantee the sale of 1000 of the stockpiled motorcycles in the UK.

Mr Reilly asked Chairman Dennis Crowder-Johnson and Felix Kean, who was responsible for Co-op PR, to welcome dealers and the press when they arrived at the factory, and asked that the other Directors accompany those who wanted to take part in factory tours. By so doing, he

The commemorative Silver Jubilee Bonneville limited edition, seen here in UK form.
(Courtesy James Crosby photography, London Motorcycle Museum)

Certificate of Ownership

This is to certify that

_____

is the Owner of a Triumph Silver 750,
one of a thousand special versions of the Triumph
Bonneville 750 motorcycle manufactured as a
Limited Edition by Meriden Motorcycles Limited
for sale in the United Kingdom, in honour of
the Silver Jubilee of the reign of Her Majesty
Queen Elizabeth II

SPECIMEN ONLY

_____
Chairman,
Meriden Motorcycles Limited

_____
Authorised Triumph Dealer
Date_____

Silver 750 Limited Edition

Silver Jubilee Bonneville certificate of authenticity. (Courtesy John Nelson's archive)

The author admires Mick Humphrey's restored US-spec Silver Jubilee Bonneville, winner of best bike on Triumph Day at the Ace Café. (Courtesy Erum Waheed's archive)

felt it would further involve the total membership in what would be a great morale-boosting opportunity to launch the Meriden Stage 2 Co-op. Brian Reilly was thanked for his fantastic contribution.

Moving on, Mr Kean advised of Ted Simon's imminent return to England following his epic four year journey around the world. This amazing adventure had taken him through 54 countries and involved riding 63,000 miles on his Triumph 500cc Tiger 100 motorcycle, a very similar model to that still used by some police forces. Ted's almost bog standard (single carburettor/low compression) Tiger 100 was one of the last to leave the factory prior to NVT's decision in 1973 to stop production of twin cylinder Triumph models and close the Meriden factory. Felix was to invite Ted Simon to attend the Earls Court show at the end of August on press preview day, and also on the high public attendance days (Saturday and Sunday). In honour of his tremendous achievement, Ted Simon was to be invited to exhibit his Tiger 100 in the exact state it arrived back in England, in pride of place on the show stand next to Triumph's sparkling 1978 model Bonnevilles and Tigers. Mr Kean would liaise with the Motorcycle Association's show organiser, Mr Ivor Davies, who probably already had plans for Ted Simon's involvement at Earls Court. Ted Simon was also to be invited to ride his trusty Triumph back home to the Meriden factory in September to enable the Co-op workforce (suitably covered by the media) to give him the rousing welcome he so richly deserved. A presentation to mark the homecoming would also take place.

Brian Reilly's Silver Jubilee model launch performance (because that's what it was) for the Co-op membership had to be seen to be believed. From the moment he discarded the microphone in preference to "booming it to them," (his description of his unique sales presentation technique), he held the gathering captive in the palm of his hand. The Triumph workforce, over generations, had never witnessed such a brilliant performance by a senior Sales Executive; the boost to morale Brian Reilly had forecast was instantaneous.

It was not long before the membership, having returned to its normal Co-op duties, came up with a traditional Triumph response in appreciation – "Brian Reilly's selling performance was said to be almost as good as Geoffrey Robinson's when he sold the idea of supporting the Co-op to Sir Arnold!"

An increase in the ECGD export finance facility would be required to cover shipment of 1000

Silver Jubilee models to the USA. Mr D Martin would soon be appointed Financial Controller/ Company Secretary.

To help us to understand the engineering development work being undertaken on the engine vibration problem, Mr J Chaplin presented a production engineering overview.

a) Engine isolation proposal – Mr Phil Love (Consultant)

Mr Chaplin advised the Directors that there was nothing new about the engine isolation design proposal, which in his opinion was unattractive from a sales point of view, and added to this was the fact that it would not solve oil leaks; they would still remain, as would other machining problems. Whilst costs would be relatively low compared with Mr Morton's contra rotating balance shafts proposal, if the isolation proposal was to fail, especially in the USA, product liability costs would be extremely high.

b) Contra rotating balance shafts proposal – Mr P Morton

Mr Chaplin was of the opinion that Mr Morton's contra rotating balance shafts proposal was a very sound project; in his view that was what the Co-op should aim for, possibly in two years' time, since it would take that long to achieve the tooling requirements. This proposal, he believed, was for the next generation of bikes, rather than a solution to the problem of the current machines.

Costs of tooling and manufacture of components for this proposal would be in the region of £50-60,000. In addition, the cost of new crankcases and crankshafts (together with families of tools), primary chain covers, and timing covers would push the total up to £500,000.

SUMMARY

Mr Chaplin was of the opinion that the previously discussed

Prototype contra rotating balance shafts Bonneville engine (known as the 'pigs in space') cured all the police bike problem vibrations, but tooling costs prevented its production. (Courtesy James Crosby photography, London Motorcycle Museum)

spend on improved tooling and manufacturing methods (£4000 to £5000 per month) would bring vastly improved consistent quality standards, and the vibration solving contra rotating balance shafts proposal should be incorporated in the next face-lifted generation of Co-op motorcycles.

Mr Chaplin was thanked for his assistance in helping us to gain further understanding of the vibration problem.

Dennis Crowder-Johnson had become very enthusiastic about the possibility of alternative products for the Co-op, especially a moped incorporating a Steyr-Daimler Puch engine and cycle parts in a Meriden-produced frame. If we could find a way of pursuing this project, it would provide alternative factory production during the difficult winter months. Mr E J Butler of New London, Connecticut, USA had been showing great interest in this project. The proposal was that the Co-op would manufacture and he would sell in the USA. Mr Craddock had advised against becoming involved in this venture; as it was presently proposed, it was very similar to the NVT marketing arrangement – accordingly the project was shelved. Mr Butler was advised of the decision, but indicated that he would be prepared to order 30,000 of the sample moped at $400 to $425 each. However, without any production costs it was impossible to decide if the moped project was a viable proposition.

On 1st August 1977 the Chairman reported progress in the recruitment of professional management, as agreed for Stage 2 of the Co-op.

a) Managing Director – Mr John Nelson

Mr Nelson, whose background was largely in motorcycles, was a very strong and sincere person who the Chairman believed would have the courage to undertake the challenge that would be provided by Meriden. Mr John Nelson had now accepted the position of Managing Director, and would be able to attend the Silver Jubilee dealers' meeting on 3rd August 1977.

b) Financial Controller/Company Secretary – Mr David Martin

During his secondment from the Co-op's auditors Coopers and Lybrand, Mr Martin had demonstrated the qualities required to undertake this managerial role. Mr David Martin accepted the above position with the Co-op.

c) Chief Engineer – Mr Brian Jones

Mr Jones had undertaken a senior design role at Triumph for many years, and was well respected within the motorcycle industry. Mr Brian Jones had been approached by the Chairman in connection with the position of Chief Engineer.

d) Sales and Commercial Function

Miss Brenda Price had indicated her acceptance of the Sales and Commercial role on her return from America, and it was believed she possessed many qualities that would make her ideally suited.

It was unanimously agreed that we would proceed with the indicated recruitment of the Co-op's own management team, which met that recommended by GEC and the HMG agreement.

With our own professional management being recruited, GEC involvement would inevitably begin to decline. Other than initial GEC Board meeting 'shock tactics', which I felt were counter productive and may have had a more lasting impact than intended, I had nothing but praise for the calibre of the individual seconded managers, and the way they tirelessly pursued the desired Co-op improvements.

The bombshell that no-one could have foreseen was when we learnt of the intended resignations by Geoffrey Robinson as Commercial Advisor to the Co-op, and Dennis Crowder-Johnson as Chairman of the Co-op Policy Board of Directors – Geoffrey, who had given a personal commitment to Harold Lever that he believed the Co-op in its new form "had a good chance of

Very experienced in the motorcycle world, John Nelson accepted the position of Co-op Managing Director. (Courtesy John Nelson's archive)

Highly experienced in Triumph motorcycle design, Brian Jones accepted the role of Co-op Chief Engineer. (Courtesy John Nelson's archive)

success," and Dennis, who had agreed "subject to re-election to remain the Chairman of the Policy Board for at least two years." They were both now to resign just as their negotiated HMG agreement was to be implemented.

6

STAGE 2 CO-OP IDEOLOGY REVISITED

We all knew that coming to terms with the commercial reality of the Stage 2 Meriden Co-op without Geoffrey Robinson and Dennis Crowder-Johnson, two of the main architects who had negotiated the further HMG support, would be difficult.

The press speculation regarding Dennis Crowder-Johnson's resignation ranged from him being fed up with 'eating and sleeping' the Meriden Co-op, to the appointment of professional management meaning he no longer had a role to play. Many of the Co-op membership drew their own conclusions that both his and Geoffrey Robinson's resignations were due to an ideological disagreement regarding the future involvement of professional management. This issue had previously been discussed on 18th June 1976 (see chapter 4), when the Co-op, having lost £1,000,000 in its first year of operation, considered a further application to HMG. The three key participants in that discussion at the time were Geoffrey Robinson, Dennis Crowder-Johnson and Bill Lapworth.

With the successful outcome of the HMG negotiations and purchase of the marketing rights from NVT, the ideological dispute seemed to have been resolved in favour of the Co-op continuing in business. Especially as that future HMG support of the Stage 2 Meriden Co-op was based upon Geoffrey Robinson's 13th January 1977 personal commitment to Harold Lever/ HMG.

Harold Lever asked for Geoffrey Robinson's personal commitment that with the changes now being proposed, there would be a good chance of Co-op success. Geoffrey agreed. providing his conditions outlined in a 13th January 1977 letter to Harold Lever were met by HMG, NVT, and the Co-op:

As far as the Co-op is concerned the following will be required:

Dennis Crowder-Johnson will continue as Chairman of the Policy Board, subject to re-election, for a period of at least two years.

A reconstruction of the Policy Board to include at least two Non-Executive Directors (initially Geoffrey Robinson and Mr Jim Houlston – Managing Director of HPL Consultants Limited) and a Managing Director to be appointed who will be responsible for execution of the policy and objectives of the Policy Board.

A formally constituted Management Board, headed by the Managing Director, will be established to carry out the objectives of the Policy Board.

The Management Board will be constructed as follows:
Managing Director – TBA
Company Secretary and Finance Director – Miss B Price
Supply Director – Mr B Baldwin
Sales Director – TBA
Engineering Director – TBA

The Advisory Board of Directors had endorsed the revised Stage 2 Meriden Co-op proposals on Sunday 16th January 1977, but did not fully implement them. The resignations of the two individuals expected to play such key roles in the quest for long-term viability had a destabilising effect on the Co-op. The uncertainty created caused the membership to divide into two opposing camps. The minority, mostly skilled trade union Co-op members who totally agreed with the need for 'professional management', and the dominant majority T&G members, who did not. Most members now believed the decision to recruit professional management had been wrong, and the main reason for Chairman Dennis Crowder-Johnson's resignation.

The other very contentious issue dividing the two groups was the fact that the recruitment of professional managers at the market's going-rate of pay was seen by the majority to be the thin end of the wedge, which would inevitably lead to granting the known wish of the skilled members: the introduction of a differential pay structure. This would change the equality pay principal that had been a fundamental part of the Co-op since its formation.

The total unity of purpose during the seven-week layoff, which previously had focused minds on trying to ensure the Co-op's future with HMG support, was now lost. We hoped this would prove to be only temporary, and that as we rectified the failings of the original Co-op, it would return. At this moment, however, the discussions and consultations the Directors had with the membership prior to acceptance of the HMG support were forgotten. Also forgotten was the HMG support that had been achieved only following the vital last minute intervention of the T&G General Secretary, Jack Jones, with Harold Lever. Disunity now threatened the Co-op for the first time, and we had to face this threat without Dennis Crowder-Johnson and Geoffrey Robinson, two of our strongest leaders and supporters. So much for my earlier thoughts that with the new HMG agreement establishing the Stage 2 Meriden Co-op, we seemed to be reaching calmer waters!

An insight can be gained into how some of the Co-op Directors were feeling at this time, from the fact that only five of the remaining seven trade union Directors were prepared to sign the notice for the membership wishing the departing Chairman Dennis Crowder-Johnson well, in whatever he chose to do in the future. Of course, at this time it was not generally known that he was to become a full-time T&G trade union official on the south coast of England. If it had been, I am not sure what the Directors would have felt.

However, life goes on, and the T&G trade union elected itself a new Director, Mr Ron Atkinson. The Advisory Board then met informally to discuss the election of a new Chairman.

There were two obvious candidates: John Grattan of the small Co-op membership electricians' union, the EPTU, and John Williams of the second largest Co-op engineering union, the AEUW. Unfortunately, in this time of Co-op disunity neither individual was particularly well revered by the membership as a possible successor to Dennis Crowder-Johnson, because of their known forceful personalities. Accordingly, the Directors were unable to agree on a new Chairman, albeit informally! Out of this total impasse the Directors looked for an independent compromise candidate, who could perhaps unite the Board in these extremely difficult times of the early Stage 2 Meriden Co-op. The Directors chose me, John Rosamond, from the small Co-op membership Sheet Metal Workers' Union. A Board meeting was called on 6th September 1977 to accept Dennis Crowder-Johnson's resignation, and then I was formally elected as Chairman of the Advisory Board of Directors.

One of my first duties as Chairman was to reassure the professional managers that regardless of what some outspoken Co-op members were saying, the policy agreed by the Board of Directors and fundamental to retaining HMG's support was the retainment of the professional management team that had been appointed to run the Co-op via the soon to be established Management Board.

The second important meeting I had as the new Chairman was with Mr Morgan and Mr Craddock of GEC; they too were also obviously very concerned at recent developments. Following my reassurance that the Board policy remained exactly as agreed with HMG and GEC, they seemed a little more relaxed!

A third, perhaps even more important meeting that had been requested by HMG officials followed. Mr Nelson (Co-op MD), Mr Morgan (GEC), Mr Craddock (GEC) and Mr Rosamond (Co-op Chairman) met Messrs Suich, Panton, Troake and Hennessy-Brown from the various HMG departments involved with the Co-op, in what could only be described as a frank exchange of views concerning the new problems both sides were experiencing! This led to a much clearer understanding being established.

I found my first mass meetings of the membership as Chairman particularly difficult. Dennis Crowder-Johnson had become an excellent public speaker and as such was a difficult act to follow. However, with the plenty of practice I was soon to receive, the membership certainly understood exactly what I was saying.

**Ted Simon's Triumph Tiger 100, the fantastic global explorer, seen here on display.
(Courtesy Coventry Transport Museum)**

With the Co-op's first very successful Earls Court Motorcycle Show over, Ted Simon was pleased to take up our invitation to ride home on his Tiger 100 to the Meriden factory, from whence he had left some four years earlier. Ted was now truly at the end of his 63,000-mile circumnavigation of the globe. As expected he was greeted with a very enthusiastic welcome from the whole Co-op workforce, who fully recognised that his fantastic achievement was the best possible endorsement their motorcycles could ever receive. As a token of Triumph's appreciation, Ted Simon was presented with a 750cc factory run-in replacement for his trusty steed, suitably equipped with Craven-provided boxes and screen. The history-making Triumph 500cc Tiger 100-P (serial number DH 31414) that had served Ted Simon so well was now destined to occupy pride of place in the local Coventry Alfred Herbert Museum (later to become the Coventry Transport Museum). Triumph's factory celebrations over, Ted started a new era of his life aboard his unfamiliar 750cc replacement (left foot gear change/right foot brake pedal). It was bound to take some getting used to after 63,000 miles in the saddle of his Tiger 100! (Ted Simon's delightful book *Jupiter's Travels* describes the journey aboard his Triumph).

One of the first Directors' Board meetings that took place under my chairmanship formally accepted the appointments of Mr B Jones as Chief Engineer and Mr F Baker as Quality Controller, and elected Mr F Kean as Vice Chairman of the Board of Directors. A major concern I soon developed was the length of time Board meetings were taking. At one particular meeting, Directors raised eighteen items for discussion under any other business. They ranged from the possibility of an additional security guard dog, to the appointment of a Director with responsibility for the Co-op Social Club! There was a danger of the Advisory Board becoming a full-time occupation, totally reflective of the time the membership was now involved in debate, often at the expense of quality and production.

To try and improve this situation, various sub-committees of the Board were set up to resolve personnel issues, such as a productivity pay scheme with a skill differential element, a Co-op health and safety policy, a statutory required training policy, measures to stop abuses of the staff status, terms and conditions of employment, and the introduction of a Co-op pension and a life insurance scheme. An ad hoc '21 Club' committee that would have considered such matters under the previous Chairman was in the process of being disbanded.

The Managing Director, John Nelson, was now communicating Co-op developments to the membership via John Grattan's excellent idea, *Nelson's Column*. Published regularly, it appeared on notice boards whenever items of note occurred.

On 1st November 1977 we received a very disturbing report from the Sales Director, Miss Price. The financial situation at the US subsidiary company acquired from NVT earlier in May, Triumph Motorcycles (America) Inc (TMA), was giving major concern. Sales to dealers were falling considerably below budget, and consequently TMA was running out of operating cash, making it doubtful that it would be able to meet bills of exchange due in the immediate future. It appeared that TMA's President had not taken effective control of the new company. There was also concern regarding the Sales Vice President and Technical Services Vice President.

The first three TMA dealer meetings were due to take place in less than a week, starting 7th November in Philadelphia, with Chicago and Los Angeles to follow. Positive decisions needed to be taken in order to safeguard the livelihood of the Meriden membership and the future of the Co-op, with the authority of the Board to take whatever action was required. Miss Price, Mr Nelson and Mr Rosamond would leave for California the following day, 2nd November 1977, in order to urgently assess the situation first-hand.

On arrival in California, the Directors found the TMA situation was exactly as reported and discussed by the Board. Accordingly, having first received American legal advice regarding the correct procedure to adopt in these matters, the TMA President and two Vice Presidents were dismissed.

Mr Jack Hawthorne, the original 'second choice' candidate when interviews for TMA President took place, was re-interviewed. In view of his National Field Sales Manager's experience with Honda and him being totally motorcycle sales/dealer orientated, he was felt to be ideally suited to immediately address the TMA sales crisis, and was appointed.

The TMA dealer meetings were well attended, with 182 individuals at the first one in Philadelphia. The dismissals at TMA and appointment of Jack Hawthorne as the new President headed off a planned dealer revolt, at which mass Triumph dealer resignations were to have taken place. As it was, the announced parent company action met with warm applause. The 1978 Triumph models displayed to the dealers were well received, as was the floor planning programme and free telephone WATS (wide area telephone service). The parent company personnel present still took a great deal of stick, especially regarding the availability of spare parts, which to date had been only a little better than when NVT handled Triumph US distribution; very few of the supply improvements that had been promised when the Co-op took over had occurred. John Nelson, who was well known to many of the US dealers because of his previous Triumph spare parts and service experience, was able to reassure the dealers that things were now being set up to ensure the promised improvements would happen.

Based upon our reassurances, we secured from the dealers what they described as a "final last chance" for Triumph. The US dealers told the Directors and the new TMA President that they considered Triumph to be different to the 'normal' American motorcycle company. In the past it had always been a family business in which they actively participated, and as such, in their opinion, they were entitled to assist, criticise and suggest matters that directly affected the company. Accordingly, many suggestions were noted to report back to the factory for consideration or implementation. Surprisingly, engine vibration problems, unlike in the UK, were not even mentioned as being a dealer concern, likely to affect US motorcycle sales. It was spares, spares, spares – get their availability right or you will fail. The meetings in Chicago and California were equally challenging. It was noted that communications between dealers across the vast US were excellent. Many of the individual dealer questions raised were similar to those at the previous meeting, being changed only slightly to take account of the answers we had already given.

The press reception to launch Triumph's 1978 models, held in the TMA Placentia Californian warehouse, was very well attended by all of the major US motorcycle publications. What became known as the 'Placentia Purge' had certainly stirred the curiosity of the press, which seemed genuinely pleased that Triumph had at last returned in strength to the US market.

The Co-op Directors present in the USA were very grateful to Honda, which at one day's notice reluctantly granted Jack Hawthorne leave to join Triumph as the 'new President' at the scheduled dealer meetings. The Japanese President of Honda USA subsequently personally wished Triumph success in all our future endeavours in America.

The remainder of the Directors' time in the US was spent in meetings with the TMA staff, confirming and realigning their working functions, and in discussions with Jack Hawthorne regarding the future operation of the company and policies to be followed. Brenda Price agreed to stay on in the USA for a further ten days to help the new President settle in. Working for Triumph, the new President agreed, would obviously be different to Honda. "In future," Jack Hawthorne said, "he would have to dazzle the dealers with footwork, not new models!"

On our return to the Meriden Co-op in England, John Nelson produced a detailed USA visit Managing Director's report for the Board, following which, via his *Nelson's Column*, it was published for the members on the notice boards. Triumph humour was back in force when I returned to the factory; there were many questions from the membership asking if I had enjoyed my holiday in the States!

David Martin tendered his resignation from the position of Company Secretary due to the amount of time he had to spend involved in meetings. This was preventing him from devoting sufficient time to important financial matters. In future Mrs Hornby would be undertaking the Minutes Secretary's job. By so doing, Mr Martin's future attendance at Board meetings would only be for specific legal or financial discussion. This new approach was acceptable to Mr Martin, who amended his resignation to that of Board minutes taking responsibilities.

On my return from America on 18th November, various rumours and questions were circulating the factory. These were said to have arisen from a recent T&G trade union branch meeting. Having initially discussed the issue with the T&G Director Ron Atkinson, a meeting was arranged with Mr Lapworth, Mr Atkinson and Mr Kean on Saturday 19th November 1977.

ALLEGATIONS, ISSUES AND OUTCOMES ARISING FROM JOHN ROSAMOND'S USA VISIT AND COMMENTS SAID TO HAVE BEEN MADE ABOUT THE PREVIOUS CHAIRMAN.
Alleged US comments by the Chairman about his predecessor – Untrue.
Why is PS Motors being allowed to use the Triumph logo? – Sale of old pattern Triumph parts (p60).
Is Miss Price a PS Motors Director? – Agreed by Co-op Board.
Why can some UK dealers get spare parts when others can't? – Dependent on Co-op stock.
Dismissal of the TMA President and two Vice Presidents – Co-op Board policy.
Allegations about the MD's comments to a visiting US dealer – Untrue
USA eastern rep appointed from UK by MD not subsequently confirmed on US visit – New TMA President's decision.
Alleged statement by GEC's Sir Arnold Weinstock that the Co-op was finished – Seemed unlikely.
Productivity deal: no time to consider before voting on its acceptance – Untrue.

I felt the meeting that had taken place had cleared the air with Mr Lapworth. Satisfactory answers seemed to have been given to all the above agenda items, however Mr Lapworth's remaining specific criticism of the Co-op was its non-compliance, as he saw it, with the originally HMG agreed constitution. In particular, the way the two boards (Advisory and Management) were now set up.

Mr Lapworth would be requesting a meeting with his union members to discuss the matters at hand. This T&G mass meeting took place with the Co-op's blessing, on 23rd November. Mr Atkinson reported on the outcome of the meeting on 24th November. A recommendation was made and carried at the T&G mass meeting that "A full inquiry is conducted into the past and present running of the Triumph Company and that all unions are invited to partake in that inquiry." One of the main criticisms at the meeting, Mr Atkinson reported, was that the Board was not working in accordance with the original constitution of the company.

Following lengthy discussion Mr Peter Davis, the Company Solicitor, explained in detail the Co-op's constitution documents. Mr Davis initially studied a copy of the minutes of Mr Lapworth's meeting with T&G members, and advised that he was of the opinion that they merely questioned the constitution of the company and the way it was being run. The remainder of the questions asked at the meeting were purely innuendo.

Mr Davis then re-appraised the constitution of the company, and stated that:

"The management of the company as it now stood was much closer to the original outline of the constitution as it was proposed and submitted to Government, on 8th April 1974 than it had been during the previous two years." The original outline of the constitution was as follows:

8TH APRIL 1974 PROPOSAL TO HMG DEPARTMENT OF INDUSTRY BOARD OF DIRECTORS
The Board has the same legal status as any other limited company Board and its members will be formally appointed by the Trustees. In practice the Board will be known as the Advisory Board.
The Advisory Board will consist of:
8 representatives, one elected from each of the eight unions
1 Government representative
1 private sector representative
The Managing Director
2 outside representatives
The Government and private sector representatives are necessary in respect of the anticipated financial contribution each will make and it is desirable that they should have a strong financial background. It is envisaged that the outside representatives would come from trade union and industrial organisations in the Coventry area.
The Chairman of the Board would normally be elected by all eight plant trade union representatives but initially the Co-op's wish is that Mr Geoffrey Robinson, Chief Executive of Jaguar Cars, should be the Chairman as well as the outside representative from local industry. Geoffrey Robinson is thought to be willing to serve provided permission is obtained from the Chairman of British Leyland. The trade union representatives would have a majority on the Board and would ensure close and continuous consultations with their members who have elected them and who would constitute the entire workforce since the plant would operate on a closed shop principle.
The Main Functions of the Advisory Board will be:-
i) Appointment of the Management Board.
ii) Approval of the budget and operating plans of the Management Board.
The proposed structure and method of recruiting the Management Board is described below.
Here it is important to note that the need for capable professional management is fully accepted by the Co-op and that flexibility and speed in the direction of the day-to-day commercial operations must be available to the Management Board if it is to operate effectively.
The relationship between the two boards would be developed over a period of time along accepted lines of delegated responsibility. It is envisaged that the Advisory Board would review the Management Board's results and policy proposals on a monthly basis and would retain the ultimate sanction on major policy issues such as capital expenditure projects (above a certain level), pricing policy and model policy.
The structure and recruitment of the Management Board:
As has been said, the need for professional management is accepted by the Co-op and it is also realised that the Management Board's structure and its operational relationship to the Advisory Board must reflect the real world needs of conducting business in a competitive environment.
The proposed structure accordingly follows orthodox principles of engineering companies and would be as follows:

Managing Director

| *Finance Manager* | *Manufacturing Manager* | *Purchase Manager* | *Chief Engineer* | *Sales/Service Manager* |

The reader should compare the original proposed 8th April 1974 Stage 1 Meriden Co-op structure agreed with HMG (page 63), with the structure subsequently required of the

Co-op for Stage 2 HMG support. There is little difference, except under Stage 2 it was now to be implemented.

Having received this reassuring legal advice, it was agreed that a mass meeting of the membership would be held at 3.00pm on Friday 25th November, at which time the Company Solicitor, Mr Davis, would explain to the entire workforce the situation regarding the stage one and Stage 2 Co-op constitutions. The Chairman would answer any other questions that occurred.

On Monday 28th November we discussed the outcome of the mass meeting on the previous Friday and concluded that there was a major communication problem with the membership. Various ideas were considered to improve the situation, but in the short-term the Chairman would issue for the notice boards a brief note of what was being discussed at each meeting.

For the longer term solution to communication with the membership, a proposal emerged from the Beneficiary Co-op owners (the membership). This was that "three of the vacant places on the Advisory Board of Directors should be filled by members elected without reference to the eight trade unions," thus establishing a Policy Board of eight Directors nominated and elected by each of the eight trade unions, and a further three Directors nominated and elected by the total membership. This was a hybrid variation of the idea first proposed by the former Chairman Dennis Crowder-Johnson, prior to the previous AGM when the Directors had sounded out their members regarding dropping the original principle of one Director from each of the eight trade unions, in favour of electing the eight most suitable individuals from the total Co-op membership. At that time the change was rejected, the non T&G unions suspecting an Advisory Board takeover by the dominant T&G membership.

A letter to Mr Lapworth regarding the outcome of his T&G mass meeting and the Company Solicitor's advice was published on the Co-op notice boards. This action met with a request from him for a right of reply, and subsequently his statement that he was not asking for a meeting with Directors, he had resigned as an advisor to the Board in April 1975 because he disagreed with the way the Co-op was being run then, and he still did! His right of reply letter was also published on the notice boards.

Mr Craddock advised that there were no longer any stockpiled motorcycles financed by GEC in the magnet pool at Rugby. Should the Co-op wish to sell motorcycles direct to the UK dealers from now on, without using the GEC facility, a £27 service fee saving per motorcycle would result. It was agreed that the Company Secretary Mr Martin and GEC's Mr Morgan should draft a letter terminating the agreement between the Co-op and GEC's magnet financial facility from 24th November 1977.

The Directors then considered the recent mass meeting comments of the membership, "that they felt the Managing Director should be more involved with the day-to-day manufacturing side of the business." This was opportune, and would enable the intended Stage 2 Meriden Co-op Advisory and Management Boards structure now to be implemented.

On 30th November we considered progress being made towards implementation of Co-op life insurance and pension schemes; confirmation of a Ministry of Defence order for 79 police escort motorcycles (value £90,000) was also advised. The Managing Director also presented his assessment of the production build programme, up to September 1978. Showing targets ranging from the current 280 per week to 370 per week by September 1978, this programme would be published on the notice boards.

The Chairman reported that Mr Morgan, Deputy Managing Director of GEC, had now indicated that with the Co-op's own management team taking over the duties previously undertaken by those seconded from GEC, it was opportune for GEC to withdraw. GEC's

John Hallard trained in the experimental department, and quickly developed a reputation as the Co-op's 'wheelie king.' Here he is aboard a prototype T140D Bonneville special. (Courtesy John Hallard's archive)

Mr Craddock and the Co-op's Mr Martin had jointly drawn up a press statement to announce this fact. Following minor amendments this was agreed and issued on 6th December 1977. The press statement simply thanked GEC for its "valuable contribution," and confirmed that should further advice be required from GEC, it remained only "a telephone call away."

On 11th December we met the Under Secretary of State for Industry Mr R Cryer, Mr N Atkinson (Labour MP for Tottenham) and Mr A George from the DTI office at Birmingham. Mr Kean gave the visitors a tour of the factory so that they could witness Co-op motorcycle production first-hand. Following this, discussion concentrated upon the possibility of a Metropolitan Police Motorcycle order and research and development co-operation with Dr Geoffrey Roe's team at Manchester University. The Met Police had tested and liked the contra rotating balanced Triumph police prototype, and were now, subject to availability and specification, considering buying British instead of German.

On the 14th December, Mr Barclay announced that the T140E 1978 USA emission standard test motorcycle had satisfactorily completed the 9500 miles special cycle endurance programme. To achieve this, two test riders and support staff had been working twelve-hour shifts at the Motor Industry Research Authority (MIRA) at Nuneaton. We all breathed a sigh of relief; Triumph Motorcycles could continue to be sold in our vital US volume market in 1978.

The T140E (emissions compliant) Bonneville had to be rapidly developed to meet the stricter American EPA requirement. (Brochure picture)

At the mass meeting of the membership on 15th December the graded bonus scheme, which had taken months to devise in order to meet HMG Department of Employment productivity payment legislation, was rejected. Subsequent discussion on 19th December evolved a much simpler scheme, whereby the 255 skilled Co-op members would each receive a £4 differential out of the productivity bonus fund – all monies over and above that figure would be shared equally amongst the total membership. This was now accepted as a basis for a Co-op bonus scheme. A 'Christmas box' bonus of £25 per member was already on offer to the membership, in return for 1200 motorcycles to be built and shipped during the twenty working days run up to the festive holiday.

On 22nd December, the Chairman reported that he had been contacted by Mr Morgan of GEC, advising that a journalist at *The Financial Times* had received information suggesting the Co-op was in a state of chaos. It was believed that the information being referred to could have come from the notice board notes on the Lapworth/T&G members call for an inquiry into the Co-op. Mr A Smith intended to write an article on the Co-op, to be published in *The Financial Times* on 4th January 1978. Should the article be of a destructive nature, which seemed possible, there could be serious commercial consequences. It was agreed that the Chairman should arrange to meet Mr Smith, in an effort to try and prevent the publishing of any incorrect facts. With this on our minds it was certainly difficult to enter into the festive spirit over Christmas.

John Rosamond and John Nelson met Arthur Smith of *The Financial Times* on 29th December 1977. As suspected, he was in possession of a copy of the Co-op notice board notes. The mass meeting concerned was when questions raised by Mr Lapworth with T&G members were answered by the Chairman. Over a three hour meeting, the MD and Chairman tried to convince the journalist that the opinions portrayed by Mr Lapworth were out of touch and not representative of the Stage 2 Meriden Co-op. Today's Co-op was now moving closer and closer to that intended when the Co-op was first set up in 1975. Whether Messrs Nelson and Rosamond had succeeded, no one would know until the article was due to be published.

Mr Smith phoned John Rosamond on 6th January 1978 quoting various points as they were to appear in his delayed article about the Co-op. It now seemed that the article could be viewed as constructive criticism of recent events at the Co-op – we had succeeded in our efforts to prevent a commercially destructive broadside, and a more balanced factual story was now to be published. Since Dennis Crowder-Johnson's resignation, the Advisory Board had consciously tried to keep the amount of Co-op exposure in the media to an absolute minimum, recognising that the previous policy of mass coverage – continually promoting how wonderful working at the Co-op was – had played a major part in lowering morale; after all, the membership were living the real story, which was nothing like the public image that had been created.

Members' absences due to long-term illness were once again having a major effect on production target shortfalls. It was not only their absence that was causing problems, it was also the psychological effect that known 'malingerers' amongst the genuine long-term sick were having on Co-op members. Derrick Hudson, the Co-op's Personnel Manager, had undertaken a tremendous amount of work determining how disciplinary action could take place, and was proceeding accordingly. The long-term sick members up to this time, although absent, remained on the manning level strength. It was now agreed that in future such individuals would be placed in a long-term sick 'pool of labour'. This new policy immediately allowed recruitment of 30 replacements. On return to work, the long-term sick would be offered employment in any suitable vacancies available at that time. Production targets were now met without the previous excessive premium-rate overtime working.

The meeting on 16th/17th January was an extremely long one, even by Co-op standards. Many aspects of the present and future operation were reviewed, perhaps the most important of which was the introduction of the Stage 2 Meriden Co-op HMG commitment, the new Advisory Board and Management Board structure. Although – as mentioned earlier – this had been in the original proposals for the Co-op in 1974, the Advisory Board under my chairmanship was now going to implement it.

The Managing Director would hold Management Board meetings each Friday. Initially it was planned that the Advisory Board of Directors would then meet fortnightly to consider Co-op policy and review management performance.

On 17th January the Directors met Mr Wainwright, Mr Lewis and Mr Oakshot. These three Liberal Party MPs were very interested to hear the Director's views on the Workers' Co-op experience at Meriden.

The Advisory Board and Management Board Co-op structural change triggered a number of key personnel changes. Brenda Price resigned her Sales directorship to enable her to become a member of the Management Board. John Williams was to resign due to ill health, from both his Advisory Board AEUW directorship and his management role as Senior Manufacturing Co-ordinator. The AEUW members nominated Mr I Williams as their replacement Director on the Advisory Board. John Grattan resigned his EPTU directorship on the Advisory Board and his Training Officer position, to enable him to replace John Williams as the new Senior Manufacturing Co-ordinator. The EPTU nominated Mr D Davenport as its new Union Director on the Advisory Board.

As a result of these management changes Mr Barclay, the TASS Director, reminded the Advisory Board of the necessity to establish a pay structure policy that addressed the welcomed development where Co-op members were promoted to senior management roles, roles in which other externally recruited individuals were already paid the market going-rate for the job.

With the exception of the Managing Director, who would sit on both boards, the other members of the Management Board were to be known as Executives. Under the new structure, the Chairman of the Advisory Board would also have dual responsibility to both Boards.

The final item of discussion during this marathon meeting, agenda item 22, was discussion of the recent mass meeting's rejection of the productivity bonus scheme. It seemed to the Directors that the membership was so disgruntled by recent external interventions, that it had totally forgotten the objectives behind the proposed productivity pay scheme – a pay scheme the subcommittee of the Advisory Board had evolved over months to meet current HMG Department of Employment legislation regarding self-financing, and to achieve the two key Co-op objectives:

• Pay all members a more competitive wage in return for higher productivity.
• Pay a token £4 skill differential to approximately a third of Co-op membership, to enable retention of vital key individuals or recruitment of replacements for those who had left.

The Co-op's second Annual General Meeting was scheduled to take place on 27th January 1978. Unfortunately, the audited accounts for the 18-month period ending 30th September 1977 could not be accepted on the day; problems experienced with their preparation meant they were incomplete. In normal, calmer times I am sure the scheduled Beneficiaries and Company AGM would have been postponed, given suitable explanation, but these were anything but calm or normal times.

Accordingly, it was decided to go ahead and at least explain personally to the Trustee shareholders the circumstances of the accountancy problem. Following detailed explanation by the Company Secretary, the two attending Trustees, Mr J Haynes and Mr R Marston, agreed that the Beneficiary nominated Directors could at least deal with the company's AGM agenda with the exception of the adjourned acceptance of the audited accounts. The AGM would then be reconvened at a later date to deal with the annual accounts.

The other item of note that was dealt with at the company AGM was a special resolution to change the Co-op trading name from Meriden Motorcycles Limited to Triumph Motorcycles (Meriden) Limited. This previously held, NVT-owned name was purchased from Dennis Poore for the princely sum of £200, as was another Triumph name, also purchased at this time for £200: Triumph Motorcycles (Export) Limited.

Finally, a 'sign of the times' proposition from Beneficiary member Mrs W Wilson, was unanimously accepted:

"Anyone with suitable qualifications, volunteering to join the company at shop floor rate of pay, should be given preference to persons requiring higher salaries." Concluding the AGM, the Trustees requested that "relevant information for the reconvened AGM be forwarded to them 48 hours prior to the date of the said meeting."

Having thanked the Trustees for their AGM attendance, the new Advisory Board met for the first time. Initial business was the election of the Chairman of the Board. I was re-elected Chairman for a specified period of twelve months, with one Director voting against and one abstaining. In these circumstances, I felt it necessary to advise the Directors that the stipulated twelve-month period was "dependent on receiving the confidence of the majority of the Board at any given time."

On 1st February we met to review the Co-op's current trading position in view of the production shortfalls of the last two periods. Production had fallen short of target by 900 motorcycles, causing a heavy increase in component stocks and tying up working capital. The financial accounts now indicated a resultant loss of £266,000 over the period in question. In view of this, the following action was proposed by the Company Secretary:

In order to retrieve at least some of the shortfall in the production targets, the workforce will be offered an incentive to raise production. A bonus of £35/£40 per month will be paid across the board to all members on the basis of a 40-hour week and achieving a target production figure of 350 motorcycles per week.

Mr Nelson (MD) is given authority to decide when and where it is necessary to work overtime, i.e. in cases where sickness and absenteeism had created shortfalls in production.

A notice to this effect would be placed on the Co-op notice boards. The proposed new 'across the board' bonus system would be put to a mass meeting tomorrow for agreement by the membership and to officially rescind the two grade bonus system.

Mr Atkinson was appointed Training Officer, thereby filling the vacancy left by Mr Grattan when he joined the Management Board. Discussed at length was the proposal that had come forward from the membership that three of the presently unfilled Director positions on the Advisory Board should now be filled by the election of the three most suitable Beneficiaries, without reference to the eight Co-op trade unions. We were not opposed in principle to this proposition, feeling that it would probably help communications with the membership regarding the problems the Co-op was facing. However, it should be noted that the trade union nominated Directors also understood that this hybrid Director selection process would inevitably produce a more T&G dominant Advisory Board.

Nominations for the three vacancies were received and placed on the Co-op notice boards to allow this election to happen. Following which, on 3rd February 1978, the three new Beneficiary Directors were confirmed as members of the Advisory Board:

Mr K Anderton

Mr W Beattie

Mr R Crowder-Johnson

The Company Secretary advised the three new Beneficiary Directors of relevant information covering the legal aspects of their Advisory Board position.

On 15th February the Advisory Board met Jack Hawthorne, President of Triumph Motorcycles (America) Inc. He provided a very informative report on all aspects of the American subsidiary and the progress being made, towards what he considered could well be a promising future.

On 18th February the Directors discussed the possibility of inviting Mr Jack Jones (General Secretary of the Transport and General Workers' Union) on his retirement to accept a Director's position on the Co-op Advisory Board. Mr Atkinson agreed that he would discuss such a possibility with Jack Jones at his retirement celebration on 29th February and report back.

At this time Miss Price was experiencing staffing difficulties within the Sales Department. In particular, there were problems securing advice and information relating to export documentation; there was an urgent need for a European Sales Manager. Recent applications and interviews in connection with this post had proved unsuccessful. Accordingly, she had sought the assistance of Mr Peter Britton of Peter Britton Sales Limited. Mr Britton currently served Trusty Cycles and Steyr Daimler Puch, working largely as an agent on their behalf in the European countries. He had indicated he was interested in being employed by the Co-op in a similar capacity. His fee for providing this service would probably equate to a Co-op member's annual pay. Miss Price further investigated this possibility, and subsequently it was agreed on 22nd February that Mr Britton would be employed. Miss Price and the Company Solicitor Mr Peter Davis would draw up a contract, stating the target number of bikes to be sold during the initial seven-month trial period, following which a review would be undertaken.

The vital Daytona Show in America would be attended by Miss Price and Mr Kean in an effort to maximise US motorcycle orders. Mr Lapworth would also be attending the show at the request of some US Triumph dealers. Accordingly it was agreed that Mr Lapworth should be invited to meet the Advisory Board of Directors at his convenience, for a frank exchange of views and discussion in an attempt to resolve any outstanding differences between him and the Co-op. The Chairman, Mr Atkinson and Mr Beattie subsequently met Mr Lapworth to outline the reasons for the Directors' request, and a Directors' meeting was scheduled for 2.30pm on 24th February.

The Company Secretary reported that the Co-op, with a total ECGD facility of £5,000,000, had 'rolled over' two bills in January because the American company had insufficient funds to meet this liability. ECGD had agreed at that time to extend its terms. Triumph's American company had now requested that the Co-op roll over two further bills, making a total rolled over facility of £490,000. Having used up this amount, it meant that the total required on 15th May 1978 would be in excess of the £5,000,000 ECGD facility. This in turn, would mean that either the American company must buy some bikes through other means, or we could apply for an increase in the facility. Whilst ECGD had not been approached, the Company Secretary doubted if a large increase could be expected, although we may have been able to obtain up to £250,000 to take us out of the problem short-term. If ECGD had to be approached, the company needed to be in a position to convince them that the American company was not overstocked and had firm orders. Meanwhile the American company required 3900 bikes, but it was not certain that the Co-op would be able to produce that quantity for the US since it was already behind target. Because of this situation, the Company Secretary advised:

– That the Daytona Show was of the utmost importance, and every endeavour must be made to obtain orders from that show. To give the company credibility, it was necessary to reconsider who was to attend the show.

– That the Board must give some thought to where it was going with the American subsidiary in view of its drain on the resources of the parent company, bearing in mind that if it continued to be unable to meet bills, it would mean that ultimately the Co-op would fold.

The Company Secretary's advice resulted in the following action:

– In addition to Miss Price and Mr Kean attending the Daytona Show as originally planned, the Chairman Mr J Rosamond and Chief Engineer Mr B Jones would also attend.

– The Company Secretary would endeavour to initiate a form of early warning system from Mr D Smith, the American company accountant, with regard to the state of the TMA cashflow. It was also felt that it may be necessary for the Company Secretary to visit the American subsidiary.

The Company Secretary received a letter from the Co-op's bank, the National Westminster. This stated that its reason for the refusal to discount bills was that it was really concerned about the recent substantial losses recorded by the Co-op. The Company Secretary offered an explanation and asked if the bank would care to meet members of the Board. Its reply had been that it would prefer to await the next two months' accounts to convince itself of the true situation.

Brian Jones, the Chief Engineer, had been interviewing candidates for the Production Engineer's job. This individual would continue the vital work begun by John Chaplin of GEC. One of the candidates considered was the Co-op's own John Williams, who the Chief Engineer now recommended following his return to work after absence due to illness.

Capital expenditure estimated at £20-£25,000 spread over six months for replacement engine crankcase dies was agreed.

In view of recent press speculation that suggested the Co-op was considering a further application for Government aid, the Chairman made clear his intention to brief Mr Geoffrey Robinson MP. This would be the first official contact with the Co-op's former advisor since his resignation. Action was considered necessary to ensure that if questions were asked in the House of Commons regarding the Co-op seeking further funding, it was made clear that the Co-op was only considering development grants at this time, as these were available to all manufacturing companies! Mr A Suich (Department of Industry) and Mr P Wainwright (Liberal Party) would also be contacted on this matter.

The eleven Advisory Board Directors met Mr Lapworth on Friday 24th February 1978. It soon became clear that the critical views and opinions expressed to the T&G union membership were very deep rooted, and had been held for some time.

After two hours of intense acrimonious debate, during which Mr Lapworth criticised all the shortcomings of the Co-op, past and present, and the Board of Directors tried to defend its present attempts to remedy these failings, little or no progress was made towards achieving unity for the visit to Daytona. It was agreed therefore to adjourn the meeting over the weekend and reconvene at 4.30pm on Monday 27th February.

If the Directors had hoped Mr Lapworth's approach would have mellowed over the weekend for the reconvened Board meeting on Monday, they were to be sadly disappointed. The only change at the second meeting was the presence of the Co-op MD John Nelson. Mr Lapworth was even more critical about the Co-op's American distribution company; its location on the west coast, its staff, and performance since its acquisition from NVT in May 1977 were all severely questioned.

I had a very restless night with little sleep, continually reflecting upon the bitter, 'clear the air' meeting, which had ended with a proposal to elect Bill Lapworth to the Advisory Board as a 'man motivator' being narrowly defeated.

7

GOING OUR
SEPARATE WAYS

T he meeting with Bill Lapworth failed to clear the air or find common ground between him and the majority of the Advisory Board. What it did do, once again, was focus the Directors' minds on the following key aims that would most influence a positive change of fortune at the Co-op, without which a slide into liquidation would almost certainly follow:

• Achieve a major attitude change in order to 'rediscover' the Co-operative workforce that was capable of producing record levels of high quality Triumph motorcycles and spare parts.

• Re-establish the Triumph volume American market, with the Co-op's subsidiary company selling every motorcycle and spare part produced for it.

Jim Barclay (TASS), Felix Kean (Admin) and George Mackie (ASTMS) were the only surviving Directors of the 1975 Advisory Board from which Bill Lapworth resigned when an advisor. All three individuals played an active part in establishing the Stage 2 Meriden Co-op policy and agreement with HMG, enabling the Co-op to continue in business. Since Stage 2 began, Dennis Crowder-Johnson (T&G), John Grattan (EPTU) and John Williams (AEUW) had resigned from the Advisory Board, leaving only five original Directors totally committed having established the Stage 2 Meriden Co-op policy on the reconfigured hybrid Advisory Board of eleven.

The result of the democratic vote at the end of the 'clear the air' meeting with Bill Lapworth was further confirmation, if ever one was needed, of the likelihood of future change to Board policy.

A Vice Chairman, Mr K Anderton, was elected to serve in my absence whilst at the Daytona Motorcycle show, should it be required. The first casualty of the uncertain times through which the Co-op was now passing was David Martin, the Company Secretary, who gave notice of his resignation on 15th March 1978.

The motorcycle dealer and consumer reaction at Daytona was satisfactory, so far as the Co-op personnel present could assess. On Brenda Price and Felix Kean's return, detailed reports would be provided on sales/orders. In addition, Brian Jones would provide a product review based on American input.

The MD reported on his 1978/79 production budget on 22nd March. He believed it would benefit from two changes: weekly rather than monthly payment of the production bonus, and the employment of a further 35 to 40 people to cancel out the 'excessive' overtime being worked, overtime that presently equated to the basic weekly wages of up to 80 Co-op members!

Mr Gratton (Senior Co-ordinator) and Mr Hudson (Personnel Manager) were also involved in these discussions. Although excessive overtime was being worked, production targets were still not being achieved; attitudes, and the refusal of some members to work in a co-operative manner were said to be major factors. We agreed to the MD's request to pay the production bonus weekly (one week in arrears), but were not prepared to agree to the further recruitment of 35 to 40 individuals without a full investigation.

The MD reported that Mr Harry Woolridge (Warranty Manager) would be absent for an indefinite period due to complications following his recent accident. It was proposed to employ Mr Henry Vale on a temporary basis to cover the warranty situation. The MD further reported that the Spare Parts Department organiser, Mr J Cartwright, would also be absent for ten weeks following his recent heart attack.

On 22nd March Mr Ivor Williams (AEUW Director) tendered his resignation for personal reasons; Mr W Farndon was elected as his successor.

On 3rd April the Chairman reported that Mr Boulter, the second choice identified by the Co-op's auditor Coopers and Lybrand at the time of the original recruitment for Financial Controller, was – in the opinion of the interview panel – suitable for the job. Mr Boulter was due a 10 per cent salary increase from his present employer and was looking for a similar situation at the Co-op. Following discussion the appointment was put to a vote: 6 voted in favour, 3 against, with 1 abstention due to being provided with what was said to be a 'fait accompli' by the interview panel!

On 6th April Mr Martin reported to the Directors that he had successfully arranged a £750,000 increase in the ECGD facility – excellent news.

The recently won Sudanese military order was currently being produced in the factory. Mr Barclay asked the MD if there were any penalty clauses involved in the contract, and the MD confirmed that there was one vital one: two aircraft would await loading at Stanstead airport, London on 12th May. Should the completed order miss these flights, the contract would be cancelled.

On Miss Price's return from the United States, she reported that the visit to Daytona had been successful. Further useful information had been gathered regarding dealer and consumer requirements, the most urgent of which being the supply of current and non-current spare parts. An urgent decision was now required regarding the supply of Triumph Trident and non-current Triumph 650cc and 500cc spares. Failure to meet this major spare parts demand would dramatically affect the ongoing sales of new Triumph motorcycles in the US.

Mr Beattie reported that Mr Lapworth had brought two matters to his attention that he had learnt on his trip to Daytona. Firstly, Mr Beattie questioned the announcement of the $100 US price increase on new motorcycles, without prior endorsement by the parent company. Miss Price pointed out that having examined the revised TMA financial budgets, she had anticipated that the Board would not condone the indicated loss she had discovered, and therefore found it necessary to make an immediate decision on the price increase. Jack Hawthorne had allowed the dealers a week's grace to place orders following which the new price would apply.

Secondly, Mr Beattie questioned the alleged practice at some US public warehouses, where dealers said they were unable to obtain the particular models they wanted without offering cash bribes! Mr Beattie stated this had already been reported to TMA. Miss Price was unaware of this practice and felt that as Jack Hawthorne was also probably unaware of what was said to be happening, she would ask him to investigate these allegations.

Mr Davenport asked the Company Secretary, David Martin, whether the TMA lateness in reporting their cashflow position, advised on 22nd February 1978, had improved. The Company

The Daytona Trade and Consumer Show Triumph stand – sectioned T140E engine produced at the Meriden factory by Doug Cashmore. Brian Jones in the background wearing a black tie. (Author's archive)

Big D of Texas-Jack Wilson's race-winning Bonneville ridden by Jon Minonno featured on the Daytona stand. Brenda Price is in the background holding a piece of paper. (Author's archive)

Secretary confirmed that it was not now giving him the degree of concern that he had previously felt!

Brian Jones (Chief Engineer) provided the Board with a 1978/79 product review. Tom Hyam, the Co-op's stylist, was also in attendance. Tom had been working on the styling mock-ups with Jez Bradley, a Coventry Lanchester Polytechnic student undertaking his industrial placement with Triumph. Three alternative styling projects had been produced in order to assess the possibility of achieving additional premium priced motorcycle sales over and above the standard T140 and TR7 models.

Jez Bradley's first project, loosely based on the style of a US Yamaha flat track racer, had already been rejected. The TMA staff including Jack Hawthorne, Peter Britton for Europe, and Tony Cooper for the UK, felt that only a maximum of 200 extra premium priced sales were possible. No justification for the extra tooling costs. Tom Hyam expressed his disappointment, believing that the flat track style would have appealed to younger riders graduating to their first big bike, a market Triumph did not currently address. It was agreed with the Board, however, that the proposed flat track styling mock-up would be turned into an engineered practical runner, and tooling costs fully assessed for its production. Then based upon the public reaction gained at the next Earls Court Motorcycle Show, and if profitable volumes could be achieved, it would be produced.

The second styling project undertaken was based upon a lowrider model; styling photos of this model had also been considered by TMA's dealers in the US, who had rejected the project because of its close similarity to Harley Davidson models.

The third project code, named the D-model or T140D, had been refined further during the visit to Daytona – basically it had Lester cast aluminium wheels, a two into one exhaust system

Jez Bradley's flat track-inspired styling project was targeted at first time big bike buyers. (Courtesy Jez Bradley photography, Erum Waheed's archive)

Co-op stylist Tom Hyam was responsible for interpreting the American subsidiary's T140D requirements, shown here in prototype form with the Meriden factory gates in the background. (Courtesy Jez Bradley photography, Erum Waheed's archive)

similar to that developed for the flat track model, and it was finished in the classic, very popular black with heavy gold pinstripe lines. This project had met with wide approval, additional premium price sales of 2000 were forecast, and accordingly it was suggested we proceed with this project. Detailed costing and engineering specifications were being pursued to enable an informed decision. Brian Jones tabled the improved specifications for the 1979 T140 and TR7 models. It was felt that the proposed new aluminium cylinder barrel change could not be justified, because of the £3000 tooling cost. The Chief Engineer was asked to consider as soon as possible the introduction of an electric start option. This, it was felt, seemed to be the most often requested specification improvement.

According to Mr Lapworth, stated Mr Beattie, Bob Oswald had offered to visit the Meriden factory at his own expense, to demonstrate his belt drive design conversion – had Mr Jones taken up this offer? Brian Jones agreed that Mr Oswald had certainly mentioned visiting the factory; however, at that time he had not suggested it would be at his own cost. In the company's present financial situation, Mr Oswald had been asked to forward a set of components to TMA for it to ship to the factory for trial. Brian Jones would re-contact Mr Oswald, and if what Mr Lapworth was claiming was correct, would invite him over!

The MD had ascertained that the hold-ups in production were due to the small batch quantities being produced, which forced machine tools to be constantly broken down and reset! Concern was expressed regarding the lack of administration throughout the production areas, where organisers were often found operating machines rather than carrying out their organisational function. Absenteeism problems were about to be overcome, the MD advised, by subcontracting to outside suppliers. The MD was asked to investigate production methods and administration throughout the factory.

Mr Boulter accepted the position of Financial Controller/Company Secretary and it was hoped he would commence employment at the Co-op before the end of May. Correspondence had been received from concerned older members regarding compensation for their time spent picketing, which stated that:

Due to the new setup for retirement pensions, Co-op workers under retirement age are fully covered for extra pensions and also life insurance. Up to the present time no provisions have been made to compensate over-64s at all and there was a bitter feeling that nothing has been done.

It was certainly a fact of life that this factory would never have reopened if the older people had not dug their heels in and said "This is where we stay."

One of the reasons for this was the repeated statements that were made that when we did get back to work we would be suitably reimbursed and that we would not stand to lose out. We now think that the time has come for discussion on this subject and as a preliminary claim would suggest at least one year's salary on retirement to compensate for the loss which was incurred during picketing.

We would appreciate your urgent attention to this request.

The letter was signed by five of the individuals who were affected. A sub-committee comprising Mr Davenport (EPTU) and Mr Barclay (TASS) plus Mr J Read, one of the elderly pickets, was set up to investigate this matter and report their findings.

On 24th April the Managing Director's report on production hold-ups was discussed and the following action decided:

Investigate and if necessary, reorganise the layout of the office areas to effect efficiency between departments.

Investigate specific manufacturing areas, such as the copy lathes section, where it was known that hold-ups occurred.

Investigate whether the administrative capabilities of co-ordinators, organisers and leading hands were sufficiently adequate for the roles they fulfilled.

The Chairman and Managing Director reported on a meeting with the Co-op's bank. The National Westminster had indicated that it was prepared to regard the next six months of operation as a period of consolidation, during which the company must improve its financial position. At the end of the six months period the bank would review the situation to establish if sufficient improvement had been made to warrant continued support.

The MD then circulated a production plan, the introduction of which he believed would overcome present problems and improve administrative systems. Following discussion, it was agreed that Mr Nelson should implement his plan and inform all relevant personnel of the changes involved. The Directors undertook to meet their respective trade union members to ensure support for the MD's production plan. The members were generally supportive of it, however, they expressed concern about the new booking system, and they hoped the recording of each individual member's work would not involve the further recruitment of administrative workers.

On 28th April we reconvened to discuss the revised contract of employment. Mr Atkinson had been drafting and redrafting revisions of the contract of employment to try and establish a set of rules and regulations by which the Co-op could be run fairly and effectively, for the benefit of the total membership.

The Chairman explained that following Mr Grattan's 27th April telephone call to the Department of Trade and Industry, an individual from the local DTI Birmingham office had now arrived asking to meet the MD and Chairman. The MD was with the DTI representative at present, and the Chairman was about to join them. Mr Anderton, the Deputy Chairman, took over the discussion of the revised contract of employment.

Shortly afterwards the Board meeting was interrupted to be informed that Mr Lapworth was on the premises and asking to see the Directors. He wished to discuss a point of discipline within the terms of the contract of employment. Mr Anderton (Deputy Chairman) invited Mr Lapworth to join the contract of employment meeting.

Mr Lapworth explained that:

His support had been requested in a disciplinary action taken against a T&G member who was absent from work through illness, and he had consequently asked for this meeting regarding this matter. Whilst he recognised that disciplinary action was required, it was unacceptable that a sick person should be disciplined, especially to the stage of dismissal. In questioning the illness of a member presenting a sick note, the company was also seen to be questioning the reputation of medical professionals, who would be quite prepared to defend that reputation. He further stressed that sickness absence could not be used as an excuse for not making production targets and, whilst it was true that a section must cover a sick colleague's work, it (the section) must be held responsible for meeting targets and organise itself accordingly. Discipline should be left to the members, and action should be taken against people not meeting targets, not persons who were genuinely ill.

In view of the situation which had come to his attention, Mr Lapworth requested that the disciplinary system should include the facility for a member to ask for the support of his trade union official. Given that concession, he was prepared to accept the disciplinary rules laid down in the contract of employment.

Mr Anderton thanked Mr Lapworth for his comments, following which Mr Lapworth withdrew from the meeting.

The Chairman reported that the DTI representative he and the MD had met earlier suggested that the company should employ a production engineer in the vital role vacated by Mr Grattan, as both engineering knowledge and motivational skills were required.

The MD and Chairman were then updated regarding the meeting with Mr Lapworth, as a consequence of which Mr Atkinson was to implement further revisions to the new contract of employment disciplinary rules.

The Directors had already received a suggestion in March 1978 from a Co-op member, Carol Huntbach, who being "perturbed at the amount it was costing the company in production and money to honour the staff status sick scheme," suggested that "encouraging employees to attend work, by rescinding the staff status and making a bonus payment to people attending work for the complete 40-hour week" would be a better solution! She had gone on to suggest that if approved in principal by the Advisory Board, it could be put to a mass meeting to garner support. This idea, we were aware, had growing backing amongst much of the membership, but if this route had to be pursued, it would be a sad indictment of the Meriden Co-op. Having failed to control the malingerers, the genuine sick would be punished by removal of the welfare scheme.

The Chairman reported that the Coopers and Lybrand audit partner, Mr Whitehouse, had requested a meeting to discuss the fact that the Co-op's Accounts Department lacked people of the right experience. At the 3rd of May meeting he indicated the difficulties and extra time and cost that had been involved, when it was found that the department had not been working efficiently throughout the previous year. When the Co-op had expanded from just manufacturing into marketing its own products, there had been barely sufficient people to run this new multi-million pound business created. He stressed that the employment of a qualified Accounts Manager, who would run the Accounts Department in conjunction with the Financial Controller, was now essential. This Accounts Manager did not necessarily have to be qualified by 'letters' but should be someone who had 10 to 15 years experience in control of such a department, and would therefore leave the Financial Controller time to run the commercial side of the company. In addition, Mr Whitehouse thought that the Accounts Department also required further qualified clerks. If the strengthening of the Accounts Department in the manner he had described was not done, the company would arrive at the end of another financial year in the same situation that existed this year! Mr Whitehouse would be confirming his verbal comments in a written auditor's report and recommendations to the Chairman.

On 9th May the Company Solicitor, Mr Peter Davis, advised that he was happy with the final draft of the revised contract of employment. So far as the involvement of trade union representatives in disciplinary procedure was concerned, it was felt that this could be offered as an alternative to the existing Co-op's appeals committee system.

The Chairman met the organisers and leading hands to explain the proposed new contract of employment and welfare scheme, following which copies were circulated for the membership's consideration prior to mass meeting approval being sort and implementation.

Further consideration was given by the Board regarding the auditor's request for an Accounts Manager. Mr Beattie felt that in view of the salary level required, the membership should be consulted at a mass meeting and their agreement secured to this additional management appointment. This was the majority view of the Board.

On 18th May Mr W Farndon suggested that if in future the normal rules of debate were adopted, the time spent in meetings would be reduced. Mr Barclay added that a return should now be made to holding fortnightly meetings, the intended aim being to hold meetings once a month.

The long awaited reconvened Annual General Meeting was held on 22nd May 1978, the delay being due to finalising the audited annual accounts. Following their acceptance, Mr Whitehouse of Coopers and Lybrand advised that his detailed report would now be handed to the Directors and the Trustee shareholders.

The Chairman suggested to the three Trustees that it would be appreciated by all concerned at the Co-op if they could become more involved, possibly attending quarterly meetings. The Trustees were agreeable to this course of action subject to sufficient notice.

During the 8th June meeting, in the agenda item matters arising from the meeting held on 9th May, Mr Beattie questioned the fact that the Chairman had not put the appointment of an Accounts Manager to a mass meeting for the workforce's agreement. The Chairman replied that the appointment of an Accounts Manager enabling the company to keep accurate books of accounts was the responsibility of the Directors, not the workforce. Mr Beattie stressed that since it was a Board decision to approach the workforce, it was not the Chairman's prerogative to take a different course of action without first informing the rest of the Directors. However, it was agreed by the Board to defer the decision regarding the appointment of an Accounts Manager until the audit partner's written report was received. Mr Barclay and Mr Crowder-Johnson pointed out to the Directors that the Board should further consider matters which must be placed before mass meetings for agreement, particularly taking into account items such as this, where a high degree of personal responsibility and liability fell upon the Directors!

The Managing Director provided a report for the Advisory Board based on progress since January 1978; this report had been circulated for consideration prior to the meeting.

The main concern expressed in the MDs report was that due to the fact he had been totally involved with manufacturing for the last six weeks, he had been unable to attend to what he considered to be the Managing Director's role – the commercial aspects of the business. This was because of the constant pressure from production 'organisers' referring all of their daily problems to him. Mr Nelson felt that in trying to attend to both the commercial and production aspects of the business, he was unable to do either adequately and recommended that the Directors strongly consider the appointment of a 'Works Manager' who would concentrate on the manufacturing side of the organisation.

Included in the MD's progress report were details compiled by Mr Roger Bryant (organiser) on problems within manufacturing/production, many of which had existed for some time and did not appear ever to be resolved. The rest of the Co-op's organisers who were invited to join the meeting largely confirmed the comments. The main problems revolved around:

Problems in maintaining production flow –

• Shortages of items to production and assembly areas
• Lack of co-ordination and co-operation in departments responsible for moving and ensuring adequate supplies into production and assembly areas
• Inefficiency of systems intended to prevent track and production stoppages

Absenteeism –

• Lack of information from the Personnel Department, especially of cover where employees were absent for brief periods i.e. quarter to half an hour due to lateness
• It was impossible to reprimand absentees covered by sick notes until such a time as the welfare scheme had been abused
• Lack of notification to organisers when persons were to be absent for doctors/dental appointments (pass out permission provided by the surgery)

Discussion with the MD and the organisers regarding the problems in maintaining production flow determined that whilst they agreed a 'link man' was required, the calibre of the individual needed would have to have wider technical experience than was presently available at the Co-op.

Mr Nelson now returned to his earlier comments about the recruitment of a Works Manager, which had been very ably supported in the meeting by the production organisers. It was accepted by all concerned that there was an urgent need for a link man, experienced in production techniques and able to co-ordinate the flow of production throughout the factory. It was also noted there was opposition from the production organisers to selecting a person from the current workforce. Offers of seconded assistance had been extended by Geoffrey Robinson and the Department of Industry, but we felt that a permanent solution must be found. Mr Beattie believed it was unnecessary to employ anyone from external sources, since he was certain that there were people within the factory who had the ability to co-ordinate production. However, he stressed that anyone appointed to this job must have 100 per cent backing from the Board, especially in cases where to achieve the desired improvements an employee or head of department needed to be removed from their present role. Mr Beattie had someone in mind that he felt may be capable of carrying out this function, and requested sufficient time to approach the person concerned and return with a recommendation. Unfortunately, when Mr Beattie raised the issue with the man in question, he declined the opportunity.

Mr Jack Hawthorne, TMA's President, presented a report covering the current US sales situation. This identified an urgent need to strengthen the existing US Triumph dealer network in order to meet present budgeted sales projections. To do this, he recommended the recruitment of a further three field sales representatives to help assess the performance of some existing dealers, and identify replacements where strengthening was required.

Concern regarding the recent drop in the TMA sales and the current stock of 1500 unsold 1978 motorcycles was expressed by the Directors – this at the end of the peak US spring selling season was unacceptable. It was a known fact that if TMA was to fail, the UK parent company would almost certainly collapse as well because of its reliance on the American market. Mr Beattie commented on the minimal amount of information coming from TMA and felt a member of the parent company Board should be employed in America to monitor the running of the subsidiary. He referred to the former Company Secretary David Martin's advice (22nd February 1978) that the Board should consider breaking up TMA.

The Chairman stated that this certainly should be given further consideration, but it was not a decision to be taken lightly. New independent distributors would have to be found and appointed and the various Government departments would obviously need to be involved, all of which would take time. The MD indicated that Ruth Firman, TMA's Company Secretary, was presently on holiday in England, and that he could arrange a meeting with her, if required.

Jack Hawthorne's plan for the appointment of the three extra TMA sales representatives was agreed; however, this was on the basis that sales activity must be intensified, especially regarding the fifteen hundred 1978 motorcycles still in stock, which must be sold by the end of the current season. Mr Hawthorne also stressed that vitally important to TMA achieving its motorcycle sales targets was the parent company supplying the ordered, highly profitable current and old pattern spare parts for the desperate dealer network.

Production time estimates had now been compiled indicating that a further 5000 manufacturing hours were required to complete the outstanding TMA orders for spare parts – these orders comprised those on back order and a current forward stocking order. The present production time cycles in the factory for motorcycles did not cater for the additional spare parts quantities now ordered, so the Chairman suggested consideration should be urgently given to the introduction of a 'skeleton' nightshift. Following discussion, the MD agreed to produce a spare parts breakdown of the machine shop components, on the basis of introducing a nightshift without the recruitment of additional machinists. Target dates for completion of the spare parts programme were then agreed as: current spare parts – 1st August 1978, old pattern spare parts – 1st January 1979.

The next item at yet another marathon meeting was discussion of Mr W Farndon's plan regarding how the Co-op accommodated long-term sick members at the same time as balancing the commercial needs of running the business. The plan was as follows:

a) Sick or injured members to be visited after 1 month and periodically thereafter by the Personnel Department.

b) After 8 months the member be recommended to accept light work if necessary so that his/her job could be filled.

c) A section to be set up so that light work can be transferred to it when it becomes available, but not created.

d) The member must sign that after a period of rehabilitation he or she will be transferred to normal working when there is a vacancy available.

e) There will be no bonus payable on the light work section; this will act as a deterrent for members with a 'preference' for light work.

f) The light work section and rehabilitation period not to be extended to persons over the age of 60 years for females and 65 years for men.

g) All persons must have been employed by the company for at least 1 year before qualifying for the light work section.

h) An assessment and time study should be made so that this facility is viable.

Mr Farndon's 25th April plan was accepted and would be implemented in conjunction with the Personnel Department, organisers and leading hands.

John Nelson advised that he had written a book (*Bonnie – The Development History of the Bonneville*). This was available for the Directors' perusal and would become a must-have for Bonneville enthusiasts.

The Chairman asked Mr Atkinson and Mr Beattie for a progress report regarding the monthly staff contract of employment that they had been considering since February, also reminding them that a management salary review was now due.

Returning to the recruitment of a Works Manager, it was decided to set up a sub-committee comprising the Chairman and Mr Beattie, whose job it would be to complete an investigation into the production and administration of the company. Initially I thought I had been presented with a poison chalice, being part of a sub-committee with Mr Beattie trying to shed light on the root causes of the Co-op's production problems. I was wrong – my day job as a welder, (when I was not involved in company business) involved me working on what was generally recognised as an efficient section. This sheltered me from the vast majority of the daily production difficulties that confronted Bill Beattie as a gear cutter. The machine shop in which he worked was plagued with all the problems we had heard about from the organisers and MD. As a production welder, I had the luxury of working in a relatively happy, self-contained environment where my colleagues were contributing to the overall efficiency of the Co-op. I soon learnt from Bill Beattie that working in the machine shop, which employed the majority of the Co-op workforce, you were confronted daily with the morale destroying, harsh reality of everything that was preventing the Co-op production process functioning efficiently. Accordingly, our totally contrasting Co-op and life experiences (Bill Beattie originated from Belfast, Northern Ireland) enabled us to consider the major production problems that existed and what could be done to achieve solutions.

The MD Mr Nelson outlined for the Directors some of the duties he considered were in keeping with the role of MD. The Directors asked him to complete his job profile and circulate it for further consideration.

The Co-op's new Social Club had a very active and enthusiastic committee. Mr Barclay was its Board spokesman who had presented the Club's proposed operating intentions. Following discussion, a detailed written response was provided, specifying exactly on what basis the Social Club could proceed with its plans.

The MD and Purchase Manager Mr Brian Baldwin had visited NVT's Mr Dennis Poore to discuss purchasing his stocks of Triumph Trident T160 and old pattern Triumph 500cc and 650cc spare parts. He had agreed to supply these parts to the Co-op provided they were shipped directly to TMA, as NVT was already supplying others in the USA!

Mr W Farndon resigned on 30th June due to continuing ill health Mr H Hughes was elected as his replacement.

The Co-op auditors advised that discussions with HMG regarding the loan interest payment due in June 1979 should start as soon as possible. It was agreed that Geoffrey Robinson MP should be asked to approach the Minister, Mr Eric Varley MP.

The MD reported on the proposed retail prices of the 1979 models – these calculations were based upon factory production costs during the period October 1977 to March 1978, provided by the Financial Controller. To enable consideration of the impact of weekly production volumes on ex-works prices, examples of 300, 325 and 350 motorcycle production levels were indicated. If during the period 31st July to 30th September we could achieve the 325 average weekly motorcycle production and sales, plus continue the £60,000 per month spare parts, we would achieve an approximate £100,000 operating profit for the period.

Miss Price (Sales) and Mr Jones (Engineering) also took part in these discussions. Both indicated how difficult it was, in their opinion, to fix an acceptable ex-works price that would both achieve the desired profitability and meet the consumer's price expectations. Hopefully, Miss Price stated, the Japanese would soon be increasing their prices. The Management Board was asked to reassess the suggested 1979 motorcycle prices and put forward further proposals, which would show a profit on sales of motorcycles plus an extra margin gained from the sale of spare parts.

Plans for a UK sales advertising campaign due to commence at the time of the major free editorial publicity of the Earls Court show were scrapped as the first of a number of cost savings being proposed by the Financial Controller.

Mr Boulter reported that the current overdraft stood at £264,000. He had intensified credit control systems endeavouring to use as little of the overdraft facility as possible. This was presently achievable due to the considerable inflow of cash from home bike sales, but several large bills were falling due for payment. However, the Coventry City Council rates bill for £37,500 had already been paid.

During the previous 10 to 12 days, the subcommittee investigating company production and administration had conducted fact finding interviews with various members of the workforce, and was now able to make detailed recommendations so far as the administration side of the business was concerned. The second stage of the investigation would look at the production areas. Summarising the proposed changes, the Chairman said that he and Mr Beattie visualised Mr J Birch as Production Controller at the hub of the administration organisation, based within the production control area. He would gather and co-ordinate information from all departments, allowing production to operate smoothly. The new persons involved in the various knock on appointments had been approached with the possibility of changes in their duties, and each one had appeared willing to undertake the necessary responsibilities. It was also thought that if the above changes were seen to be taking place on the administration side of the business, it would help the second stage, a similar investigation throughout the factory. More opposition was likely in the factory unless positive reorganisation was already under way in the office areas. After lengthy discussion and slight compromise, it was agreed to proceed with the proposed administration changes. Mr Barclay considered the changes to be a package that should now be passed to the MD to implement. The MD should be given the authority to endorse and implement those parts that he considered were workable, rather than the decision being imposed upon him regardless of his opinion.

Miss Price and Mr Jones were present at the meeting when the MD distributed a further report containing the revised 1979 motorcycle sales price calculations; these were now based upon a production rate of 300 motorcycles per week, plus spare parts. The Chairman read out a letter from the President of TMA requesting that the 1979 models price increase should be kept to an absolute minimum in view of the current US market situation and the fact that there were still over 1000 Triumph motorcycles in stock. The proposed retail prices were $2399 USA, £1217 UK and £1239.50 general export with ex-works prices of £889 USA, £856 UK, and £856 general export respectively. The MD hoped these figures would generate a profit at 31st December 1978, but in the meantime various cost savings would need to be made.

The Financial Controller proposed the following areas for cost savings – direct materials, subcontracting, direct labour, variable overheads, chasing debtors and setting and maintaining minimum component stock levels. Concern was expressed, however, regarding the lower production target levels, but Mr Jones felt it was better to set achievable targets rather than producing variable numbers each day. Mr Beattie was concerned regarding reliance upon cost savings, which if they did not materialise would result in more Co-op losses, and if cost savings could now be achieved, it meant that the company must have been run in a haphazard way over the previous three years. Mr Beattie's statement was countered by the fact that for most of this period, NVT's involvement prevented positive steps being implemented to improve the Co-op's financial situation (the MD had previously advised that material costs had increased by 13.1 per cent in the period July 1977 to February 1978). Mr Jones further stated that of the 700 people employed at the Co-op, some 650 only needed to be told in a positive manner what to do, and they would willingly make every effort to achieve production. With regard to the key, production co-ordinating link man job, he believed it would be advisable to acquire someone with the right amount of technical knowledge and experience in production techniques and control to fulfil the Works Manager's role. Miss Price stressed that she currently had no firm orders for the 1979 model, and to rectify this situation and generate orders she needed a price to convey to the distributors. Accordingly, she suggested that the proposed prices should be accepted now and reviewed in October, by which time a full assessment of the market situation could be made. Agreement was reached on this course of action, although Mr Beattie abstained from the vote due to the uncertainty of possible cost savings being achieved.

The Financial Controller, Mr Boulter, reported that the company was now struggling financially, largely brought about by the payment of £167,000 bank overdraft interest charges.

The subcommittee's investigation into production and administration of the company was also now struggling, as it had been thrown into complete disarray by the receipt of a letter from Mr Birch declining the position of Production Controller. Mr Beattie stated that whilst Mr Birch, the key figure, had been in favour of accepting the appointment on 3rd July, he had reversed that decision by the 4th. The subcommittee felt that he may have discussed the matter with senior Co-op individuals who did not want any organisational changes to take place, naively content with the way the Co-op had run to date making financial losses. Mr F Kean asked for clarification regarding the terms of reference of the subcommittee's investigation into production and administration. Once it had been confirmed that the subcommittee was still working within its terms of reference, it was explained that the investigation into production was being undertaken slightly differently to that of the administration area, in that only the findings of the investigation would be put forward for consideration. No recommendations on how to address those findings would be made by the subcommittee.

A lengthy, heated acrimonious debate then took place, at the end of which 5 voted in favour of the sub-committee continuing the production investigation, and 3 voted against, with Mr Barclay abstaining for the same reason as with the administration investigation. Mr Beattie then provided an initial progress report on the investigation into production, which yielded the following findings:

a) There appeared to be a substantial lack of effort and efficiency throughout the plant.
b) There were people who had been 'accommodated' by moving them from one job to another, rather than giving them jobs which they could adequately carry out.
c) It appeared to be a general view that there were too many people employed within the plant, considering the number of bikes being produced, which indicated that people were not doing their jobs effectively.

d) There were hold ups on certain sections, sections which were constantly giving trouble and sections on which a night shift was needed.

e) 50 per cent absenteeism was tolerated on the grinding section whilst grinding work was subcontracted.

f) Machinery in certain areas was being used on the wrong type of job.

g) Criticism had been levelled at organisers and leading hands where operators were quoting better ways of doing jobs, but could not find anyone to take up their suggestions.

After a further brief outline of the manner in which the subcommittee conducted their meetings, and explanation given to the numerous points raised by personnel, Mr Beattie said that as mentioned earlier a fully detailed report would be presented in due course.

Mr Barclay reported that progress was being made regarding the investigation into paying retirement grants to the pickets who, because of their age, did not qualify for the Co-op's pension or life insurance schemes. Hogg Robinson, the consultants involved, would be providing its proposals on how such grants could be achieved at a meeting on 11th July.

A meeting took place on 14th July to receive a brief report on the Co-op's American subsidiary, TMA. The report had been compiled by Miss Price as a result of a disturbing telex she had received from Mr D Smith, the TMA accountant.

Miss Price reported TMA's cashflow projection indicated that because of a 2253 motorcycle sales shortfall during the nine months to the end of June, the cash margins showed a deficit against budget to the end of June of $346,000, with a further projected deficit of $8000 for the next three months. Financial results for the eight months to end of May showed a cumulative loss of $305,576 against a budgeted for profit of $118,797. It had been envisaged that sales figures for June and July would show an improvement, but these had also fallen well behind budget with 593 sales in June against a budgeted 1200 units, and only 32 sales in the first week of July against a budgeted 400 units for the month. Spare parts sales for the eight months to the end of May showed a betterment of $117,304 (actual $447,304; budget $330,000) whereas a shortfall of $2591 was indicated against the budget for the month of June (actual $82,409; budget $85,000).

Miss Price explained that the margins were required to pay duty, warehouse charges, product liability insurance, salaries and general operating costs, and additionally to meet ECGD bills of exchange in the period August to December for machines which were shipped during the period January to May. With projected stocks of 2000 units at 30th September, the company would not be able to meet the due bills, and would therefore be unable to ship all the 1979 models programmed up to December because of the £6,000,000 limit on the ECGD facility.

Finally, Miss Price said that the report was factually correct up to the end of June 1978, but presumed that the projection was somewhat pessimistic, although it appeared that sales of motorcycles had dropped throughout the whole US market with competitors already offering 'discounting' and 'free flooring. After discussion regarding the necessity to discount models in stock and draw up a planned forward sales campaign, Miss Price suggested that as she was visiting America from Saturday 15th July, the matter would be discussed first-hand with the TMA President Mr J Hawthorne and Mr D Smith (Accountant) when the seriousness of the situation would be stressed to all members of the American company. Miss Price would communicate details of any plans which evolved during these discussions in order to obtain the parent company approval prior to such plans being actioned. The adjourned 14th July meeting was reconvened on 25th July during the Co-op's summer fortnight holiday shutdown, because of which Mr Barclay and Mr Roberts could not attend.

The 25th July emergency meeting considered a telex that had been received from Miss Price, which gave details of the TMA's financial situation, stock figures, sales plan to sell 2000 1978 stock units during August/September 1978, and a 1979 model sales programme for Triumph Motorcycles (Meriden) Limited from 1st August 1978 to 31st July 1979. This programme was based upon average sales of 60 units per day (300 per week production/sales) for the 231 working days forecast period, totalling 13,680 units.

Major concern was expressed in respect of the immediate need for finance to be transferred to the subsidiary, in view of the financial situation of the parent company. Questions were also raised with regard to the fact of the existence of $90,000 (£45,000) in Triumph's Australian company's bank account. The Financial Controller advised that the requested transfer of $60,000 (from the factory) could, if authorised, take place immediately as requested by Miss Price, plus the $90,000 (from the Australian accounts) could also be transferred by the end of the current week, if authorised. However, he was very concerned regarding the possible ongoing situation of supplying $100,000 per month to TMA up to February 1979. This matter needed serious consideration and a decision made at a later date.

During further discussion, it was recognised that an immediate decision on the transfer of cash and approval of the sales plan was required in order to aid the company's survival. It was decided that:
a) The immediate transfer of cash ($60,000 from UK and $90,000 Australia) could take place.
b) The sales plan and forward sales programme, as recommended by Miss Price, could be accepted.
c) A full report be issued regarding TMA on Miss Price's return from America.
d) Miss Price would be required to issue weekly reports on the operating of the American and Australian companies and details of the world business.
e) The Chairman would contact Miss Price by telephone to convey to her the parent company's decision.

The Managing Director reported that Mr Suich and Mr Hawkes of the Department of Industry had visited the factory to meet Mr Boulter and discuss the factory operation. Much of the informal discussion had revolved around financial accounting, about which Mr Suich had indicated that negotiations could not take place with regard to waiving the HMG loan interest unless properly prepared accounts were produced. Mr Suich would provide his recommendations with regards to the required financial accounting.

Mr Jones (Chief Engineer) reassured the Board that production of the 1979 models would be achieved in the first week after the summer holiday shutdown, with several minor production problems with the electrics and frame overcome by then, enabling production of 240 units in the first week back.

The Chairman opened the meeting on 1st August by explaining to the Directors that because of the recently reported information regarding sales at the American subsidiary TMA, and the overall situation of the Co-op brought to light in the recent investigation into production and administration, he and Mr Beattie had decided to seek assistance from Messrs Geoffrey Robinson and Bill Lapworth.

Having explained the situation to Geoffrey Robinson and Bill Lapworth, they had offered to make preliminary inquiries from various sources with regard to the possibility of obtaining financial and managerial help on behalf of the company. It was now necessary for Messrs Robinson and Lapworth to meet the Board to discuss progress they had made, and the Chairman, in asking whether the Board was prepared to meet them, pointed out that he had stressed to both individuals that they should understand that the Board would only be willing to speak to them jointly and that any work carried out on behalf of the Meriden Co-op must be done with the agreement of both parties.

Mr Kean, one of the original three trade union Directors from the early days of the Co-op in 1975, when the two aforementioned advisors were jointly involved, was the first to respond.

If these two advisors were re-involved, no split must occur within the Board by members being in favour of either one person or the other.

Mr Hughes, the most recent union Director appointed to the Board, then asked why the decision had been made to obtain outside assistance since he was not aware that the Board had, within the terms of reference of the investigation into production and administration, authorised the subcommittee to seek advice from outside the plant.

The Chairman agreed that authorisation had not been obtained, but having received the critical TMA financial information and after speaking to various people during the course of the investigation, the subcommittee had come to the conclusion that there was little alternative but to seek outside assistance.

It was agreed that Messrs Robinson and Lapworth be contacted with a view to their attending a reconvened meeting. Mr Beattie telephoned Mr Lapworth and the Chairman telephoned Mr Robinson with the invitations; they joined the meeting at 3.00pm on 1st August 1978.

8

ADVISORS RETURN

The reconvened meeting on 1st August began with the Chairman welcoming Mr G Robinson (MP) and Mr W Lapworth (T&G official) and bringing them up to date regarding the Directors' earlier discussion. Mr Robinson said that he and Mr Lapworth understood that Messrs Rosamond and Beattie had been deputed by the Board to see how the company proposed to survive throughout a difficult winter, and had been authorised to approach them on this matter.

Geoffrey Robinson stated that he thought the key was to ensure that there would be sufficient capital to see the company through the winter, and also to obtain managerial assistance. In view of the financial position of the company, however, it would be difficult to strengthen to the extent necessary the management functions without a greater degree of financial backing and conviction in general terms. Bearing this in mind, they had approached various sources to help. They had found, so far, a great deal of goodwill towards Meriden and the wish to see it survive and grow towards success in the future, not only as a useful point of recruitment, but also with a view to eliminating the conflict within the generally known management labour situation, thereby forming something new in industrial management and recruitment.

In view of the reassuring degree of goodwill, Mr Robinson was of the opinion that a pattern could evolve for combined financial and managerial assistance to be obtained, not only for the winter but for the next 18 months. At the same time, the sources that had been approached had expressed the wish to see Meriden return to the original concept of the Co-operative, wherein there existed a Management Board totally responsible to the Supervisory Board (and to the whole of the workforce) with the Supervisory Board setting policy, overseeing the management team, and meeting once a month to review progress.

The eventuality would be that after the 18 month involvement of management people, in-house personnel would take over from them, having received training.

One further condition with regard to the provision of finance and management was that the sources concerned did not wish their commitment to be made publicly known. The employment of a management team, for instance, must appear as Meriden's recruitment of its own personnel.

Mr Bill Lapworth then largely reiterated the points made by Mr Robinson, adding that the Board must fully understand that no one would be interested in making a financial commitment just to provide bikes that would simply be placed in stock. Meriden had had assistance in running the company from several sources in the past, and no further assistance would be forthcoming without there being a viability study which would indicate an ongoing situation with prospects reaching well into the future. Mr Lapworth further stated that he would have liked to have seen the company generate the people who could oversee each management function from within, headed up by one man (i.e. the Managing Director), but it now appeared that he (Bill Lapworth) had underestimated what was required and advised that individuals must be employed for each separate function.

Following a question and answer session, Mr Robinson in summarising asked that the Board base its decision on reflection of the following:

• That it would return to the original concept of the Co-op.

• That during the 18 month involvement of outside assistance, in-house personnel would be trained to the point of taking over from the management team.

• That the Supervisory Board must be prepared to let the management team operate with the Supervisory Board setting policy, overseeing the management team and meeting once a month to review progress.

• That the assistance if/when acquired, would not be from a single source.

• That the financial help if available, would not be in the terms of £1,000,000 'thrown in' but would be combined with managerial assistance.

• That the source of any financial and managerial assistance would not be made known publicly.

After further brief discussion, the Board unanimously accepted the terms outlined and authorised Messrs Robinson and Lapworth to jointly pursue the possibility of obtaining financial and managerial assistance on behalf of the Co-op.

Mr Barclay then proposed that in view of the above decision, the terms of reference of the subcommittee investigating administration and production of the company should now be changed, and suggested that the Chairman and Mr Beattie could devote their time to formulating a policy relative to the basic management operating parameters within the Co-op.

Mr Robinson was of the opinion that this was something that could be discussed eventually with the management team when it was employed. Mr Lapworth agreed with Mr Barclay's suggestion, in view of the fact that the Board as individuals each held their own beliefs, and it was necessary for them to agree a common policy; whilst brief Board discussion took place, no decision was reached.

So there we had it. The founding advisors had by compromise managed to reunite to try and save the Co-op, and the Co-op structure remained as agreed with HMG. In addition, it was now proposed by Geoffrey Robinson to train Co-op members to eventually become part of the management team. In return, Bill Lapworth acknowledged he had underestimated the number of managers needed to run the company. He was also proposing a long-term viability study to ensure all this effort was worthwhile.

From my point of view, since the resignation of the previous Chairman and my appointment I had felt that whilst the Board's two founding advisors were no longer directly involved in the Co-op, their indirect presence was still having considerable influence with the membership – especially with Bill Lapworth through his T&G branch meetings, and to a lesser degree Geoffrey Robinson MP as a result of his constituency work. Accordingly, when discussing how the outcome of this vital Board meeting could be communicated to the membership, Bill Beattie suggested to the Directors they indicate verbally that Geoffrey

Robinson and Bill Lapworth had returned to Meriden in an advisory capacity. As Chairman I accepted Mr Beattie's suggestion as a proposition, and put it to the vote. The Board of Directors voted unanimously in favour. The united advisors were now back in their rightful place, directly involved at the heart of the Co-op; and equally as important to the Chairman, they were accountable for helping me make it work!

Mr Robinson indicated that it was hoped to present a progress report on 9th/10th August when he had a visit scheduled to the Meriden factory, accompanying the American Ambassador. The Ambassador had asked for a tour of the Co-op and meetings with the Directors and Miss Price, the Sales Executive with responsibility for Triumph's US subsidiary, TMA.

On 9th August Miss Price presented the promised detailed report on TMA. Together with this report, Miss Price brought back from America for the Directors' perusal a file containing details of the past and present operation of the TMA subsidiary.

The scheduled meeting with Geoffrey Robinson and Bill Lapworth on 10th August to receive a progress report on financial and managerial assistance failed to take place. Mr Griffiths of GKN and Mr Morgan of GEC were unable to attend. Without securing managerial help, Mr Robinson explained, progress on the financial assistance to survive the winter could not be made. Mr Robinson also reported that the Government was not, at present, prepared to make a decision on waiving of the loan interest due in June 1979. He would write to the Minister, Mr E Varley MP, expressing our disappointment. The Board then adjourned for a meeting with Mr Brewster, the American Ambassador. The Ambassador showed great interest in the concept and formation of the Co-operative, and expressed the sympathy of the American people towards the establishment. Mr Robinson left with the American Ambassador, the Board meeting reconvened, and Mr Lapworth remained with the Directors. The Directors agreed that they would communicate to the membership that today's meeting was one of a series that would take place between the Board and the Co-op's two advisors. Mr Beattie asked Mr Lapworth for his suggestions with regards an alternative to the American subsidiary TMA, and Mr Lapworth stated that his original idea had been to create a deeper commitment on the part of the US dealers, thereby giving them a closer interest in the wellbeing and continuity of the whole Triumph company. At the same time, he pointed out the necessity to intensify confidence in the dealers and the workforce at Meriden, in order to promote ongoing sales of the product.

On 28th August the Financial Controller, Mr Boulter, provided the third draft of the budget for 1978/79; when agreed, it would be presented to the Department of Trade and Industry indicating the ongoing position visualised by the company. The budget showed monthly calculations to September 1979. Following discussion, the Directors accepted the draft budget and authorised the Financial Controller to present it at the forthcoming meeting with the Department of Trade and Industry.

On 1st September 1978, the subcommittee of the Board tabled its finalised investigation of the production areas of the company:

The Advisory Board Directors were told that the meetings with production organisers, leading hands and operators had brought the subcommittee to its final conclusion. An imbalance of labour existed throughout the manufacturing and ancillary areas, resulting in a shortage of productive capacity on sections within the machine shop. One of the reasons for this was that when job vacancies had occurred in ancillary areas, the majority who applied were machine shop personnel that were subsequently accepted and transferred. The second contributory factor to the imbalance was the high rate of absenteeism by a known quantity of employees abusing the sick scheme. Finally, the attitude on certain machine shop sections was a major factor in creating hold-ups at crucial points in production. In addition to the personnel factors, first operations in the machine shop process were not correctly labour loaded to produce large enough batch sizes to allow components to flow to the follow up operations, and through to completion. This then restricted engine and motorcycle assembly.

Bar Autos, 3As and Junior Auto machines with fixed operating time cycles required additional nightshift manning to enable sufficient capacity for production continuity. The subcommittee's conclusion was therefore that the labour imbalances had to be corrected if the shortfalls on budgeted production programmes were ever to be rectified. To achieve this correction, the subcommittee was proposing that 30 employees from ancillary areas (especially those with the required machine shop experience) be moved back into the machine shop.

To determine how this proposal would be received, the subcommittee had held a meeting on 30th August with members in the areas concerned, outlining the fact that "if production budgets were not achieved, it would lead to the closure of the Co-op," and that to rectify the situation there was a need to rebalance labour from ancillary areas back to the machine shop. On 31st August, a meeting was held with the respective organisers to ascertain the number of employees who could be released for transfer to the machine shop; 14 employees were identified, leaving a further 16 to be selected for movement. To achieve this selection and movement, the subcommittee was proposing mobility under the terms of the contract of employment.

The reaction of certain employees following the meetings had been one of total rejection of redeployment of labour. In view of this, the subcommittee was of the opinion that movement of labour should be enforced utilising the contract of employment to the full.

The Directors discussed at length the findings and proposed solutions contained in the subcommittee's investigation, particularly concentrating upon how the movement of personnel from ancillary areas back to the machine shop would be achieved. Following this a vote took place to accept the investigation's findings in principle; 6 Directors voted in favour – 3 against.

Mr Barclay, who voted against, wished to record that he felt the report presented by the Chairman and Mr Beattie exceeded their terms of reference. The original intention of the investigation had been to determine the need for a Works Manager. Mr Barclay considered the report confirmed the need for such an individual who would have sufficient knowledge and experience to make decisions with regard to production. Having carried out the investigation, he felt the subcommittee was now working in a Works Manager role.

The Directors had further detailed discussion regarding the enforced movement of labour utilising the contract of employment, and it was felt that a more 'humane' way should be determined to correct the machine shop labour imbalances.

The Chairman further explained that the subcommittee had visualised that individuals would first be asked to move; only if that request was met with a refusal was action based upon the contract of employment envisaged.

Mr Kean proposed that a vote should be taken by the Board for or against the enforced movement of labour. Before putting it to a vote, the Chairman reminded the Directors of the importance of achieving production targets, without which, as the Board was totally aware, the Co-op would face closure. The proposal for the enforced movement of labour was defeated – five Directors voted against, and the MD abstained on the basis of whatever was decided by the Board, he would have to implement.

Mr Hughes, one of the Directors who voted in favour of acceptance, then proposed that the five Directors who voted against should come forward with an alternative proposal on how the labour movement was to be achieved! This action was agreed by the Board; Mr Anderton, Mr Barclay, Mr Kean, Mr Mackie and Mr Roberts were to return with an alternative 'humane' proposal as soon as possible.

The MD reported briefly on the meeting on 30th August 1978 with the HMG Department of Industry senior official, Mr A Suich. Following presentation by the Financial Controller of the 1978/79 budgets, Mr Suich had asked for Triumph's proposals regarding the June 1979 loan interest payment, initially with a view to consolidating the interest with the capital. Triumph agreed that proposals would be made before the September accounts were finalised, but it was pointed out to Mr Suich that to capitalise the interest would cost the Co-op in the region of £100,000 per year.

On 5th September, the revised humane proposals for the movement of labour back to the machine shop were discussed by the Board. It was now proposed that meetings would be held with members of the ancillary areas in order to request volunteers to come forward (particularly those with machine shop experience); these meetings would be conducted by the MD with the full Advisory Board in attendance. After assessing the number of volunteers, if this was not sufficient to cover the requirement, organisers would be requested to nominate personnel who they considered could be released from their sections. Full consultation would then be entered into, firstly with the volunteers and secondly with the nominees to explain fully and persuasively the need for their movement into the machine shop. In the event of a nominee refusing to move, a member of the Board would be called upon to assist in persuading that member to accept his/her transfer into the machine shop. Only if a member then persisted in his/her non co-operation would procedure under the terms of the contract of employment be entered into.

The Directors who put forward the 'humane five-step' approach stated that the implementation of the transfer of labour would be carried out totally by the Managing Director, with members of the Board being called upon in order to show a united front. They also felt that if this plan was adopted, it would enable the transfer of labour to take place with a minimum amount of conflict and disruption.

The Chairman, Mr Beattie and Mr Hughes commented that this was a more elaborate version of the original plan, whereby individuals would be requested to move, and only if this was met by refusal would the contract of employment be implemented to the full. Following discussion, the more elaborate plan was adopted, with the MD to draw up a timetable for implementation.

Mr Beattie, who had voted against the five-step plan, said that in his opinion the MD should not be implementing the movement of labour, since he considered that as an elected Advisory Board Director he and the other Directors should be conducting such matters involving the workforce. The Chairman agreed with Mr Beattie, stating that the Board should influence the workforce in order to affect an improvement in labour relations, which would then enable the management team to operate in a normal and compatible atmosphere. These views had been reinforced during the subcommittee investigations, when it became clear that appeasement and lack of a clear personnel policy had been major contributory factors in the production demise of the Co-op. Messrs Rosamond and Beattie were also totally agreed, that to change this position amongst the membership who the Directors represented could only be achieved by confronting them with the reality of commercial life. This was unlikely to be accomplished by worrying too much about hurting their feelings or adopting a more humane approach!

On 8th September, the MD reported to the Board on the movement of labour into the machine shop. He was disappointed that only eleven volunteers had come forward, and the organisers were reluctant to release six of these. However, he was of the opinion that the fact that a few volunteers had come forward would make it less difficult to ask other members to accept their transfer; the second stage of the movement proposal would commence following this Board meeting.

The Chairman reported that he was awaiting a telephone call from Mr Robinson to confirm a meeting in London with Mr G Griffiths of GKN, at which their possible financial and managerial assistance would be discussed. Continuing, the Chairman indicated that he would attend with the MD and Mr Beattie. Whilst the Board agreed to this representation, it was stressed that these Directors should be extremely careful not to return to the situation that allegedly existed previously under Dennis Crowder-Johnson's chairmanship, at which time Board members accompanied others to meetings without reporting back. John Rosamond gave the Board his assurance that if this occurred previously, he would not allow this situation to occur again under his chairmanship.

The Chairman then reported that the Co-op Personnel Manager, Mr Hudson, had resigned his position and would leave the company at the end of the week; he was to undertake a ten week training course. Board discussion then took place regarding the personnel function in light of the subcommittee's production investigation findings, and it was agreed that the systems that existed within that department needed to be thoroughly examined to determine whether they were appropriate. Mr Hudson had found it necessary to devote the greater part of his time to industrial relations; this should not have been necessary in a workers' Co-op! Whilst the examination was taking place, Mr Atkinson would undertake the role of Personnel Manager.

The Directors then entered into lengthy discussion regarding the general production situation on 19th September. There was a shortfall in the build programme of 200 units, and the factors contributing to this shortfall were thought to be widespread throughout the factory.

The Chairman was of the opinion that the major problem was the present disgraceful attitude of certain members of the workforce, and he asked if any of the Directors knew the cause.

The MD commented that the movement of labour into the machine shop – in which he was currently involved on the instructions of the Board – had proved extremely difficult and had a marked effect on both production and morale. Of the people who had been nominated to move, several had returned to work with doctor's notes stating that they were unable to work on machines, and two people had left the company. Where personnel had been moved and machining operations had to be learnt, the normal free flow of work could not immediately be achieved. Mr Nelson had anticipated there would be difficulties to be faced in the movement of personnel, and now considered that the whole exercise had created uncertainty and unhappiness throughout the workforce.

The Chairman advised that he had spoken to members on the assembly tracks, whose production levels had for a long time been constrained by lack of component supplies from the machine shop. They were now claiming that as assembly workers had been moved into the machine shop, they could no longer achieve their targets.

Mr Beattie pointed out that, in his opinion, the problem was wholly due to uncooperative attitudes; it would seem that some members had no desire to make a success of the company. Accordingly, he requested that the matter be put before a mass meeting at which the whole workforce be made aware of the facts of the situation, and told that if they so wished they were at liberty to elect a new Board of Directors. The Chairman was in total agreement with Mr Beattie's proposal for holding a mass meeting, and following Board discussion, the agenda for that meeting was decided.

The Chairman was to put the following matters to the mass meeting:

• To appeal to the silent majority to come forward with possible reasons for the dissatisfaction of the workforce.

• To convey the facts of the current situation of the company.

• To offer the opportunity for the workforce to elect a new 11-member Beneficiary Board of Directors.

It was finally agreed – 9 votes in favour, 1 against – that a mass meeting would be held in 15 minutes. Mr Mackie, who had voted against the proposition, stressed that he did not think a mass meeting would serve any useful purpose. The Financial Controller expressed concern regarding continuity, should the Directors be changed! With the worsening workforce attitude, attendance of recent mass meetings by the membership had also declined, and not everyone was present.

As agreed by the Directors, the Chairman informed the members at the mass meeting of the very serious position the Co-op was in. The impact on the workforce was obvious – being totally unexpected, you could hear a pin drop! One or two individuals attempted to suggest they were being blamed for the demise of the Co-op, but it was quickly pointed out to them that their Directors could not force them to keep a job. All that could be done to represent the membership's interests was to provide information on what was required to give the Co-op the best possible chance of survival. If the membership did not agree with what its Directors were asking it to do, then it should elect a new Board that it felt it could support. The Directors who were legally accountable for the Co-op were not prepared to continue without the membership's total support in achieving Board policy.

The silent majority certainly did respond, and all the Directors remained in office.

One of the silent majority offered a reason for some of the shop floor's dissatisfaction. He had overheard office conversations that appeared to suggest a member of the admin staff working for Miss Price had unofficially been paid overtime for undertaking work at home. On investigation, it was determined that in fact there were three individuals who had been paid for such work (two persons from the wages department, and Miss Price's secretary on several occasions). It was agreed that this practice must cease and if this meant urgent work was delayed until the required members were available to work on the factory premises, then this is what would have to happen. In future all overtime working would be sanctioned by the MD.

Geoffrey Robinson addressed the Board on 21st September 1978 regarding financial and managerial assistance.

Mr W Morgan had now indicated to him that GEC would not be prepared to provide financial assistance to the company. GEC had no further legal obligation to Meriden with regard to the £1,000,000 loan made in May/June 1977.

Mr Robinson had made a further approach to Mr G Griffiths (GKN), who had reconsidered the possibility of providing managerial assistance and agreed to attend a meeting with the Directors, following which he would visit the shop floor to make an assessment of the situation. Should he then be convinced that the provision of managerial staff was a workable proposition, he would attempt to provide a good team.

Mr Robinson then stressed that whilst he was now aware that the Board was willing to face up to its responsibilities, a repetition of the difficult situation that had occurred when GKN personnel were previously made available to Meriden could not be tolerated. Meanwhile, he was very pleased to hear that every endeavour was being made to create a receptive atmosphere on the shop floor.

Mr Robinson asked Messrs Nelson (MD) and Boulter (Financial Controller) to pursue their proposals with regard to the HMG loan interest, which would be presented to the Department of Industry, and he offered to give any necessary assistance. Meantime, he requested that details of the company's bought out component costs were provided to him, to enable him to assess the movement of supplier price increases over the past two years. However, a meeting with Mr G Griffiths of GKN did not take place, and Mr Robinson was subsequently advised that like GEC, GKN was not interested.

A further member of the silent majority, Mr F Sherwood, was also stirred into action by the recent mass meeting, writing to the Advisory Board as follows:

Once again at an open meeting of the workforce the blame for failure to achieve and maintain production targets has been put onto production workers, mainly in manufacturing areas. Once again the whipping boy of the welfare scheme and persons not pulling their weight has been publicly flogged along with a new one of 'attitudes'.

Once again the 'myth of Meriden' has been raised, that is 'one complete motorcycle per week for each production worker'. This was never achieved under previous management, either with the incentive of a piecework scheme or under the BSA/Triumph management who tried to 'buy' production with inflated earnings.

Once again no recognition has been given to the dilapidated condition of the plant and the buildings that house them. This particularly applies to the majority of the machine tools and jigs and fixtures, which continue to produce solely due to the efforts of the toolmakers, the machine tool fitters, the jig repairers and the maintenance men. Twenty years ago under the Triumph Engineering Management, some of these machines were reaching the end of their economic productiveness. But in the words of that management "they were good enough to do the job we want."

Since the recommencement of production at Meriden several surveys of condition of the plant in various areas have been carried out on behalf of GKN and GEC and over 2 years ago, consultants Price-Waterhouse suggested that capital investment of £12,000,000 was necessary to replace and refurbish plant and equipment to bring it up to an economic condition. The idea of 'double shifting' in certain areas would possibly increase man hours and production but would be at the risk of longer machine downtime due to breakdowns. To paraphrase the words of a wartime leader "give us the tools and we will give you the job."

The recent extensive discussions regarding how production problems could be solved – reorganisation and relocation of the assembly tracks – was suggested. During GEC's involvement, a consultant Mr Holloway had undertaken some preliminary work on this possibility. Mr Holloway had indicated he could complete these planning proposals on a part time basis over the course of a month, at the cost of £300/£400. The MD and Financial Controller were asked to identify from the completed proposals the savings to be gained from vacating the large Butler Building, and present the finalised report for consideration and approval.

Mr Barclay and Mr Davenport, the subcommittee looking at how elderly pickets could be financially compensated, circulated a report based on advice from consultants Hogg Robinson. Hogg Robinson had indicated how individual retirement grants of up to £3000 (the picket's aspiration) could be realised. The Directors decided that in the company's present financial situation, regrettably the premiums required to gain the compensatory cash benefits could not be agreed. However, the proposition was to be kept in mind as there may be other possible ways of meeting the requested compensation in the future.

On 12th October 1978 we were made aware by the Financial Controller that the company was holding raw material and component stocks, including unfinished bikes, to the value of £2,000,000. Mr Boulter explained how this impacted on the current and budgeted financial position, and reported that the cashflow situation would be critical through the months of October 1978 to January 1979. The cash shortfall at the end of the next four months would produce a bank overdraft in excess of the £500,000 limit. The company would feel the benefit of increased retail prices in January 1979 when it would enter a credit situation until April, following which the position would again decline in July. He expressed his concern regarding the excessive £2,000,000 stock figure. Every effort must be made to reduce this, by increasing production to 330 bikes per week and recovering previous shortfalls. These production shortfalls had contributed to the present overstocking situation. In the meantime, steps were already being taken by the Purchase Department to reduce scheduled order quantities, and a stricter control would now be kept according to lead times on all components.

The Financial Controller pointed out that because of lack of time on his part and the inadequacies of the accounting systems, he had not been fully aware of the developing overstocking situation until it had reached its present state. The appointment of an Accounts Manager – recommended to the Board by the auditors – had not taken place. The Board agreed that the Financial Controller should obtain an Accounts Manager with sufficient experience to run the Accounts Department and attend to the accounting systems generally. Mr Boulter felt such an individual would probably require the normal commensurate salary with this position. Mr Kean abstained from voting on the recruitment of an Accounts Manager.

Along with the MD, the Chairman and Mr Beattie had been reviewing the bonus and sick schemes following the views expressed at the 19th September mass meeting, i.e. the workforce should be given a choice of either being part of the bonus scheme or the sick scheme! In the present financial circumstances the mass meeting's suggestion was well worth considering, as the budgeted cost to the Co-op of the sick scheme in 1978/79 was £115,000. The proposal would be circulated to the workforce for future mass meeting discussion and agreement.

We were very concerned at this time regarding a proposed meeting of skilled trade union Co-op members that had been organised to take place outside the factory premises. It was agreed that if we were invited to attend, it would be made clear that we were doing so as a trade union member, not as Directors of the Co-op!

Geoffrey Robinson advised that with GKN and GEC not being prepared to provide further managerial or financial assistance, it was now necessary for the Co-op to face the coming year alone. Whilst the task appeared difficult in all aspects, he thought that given the right attitudes and determination throughout the workforce, it was possible. If every effort could be made to succeed by achieving at least the departmental budget/production targets of 300 motorcycles plus spare parts per week, Triumph could enter into a further year. Mr Robinson stated that in these circumstances he would give the company every support, and would like as much financial information as possible to assess the situation in detail.

Three days later, the Chairman was able to advise the Directors that Geoffrey Robinson had indicated he would shortly put forward for consideration details of his own possible managerial assistance! He would be visiting the factory on 18th/19th October to meet some of the company's suppliers with the Buying Department, and speak to members of the workforce with a view to raising morale and increasing their productive effort. Mr Lapworth was currently being kept up to date with developments, and would be requested to join Mr Robinson on his forthcoming visit.

9

INHERENT AND IRRECONCILABLE CONTRADICTIONS

It came as little surprise to the Co-op Chairman that GKN and GEC were not prepared to offer further managerial or financial help. GKN's previous seconded managerial assistance had been less than enthusiastically welcomed by the workforce. GEC's commercial experience with the Co-op was also less than memorable. Having provided seconded senior management advice and a £1m factoring finance facility to enable the Stage 2 Meriden Co-op deal with HMG to go ahead, I am sure it felt it had been left 'holding the Co-op baby' when it discovered the two main Co-op architects of the deal, Geoffrey Robinson MP and Dennis Crowder-Johnson (Chairman), had resigned and would no longer be involved.

As Dennis Crowder-Johnson's replacement, I had to try and reassure GEC that it would be business as usual – the agreement with it and HMG would still be fully implemented. When Geoffrey Robinson became re-involved as an advisor, he was critical of the decision to let GEC off the £1m financial hook. Ironically, that Board decision was one of the few occasions when the Directors accepted professional management's advice at face value! The GEC factoring finance was costing the Co-op £27 per bike; a £27 per bike saving could be made by no longer using the facility, so the recommendation to terminate the deal early was accepted by the Board. So there we had it – GKN was not prepared to provide management help and GEC would not reactivate the £1m loan agreement. They were both out.

I felt the senior GKN and GEC executives may well have thought that the ex-Chief Executive of Jaguar Cars, Geoffrey Robinson, was ideally qualified to provide the Co-op with the management leadership it so desperately needed. If this was the reason Geoffrey Robinson had now indicated he was prepared to become directly involved in a senior managerial role, no-one at the Co-op was happier than I. I saw his courageous decision as probably representing the only possibility of the Co-op surviving the winter. We were no longer alone.

Geoffrey Robinson reported on 25th October 1978 that his meetings with the workforce, conducted on a section by section basis, had left him very concerned about the overall situation, which was even worse than he had thought! There were major problems in the skilled areas, not only regarding money, but also about recognition of skills and the backing of vital actions that skilled workers were trying to take for the benefit of the company. There was also bitterness amongst skilled workers that clerical workers, because of the Co-op equal pay policy, were receiving district and above district average wage rates, whilst they were paid below – he felt this needed to be urgently addressed. Even though the admin workers were few in number, psychologically it was important to make this pay adjustment, and this could be done by varying the productivity bonus levels paid.

Following lengthy discussions, the Board agreed that the proposed bonus scheme changes would be placed before the scheduled mass meeting as part of the package of changes that would secure Geoffrey Robinson's involvement in management of the Co-op.

The other changes in this package related to the suspension of the sick scheme for a period of six months – reintroduction being dependent upon affordability on review, and restructuring of the Co-op's management to fully implement the Stage 2 Meriden Co-op Advisory Board to Management Board structure agreed with HMG. This change involved monthly Advisory Board meetings that reviewed management's progress towards achieving company policy, as had always been planned.

The management restructuring proposal enabling this action to take place would involve a new role for John Nelson, who was thanked for his important contribution to the Co-op whilst he was MD. John Nelson, recruited by Dennis Crowder-Johnson – the previous Advisory Board Chairman – to undertake a commercial role in the new Stage 2 Meriden Co-op, found that he became more and more involved in daily production management; not his forte. Without John's commercial contribution during the early, very difficult months of the Stage 2 Meriden Co-op, survival till now would have been impossible. Due to the Co-op's desperate position, John accepted a new role as Spares and Service Executive, where his knowledge and past experience would allow him to make a further fundamental contribution to the Co-op's survival under Geoffrey Robinson's leadership. Directors raised questions regarding the new management structure, particularly about heads of departments selecting or recruiting their own support teams, and the salary levels that may be required, commenting that at the last Beneficiaries' AGM it had been confirmed by resolution that wherever possible, recruitment at Co-op pay rates should take place.

There was obvious Director concern regarding their diminishing role with the proposed monthly Board meeting structure. However, the Chairman was able to reassure them by confirming that whilst he was sure the Directors did not wish to be involved in the day-to-day running of the company, in the event of any problems he would call a meeting to resolve them. In the meantime, John Rosamond stated that he was convinced the Advisory Board was prepared to show confidence in the restructured management team.

PACKAGE TO BE PLACED BEFORE THE MASS MEETING FOR AGREEMENT ON 25TH OCTOBER 1978
    1) Revised bonus scheme
    • The sick scheme would be suspended for a period of six months, after which time it would be reviewed, taking into consideration the financial situation of the company at the time.
    • A two tier bonus would be paid at rates of:
£9 to direct production and certain indirect workers and £6 to the remainder of indirect and administration workers.
    • Payment of the bonus would be based on production of 300+ bikes per week passed to dispatch, plus £25,000 worth of spares.
    • In order to retain flexibility in the amount of 300 units, any number produced over that figure would be placed into a 'bank' that could be used in the event of unforeseen shortages.
    2) Management restructure
    • Co-op co-ordinating capacity – Mr Geoffrey Robinson (in addition to his parliamentary duties).

• Manufacturing and Engineering – Mr Brian Jones.
• Sales Executive (remains as is) – Miss Brenda Price.
• Financial Controller (remains as is) – Mr John Boulter.
• Spares and Service Executive – Mr John Nelson.
3) HMG agreed Advisory Board and Management Board structure
• Monthly Advisory Board meetings to review management's performance.
• Advisory Board Directors to return to their normal duties.

Finally, Geoffrey Robinson requested united support from the Directors, stressing that should he find the situation throughout the factory was such that he met with a refusal to accept the package, then he would feel disinclined to offer continued assistance.

The Geoffrey Robinson statement was music to the ears of at least two Directors, fully justifying their extensive efforts. Subject to receiving the expected mass meeting support, he was in, although initially still only in an advisory capacity, accountable not only to the Directors but also to the workforce – many of whom were his constituents.

The mass meeting on 25th October overwhelmingly voted in favour of the package of changes. Geoffrey Robinson took up the reins of his co-ordination role the following day. There was an immediate boost to morale, and a change in attitudes; belief in the Co-operative workforce was once again achieved, giving 30 per cent improved productivity levels. I was able to return to my day job, and evening round-up meetings with Geoffrey Robinson became the norm, enabling an 'at arms length' Advisory Board overview. No Advisory Board meetings were asked for or took place until the scheduled one on 11th December, to review progress since the October changes.

Geoffrey Robinson and his management team produced a detailed department by department report of over 80 pages, meeting Bill Lapworth's request for a comprehensive review. This outlined the generally improved situation achieved from the end of October to 26th November (the period under consideration). A further package of proposals at the end of the report outlined planned future changes, and the reasons for their implementation. The report was circulated on Saturday 9th December to all those who would attend the Advisory Board meeting, enabling consideration over the weekend for Monday's meeting.

The report, covering all aspects of the business, was discussed and accepted by the Advisory Board, leading to Mr Robinson's package of proposals. These represented the immediate actions he considered necessary to effect continuing improvements towards the company's survival from its current situation. Upon acceptance of the proposals, Mr Robinson would be prepared to undertake the role of Chief Executive.

Mr Robinson commented about his proposals as follows:

The specific proposals here were identified in the main body of the circulated report; they are presented as a package to be accepted or rejected as such. Presenting them as a package is in no sense meant to be an ultimatum, or take it or leave it approach. They are so presented because in total they represent what is felt is the absolute minimum for Meriden to stand any chance of survival from its present desperate financial situation and lack of management.

a) The Directors continue as present to work at their positions in the factory; to attend Board meetings out of working hours once a month in order to review the management of the company.

b) The automatic entitlement to 4 hours overtime each Saturday for each member to be withdrawn.

c) The following management recruitment (the minimum for the current year) would take place and appointments would be made at current market rates.

1 Financial Accountant
1 Facilities, Methods and Planning Engineer
1 Production Engineer
1 Senior Design Engineer
1 Senior Development Engineer
2 Senior Draughtsmen
1 Chief Inspector
1 Senior Sales Administrator

d) The management structure would be realigned and a common salary level established, applying to both designated Senior Executives – Mr B E Jones and Miss B M Price.

e) Offices would be relocated as follows: Spares and Service to space occupied by Sales; Sales to the space occupied by the old Buying office; the offices for Finance, Purchase and Production control would be converted according to the original layout plan.

f) The flat rate payment system would be modified to incorporate a simple grading structure; the basis for this can be either a review carried out by a qualified external organisation, or an internally conducted grading review, or it can be decided by reference to grouped district averages.

The manner of doing this is open for discussion and decision by the Board; the Board's decision on this point would be subject to approval by the workforce.

g) The next pay round scheduled for March 1979 should provide for the introduction of some part of the grading system.

h) The Butler Building should be cleared and steps put in hand to relocate its stores and assembly activities to the main building by the end of August 1979.

A large part of the reasoning behind these proposals is in the main text of the Board report. I am prepared to go through the whole of the report with all the sections of the Co-op out of work hours. There is nothing much more I can say. If the Board kick out the package of proposals, and myself with it, then it will be a relief for me; if they accept it, I'll take the job on but to make a go of it I'll need the active co-operation of the whole Board and all at Meriden. In a Co-op I can only be as effective as the members wish; it is up to everyone to put the Co-op's interests first and work as a team.

Geoffrey Robinson had considered in some depth in the management report the contentious issue that had challenged the Advisory Board of Directors since the formation of the Co-op. Once nominated and elected by one of the eight Co-op trade unions, Directors were expected to act totally in support of democratically agreed Board decisions, not the interests of their own union members. In the report, he precisely identified the dual role of Board member and shop steward as succumbing to inherent and irreconcilable contradictions.

Bill Lapworth, when the Co-op was formed in 1975, commented in the press as follows: "Critics say we are trying to make capitalism work; they're right, for if this comes off both managers and workers will share the benefits. The Meriden Co-operative, with scrapping of restrictive practices and over-manning as well as willingness to accept the linkage of pay to productivity, could demonstrate one of the answers to the deeper problems of British industry. It was well worth paying a small sum of taxpayer's money to find out whether it does."

GKN and GEC had decided against further involvement as a result of their brief experiences with the Co-op's 'new labour' involvement. The different issues that had to be dealt with in a Co-op were not for them!

The forthright debate that took place between Mr Robinson and Mr Lapworth throughout this Advisory Board discussion of Mr Robinson's package of proposals indicated their opposing respective management and trade union views on the way forward, and vividly reminded the Directors that in the past, such contrasting advice had contributed to the "inherent and irreconcilable contradictions" of the Co-op. I wondered if this could have also been one of the reasons my predecessor, Dennis Crowder-Johnson, had chosen to walk away from his Co-operative dream.

After detailed discussion and clarification to the Directors' satisfaction, each of Mr Robinson's proposals and the overall package was finally accepted by a vote of 7 in favour and 3 against; a clear and unequivocal indication of Advisory Board support.

The four hour Advisory Board meeting ended at 8.30pm. If ever justification had been needed for the direct re-involvement of the Co-op's two founding advisors, it was certainly evident in the discussions that had just taken place.

Jim Barclay, the TASS Board Director since the formation of the Co-op, indicated his intention to resign over recent developments. His reasons would be provided in his written resignation for discussion at the next meeting.

Geoffrey Robinson formally accepted the position of Chief Executive in a letter to the Chairman, stating:

Following the proposals that were agreed at the mass meeting on 25th October 1978 and following the acceptance of my proposals as set out in the report presented to the Board at the meeting held on 11th October 1978, I confirm my acceptance of the position of Chief Executive to Triumph Motorcycles (Meriden) Limited.

I am sure you and your Board colleagues will appreciate that the speedy and complete implementation of these proposals is essential to the success of Triumph, and that my continuance as Chief Executive will be dependent upon our achieving them.

My appointment will also be dependent upon Government's decision, effectively to remove their interest charge from this year's trading, as requested in my letter of 15th December 1978 to the Secretary of State for Industry (a draft of this proposed letter was included in Geoffrey Robinson's report to the Board of Directors).

I will do everything in my power to help Triumph succeed but must of course make the reservation that my appointment is subject to my parliamentary and constituency responsibilities.

Geoffrey Robinson.

Geoffrey Robinson was now well and truly in as Chief Executive. The following is his letter to the Secretary of State for Industry, Rt.hon. Eric Varley Esq. MP.

Dear Eric
Meriden
I am addressing this letter directly to yourself since the points it raises will require decisions from yourself and probably Cabinet colleagues. Of course I am copying it to Alan Williams and the relevant officials.

You will find attached some detailed financial information, together with my report to the Board following which my appointment as Chief Executive of Meriden was formally taken.

The financial information gives the revised budget for the period 1st December 1978 to 30th September 1979 for Triumph Motorcycles (Meriden) Limited and for Triumph Motorcycles America Inc. the US subsidiary. The Meriden budget supersedes the one previously forwarded to Alfred Suich by John Boulter, Meriden's Financial Controller, in early September.

The differences between the two budgets are clear from the detailed list of assumptions for the revised budget; by far the most important of these is of course the difference in the dollar/sterling conversion rate it has been found necessary to use since the original budgets were prepared in August this year. It is impossible to exaggerate the crippling effect the dollar exchange rate has had on Meriden which, as you know, in the financial year 1977/78 exported over 60 per cent of its output to the USA and which this year, despite efforts to develop new markets, will still be 57 per cent dependent upon the USA; we have spelled out the implications in our letter to suppliers.

As you can see, Meriden has taken considerable opportunity to increase its retail prices, but despite a 40 per cent reduction in the yen this year to August, Honda has only increased retail prices by 15 per cent. They have even been convicted by the US Treasury of dumping! How topsy turvy a world can you get? I also understand that Honda lost $50m in the last year. Conservatively the dollar devaluation can be said to have cost Meriden £0.4m in the financial year 1977/78.

The Meriden figures tell their own story; if full provision is made in 1978/79 for the payment of Government interest then there will be a loss of £1million. We have taken immediate action to reduce the budgeted loss, and feel acceptably confident that we have sufficient scope for some £600,000 profit improvement. Of these opportunities, the most important relate to savings in material and labour costs but even with these savings, and heaven knows they are going to be difficult enough to achieve, it remains quite clear that we cannot entertain any realistic expectations at all of meeting Government interest.

The detailed up to date product cost breakdown expresses the same problem in a different way and shows Meriden's current trading position is not profitable if interest has to be paid. Against this background it is not so bad an outcome that Meriden last year turned in a loss of around £500,000 (a provisional figure), an improvement over previous years, it should also be noted. But given the budgets exchange rate of $2:£1, this year's budget (1978/79) is bound to present a difficult trading position and it is against this background, over which it has no control, that Meriden at least for 1978/79 is going to have to trade.

The implication for the legal trading position of the Co-op is self evident and cannot be brushed aside. But quite apart from the serious legal considerations I cannot stress enough to you the everlasting effect of a prolonged period of uncertainty and the damage this does to the Co-op's credibility with suppliers and to the morale of those who work at the Co-op. The sort of article in The Financial Times has devastating repercussions in all the above areas.

These conditions are in themselves all compelling enough reasons for the waiver of interest, but there is a further fundamental point; the Co-op will not be able to recruit the key management it needs to survive unless there is some prospect of a future. This is precisely the point I put repeatedly to the Department during the negotiations for the acquisition of the selling rights. The negotiations took seven months, November 1976 to May 1977, an inordinately long period due to the Government's initial rejection of our proposals, then its reluctant acquiescence in the scheme we had originally put up. The only difference at the end of the negotiations was the £1million stock finance from GEC and their offer of managerial advice. Neither of these would have been necessary if the Government had accepted our plans at the beginning; the GEC finance was only needed because of the build up of stock caused by the delay, and the fact that the money is now repaid and the facility is terminated substantiates this point. As far as management goes, had the Government gone along with our plans in the first place, we had a management team ready to start on 1st January 1977 which would have provided a much sounder basis for running the company than through GEC's 'management advice service'. We had previously tried this way; you cannot run a business on advice, there must be a dedicated team directly responsible if you want it to work.

Please do not feel I am trying to rake over the coals; I have written the above because it is directly relevant to our previous position. The management at Meriden needs urgent strengthening; I have proposals for this (see my report to the Board), and have taken full personal responsibility as Chief Executive with the intention of getting Meriden on a firm footing. I have spoken to 5-6 people necessary to fill the gaps in the management team and they are prepared to join the Co-op as from 1st January 1979, but I cannot ask them in all conscience to do this unless HMG is prepared to waive interest to give us at least a fighting chance.

The strengthening of the management team is fully supported by the Board that have progressively come to realise the need for it. This is perhaps one of the most important changes to have taken place at Meriden; it is at their request that I myself have become directly, personally involved in the running of the business.

Turning next to the product itself; as you know this is at the heart of any business. The great failure of the past Triumph management and of many more managements in the private sector was a failure to invest in product development and in new plant and machinery to make the product efficiently and to a high standard of quality. In this report to the Board we have given an outline of what we think is necessary and feasible to keep the Bonneville going for the next five years. The plan, obviously, has got to be developed and costed in detail and this means the expansion of the Engineering Department. In addition to our own plans, we are working with Manchester University with the aid of £150,000 grant from the Wolfson Foundation on more fundamental developments. Obviously this is small beer and much more will be needed, but at least it is a start and it is surprising what can be achieved with a small dedicated team of really good engineers.

May I lastly turn to some general political and philosophical considerations, I personally do not subscribe to the view that the Civil Service do not want Meriden to succeed, but Governmental bureaucracy and the consequent dealings have on previous occasions cost us dear. It is vital therefore that we avoid delay this time. Two Co-ops have already gone under. There is a real risk that the whole concept will be destroyed with perhaps irreparable damage to some of the most deeply held principles and values of our movement.

No one can guarantee you that we can make it through at Meriden, but we have a chance and Government owes it to the men and to itself to give us that chance especially since the reality of the situation is that Government is giving up nothing; Meriden cannot pay interest and that is that.

In reaching your decision, you and your colleagues in the Cabinet may wish to consider what has been achieved at Meriden to justify continued support. Perhaps I can put a few points to you.

Meriden has paid £128,000 interest.

Meriden has not applied for TES.

Meriden has provided continuous employment for some 700 people for three years.

Meriden has generated over £10m pounds of exports.

Meriden, despite all the traumas of 1975-76 sold 13,400 motorcycles last year, more than the Boston Consultancy group thought possible.

Meriden productivity is now some 30 per cent higher than it was under private ownership.

Meriden's Board of Worker Directors is proving the worth of co-operation against conflict.

Meriden has progressively established a competent management team accepted by all and working with all.

Of course, none of this one can easily object has generated profits. That is a valid point to which, however, there are two equally valid rejoinders. In the period March 1975 to May 1976, Meriden was at the mercy of Dennis Poore who had the exclusive selling rights. We have no direct access to his files, but are convinced that he made profits, at least equal to Meriden's losses. Secondly, as has already been said, the devaluation of the dollar against sterling has cost Meriden very dear; some £0.4million on our estimates – far more than our last year's losses.

For my part I can do no more than put my name to Meriden and to take on the Chief Executive's responsibility as I have; however, my continuance in this function is dependent on an early waiver of interest being granted or some other means being found to remove the charge from this year's trading.

Yours sincerely
Triumph Motorcycles (Meriden) Limited
Geoffrey Robinson MP
(Chief Executive)

The Meriden workforce was once again totally committed, content in the knowledge that at last, in Geoffrey Robinson, they had a proven Chief Executive they could trust to eat, sleep and breathe Triumph until the desperate position their Co-op was in was resolved; whatever was required of them to support his actions in 1979, they were totally prepared to give!

10

FREEDOM OF THE PRESS

The festive season provided quality time for all Co-op members to spend with their families, and I was no different. Later in the new year Brian Sedgemore MP's forceful speech on the 15th January in the House of Commons debate on the Civil Service, certainly shocked me. The press allegation that followed about Civil Servants at the Department of Industry having attempted to close the Meriden Co-op as part of a secret deal with Japanese motorcycle company Kawasaki to bring its manufacturing operation to Britain was devastating news for all Co-op members.

Thank God for the freedom of the press. It had long been a generally held view of the Meriden membership that whilst the political complexion of Government and Ministers changed from time to time, the Civil Servants remained exactly the same, doing everything they could, it would seem, to obstruct the Co-op; but without the press we would not have known of this alleged treachery.

There was never any doubt in my mind that Geoffrey Robinson was a very well educated (Emanuel School, Clare College Cambridge and Yale University) 'man in a hurry', and as such exactly what the Meriden Co-op needed. A solution to our commercial problems had to be found, and found quickly, if long-term viability was to be pursued. I was also in no doubt that our new Chief Executive had the ability and drive to find that solution, if there was one to be found.

No-one forced him to become the Co-op's unpaid Chief Executive; according to the press he took the job at the request of the Department of Industry – extremely good news for me, as it suggested that if an acceptable formula could be found, the socialist Department of Industry Ministers would be supportive.

Putting his Meriden Co-op 'baby' on a better financial footing was obviously only a short-term personal objective for Geoffrey Robinson, who had already achieved industrial career success as the Chief Executive of Jaguar Cars prior to beginning his political career as socialist MP for Coventry North West. Making the courageous personal decision to become directly involved in saving the Co-op indicated to me that he believed it was saveable; a massive boost to morale and the basis of my personal support and commitment to him. I was totally aware that his involvement in the Co-op would be extremely beneficial to his left-wing socialist credentials, advancing him from one of many Labour party back benchers to 'the socialist', using his commercial ability and experience to advance the Co-operative concept so revered by the Labour movement, and in so doing assisting his obvious political ambition to climb to high ministerial office within Government.

A more humorous side to increasing Geoffrey Robinson's political profile was provided by the Co-op's Social Club. They had recently started selling very distinctive red, white and blue Triumph quilted paddock jackets. Geoffrey was provided with a special three quarter length one, which he often wore whilst in the House of Commons, causing his immediate recognition. Whenever I or Bill Beattie accompanied Geoffrey on Labour party activities, our dress code was always 'smart casual with Triumph jacket'! Bill Beattie and I were often initially mistaken for Geoffrey by other political dignitaries, who on recognising the Triumph jacket would say "Hello Geoffrey, how are things at the Co-op? Oh sorry, I thought you were Geoffrey Robinson." Geoffrey Robinson certainly now stood out from the other back benchers, and was already respected for fighting to keep the Co-op alive.

At our first meeting of 1979 on 22nd January, the Chief Executive thanked everyone for the team effort made during the 19th January meeting with the DOI and IDU. The main reason for the meeting today was for him to seek approval for further strengthening of the management team. Brian Jones, who had assumed responsibility 3 months earlier for manufacturing in addition to his Chief Engineer's design duties, had done a magnificent job achieving both motorcycle production and spare parts targets. However, as had been foreseen, this came at the cost of adversely affecting the engineering effort that was also vital to the Co-op's survival. Accordingly, in line with the agreed Board policy it was now necessary to appoint a fully qualified and experienced Manufacturing Executive. From recruitment activities during the last three months, Geoffrey Robinson had shortlisted two individuals, Mr N Yarrow and Mr R Lindsay. His recommendation was Mr Lindsay, who had worked for him in this manufacturing role when he was Chief Executive of Jaguar Cars.

The Chief Executive gave a full account of Mr R (Bob) Lindsay's personal background and detailed his extensive knowledge and experience in manufacturing. He had previously been Director in charge of Ford Dagenham Engine Plant and then Director of Manufacturing for Jaguar Cars.

The Directors approved the Chief Executive's recommendation, although Mr Mackie, who voted against, was concerned at the prospect of a salary 'leapfrogging' situation developing so far as future executive recruitment was concerned. Mr Robinson stated that he would make sure this did not occur.

The Chief Executive's management report for the period end-November 1978 to 26th January 1979 was circulated for consideration prior to the meeting on 2nd February 1979. It was evident from the details provided that Geoffrey Robinson was now totally in control of his management team, whose collective efforts he was leading. His two deputies, Brenda Price and Brian Jones, were proving to be excellent choices. The management team's strengthening with the appointment of Mr R Lindsay (Manufacturing Executive), Mr V Gupwell (Chief Inspector), Mr I Rush (Senior Sales Administrator) and Mr B Gathercole (Accountant) further increased its effectiveness. Mr R Atkinson, who had indicated his intention to resign as a Board Director in order to take on the role of Personnel Manager, was asked to delay until the Co-op's AGM. He was currently totally involved with Mr Beattie and the trade union movement in securing right of passage for the Co-op's motorcycle export containers through the national dock's strike pickets. Mr Barclay's reasons for resignation were discussed by the Board prior to being appended to the minutes as he had requested.

Geoffrey Robinson disputed Mr Barclay's claim that the Co-op management now being recruited was additional to that proposed in the original 1975 constitution. The Chief Executive also tried to persuade Mr Barclay to reconsider his resignation, but it was clear that he was suffering deeply from the "inherent and irreconcilable contradictions" of being a Meriden Co-op Director.

The strengthening of the management team agreed by the Board in order to address commercial reality was vital if long-term viability was to be pursued. Unfortunately, although there were already able and qualified individuals in the company working for the Co-op rate of pay, the reality was to recruit the additional able and qualified managers, we had to pay competitive market rates. Perhaps Mr Barclay's TASS trade union members were to recognise this idealism versus realism conflict when they later re-elected him as their most able person to serve on the Advisory Board.

The Chief Executive advised on the 15th February that all the documents requested by Mr A Suich (Senior DoI Civil Servant) had now been supplied, with the exception of a 3-year forecast which was impossible to produce prior to the commencement of the selling section. Mr Suich had put forward the suggestion of a deferral of the HMG loan interest, basically on the grounds that a) the Government was not convinced that Triumph would sell the bikes, and b) by granting a deferral it meant that the Government would not relinquish its right (as would be the case should they agree to a waiver) to the £1.2m interest should the company close down.

Mr Robinson's reply to Mr Suich's interest deferral suggestion was that unless a total waiver was granted, the Co-op would request the Government to appoint a receiver.

Whilst a meeting took place on 23rd February, at which important issues such as the March pay review (based upon Coventry district average differentials) were discussed in depth, it was hard to get away from the fact that without a solution to the HMG loan interest, the future of the Co-op looked bleak. The company's auditors had already advised that without the interest waiver they would be obliged to qualify the now due annual accounts. Mr Lapworth (Advisor) was present at this Board meeting, the first one he had attended since Mr Robinson's appointment as Chief Executive.

Mr Lapworth registered his opinion that the Board members were not interested in receiving advice from the trade union, this impression being borne out by the fact that proposals had been put forward and times of Board meetings (at which important decisions had been made, such as management recruitments) changed at short notice, making it impossible for him to attend. The Chairman and the Chief Executive both objected to Mr Lapworth's claim that changes to the times of Board meetings were intentionally made to prevent his attendance! The Chairman pointed out that he had always tried to contact Mr Lapworth on such occasions. The Chief Executive reminded the Directors that he had an understanding with the Board that meetings had to be arranged to take into consideration his parliamentary commitments. The Chairman stated that in future the Company Secretary, Mr Boulter, would undertake to notify Mr Lapworth of meetings in writing via recorded delivery, and he was sorry if Mr Lapworth had gained the impression that he was not required at the Board meetings since all of the Directors always welcomed and appreciated his advice.

On 8th March the Board agreed that Messrs J Rosamond, W Beattie, G Mackie, H Hughes, G Robinson and the Company Secretary would represent the Co-op at a meeting with Mr A Williams, Minister of State, and colleagues at the Department of Industry, London, to be held at 4.00pm on Friday 9th March. It was further agreed that the aforementioned Directors should be empowered to act on behalf of the Board in pursuance of a complete waiver of all HMG accrued interest to date.

On 10th March, the Chairman and the other Directors present at the Department of Industry meeting the previous day reported that only a deferral of interest due on 31st December 1979 had been offered. In line with the authority invested in the representative Directors, this offer was rejected as being of little use if qualified annual accounts were to be avoided. At the end of the Department of Industry meeting, the Chief Executive confirmed the Board's position in a handwritten letter (on House of Commons note paper) to the Minister of State.

Mr Alan Williams, Minister of State, undertook to reply within 4 to 6 weeks regarding the Co-op's request for a complete waiver of all interest.

The Chief Executive told the Directors that since our DoI meeting he had spoken with Sir Peter Carey, Permanent Under Secretary at the Department of Industry, and with Mr Alan Williams, Minister of State, reiterating the commercial, political and psychological reasons a waiver as set out in the 9th March 1979 letter was the minimum that we could accept.

We never did find out why the offered 6-month deferral of interest would have been beneficial to us. Perhaps within the minority Government it was felt to be the best that could be done with a possible General Election being contemplated, the results of which, if it went against Labour, would leave the Co-op fighting not only the Civil Servants but also an ideologically hostile Conservative Government. If this was the reason, then in my view it would have been an ideal time to take the waiver decision and further support the Co-op in its hour of need, especially in view of the Department of Industry's alleged involvement with Kawasaki for which taxpayers' money was supposedly available! Without the HMG interest waiver, the future looked very bleak, not least because Geoffrey Robinson had made it clear from the outset to both the Co-op and HMG that he would only undertake the Chief Executive's role on the understanding that an acceptable solution was found for non-payment of the loan interest.

On 23rd March, the Directors received a copy of the Chief Executive's latest management report for the period up to 23rd March; because of the available time before the Board meeting that afternoon, Geoffrey Robinson would go through every section in detail. Once again it was a very comprehensive report, covering all aspects of the business during the period under review.

An impressive turnaround in the cash situation had been achieved due to the management actions that had been taken – as at 23rd February, the bank balance stood at plus £169,500, compared with a forecasted overdraft of £667,700. The improvement over budget of £837,200 demonstrated that the company had avoided the cash crisis it was facing at the beginning of the financial year.

Summarising the overall financial report, the Chief Executive commented that the losses in the United States were at present at their worst; budgeted pricing action would reduce them by at least 50 per cent. So, with the losses budgeted for, and as the mix of production and sales moved from the USA, profitability would improve and a break even on profit and loss was still envisaged as per the DoI February 1979 submission, in pursuit of the HMG loan interest waiver.

Despite the devaluation in the dollar and despite the current stocks, Mr Robinson reiterated his aim was still a break even, with HMG loan interest waived. What was required in the States was a lower volume of sales at a consistently higher price.

A mass meeting had approved the four proposed wage groupings based broadly in line with Coventry district averages. The productivity element would be paid by cutting back 50 per cent on overtime and bringing back £10 per bike on subcontract work currently done outside the Co-op.

New organisation for the manufacturing areas was being pursued by Mr Lindsay, and a firm commitment had been given to introduce a pay differential unlinked to production by no later than the next review. Whilst not all members were fully in agreement, it was thought the grievances would subside as the new payment system bedded in. Mr Beattie raised his concern that if Mr Lindsay was unable to recruit all the planned senior organisers from within the plant, he may have to consider recruitment from outside at market rates, in which case he felt it would be morally wrong to expect individuals recruited from within the Co-op to continue their senior organiser roles without increasing their wages to the same market rates of pay. The Chief Executive replied that initially the intention was to pursue the internal recruitment route at the Co-op's current top rate of pay, and if there was any change to this he would re-approach the Board. Having considered the management report in detail, it was accepted.

Whilst Geoffrey Robinson was still deeply involved at the Co-op during the early part of April, particularly in an attempt to achieve a more efficient running of the factory by altering the tea break times (these changes ended up with the final decision being taken by ballot), more and more of his time was being focused on political matters in the run up to the General Election on 3rd May 1979. Many of the Co-op members, including Bill Beattie and myself, were helping outside works hours in Geoffrey's campaign for re-election as Labour MP for Coventry North West. The campaigning volunteers, suitably decked out in Triumph jackets with Labour party rosettes, were delegated to knocking on constituency doors amidst the leafleting action taking place. The response we got on the doorsteps left us in little doubt that Geoffrey was a well liked, good constituency MP, and certain to be re-elected.

JJ Burnell, song writer, bass guitarist and occasional lead vocalist with the highly acclaimed rock band The Stranglers, released his solo debut album *Euroman Cometh* in 1979; by April it had reached number one in the charts. JJ, a Triumph enthusiast, noted the battle taking place to save the company with the following inside-sleeve declaration:

"The Triumph Worker's Co-operative at Meriden has proved that personally motivated enterprise coupled with group interest is a necessary ingredient in successful socialism and that the sham they call National Socialism could only be suggested and perpetrated by enemies of the people."

The *Euroman Cometh* album track *Triumph of the Good City* featured the iconic engine sound of the Bonneville.

All the Labour party faithful were gathered with Geoffrey Robinson on the evening of 3rd May to hear the Coventry North West result, and we were not disappointed. Geoffrey Robinson was re-elected and the celebrations began. These were short-lived, however, when it became clear that Geoffrey's local success had not been repeated across the country and there was to be a change of Government. The Labour party was out and the Conservatives had been returned to power. The party faithful were devastated – those who also worked at the Co-op doubly so. The difficult task of trying to persuade a Labour Government Minister to waive the loan interest had just become almost impossible. Whatever understandings Geoffrey Robinson may have had with the previous socialist Department of Industry regime no longer existed. The believed to be anti Co-op Civil Servants were now to be supervised by Tory Ministers who were hostile to Co-ops. Geoffrey Robinson's personal political ambition had also taken a big hit, as ministerial office was now obviously years away whilst a period in opposition was served. The Co-op's first really effective Chief Executive, who I have referred to previously as a man in a hurry, was now going to have to 'mark time' politically, which I knew he would not take to kindly!

Geoffrey Robinson's immediate reaction was to refocus on the Co-op. Over the next week the Chief Executive took stock, forced now to operate in a totally new political environment. He reassessed the Co-op's desperate commercial situation, especially motorcycle sales performance, now that the selling season was well under way. What he found was not good – stock was building up and this situation had to be addressed. The Chief Executive told me that he was working on the details of a management report for the Board which would indicate the need to cut back on factory production to destock the market, and inevitably this meant a reduction of the workforce.

Keeping it in the family; biker sister-in-law to be Rose aboard a US-spec T140V Bonneville. (Courtesy Rose Tolley)

Brother-in-law to be Ted (left) and his brothers Bob and Chris (in the tent) were also into the British motorcycle rider scene. (Courtesy Rose and Ted Tolley)

The Board report indicating the problems we faced was being compiled in the normal way by the management team under the Chief Executive's supervision, and now required the additional input of the Personnel Manager, Ron Atkinson, regarding Department of Employment legislation that needed to be adhered to. The confidential management report for the Advisory Board, when complete, would give details of the motorcycle overstock situation and provide commercial options and recommendations from the Chief Executive for the Director's consideration, before deciding upon the policy to be put before the workforce for agreement. The detailed information contained in the management report would also provide the basis on which to speak to the Co-op's bank and HMG, it being vital to retain their continued support whilst these difficult measures were implemented. Unfortunately, before the management report was complete a leak to the *Coventry Evening Telegraph* forced the calling of an urgent Advisory Board meeting. Bad news was about to break in the same publication that carried the story of Triumph factory closure before the workforce had been consulted in 1973!

The emergency Board meeting on 17th May 1979 opened with the Chairman explaining to the Directors that because of this leak to the press, there was a likelihood of a report concerning Meriden appearing in the *Coventry Evening Telegraph* with regard to:
a) Redundancies
b) The return of motorcycles from the States
c) The renting out of the Butler Building

The *Telegraph* had telephoned Mr Robinson, giving details that had been made known to it and which included exaggerated figures regarding the number of redundancies and bikes to be returned from the States. Mr Robinson had been forced to correct the details, at the same time confirming that such proposals were to be placed before the Board. Mr Robinson had also spoken to the Department of Industry regarding the situation and would be meeting with representatives of the National Westminster Bank on 18th May.

The Chairman further explained that whilst the Board (with the exception of himself and Ron Atkinson, Personnel Manager) had no knowledge of the proposals, which included redundancies and short-time working, they were contained in a report for discussion by the Directors at tomorrow's meeting, Friday 18th May, following which recommendations would be put to the workforce at a mass meeting. Meantime, whilst preliminary discussions had taken place on the proposals during the last two weeks, the Chairman advised that the only persons with knowledge of the details were himself and Mr Atkinson, Messrs Robinson, Jones, Lindsay, Boulter, Baldwin and Miss Price.

The Directors were very concerned at the effect such a press report would have on suppliers, dealers and the workforce, and critical of the fact that they themselves had no knowledge of what was being considered. It was therefore agreed that a notice would be immediately posted on the boards referring to the possible publication of the report in the *Telegraph* and explaining that management's proposals had not yet been discussed by the Board, and that recommendations would be the subject of a mass meeting to be held on Monday 21st May. Mr Kean raised the question of the rights and possible claims that could be made by Co-op Beneficiaries against the company in the event of members being dismissed, and it was agreed that Mr P Davies (solicitor) would be requested to join the Board meeting arranged for the following day, in order to clarify the legal implications of the situation.

The 18th May Board meeting opened with the Company Solicitor, Mr Peter Davis, providing the required Beneficiary clarification. This matter was not covered in the original trust document; whilst the Beneficiaries had an interest in the ownership of the company, they were also employees and it would be the contract of employment which would be terminated on the grounds of redundancy. At the same time, anyone considering that he/she had a claim for wrongful dismissal would have the normal rights to appeal to a tribunal. The consequence of being dismissed, however, was that one ceased to be a Beneficiary; what the trust document did not cover was the situation in the event of a member's notional interest being of value.

The company being in a deficit situation meant that the Beneficiaries' notional interest was of no monetary value, but only gave the Beneficiary the right to control. The matter was one to which the company should, perhaps, give consideration in the future in order to cover the event of the company becoming profitable, at which stage problems could arise regarding anyone joining or leaving the company; individuals would then be required on joining to provide a sum of money to become a Beneficiary, whereas individuals leaving the company would have to be paid a cash sum equal to the value of their notional interest.

The Chief Executive then outlined his proposals regarding redundancy and/or short-time working, first reminding the Directors that when he came to Triumph in October 1978, he had said that he would not know what action would finally be necessary until the start of the selling season. The season having now commenced, it was apparent that the company would be unable to sell more than approximately 11,150 motorcycles in the current year. Various factors had contributed to the recent over-stocking situation, the decline in sales (in part due to adverse weather conditions during winter months) and the revaluation of sterling, which resulted in extensive monetary losses due to the high percentage of export trade. Mr Robinson's proposal in respect of sales was to sell a total of 11,140 units in 1979/1980, which would in fact be a 10 per cent increase in sales over last year and this should ensure a break even position before HMG interest payment. If the figure of 11,140 sales was not accepted, it would mean (because of the present high stocking position and the declining trend in sales) that the company would accumulate a total stock of 8208 motorcycles by the end of the year.

The Chief Executive explained that it was therefore necessary to destock the market, and in order to achieve this it was proposed that the weekly production rate be cut back from 300 to 200 motorcycles per week by either:

a) A period of 18 months of short-time working at 3 days per week.

b) A period of 2 months of total factory closure.

c) A reduction in the labour force equivalent to 200 employees, requiring:

– 150 redundancies incorporating immediate retirement of employees over retirement age.

– The elimination of paid overtime; time off would be granted in lieu of overtime worked.

– The in-sourcing of an additional £10 per bike of sub-contract work.

Because of the disadvantages that would be incurred by options a) and b) in respect of cost and the loss of skilled employees, the Chief Executive's recommendation was option c), which he visualised should be implemented immediately with the selection of the 150 employees involved being balanced throughout the factory in order to achieve the required lower production targets.

The Directors were not in agreement with the implementation of this action at such short notice, and it was pointed out that notification must be given to both the Department of Employment and the trade unions.

Mr Atkinson, the Personnel Manager, reported that he had contacted the Department of Employment whom he thought would accept the situation, provided it was also agreeable to the trade unions. In the case of the latter, for whom the stipulated notice period is 90 days, it was agreed that representatives from the 8 trade unions involved would be invited to attend a meeting with the Board of Directors as soon as possible.

It was agreed by the Directors that further time was required for consideration before arriving at a decision. Having slept on the resolution to dismiss fellow members because they were now surplus to requirements – probably the most difficult decision a Director of a Workers' Co-operative could ever have to make – the Board meeting reconvened at 8.15am on Saturday 19th May, when the Chief Executive requested that the following points of principle be minuted:

a) If the Board felt that he had not been consulting with it as fully as he should over the past five weeks, he would remind it that during that time he had been fighting a General Election, which had required his full attention, and it was in no way his intention to boycott the Board.

b) Furthermore, full reports had been presented to the Board previous to the election, and it was his intention that these would continue. Between Board meetings he would be consulting with the Chairman, and this was the way a Chief Executive would normally work.

c) Finally he wanted to get away from the idea that it was he who was running the company as Chief Executive in his own right, and stressed that it was the whole team (Board and management) who was running the company. At the same time, he also wanted to eliminate the 'us and them' situation between those earning salaries and the rest of the members.

The Chief Executive then repeated the options that had been proposed for destocking the market.

Voting then took place on the market destocking proposals, which resulted in 1 Director voting against and 9 Directors voting in favour of redundancy.

The redundancy would be consistent with achieving the following:

a) 200 bikes per week.

b) £1.5m spare parts per year.

c) Selling 10 per cent more motorcycles next year than this year.

Additionally, to equate with a total redundancy of 200 employees, a further £10 per bike of subcontract work would be resourced in-house and all paid overtime would be abolished (proportionate time off in lieu of overtime hours worked would be granted).

Mr Barclay recorded his reasons why he had voted against redundancy. Whilst he recognised that some action must be taken to reduce both the workforce and output because of the sales position, and at the same time accepted the Chief Executive's views regarding advertising, he was not satisfied that enough was being done to maximise sales of bikes. The Chief Executive stated that he was satisfied with the sales performance.

Mr Kean recorded that in light of the facts that had been placed before the Board, he could see no alternative but to vote for redundancy.

Following further discussion the Directors agreed the order in which redundancy would take place:

a) Everyone of retirement age and over (60 years female – 65 years male) would be requested to retire, and it would become company policy for employees to retire at normal retirement age. All founder members (pickets) compulsorily retired due to being over retirement age would receive a sum of either £500 or whatever the maximum was paid to other employees who may be made redundant. This commitment to continue through to 10th March 1980 in respect of founder members reaching retirement age.

b) Part-timers: Toilet cleaners to be retained.

All part-timers in manufacturing areas to be made redundant.

In administration areas, when anyone was to be made redundant part timers would be given notice first.

Work experience personnel would cease immediately.

Temporary personnel would cease immediately.

c) Following retirement (approximately 40 employees), the company would pay the minimum legal requirement to the remaining 110 employees to be made redundant.

d) Mr R Lindsay and his organisers would be charged with coming forward with a list of redundancies from manufacturing areas. Mr G Robinson would attend to administration areas.

e) Meetings with the workforce, on a sectional basis, would take place during Monday 21st May.

f) All information explaining and justifying the course of action would be produced for the trade union officials who would be invited to attend a meeting on Tuesday 22nd May.

g) Security measures would be arranged in order to avoid losses of tools, equipment and overalls.

When the Advisory Board supported Geoffrey Robinson's appointment as Chief Executive, it was in the full knowledge and belief he would implement commercial policies agreed by it to try and achieve long-term viability for the Co-op, everything else that had been tried to date having failed. Accordingly, it was only right that however painful and difficult the Chief Executive's recommended commercial action was, the Directors supported him.

11

RETIREMENTS AND REDUNDANCIES

The distressing 17th May 1979 article by David Fuller in the *Coventry Evening Telegraph* confirmed everyone's fears – "Jobs Shock for Meriden Men." Months of constant investigation and rebalancing the workforce to try and achieve the vital 300 motorcycles plus spare parts each week had only partially succeeded. Geoffrey Robinson becoming the unpaid Chief Executive with his additional management created the organisational, attitude and pay structure changes that guaranteed production targets were met on a regular basis. Having finally achieved manufacturing targets, overstock had been created in the market that would now have to be corrected by reducing production capacity with enforced retirements and redundancy – devastating news.

The Advisory Board, which had been totally involved with the Chief Executive in the commercial changes that had secured the Co-op workforce's confidence transformation, reacted badly to the news of the market overstock situation and the proposals to resolve it. So much so, that having initially discussed the position, we adjourned overnight before making any decisions. The following day I understood exactly why Geoffrey Robinson felt obliged to record his three points of principle at the beginning of the reconvened meeting.

The points of principle reminded the Directors of their collective responsibility for the realistic commercial policy that had been established, and also ensured that they spoke in support, however difficult, at the meetings with the membership. The Chief Executive's stinging criticism of the Board when defending the missed sales targets that had caused the overstock situation was unfair. He pointed out that sales the previous year had only been achieved whilst selling at a loss in all markets. Whilst this was true, the Directors' guilt was from believing professional management regarding the calculated motorcycle sales prices! Not the most reassuring of thoughts when the Directors contemplated how they would explain to their trade union members that having done exactly what had been asked of them, nearly a third would now lose their jobs. Yet again, the inherent and irreconcilable contradictions of being a trade union shop steward and an Advisory Board Director were to be exposed, on this occasion to the total workforce. It was not at all surprising that faced with this terrible dilemma, some of the Directors started to wobble under pressure from their members, who on seeing the *Telegraph* article turned to their full-time trade union officials for advice and representation.

The section meetings with the workforce on 21st May were, as anticipated, extremely hostile. The Chief Executive's points of principle had succeeded in reminding the 11 Directors of their collective responsibility for the agreed market destocking policy. However, convincing the already aware workforce that nearly a third of their number were likely to lose their jobs, when they were of the opinion that it was those who had failed to sell the bikes that should be dismissed, not those who had finally succeeded in producing them, was going to be more difficult.

One lasting memory I came away with from those extremely painful section meetings was the muttered comment in my ear of Sir Walter Scott's *Marmion* epic poem quotation "O what a tangled web we weave when first we practice to deceive." This pretty well summed up the general feelings of the workforce. The section meetings completed, the workforce was now in full possession of the details of the Board's destocking proposals recommended for their acceptance. It was now also able to determine exactly who would be affected by way of retirement or redundancy, should it vote in favour. Once again, the well informed *Coventry Evening Telegraph* carried the story by David Fuller of the day's section meetings. "Meriden boss spells out crisis plan – axe on jobs is only chance."

On 22nd May, the full-time trade union officials met the Chief Executive and the Advisory Board of Directors. What can only be described as a very acrimonious meeting took place, at which the officials found it impossible to come to terms with the fact that they were trying to negotiate with their own factory trade union representatives, who at the Co-op were also company Directors.

Accordingly, Geoffrey Robinson the Chief Executive was the main focus of their total opposition towards any enforced action to reduce the workforce, regardless of the seriousness of the financial situation.

A workforce mass meeting with the trade union officials took place on 24th May, before which the early editions of the *Coventry Evening Telegraph* had a story by Andy Grice reporting further bad news for the Co-op – "Trouble-torn Meriden Co-op face rates crisis."

The 24th May mass meeting of the workforce, addressed by the trade union officials, took place in the company's soon to be vacated Butler Building, chaired by Ray Lissaman, District Official for the Co-op's second largest trade union membership, the AEUW. The three options to cut production, put by the Chief Executive to the Board, were now reconsidered by the total workforce.

The union officials were speaking against the Board's commercial recommendation to reduce the workforce, and in favour of an alternative investigation by the trade union officials to determine the most acceptable method of short-time working. During an extremely rowdy meeting – at which an attempt was made to present a petition to Chairman Ray Lissaman demanding Geoffrey Robinson's presence to put across the commercial view (which was refused) – a vote in favour of the union officials' short-time working investigation was carried.

After the mass meeting, the trade union officials advised the Chief Executive of the workforce's decision for them to further investigate short-time working possibilities. The legally accountable Advisory Board Directors' recommended policy for saving the Co-op had been hijacked in favour of a trade union option that was not commercially viable. The Chief Executive and Directors had a choice: resign, or fight back to regain control – they chose the latter. Geoffrey Robinson can only be described as being extremely angry. He recalled the workforce to another mass meeting and very forcefully spelt out the commercial facts of life that the Co-op faced if it was to survive. Directors, who were felt not to have stood firm on the agreed Board policy, incurred the Chief Executive's wrath. The outcome of this blistering performance was that the trade union officials' short-time working proposal was thrown out in favour of the Advisory Board's recommended destocking programme, to be achieved by retirements and redundancies – the only commercial option, Geoffrey Robinson had indicated to the mass meeting, that he believed gave the Co-op the slightest chance of survival. A wily old Brummie (man from Birmingham) from the stores was heard to comment about the Chief Executive's performance to get the trade union officials' decision reversed – "You'd have paid a tenner to see that at Stratford." I wondered if he knew Geoffrey loved Shakespeare! Once again, the *Coventry Evening Telegraph* carried a detailed story by David Fuller in the final edition on 24th May: "Meriden about turn on jobs."

The Advisory Board of Directors, legally accountable for the Co-op, was once again in control ... well, almost! When consulted regarding the destocking proposals, the Department of Employment had indicated that it would fall in line with whatever the trade unions agreed regarding the enforced retirement and redundancy programme.

Accordingly, without agreement with the trade unions, the statutory 90 days' notice period had to be served on a short-time working basis. Morale, so vital to the Co-op's existence, can only be described as now being at an all time low, with the workforce suffering acute depression from the destocking production rate cut that forced short-time working. Having agreed to the Boards' recommendation, the workforce now had to face 90 days before the plan could be implemented. However, those who knew they were destined to lose their jobs took the matter into their own hands, taking the job offers the Chief Executive had managed to secure for them.

Predictably, however, there were a number of very genuine Co-op members who were deeply troubled by the events they had witnessed, decided they had had enough, and also departed.

Geoffrey Robinson, who had briefly left the Advisory Board meeting that followed the mass meetings, returned to collect a draft letter to Sir Keith Joseph at the Department of Industry. The letter outlined future relations between Triumph and the new Tory Government. The Chief Executive took the opportunity to apologise to Mr Barclay, Mr Kean and Mr Williams for the events that had occurred during the earlier mass meetings, when he had attempted to try and regain control. Two Directors, Jim Barclay and Felix Kean, subsequently resigned as a direct result of what had happened. Ken Anderton and David Davenport were to follow shortly afterwards. Geoffrey's political standing in the eyes of his constituency Labour party also took a knock as a result of the highly publicised Co-op workforce cut backs. They were concerned regarding the impact on his constituents. In a few days, Geoffrey had gone from the socialist hero battling to save the Co-op, to appearing to be making the Co-op members redundant. It was therefore understandable that the Chief Executive was in favour of allowing the BBC *Man Alive* programme to make a documentary explaining the problems of the Co-op, and the forced commercial steps to try and solve them. I knew the workforce would not be as enthusiastic about returning to the 'goldfish bowl' media coverage that existed under Dennis Crowder-Johnson's chairmanship. However, as the BBC documentary would be factually correct and the workers would play their part in its contents, I believed they would agree to it.

I was extremely worried about Geoffrey's health at this time, concerned he might crack up under the tremendous workload he was undertaking on our behalf. He often commuted between London and Coventry, taking part in high pressure meetings in his constituency, at the Co-op and in Parliament. On one occasion, Bill Beattie and I were to accompany him to a meeting in London. We had arranged to meet at Coventry railway station to undertake the journey together. Geoffrey Robinson, having already completed his early meeting in his

Coventry North West constituency, arrived at the station to see me queuing for train tickets. "I've got the tickets" he shouted, and we all boarded the train. Finding out that, with so many things on his mind, he actually did not have the right tickets led to some embarrassment upon arrival at Euston Station.

In anticipation that the Government would shortly make a clear decision on waiving the loan interest, it was necessary with production cut back to 3 days a week that other key areas of the Co-op continued to function as normally as possible on 5-day working. These key areas, vital to the Co-op's future, demonstrated a tremendous act of faith and commitment in answering the Chief Executive's appeal for this, doing so whilst in receipt of only 3 days pay. Quite remarkable in the circumstances.

The key sections continuing on 5-day working were the Engineering and Experimental departments (working on the 8-valve cylinder head, electric start and balanced engine projects, plus the 1980 model introduction updates), Spare Parts and Motorcycle Sales (highly profitable sales of spare parts and destocking sales of motorcycles), Wages (making sure the workforce on short-time received its 3 days' wages, plus statutory guaranteed payments for their two laid-off days), and Accounts Payable (ensuring suppliers were treated in line with the Chief Executive's agreements with them to retain their continued support).

Four weeks after the mass meeting with the trade union officials, over 80 Co-op workers had already left, usually for higher paid, more secure jobs in local industry. Ex-Meriden Co-op workers were certainly seen as very employable individuals. Unfortunately for the Co-op, not all those who had chosen to leave would have been destined to depart in the retirement or redundancy programme. In some production areas whole sections had been wiped out, making achieving 3-day week production targets impossible. Once again, a further painful labour rebalancing exercise was required.

On 2nd July the Financial Controller reminded the Board that the Co-op's Annual General Meeting was now due, notice needed to be given if it was to take place by 31st July 1979. However, discussions with Coopers and Lybrand the auditor regarding the completion of annual accounts to be presented at the AGM indicated that, because of the uncertainties surrounding a final HMG interest decision, it would be impossible to proceed within the proposed time scale.

John Boulter, the Co-op's Company Secretary, indicated to the Board that he was in trouble regarding his professional responsibilities, and in view of the present financial situation he felt he must resign. He was prepared to continue as Financial Controller if the Board so wished. Three of four Directors' vacancies, created by the recent resignations, were filled at this time. Mr J Barclay, the TASS Director, was replaced by Mr J Inglesant, Mr F Kean, the ACTSS-Admin Director, was replaced by Mr L Hambridge, and Mr D Davenport, the EEPTU Director, was replaced by the return of Mr J Grattan.

The Chief Executive advised on 13th July that all information had now been sent to the Government, but he did not think a deferral or waiver of interest would be granted. A meeting had been arranged in London with Lord Trenchard, Minister of State for Industry, on 18th July and he would attend with the Chairman. In the event of HMG deciding against a deferral or waiver, Geoffrey Robinson considered the following options were open to the Co-op:

a) Accept the decision and approach the bank to appoint a receiver/manager.

b) Go into voluntary liquidation.

c) Call a meeting with all creditors to obtain a decision that Triumph continues to trade in their interests.

d) Make a public appeal for money with which to pay Government.

e) Offer to issue the three shares of the company to see whether they would be taken up by the public.

During discussions that followed, the Chief Executive recommended that a meeting with creditors be held, followed by meetings with companies possibly interested in acquiring the business, after which an approach could then be made to Government for its agreement for continuing to trade, and/or the appointment of a receiver/manager. After fully considering the five options, it was unanimously agreed that the Chief Executive should pursue option c, calling a meeting of creditors at which the situation would be fully discussed and a request made for their continued support.

The Directors were obviously concerned regarding their personal liabilities in the event that the Co-op went into liquidation, and it was agreed that Mr Peter Davis, the Company Solicitor, should be invited to attend the Board meeting to clarify this situation. His advice was that should the company continue to trade and to incur debts and appoint new creditors, whilst knowing it was unable to pay its liabilities, it would be considered to be trading fraudulently. If, however, the creditors were made fully aware of the situation and agreed to support the company in its continued trading, this would not be considered fraudulent.

The Directors' decision to hold a meeting with the creditors was thus confirmed as the appropriate legal option to pursue, and was arranged to take place on 16th July. As this date was during the annual two weeks summer holiday period, some Directors who would be unable to attend agreed to accept any decision taken by the quorum of Directors present at the creditors' meeting.

The only other positive news the workforce was to receive when it returned from holiday was that agreement was at last now likely with the trade unions, allowing the retirement and redundancy programme agreed on 24th May to be concluded on 23rd August 1979 – the 90 days statutory notice period over! The trade unions' requirement for completion of the retirement and redundancy programme would be first discussed by the Advisory Board, and then full consultation with all those involved would follow prior to implementation. The only changes from that agreed by the workforce 90 days earlier were that fewer would now need to be made redundant because of those who had already left, and a specific reference had been added to the Co-op's new retirement policy so that it also applied to professional management.

The BBC *Man Alive* documentary was to feature these consultations. The meeting with the elderly pickets was a particularly harrowing and emotional occasion, one I will never forget. I was asked by one elderly lady picket, as the Co-op Chairman, how I could possibly treat her and the other elderly pickets in this way after all their sacrifices and the promises that had been made to them about jobs for life, now they were being forced to retire. I could only ask for their understanding of the Co-op's desperate position.

An unidentified poet summed up the feelings of those founder member pickets facing retirement:

DIRGE FOR THE TRIUMPH LEGEND
The call was loud in '73 to man the gates and stay.
The Midlands heard the stewards call that memorable day.
"Stand fast" the stewards cried aloud "and we shall stay with thee"
"Stand fast in sun and ice and rain for all the land to see."
But those who called the loudest on that brave and righteous day
Picked up their coats and tools and slowly slunk away.

And there was left a band of men who simply would not go
Who watched the gates for eighteen months in sun and rain and snow.
For some were young and some were old who fought that waiting game
Who carved themselves a legend and "TRIUMPH" was its name.
Then in the year of '75 the battle had been won
And from the ice and snow they walked into the sun.
Each worker then took up his tools and promises were made
"Produce the legend now let each one to his trade.
Age shall not be a barrier till you falter on your way
Even then we shall protect you, we promise you this day."
Then rules were made and each one swore that there would be no strife
The legend would be honoured the remainder of your life.
And then the chains were taken off, the gates were opened wide
For those who wished to keep the rules, to come right on inside.
Then back they crept, the faithless ones who wouldn't stand and fight
And started back where they left off as if it was their right.
And slowly wormed their wretched way to head the workshop rules
To oust the ones who had stood and fought and make them look like fools.
It needed guts and brains to win the legends race
And sacrifice galore to set the legends pace.
Not mouths that called in '73 to slam the gates and stay
That couldn't last a little while without receiving pay.
No brains were there – the debts piled high, professionals were brought
Not for the pittance of the men who had so bravely fought.
But high awards and little skill and nothing else to show
"Five hundred workers more" they cried, "to make the legend grow."
By '79 the rot had won, "too many men," they cried
"We'll sack the old who picketed and many more beside."
And some who left (the choice was theirs) 8 hundred pounds to leave
The older ones with many skills 5 hundred did receive.
All promises now broken, the legends dead at last
Act decent now and bury it, this legend of the past.
No longer trust the words of men who would not stand and fight
Or some who picketed by day, and not the chill of night.
The battles lost, the legends done, the sacrifice in vain
If resurrection does occur, "DECEIT" shall be its name
Not "TRIUMPH" which lies buried, beneath the lies of men
So having wept upon the grave, I lay aside my pen.

Source: London Motorcycle Museum.

Much of the filming of the *Man Alive* documentary was memorable, not least because the programme's producer, Terry O'Riley, believed the research he had done suggested that, promoted correctly, the programme could form the basis of a public appeal for funds to help save the Co-op. The first interview I did to camera involved answering a question relating to 'not knowing our costs of production and selling motorcycles at a loss' – a variation on the Chief Executive's criticism levelled at the Directors selling motorcycles last year at below cost.

I wonder where that question came from! Although as at the Board meeting I believed the criticism to be unfair, the Directors having done all in their power to ensure the professional managers had set realistic sales prices, it was not the time or place to show disunity in front of millions of potential 'donors'. So, as Chairman I accepted the collective criticism on behalf of the company. I was sure there would be many other occasions for the strengths of the Co-op to shine through during a one-hour documentary, made by the world renowned BBC. I was not to be disappointed.

12

GOVERNMENT SWORD OF DAMOCLES

I t wasn't only the Chief Executive that was now eating, sleeping and breathing Triumph. Even so, although there were vital survival meetings to take place with the Co-op's trade creditors and the Government during the first week of the factory summer shutdown, I was determined that I was going to spend some quality time with my family during the remainder of the break.

It was the families of all the senior people who suffered most from their loved ones' long working days, missed weekends and interrupted holidays. At least on this occasion I had not planned a trip away from home with my family ... unlike in the spring. The memory of that week's caravanning holiday in Cornwall, and the interruption for a London meeting, although stressful at the time, still brings a smile to my face.

The experience had resulted in a classic Triumph humour occasion – unfortunately humour I could not share with anyone else at the time! Realising the difficulty I had been placed in through having to attend an important London meeting whilst on holiday in Cornwall, Geoffrey Robinson offered the overnight use of the London flat he often stayed in at the Grosvenor House Hotel. He suggested I travel up by train from Cornwall, stay overnight at the flat, attend the meeting with him the following day, then return to my family in Cornwall. I accepted his suggestion, and he said that he would make the arrangements.

Geoffrey's use of the Grosvenor House flat was as a result of the consultancy work he did for owner Joska Bourgeois, the wealthy proprietor of the successful Belgian Motor Company, the Jaguar and Toyota distributor. In 1975, Geoffrey had resigned from his position as Chief Executive of Jaguar Cars, unable to support the Ryder Plan that effectively destroyed, as he saw it, the specialist nature of Jaguar, amalgamating it with Austin, Morris, Triumph and Rover. Fluent in French and German and highly experienced in the commercial world, Geoffrey accepted a consultancy offer from Joska Bourgeois. As with the Chief Executive's role at the Co-op, his acceptance was subject to his parliamentary duties always taking priority.

I arrived at the luxurious Grosvenor House Hotel, Park Lane, London and introduced myself to the Duty Manager, requesting the keys to the flat. To our surprise, he had no knowledge of my intended overnight stay and without personal authorisation from Joska Bourgeois, whose name the flat was in, he could not provide the keys. Over the next two hours efforts were made to contact Joska Bourgeois and Geoffrey Robinson, without success. The only respite for me from this tense and embarrassing situation was the repeated sounding of the hotel fire alarm system,

146

triggered by the particularly hot spring evening temperatures. Each time the alarm sounded, wealthy Arabs were sent scurrying to all the hotel exits to the amusement of all the English people present. The cabaret over, I decided I had just enough time to catch the last train back to Cornwall, and told the Duty Manager of my intended departure. He explained that whilst he did not doubt my story, the flat was not in Geoffrey Robinson's name and without authorisation from Joska Bourgeois it was more than his job was worth to allow me to use it. However, he would provide me with a room for my overnight stay and bill Mr Robinson for its use. Just as well; whilst I enjoyed my night's sleep, the stay cost the equivalent of over one week's wages for me at the Co-op.

When I met Geoffrey for the meeting the following day, he asked if I was well. I said "yes very well," and graciously he never mentioned the bill when he received it. The meeting over, I smiled, bid Geoffrey farewell, and returned to Cornwall to enjoy the remainder of my family caravanning holiday.

The first of the vital survival meetings during the summer holidays took place with the Co-op's trade creditors on Monday 16th July. Representatives of approximately 75 per cent of Triumph's trade creditors attended. The Co-op's Company Solicitor, Mr Peter Davis, was present, as was the Chief Executive, Chairman and other Executives. In line with the Advisory Board's decision, the purpose of this meeting was whether the creditors were prepared to continue supporting the company, given full disclosure of Triumph's present critical situation.

The Chief Executive explained to the trade creditors the position regarding the Government decision on whether or not to grant either a deferral or waiver of interest, and stressed that Triumph considered its major commitment to be to the creditors and employees. Various plans for survival of the company, including the possibility of linking up with a larger internationally-based concern, were already under consideration, but a proposition allowing the company time to negotiate all the possibilities would have to be put to Government for approval. To present such a proposition first required that the creditors declare their support for Triumph in its continued trading. Should the creditors give their support, and in an attempt to avoid losses which would inevitably be incurred by creditors should a receiver or liquidator be appointed, the Chief Executive proposed that in the event that Government granted a deferral:

"The creditors would maintain Triumph's present level of indebtedness for a period of six months."

Or in the event the Government refused either a deferral or waiver:

"The creditors would form a Trade Creditors' Committee (which could, perhaps, include a representative of the dealerships – one UK, one US) to consider Triumph's trading situation."

Should it be the wish of the creditors to form such a committee, Triumph would:

a) Provide all the required information to enable such a committee to arrive at a conclusion regarding the continued trading of the company, and

b) For a given period of time, convert a given amount of company cash outstanding to the creditors into redeemable preference shares, in exchange for which the Government would be offered payment of the £1.2m interest.

Following discussion on the foregoing, it was agreed that a Trade Creditors' Committee be appointed to conduct a search into Triumph's situation, and return with recommendations as to whether it was considered a viable proposition for Triumph, with the support of its creditors, to continue to trade.

Mr F Tippets of the Wholesale Traders' Association was elected to act as Chairman in the ensuing meeting between the creditors. The appointed committee would, after brief discussion, report to Mr Robinson's office.

The Trade Creditors' Committee first confirmed that approximately 75 per cent of Triumph's creditors were present, and agreed that the committee, which would include a fully qualified accountant, be appointed from volunteers who would be prepared to conduct the investigation.

VOLUNTEERS FOR TRADE CREDITORS' COMMITTEE
Mr F Tippets: Wholesale Traders' Association
Mr P Phillips: Gaudie and Strapper (London) representing various creditors
Mr Howard: Aeroplane and Motor
Mr F Ashley: F J Ashley Limited
Mr Orr: Phoenix Castings
Mr Bottomley: Automotive Products
Mr Pulley: Pulley Brothers Limited
Mr N McLuskie: GKN Group Companies
Mr Laptmorne: Lucas Electrical Limited
Mr E Fearne: Thornton Baker and Company (Accountants) representing various creditors

The meeting with the trade creditors went well, and indicated that there was still support from them for Triumph. The appointed Creditors' Committee would investigate the viability of the Co-op continuing to trade. Following our meeting in London with the Minister of State for Industry, Lord Trenchard, on Wednesday 18th July, we would meet the Trade Creditors' Committee the next day.

It now seemed a widely held opinion that the Government's 'Sword of Damocles' would shortly fall on the Co-op. This was not my view. Based on Geoffrey Robinson's previous record of securing deals for the Co-op, I still retained total confidence that given full backing he would succeed again.

I was never more convinced that the Advisory Board's decision to appoint Geoffrey Robinson as the Chief Executive of the Co-op had been the right one, and would play a fundamental part in our survival. Geoffrey's whole approach to business following his resignation from Jaguar Cars was a simple one: if you were employed as a consultant, as with the Belgian Motor Company, advice was provided that could be accepted or rejected; If you were the Chief Executive, as at the Co-op, and accountable for achieving company policy, you had to have total control of and belief in the policy the company was pursuing. If you were unable to convince the Board of Directors to back what you believed, as had been the case when Jaguar was fundamentally changed by the Ryder Plan, you must resign. With Geoffrey Robinson's business rationale of total control of policy rightfully came accountability – an extremely strong additional motivating force when it came to negotiations.

In the past, when everything had appeared to be at its bleakest and everyone believed it would be impossible to secure a deal, Geoffrey had come good. He would not fail this time for lack of support. To date, it had been as if none of the opposing senior individuals negotiating with Geoffrey Robinson wanted their legacy to be the killing of the Meriden Co-op. Our absolute weakness, following the many sacrifices made by the workforce to try and save its Co-op, seemed to be our strength. This 'British bulldog' spirit was certainly what attracted much of the extensive media coverage that influenced general public opinion and support. The blow-by-blow documentary coverage now to come from the BBC *Man Alive* programme would further focus that opinion on negotiations to save the Co-op.

MEETING WITH LORD TRENCHARD – MINISTER OF STATE FOR INDUSTRY AND OFFICIALS

The meeting was arranged in the light of the Government's decision not to defer or waive interest due from Meriden on the Government loan.

Mr Robinson began by asking whether, if Meriden were to pay to the Government £1m, the Government would be prepared to write off the rest of the outstanding interest and principal on the loan. Because of the decision that had been taken, Meriden was finding it impossible to sell motorcycles. If Meriden was to go bankrupt, then he believed that everyone would lose. Lord Trenchard said he accepted that if in the next three weeks Meriden could formulate some definite offer, then it would obviously be the Government's duty to consider it. Mr Bell added that whatever happened, the interests of ECGD would need to be safeguarded.

When Mr Robinson suggested that to ensure viability the Government would need either to write off the outstanding loan and interest or convert to deferred equity, Lord Trenchard said that the Government had decided that the interest should not be waived or deferred. The loan obligation therefore still stood, and it would be misleading for him to suggest that there might be some form of waiver or deferment.

Mr Robinson then said that he had put a number of options to the creditors at the meeting, and had given them copies of the submission which he had put to Government, explaining that it was now obsolete in light of the budget, and that he would update it. The creditors had decided that Meriden should go on trading. Mr Robinson then reiterated that the Co-operative was now unable to sell motorbikes, and suggested that the way forward might be to pay off the outstanding interest in two instalments. Lord Trenchard said that the department would consider such an offer, but would have to ask how Meriden might meet its future obligations.

Returning to his point about lack of sales, Mr Robinson said that the Co-operative needed some form of statement from Government that would encourage people to start buying its product again. He then added that he could not see how Government had reached the decision it had, in view of Meriden's possible link up with another company. Lord Trenchard said that although Mr Robinson had mentioned the possibility, he had given the department no details, except to say that discussions were at a very early stage. When Mr Robinson suggested that the Co-operative needed to keep going for six months if it was to find a long-term solution. Lord Trenchard said that if it could make some sort of offer of payment of outstanding interest and also substantiate the claim that a third party was interested, it would be perfectly right for the Government to consider the position.

Mr Robinson then suggested that in view of the Kawasaki leak, he was not sure his Board would allow him to discuss possible third party interest in any detail. When he asked whether he could have more than three weeks in which to put a proposition to the department, Lord Trenchard agreed to look at the possibility.

Mr Rosamond asked whether he was right in thinking that the Government believed it would get nothing back from Meriden, and Lord Trenchard agreed that it looked extraordinarily unlikely. Mr Robinson said that he could still not understand the Government's decision and Lord Trenchard said that, in short, there was a serious risk of things at Meriden getting worse rather than getting better, and that the Government's view of this likelihood was different from that of the Co-operative. Mr Robinson believed that it would have helped the Co-operative to have had an earlier decision from Government, and that there was an air of inevitability about the final decision; to some extent, Meriden had brought it upon itself. Lord Trenchard recognised that the final decision had been made very close to the due date for interest payment, and that the change of Government had not helped. In this context, Mr Robinson said that it had applied to the previous administration for a deferment or waiver of interest, and that the former Minister of State had offered to defer interest on the grounds that it would be much easier for the Co-operative that way; the former Minister would not, however, explain the reasoning behind this to Mr Robinson. Mr Bell said that no formal offer of any kind had been made to Meriden by the previous administration. They had simply been told that deferment would be an easier route and were asked to think about it.

Mr Robinson reiterated that if he had 6 weeks in which to come up with a proposal, it would be more realistic. On the question of press relations, he proposed to tell them that he had indicated alternative proposals to the Government and that the Government was willing to receive them. Lord Trenchard said that he was not willing to confirm such a statement. He was, however, prepared for Mr Robinson to say that since the final decision had been communicated to Meriden only a few days before the due date for interest payment, the Government was prepared to give them a little time to consider what their next move should be. Mr Robinson insisted that he needed to be able to say something positive to the press, and after the Minister had left the meeting he indicated that the line he would take would be that the Government was not pressing for immediate payment of the interest, that it was aware of possible plans that Meriden had for the future, and that it believed the Government would look at the plans. Officials made it clear that the Government would not be able to confirm anything about future plans.

The meeting with Government had gone very much as expected, with the exception of Lord Trenchard's statement that it would be "extraordinarily unlikely" that the Government would receive anything back from Meriden, thus confirming the Chief Executive's point that nothing could be lost from writing the interest off. Mr Bell's point that whatever happened to the loan interest, "ECGD's position would need to be protected," was also a useful contribution towards future negotiations.

As agreed on Thursday 19th July, we met the Co-op Trade Creditors' Committee. Geoffrey Robinson reported that Lord Trenchard had now indicated that Government had consented to allowing Triumph a short period of time (as yet unspecified) before payment of interest, during which time the company would pursue negotiations with potential partners and thereafter put forward a proposal for continued trading in partnership with a larger concern.

Meetings were already taking place with interested parties, and full reports were being drawn up for their appraisal. The Chief Executive assured the creditors that the best possible deal would be negotiated to ensure the security of both the creditors and Triumph's employees. It was therefore necessary to obtain the approval of the committee with regard to Triumph entering into partnership with a larger concern, and meantime ensure the company would continue to trade at its present level of credit. Mr Robinson also pointed out that it may be necessary to raise money against security of bikes, but at this point he would refer back to the committee for approval before acting.

Following the current holiday period, the factory would be able to commence production of spare parts. Whilst it was thought that no further credit or materials would be required, it would, however, be necessary to ship goods, and Triumph was experiencing difficulties. These necessitated that alternative shipping arrangements be obtained, with the approval of the committee.

After discussion, during which the Chief Executive assured the committee that it would be kept as fully informed as possible during current negotiations, the committee gave its approval of the foregoing:

a) That Triumph conduct negotiations to enter into partnership with a larger concern, whilst continuing to trade at the present level of credit.

b) That Triumph should, if necessary, make alternative arrangements for shipping goods.

It was further arranged that points of contact for information would be:

Mr J A Rosamond: Triumph

Mr F Tippets: Wholesale Traders' Association

It was agreed that the next meeting would be held at the Meriden factory on Monday 30th July, at a time to be arranged. It was also agreed that a brief press statement would be made to the effect that the creditors' committee was fully in support of Triumph's negotiations with potential partners, in pursuance of a deal that would secure both their interests and those of the employees at Triumph.

With the workforce returning to work on Monday 30th July following the summer holiday, I called a Board meeting on the Sunday before to bring the Directors up to date on developments during the break. A mass meeting of the total workforce would take place the following day. All current information would be put to the meeting, and a vote would be taken on the way in which negotiations with potential partners should be carried out.

Arrangements had been made through the Chief Executive for BBC's *Man Alive* team to gather material for a film that would be released in September 1979. An undertaking had been received that Triumph representatives could review the film prior to its release. A suggestion had been made that Monday's mass meeting could be filmed, and it was thought that cameras could be set up in readiness for the filming prior to the meeting, with the workforce being asked whether or not it agreed to the *Man Alive* team being present. The Directors agreed that, with the provisos mentioned, the TV team could be invited to attend to obtain the necessary material.

The mass meeting took place on Monday 30th July, with the cameras set up and ready to roll. The crew withdrew whilst the Chairman consulted the members regarding their agreement to the filming; they agreed, and the meeting went ahead. The Chief Executive brought the workforce up to date with a detailed report on the Co-op's meetings with trade creditors, Government and negotiations with potential partners, following which a unanimous vote in support of the Advisory Board's survival policy was received.

On 24th August Mr John Boulter confirmed his resignation as Company Secretary. I had discussed Mr Boulter's proposed resignation with the Chief Executive, who had indicated that suitable provision would now be made regarding the position of Company Secretary.

In the present highly volatile situation, Mr Dennis Poore was attempting to serve an injunction against Triumph for recovery of debts of approximately £50/£56,000 in respect of Triumph name royalties. An agreement drawn up by Mr Poore was currently under consideration by the Chief Executive and the Company Solicitor. At the same time, the Chief Executive considered that it may be possible for the Triumph name to be purchased from the liquidator of NVT, under an agreement with one of Triumph's prospective partners. A royalty payment of £6000 had been made, since not doing so may have affected the proposed agreement now under consideration.

The Chairman advised the Directors that the fantastic, highly profitable Nigerian police/military order for 1300 Triumph Tiger 750cc motorcycles had been secured by the Sales Administrator, Mr Ian Rush. In addition to the motorcycles was a substantial spare parts stocking order, service tools/manuals, and an Nigeria-based mechanics' training programme to be undertaken by four Triumph personnel. Ian Rush secured the order against fierce competition from German and Japanese companies. It was believed that Triumph motorcycles were preferred because of their rugged qualities, simplicity of engineering design and ability to continue to operate in the most hostile environments, even when subjected to severe abuse – the very qualities Ted Simon had found vital during his historic 63,000-mile circumnavigation of the globe on a Triumph Tiger 100. Finally, the ability to meet a very tight delivery schedule

John Rosamond and Brian Jones discuss production of the initial 300 batch of the vital
Nigerian order. (Courtesy *Coventry Evening Telegraph*)

was also believed to be a vital consideration in obtaining the order. The letter of credit in respect of the order for Nigeria was not yet to hand, although an offer had been made by Integration Limited (the UK representative of the agent involved) to provide £150,000 to enable Triumph to commence the initial build of 300 motorcycles. Completion of the initial build was covered by a two-week deadline, about which we were all very concerned.

The Chairman then read to the Directors the latest letter from Lord Trenchard, confirming the negotiations that had been taking place with Government:

Dear Mr Robinson
I delayed answering your letter of 2nd August 1979 because of your meeting with Mr Suich and I am now writing in relation both to that letter and your letter of 10th August 1979 to make clear the Government's current position. I have to tell you that I do not accept as accurate some of the alleged quotations or statements which you attribute to me at our meeting on 18th July 1979. They are not in accordance with my recollection or with the record of the meeting in a number of important aspects. In particular I do not accept the implication that I had indicated that the Government is prepared to forego its rights to recovery of the money owed to it to enable an agreement with a prospective partner. I enclose a copy of our record of that meeting [readers will recall that this appears earlier in this chapter]. *You already have my letter of 24th July 1979 written after our meeting which clearly sets out the Government's position. The period of deferment which I granted in my letter of 24th July 1979 before setting in hand normal proceedings should your company continue to be in default on payment of interest has now elapsed. The Government's position now is that the whole of the money outstanding against the loan agreement is due, but in view of your statement about negotiations with possible partners who as I understand it might take over the responsibilities for the continuation of the Meriden business, I have instructed my officials to delay further until the middle of September 1979 the legal proceedings for recovery of the debt owed to us, unless before then there is a change in the circumstances which I consider material. My offer to meet you and any prospective backer still stands but only up to the middle of next month.*
Yours sincerely
Lord Trenchard

During this period, John Nelson, who had achieved major improvements in Triumph's Spare Parts and Service operation since he accepted these new responsibilities, departed. He returned, with the Co-op's good wishes, to Steyr-Daimler Puch GB Ltd as its Technical Service Manager.

We had an excellent Earls Court Motorcycle Show. A sign of the times was that there were only minor engineering specification updates to the three Triumph models for 1980 – the T140E Bonneville, the T140D Bonneville Special and the TR7V Tiger:
a) Four-valve oil pump
b) Stiffer swinging arm with improved chain adjuster
c) Lifted exhaust system, prop stand and centre stand to improve ground clearance
d) Improved petrol pipe material
e) Tool tray enlarged
f) Improved primary chain adjuster for easier servicing
g) Relocated rear brake calliper for improved braking in adverse weather conditions
In addition, electric start and 8-valve cylinder head model options were planned for introduction in the spring and summer of 1980.

Tremendous goodwill was expressed by the motorcycling public attending the show, aware of the extreme situation the Co-op membership was trying to survive due to the wide publicity. This response suggested that if all else failed, perhaps a public appeal may succeed!

On 30th August, an Advisory Board meeting took place (filmed by the BBC) to enable the Chief Executive to bring the Directors up to date on the potential partnership negotiations. Geoffrey Robinson first apologised for the absence of a written report.

Almost daily developments in the situation made it difficult to produce an up to date report; a verbal report on progress was therefore given. In connection with potential partner negotiations currently under way, the Chief Executive was considering the inclusion of a proposal for the purchase of the Triumph name, of which the company had the use only through the NVT liquidator (under an agreement with Dennis Poore) for a payment of royalties of 1 per cent on sales or an annual minimum payment of £75,000. Mr Poore had said that he was prepared to forego his claim to the name on receipt of the whole (except for a £10,000 contribution from himself) of the outstanding liability, if a purchaser could be found who would acquire the name on Triumph's behalf, probably as part of a partnership deal. The effect would be to ensure the security of the name in the event of Government deciding to place the company into liquidation.

The Directors agreed with the Chief Executive's proposition and asked whether this would be acceptable to the creditors under the present circumstances. The matter had been discussed with the creditors' committee on 15th August, and it had agreed to the name purchase by a third party provided that the terms involved would not worsen the position of the company and its creditors.

Geoffrey Robinson stated that with regard to the partnership deals, the terms upon which Triumph would negotiate had been made clear to all parties and the Government had been given details of all negotiations to date. Whilst all prospective partners were insisting on control, one firm offer had been made which would give the membership a 33 per cent share in the equity and included all the basic criteria acceptable to Triumph.

The terms under which Triumph would negotiate:
a) Re-capitalise the company
b) Write off Government interest
c) Retain the present product and workforce
d) Keep creditors at their present levels

Other potential partner openings which had been pursued:

Japanese – The terms negotiated, whilst basically the same as with all parties, included the possibility of the company concerned manufacturing a new product. No indication had as yet been made as to their continued interest, but the agents involved had requested that the Chief Executive now make a direct approach.

UK a) – One company, from a group of consultants, was interested in Triumph's facilities, but holidays prevented further contact at the present time.

UK b) – To be considered as an alternative, one firm that was aware of the people's commitment to Triumph and would like to see the company succeed was prepared to inject £200,000, which was one fifth of what was required to pay Government. If several such partners could be obtained on a similar basis to give the company the sum total of the equity, the Chief Executive considered such a proposition worth pursuing.

Europe – Proposals for joint marketing had been made, but the Chief Executive did not consider such a proposition worth pursuing.

Having reported verbally and discussed the implications of the firm offer that had been received, particularly with regards the retention of one third of the equity and the role of Directors, who may participate in the operation of the company, the Chief Executive undertook to circulate to Directors full details of any proposal prior to an agreement being signed. Meantime, progress reports would be made as the negotiations developed.

The Chairman and Mr Beattie reported upon section meetings (filmed by the *Man Alive* TV crew) with production workers, to explain the need to produce the initial batch of 300 Nigerian military/police motorcycles to a very tight two-week deadline.

It should be noted that 110 workers had agreed to work during the weekend without pay, utilising the £150,000 Integration upfront money to produce the first 300 batch of the 1300 Nigerian order. This positive action, it was hoped, would secure full letter of credit confirmation of the remainder, obviously strengthening Triumph's position with Government and any prospective partner negotiations.

The Chief Executive reported briefly on TMA's current trading position and with regard to spare parts in particular, pointed out that the performance was 60 per cent up on last year. The Spares Manager in America had recently been dismissed and a new parts ordering system introduced, which would ensure that the company would not face an over-stocking situation at the year end. In reply to criticism by the Directors regarding the operation of the American company, the Chief Executive asked that any such opinions with regard his management team must be directed towards him, since he considered it to be his responsibility to deal with such matters. Furthermore, in view of the fact that the company was still on target for a break even position, he was satisfied with management's performance.

When the BBC *Man Alive* crew had withdrawn from the Board room, discussion took place regarding Mr Boulter's resignation from the position of Company Secretary. The Chief Executive could not understand the reasons given, since the company was continuing to trade with the consent of the creditors, the Government and all concerned and was therefore not trading illegally. He was, however, confident that full provision could be made to cover the situation. The matter was left in abeyance until the next Board meeting, by which time the Chief Executive undertook to make the necessary arrangements.

The Chief Executive's workload was now even more colossal; constant negotiations on many fronts with prospective partners to try and find a solution acceptable to Government and creditors, and save as many Co-op jobs as possible. Inevitably, a lot of these confidential negotiations took place in London, and there was no way he could have coped if it had not been for his very able commercial deputy and assistant, Miss Price. Brenda was the long-term link with all things commercial at Triumph. Whilst at times she enjoyed a difficult relationship with some of the Co-op membership, I always found her an extremely hardworking, reliable and dedicated individual, highly trusted in the commercial world in which the Co-op had to function.

The Triumph Bonneville won the prestigious *Motor Cycle News* 'Machine of the Year' title voted for by *MCN*'s readership, a further indication of public support for the Co-op. I took the opportunity at this time to make a small gesture to show Brenda Price she was appreciated, by asking her to accept the award on behalf of Triumph. The presentation by Murray Walker at the packed out *MCN* awards bash in London was enthusiastically cheered on by a coach-load of Co-op members, two of whom won Kawasaki motorcycles in the raffle. The memorable champagne celebrations went on well into the night.

In preparation for the vital meeting with Lord Trenchard on 7th September, Geoffrey Robinson prepared a decisive letter indicating Triumph's improved position based upon developments that had taken place since 18th July. The 7th September letter (on House of Commons notepaper) formed the basis of discussions that day with the Minister of State at the Department of Industry.

Dear Lord Trenchard

Thank you for your letter of 23rd August 1979. I understand you have seen my letters of 23rd and 28th August to Alfred Suich.

It was kind of you to copy us your record of the meeting of 18th July 1979; in fact this record follows closely on most points of our own account and recollections of the meeting [the reader will recall this from earlier in this chapter]. With regard to point 5 and Mr Rosamond's question to you whether "the Government believed it would get nothing back from Meriden"; you are quoted as saying "that it looked extraordinarily unlikely". That is correct, but you went on to make the explicit statement "that you were not expecting anything back". I can easily understand that David Rowlands felt it otiose to include your subsequent remark since it followed from the first.

There are one or two other small amendments we would suggest, but these are not material.

Our disagreement is rather fundamental, however, on the point you make as follows in what you say in your letter of 23rd August 1979 "in particular I do not accept the implication that I had indicated that the Government is prepared to forego its rights to recovery of the money owed to it, to enable an agreement to be concluded with a prospective partner."

If that was not the implication of your remarks at the 18th July 1979 meeting – the one quoted in the Department's record of the meeting – then we are in a rather unusual position. For in the pursuit of the "extraordinarily unlikely" it would seem that the department is prepared to frustrate a positive and long-term solution to Triumph's problems. A solution, furthermore, that would continue employment, promote exports and enable us to honour large current orders for such important customers as Nigeria, Egypt and Libya; Mr Suich had been informed about these recent developments.

The effect of the 1300 order for Nigeria, the nearly 200 order for Libya and Egypt together with 400 orders on hand (which include those taken at Earls Court) is that we have orders covering production for the rest of this calendar year. It seems to us, therefore, that this is a 'material change' in the situation and certainly a change that invalidates the Department's view "that there was serious risk of things getting worse rather than better." Again, this is an important point since this appeared to be the only reason for the Government's decision, apart from your lack of knowledge about prospective partners.

Given now that these two arguments central to the Government's decision have been materially changed, we feel that a more realistic timescale should be agreed between us for the conclusion of a partnership deal, or to find some other long-term solution for Triumph. We say this not least because we would ourselves like to get something back for the Government – however extraordinarily unlikely this may be – and we are finding the timescale to which we have to operate, a fundamental weakness in our negotiations.

*As you will see from the attached notes, the negotiations are progressing well and the prospects of a deal look increasingly good; but it is only fair to consider that August is usually a dead month and this has further slowed up progress. However, we are hopeful we can now reach a realistic understanding with you on a timescale, and look forward to our meeting on Friday 7th September 1979.

Yours sincerely

Geoffrey Robinson MP

PS. I am enclosing a copy of the previous administration's offer to us; this again we feel substantiates our view of what previously transpired.

*These are separately in the post to you and if you have not received them, I will give you a verbal report.

I am not sure if this outcome was quite what Geoffrey Robinson had in mind when he suggested to me that I should get involved in the Government negotiations, as he felt it was more likely that answers given to my questions would probably be less guarded and as such, I might even succeed in exposing the Government's soft underbelly! Geoffrey's intuitive strategy certainly worked, the "extraordinarily unlikely" achievement allowing more time to pursue a partnership or some other long-term solution for the Co-op.

13

PARTNERSHIP NEGOTIATIONS

The Government agreeing to be more flexible in allowing a realistic period of time to find a partner and organise a long-term solution was a vital step forward. However, this is where Government's flexibility ended; full payment of accrued interest and loan capital still needed to be achieved!

Initial happiness at the Meriden factory was soon to be replaced in the battle weary minds of the Co-op membership with the realisation that the uncertainty about the future was to continue. As the weeks passed and the procession of potential partners visiting the factory escorted by Messrs Rosamond and Beattie grew, so did the level of concern amongst the membership. Not knowing just what the future held for Triumph was certainly taking its toll on morale.

Aboard Triumph 750 Tigers, the Royal Signals White Helmets display team always impressed, and had a positive effect on Co-op morale. (Author's archive)

Some pride was temporarily restored in the membership when the excellent BBC *Man Alive* documentary was aired. It certainly fulfilled all our expectations when it portrayed a true account of the workforce's efforts to try and secure a future for Triumph and its employees. Inevitably, there were the heartbreaking moments when the elderly pickets were retired and redundancies occured. But there were also many other occasions that vividly demonstrated to the viewer what Triumph meant to the Co-op membership. The workforce's behaviour in the documentary was such a total contrast to the 'normal' industrial disruption common in engineering manufacturing companies at the time that the programme generated rave reviews for the BBC and unsolicited small cash donations for the Co-op. The only person not totally convinced by the documentary's coverage was Geoffrey Robinson, the person who organised the BBC's involvement. He felt his constituency electorate would still probably see him as the Chief Executive, disregarding the members of the Co-operative. My experience, campaigning on doorsteps for Geoffrey at the last General Election, suggested that his constituents were a lot more supportive of their MP than perhaps he realised.

With no Board meetings for many weeks, the membership turned to its Directors, demanding information regarding the partnership negotiations. It wanted answers to the question "How and when would a partnership securing the future be achieved?" Even the negotiating team of Geoffrey Robinson, John Rosamond and Bill Beattie could not answer those questions, or indeed, whether some other solution would be found that achieved long-term viability for Triumph. Although confidential negotiations were under way with several potential partners, it was totally unrealistic to expect quick results in what had been a relatively short period of time. Even the Government finally had to acknowledge this reality!

Bob Haines takes the picture of (left to right) Brian Durrant, Cyril Miller and John Inglesant relaxing on arrival at their Lagos Hotel, Nigeria. (Courtesy Bob Haines' archive)

Brian Durrant (middle) and Cyril Miller (right) make some friends at the bush army camp bar. A fire engine service engineer is doing the same. (Courtesy Bob Haines' archive)

Some Triumph humour helped reinvigorate the membership a little at this time. As was usually the case, it was at someone else's expense. The magnificent workforce effort that achieved the very tight production deadline and shipment of the initial 300 batch of the Nigerian order now needed to be followed up when the motorcycles reached their destination, by the visit of a four-man team of Triumph fitters. The fitters' job was to teach army and police mechanics how to assemble the bikes out of the packing crates, and to maintain them in their ongoing service life. John Inglesant was one of the highly skilled Triumph fitters involved in production of police and military motorcycles at the factory. As such, he was an obvious candidate for the field commissioning and training programme in Nigeria. John, also the TASS Advisory Board Director, was an inspirational example to us all. Although he was disabled (having an artificial leg), he insisted on and received exactly the same treatment as any able-bodied person. So when Brian Jones, the Engineering Senior Executive responsible for selecting the four-man team for Nigeria, did not choose him because of the likely primitive conditions that would have to be faced, he was very aggrieved! He forcefully argued with Brian Jones that it was unfair to exclude him because of his disability, when he was confident he would be able to play a full part in the four-man team's work. Brian changed his decision and John was happy. John Inglesant was known for being more than prepared to fight his corner when he believed he was right. Most at Meriden knew what had happened to achieve Brian Jones' change of mind – exactly the situation required for classic Triumph humour at its best.

On arrival at the Nigerian Army camp compound, in the bush outside the capital Lagos, conditions were exactly as Brian Jones had predicted – primitive! In discussions with the Nigerian Army Commanding Officer in his very basic office, John Inglesant asked for directions to the lavatory. The officer's reply brought hysterical laughter from John's three colleagues. He simply said, "there's the spade man, pick your spot!" So the four-man Triumph team's first assembly job was to fashion John a commode from one of the wooden motorcycle packing crates. This hilarious myth soon found its way back to those Meriden factory members who were prepared to believe the tale of the Nigerian Army Triumph packing crate commode.

Unfortunately, however, Brian Jones' predictions regarding the primitive conditions to be faced were correct, and John Inglesant had to return home after only 3 weeks.

The Chief Executive was continuing to perform a massive juggling act in an effort to keep the Co-op in business for sufficient time to find a solution that would provide long-term viability. To do this, Geoffrey Robinson used all the resources at his disposal. Meetings in London with prospective partners and trade creditors over lunch or dinner at the Grosvenor House Hotel or House of Commons never failed to impress. The offer to prospective partners of ministerial involvement, at the appropriate time, confirmed Triumph's Chief Executive as a very serious player in the commercial world with which he was so familiar. Bill Beattie and I assisted when appropriate, specifically on Co-op membership related issues, and with less likely potential partners. Surprisingly, we secured the first firm offer in July 1979, but Geoffrey was always very clear that the best possible long-term solution by way of partnership would be with the Japanese. However, because of their attention to detail, they would also be the most difficult to reach agreement with! The previous press coverage of the Civil Service Kawasaki/Triumph fiasco made confidential negotiations imperative.

Chief Nigerian police/army fitter in charge of training personnel and ongoing servicing of Triumph motorcycles. (Courtesy Bob Haines' archive)

Bob Haines and Cyril Miller relaxing on the Lagos beach before returning to the bush army camp. (Courtesy Bob Haines' archive)

The receipt of the Nigerian order letter of credit, enabling completion of the 1300 bike order, would be critical to buying the necessary time to keep Triumph in business and find a solution. The Directors now needed to be apprised by the Chief Executive of the precarious financial situation the Co-op was in, as it awaited the letter of credit.

A meeting was called for 4.30pm on Friday 26th October. Geoffrey Robinson reported that a full financial update would be in the comprehensive year end report he was in the process of compiling. This would be available for the Directors' consideration prior to the next meeting. It appeared from collating this report that, whilst the company had weathered the £90,000 loss, which at one time was anticipated, it would be hard-pushed to break even. If, however, the letter of credit from Nigeria was to hand, the accounts should show a significant improvement with the cash situation. The purpose of today's emergency meeting was to inform the Directors that the company was now in a critical financial situation, brought about by the fact that the first part payment letter of credit for £510,000 from Nigeria had not yet been received. Because of this, it would be necessary to lay off the factory unless alternative financing arrangements could be made. The Chief Executive undertook to investigate the possibility of arranging sufficient finance to continue production for the next few weeks.

Geoffrey Robinson was still confident that a partnership deal could be achieved, and considered the best course of action would be with the Japanese Motorcycle Company, which had already visited the factory. Assuming that a favourable reply was received, a visit would be made to Japan in November. The next best course of action amongst the existing contenders would be a deal with a strong Midlands-based company. Failing that, it would be necessary to approach Government with a view to it backing Triumph in going public. With regards the Midlands-based company that had visited the factory that day, it was a reasonably strong concern with large cash reserves. Arrangements were also being made for the visit of a Canadian company, and the first firm offer that had been made in July was still open for consideration.

Mr Hughes asked the Chief Executive if alternative arrangements had been made to cover the position of Company Secretary, since Mr Boulter would leave the company during November.

The Chief Executive offered to undertake the position himself if it was legally possible for him to do so. Advice on the matter would be sought from the Company Solicitor, Mr Peter Davis. Meantime, to also ensure that accounts were kept up to date, arrangements were being made for two or three people with financial qualifications – who had offered their services free of charge – to be drafted into the Accounts Department.

Mr Hughes then expressed concern at the short notice (36 hours) given for attendance of this Board meeting, and further questioned the need to commence the meeting at the end of the working day, 4.30pm, especially during a period when it was difficult to keep the factory workforce fully occupied during normal working hours. He further pointed out that he and other Directors had commitments after leaving work, which in turn had to be rescheduled at short notice. The Chief Executive replied that this Board meeting had been called as an emergency, and only for the purpose of informing the Directors of the Nigerian letter of credit situation, which he had covered in the first few minutes of the meeting. It had been previously agreed that meetings would be held out of working hours, and he considered it was still preferable to do so.

Mr Inglesant then questioned the lack of information available to the Directors, and stressed that personally he found it extremely embarrassing that he could not answer any questions put to him by members of the workforce. The Chief Executive pointed out that it had also been agreed that no one other than the negotiating team would be informed of progress, given the present highly confidential situation. Everything would, however, be reported at the next Board meeting on 9th November, at a time to be advised. The Chairman suggested that to aid communications with the membership an abridged version of the year end report could, after discussion, be published on the notice Boards. The Chief Executive and Directors agreed to this course of action.

Although there was now great uncertainty regarding the future, this did not stop the Royal Signals White Helmets display team's annual factory refit. With a nonexistent advertising budget, the team provided the majority of Triumph's yearly promotional exposure. The refit of the team's bikes was Triumph's sponsorship contribution. After a year of extremely challenging displays, the 24 White Helmets' 750cc Triumph Tigers arrived back at the factory in need of a serious overhaul and restoration. However, as every Meriden Triumph owner knows, it's amazing what can be done if you know how! When the team's Tigers left each year just before Christmas they were in pristine showroom condition, ready for a new season of fantastic displays. I had commented to the Royal Signals Commanding Officer how pleased Triumph was with the promotional work it was doing – a factory-front lawn team display had featured in the recent BBC *Man Alive* documentary. The CO asked me if I would write a piece for the team magazine, which I did.

Our team on our bikes
When the Demonstration Team Commanding Officer first approached the Meriden Co-operative approximately four years ago and expressed the wish that the previous long association which had existed with the old Triumph Engineering Company should continue, we were all very excited by the prospect. The tremendous measure of skill and teamwork, as shown by the White Helmets Display Team, demonstrated our world-renowned Triumph motorcycles to the general public in the best possible manner.

So an immediate start was made. Twenty four standard single carburettor 750cc twin cylinder Triumph Tiger motorcycles were produced in double quick time to enable the White Helmets team to commence practising for the new season.

Three very successful seasons of displays had now passed. The team's Triumph Tigers return to the Triumph factory at Meriden, in the heart of the West Midlands, at the end of each year for a period of eight weeks, during which time the bikes are stripped, refurbished and completely rebuilt. When I wrote this piece for the team's magazine we were, in the first week of November, two weeks into this exercise. John Inglesant, organiser of our Experimental Department and a Company Director of Triumph, was responsible for liaising with the three team members carrying out this exercise and making sure that all that was required was available. All at Triumph thoroughly enjoyed their involvement in helping the team to prepare the bikes for a new season of displays. It is always an extremely proud moment for all concerned when, the job completed, the bikes are lined up ready for loading into the team's transporter.

Having seen the bikes suitably dispatched, we will not see the White Helmets team back at the factory until next September when, as has become the custom each year, a special display will be given. The display takes place on the lawn in front of the factory in an extremely confined space, overhanging branches on trees having been pruned back sufficiently to enable all but the top three blokes in the 22-man fan to pass under. All of this seems to add to the enjoyment of the team and spectators alike. The success of this display at the factory can only be judged by the fact that it is always tremendously well supported by Triumph people, their families, friends and passing motorists who stop to join in the fun. In fact, all concerned with Triumph never cease to be thrilled by the tremendous teamwork and skill of 'our team on our bikes'.

There was no doubt that the factory presence of the Royal Signals White Helmets, whether it was just the three members of the refit squad or the whole team for a factory display, always provided a boost to Co-op morale.

Although the date of the next eagerly awaited Board meeting had been set for 9th November, it was cancelled, partnership negotiations taking priority. However, the detailed year end report was circulated to the Directors on that day, allowing a week to thoroughly digest its contents before the rearranged meeting on 15th November. The meeting started at 1.30pm, and turned out to be a marathon, having to be adjourned at 6.45pm and reconvened the following day at 3.00pm. We first considered the solicitor's advice regarding the Company Secretary, requested at the previous meeting:

a) The appointment of a Company Secretary was essential.

b) Anyone (including a Director) could undertake the role provided he/she was not involved in the management of the company. Furthermore, anyone acting purely as Company Secretary would not be held responsible in the event of there arising a question of fraudulent trading.

c) It was not possible for either Miss Price, as a Senior Commercial Executive, or Mr Robinson, as Chief Executive, to legally undertake the position.

Unfortunately, Mr Davis had further pressing engagements forcing him to leave the meeting during the Board discussions. As there was some doubt regarding the exact responsibilities involved, it was agreed to seek further clarification from the Company Solicitor for consideration at the next meeting.

The Directors now briefly discussed the Co-op's retirement policy, established when the reduction of the workforce took place. Personnel Manager Mr Atkinson's detailed notes, which had been circulated, confirmed exactly what the mass meeting of the membership had agreed on 15th August 1979, namely that anyone retiring from the company after 1st January 1980

**The Royal Signals White Helmets display team, seen here performing at Meriden.
(Author's archive)**

would be given one week's notice, which would terminate on the Friday following their (60th women/65th men) birthday. No ex-gratia payments would be made.

Having received the clarification, the Directors confirmed the retirement policy would continue exactly as agreed on 15th August 1979. The Chief Executive now moved on to his presentation of the 1978/79 end of financial year management report. Part of the report was the detailed update on negotiations with prospective partners, requested by Directors at the previous Board meeting. As with all Geoffrey Robinson's management reports, it was detailed and comprehensive; the Directors had certainly needed the week they had received to fully consider its contents.

The end of year management report comprised 15 sections plus appendices, indicating the commercial progress that had been made during the 1978/79 financial year and the steps taken to achieve this progress.

END OF YEAR MANAGEMENT REPORT – FINANCIAL YEAR 1978/79
Negotiations with Government
Triumph name and agreement relating to Triumph Meriden's use
Negotiations with potential partners
Creditors' Committee
ECGD
Nigerian order
Finance
Manufacturing

Purchasing
Spare parts
Sales
Triumph Motorcycles (America) Inc. (TMA)
Engineering
Personnel
Organisational changes

Much of the report's contents have already been covered in earlier chapters, so I will concentrate upon section 3, *Negotiations with potential partners*, which partially answered the questions the Co-op membership and Directors were asking – "How and when would a future securing partnership deal be achieved?"

The basic Advisory Board of Directors agreement governing the negotiations were summarised as follows:

i) Triumph's negotiating team would comprise John Rosamond, Bill Beattie and Geoffrey Robinson.

ii) In any deal involving a partner acquiring a majority shareholding, Triumph should aim to achieve a substantial minority holding, there being three shares i.e. 33 per cent for the membership.

iii) In any deal such as ii) above, a recapitalisation of Triumph would be desirable; for example, two thirds of the equity would be valued at £1m which would be injected as new capital.

iv) A prospective partner would be required to commit to maintaining the present workforce for a given period of time.

v) A prospective partner would be required to reduce creditors, with whom Triumph was still trading, to normal levels.

vi) The Government's position would be a matter of negotiation.

vii) The negotiating team was authorised to pursue other possibilities than a partnership arrangement that would enable Triumph to continue on its own, whilst meeting whatever requirements would satisfy the Government.

viii) The negotiating team was authorised to negotiate terms, but not commit Triumph, it being understood that any deal would be subject to the approval of the Board and a mass meeting.

ix) The Board has been regularly informed about the negotiations with potential partners, with due regard only being taken as to hiding the identity of the organisations in question.

Summarised below are the companies involved in negotiations, together with the state of each prospective deal:

Honda:
Honda has decided that it would not go ahead with either marketing or partnership.

Kawasaki/Yahama:
Kawasaki turned down the proposition. No response has been received from Yamaha and it is thought unlikely that it will be interested, given its tie-up with NVT.

Harley Davidson:
Whilst the advantages were put to it in terms of marketing rationalisation in USA, UK and Europe and of Triumph's complementing its product range with a 750cc model, no definite reply has yet been received.

Richard and Wallington Industries:
A Birmingham based company operating in construction equipment leasing, Mr Roy

Richards, a main shareholder, is founder of the Motorcycle Museum near Meriden; he and his Finance Director favoured partnership, but the Board of Richard and Wallington decided against.

Quadrant Associates:

A member of this group was interested in acquiring the premises of Triumph; the intention was to invest £10-15m for a new, different product. Mr Robinson had indicated that he would be prepared to talk on the basis of retaining the membership, but no further reaction has been forthcoming.

CGCIM Cycles Peugeot/Seudem (Motobelane):

CGCIM is a 100 per cent subsidiary of Peugeot and is interested in the distribution of Triumph in France, but because of its recent connection with Chrysler, is not contemplating further investment in the UK.

Seudem is a 100 per cent subsidiary of Motobelane (part of the Renault group) and is also interested in distributing Triumph in France, but not in partnership.

Steyr Daimler Puch:

A strong Austrian-based group with headquarters at Nottingham. Marketing possibilities in USA, UK and Europe are mutually attractive. However, Puch is not interested in a partnership, but only envisaged co-operation in marketing.

Rapport International:

A small company owned by Mr Ian Leaf, who so far has a record of success. Rapport approached Triumph and to date this is the one firm offer made. There is at least one potentially much better deal still under negotiation; however, this definite prospect for partnership has been referred to Government and has helped to gain time.

Pioneer Chain Saw (Canada):

This company has evaluated the information supplied by Triumph and is still interested. A visit is planned, to see whether the basis for a partnership can be evolved.

Armstrong Equipment:

The company approached Triumph and a visit took place on 22nd October. Its negotiator has since said that the company is still very interested and would refer back to Triumph within one month after completion of a current acquisition.

Penarth Commercial Properties:

A Welsh-based company with diversified interests in property, land, distribution and some manufacturing. A visit took place on 26th October. A condition of its proposition may be 100 per cent ownership, however, but the possibility must still be explored.

Marubeni Consultants:

MBC is the code name for the remaining large Japanese motorcycle company. The approach was made to Triumph by Marubeni (a large trading company) and a detailed set of documents sent to MBC via Marubeni in August 1979. A visit took place on 3rd October attended by the Technical Director of MBC and the head of its four wheel division. It was left on the basis that MBC would give a decision within two months. If there is interest, it is possible that Triumph's negotiating team would be requested to visit Japan in November.

The Chief Executive believed that:

• A further possibility had arisen in terms of a joint venture with Rapport International and Penarth Commercial Properties.

• There remained the two firm offers (Rapport and Penarth), though at this stage neither were considered large enough for immediate decisions to be taken.

Responses were awaited from the remaining three possible proposals, i.e. Armstrong

Equipment, Pioneer Chain Saw, and MBC. In the case of MBC, the most favourable proposition, it was thought that its initial interest may have reduced due to the alleged intervention of the UK importers. Efforts would take place to reactivate its interest. It was anticipated that further positive information would be secured from a meeting due to take place on 22nd/23rd November.

Meanwhile, it was not possible at this stage to make a definite recommendation in respect of any one proposition.

The Chief Executive recorded his appreciation and tributes to:

a) The Chairman and Mr Beattie for the positive contribution in negotiations with potential partners and Government.

b) The fitters who had visited Nigeria to work on the motorcycles on delivery and to the workforce who had worked voluntary overtime in order to meet the deadline for shipping; also to the sales department, in particular Mr Ian Rush, who initially had obtained the Nigerian order. Without the efforts of the members involved, the Chief Executive said that he was almost certain the company would by now have gone into liquidation.

c) The Board, for its courage and realism in administering the redundancy programme, which he said reflected against what had happened at the Kirkby Co-op where similar problems were not faced with realism.

The report on partnership negotiations was then duly accepted by the Board.

The Chief Executive's year end report demonstrated all his presentational skills. Much of the information contained was that which he was using extensively in the potential partnership negotiations. Accordingly, he was well accustomed to answering the resultant questions. However, during the marathon Board meeting, I detected Geoffrey Robinson starting to feel that some of the Directors did not appreciate the lengths to which he was going to try and keep the Co-op in business long enough to find a solution, whilst simultaneously, those same Board Directors seemed to feel they were not being consulted sufficiently on developments! The tense Board meeting atmosphere came to a head when discussing the last section, section 15 of the management report – *Organisational changes*. The Chief Executive proposed to formalise a third centre of executive control within the Triumph Meriden management structure, with Mr Lindsay appointed Senior Manufacturing Executive, reporting directly to the Chief Executive. Mr Alec Bottrill would be appointed Production Executive, reporting directly to Mr Lindsay, and Mr Brian Baldwin would be confirmed as Purchasing Executive. The new organisation would provide a more even spread of responsibility, and in particular relieve the excessively heavy burden on Miss Price and Mr Jones. In view of these changes, the Chief Executive proposed to increase the salaries of Mr Baldwin and Mr Bottrill. The Chief Executive said that this was in accordance with undertakings he had previously given to the persons concerned.

In the Board discussions that followed, it was pointed out by the Directors that salary increases could not be considered until the wage structure for the total workforce was reviewed, thereby fulfilling the commitment made at the mass meeting in May. Furthermore, it was regrettable that the Chief Executive had given undertakings without first notifying the Board. In view of the present partnership negotiations, it would be unfair to increase the salaries of two individuals when the whole pay structure required adjustment. Meantime, whilst it may cause some embarrassment to the Chief Executive, the Directors' views should be conveyed to Messrs Baldwin and Bottrill.

The vote which then followed resulted in a unanimous decision against the increase in salary for Mr Baldwin and Mr Bottrill.

The Chief Executive then pointed out:

a) That he had authority within the agreement of 11th December 1978 to recruit 10 management personnel.

b) That all of the Co-op's workers had had increases year on year of between 11 per cent and 26.5 per cent since November 1978.

c) That the commitments given for the next pay round (March 1980) would be carried out.

d) That this was therefore in effect discrimination against Mr Baldwin and Mr Bottrill.

e) Further discussion was therefore pointless since any vote was a foregone conclusion.

The Chief Executive left the Board meeting at 6.30pm and requested the meeting continue without him.

The Board now discussed a review of overtime payment rates previously requested by Mr Hughes. Confirmation had been received from the Department of Industry that the Co-op was no longer covered by any wage legislation that prevented a review taking place. Mr Hughes pursued a proposition that overtime premiums should be based on current basic rates of pay.

Mr Beattie raised an amendment to this proposition, suggesting that whilst Triumph was in the process of seeking a partner, it was inappropriate to review overtime rates. But assuming the company entered into partnership, consideration would be sought for payment of overall district average rates of pay, in which would be included overtime rates.

The amendment was carried. The meeting was then adjourned at 6.45pm to reconvene the following day, Friday 16th November, at 3.00pm.

The first business of the reconvened Board meeting, without the Chief Executive's participation, was to decide upon formal acceptance of the 1978/79 end of financial year management report. In view of the decision to rule out the salary increases for Mr Baldwin and Mr Bottrill in section 15, it was proposed by Mr Beattie that the report should be accepted with the exception of this – the Chief Executive being requested to further explain his managerial strategy relating to the new structure; this was agreed.

The Co-op's three Trustees were very concerned that the overdue Annual General Meeting had not taken place. The Company Solicitor and the Chairman had met the Trustees on 15th November, when it had been explained to them that whereas it was their prerogative to call an AGM, it would be inadvisable to do so under the present circumstances. The Trustees had also been advised upon their position in the eventuality of a partnership deal, when a meeting of the workforce would take place at which they would accept the instructions of the Beneficiary owners of the company. Mr J Tomlinson (Trustee) agreed to accept for information in the strictest confidence a copy of the Chief Executive's 1978/79 end of financial year management report.

This marathon Board meeting should have ended with a resounding vote of thanks for the Chief Executive, acknowledging his tremendous commercial efforts to keep the Co-op alive whilst trying to find a solution that would provide a chance of long-term viability. Instead, Geoffrey Robinson had been criticised for exceeding his executive authority regarding proposed organisational changes.

For the first time since Geoffrey's appointment as Chief Executive, I was extremely concerned that we would not survive. Not because he would fail to find a solution to the Co-op's problems, but because of Board disunity. We would all need to refocus very quickly, or there would be nothing to disagree about!

14

LEGAL PROCEEDINGS

The Directors were surprised when having had only three days for reflection since the previous Board meeting, the Company Solicitor called for another! Initially they thought there had been further developments regarding their disagreement with the Chief Executive, but they were wrong. Peter Davis needed to advise us of the threat of imminent legal action by Integration Limited, in order to recover its £150,000 upfront payment. It was this payment that had enabled production of the initial 300 of the 1300 Nigerian order, so vital to the Co-op's survival.

The Company Solicitor advised that a trust document covering the £150,000 Integration loan had originally been drawn up. This stated that on receipt of payment from Nigeria for these 300 motorcycles, the loan would be repaid. This loan was therefore not paid to Triumph Meriden to fund working capital beyond the purchase of materials for the first 300 motorcycles. Having not received its repayment, Integration was now concerned that in the event of the Co-op going into liquidation, the £150,000 loan would become untraceable in Triumph's bank account. It was understood that Integration's legal action would not be to sue for recovery of the money, but to file a petition for the immediate winding up of Triumph Meriden on the grounds that the Co-op was unable to pay its debts. Thereafter, Integration would commence proceedings against each Director, in respect of their breach of duty and trust under the terms of the trust document. Any other thoughts the Directors may have had about discussing the previous advice on the duties and responsibilities of the Company Secretary, completely disappeared – the Company Solicitor's advice on the Integration situation certainly reminded the Directors of the precarious legal position they and the Co-op were in, and this potential personal liability now had the Directors' full attention. To provide a little perspective for the reader, my average family house mortgage at the time was for £5000 repaid over 25 years. The personal liability of each Director to Integration was one twelfth of £150,000, i.e. £12,500 plus costs!

John Rosamond advised that the Chief Executive was presently regarding Integration's demand as only a threat, and recommended that we take no immediate action. The Board thoroughly discussed this situation, particularly with regards the following:

a) Paying the £150,000, assuming the money was available, would not meet with the approval of the Trade Creditors' Committee and could lead to further immediate demands from other creditors. This would close the Co-op.

b) Accepting the Chief Executive's recommendation not to pay the £150,000, which in turn could also lead to closure of the Co-op if the legal threat to petition was carried out.

c) The position of each individual Director, in the event of proceedings being taken against them for breach of trust.

d) The Chief Executive's knowledge of the people involved, with whom he had been in close contact throughout the negotiations on the Nigerian contract.

Following discussion, it was resolved by a vote of 5 in favour and 3 against that "The Board of Directors would endorse the Chief Executive's recommendation to take no immediate action to repay the £150,000 as demanded by Integration."

Peter Davis was asked to inform Mr Tippets (Chairman of the Creditors' Committee) of the present situation regarding Integration.

The £150,000 was not repaid to Integration at this time, and its threat of legal action for its immediate recovery turned out to be exactly that! The Chief Executive's assessment of the situation – and in particular the people involved – had been correct, and the Board's confidence in him totally vindicated.

Geoffrey Robinson's year end management report had already provided the Directors at the previous meeting with details of exactly how difficult it had been to secure the vital Nigerian police/military order. Getting paid was to prove just the same. The tremendous pressures borne by Geoffrey Robinson in achieving the 'Co-op saving' Nigerian order were now to be shared with the other Directors, as renegotiations of the payment terms took place.

The scheduled December meeting with the Chief Executive had to be cancelled at short notice. Geoffrey Robinson had been delayed in London because of parliamentary commitments, and requested that the meeting be postponed until 1.00pm tomorrow, Friday 21st December, at which time he would be available for one hour – Geoffrey certainly knew how to be provocative. He obviously had nothing further by way of negotiation progress to report! Harry Hughes rose to the bait, considering it deplorable that once again we had been inconvenienced by cancellation of a meeting at such short notice. Added to which, he commented, meetings were still being held out of works hours when our time could easily be devoted to meetings between 8.00am and 4.30pm. Furthermore, he and other Directors with supervisory duties in the factory were reluctant to attend a meeting on the last day prior to a holiday, and as meetings were so infrequent, lengthy discussions inevitably took place. In view of the agenda prepared for this meeting, the restricted time of one hour was insufficient. Accordingly, the Directors agreed to postpone the meeting until the first date in the New Year when the Chief Executive was available.

What a difference 12 months makes! As the Co-op membership once again began its festive break, the escalating uncertainty about the future was massive, and we were all left wondering whether the sacrifices and effort involved in pursuit of long-term viability would be worthwhile. Bill Crosby of Reg Allen in London organised a UK dealers' collection for the Co-op membership in recognition of its commitment, which provided much-appreciated Boots Christmas gift vouchers for all concerned.

Back to work following the Christmas/New Year holiday with our families, we couldn't imagine what further surprises 1980 would bring for Triumph. On the frame section we were still busy with production of the Nigerian order, both for complete Tiger 750 motorcycles and back-up spare parts. My day job as a welder helped keep me in touch with the production realities confronting the Co-op membership on a daily basis. On the first day back, the Chief Executive did not make contact regarding his availability for the rearranged December meeting; however, the Company Solicitor Peter Davis did. He required a Board meeting the following day to bring

Brenda Price and John Rosamond receive details of the UK dealers' Christmas collection for Co-op members, from Bill Crosby of London dealer Reg Allen. (Courtesy London Motorcycle Museum)

the Directors up to date on legal developments with NVT. These would result in the Directors being served with a court order during tomorrow's meeting.

The meeting at 3.00pm on Thursday 3rd January 1980 started with Peter Davis providing a detailed account of events dating back to 1975, in relation to agreements then made concerning the use of the Triumph name and the recent action taken by NVT to recover outstanding payments of royalties from the Co-op. In the negotiations to purchase the name, it had been revealed to Triumph Meriden that variations to the 1975 agreement had been made as a consequence of further agreements drawn up between NVT and the receiver or liquidator in 1978/79.

This action was claimed to be in breach of trust after Triumph Meriden's 1975 agreement, and gave rise to a claim in respect of tax implications, which could reduce Triumph Meriden's percentage of royalties payable from 1 per cent to 0.48 per cent of the retail price of each motorcycle sold. On these grounds, Triumph Meriden was permitted to withdraw from a court hearing in October 1979, when a judgement had been applied for by NVT in relation to recovery of outstanding royalty payments amounting to £55,447.

A further court hearing would take place on 23rd January 1980, at which it would be resolved whether in view of the said variations to the 1975 agreement, a breach of trust had been committed against Triumph Meriden and whether the percentage royalty payable by Triumph Meriden should have been reduced to 0.48 per cent. In the event that the case was successful, a claim could then be made for recovery of any monies already paid by Triumph Meriden into a deposit account at National Westminster Bank Limited (referred to in point b below).

Meanwhile, at a hearing on 7th December 1979, NVT was granted an injunction restraining Triumph Meriden's use of the Triumph name, stipulating the following conditions:

a) Triumph Meriden would not use the name unless it provided NVT with a statement of sales of motorcycles and relevant sales prices each Friday, and

b) Triumph Meriden place into a joint bank account, in the names of Slaughter and May (solicitors for NVT) and Ward and Rider (solicitors for Triumph Meriden), a sum equal to 1 per cent of the selling price in relation to the statement required by a) above.

Copies of the court order were now to be served on each Director individually, to make certain they were aware of it and would ensure payments were made. Non-compliance with the order would render the Directors liable for penalties.

Messrs Hughes and Inglesant asked by what means they could ensure that payments were made into the bank account, since such matters were completely in the hands of the relevant management personnel. John Rosamond replied that the Chief Executive did not wish the Directors to involve themselves in managerial procedures. However, at the same time the Chief Executive had given his assurances that the matter would be dealt with. It was further pointed out by Mr Grattan and Mr Beattie that they considered the Chief Executive, whose actions to date had been for the benefit of the company, should be given the full confidence of all the Directors, and that they personally had no reason to doubt his advice in the current situation.

Mr Millen of NVT's solicitors Slaughter and May joined the meeting at 4.10pm for the purpose of serving the court order on each Director – with the exception of Mr L Hambridge and Mr G Robinson, who were not present – and on the company of Triumph Motorcycles (Meriden) Limited. Mr Robinson and Mr Hambridge would be served with the order in due course. Following Mr Millen's withdrawal from the meeting at 4.25pm and having read the order, the Directors agreed that to ensure the continued use of the Triumph name, action must be taken in accordance with the terms and conditions of the order, and that they, the Directors, expected this to be carried out by the management personnel responsible for such transactions.

The only other pressing business the Chairman then reported was that the Trustees had recently approached him with a view to holding a meeting with the Board, so that a useful exchange of views may take place. The Directors considered that nothing could be gained from such a meeting at the present time, since they required an update themselves from the Chief Executive. He was therefore requested to withhold arrangements for a meeting with the Trustees for the time being.

At last there were developments with the partnership negotiations, and a meeting was called on 18th January to deal with a Telex communication from Marubeni, detailing a series of questions. Replies to the following two were required from the Advisory Board Directors:

• Marubeni question no. 76

Explanation is required on Co-operative i.e. legal status and how it is operated and functioned; as an example, you are requested to explain how management decisions would be made.

It is stated that no connections with the trade union have existed, but there are trade union members on the premises; they want to know where they are placed in the company organisation and what degree of right to speak they have.

• Marubeni question no. 77

What degree of authority does the Chief Executive have in connection with the Co-operative?

Discussion had already taken place between the Board's negotiating team, Geoffrey Robinson, John Rosamond and Bill Beattie with regards the content of the replies to be relayed to Marubeni. The Chief Executive considered it necessary to indicate a form of control within the Co-operative that would be recognisable to Marubeni, and show there was a degree of experience behind the manufacturing side of the business. In accordance with his interpretation of the questions, he had suggested the Board should be reformed to consist of either eight Directors with eight Senior Executives, plus the Chief Executive having the casting vote; or eight Directors elected to a Works Council, five elected to the Board, with five Senior Executives, and the Chief Executive having the casting vote.

The Directors were unable to understand why these questions had now been raised, since previous negotiation reports had indicated that Marubeni had already been informed of the functioning of the Co-op, and was suitably impressed. Furthermore, they considered the wording and interpretation of the questions difficult to comprehend, and were equally concerned that any replies given may be misinterpreted in translation. As a consequence of which, any decisions made now may have adverse repercussions at a later date.

Mr Beattie explained that Marubeni required further reassurance because of a third party's alleged contradictory reports on the Co-op. In the ensuing discussion related to the reformation of the Board, the following points were considered:

The degree of control on the part of the Directors, under either of the options mentioned, would be no different from the present format since the management was already in total control of the factory, under the jurisdiction of the Chief Executive. Furthermore, the Directors had complied with every proposal (with one exception) that had been put forward by the Chief Executive during the last year.

It was the Board's intention to offer full co-operation to any company with which Triumph entered into partnership. The new format would require the appointment of management personnel to the Board of Directors; names of the people involved were requested.

Mr Grattan suggested that, if it was agreed to adopt the Chief Executive's option ii), it may be possible to apply a system of rotation for the three members elected to the Works Council, who would not be appointed to the Board. Whilst it was thought that the system of rotation would not give the required continuity, Mr Grattan's suggestion was pursued, and it was decided that in adopting option ii), the three Directors who were not appointed to the Board could be given the right to participate in Board meetings without the entitlement to vote.

The Chief Executive was then contacted by telephone with regard to the above, and he agreed that this was an acceptable proposition. It was then agreed by the Directors that the reformed Board could consist of eight Directors elected to represent each of the Co-op's trade unions, five of whom would be appointed to the Board, with the remaining three being given the right to participate in Board meetings, but without voting privileges. A system of rotation would be established: five Senior Executives, with the Chief Executive having the casting vote.

Messrs Hughes and Inglesant voted against the proposition. Mr Hughes stated that, if he was elected as a member of the Board, he would not agree to take part in discussions without the right to vote; Mr Inglesant's views were the same as those of Mr Hughes.

Further points were raised, which would also be included in the replies sent to Marubeni, and with which the Directors were in agreement. These were as follows:

• There would be an integrated membership, with everyone including management personnel becoming members of the Co-operative. A fully comprehensive grading system would be implemented, with everyone including management personnel being subject to a graded payment structure.

• Training schemes would be introduced to enable employees to progress to executive levels.

• Wherever possible, all trade union problems would be settled internally without reference to outside officials – this was considered acceptable in all but isolated cases where individuals, having the right as subscribers to the trade unions, may wish to seek advice from their district official.

It was further agreed that the Trustees of the company would be consulted with regard to their position, changes in the shareholding arrangements and the constitution of the company. Discussions would take place on all these subjects at a Beneficiaries' meeting. In addition, the Chief Executive had suggested that the Board should, in relation to specific instances, reserve the right of veto. This point was left open pending further discussions relating to the constitution of the company.

Mr Beattie suggested that should a positive reply be received from Marubeni, a mass meeting should be called to inform the workforce of the exact position, preceded by a meeting of the Directors.

The Advisory Board met the Chief Executive on 1st February 1980. He gave a brief verbal report on the financial situation, stating that in the circumstances, the company had traded satisfactorily to the end of December 1979, and sufficient resources were available for the month of February. The National Westminster Bank had agreed to continue the overdraft limit of £850,000. Whilst the Export Credit Guarantee Department had again been approached, the facility had not been renewed, and discussions were therefore continuing with a view to obtaining alternative finance. Moving to the creditor's situation, Geoffrey Robinson reported that Mr Tippets (Chairman of the Creditors' Committee) had been contacted and had reported that the situation with creditors generally was under control. The arrangement previously made with regard to payment of local rates was still satisfactory, and a meeting with the Coventry City Council was due to take place later that day.

Reporting on the Triumph name, the Chief Executive stated that a court case had been heard during 7th/9th January 1980 at which judgement had been reserved – it was assumed that it was still being read, and further information on the outcome was expected from the Company Solicitor. Meanwhile, the restrictions on the use of the Triumph name remained, with Geoffrey Robinson continuing to pursue a purchaser for it. The terms of acquisition, which would include a requirement for the name to revert to the company, would be put before the Board for consideration in due course.

Moving on with his report, he stated that he had reached agreement with the Personnel Manager, Ron Atkinson, on the implementation of 'staggered' holidays during the year 1980. The closing date for holiday requests would be 1st March, after which it would be necessary for employees to seek permission for specific dates from their organiser.

Discussions then took place on a proposition moved by Mr Beattie that, for a trial period of one month, the Social Club be permitted to sell alcohol during the half hour lunchtime opening period. He considered that the committee had proved its sense of responsibility through its efforts in opening the club, and through recent events in which it dealt positively with people who had interfered in the club's business. The Chief Executive registered his disagreement with the sale of alcohol on the premises, and considered that if permission were granted, the Social Club should bear the entire legal responsibility. He further advised the Board to consult the Company Solicitor with regard to the legal aspects being written into the articles of the club. Messrs Hughes and Atkinson also recorded strong opposition to the sale of alcohol, both in view of the possibility of serious accidents which may occur within the factory, especially to the younger employees, and the probability of encouraging an increase in the number who consumed alcohol at lunchtime, which at present was minimal. The proposition was again moved by Mr Beattie, who added that if the Board was agreeable, he would be responsible for monitoring the situation during the trial period, and would subsequently present the Board with a report.

The Board's agreement was subject to the following conditions:

a) For a one month trial period, the Social Club is granted permission to sell alcohol during the lunchtime opening period i.e. 1.00pm till 1.30pm.

b) The Board reserved the right to rescind this decision following a review of the situation at the end of the trial period.

c) The legal responsibilities of the Social Club be confirmed through the Company Solicitor, Mr P Davis.

d) Mr Beattie should undertake the responsibility of monitoring the situation during the trial period, and submit a report to the Board.

e) Opening for the lunchtime sale of alcohol would not commence until a meeting between the Chief Executive, Mr Beattie and the Social Club had taken place, and the relevant legal details had been confirmed.

Four votes were recorded against the proposition, and Mr Hughes recorded his disagreement.

The Chief Executive now provided a progress report on the partnership negotiations. Two distinct possibilities remained:

a) Marubeni – with whom a partnership would give Meriden access to sales and technical expertise, in addition to an injection of capital. In the case of sales, the Chief Executive explained that it appeared the intention was to set up a separate sales company that would have no link with the Co-operative i.e. by way of manufacturing and engineering functions.

All relevant information requested in recent telexes had now been provided to Marubeni and negotiations continued. Miss Price was currently visiting Japan in order to clarify points related to Triumph's American subsidiary (TMA).

It was intended that the Chief Executive and Mr Murison (Accountant) would also visit Marubeni, mainly to substantiate financial statements (Mr Murison was the Commercial Executive/Accountant Geoffrey Robinson had recruited to help after John Boulter resigned). The Chief Executive considered it advisable for the visiting party to be restricted to three people, with Miss Price and Mr Murison checking each other's work, and him answering any queries that may arise regarding the Co-operative. The Chairman explained that he and Mr Beattie considered the costs too great for their involvement at this time. The first meeting in Japan was due to take place on Monday 4th February, with reports telexed back to Triumph as negotiations progressed. The Board sanctioned the release of cash for expenses that may be incurred by those visiting Japan.

b) Armstrong Equipment – the Chairman and Mr Beattie had so far undertaken the negotiations with this company, and reported that to date discussions had concentrated on engineering matters and employees' wages. Miss Price's return to Meriden was now awaited to discuss the American motorcycle market. Mr Hooper of Armstrong Equipment had also had a meeting with Government regarding Triumph.

Mr Atkinson, the Personnel Manager, advised that in view of the imminent wage review in March, informal preliminary discussions involving Mr Lindsay (Manufacturing Executive), Mr Hughes and himself had taken place. The results of those discussions would be passed to the Chief Executive. Geoffrey Robinson requested that this subject be held in abeyance pending a further meeting to be held on his return from Japan, at which time the matter could be considered in isolation.

A 21st January letter from the Co-op's Trustees, issuing the Directors with an ultimatum, forced a meeting to be held with them at 3.30pm with the Chief Executive and Company Solicitor in attendance. The Trustees' letter was on Transport and General Workers' Trade Union headed note paper, and read as follows:

Dear Mr Rosamond
I refer to my telephone conversation enquiring whether a joint meeting could be arranged between the Directors of the Board and the Trustees, together with the Finance Committee. You did indicate that you had taken a consensus of opinion from the Directors and the request would be put before the next meeting of the Board, and that the meeting would take place based upon the availability of Mr G Robinson. I have consulted with the other two Trustees and it is the joint opinion of all Trustees that we should indicate to you as Chairman, that unless a mutually agreed date can be arranged for the above mentioned joint parties, within seven days of receiving the correspondence, the Trustees would reserve their right to meet the full meeting of Beneficiaries.

I trust that you will give this matter serious consideration and let me have your reply.

Yours sincerely
R Marston, on behalf of the three Trustees
cc Mr J Tomlinson
Mr J Haynes

John Tomlinson (the local Meriden Constituency Labour Party MP 1974-1979), John Haynes (a Labour Party Local Government Councillor) and Ron Marston (a Transport and General Workers' Trade Union official) were all very sympathetic supporters of the efforts to establish the Triumph Meriden Workers' Co-operative. Accordingly, in 1975 they were obvious choices as Trustee holders of the three company shares, on behalf of the Beneficiary owners of the Co-operative. The three Trustees' largely symbolic independent role was usually only activated at the times of Co-operative Annual General Meetings. However, as recognised personalities in the local community in which many of the Beneficiary owners lived, it was not surprising that members approached them for information, especially in times of great uncertainty.

A meeting had previously been held with regard to the time which had elapsed since the last Annual General Meeting (22nd May 1978), at which the Trustees had accepted the reasons given and had also recognised the need to allow considerable time in which to enable partnership negotiations to take place. They (the Trustees) had since spoken to the remainder (five people) of the last appointed Beneficiaries Committee, who had shown concern regarding the lack of information available, and indicated that they had only heard rumours in relation to the present situation of the company.

In view of the Trustees' responsibilities to the Beneficiaries, and because of the attitude of the Beneficiaries to whom they had spoken – which was one of depression brought about by lack of knowledge and understanding of the present position – the Trustees now required further assurances regarding the company's situation, and the alleged lack of information passed to the Beneficiaries.

The Trustees were reminded by the Company Solicitor, Mr Peter Davis, of the role of the Beneficiaries' Committee, which was elected by the workforce at the time of the Annual General Meeting for the sole purpose of taking a casting vote at that meeting, should the required majority not be produced.

The Directors then advised the Trustees that, as far as possible, all available information regarding the present situation of the company had been relayed to the workforce. For example, in the case of the members of the Transport and General Workers' Union, three meetings had been held at which reports had been made on the progress of the partnership negotiations. In view of this, it was not possible to fully understand the present concern of the people to whom the Trustees had spoken. However, as there were only a small number of people involved, it was conceivable that five people out of the total workforce could probably hold the opinion that they were not fully informed. It should also be taken into consideration that all negotiations were left to the appointed negotiating committee (Geoffrey Robinson, John Rosamond and Bill Beattie), and as yet, no concrete proposals were available to put before the Beneficiaries. As far as the Annual General Meeting of the Co-operative was concerned, it was further explained by the Company Solicitor that at the time the AGM was due, it was considered inadvisable to publish the company's accounts (as the Trustees were already aware). However, with the consent of the auditors and all other relevant parties it had been agreed that, because of the interest being shown towards a partnership and the need to encourage such interest, the AGM would be postponed until negotiations were concluded.

The Chief Executive enlarged on the points made by the Directors, and further explained the detrimental effect that the holding of an AGM may have had on the negotiations taking place. It was necessary at that time for the company to continue trading, and this involved negotiations with creditors, the bank, Government and ECGD, all of whom agreed to support Triumph until such time as a partner could be found. Meantime, whilst the Chief Executive expressed his appreciation of the tolerance and patience shown by the Trustees, he pointed out the problems faced by everyone during the period since May 1979, and most particularly the Directors, who had held the situation together at the factory under extremely difficult circumstances.

The position at the present time was that whilst it was thought definite proposals may be available by the end of March, partnership negotiations still continued, and although the ECGD facility had not been renewed the company was in a financial position to continue producing until the end of February.

Peter Davis, the Company Solicitor, then confirmed that although the company was at fault in not holding the AGM, the Directors had taken the decision to postpone it in view of the circumstances prevalent at that particular time, and to continue trading because the support of all creditors had been obtained for them to do so. Triumph's continued trading was therefore not fraudulent, but in the interest of all creditors and employees. Furthermore, since the Directors had not issued a notice for the winding up of the company, nor had they requested that an AGM be called, the Trustees, as nominal shareholders, were in a legally sound position.

Mr Tomlinson then indicated his acceptance of the situation, and requested that the Chairman contact the Trustees as soon as any positive information became available.

The Chief Executive assured the Trustees that they would be made aware immediately of any concrete proposals that may materialise, at which time, of course, a General Meeting would be called for the purpose of acceptance by the Beneficiaries.

The Directors further confirmed that all available information would continue to be passed to the Beneficiaries, and suggested a meeting with the members who had approached the Trustees. Mr Marston indicated that he had intended for the remaining five members of the last AGM Beneficiaries' Committee to attend today's meeting. Because of an error in Mr Marston's letter of 21st January, when these individuals were referred to as members of the Finance Committee (pointed out by the Chairman), an invitation had not been extended to those members concerned!

With all the aforementioned interested parties now apprised of the negotiations in Japan, Mr Hooper – the Chairman and Managing Director of Armstrong Equipment – also awaited the outcome. He had certainly demonstrated to John Rosamond and Bill Beattie that he was also a man in a hurry, with a number of recent successful company acquisitions behind him. When time available for a meeting to discuss partnership became a problem, he sent the company aeroplane to transport Bill Beattie and myself to Armstrong Equipment's headquarters on Humberside. Our enquiries regarding Harry Hooper's business takeover strategy suggested he was an extremely shrewd and tough negotiator, a side we felt we may only see if his company became a real contender for partnership with Triumph. Everyone now awaited developments in Japan.

15

JAPANESE
NEGOTIATIONS

On 19th February 1980, the Chief Executive gave a verbal report on the visit to Marubeni/Suzuki in Japan (this largely confirmed the details in the 11-page telexed report that he had provided for the Chairman to read informally to Directors on 13th February). The key points were as follows:

• Marubeni is keen to do the deal.

• As a result of Brenda Price's first week's work, supported by Rob Murison in the second, Marubeni also has greater confidence in our organisation, so many of the problems were simply ones of language, terminology and concepts.

• The problem is to get Suzuki aboard – the visit can only have helped in this respect, but it is simply impossible to tell the real situation at the moment.

• At times the Assistant General Manager of Marubeni's machinery division 3 seemed to let slip hints that Suzuki, to all intents and purposes, was set for the deal with Triumph.

• Both Marubeni and Suzuki are playing it very close to their chest.

• All that happened during the visit should have helped the deal along.

• What we need to do now is last out till March, somehow!

• All of the requested information has been clarified to the satisfaction of the representatives of Marubeni, and they will draw up proposals for presentation to and discussion with Suzuki.

It was anticipated that informal proposals would be forthcoming by mid-March, with a formal decision from the Japanese at the end of the month. It was thought further negotiations would be unlikely, with a final proposal simply being presented to Triumph for acceptance or rejection. Full details of any such deal would be related to the Advisory Board for approval prior to finalisation. Whilst awaiting further information from Marubeni, the Chief Executive would contact Armstrong Equipment and Penarth.

Geoffrey Robinson advised that to generate the cash to continue trading until the end of March, sales promotion needed to be strengthened in the UK and European markets. Whilst there would be no US motorcycle build, five-day working would continue throughout the factory during this period. At the same time, production had to be cut back to 100 motorcycles per week, and component supplies rescheduled accordingly.

On the Triumph name legal situation with NVT, the Chief Executive indicated that preliminary points of the proceedings against Triumph Meriden had been concluded in the company's favour, thereby reducing our royalty payment to 0.48 per cent of the unit price of each motorcycle sold. We would continue to pursue the possibility of purchasing the Triumph name and associated rights.

Whilst documentation had been compiled in relation to a new wage structure in line with previous Board discussions, it was considered by the Directors to be inappropriate for such proposals at this time. Any movement would involve negotiations with whoever was the eventual partner. It was agreed, however, that the Board would discuss the wage structure again prior to any partnership being entered into. Meanwhile, a notice would be posted to inform the workforce of the reasons for delaying detailed discussions, and advising that any subsequent agreement would aim to have the settlement backdated.

Finally, the Board was informed that Miss Price had returned to Triumph's American subsidiary TMA to conclude business, and was interviewing candidates for the position of National Sales Manager.

The Chairman told the Directors that the negotiating team had been requested to stand by in readiness for a further visit to Japan, possibly leaving England on Saturday 22nd March. Mr Mackie expressed the hope that no agreement would be signed during the visit. The Chairman confirmed that he had already given an undertaking that the finalisation of any deal would be withheld until full discussions had taken place at Meriden. At the last Creditors' Committee meeting, the Chairman continued, the committee had expressed the wish for a definite settlement in the partnership negotiations by the end of March, although it was satisfied with progress to date. The next Creditors' Committee meeting had been arranged for 2nd April. The Chairman then informed the Directors that Mr Hooper, Chairman and Managing Director of Armstrong Equipment, would make a further visit to the factory on Friday 21st March.

An unexpected development resulted in a brief Board meeting the following day (20th March) to inform the Directors that Marubeni representatives would now be visiting the factory on Monday 24th March. Accordingly, the negotiating team's visit to Japan had been postponed.

At 8.30am on 25th March, the Directors attended a meeting to receive a report from the Chairman on the previous day's negotiations with Marubeni. Those taking part in that meeting were as follows:

Messrs Matsuda and Sato – representing Marubeni.

Messrs Robinson, Baldwin, Jones, Bottrill, Rosamond, Beattie and Miss Price – representing Triumph.

Mr Brian Whitehouse (Coopers & Lybrand) – Auditors.

Mr Peter Davis (Ward & Ryder) – Company Solicitor.

The original proposals had been that Marubeni would take control of the Sales/Marketing aspect of the partnership, with the Co-operative being retained in its entirety and responsible for manufacturing and engineering. The latter proposal had, however, been rejected by Suzuki after a review of information presented to them by Marubeni. This information had indicated to Suzuki that more intensive action was required to affect the recovery of Triumph.

Alternative suggestions had now been put forward by the Japanese company:

a) That Suzuki take total control of the business in respect of manufacturing and engineering.

b) That union representatives would not be acceptable as Directors of the Board.

c) That the motorcycle range be extended to three models – 250cc, 500cc and 750cc – thereby increasing market penetration, especially in the USA.

d) That production be increased to 10,000 of each of the three models, totalling 30,000 units per year.

e) That the HMG debt be waived (this matter to be negotiated by the Chief Executive).

f) That some form of membership shareholding could be considered.

To further examine the possibility of Suzuki's taking control of the business, the following were now required and were being drawn up:

• A cost analysis of Triumph's components, both manufactured and bought out, for comparison with the cost of similar items produced in Japan.

• Audited accounts for the year ended 30th September 1979. (These had not been required for consideration under the terms of the original proposals.)

A decision from Suzuki was now dependent upon the efficiency of these, evident by the content of the financial information requested.

The Chairman expanded briefly and invited the Directors to express their views, but at the same time stressed that the aforementioned conditions as listed (a to f) were merely suggestions, and in no way constituted a definite proposal. It was understood however, that Triumph's negotiating team would not be called upon to visit Japan until such time as Marubeni/Suzuki had decided the terms of their offer to Triumph. The points mainly highlighted in the Directors' discussion were with regard to the refusal of trade union representation on the Board. Whilst it was widely acknowledged that Suzuki would wish to take complete control of its investment, it was felt consideration should be given to the fact that during the life of the Co-op, such Board representation had proved its merits by way of the very good industrial relations throughout the plant. At the same time it was considered inadvisable to strongly pursue this point in case such emphasis was to jeopardise a deal.

John Rosamond and Bill Beattie then explained the difficulties experienced in the negotiations, with Mr Beattie requesting Board confirmation of the brief given to the negotiating team – which he believed had been 'get the best possible deal'! Some of the Directors, however, emphasised that any proposal would be subject to approval by the Board, and would require final acceptance at a general meeting of Beneficiaries. John Grattan expressed the view that he had never thought the companies involved would countenance union representation on the Board, and also considered that the suggestions presently put forward were probably the least contentious of what would finally be offered! Furthermore, as had already been stated by the Chairman, the Japanese had indicated that they would not call on the negotiating team again until they (Marubeni/Suzuki) had decided on the terms under which they would enter into partnership, at which time it was evident that Triumph's representatives would no longer be in a negotiating position.

The Chairman then reiterated his previously given undertakings that there would be ample time for discussion prior to finalisation of any deal, going on to explain that because of Suzuki's requirement of audited accounts and cost information, the timescale of negotiations would now be extended by approximately four weeks. The Chief Executive had suggested that in order to stretch the cash resources of the company over this period, it would be advisable to manipulate certain of the scheduled holidays for everyone other than those who were directly involved in the generation of cash. In so doing, the company would, by payment of holiday money, generate cash from sales of motorcycles and spare parts whilst eliminating the cost of overheads and material purchases.

A factory notice was then compiled, which explained the situation and requested that the workforce, other than nominated personnel, accept the following rearrangement of holidays:

a) The Easter Holiday (2 days) would be extended by 3 days.

b) The September break (5 days) would be brought forward to be taken immediately following a) above.

This would close down production for two weeks from 4th to 21st April, with payment at normal rate during this rearrangement of holidays. Anyone requested to work the additional 3 days at Easter would be given the opportunity to take the holiday at a later date. In the event that some personnel had already booked holidays in September, every effort would be made to honour those arrangements, and as an alternative, consideration could be given to bringing forward the spring break.

The Chairman then reported that Mr Hooper (Chairman and Managing Director) of Armstrong Equipment had visited the factory on 21st March, and continued to show an interest in partnership negotiations. A senior accountant from his company would visit today to review financial information.

John Inglesant asked how the present situation regarding the Triumph name would affect any partnership deal. The Chairman replied that the name would be purchased as soon as it could be seen that a deal was reaching fruition. Meanwhile, it was reported that NVT had appealed against the court's judgement on 7th/9th January, and proceedings were continuing.

The next Board meeting took place on 21st May. Mr Dowling and Mrs Sara attended the meeting on behalf of Messrs Hughes and Hambridge, who were indisposed. Prior to the 10.00am meeting starting, the Chief Executive explained that whilst negotiations with the Japanese were progressing, in the event that a deal did not materialise it may be necessary to seek general public support, and for this reason he had invited the crew of BBC's *Newsnight* to film this meeting. Transmission would take place that night at 11.00pm (filming took place from 10.15am to 11.00am).

The Chief Executive opened the meeting by reading out a telex received from Japan. It requested that a further meeting be arranged to take place in Japan mid-June, at which time a party of five representatives from Triumph would enter into discussions with Marubeni and Suzuki representatives to formulate joint proposals. Board authorisation was requested for the negotiating team's visit, and was given.

The Chairman reported that he and Mr Beattie had continued negotiations with Armstrong Equipment Limited. Mr Hooper, the Chairman and Managing Director, had stated that because of other commitments he was not ready at the present time to put forward a definite proposal; there was, however, a strong possibility that a proposal would be forthcoming in due course.

It was suggested by Geoffrey Robinson that a letter be sent by the Chairman to Mr Hooper, expressing the hope that a proposal be drawn up and that the possibility of a Japanese link would not be ruled out.

The Chief Executive went on to report on finance, stating that the company was still operating within its overdraft limit, although because of the extended time required for negotiations, the measures previously discussed would need to be implemented in order that the company could remain open for a further six weeks. In this respect, the following action was required:

a) Spare parts order

A large spares order was under consideration which would ensure an income in the region of £25,000 per week for the next 6-8 weeks.

b) Launching of new models

Arrangements had been made to launch the Bonneville Electric Start and Executive models. Messrs David Essex and James Hunt had agreed to attend the launch, which would take place at the Grosvenor House Hotel, London on Friday 23rd May.

It was anticipated that sales of the new models (orders for which were already on hand), together with the spare parts order would generate sufficient cash to cover the period to the end of June.

The Board adjourned at 11.10am to allow a meeting with the Trade Creditors' Committee at 11.30am.

The Board meeting was reconvened at 2.00pm, at which time the Chairman reported that a successful meeting had taken place with the Trade Creditors' Committee, which had indicated its continued support for Triumph to enable the final stages of the Japanese negotiations to proceed to a conclusion.

Further Board discussion then took place regarding the forthcoming visit to Japan, during which it was explained by Geoffrey Robinson that the visiting team would consist of the Chief Executive, the Chairman, Miss Price, Mr Lindsay and Mr Jones.

The Chief Executive was asked whether it was advisable that Miss Price should be included in the team, in view of her intention to leave Triumph. (Miss Price had made the decision to seek alternative employment when she became aware that the Japanese companies did not employ female Senior Commercial Executives; a terrible shock for Brenda and a major problem for Triumph, about to lose one of its most valuable and loyal Senior Executives.)

The Chief Executive explained that the Triumph people concerned would be taking part at the request of the Japanese companies, and that whilst they had been made aware that Miss Price was leaving Triumph, they preferred that she should remain involved until negotiations were concluded. (Brenda Price's Senior Executive employment was now to be at Mercia Sound, the new Coventry-based commercial radio station.)

Factory preparations for the London launch of the Bonneville Electric Start and Executive models were now well advanced. The Executive model – with its 3.9 cubic feet luggage carrying capacity in two quality, quickly detachable sigma suitcase panniers and a matching top box – provided potential Triumph customers with a touring option. The Brearly Smith headlamp fairing completed the package, offering surprising weather protection for the rider. However, the crowning glory of the Executive model was the luxurious, 'smoked' colour co-ordinated rich maroon finish on all of the aforementioned new touring accessories. The choice of one of London's premier hotels, Grosvenor House, to launch this model was inspired, as no-one would be ashamed to arrive at this venue on a Triumph Executive!

At last, the most requested option – the Electric Start model – could be provided on all Triumph models in the range. UK and US specification Bonnevilles were to be shown at the launch. It is said that nothing worthwhile comes easily, and this was certainly the case regarding the design and development of the Triumph Electric Start.

On seeing the highly publicised setbacks with the Government and the partnership negotiations, major suppliers of key specialist components had on several occasions feared the worst and ceased production of the new casting dies and electrics. Similar delays had also occurred at the factory during this very difficult period of first redundancies, and then excessive overtime without pay in engineering design and development areas. Because of the massive uncertainty about Triumph's future, there was also similar concern in the marketplace. At times, the only orders for motorcycles we had were for the Electric Start Bonnevilles, which we could not supply. In view of the delays, liberties were initially taken in the development testing programme, which led to failures and a series of late modifications in order to finalise the design. These failures severely knocked the credibility of the Chief Engineer, Brian Jones, and led to some Directors criticising him at Board level. In particular, Brian was accused of having a 'not invented here' design complex, unprepared to listen to other individuals' suggestions or ideas! Geoffrey Robinson forcefully defended Brian Jones, stating that in his experience "he had never known a Chief Engineer who did not have a similar reputation."

After further extensive electric start rig testing, it was finally believed that the latest design

Triumph's first limited edition touring option, the Bonneville Executive, was launched at the same time as the Electric Start models. (Brochure picture)

was man enough for the job. Aesthetically, the Electric Start design could not have worked better from the start, perfectly suiting the iconic Triumph vertical twin cylinder engine design.

On 23rd May, the launch of the Bonneville Electric Start and Executive models took place at the Grosvenor House Hotel in London.

Geoffrey Robinson had secured the services of two fantastic personalities, David Essex (pop superstar and longstanding Triumph owner/enthusiast) and James Hunt (McLaren's 1976 Formula 1 Grand Prix World Champion), to promote Triumph's new models at the expectedly large media gathering, with representatives from both specialist publications and national dailies. Safety issues surrounding motorcycle riding had occupied many column inches in the press, so when James Hunt turned up for the launch on crutches, with one leg in plaster (from a skiing accident), there was understandable but unwelcome laughter.

However, with judicious diplomatic staging – David Essex riding and James Hunt on pillion – the plastered leg was hidden from the camera lenses on the side of the bike not in shot. Many excellent media photographs were taken, and one was turned into a promotional poster for the dealer network. All in all the launch went very well, with Triumph receiving excellent press copy promoting the new models, and in addition, positive coverage of the delicately poised partnership negotiations. Geoffrey's connections at the fabulous Grosvenor House Hotel certainly did an excellent job, which was much appreciated by the well-fed and watered journalists and London Triumph dealers present.

Several of these very supportive dealers, Reg Allen and Roebuck to name just two, provided the Triumph promotional materials for this event, with the factory being completely out of stock in these frugal times. The only one of the attending Triumph Meriden Executives and Advisory Board Directors who was not totally convinced about this excellent promotional occasion was John Inglesant, whose disabled car parking blue badge was snatched during the event!

The excellent launch of the new models certainly boosted morale and stimulated a more positive feeling amongst Triumph dealers, employees and the motorcycle-buying public. Unfortunately, this was not to last long.

On 17th June, an Advisory Board meeting took place to enable the Chief Executive to

The Grosvenor House Hotel launch of the Electric Start Bonneville, by personalities David Essex and James Hunt, was captured on an advertising poster.

provide an update on the partnership negotiations. (Once again Mrs Sara was deputising for Mr Hambridge.) Initially, the Chief Executive pointed out that because of the present Government's policies, the country as a whole would probably be plunged into the worst recession since the 1930s with prospects of unemployment increasing to some 2.5 million by the end of next year and the possibility of spectacular bankruptcies throughout industry. In view of this, any idea that the company could survive against the general trend was illusory. Added to which, Triumph's problems were compounded by its unique position with its large percentage of exports into the USA market, where as with other countries the Japanese had taken the market. This had occurred whilst both the dollar and the yen devalued heavily against sterling. The various negotiations can be summarised as follows:

i) Japanese

Geoffrey Robinson reminded the Directors that the original concept in negotiations with the Japanese was that Marubeni would take over marketing, and Suzuki, with its technical and financial strength, would also enter into partnership.

By January this year there was every indication that a deal was almost certainly possible. In January/February the estimated odds were 90:10 in favour, and in May negotiations had reached the point where even if Suzuki would not directly enter partnership in terms of product investment, Marubeni alone was prepared to do so. Thus for six months, having received these assurances, the negotiating team had depended upon a deal with Marubeni and Suzuki in terms of marketing, technology and finance.

David Essex goes solo on the Electric Start Bonneville, also at the launch event. (Advertising picture)

On Friday 6th June, the Chief Executive was made aware that the Japanese deal was off for the following reasons:

a) Devaluation of the yen by some 40 per cent – it was obvious after consideration of British product costs that the Japanese were able to produce more effectively than Britain in terms of product design and marketing.

b) Negotiations were conducted through Marubeni, which was in favour of partnership.

c) No real direct contact was possible with Suzuki in order to put forward a convincing statement on Triumph's behalf.

d) It was now thought that if it was Suzuki's wish to enter the Common Market, it would prefer – as had been done in other cases – to go into a 'green field' site rather than enter into an existing situation. By so doing, it could recruit its own employees and educate them into its particular methods of operation.

e) Some of the millions of dollars recently lost in Indonesia undermined Marubeni's ability to push the deal between Triumph and Suzuki.

f) UK importers had allegedly worked to present the worst picture of Triumph.

The Chief Executive went on to say that on reflection, whilst he had considered a Japanese partnership to be the best proposition theoretically, he could now see that culture clashes could have arisen in the future. Meanwhile, he had continued to contact Marubeni since 6th June, but had been unable to persuade any change of direction.

ii) British

Regarding the British company Armstrong Equipment, a meeting had taken place at which Messrs Lindsay, Murison, Rosamond, Beattie and Miss Price were involved in discussions. Whilst there was a strong commitment to a partnership on the part of the representative concerned, it was necessary for him to present the proposition to his Board. It was indicated, however, that an answer would be given to Meriden within the next week.

In the event that a deal could be formulated, it would be necessary to include a period of short time and redundancies, since it had been made clear that the British company concerned would not subsidise Meriden at the expense of its other employees. In addition to which, the Meriden workforce would need to be trimmed according to what was considered to be the market requirements. As soon as a reply was received from Armstrong Equipment, a Board meeting and mass meeting would be held to discuss the situation.

The Creditors' Committee had been contacted by Miss Price as soon as the announcement regarding the Japanese deal was received. Further contact would be made with the committee following the Board meeting.

In reply to a question raised by Mrs Sara with regard to Miss Price's position, the Chief Executive said that Miss Price had agreed to see the partnership negotiations concluded.

A notice detailing the outcome of the day's discussions was dictated, to be posted on the factory notice boards immediately after the meeting.

16

BRITISH NEGOTIATIONS

The Co-op membership, now totally aware from the factory notice boards of the breakdown of negotiations with the Japanese, knew there remained only one realistic potential partner – Armstrong Equipment.

Developments required a further meeting on 23rd June. Apologies were received from Messrs Robinson, Hambridge and Atkinson (Mrs S Miles and Mr R Boller deputised for Mr Hambridge and Mr Atkinson).

The Chairman reported that since 19th June, together with the Chief Executive, Miss Price, and Mr Beattie, they had relentlessly pursued Marubeni/Suzuki in an effort to rescue the Japanese partnership, but to no avail. The only positive to be achieved was the indication that should Triumph manage to stay in business, there was still an opportunity for future technical collaboration.

Accordingly, it was now necessary to consider either a deal with the remaining British company or receivership. A formal proposal was not yet available from Armstrong Equipment, as it first required an indication from the Triumph workforce that it would be prepared to accept the following pre-conditions:

• A redundancy of approximately 300 employees (to be carried out on a 'selective' basis).
• With the 150 (maximum) remaining employees, the rate of production to be 100 motorcycles/week plus 10 per cent spare parts.
• Wages to be reviewed, and rates of pay to be in accordance with those paid by Armstrong Equipment Limited i.e. skilled – £100 per week; semi-skilled (3 grades) – £92, £88, £81 per week. Armstrong's own job evaluation team would assess the skills of the employees retained.
• The Armstrong Equipment/Triumph operation would be housed in the Butler Building and the main factory buildings would be retained for further use. No information had yet been obtained in respect of staff/administration employees.

An assurance from Triumph that the workforce would accept the aforementioned pre-conditions would enable Armstrong Equipment to have meetings with the Department of Industry and other interested Government departments. Following which, a full proposal could be formulated for presentation to the Triumph Board.

Various observations were made by the Directors with regard to expected production levels from a total workforce of 150. Queries were also raised on the type of production to be retained at the factory; would manufacturing be carried out elsewhere, leaving Meriden purely as an assembly unit? It was further pointed out that legal procedures laid down in cases of redundancy included the statutory right to 90 days' notice. The Chairman stated that the question of 90 days' redundancy notice would be raised, although it had already been indicated by Armstrong that redundancy payments would be in accordance with legal requirements.

It was finally agreed by the Directors that a mass meeting should be held immediately to ascertain the views of the workforce. As insufficient information about the Armstrong Equipment proposal was available, it was considered that the workforce should only be asked if it wished to authorise the negotiating team to obtain further information.

The mass meeting was similar to the Board meeting – a very difficult one! The members, stunned by the failed expectations of a partnership deal with the Japanese and still in a state of shock, were now having to consider the possibility of a British deal that, if agreed, appeared to provide only slave labour employment for a third of their number. However, having left the Directors in no doubt as to what they were thinking, the mass meeting authorised the negotiating team to obtain further information and report back.

On 26th June a further Board meeting took place to consider partnership negotiations with Armstrong Equipment. On this occasion, Mrs F Robbins and Mr R Boller were attending the meeting on behalf of Messrs Hambridge and Atkinson.

The Chief Executive apologised for his absence from the previous Board and mass meetings, also expressing his regret that the Japanese negotiations had irretrievably fallen through. He went on to say that if it was thought the negotiating team had made mistakes, he could only consider these to be his responsibility. At the same time, it was always apparent that the Japanese negotiations had to be pursued, since involvement with such a large concern would have sustained employment at its present levels and ensured debt settlement for both ECGD and trade creditors.

It was unfortunate that the British deal negotiations would be surrounded by such an adverse economic climate that not only affected Triumph, but the country as a whole. Negotiations with Armstrong Equipment to date had been undertaken entirely by the Chairman and Mr Beattie. The company concerned was a large, profitable engineering group, which was prepared to take on Triumph under its own terms; a tremendous commitment on its part, in view of Triumph's financial position and comparable lack of assets. Any idea within the factory of the deal being an asset-stripping exercise needed to be dismissed immediately. It also had to be recognised that the planned redundancies of 300 employees would have been inevitable, should Triumph have attempted to continue without a partner. It was only by carrying out such a large redundancy that breaking even could ever be achieved.

With regard to the redundancies, the Chairman then explained that following the instructions of the mass meeting, he and Mr Beattie had asked Armstrong Equipment whether it was prepared to pay for the entitlement to 90 days' notice. This was refused, and it was stated that if the 90 days period of notice was not waived, the deal would no longer be pursued. In view of this, the Chairman had asked what offer could be made to lessen the hardship of those who would face redundancy, and it was requested that Triumph draw up an estimate of redundancy costs involved.

Redundancy calculations were undertaken with the assistance of Mr R Lindsay (Senior Manufacturing Executive). These resulted in the following being put forward for consideration by Armstrong Equipment:

To lessen the hardship for those facing redundancy the company would pay –

• One week's salary for each years service in lieu of notice (in accordance with the present contract of employment).

• Redundancy payments in line with the legal requirements.

• An ex gratia payment of 4 weeks' wages for each employee regardless of length of service – the latter being dependent upon the waiving of the 90 days' statutory notice (for instance, for an employee over the age of 41 years, at a weekly average wage of £81 and with 5 years' service, payment would total approximately £1300, or 16 weeks' pay).

In the case of employees being retained by the new company, their service would be regarded as continuous. The foregoing redundancy settlement details were confirmed by Armstrong Equipment's Director of Industrial Relations.

Mr Beattie stated that questions had also been raised with regards the possibility of retaining more employees on a part time basis, rather than the intended 150 on full-time. However, this was not considered feasible, since it was anticipated that by doing so, further redundancies would inevitably arise at a later date. Therefore it was definitely not proposed to commence the new operation with more than 150 employees. Regarding the scaling down of the workforce, it had been requested that Triumph personnel assess and balance the required manpower. The applicable rates of pay would be evaluated by Armstrong Equipment in due course. No further information regarding future operating plans was requested at this point, both members of the negotiating team feeling that any acceptance of the detailed conditions could not rest with them, and it was now necessary to consult both the Board and the workforce.

It was pointed out by the Directors that some employees may wish to leave the company and may be selected to stay, thereby being left with a job which they did not want, whilst others may wish to consult their trade union officials about the waiving of their statutory right to 90 days' notice. Mr Boller reminded the meeting that the procedures laid down to cover redundancy should be adhered to.

John Rosamond commented that the Chairman/Managing Director of Armstrong Equipment had indicated that the following conditions would govern the redundancy:

• Employees would have to take the chance of remaining employed, even against their wishes.

• If employees were to pursue with their trade union officials the entitlement to 90 days' notice, this action would terminate any further negotiations, and Triumph's only alternative would be to appoint a receiver.

• Following a meeting with the workforce, depending upon its decision all procedural requirements involved in cases of redundancy would be observed.

The Chief Executive further reminded the Directors that the deal under consideration was infinitely better than receivership, and should the workforce not agree, there would be no option but to bring in a receiver. He then expressed the hope that the Directors would be unanimous in their support of the package.

The Directors agreed that a mass meeting would be called for 2.15pm, at which the terms of the package would be outlined i.e. redundancy, retrenchment of the company, and balancing of the workforce.

The mass meeting was a highly charged occasion, and at times acrimonious exchanges of views took place on the position Triumph was now in. At the end of the discussions it came down to a simple choice – call it a day or fight on! If we called it a day, every one at the Co-op was treated as equal and was out of a job. If we decided to fight, 300 members would have to be made redundant to provide the opportunity for 150 to carry on, hopefully securing a better future for Triumph. Obviously there was much discussion regarding exactly how the selection of the balanced 150 workforce would be undertaken. In the end it came down to the statement of Harry Hooper, Armstrong Equipment's Chairman and Managing Director: every member would have to take their chance of remaining employed!

As with all big decisions since the Meriden Co-op's formation, the membership had the final democratic vote. No decisions, however, were more difficult or bigger than this one. Agreeing to pursue the British takeover package provided a chance for Triumph to continue, but only after sacrificing the jobs of two thirds of the membership. Remarkably, the members overwhelmingly agreed in principle to pursue the British takeover.

An account of these takeover developments appeared in the 27th June *Coventry Evening Telegraph*."Meriden – new era at a price."

On 10th July the Chairman reported to a Board meeting called to indicate progress. Armstrong Equipment had approached the Government two days earlier, and its takeover proposals were now under consideration by the relevant Minister. In view of Triumph's critical financial position, the urgent need for a decision had been strongly emphasised.

The Co-op Trustee Mr John Tomlinson had suggested to the Chairman that a provisional date for an extraordinary general meeting of Beneficiaries be arranged in order to avoid delay. Whilst telephone and written contact had been made with the three Trustees to this effect, the Company Solicitor, on his return from holiday, had advised against doing this; seven days' notice of a general meeting were required, at which time notification must be given of the takeover motion and any other matters for discussion. The Trustees were re-contacted and told of the formal legal requirements. They would endeavour to give Triumph every assistance in the fixing of a date for this meeting, as seven days' notice could not be avoided. The Chairman pointed out that given the financial position of the company, it would not be possible to purchase raw materials for the first week back at work following the fortnight's summer holiday, which started the next day, 11th July. It had therefore been suggested by the Chief Executive that a mass meeting should take place on Monday 28th July (the day members returned) to inform the workforce of developments.

Mr Atkinson reported that the Social Club Committee had stated its intention to extend the lunchtime opening of the club on the final day before the holiday. The Board agreed that notification should be given to the Social Club Secretary to the effect that opening time must be restricted to the normal half hour, 1.00-1.30pm, as previously agreed in June 1978.

On 28th July we returned from summer holiday, and the scheduled Advisory Board meeting attended by the Chief Executive took place. Geoffrey Robinson reported that during the last six months of negotiations with the Japanese the net worth of the company had proceeded to run down, largely because at a time when sales were worsening, no redundancy had taken place. This had been insisted on by the Japanese, it being considered unwise to enter into redundancy or layoffs whilst negotiations were under way. The current net worth of the company had, however, been made clear at the commencement of the negotiations with Armstrong Equipment, which had subsequently made proposals to Government. The Chief Executive had been in touch with ECGD during the last two weeks, and found the department to be not entirely unsympathetic towards Triumph. However, the possibility of ECGD waiving Triumph's debts, as required by the British company's takeover proposals, was doubtful. A letter had been sent by ECGD to Armstrong Equipment requesting further negotiations at a meeting to take place this week.

It was thought that the outcome of this meeting with Government would not be conclusive, the matter having to go to a full Cabinet meeting from which a decision may be issued within the next two to three weeks.

The Chief Executive was now giving consideration to alternative proposals in the event that a deal did not materialise from the current British company negotiations. These proposals would be difficult to negotiate, and would require further agreements with the trade creditors and all other parties, particularly the Department of Industry and ECGD. The Chief Executive reported that Miss Price, who was on holiday in the USA, would spend two weeks at TMA and had been requested to draw up plans for a drastic reduction of the American operation. As Triumph was in difficulties in the States due to currency problems relating to the yen/dollar and pound sterling, a number of bikes would probably have to be returned to England. One further US problem would be the disposal of the spare parts stocks. Consideration was being given to this matter, and to the eventual organisation that Triumph Meriden should have in the USA. Geoffrey Robinson stated that he saw no reason why the company accounts for the 1977/78 and 1978/79 financial years should not now be published. The 1978/79 accounts had shown a break even, representing an improvement of over £3m from 1977/78. This result had been a clear commitment in the submission put to Government in June 1978, and it was gratifying to see it had been achieved, despite all the difficulties. The Chief Executive then went on to say that in the present situation, given the negotiations that made it necessary for the factory to remain functional whilst awaiting the outcome of Armstrong Equipment's meeting with Government, a decision had to be taken by management to reduce motorcycle output to 50 per week. This output was in accordance with the estimated sales potential as assessed by Mr Lindsay, who together with the Chairman had now assumed responsibility for sales. In view of the reduced production figure, and bearing in mind that the factory was manned to produce 200 motorcycles per week, a two-day working week was proposed.

Mr Lindsay explained to the Board the short-time working pattern for production. This involved the machine shops and assembly tracks alternating over three days, thereby giving two days' working per week to each section. The two-day week would apply in all departments, with offices and other areas probably also adopting rotational systems. Payment of the guaranteed week at average earnings rate of pay would be observed, and full details of the working pattern would be posted on the notice boards, after acceptance by the Board. The Board agreed that a mass meeting would be arranged to take place at 1.45pm, when the situation would be fully explained to the workforce.

As soon as the Government's refusal to support the Armstrong Equipment takeover of Triumph by writing off the outstanding debts became known, it sparked spontaneous nationwide outrage amongst British bike enthusiasts. The Worcestershire branch of the British Motorcycle Riders' Club organised a 'ride the flag' demonstration from the Meriden factory to the heart of Government, 10 Downing Street. By the time the 700 bike column from the Midlands reached the London gathering point at Aldenham Country Park in Elstree it had more than doubled in size, with an estimated 2000 motorcyclists completing the protest to Downing Street on foot. There, a 5000 signature petition from riders all over the country was handed in for the Prime Minister. This fantastic fillip to sagging Co-op morale was certainly very welcome to the membership, who vowed to fight on.

Although the Co-op was now on short time, we were also entering the build-up to the annual August Earls Court International Motorcycle Show. Not taking part would have confirmed the many rumours that were circulating about the end of Triumph Meriden. Show expenditure had long since been committed, so there was never any doubt in our minds that the launch of the 1981 Triumph model range would go ahead. The 1980 show stand theme this year was "Triumph Bonneville – *MCN* machine of the year."

A full complement of 1981 models was to be shown:
• UK and US-spec Bonneville Electro (T140ES)
• UK and US-spec Tiger (TR7V)
• US-spec Bonneville Special (T140D)
• UK Bonneville Executive – Touring

Geoffrey Robinson, MP, Chief Executive of the Co-op, meets a very concerned delegation of Triumph supporters outside the Department for Trade and Industry, London.
(Courtesy Bob Haines' archive)

The Triumph Bonneville's prestigious *MCN* Machine of the Year award was also celebrated with an advertising poster.

194

Contained within these 1981 models were the ongoing evolutionary engineering developments and upgrades. There was also to be a surprise exhibit to assess rider reaction to the Triumph factory's take on the lowrider style of motorcycle, dubbed the Triumph Phoenix (T140PE). This much more radical development to assess market reaction had been brought about as a result of the less than hoped for sales success of the T140D Bonneville Special. The Phoenix was the design creation of Jim Barclay. When Jim resigned from the Co-op Board of Directors on a point of principle, Geoffrey Robinson eventually persuaded him to take up the vacant Development Engineer post in the Experimental Department, where his main project was the Phoenix. Until Brian Jones' recruitment as Chief Engineer, Jim Barclay steadfastly led Triumph's engineering effort, being a veteran of design developments to convert to left foot gear change/right foot braking during the factory occupation, and more latterly noise and emissions modifications to meet new US EPA legislation. Probably Jim's most memorable previous creation from an aesthetic point of view was the Premium Bonneville, with its striking three spoke alloy wheels. Like the Premium Bonneville, the Phoenix Lowrider was radical for Triumph, with many serious design changes as well as the obvious cosmetic ones. After many months of work, Jim's creation came together just in time for dispatch with the other show models to Earls Court. In addition, there was an impressively detailed specification board to show visitors all the important new design features on the Triumph Phoenix (T140PE). This created a humorous stir amongst female members of staff at Triumph – as lowrider models are more popular in the US, the highly

Bob Haines discusses the touring qualities of the Bonneville Executive with a visitor to the Earls Court show stand. (Courtesy Paul Golledge's archive)

The TR7V Tiger 750 on the now almost deserted Triumph stand, at the end of another long day at Earls Court. (Courtesy Paul Golledge's archive)

stepped pillion pad was described using an American term, which had quite a different meaning for us ... The specification board had to be amended to a more appropriate British pillion seat description!

A Board meeting took place at the request of the Trustees on 20th August to enable questions raised by Beneficiaries about the present and future position of the company to be answered. Two of the three Trustees, Mr Marston and Mr Tomlinson, had visited the factory on 4th August when discussions had taken place with Messrs Lindsay and Atkinson. In a subsequent telephone conversation between Mr Marston and the Chairman, a time and date had been agreed for the day's meeting.

In his introductory remarks, the Chairman stated that during the past few months the Trustees had been under tremendous pressure, as had the Directors, and as negotiations had continued it had become increasingly difficult to keep control within the factory. Mr Marston explained that the Trustees had been approached by members of the press following Government rejection of any further assistance to support the Armstrong Equipment/Triumph deal. Several employees had complained to the Trustees with regard to short-time working arrangements and lack of communications relating to what the future now held for Triumph.

The Chief Executive considered the complaints regarding lack of communications to be unfair, but agreed that the two-day week, short-time working could not continue. He went on to say that he was disappointed that Messrs Haynes and Tomlinson could not attend today's meeting, during which he would require a decision from the Board. Should any consent also be required from the other two Trustees, then Mr Marston would be at liberty to consult them.

The Chief Executive continued by explaining that once the Armstrong Equipment takeover proposal had been turned down by Government, the negotiating team had approached it with alternatives. Whilst discussions had also taken place with several other interested parties, none had offered a proposal that could suitably recompense Government, ECGD and the creditors. It had become clear that Triumph could not at present sell in dollar markets and the operation would therefore have to continue on a much reduced scale, which would consequently require a reduction of the workforce. It was therefore proposed that in order to reduce Triumph's debts to ECGD, some of the US motorcycle stock would be returned to England. Every endeavour would be made to sell them in the UK and other markets, thereby offering ECGD possibly 50p in the pound against outstanding debts. This action should also enable Triumph to make an initial payment to creditors of 10p in the pound as part of a schedule of repayments, to be drawn up in due course. At the same time, if this proposal was to go ahead a redundancy would need to be carried out similar to that proposed by Armstrong Equipment, to which the workforce had agreed to in principle on 26th June, in the event of that company taking over Triumph. The number of redundancies required would be in the region of 300, retaining approximately 150 employees initially producing 50 motorcycles

The 1980 Earls Court show team: (clockwise) Len Hamilton, Guy Sanders from Australia. Brenda Price, Jock Copland, Bob Haines, Margaret Wright and Doug Cashmore. (Courtesy Bob Haines' archive)

per week, but with a manning capacity of 80-100. Severance payments to be made to those selected for redundancy would be the minimum legal entitlement, plus any monies due in lieu of notice i.e. one week's wages for each year of service. No ex gratia payments could be made such as had been offered by the Armstrong deal, which had previously been accepted on the understanding that the employees waived their right to 90 days redundancy notice. In selecting the redundancies, it was intended to retain a workforce of people with varying skills who could undertake a number of jobs, rather than being employed in a single role. Grading of wages would be up to the levels quoted in the Armstrong deal, and the whole operation might in due course be contained within the Butler Building. It was further pointed out by the Chief Executive that even with the reduced workforce, there was no guarantee of full-time working, and the uncertainty surrounding the company would continue for some time.

The Chairman said that whilst he would not wish to be seen to be carrying out the proposed redundancies with indecent haste, he considered it necessary to inform and consult the workforce regarding developments at a mass meeting the next day, 21st August. Mr Marston, on behalf of the Trustees, agreed that the employees should be told as soon as possible.

After further discussions it was finally moved by Mr J Grattan, seconded by Mr R Crowder-Johnson, and agreed by the Board that a mass meeting would be held at 8.30am, at which time, following full discussion, the proposal for a selective redundancy of 300 employees would be put to the workforce. All sections of the company would be notified by their respective organisers of the time of the meeting, with official notices also posted on the boards. Those persons who would not normally be attending work because of the short-time working arrangements, would be offered travelling expenses.

Mr Marston then inquired about the date of the Annual General Meeting. The Chairman stated that because of recent developments, the provisionally suggested AGM date of 12th September had to be changed by Mr Murison. Written confirmation would be sent to the Trustees as soon as new arrangements could be made.

The 21st August mass meeting was, as expected, attended by the total workforce.

Understandably the members were all fully aware of exactly what was to be discussed, the workforce having already agreed in principle to a selective redundancy as part of the Armstrong Equipment takeover proposal.

As that takeover proposal was unacceptable to Government, it was now subject to the workforce's agreement to implement a 300-employee selective redundancy programme, thus allowing a dramatically reduced Meriden Co-op to continue its pursuit of long-term Triumph viability. As anticipated, the mass meeting was extremely emotional; after 4 weeks of short-time working – 2 days each week – reality had certainly hit home. Everyone present knew redundancy was the only possible option if Triumph and the Co-op were to continue. Ever since Triumph Meriden reopened as a workers' co-operative in 1975, there had never been any easy options for the members. All of the hard decisions that they had to take to keep Triumph in business had involved sacrifices and hardship for them and their families. It was not surprising, therefore, that with the proposition to make two thirds of the total Co-op membership redundant, members were questioning at least in their own minds if this sacrifice was one too many, and whether the time had now come to call it a day for everyone. This terrible decision had to be taken in the week UK unemployment reached 2,000,000.

In these circumstances as Chairman, I was determined that the democratic vote would not take place until everyone present was fully aware of all the facts, including the financial settlement on offer to those unfortunately selected for redundancy. Once all the redundancy information had been provided, there were many detailed questions. These were answered by Directors and management alike, following which the proposed redundancy was put to the vote. Remarkably, the proposal for a selective redundancy of 300 Co-op members was overwhelmingly carried, with only 5 votes against and 20 abstentions. The worst Co-op mass meeting that had ever taken place came to a close, and the terrible task of selecting a balanced, multi-skilled labour force of 150 began.

By 1.45pm the following Tuesday 26th August, the redundancy selection task was complete, and the identified list of the 300 members to be made redundant was in the hands of the Personnel Manager.

A meeting was called, and the Chairman advised the Directors that following the workforce's acceptance of the selected redundancy of 300 employees, he had written a letter informing all eight Co-op trade unions of the decision.

Dear Sir,
Further to our letter dated 27th June, we have to advise you that the trading position of the

company has not changed significantly since that date. As you are aware, Armstrong Equipment has now withdrawn from taking over, due to their proposal not being acceptable to Her Majesty's Government.

The company has been working short time, two days per week, for the last four weeks. At a mass meeting today, 21st August, it was agreed by an overwhelming majority (5 against, 20 abstentions) that the Armstrong Equipment redundancy plan be effected immediately, with the following exception; full redundancy entitlements plus an agreed ex gratia payment were accepted on the understanding that the 90 days consultation period would be waived by the membership. The redundancy will be on a selective basis, members will be notified on Tuesday 26th August of those affected. The redundancy will be effective from Friday 29th August.

The Director representing your union intends to visit you as soon as possible to discuss the members in your union, who are affected by the redundancy.

The aforementioned action will not, in itself, secure the company. Triumph's continued existence will still totally depend upon the present support from Her Majesty's Government and trade creditors regarding outstanding debts remaining, for sufficient time to allow us to solve our present critical financial problems.

Yours sincerely
For Triumph Motorcycles (Meriden) Limited
J A Rosamond
Chairman

The Chairman further advised the Directors that the Personnel Manager, Mr Atkinson, had drafted two letters for employees, stating the company's intention to either continue or terminate their employment.

1ST LETTER CONFIRMING CONTINUED EMPLOYMENT
26th August 1980
Dear
Please be advised that your employment at Triumph Motorcycles (Meriden) Limited is to be continued.

You are requested to collect your pay for week ending 29th August on either Thursday 28th August between 1.00 and 1.30pm or on Friday 29th August between 9.00 and 11.00am. You will be paid week ending 29th August for 2 complete days but you will not be expected to attend work on Friday 29th August.

Week commencing 1st September you will attend for work at 8.00am on Tuesday 2nd September. Payment of wages on Thursday or Friday will be in the new canteen upstairs.
For and on behalf of:
Triumph Motorcycles (Meriden) Limited
R Atkinson
Personnel Manager

2ND LETTER TERMINATING EMPLOYMENT
26th August 1980
Dear
It is with regret that we must inform you that due to the trading difficulties of the company we must make you redundant. Your in lieu of notice will terminate on Friday 29th August.

This is in accordance with the decision of a mass meeting held on Thursday 21st August and the previous notice of intended redundancy on 27th June issued to the Department of Employment and the trade unions. You will be entitled to your redundancy pay according to your service; in addition you will receive a gratuitous bounty as consideration of your past service. This payment does not represent compensation for loss of future income of any kind, or any such loss in lieu either of notice or of remuneration which you would otherwise have received had your employment not been terminated.

All payments will be made in the new canteen upstairs on Friday 29th August between 9.00 and 11.00am.

Adjustments for holidays will be deducted from the gratuitous bounty.

You will be paid week ending 29th August for two complete days but you will not be expected to attend work on Friday 29th August.

We would like to thank you for all your efforts in the past and assure you that should Meriden in the future require additional members you will certainly be considered.

For and on behalf of:
Triumph Motorcycles (Meriden) Limited
R Atkinson
Personnel Manager

The aforementioned letters from the Personnel Manager would be handed to each employee by their organiser from 3.00pm onwards that day. A notice referring to personal belongings and holiday adjustments of individuals made redundant had also been drafted by the Personnel Manager, and would be posted on the boards.

The Chairman then went on to say that a lot of good people would now be leaving the company, and selecting a balanced, multi-skilled, 150-member workforce in these difficult circumstances had been very arduous. Those individuals who had carried out the selection process had done so in as unbiased a manner as possible.

In answer to Mr Mackie, the Chairman indicated that detailed operating plans for the scaled down Co-op had not yet been completed. Mr Mackie then questioned the case of Mr R Bryant (a salesman) who, being redundant from the sales function, was to be retained in charge of the assembly tracks. The Chairman replied that Mr Wozencroft, the assembly tracks organiser, had volunteered for redundancy; accordingly Mr Bryant, who had undertaken this responsibility in the past, had not been made redundant and would return to his former position. It was agreed by the Board that a mass meeting to discuss the Co-op's forward operating plans would take place following the redundancy; a Board meeting would precede this.

The Board now discussed the public appeal fund, which currently stood at £4000. Some members of the workforce had been seeking a 'share out' amongst the 300 redundant members. Objections were raised by some Directors on the grounds that the appeal fund had been donated by independent members of the public in an effort to keep Triumph going, and should be used for that purpose. It was further suggested that perhaps it could be used for the purchase of equipment or a piece of machinery. It was agreed that this matter would be left in abeyance, to be decided by the Board in due course.

The Advisory Board then accepted the resignations of Mr R Crowder-Johnson and Mr J Grattan, who were to be made redundant. Both individuals were thanked by the Chairman for their past contributions.

There were certainly more than a few tears shed on the afternoon of Tuesday 26th August, as 300 redundant members said farewell. Many came to see the Chairman and the rest of the

Directors to shake their hands and to say thank you for all the efforts on their behalf. We were gutted; what do you say to a friend and colleague you have just made redundant? The measures implemented, any thoughts that there would be a quick return to normality were soon forgotten. With 300 members missing from the Meriden factory it was just like a vast empty mausoleum, housing 150 guilt-ridden mourners taking part in a family wake.

Of course, it wasn't only the 150 whose employment at the Meriden Co-op was to continue that were upset – nearly 70 of those selected for redundancy were now protesting and calling for a public enquiry through the local press.

Those very long days that followed the redundancy were extremely difficult within the factory, as the chosen few who remained struggled to adjust to the loss of so many good friends and colleagues, with whom they had gone through so much. The negotiating team was determined that such sacrifices would not be for nothing.

17

NEW BEGINNINGS

owever difficult, the negotiating team had no alternative but to continue the detailed work on the plans for future operation of the Co-op.

It took the remainder of the membership almost two weeks before anything like normality returned, and operation of the factory under the new circumstances could begin in earnest. As expected, it was not going to be easy; it quickly became obvious to all concerned that there would be many new production challenges to overcome. The more inter-dependent members soon realised that being one of the 150 chosen to continue the battle for Triumph brought much greater responsibility. With that responsibility, and the variation of jobs now to be undertaken, the life of production workers at Triumph Meriden had never been more interesting!

The Advisory Board Directors not selected for redundancy – Messrs R Atkinson, W Beattie, H Hughes, J Inglesant, G Mackie and W Roberts – met under J Rosamond's chairmanship on 9th September 1980. The Board decided that in keeping with the company's regrouping operations, meeting minutes would now be minimised to reflect only the basic legal requirements. In future, only decisions taken would be recorded. Finally, the Board discussed the role of the Chairman, recognising his present additional workload in connection with preparations for the AGM. Accordingly, it was decided that John Rosamond's manufacturing responsibilities should now be of secondary importance.

On 12th September a further meeting had to be called. Each Director had received a letter from the company's registration office regarding the overdue audited annual accounts for the two financial years 1st October 1977 to 30th September 1978, and 1st October 1978 to 30th September 1979. Following full discussion of these with Mr Murison, the Company Accountant, the Board authorised the appropriate Directors to sign them. The Directors placed on record their gratitude for Mr Murison's explicit explanation of these annual accounts. The Chairman then advised that it was now proposed to hold the AGM at 3.00pm on 8th October 1980, and he would contact the Trustees accordingly. Finally, it was reported that there would be a meeting in London with ECGD and Department of Industry officials at 3.00pm on 17th September.

On 28th July, the Chief Executive had reported to the Directors and Trustees the intention to pursue alternative proposals to try and resolve the Co-op's HMG debts. During these discussions, it became apparent that ECGD had been investigating how it could secure the best financial return for the stockpiled Triumph motorcycles in America. Various companies had been approached and had quoted their costs for undertaking the discounted disposal exercise, following which it was possible to arrive at a 'so much in the pound' return for ECGD. Once the Co-op became aware of what was being contemplated, it was determined that if Triumph, with its established sales distribution network, undertook the job, a greater financial return could be secured for ECGD. However, to do this successfully, Triumph felt the great uncertainty about the company's immediate future would have to be removed. Having established that there was a mutual benefit in Triumph undertaking the disposal exercise for ECGD, the Department of Industry agreed that on satisfactory completion of the job, it would eliminate the uncertainty by writing off Triumph's other HMG debts. (From chapter 12, the reader will recall Lord Trenchard's 12th July 1979 answer to John Rosamond's question about whether the Government believed it would get nothing back: "it looked extraordinarily unlikely.")

By acknowledging what the Department of Industry had already accepted – the money was lost – and allowing Triumph Meriden to continue in business, ECGD was able to secure the best possible return on its export credit finance. We were led to believe that this non-political commercial decision regarding the debt write-off had been taken by HMG at cabinet level! Shortly before the announcement, the Department of Industry provided Triumph Meriden with a copy of its intended press notice. This had an embargo on publication until the morning of 26th September 1980:

123 Victoria Street
London SW1E 6RB
TEL: 01 212 5492/3
Ref: September 26, 1980

TRIUMPH MOTOR CYCLES (MERIDEN) LTD
Lord Trenchard, Minister of State for Industry, today announced that if and when Triumph Motorcycles (Meriden) Ltd fulfil the terms of an agreement with the Export Credits Guarantee Department (ECGD) he would write off the company's outstanding loan and accrued interest.

The sum involved currently stands at £5.887m.

Lord Trenchard stated that in the present circumstances of Meriden there is no possibility of recovery in whole or part. He stressed that his Department's decision did not represent any further financial assistance to the Co-operative.

"I hope", he said, "that the removal of this shadow from Meriden will help it fulfil its undertakings to ECGD and I wish them well."

The decision follows discussions between ECGD and Meriden in which an agreement has been reached for the Co-operative and its United States subsidiary company to arrange for the early sale of those motor-bicycles for which ECGD supported the financing by Meriden's bank.

The USA is Meriden's major overseas market. Meriden feels that sales there have been hampered by uncertainty about the Co-operative's future, and the appreciation of sterling against the US dollar has left the Co-operative with substantial losses; foreign competition has limited the Co-operative's ability to react and curtail these by raising prices in the market.

ECGD, who guaranteed repayment of the finance to Meriden's bank, have agreed that, on satisfactory completion of the agreement, they will release Meriden from their obligation to repay to ECGD the difference between the sterling amount advanced by the bank and that realised from sale of the motorbicycles.

NOTE TO EDITORS
The Department of Industry gave a loan in 1975 to the Meriden Co-operative of £4.2m together with grants of £0.75m under Section 8 of the 1972 Industry Act.

The successful Co-op negotiating team. Left to right: Geoffrey Robinson MP (Chief Executive), John Rosamond (Chairman), Bill Beattie (Director). (Author's archive)

So there we have it. The negotiating team, brilliantly led by Geoffrey Robinson, had secured the write-off of the remaining HMG debts once the ECGD motorcycle stocks had been sold. Encouraged by this success, the three-man team of the commercially inspired socialist, the welder and the gear cutter, with the help of Peter Davis (Company Solicitor), gave further consideration to detailed proposals for a more appropriate operating structure for the Co-op. The new structure was to be based upon all the experiences and hard-learnt lessons we had endured since the Co-op's formation in 1975.

An Advisory Board meeting took place on Thursday 25th September (the day before the HMG announcement) to consider the proposed new operating structure. Following lengthy and detailed discussions, the Directors agreed to the following:

It was essential to retain the aims of the Co-operative as set out in the letter of 8th April 1974 to the Government, but the structure of a legally constituted Advisory Board and a separate Management Board was no longer considered appropriate in the changed circumstances.

A new arrangement should supersede the Supervisory and Managerial organisation outlined in the letter of 8th April 1974, although the shareholding would remain unchanged. The company would now best be served by a Board that would consist of the four persons occupying the executive positions responsible for Manufacture, Engineering, Sales and Finance, together with five elected representatives from among the Beneficiaries. Where the Board considered it in the interests of the company to appoint additional Directors, it would make such appointments necessary to ensure that the elected representatives of the Beneficiaries continued to constitute half of the Board.

It was proposed and agreed that Messrs R Lindsay, B E Jones, P L Britton and R W Murison be appointed Directors. The positions the newly appointed Directors would occupy were as follows:

Mr R Lindsay: Managing Director
Mr B E Jones: Engineering Director
Mr P L Britton: Sales Director
Mr R W Murison: Finance Director

Written resignations from W Roberts and R Atkinson were produced to the Board. These were unanimously accepted with immediate effect. The Board extended its thanks and appreciation to Mr Roberts and Mr Atkinson for their outstanding and dedicated services.

Geoffrey Robinson tendered his resignation as unpaid Chief Executive, since he considered he had fulfilled his original undertaking to put the company in a potentially solvent position. The Board accepted his resignation, and having expressed its thanks for his work, requested him to continue as a Non-Executive Director for the time being. Mr Robinson accepted.

It was decided that in the new circumstances of the company, the flat rate wage system was no longer appropriate. Therefore the intention would be for all employees in the company to be paid in accordance with the Coventry District average rates applicable to the functions performed, although the movement to achieve this must be governed by the company's ability to pay.

It was further agreed that Mr J A Rosamond should be confirmed in the position as Chairman of the Board, and in future the Board would meet monthly under his chairmanship. The Chairman should be appointed by the Board from among the Director representatives of the Beneficiaries, which the Board recognised as including any persons that had completed one year's service with the company in any capacity. The purpose of the monthly Board meeting would be to receive management reports and accounts, which would be reviewed by the Board as a whole, and to make policy decisions affecting the operation of the company.

In future, the Board would fill casual vacancies of Director representatives of the Beneficiaries; the remaining Director representatives would co-opt, at their discretion, the relevant number to maintain the full complement of five, or such additional number as necessitated by other Executive or Non-Executive appointments. Further appointments to the position of Engineering, Sales and Finance Director would be made by the Board on the recommendation of the Managing Director. Any future appointment to the position of Managing Director would be made by the Board.

The Director representatives of the Beneficiaries would act as a grievance committee at the meetings, at which the Managing Director would be present. This committee would review and adjudicate on grievances arising from contracts of employment. The Managing Director would hold a weekly management review session, at which the Chairman would be present.

Although time was very short, Geoffrey Robinson still managed to organise a Co-op press conference at the Grosvenor House Hotel the following day, Friday 26th September. Geoffrey believed the media/political interest would be massive once HMG made the debt write-off announcement, which he felt would appear to be a softening of Tory party policy regarding support for manufacturing industry. He was correct. All the national dailies and serious weekend publications were well represented at the press conference, plus most of the specialist motorcycle journals. Geoffrey Robinson answered many questions on behalf of the Co-op, at what could only be described as a very positive press conference. Brenda Price, back from the US, was also present. She had done a tremendous job in America putting together the discounted sale ECGD disposal plan.

Once the HMG debt write-off story broke on Friday 26th September 1980, the Meriden factory was inundated with messages of congratulations and good wishes for the future from many of its greatest supporters.

GREETINGS
TRIUMPH MOTORCYCLES LTD MERIDEN WORKS
ALLESLEY– COVENTRY

WHOOPEE YAHOO CONGRATULATIONS ALL THE BEST
FROM ME AND MY TRIUMPH
TONY (BENN)

GREETINGS
GEOFFREY ROBINSON, STAFF AND CO-OPERATIVE MEMBERS TRIUMPH MOTORCYCLES MERIDEN COVENTRY
CONGRATULATIONS I AM THRILLED AT THE NEWS OF GOVERNMENT ACTION. MY BIKE IS STILL GOING STRONG TO PROVE IT.
BEST WISHES
DAVID ESSEX

GREETINGS
MISS BRENDA PRICE AND ALL STAFF – TRIUMPH MOTORCYCLES
ALLESLEY MERIDEN – COVENTRY

CONGRATULATIONS ON GOOD NEWS FROM ALL MEMBERS
MIKE THOMPSON CHAIRMAN TOMCC

GREETINGS
TRIUMPH MOTORCYCLES MERIDEN LTD – SOCIAL CLUB MERIDEN WORKS ALLESLEY COVENTRY
WELL DONE EVERYBODY GOOD LUCK FOR THE FUTURE
GEOFFREY (ROBINSON)

GREETINGS
TRIUMPH MOTORCYCLES SOCIAL CLUB MERIDEN WORKS ALLESLEY COVENTRY
THIS IS YOUR DAY STOP HAVE A GOOD TIME
YOUR DIRECTORS

As we had come to expect, the local evening newspaper was first into print, publishing on its front page the story of the Meriden Co-op debt write-off on the day of the HMG press release! In the same edition of the newspaper was a review of T&G leader Jack Jones' "Tom Mann' lecture in Coventry the previous evening (famous Coventry Labour activist and veteran trade union campaigner, 1856-1941). Surprisingly, whoever wrote the review failed to highlight the connection between their front page story about the debt write-off and one of the Co-op's greatest supporters, Jack Jones. The majority of the press coverage regarding the proposed agreement by HMG appeared on Saturday 27th September 1980, with the story featuring in all the national dailies.

Geoffrey Robinson's dedication to putting the Meriden Co-op and Triumph in a potentially solvent position must never be underestimated. When he first became the Co-op's unpaid Chief Executive in October 1978, we were in dire straits, destined for receivership and liquidation. He took a hard commercial look at the business, and based upon what he found, drew up a plan and negotiating strategy to achieve solvency. Geoffrey is a tough, shrewd, commercial negotiator, but we would not have succeeded if it had not been for his total commitment, often at the expense of everything else in his life. Failure was never an option in his mind, but often was in the minds of others outside the Co-op's negotiating team. It's difficult to think of a similar achievement that comes close to what Geoffrey Robinson accomplished for the Co-op and Triumph.

It took almost two years of extremely difficult, high pressure negotiations to get to our goal, during which the constant threat of personal liability hung over the Co-op Directors, who steadfastly maintained their support. We could not have achieved this success without the sacrifices and support of the unique workforce and their families whose belief in Triumph remained total.

For the first time since the underfunded Meriden Co-operative was set up in 1975, the company would no longer be on a war-like footing, continually battling in day-to-day negotiations to survive, with such wranglings inevitably distracting the Co-op's senior people from running the motorcycle business. Now confronted by fierce competition, in the depth of an economic recession, with the dollar to sterling exchange rate problem preventing motorcycle sales in Triumph's main mass market, the USA, the 150-member Meriden Co-op would start again. For the foreseeable future, the business would have to be based around the manufacture and sale of the vastly improved Triumph twins that Dennis Poore had destined for the scrap heap when he closed the Meriden factory in 1973.

Perhaps the most astute article that was published at this time came from the well respected journalist and editor of *Motor Cycle Weekly*, Mick Woollett. His story summed up almost exactly the Meriden Co-op and Triumph's new position, when it challenged Triumph supporters to buy a new bike if they wanted Meriden to survive!

18

OPTIMISM OR FALSE DAWN?

With the euphoria of the HMG debt write-off barely over, the Meriden Co-op had further reason for celebration at the beginning of October 1980. The design team at Triumph had been considering a trail model for about six months, when the French importer indicated it felt sales of 250 were possible in its market. Display of a prototype at the Paris Motorcycle Show, taking place in two weeks' time, would confirm whether the public shared the importer's enthusiasm. Meriden's fantastic design and development team rose to the challenge, and completed the prototype in record time. As predicted by the importer, Triumph's Tiger Trail TR7T received a fantastic public reaction when unveiled on 2nd October. It's specification was as follows:

Engine type OHV parallel twin, four stroke (low compression)
Bore 76mm (2.992in)
Stroke 82mm (3.228in)
Capacity . . . . 744cc (45cu in)
Carburettor . . . . single amal
Tyres . . . . front 3.00 x 21
                                       rear 4.00 x 18
Brakes . . . . front 10in (254mm) disc
                               rear 7in (178mm) drum
Gearbox type 5-speed
Wheelbase 56in (1420mm)
Seat height 32.5in (828mm)
Dry weight 383lb (173kg)
Fuel capacity . . . . 2.3 imp gal (10.45 litres)
Electrics . . . . 12 volts/alternator
Ignition system . . . . Lucas Electronic
Instruments . . . . Speedo/no tachometer

The new Triumph Tiger TR7T certainly captured the Trail bike look with its plastic mudguards, engine bash-plate, smaller seat and braced handlebars. Extensive use of black wherever possible on the forks (fitted with rubber gaiters), high level exhaust system and handlebars contrasted the bright yellow finish of the petrol tank, side panels and mudguards.

Lightweight, with easier response, tractability and handling bred from years of experience

The Tiger Trail certainly met the expectations of those attending the Paris Show, and admiring glances at the Ace Café suggest it still has a similar effect! (Courtesy Erum Waheed's archive)

with its predecessors in ISDT events were the qualities it was felt would produce a rare experience for the rider on road or trail. Meriden's resident enthusiast Robert (Bob) Haines' detailed input guaranteed this was achieved. The show over, the bike was returned to the Meriden factory for further development and production in June of 1981.

Financial Director Rob Murison's excellent comprehensive budgets indicated exactly what

Triumph had to accomplish in the new operating circumstances, and to achieve the ECGD stock disposal that would secure the HMG debt write-off. These budgets were based on the market-forced reduction of manufacturing capacity. Having cut the labour force by two thirds through redundancies, only one third of the 300,000 square feet Meriden factory space was now required to meet the projected sales demand. The unused space would be cleared and sublet to generate income. Once vacated, local Coventry Council rates of £50,000 per half year were budgeted to fall to £20,000 during the second six months of operation. Utilities (heating, light, power, water, waste disposal and other services) were also expected to achieve similar proportionate savings. On the debit side, we had to operate on a bank overdraft facility secured against Triumph's assets. The overdraft usage was expected to average £900,000, upon which 16.5 per cent interest would have to be paid. We also had an informal arrangement with our trade creditors to repay, over time, a frozen moratorium debt of approximately £1.2m. An initial 10p in the pound repayment had been made to creditors from the bank overdraft. In order to retain the trade creditors' continued support, we needed to trade positively with them. However, that mutual benefit effectively removed the normal manufacturing industry opportunity to resource components in order to make cost savings or quality improvements. Such action, however desirable, would trigger demands from the company concerned for immediate settlement of its total moratorium debt. To achieve a satisfactory trading position, we had to produce and sell 79 new motorcycles and £19,500 worth of spare parts each week, in addition to disposing of the ECGD stocks. Obviously, some of the discounted ECGD motorcycle sales would be at the expense of sales of current, higher-priced motorcycles, at a time when Triumph's sale price was under great pressure from competitors in recession-hit markets. On the positive side, Triumph's customer base liked the longevity of the brand, and purchased many spare parts – parts upon which we made an approximate 50 per cent gross margin.

The reader will appreciate from the operating budget points mentioned, why there was no doubt in our minds that the immediate future of the Meriden Co-op was going to be challenging. Just how challenging only time would tell. But at least we now had a fighting chance – before the agreement with HMG there was no chance!

Geoffrey Robinson's direct involvement as Chief Executive would certainly be missed, but his continued, non-executive participation in the vital areas he had personally dealt with in the past would ensure continuity and ongoing guidance.

The appointment of a highly competent Managing Director was obviously vital. Experience regarding this key role had already taught us that the MD at Meriden needed to be highly biased towards manufacturing. Geoffrey Robinson's nominee, Bob Lindsay, was ideally qualified for the position. Bob, Geoffrey's Director of Manufacturing at Jaguar Cars, had certainly made an excellent contribution since his executive appointment at the Co-op in January 1979, and was promoted to become the new Managing Director.

The holding of the long overdue Triumph Motorcycles (Meriden) Limited Annual General Meeting on 8th October 1980 enabled Trustees, Beneficiaries and Directors to return the company to its proper status, and discuss collectively the changes that were now taking place. Having satisfactorily dealt with the formal AGM business of accepting the outstanding annual accounts for the financial years 1st October 1977 to 30th September 1978, and 1st October 1978 to 30th September 1979, these were submitted to the official Companies Registration Office. Mr Atkinson and Mr Roberts' resignations as Beneficiary Directors were formally accepted. Of the remaining five Beneficiary Directors seeking re-election at the AGM (now to be chosen by the Beneficiaries without reference to individuals' trade union membership) only Mr Mackie was unsuccessful, his place being taken by Mr K C Miller.

Co-op Directors' celebratory meeting. Standing (left to right) Messrs Mackie, Murison, Jones and Roberts. Seated (left to right) Messrs Britton, Beattie, Lindsay, Rosamond, Robinson and Hughes. (Author's archive)

A Directors' meeting was called the next day at which the following Board appointments were agreed:

1) Board appointments

Mr J A Rosamond – Chairman

Mr W A Beattie – Deputy Chairman

Mr R Murison – Company Secretary

A proposed organisation structure for the company was outlined to the meeting by the MD, and the following points noted:

a) TMA had to report directly to the MD, who was responsible for monitoring its performance and arranging for disposal of ECGD stocks in markets other than the USA.

b) Miss Brenda Price, as unpaid President of TMA, was responsible for disposal of ECGD stocks within the USA.

c) Mr G Robinson considered more staff were required in Sales and Engineering, on the basis that the company needed sufficient representation in those areas for it to survive.

d) The staffing levels for the Spare Parts Department were also considered low. But it was explained that an approach had been made by P S Motors for a joint marketing operation, details about which would be provided at the next Board meeting. It was agreed that the sales of Triumph factory spare parts required much more effort.

Regarding the wage settlement, after the total value of it had been agreed by Mr Lindsay and Mr Murison, it would be discussed with the Chairman before implementation.

Mr Robinson's non-executive role was summarised as follows:

• Continuing negotiations regarding purchase of the Triumph name.
• Assisting in any negotiations on institutional links.
• Pursuing the next Nigerian motorcycle order.
• Assisting in regaining UK police business.
• Participation in further negotiations with Government.
• Performing such tasks, particularly of a public relations nature, and as individually agreed by the Board.

Mr Robinson updated the Board with the present situation on the Nigerian order and the Triumph name purchase, which he was dealing with. Other points raised at the meeting were:

Australian sales – the Triumph Australian subsidiary was to report to the Sales Director, Mr Peter Britton, who would present a report on present activity in due course.

Extracted budget details – Mr Murison (Company Secretary) would provide breakdowns on specific budget areas for discussion at the next meeting.

Monthly reporting strategy – Mr Lindsay (MD) outlined the monthly management reporting strategy, which was to be introduced for future Board meetings.

Employee welfare – the need to improve the provision of employee welfare was agreed. The Chairman was to take a special interest in improving the situation, with general responsibility lying with the Personnel Officer, Mr Atkinson.

Workforce communications – the MD was to arrange regular group meetings with the workforce in an effort to improve communications between management and employees.

Formal thanks to be provided to retired Directors – the Chairman was asked to formally thank those Board Directors who recently retired, at the company's Annual General Meeting.

On 3rd November the Directors reviewed the management performance report for the three weeks ending 31st October. Dispatches of both motorcycles and spare parts had declined in each of the three weeks under review, and were considerably below budget. Production off-track had consistently exceeded dispatches, although still below budget. As a result, stocks of assembled bikes were excessively high. Sales orders averaged 60 per week, including abnormally high sales (106) arising from the dealer meeting. This was well below the 79 budgeted weekly averages required to keep the 'order bank' at a desirable level. Overtime payments were steadily increasing. An excessive amount of debts were outstanding.

The bank overdraft was dangerously high, and the cash outflow of £29,000 over the period was in spite of non-trading receipts of £65,000 generated from the disposal of surplus machine tools.

The following corrective action was agreed:

a) The MD would personally monitor stock levels of built motorcycles to ensure that they were permanently reduced to less than 40.

b) To match production capacity more closely with anticipated demand for the year, it was agreed that –

i) The Christmas holiday will run from 19th December 1980 to 4th January 1981.
ii) The Easter holiday will run from 17th to 26th April 1981.

It was proposed that the two weeks summer holiday should be from 11th to 26th July, and the September break from 19th to 28th September 1981, subject to approval at a mass meeting.

c) To reduce the seasonal discrepancy between production and sales demand over the winter, it was agreed that the weekly working pattern be changed to 3 days of 9 hours and 1 day of 8 hours, equalling 35 hours followed (or preceded) by a 4-day 'long' weekend.

The reduced working week now equated with a budgeted motorcycle production of 70. It was to be emphasised to the workforce that the company may adjust this working pattern over the period, and that the time and lost production would need to be made up during the summer. This was in an attempt to alleviate the financial hardship short-time working would cause, but which may prove unavoidable.

d) Overtime, debts outstanding and the overdraft situation were to be closely monitored by the Management Board.

e) Poor sales performance of spare parts was discussed, and it was agreed that the company should consider advertising for a Spare Parts Manager; details regarding this were left to management's discretion. John Rosamond was asked to evaluate possible means of improving spare parts performance.

The American subsidiary TMA was briefly discussed. It was agreed that performance to date was disappointing, but no decisions were taken pending full discussions with Brenda Price's recent appointment, Mr Wayne Moulton, who was to arrive at the factory later in the week. Brian Jones outlined product development plans, indicating that a preliminary review had enabled a 10 year programme to be drawn up. It was agreed that the establishment of long-term product objectives was vital in order to secure the future of the company.

When the adjourned meeting reconvened on 6th November, we were advised that all appeals associated with the recent pay review had now been resolved. The circulated new contract of employment was amended to include the Co-op welfare scheme, and was duly accepted. The contract of employment under consideration for the Executive Management would be placed before the Board in due course. The documents headed *Holiday entitlement, Appeals Council* and *Disciplinary rules and procedures* that had also been circulated were all agreed, and would be appended to the notice boards prior to section meeting discussion, and a mass meeting decision on the Wages and Conditions package. The documents headed *Guidance notes for management and supervisors* were amended to indicate that "an independent member of the Appeals Council should be present when any disciplinary warnings are given," following which they were accepted.

The circulated document headed *Sick scheme and casual days* was discussed extensively, welfare for members being of prime importance. However, the Directors decided unanimously that the introduction of any further benefits would totally depend on the financial strength of the company improving considerably. The Chairman was asked to put the proposed new *Sick scheme and casual days leave* document on the notice boards to indicate to the membership that possibilities lay ahead in welfare, providing the company became financially stronger. The MD suggested that perhaps the present Co-op Social Club could be developed to include a benevolent facility to look after cases of special hardship amongst the members. It was agreed to research fully the implications of this.

As previously mentioned, Wayne Moulton visited the Meriden factory for the first time since being recruited by Brenda Price. I found him extremely knowledgeable regarding the

American motorcycle market, which was not surprising considering his background – early years with Triumph, and then Kawasaki's Director of Technical Operations from 1964 to '77. No punches were pulled by Wayne or Meriden personnel during these detailed discussions on the size of TMA's task: disposing of the ECGD stock and finding a way of financing and selling 1981 Triumph motorcycles, which because of currency problems were totally uncompetitive in price. Whilst with Kawasaki, Wayne had been responsible for the very popular Ltd range, which successfully extended product life by way of new custom styling of aging models. Accordingly, he had noted with interest what Triumph had attempted with the T140D Bonneville Specials; whilst recognising that the concept was right, it had been less than well executed, and therefore failed to capture the imagination of potential US buyers. On his return to California, in addition to his major commercial task, he would start a project to produce a styling model based upon his and others' local US knowledge, one that would meet exactly what was required from the customer. (Once complete, this TMA model was shipped to the factory and produced exactly as styled, becoming the TSX.)

Shortly after Wayne Moulton returned to the United States, the Chairman received an extremely disturbing letter from Mr M G Stephens, Under Secretary at ECGD, querying the operation of the TMA stock disposal agreement.

The queries had arisen in the weeks ending 17th and 24th October and 3rd November. The Under Secretary was very concerned that all details of the way the agreement between HMG and Triumph was put into practice should be clear and demonstrable, particularly because of the degree of public and parliamentary interest and the very real possibility of the involvement of the Public Accounts Committee. It was obvious from the queries raised that those at TMA responsible for administering the ECGD agreement had not fully understood exactly what was required – especially when the first related to providing an explanation of the circumstances surrounding the sale of a motorcycle described as secondhand! Unfortunately, Brenda Price, TMA's President, was away on a short holiday at that time so an immediate detailed explanation was not possible.

Geoffrey Robinson, who received a copy of the ECGD letter, was concerned at the Chairman's involvement in what was a management matter, and pointed out that he had already received workforce complaints at his constituency surgery regarding my recent lack of involvement in the welding department. He felt it was important for me to remember that the Chairman's role was a non-executive one. This was certainly a time of great personal pressure for me as Chairman, trying to reconcile the conflicting requirements of the job. This pressurised state of mind manifested itself in several ways. My mind was often in a state of great turmoil, causing difficulty sleeping, and on one occasion when driving home deep in thought, I came extremely close to involvement in a very serious road accident. The other four Beneficiary Directors, now limited to Board meetings on a monthly basis, were very concerned about the Co-op's poor performance and were keen that the Chairman should maintain a very active involvement with management on their behalf. Unsure that the other Executive Managers were taking the worsening situation seriously, Rob Murison, the Financial Director, was also leaning heavily on the Chairman to support his concerns in management meetings. At the last Board of Directors meeting, I had been asked to investigate the vital spare parts situation and report back.

It would have been so easy to respond to Geoffrey Robinson's comments and bury myself in my day job on the welding section until the next meeting. However, the amazing statement at the last Board meeting declaring that a joint marketing operation with another company was required, because more sales effort was needed to sell Triumph spare parts (spare parts the factory never produced), had confirmed to me that the Directors needed more in-depth commercial information before making such important decisions that affected the only really profitable part of our business. Having checked with my welding shop colleagues and explained the situation that was keeping me away, they were more than happy for me to continue to investigate how we could improve the Co-op's poor supply performance on spare parts. With a 50 per cent gross margin even our welders' logic suggested we must do better! My intention was to provide an overview with recommendations on how spare parts performance could be improved.

The meeting on 1st December was a continuation of the previous Directors' meeting in November and included the approval of management contracts of employment. The detailed management reports indicated the continuing worrying trend of not achieving production, sales and consequentially financial budgets.

Geoffrey Robinson outlined the procurement difficulties presently being encountered by the Nigerian Government departments, and concluded that the prospects of another order in the immediate future appeared poor.

The Co-op had been notified that the five unfair dismissal claims that had arisen as a result of the August redundancies would now be held at a tribunal on 15th December. The only really encouraging Board meeting developments were reported by Geoffrey Robinson, who provided detailed notes and a copy of the proposed draft agreement for the outright purchase by the Co-op from the NVT liquidator of the Triumph name and associated rights.

The agreement had been passed to Peter Davis (Triumph's solicitor) who was discussing certain aspects of it (referred to below) with Mr A Boyce of Slaughter and May, NVT's solicitor. Turning first to the financial implications, these meant that:

a) Triumph and NVT would drop all outstanding litigation against each other.

b) Triumph and NVT would each settle their own legal costs that had been incurred in the litigation so far.

c) NVT would take over the amount currently in the deposit account, approximately £4200.

d) Triumph would have no obligation to pay royalties that would have been due for payment at 31st January 1981, amounting to over £20,000.

e) Triumph, for the outright purchase of the Triumph name and all associated rights, would make, apart from what has been stated above, a payment to the liquidator of £50,000.

The effect of this was that we would avoid any further legal costs and the danger of having the previous decision – which went in our favour – reversed. If the previous decision was to be reversed we would be liable to a royalty of 1 per cent, as opposed to the 0.48 per cent we were presently paying, and it would also be subject to a minimum annual payment of £75,000. This would mean that by 31st January, for example, as opposed to the £20,000 mentioned above, we might well have to find £57,000, and to that we might also have to add further legal fees. Instead of this prospect, we were in effect buying the name outright, and all associated copyright and other rights for a net figure equal approximately to one years' royalty at the lower figure of 0.48 per cent, or a minimum annual payment of £36,000.

In the circumstances it was the considered view of Peter Davis and Geoffrey Robinson that arrangements should be made with the National Westminster Bank to provide approximately the extra £30,000 we needed to carry out the purchase. Initial soundings with the bank suggested that this could be done, and Board approval for that course of action was urgently required.

Once again Geoffrey Robinson's perseverance and brilliant commercial ability had paid off and enabled him, with Peter Davis' help to secure an excellent deal for the Co-op. Geoffrey Robinson was thanked and empowered to conclude the negotiations.

The Directors now reviewed the interim spare parts information provided by John Rosamond.

PERFORMANCE AND HISTORY TO DATE

During the eighteen months of occupation which led to the formation of the Co-op, the non-availability of Triumph genuine factory parts allowed pirate suppliers to establish themselves. This period was followed by a further two years when, although the Co-op was in operation as a manufacturer, all marketing of motorcycles and spare parts was undertaken by NVT whose orders of spare parts were pitiful. Triumph's spare parts approach since the acquisition of the marketing rights from NVT had been based upon a feeling that if we indicated that we were prepared to supply some non-current parts, then as a manufacturer we would be obliged to supply all non-current parts. Accompanying this feeling has been Triumph's inability to supply in sufficient quantities spare parts used in current production. Put the two together and it can be readily seen how we have reached our present position, where pirate suppliers not only supply non-current spare parts, but have also found it worth their while to supply current production spare parts. It is a well known fact that any item in short supply for production has been virtually impossible to supply to the spare parts market.

SUPPLY FACILITY

It is of prime importance that we first establish that the supply of spare parts is both a legal and moral responsibility. If not undertaken effectively, it tarnishes Triumph's reputation and restricts sales of motorcycles. Whilst the manufacture and sale of motorcycles will always provide Triumph with the bread and butter revenue, if undertaken correctly spare parts sales will provide the icing on the cake.

When expenditure is severely restricted, a battle is waged between parts required for production and parts required to supply to the spares market. The spares department's job is to supply, without the parts it cannot function. If Triumph had unlimited cash resources which enabled large stocks of parts to be stored, a rapid improvement of supply and sales could be achieved overnight. This is never likely to be the case in the near future and the disciplines that we now have to learn should be continued as there will always be a better place for investment than tying up our finance in stock. The historical records of spare parts demand are very sketchy and in some cases totally out of date, accordingly effective planning of future requirements is very difficult. Even so, I think it is reasonable to expect that we could set a target to achieve 90 per cent availability of current model spare parts by the spring; after all we are achieving 100 per cent availability of parts to produce motorcycles. To meet this objective I believe we have to undertake the following:

1) Re-introduce a back ordering system for spare parts.

Place the responsibility for planning the purchase, manufacture and availability of spare parts in the same facility which has the responsibility for planning the purchase, manufacture and availability of parts for building motorcycles.

PRICING, PAYMENT TERMS AND FINANCIAL IMPLICATIONS

There is an immediate necessity for a complete price review of all spare parts, the last blanket price increase of 15 per cent has caused anomalies which if not corrected, will restrict sales of grossly overpriced items, when if they were realistically priced, they would provide good profit generation. Steps have already been taken to involve the stockists in spotting parts which appear to have been priced incorrectly. The previous Triumph system of pricing spare parts should be re-introduced. A review of spare parts prices should be undertaken at 3 monthly intervals, the dealers appearing to prefer a little and often strategy which encourages them to try and stay one step ahead of price increases and stock spare parts. The component suppliers to Triumph of proprietary parts such as

Amal, Lucas, Girling and Automotive Products, have their own spare parts organisations. They presently sell through these organisations to Triumph spare parts stockists and ordinary Triumph dealers at prices which significantly undercut Triumph. Accordingly the amount of business Triumph receives in supplying these proprietary items is relatively small. As Triumph is the prime user by way of volume ordering for original equipment, this situation should be reviewed immediately to ensure that Triumph receives its rightful share of the proprietary spare parts business. The Triumph spare parts stockists have indicated that they would be prepared to deal solely with Triumph for these parts if the pricing was correct as it would be more convenient for them to do so. It may also be worthy of consideration as to whether the Triumph spare parts stockists could be contracted to supply only spare parts supplied by the Triumph factory from whom they earn their bread and butter. The agreements that Triumph have with their twelve stockists were arrived at sixteen months ago and therefore the minimum agreed turnover figure of £12,000 per year has been significantly eroded due to both price increases and inflation and therefore needs immediate review. The fact that the two best stockists achieved annual turnover of £60,000 shows perhaps how much the figure needs reviewing. Stockists who are not on target for achieving even the £12,000 should be replaced from those begging us for a stockist agreement.

The payment terms that Triumph offer to UK stockists must be reviewed immediately if continued loss of revenue is to be prevented. If this is not possible, prices of parts financed by the overdraft will have to be increased accordingly to offset the 16.5 per cent overdraft interest paid by Triumph. The financial implications of the previous items mentioned are self explanatory, but unless the whole financial situation surrounding spare parts is considered collectively we can increase our turnover progressively without increasing profits. In which case we have only become busy fools and it therefore follows that all items regarding the financial implications of spare parts should be totally overseen by the Financial Director.

GENUINE TRIUMPH SPARE PARTS
Even though the pirate suppliers of Triumph spare parts have made vast inroads into Triumph's market, there is a glimmer of light at the end of the tunnel. The average Triumph rider is very aware of pirate spare parts, many of which fall into the category of 'cheap and nasty' pattern parts. These are not only very inferior in quality but some are also dangerous. In the medium term Triumph should therefore aim to stamp or etch the Triumph logo on every spare part to identify it as a genuine factory item, prior to it leaving the factory. In the short-term however, Triumph can only rely upon distinctive packaging readily identifying the contents as genuine. The extra cost involved in both this move and medium term action will be recovered many times over as Triumph's spare parts market expands causing the pirate suppliers to lose ground.

Accompanying positive action to try and recover the market for Triumph spare parts should be an advertising campaign which promotes the use of only 'genuine Triumph factory spare parts' on one hand and compares the use of 'pattern spare parts that can kill' on the other. There is an added bonus to be gained by promoting genuine factory spare parts in that they will, when identified as such command a higher price.

NON-CURRENT TRIUMPH SPARE PARTS
Any mention of supplying non-current spare parts, because of the difficulties experienced with supplying current parts has always met with screams of horror. The fact that about 30 per cent of parts currently used in motorcycle production will fit or can be made to fit these older models seems to have been overlooked. A 1979 survey of Triumph motorcycles still in use in America suggested that there were approximately 200,000 predominantly Triumph twin cylinder models, all of which needed

servicing with fast and slow moving spare parts. Pirate suppliers of spare parts for the non-current motorcycles have in some cases acquired engineering drawings from BSA, NVT or the Co-op and subcontracted the manufacture of these parts to light engineering companies or the Co-op for them to then market. In so doing, the pirate suppliers have a facility and reputation of being able to supply any Triumph parts on a 'cost plus' profit margin basis. Accordingly, the pirates have established a very profitable business. There is no reason why, in the medium term, Triumph should not expand into the area of supplying non-current Triumph spare parts, even if it also means subcontracting their manufacture. Triumph possess a complete set of engineering drawings and if every non-current spare part was also identified as a genuine factory Triumph part, I believe we can give the pirate suppliers a good run for their money and eventually beat them at their own game. The supply to any third party of Triumph drawings for their production and sale of spare parts, represents giving away our 'seed corn' and has been stopped. This practice should only be allowed to take place in the future with prior Board of Directors' approval. It can be seen from this interim spare parts report that there is tremendous scope for change and improvement. It is now a matter of judgement as to what Triumph can or cannot afford to do.

Following discussion, it was agreed that the investigation had provided some valuable if disturbing information regarding the Co-op's poor performance with supply of spare parts. It was further agreed that the recruitment of a Spare Parts Manager was of immediate importance, and that efforts should be made to find a suitable candidate from among the existing employees.

The meeting over, I reflected further on Geoffrey Robinson's comments regarding the Chairman's role being a non-executive one, and returned to my day job on the welding section. Welding was a hot and sweaty job at Triumph, and when swinging frame assemblies around all day long, quite physically demanding. But having perfected it by way of repetition, there was something quite satisfying about the welding operation; you could allow your mind to wander on to completely different issues. Most of my deepest thinking about the Co-op's situation was often done when undertaking my day job, and it was during one of these moments whilst on autopilot that it struck me: the danger of the non-executive Chairman's role in the Co-op's structure was that I became extremely familiar with all the problems and reasons why management was failing, when their expertise as professional managers had been sought in order to succeed. As Chairman, when questioned by the other four Beneficiary Directors I was obliged to explain these reasons, and this routine inevitably began to sound like the Chairman making excuses for management. Geoffrey Robinson's timely reminder of my non-executive status gave me the wake-up call I needed. The Co-op had decided to employ qualified managers to run the company successfully; after all, we had managed to run the company unsuccessfully ourselves in the past!

In my own time, I worked on a review of the company's commercial performance since October 1980. I analysed the achievements and failures of the Executive Management in finance, manufacturing, engineering and sales, which had led to the Co-op's below budget performance. There was no doubt a tremendous amount had been achieved in a short time, but not sufficient to meet the budgeted requirements that would guarantee the Co-op's survival. This investigation enabled me to highlight some glaring weaknesses, about which I would question the appropriate Executive Directors at the end of the next management meeting. By way of introduction, I first pointed out that at our meeting on 12th January 1981, the Trustees would be in attendance. In view of the worsening financial position of the company due to our failure to achieve budgeted performance targets, I had prepared a list of questions I anticipated the Trustees would ask on behalf of the Beneficiary owners of the Co-op. The Executive Directors put up a spirited defence as to why they were not achieving the required engineering, production, sales and financial targets. However some of my questions had raised issues that were difficult to defend. So after this highly charged management meeting I spoke alone to Bob Lindsay and asked him if, as MD, he intended to make any changes. He replied "if you want answers to all of those questions nothing will ever get done!"

Our MD was the most experienced Executive Director at Triumph, with extensive service with the Ford Motor Company and Jaguar Cars. A likeable and shrewd operator who had survived the massive pressures of being accountable for achieving results over many years, I was acutely aware that what I had been asking would not have been the first time in his industrial career that such difficult questioning had taken place. I also knew not to take too much notice of his initial knee-jerk reply, that if I wanted the Executive Directors to answer all my questions, nothing would get done! For a long time I had known it was far better to pay attention to how individuals reacted not what they said, actions always speaking much louder than words. It wasn't only the MD who reacted positively to the Chairman's criticism.

The Sales Department under Peter Britton's direction had started poorly following the HMG/ECGD debt solution, failing to maintain Triumph's market share in the UK due to what was said to be the recession. However, little effort seemed to have been put into trying to recruit new dealers, who would have been obliged to place orders to secure the franchise. What did happen was dealers were allowed to place orders for new models that were months away from production, and this situation now had to be quickly corrected. Also, nothing seemed to have been done until now to try and open up new markets using the relatively cheap ECGD motorcycles. By not pursuing this approach, sales of discounted Triumphs in existing markets made it more difficult to achieve sales of current, higher priced motorcycles.

For a long time, the Service Manager had been complaining to Brian Jones regarding the lack of analysis of warranty returns. This prevented reoccurring quality problems being addressed, so a start was now made. The long-term product plan for the 1980s and '90s was also further developed. Initial evolution of existing designs would lead to an all new ultimate parallel twin design. Equally as important was that planning was now to be undertaken to establish realistic model introduction dates. Co-ordination with the other departments in the company was also to be implemented.

Perhaps the most dramatic sign of positive change was demonstrated by the MD, who became more directly involved in manufacturing. Bob Lindsay held factory section meetings at which he acknowledged that whilst there had been component shortages preventing the achievement of targets, he had taken steps to improve the situation. Rob Murison had agreed to provide an extra £15,000 for more work in progress; this would now enable production budgets to be achieved. The Finance Director had also reacted, finding extra working capital. In addition, Rob Murison started to address the financial weaknesses recently highlighted in the Co-op's spare parts operation.

Although we had continued the adjusted hour working pattern with a 4-day weekend through December (3 days x 9 hours and 1 day x 8 hours = 35-hour week), thus avoiding the dreaded short-time working, Co-op morale in the run-up to the festive holiday was not good. Everyone knew that unless there was a dramatic improvement in the company's fortunes, short-time working would be inevitable in the New Year.

During December 1980, morale was very low throughout the engineering industry in the Coventry area, when great uncertainty prevailed. Many of the major employers were already working short time as a preliminary to redundancies or factory closures. Although nationally annual inflation had fallen slightly to 16.3 per cent, unemployment had now reached 2.5m and was forecast to rise further, especially in the engineering industry in the West Midlands.

Following a pay review (the first for a long time), the Co-op membership was at least now being paid the Coventry and District rate for the job. This enabled them to weather the period of raging inflation and to enjoy the festive holiday with their families; thoughts about an uncertain 1981 could wait until the New Year. Unfortunately, the early start to the Christmas holidays was disturbed by shocking news from the redundancy unfair dismissal industrial tribunal that the Co-op sacking policy had been wrong.

Having received only an oral tribunal judgement, the Co-op's legal advisor decided to await the written judgement before deciding if there were grounds for appeal. The possibility of late unfair dismissal claims being successfully brought was believed to be very unlikely, because of the statutory three months limit. This was only one of the challenges we were to face in 1981.

19

CONFRONTING REALITY

The extended festive holiday over, the membership returned to the Meriden factory on 5th January 1981. Everyone recognised the massive new challenges we now faced, these having been quantified by our experience operating the restructured Co-op over the last 3 months of 1980, when we dramatically underperformed in all areas of the business. The MD's management report for the 12th January meeting identified the size of the problem. The following is a summary of the operating budget performance, October to December 1980:

Motorcycles ordered: . . . .-340
Motorcycles assembled on track: . . . . .-254
Motorcycles sold: . . . .-248
Spare parts sold: . . . . -£31,017
Spare parts orders: . . . .-316
Overdue debt payments: . . . . . . +£149,000

The Financial Director's report stated that as an inevitable result of continuing below budget performance, the company's cash position over the coming months would be extremely grim. The latest forecast suggested that by 13th February, our overdraft would be £100,000 over the limit if we failed to take the following measures to secure our survival:

• Produce and dispatch at least 70 motorcycles every week.
• Invoice and dispatch £15,000 worth of spare parts every week.
• Rigidly maintain restrictions on expenditure by all departments including payroll. The detailed limits of expenditure for each department were being discussed with department heads.
• Continue to strengthen credit control.

These measures would make life uncomfortable for everyone, but no one should have been surprised that they were necessary. Our poor performance since the Government debt settlement agreement had been obvious to all of us, and now it had come home to roost.

The Meriden factory's below-budget performance was as worrying as TMA's achievements in implementing the ECGD discounted stock sales agreement in America:

Model	Budget	Actual Sales	Deficit
T140D	285	115	-170
T140E	335	336	+1
	620	**451**	**-169**

The Chairman had had a forthright discussion with the Executive Directors before Christmas to determine actions planned to rectify the situation. Further consideration would be given to this situation by the Directors and Trustees at their meetings on 12th January.

Commenting on his report at the meeting, MD Bob Lindsay summarised the failure to meet production targets as being largely due to material supply problems. Whilst some shortages had been due to a failure by the Buying Department to obtain the required supplies, the greater part of the shortages were caused by factors beyond our control. A number of our recession hit suppliers were either working short time, or in the process of going out of business. The resultant disruption aggravated supply problems, which we would have had anyway as a result of our financial policy of holding minimum stocks. Compounding this was the failure of several new suppliers to achieve required quality standards.

The situation regarding the sale of D-model Bonneville Specials by TMA, the MD advised, continued to cause grave concern. Whilst every effort was being made to find new markets for these discounted ECGD motorcycles, there was considerable difficulty being experienced in locating markets for them where no significant substitution effect took place i.e. losing the opportunity to sell 1981 models.

In view of the seriousness of the situation, a subcommittee of the Board was set up comprising John Rosamond and Geoffrey Robinson, together with whoever else they felt should be co-opted to consider what could be done to improve the situation.

In response to a request from ECGD for "greater comfort," so far as the returns detailing the TMA stock disposals were concerned, John Rosamond and Geoffrey Robinson would in future sign them off on behalf of the Board of Directors.

Perhaps the most important new development at this meeting was Bill Beattie agreeing to act in the capacity of Spare Parts Manager for the next three months. My experience of working with Bill suggested to me that he would make a major impact, guaranteeing that Triumph's supply of spare parts to the market would dramatically improve, and with it the Co-op's profitability. Continuing the work started with the interim spare parts Board report, he would draw up a list of recommendations based upon his hands-on findings over the next few weeks.

We then adjourned to convey to the membership, through section meetings, the seriousness of the financial situation and the required measures indicated by the Financial Director to secure the Co-op's survival. With these completed, we met the Trustees for the quarterly meeting.

As the Chairman had predicted, the Trustee's present (Messrs J Tomlinson and R Marston) wanted answers and reassurances, in particular confirmation that there was a market for the Co-op's products. Mr Tomlinson noted the critical financial position and requested details on progress towards making the repayments to ECGD. Mr Marston questioned whether there was a market for Triumphs, to which the Sales Director, Peter Britton, emphatically stated that he believed there was. The Trustees were provided with the only real piece of good news regarding the purchase of the Triumph name and associated rights, on what were considered favourable terms. Although asked, Mr Marston was unable to comment on the outcome of the unfair dismissal tribunal because of the ongoing involvement of his trade union, the T&G. Mr Tomlinson referred the Directors to Messrs Anderman and Foster at Warwick University, should advice regarding an appeal on the tribunal judgement be required. The next meeting with the Trustees was scheduled for 4pm on 6th April 1981.

From the MD's comments, I felt I knew that his vast manufacturing experience told him if we could at least improve the home market sales demand to somewhere near forecasted levels, sufficient breathing space could be secured to solve the factory production problems. To this end, Bob Lindsay continued the dealer visits that had started before Christmas, joining Peter

Britton and the two sales representatives. They were investigating a possible change in the way we marketed our motorcycles that would achieve the desired sales improvement.

As Co-op Chairman I was also embarking on a mission. I was not prepared to sign off TMA-ECGD returns on behalf of the Board of Directors, without having a much clearer understanding of exactly what I was confirming. This could only be achieved by visiting our subsidiary company in California, which I subsequently did with Brenda Price on 17th January. During our visit, I was also determined to discuss in detail how increased ECGD discounted sales could be accomplished in the United States. Such a plan was vital to stop the substitution effect that would rob the factory of potential 'new' 1981 sales. The other key issue to be discussed with Wayne Moulton was how he proposed to make TMA a financially self-sufficient operation. To this end, I was to confront him with the issue that had induced many hours of debate around the Meriden boardroom table; finding a way to get rid of the TMA millstone from around the Co-op's neck! There had always been a majority of Directors and members favouring this action, if a way could be found. In view of the potential size of the American market, I continued to believe that such action was the absolute last resort. What I already knew about Wayne Moulton led me to believe that if there was a commercially viable way of retaining the US subsidiary, he was the man to come up with it.

On arrival at TMA we exchanged pleasantries with the staff and got down to business. Brenda Price started preparation of a report that would show the cash-received procedures in daily detail from 28th July 1980 to 5th February 1981. This documentary evidence would confirm the ECGD-required procedures that had been adopted. When complete, the report would enable Geoffrey Robinson and me to decide if it was right and proper to sign off TMA-ECGD returns on behalf of the Board.

Not surprisingly, Bob Lindsay and Rob Murison had requested ongoing detailed TMA cashflow projections (p221) from Brenda Price, as a result of the ECGD agreement, below-budget performance, and the implications for the parent company.

For my part, I made Wayne Moulton aware of my objectives and we made a start, initially reviewing the ECGD position in detail. It soon became clear that some of the key assumptions made under pressure of time had turned out to be wrong due to the deepening recession, fierce competition from the major Japanese motorcycle competitors, and currency exchange rates. As ECGD sales were down, so was the operating margin needed to run TMA. However, who could argue that the most important priority when the deal was negotiated was to secure a deal providing a chance for Triumph to survive, which it did, and once the discounted stock had been disposed of, the opportunity to write off all HMG debts? Accordingly, rather than spending a great deal of time on the whys and wherefores of what had gone wrong, we moved on. We were where we were; we now had to find a way of making it work for ECGD, HMG, TMA and the Co-op.

It was extremely clear that since he joined TMA, Wayne Moulton had spent a great deal of time exploring in detail every aspect of the company's operation. Having amassed this knowledge of the organisation, he certainly inspired confidence regarding what he believed could or could not be achieved. He immediately focused on the 600 ECGD bikes planned to be returned and sold in the UK. Retailing at higher prices than in the US, these bikes would make a better return for ECGD and a bigger dent in the total debt repayment. If it was now proposed that these 600 bikes were to be sold in the US instead, money would have to be found for US import duty to withdraw them from the bonded warehouse facilities. The proposed return of these bikes to the UK avoided import duty payment of $15,000 per 120 bikes. TMA was already suffering shortfalls on projected ECGD D-model sales, so these had not generated contributions towards the subsidiary's operating expenses. The subsidiary's total fixed costs had to be met out of spare parts profits. Instead of being in a position to meet half-yearly expenditure such as product liability insurance premiums of $41,000 in February, there was now a shortfall of over and above that amount.

Only a few dealers then holding stock had ordered further ECGD bikes that would qualify them for the $200 (per stock bike) discount they would receive when ordering bikes covered by the agreement. This would change in February and March as the new sales season started, and there would therefore be a further cash injection required, with the amount concerned not known at the time. Wayne believed that February's operating budget shortfall could possibly be met by a 'robbing Peter to pay Paul' strategy. Ongoing warranty payments on ECGD agreement sales after the completion of the deal were also a worry. It was not possible to delay payments of warranty to dealers, as if not punctually paid, they simply deducted the owed amount from their next spare parts payment to TMA. Fixed overheads and expenditure were being explored for savings, but to date none had been found that significantly altered the immediate overall TMA position and the need for cash injections from the parent company. Expenditure appeared to be fairly fixed, and salary payments were predominantly accounted for by the three top earners: Wayne Moulton, Ruth Furman and Gene Cox. It would have been possible to reduce expenditure by a third here, Wayne agreed, but it was a matter for difficult discussion and deciding which of these most loyal and able people should be sacrificed. In the lower salary bracket it would also be possible to reduce staff by one, but such considerations would not be sufficient to stop the financial demise of TMA.

Moving out of the Placenta premises, which were too large for present needs (office facilities and spare parts warehousing), would bring little or no benefit to TMA's cash position. Removal costs, installation costs (computer system, burglar alarms, and telephone telex charges) and complete shutdown of the spare parts operation for two weeks during the peak supply and profit period would likely make matters worse. Whilst Wayne Moulton did not like these premises because of their size, layout and lack of service facilities, he believed that if TMA was ever to be profitable, the space would be required in the future.

The TMA warehouse held $700,000 worth of good spare parts stock, some $300,000 of which was slow moving overstock – accordingly, some was available to ship back to Meriden. This would part-fund TMA purchases of 1981 model factory production. The availability of which, when announced at the forced dollar to sterling high retail prices, would make the ECGD stock disposal bikes look cheap in comparison. Once returned to the Meriden factory, the TMA spare parts overstock would represent significant component purchase saving for the Co-op on manufacture of 1981 models. A full overstock list had been telexed to Meriden, to enable a priority list of those to be returned to be drawn up.

As previously mentioned, Wayne Moulton had ideas for the present "too large" TMA premises. I asked him to work these ideas into an operational plan for Executive Management and Board consideration by the parent company. He believed that one way of reducing the cost of Triumph motorcycles for sale in America would be to undertake a CKD (completely knocked down) operation at TMA. A track would be set up to enable assembly of engines, frames, swing arms and front forks supplied by the factory. The remaining component parts to complete the motorcycles would be purchased in the United States at significantly lower prices, and specifically for sale in dollar markets.

The supply of TMA, US-sourced cheaper parts would also be available to the Meriden factory if required. Remaining warehouse space would be utilised to house accessories and stocks of parts not currently distributed, such as tyres. It was also felt that whilst supply of genuine spare parts for 1973 to 1981 models should be optimised through the official US Triumph dealer network of 450, there was a vast, untapped market for 650-500 twins and Trident triple parts, plus the 'cheap and nasty' non-genuine parts that were sold in vast numbers to both the genuine Triumph dealers and thousands of motorcycle repair shops. Because of the recent factory financial position, there was big business in keeping old Triumphs on the road. To be able to supply the thousands of repair shops with 'cheap and nasty' parts, many of which (chains, tyres, pistons, valves, etc) were Japanese in origin, a separate company would have to be set up, owned by Triumph – possibly called Brit Bits Ltd, operating from the same TMA facilities, but not infringing the official dealer's rights to the genuine Triumph spare parts franchise. By so doing, we would be greatly increasing TMA turnover and therefore profit potential. At the time, the TMA spare parts turnover was not sufficient to break even, if product liability insurance premiums had to be paid by the subsidiary.

Wayne Moulton had experience in setting up an operation similar to the one mentioned, being responsible for the successful Top Gear Triumph line before the BSA/Triumph whizz kids got hold of it. They destroyed it, Wayne commented, by allowing the original tight stock controls to go out of the window.

The projected TMA cashflow indicated that if the 'rob Peter to pay Paul' strategy was not adopted to cover the February shortfall, an immediate cash injection of £25,000 from the parent company would be required. The next crunch month would be August, when the annual renegotiation and premium payment for product liability occured. The likely premium for $1,000,000 cover (Triumph to pay the first $25,000 of any claim) was $97,000. Even if the premium was paid in two halves, TMA would not be able to find that amount. It was Wayne Moulton's view that, as in previous years, product liability insurance was a company responsibility, and therefore should be borne by the subsidiary and parent. It was also his view that any savings made on the renegotiated renewal premium as a result of no longer having to cover Norton's (an NVT requirement) should be spent in increasing Triumph's overall cover to $5,000,000. The increase in premium to cover the extra $4,000,000 was likely to be relatively small, and worthwhile if it prevented a single 'fatal' claim wiping Triumph out. Ruth Furman was the very knowledgeable long-term commercial specialist in this area.

Borg Warner short-term finance had been requested to enable TMA to purchase 1981 models in container shipments of 28 from the factory, but was refused. Orders were about to be taken for 1981 models, so dealers would be circulated with photographs and prices. The dealers would be told that initial supplies of 1981 models were severely restricted, with the factory concentrating only on firm orders for other markets, but that TMA had some relatively cheap carry-over motorcycles that were still available! Borg Warner held a $250,000 bond and recourse agreement with TMA, which was required in the past when approximately $3,000,000 worth of Triumph bikes were floor-planned at the dealers pending their sale. The bond (the only one in the US motorcycle industry) represented a risk view taken by Borg Warner at the time, based on the $3,000,000 floor-planning finance. Since the Government agreement and change in Triumph circumstances, Wayne Moulton had tried to renegotiate the bond to a level more in keeping with the now greatly reduced risk, but to no avail. Borg Warner still considered that Triumph's financially weak position, and possible inability to repurchase the floor-planned motorcycles, justified it retaining the $250,000 bond. There was no point pressing this matter any further at the time, because if the ECGD bikes didn't start to move in the spring, Wayne Moulton's fall back plan was to 'free' floor-plan them for up to 3 months, based on the Borge Warner facility, at a cost of $50 per bike per month. One of the major concerns to be borne in mind was that when the 1981 prices were announced, some dealers holding stocks of Borge Warner floor-planned motorcycles might decide to throw in the towel, because of what they saw as excessively high prices for the new Triumph models. Under the Borge Warner recourse agreement, TMA was obliged to buy back all the floor-planned bikes from those dealers. However, experience to date when dealers had gone bust showed such bikes had been successfully resold at only a small loss. It was Wayne Moulton's view, from the dealers he had spoken to, that the number who chose to quit would be handleable, with most dealers only stocking one or two bikes and sticking with the franchise because of the business they were doing in spare parts supply and service work. Borge Warner was not the only one holding a Triumph bond; the State of Maryland held a bond of $50,000 – the cost of doing business in that region.

Triumph's public image in the United States continued to be very weak indeed. Whilst all the dealers had been told about the agreement with the British Government that would remove the debts and secure the future, the motorcycle buying public was still not aware of any change to Triumph's circumstances. The recent six-page article in January's American magazine *Motorcyclist* would help, featuring interviews and photographs at the Meriden factory, and road tests presently being undertaken. But the fact remained; the generally held view was that Triumph went out of business. Wayne Moulton even heard a story about Triumph's debt write-off being a lie, only put around to help sell off all the old bikes! Advertising, even if it could be afforded (and it couldn't), would not help influence spring sales – the 3-month lead time to publication would mean copy would appear after the main spring sales had taken place. However, the same motorcycle magazines that killed the D-model Bonneville Specials 2 years ago were now raving about the 1981 models they were testing, even talking about featuring a photograph on the front cover! Ironic this may be, but these magazines did influence buyers tremendously. The only problem was that the road test articles were likely to appear too late to significantly influence spring sales. Supplying dealers with reprints of these good road tests would push sales in the right direction, as would the production of a 1981 brochure if cash were available, even if it was only a single sheet flyer. Wayne Moulton intended to try and use precisely targeted short sharp bursts (rifle shots) of publicity, if money could be generated.

On the middle Sunday of our trip to California I visited the Anaheim Motorcycle Show with Wayne Moulton and Gene Cox. About half the size of Earls Court in the UK, it was well laid out, with Harley Davidson, Kawasaki, Suzuki and Yamaha well represented – although surprisingly no Honda! Wayne was widely known by many of the company representatives present, having worked with most of them either in the old days at Triumph or more recently at Kawasaki. Genuine interest appeared to be shown in Triumph – particularly why we were not exhibiting.

The four-day show was divided into two days for dealers and two days for the general public. Everyone we spoke to was excited by the positive interest in motorcycles being shown by the general public. This was felt to be due to the imminent American presidential election, at which it was forecast a change for the better would occur, ensuring more spending money in people's pockets. The press we met were also very positive. Wayne summed this up as being good feelings towards Triumph and all other non-Japanese manufacturers. Readers had become alienated by the motorcycle magazines, accusing them of working for the Japanese on the basis that they were all the journalists ever wrote about! Any opportunities to write stories about other motorcycle manufacturers were welcomed, as they demonstrated that the publications were not in the pay of the Japanese. *Road Rider* magazine invited us for an interview, and Wayne Moulton was to pursue interviews with all California-based magazines.

Gene Cox made an important comment regarding possible factory component changes that would impact on 'fast moving' spare parts. If such changes were made, like reduced diameter wheel spokes or changes to the finish on drive sprockets, customer demand for some of TMA's high-profit earners would immediately stop – small cost-savers at the factory could cost the US subsidiary dearly! John Rosamond would advise Brian Jones of this situation, and he would be asked to refer planned original equipment cost-savers to TMA for comment, before implementation. We met the sprocket manufacturer that supplied Harley Davidson with its current 'original equipment' production parts, and was interested in quoting for Triumph's business.

Back at TMA the following day, we discussed in some detail new US model possibilities. I had glanced at the TV in the hotel room to watch the early morning news and noted an item on the forthcoming wedding of His Royal Highness the Prince of Wales to Lady Diana Spencer. In view of the success of the Silver Jubilee models in 1977, I put it to Wayne Moulton, was there a possibility to produce another Triumph limited edition for the United States? Perhaps reworking and updating, say, 200 certificated ex-ECGD bikes with enhanced specifications that would command a price of $4500? The idea was considered a non-starter, on the basis that no-one else in the motorcycle industry intended to do a commemorative edition, and also, how would we get around the known fact that the reworked motorcycles were 1979 models?

"There's nothing wrong with the limited edition idea," Wayne commented (not surprising – he perfected the idea whilst at Kawasaki), "it just has to be precisely specified and targeted." The Bonneville Specials (D-models) never really had a chance to succeed; the forced mid-season price increase together with the halt in advertising killed them. Wayne Moulton advised that there was still fairly strong dealer resistance to them mainly because of the muffler (silencer) design, so he had come up with an attractive replacement. The new muffler would be sold to the dealers on future sales of D-models, and also for the dealers existing stock; a win-win situation. We then discussed new models for the United States, in terms of the priorities of the American motorcycle buying public:

• Value for money based upon $ per cc
i.e. 750cc $2995 maximum
850cc $3495 maximum
950cc $3995 maximum
NB Investigate possibility of CKD 1000cc Lowrider project; US sourced parts and assembly of engine/frame/forks/swing arm from the factory in England; target price $3995.
• Quality control – engine life 50,000 miles, after which major service work is required, even if at this mileage all component parts need replacement.
• Full spare parts back up, even at high cost.
• Full dealer service back up.
• Ability to ride at between 50 and 70mph, at about 2500rpm; top gear riding with a non-stressed engine; 400 miles per day and the same again for the next 5 days; 135mph top speed potential.
• Riding position/controls/seat to be extremely comfortable; front forks and rear shock absorbers to be on the soft side, but equal to providing good handling properties.
• Petrol tank to be styled to give good looks and petrol capacity to equate with riding 240 miles, 5 gallons including reserve.
• Lighting – head lamp to be quartz halogen, rear twin bulb.
• Full set of accessories to be available at time of model introduction.
• Priority – to resource on new models all Lucas electrics.
• Dealers are requesting a larger engine capacity motorcycle to return Triumph to its old image of high-powered performance sports bike, presently lost on the Bonneville.

227

We were just coming to the end of our product meeting when Jack Wilson of Big D Cycle in Dallas called at TMA. Wayne Moulton introduced me. Previously I had only known him by his reputation as one of the finest Triumph engine tuners in the world. We got chatting about the performance potential of the new 8-valver that was being introduced next year. I found Jack Wilson's enthusiasm infectious, and soon agreed to ship over a well-worn works development 8-valve motor for Big D's BOT (Battle of Twins) entry. Factory involvement at Daytona would certainly cause a stir in the motorcycle magazines, and hopefully confirm that Triumph was still alive and kicking. (Jack Wilson's entry was to show the potential; ridden by Jon Minonno, it was clocked at 152mph on the Daytona banking in qualifying.) The increased performance discussion also stirred Wayne Moulton's imagination – immediately after our product meeting regarding the dealers' wish to rectify the Bonneville's performance deficit, he enquired about the possibility of the 8-valve engine powering the American TSX Triumph model his team was working on. The TSX was gradually taking shape under Wayne's guidance, and when finished would be shipped to Meriden. I stressed to him that when the TSX model was ready for the factory's consideration, it would be important for him to provide a full presentation.

On 28th January I received a very disturbing telephone call from the factory. Earlier that day an emergency Board meeting had taken place to review the company's worsening financial situation. The MD had pointed out that since October 1980, motorcycle orders received were very similar in number to those of the previous year, if sales to Nigeria and America were excluded. However without access to these two important markets, orders were insufficient to sustain even the seasonally adjusted 35-hour week presently in place. Accordingly, the Directors were obliged to agree to the dreaded short-time working, with the bulk of employees to work a two-day week. It was further agreed that in certain critical areas, hours worked would have to be increased as necessary. Overtime would be rigorously controlled to ensure the absolute minimum. After all our efforts with the forward thinking, seasonally adjusted 35-hour week to minimise economic pain for the membership whilst optimising annual performance of the company, we had still failed due to lack of orders! The hardship we would now feel would inevitably lower morale even further.

I knew that I would have to be extremely diplomatic when reporting the findings of my TMA visit. The Directors and membership would be even less inclined to understand why TMA's workforce had not been reduced further last August, when two thirds of the Co-op membership was made redundant. TMA's $300,000 of Meriden-provided, slow-moving overstock spare parts was also going to be very difficult to explain to the factory Purchasing Department and Financial Director, who fought a daily battle juggling overstretched financial resources to ensure new supplies of those same parts for motorcycle production. The Meriden factory and TMA were not only worlds apart geographically!

In the short-term, there was still no doubt in my mind that TMA should remain an integral part of Triumph's future. Wayne Moulton's lateral thinking, based on many years' experience in the American motorcycle industry, suggested to me that under his guidance TMA could become financially self-sufficient in the short-term, and profitable in the long-term. It was now a question as to how I could best ensure that this sort of policy could be pursued. Having first double checked my findings, I decided I would produce a TMA report for the Directors, and verbally provide imminent TMA cashflow concerns for the MD and Financial Director, subsequently expanding on the background to my findings. Brenda Price, TMA's Chairman, completed her detailed review of the returns submitted to ECGD for the period 25th August 1980 to 30th January 1981, confirming that they were a correct record of TMA sales, cash and stock position.

CHAIRMAN'S TMA REPORT
During my visit to America, I had two main objectives:

– To satisfy myself that it was right and proper to sign off the weekly TMA ECGD returns on behalf of the Board of Directors – this I was able to do.

– To return to Meriden with a better understanding of the American subsidiary and any remaining opportunities left open to Triumph that would influence future operations in the US market.

It would be wrong not to point out that prior to my visit I believed that on conclusion of the disposal of the ECGD bikes, projected future levels of operation in America indicated that distributors could quite possibly cover Triumph's requirements. Having analysed the situation at first-hand however, I have found this not to be the case. There is a need for a top level meeting between representatives of Triumph on both sides of the Atlantic to try and sort out the 'operating strategy' regarding just what TMA is expected to be capable of doing in the short-term. Their present performance is almost totally influenced by Triumph at Meriden.

There remains tremendous scope to expand the spare parts side of the business. The potential, I believe, for exceeding the point where TMA can become self-financing and profit-making even with the considerably reduced level of motorcycle sales; this makes it more than worthwhile to retain the company. Retaining our own subsidiary in America and continuing the current amount of effort, even at the present capacity, will enable the severely tarnished Triumph name to be restored to its past status. So that, at a date in the future, volume sales of Triumph motorcycles can be resumed with a vengeance!

J A Rosamond – Chairman

In addition to this report for the Board, as previously mentioned I also had to provide the Executive Directors with a confidential verbal overview of the ECGD disposal operation, and Wayne Moulton's thoughts on how the present situation could be improved, my thinking being that the implications of the TMA cashflow position would certainly grab the Executive's immediate attention. Possible solutions, however, would only be thrashed out through co-ordinated efforts involving senior management from both the subsidiary and the parent company.

From what I had heard in America, it was clear that a sales miracle would have to occur if the 31st May 1981 deadline for the ECGD disposal agreement was to be achieved, especially if those bikes previously scheduled for return to the UK were now to be sold in the US. Wayne Moulton's view was that immediate steps should be taken to try and renegotiate an extension to this deadline. This would be a matter for Geoffrey Robinson and Brenda Price's attention. Brenda Price had done her usual dedicated, efficient job during our visit to TMA. Whilst her paid employment lay elsewhere, her heart still remained in Triumph.

Back at Meriden, the monthly meeting on 11th February enabled Geoffrey Robinson to advise that contact had been established with the motorcycle division of BMW, enabling possible future reference to them by Triumph's engineering department. A noncommittal letter proposing an informal meeting in London with the Triumph MD would be sent.

The Chairman provided his brief report on TMA, also stressing the continuing need for supply of fast-moving spare parts to TMA, even though slow-moving overstocks were being returned to the factory, and adding that the current dollar to sterling exchange rate made the US an attractive source to purchase component supplies for the factory. Following discussion, the Board agreed that TMA must prove its viability as presently constituted, in order to justify maintaining the status quo after 31st May 1981.

TMA'S POSITION WITH REGARD TO ECGD (AS OF 30TH JANUARY)

Model	Budget	Actual	(+ or -)
T140D	325	132	-193
T140E	375	427	+ 52
	690	**559**	**-141**

TMA TOTAL ECGD STOCK POSITION

T140D	1285
T140E	438
	1723

Bob Lindsay explained that the return of slow-moving spare parts to the value of $50,000 would help finance the first 20ft container of 28 1981 models to TMA. He added that the arrival of these models at their much higher retail price should help sell the residual ECGD stocks. Bob Lindsay reported that as yet no firm sales plan had been received from TMA covering the below-budget ECGD D-model sales.

Geoffrey Robinson cautioned that Triumph would continue to incur ongoing product liability insurance premiums and warranty liabilities estimated at $200,000 in 1982, irrespective of what happened to TMA. He also stated that our present insurance cover of $1m should be increased to $5m, and that this cover must apply for 7 years forward, expressing the view that TMA must continue in order to fund this. John Inglesant made the observation that the cost of achieving EPA American legislation standards for the 1981 Bonnevilles was disproportionately high, on such a low sales volume.

The rest of the MD's report was discussed by the Directors – sadly, it confirmed the continued below operating budget trends. The Financial Director's comments on the situation were a little more positive as a result of the prompt introduction of short-time working.

On the basis of Harry Hughes' Board meeting comments regarding the company's present situation, and how best this could be communicated to the members, it was agreed to hold section meetings without delay in order to explain in detail the current position.

On 16th February, the MD wrote to Wayne Moulton at TMA. As shown here, the letter essentially indicated that TMA would be expected to continue to operate in the same manner until 31st May 1981, by which time ECGD stock should be sold.

TMA's performance is at present below budget and a retrieval exercise must get under way. A further review of TMA's performance will be undertaken with you at the Meriden factory no later than 30th April.

We will ship to TMA a container of 28, 1981 model Bonnevilles week commencing 23rd February, payment being offset against TMA's returned 'slow moving' spare parts. Further motorcycle shipments will take place as soon as finances can be arranged. Money generated by the first shipment to be used to fund the second shipment etc.

The scale and nature of operations after 31st May 1981 will depend on TMA having demonstrated in the intervening period the viability of it continuing at its present size with the sale of spare parts and motorcycles, on the same basis that is currently happening for both.

We are pleased to advise you that, effective immediately, you are appointed President of Triumph Motorcycles (America) Inc. For the purpose of ECGD you will report to the Chairman of TMA, Miss Brenda Price. However on certain operational matters you will report to the Managing

Director of Triumph Motorcycles (Meriden) Ltd, Mr Bob Lindsay. The above has been cleared with ECGD. For the present there will be no change in your conditions of employment.

Once again may I say how grateful I am for your efforts over there. You can count on our full support and any requirements (which are within our capability) that are needed to assist you in your difficult task.

R Lindsay – Managing Director

Our visit to TMA had been worthwhile. We now had in Wayne Moulton a very knowledgeable, experienced President, in daily control of the subsidiary and capable of planning and effecting Triumph's future for the better.

20

COMING OF AGE

With the seeds sown for positive change in America, it was now time to focus on how motorcycle orders could be dramatically improved in the UK. The dealer charm offensive and fact finding mission, started before Christmas by the MD, Sales Director and sales representatives, now needed to bear fruit. One of the major multi-franchise dealer outlets offered a suggestion that it could take over responsibility for Triumph's complete sales and marketing operation, but this fell on deaf ears, reminding us too much of the previous experience with NVT. Initial reports on the dealer visits indicated that there was a keen desire amongst most to continue with the Triumph franchise, and a pleasing acknowledgement of improving product quality; however, very few orders were being placed, with most dealers having stock. This suggested destocking would have to occur before new orders were placed! The Sales Department was therefore looking at methods of increasing retail sales whilst introducing incentives for dealers to reorder.

The MD Bob Lindsay's management report for the 9th March meeting concentrated heavily on the sales situation:

> Motorcycle orders received in February – 159
> The order bank as of 3rd March was as follows:
> Bank   182
> Stock   50
> To build   132
> The projected intake of orders for UK and Europe during March was 15 per week. The Sales Department had achieved 10 of these by 4.30pm on 4th March.
> The 114 TMA 1981 models ordered on 27th February (96 T140E and 18 Executives) was a welcome achievement. We are now able to finance the initial 56 by a combination of returned overstock spare parts and a rearrangement of funds. The revenue generated from the first TMA shipment will be used to part-fund subsequent shipments. Alloy wheels are now available and the TMA build will commence.
> TMA position regarding ECGD

Sales	Budget	Actual	Variance
T140D	525	201	-324
T140E	525	582	+57
	1050	**782**	**-267**

Sold in February   *224*
Orders on hand   *117*
In stock:
T140D   *1216*
T140E   *283*
Total   *1499*

Wayne Moulton, TMA's new President, will visit Meriden in April to discuss the future of the US subsidiary.

(In addition to the above, the MD's sales report indicated that an order for 12 police motorcycles had been received from Uganda and was now in production. Having considered the order bank it was decided to plan production at a volume of 48 motorcycles per week for at least the next two weeks. This would involve 3-day working for the majority of members, with additional hours to be worked where required. The first press release from the new PR firm Charles Barker and Associates had a favourable impact.)

• *Sales organisation – Europe*
Mr M J Elvidge has been transferred to full-time responsibility for sales (motorcycles and spare parts) to European markets, he would be designated European Sales Executive.
• *Sales organisation – UK*
Our present sales resources are insufficient to support the professional approach that is required for the UK market therefore the following changes are proposed:
i) Recruit a UK Sales Manager.
ii) Retain one of the existing sales representatives.
iii) Re-designate the other representative to technical sales.
This action will enable Triumph to provide improved technical sales support to the dealer network, and also organise mechanic training, for which we are receiving requests.
• *Change to UK retail motorcycle sales outlets*
After careful consideration of the facts gained from the dealer visits, it is felt there is a necessity to reduce the number of UK dealer outlets. These currently number around 250.
It is therefore proposed to appoint a mixture of main, single and sub-dealer outlets, with the main dealer normally having a clearly defined territory, in which they supply motorcycles. The single dealer will usually be a current dealer with a good sales track record, who will be retained and have direct access to the factory for motorcycles. The remainder of the current dealer network will be advised that they no longer have the Triumph franchise with direct access to the factory, but if considered suitable by a main dealer may be given the opportunity to become sub-dealer.
While arriving at the above decision, we have reviewed motorcycle sales over the whole of the UK with the sales representatives, based upon visits to dealers of all sizes and locations. The dealer visits indicated a good interest in Triumph and an excellent reaction to these visits.
The large dealers are not generally considered to be good on after-sales service or warranty, possibly lacking the personal touch that Triumph owners expect.
However, many of them have excellent premises and workshops. A large percentage of these dealers admitted that they had not really tried to sell Triumphs due in part to the uncertainty regarding the company's future. After discussions we felt we had regained their confidence and most of them are prepared to sign agreements for an acceptable number of sales per year, on the basis of being given a fixed territory.
The small dealers often have dismal premises and poor presentation. They generally have

a very good mechanic and personally run the operation, giving excellent PDI (pre-delivery inspection) and after-sales service thereby building up a clientele and reputation enabling them to make good sales. They often carry large stocks of spare parts, tying up their working capital. There are of course exceptions to the above and some small dealers have excellent premises.

In the main the small dealer deals only in Triumph, which of course must be considered in our selection of dealers to be retained. Most dealers, large and small, complained at the lack of advertising and other promotional aids, and many wanted Triumph to get back the police business. It became apparent that very little effort had been made in recent times to improve our dealer network and appoint better dealers. Since we commenced the dealer network review, we have had requests for dealerships. The Co-op's own sales representatives initiated the review.

The above proposed structural change to the UK dealer network occupied a large part of the MD's monthly management report and subsequent meeting discussion on 9th March.

Bill Beattie asked what commitment on sales volumes dealers would be required to make. Bob Lindsay indicated that main dealers would need to attain at least 1 per cent of total motorcycle sales in their territory. In the past, such high volume dealers had tended to avoid Triumph because of lack of confidence regarding the company's future. Bill Beattie then commented on the difficulties he was experiencing as acting Spare Parts Manager, where there was considerable resistance from dealers to buying from distributors rather than having direct factory access. The MD considered this to be only a small problem so far as motorcycle sales were concerned, estimating that approximately only 200 bikes a year were sold through small dealers, and that these sales would probably be taken up elsewhere if the small dealers refused to co-operate with the new plans. The Financial Director, Rob Murison, commented that it would be important to confirm that the estimate of 200 bikes a year sold through small dealers was accurate; as these sales were potentially jeopardised by the new arrangements, we needed to be sure that our quantification of this risk was correct.

The Accounts Department would need to approve the proposed list of main dealers, as the average outstanding debt from each of these would be considerably higher than in the past. The MD stated that main dealers would receive an additional 2.5 per cent discount on stocks sold to sub-dealers, and this wholesale business would be limited to 10 per cent of their total Triumph motorcycle sales. No effort would be employed to encourage retail price maintenance by the larger main dealers.

John Inglesant raised the possibility that sales might be lost through the disappearance of the close personal relationship between the dealer and the customer. Bob Lindsay agreed that this was a possibility, but believed that rationalisation of the retail trade was a trend of the future, and as large outlets already sold the majority of Triumph's output, there was little risk. Furthermore, it was impossible to generalise, as some smaller dealers had poor customer relations, whilst some larger ones were excellent. Brian Jones, the Chief Engineer, cautioned that care would have to be taken to ensure our new retail sales structure did not contravene existing fair-trading legislation. Bill Beattie asked for and received confirmation that the proposed new motorcycle sales structure would not effect in any way what was being planned by way of changes to the distribution and sale of spare parts.

The Directors agreed that subject to satisfactory clarification of the points raised during the discussion, they would approve the proposed changes to the structure of the UK dealer network.

Board discussion now moved to product development, and in particular the lack of any mention in the MD's report of the Ian Dyson project, one that Bob Lindsay had been enthusiastically supporting. The MD reported that progress to date had been disappointing – it had probably been a mistake to have left Dyson to his own devices for so long. However, he had now been given assurances that the prototype TS8-1 would be ready for exhibition as the Triumph flagship model at the NEC Motorcycle Show, and there was no reason to doubt his efforts to meet that deadline.

The next item discussed by the Board was the MD's proposal to recruit a Product Planning and Timing Manager. The TS8-1 was only one of the new projects (Thunderbird, Police AV Special and the totally new Diana design) that would impact upon design, production, sales and finance at the Co-op. Bob Lindsay's extensive manufacturing experience had been reawakened with a jolt by what happened with the TS8-1 – there was an urgent need for a person capable of maintaining an overview of new project developments for the MD. Bob Lindsay therefore proposed to appoint the Product Planning and Timing Manager by the 'job opportunity' method, from amongst the Co-op membership. A notice would be posted indicating the qualities and expertise required, stating that the new manager would be recruited at the appropriate market salary. It was agreed by the Board that this appointment could be critical to Triumph's future; to date, the only actions that had stimulated market interest and orders had been the introduction of new models. However, with each new model came a more complex and higher level of component parts. Along with new parts that would have to be purchased or manufactured, the anticipated demand for these new models would generate additional manufacturing and assembly challenges for the membership. Perhaps the greatest risk of all was that the Co-op would end up with an acceptable order bank for the new models, the production of which could not be financed because stretched financial resources had become tied up in part-finished, difficult to produce motorcycles. The Product Planning Manager's job was indeed an important one!

The Directors next considered the Financial Director's review of management performance.

Immediate prospects:
The next six weeks will probably be the most testing period we have yet experienced. Expenditure must be held to approximately three quarters the average level of spend to date. All budgeted motorcycles must be built, and strenuous efforts must be made to ensure extremely prompt payment of outstanding debts to the Co-op. If we survive the winter, all our efforts will have been wasted if we go broke next winter. We must not therefore start next winter worse financially than we started this one. This means that we must break even for the year and to do this means we have an enormous amount of catching up to do.
Summary:
As we anticipated, we are now extremely weak. Survival will require continued hard work and an understanding that we must take whatever steps necessary to stay within the limits of our resources.

John Rosamond asked Rob Murison the number of motorcycles required to regain the budget by the end of the year. The Finance Director stated that to obtain our budgeted target of 3640 units, production would have to be increased to a level of approximately 110 motorcycles per week. The MD said that he did not consider this feasible, estimating maximum capacity at present to be 96 units each week, including the use of overtime.

The Financial Director was asked to produce a budget projection of our position in 6 to 12 months' time, based on realistic figures for output.

Shortly after the end of the meeting the job opportunity vacancy for Product Planning and Timing Manager was published on the notice boards. It certainly created a stir amongst the membership, particularly the reference to the salary being commensurate with the responsibilities of the job. This promotion of one of the Co-op's own to a salaried managerial role would be fulfilment of the commitment always reaffirmed with each change to the Co-op's management structure. I only hoped the overheard, derisive comments about this vital job opportunity would not put off good candidates from applying. If this happened, it would force external recruitment to take place. By the time an external recruit became familiar with exactly what had to be done to achieve the desired results at the Co-op, any planning input to help the MD cope with the new product developments would be lost.

The more I thought about the Product Planning and Timing Manager's job and the negative comments from some vociferous members ("another management job being created for those prepared to creep to the MD"), the more determined I became to see if the Co-op was up to coming of age. I applied for the job myself in the full knowledge that if I got it, I would confront the membership by resigning as a Director of the Board, enabling them to decide if they wanted me to also continue in that additional non-executive role. I was extremely pleased to hear that there were two other candidates who had applied for the job. We were to appear before an interview panel comprising MD Bob Lindsay, Chief Engineer and Engineering Director Brian Jones, and Personnel Officer Ron Atkinson.

Obviously I was able to answer the panel's first question in some depth: "What do you consider the Product Planning and Timing Manager's role to be?" My Board knowledge meant I recognised exactly why the MD needed this important assistant. My detailed practical involvement in R&D work at the Co-op since its inception, with the conversion to left foot gear shift/right foot brake, Premium Bonneville, Trident in Bonneville frame, Bulmers flat track, Tom Hyam moped, Puch jogger, Phoenix Lowrider, Tiger Trail, Bonneville Executive and the police anti-vibration developments, demonstrated that I was very familiar with that side of the business. This experience, I commented, also gave me an insight into and appreciation of exactly what the factory was capable of producing, and what had to be outsourced. Perhaps even more important, though, was the amount of time involved in moving from prototypes to production. Even with the tremendous goodwill I knew I would be able to call upon from most of the Co-op membership, I was aware this transition would be the most difficult to achieve. To the panel's question, "Why do you want to take the job on?" I simply replied "I think it's a massive task, one which I feel I could accomplish, and as Chairman I want to know that everything that can be done to help the Co-op survive is being done." The interview over, I returned to my day job on the welding section.

The motorcycle order bank had increased to 350 by the middle of March, allowing a return to full-time working. This was mainly due to orders from Europe and the UK. In the UK, the imminent introduction of 10 per cent car tax (also to be applied to motorcycles) from 1st April stimulated a little Triumph demand. The financially strong sales organisations of the big four Japanese manufacturers tried to counter the ongoing negative impact of the car tax price increase by pre-registering their stock, in what was already a very depressed UK market. This enabled the stock to be sold to customers after 1st April at pre-car tax prices. Unfortunately, this action was only partially successful, and completely distorted the apparent UK retail sales registration figures for months to come.

The 10 per cent car tax calculation was based upon the notional wholesale value, and would increase Triumph's lowest priced model, the TR7V Tiger, by £120.78p! The MD informed the membership of the return to 5-day working with the following notice:

Notes on return to 5-day working 19th March
It has become possible to return to normal 5-day working from Monday 23rd March.
The minimum production programme will be:
Week commencing 23rd March – 48 motorcycles + spare parts
Week commencing 30th March – 60 motorcycles + spare parts
Week commencing 6th April – 70 motorcycles + spare parts
Week commencing 13th April – 80 motorcycles + spare parts
The above must be considered a minimum track build and spare parts supply programme.
The machine shops and associated areas' target should be 85 sets plus spare parts for each of the four weeks. This will enable us to re-establish floats and build stock against the engine and motorcycle track assembly lines.
We will probably have shortages of raw materials due to suppliers being unable to immediately react with increased supplies. However, we should then over-produce parts where material is available, thus making the most effective use of the man hours available. This will require good planning and communications and quick reaction to difficulties. Supply of bought-out finished parts could also present some difficulties initially, so our programme indicates a minimum number. We must produce every bike we can before Easter otherwise orders will be lost!
The above has only been made possible by us obtaining an additional 160 orders from Europe and the effect of the Chancellor's Budget in pulling forward some UK orders to before 1st April. We hope that we will be able to maintain normal working after the Easter break, but this will depend on the acceptance of our new models at the NEC Motorcycle Show commencing 16th April. Also, if the Chancellor's Budget has any lasting effect on sales, we would need to review our position.
Finally, the next few weeks are critical and we must insist on a maximum effort from every member. We have come so far – don't lose the opportunity for success which we are sure is available if we get on with the job. The motorcycle track will have the priority over spare parts for this four week period.
Bob Lindsay – Managing Director

On 31st March I received a letter offering me the position of Product Planning and Timing Manager commencing 1st April 1981, initially subject to a six-month trial period. Bill Beattie received a similar letter offering him the Spare Parts Manager's job, also on a salary commensurate with the responsibilities involved. The membership would now have to come to terms with two of their number becoming management! I indicated to Bill Beattie my intention to resign my Director's role at the next Board meeting, by so doing enabling the anticipated concern of some members and Beneficiary Directors to be confronted via a mass meeting. Bill was of a similar mind, and we decided that joint resignations would be offered at the meeting on 6th April.

The Board meeting on 6th April began at 11.00am. Contained within the MD's circulated monthly management report were copies of the letters of appointment for John Rosamond and Bill Beattie, so the other three Beneficiary Directors were fully aware of the developments concerning the new appointments of the Spare Parts Manager and the Product Planning and Timing Manager. The Board confirmed the appointments and that remuneration would be commensurate with the responsibilities of the jobs. John Inglesant indicated that there was now 'constitutional uncertainty' regarding these two management appointments, as it was generally believed that no Beneficiaries of higher than Foreman status were eligible for a seat on the Board. While it was not the view of the whole Board, John Rosamond and Bill Beattie had anticipated this view would be expressed and offered their resignations. It was agreed that the Board meeting should adjourn whilst the view of the Beneficiaries was sought at a mass meeting.

The mass meeting discussed the situation and a vote was taken regarding John Rosamond and Bill Beattie's continued presence on the Board. Only 106 votes were cast – 50 in favour, 56 against. In view of this, the Board accepted the offered resignations, having first taken advice from the Trustees on the procedure to adopt. The Board meeting was once again adjourned to enable the remaining three Beneficiary Directors to co-opt two further Beneficiaries to the Board, in line with the 'Co-op operating structure changes' policy, made following the ECGD/HMG debt write-off agreement (chapter 17).

Messrs Beattie and Rosamond were re-nominated for selection by the Beneficiaries. Clarification was sought by the remaining 3 Beneficiary Directors on the legality of this taking place. Peter Davis, the Co-op's Company Solicitor, advised that this was in accordance with the present constitution.

The adjourned Board meeting was reconvened and Company Secretary Rob Murison outlined events that had now taken place. He noted the three remaining Beneficiary Directors had co-opted John Rosamond and Richard Horton to their number. It then fell to the Board to select a Chairman, and John Rosamond was unanimously chosen for that position.

It was now agreed by the Board to be of great importance that the membership as a whole was aware that the Board was united. Chairman John Rosamond agreed, arguing strongly that the best way of achieving this was by way of a mass meeting. It was further agreed that Board members should give careful consideration to ways in which communications with the membership as a whole could be improved, and that this should be discussed at the next Board meeting.

The Chairman asked the Directors to consider posting minutes on the notice boards after each meeting. (I was always of the opinion that getting the total involvement of the Co-op's owners, the membership, by publishing details of the commercial reality we faced would solve the problems of communication.) It was agreed that these matters, together with the selection of a Vice Chairman, should be on the agenda of the next Board meeting.

The quarterly meeting with the Trustees also took place later the same day, Mr J Tomlinson and Mr R Marsdon in attendance. Having been circulated with copies of the Board reports prior to the meeting, the Trustees asked for the following information:

a) Mr Tomlinson enquired about the basis of the unfair dismissal tribunal's judgement. This was summarised by Bob Lindsay. Mr Tomlinson noted that if any of the claimants were re-instated and were then subject to apparent hostility or prejudice they might succeed in a claim for constructive dismissal.

b) Mr Tomlinson also enquired into the future outlook of the company, and was told that whilst we were making considerable strides in product development, the financial situation was extremely shaky.

c) Mr Marsdon enquired as to whether the cost of the motorcycle show justified our presence. He was told of the vital necessity of ensuring the public was aware of our continuing strong presence in the market, and informed that our absence from the show would be interpreted as a sign of great weakness.

The following day there was an interesting letter in my post – a reply from the Prince of Wales' Equerry. I had written to His Royal Highness the Prince of Wales regarding the Commemorative Limited Edition Triumph Bonneville Royal. Styling, samples of which in UK and US specification variants were presently taking shape for consideration. I had suggested in my letter that Triumph wished to present the first one of the Limited Edition to the Prince of Wales and Lady Diana Spencer as a gift for the forthcoming 29th July 1981 wedding. The reader will have already noted that I favoured limited edition models as a way of stimulating sales demand when orders were scarce. Although this was the Chairman's view, TMA had indicated little interest in the possibility. This was also the view of the Sales Director, Peter Britton, so far as the UK and Europe were concerned. However, I felt the opportunity to mark this royal wedding was too good to miss, especially in view of the success of the 1977 Silver Jubilee models. We had already marked the engagement of the royal couple, announced at almost the same time the new Ultimate Triumph Vertical Twin design project began, by codenaming the model 'Diana'.

Unfortunately, the Prince of Wales' Equerry said that it was felt by the Royal couple they could not accept the offer of the wedding present, but would rather the monetary value was donated to The Year of the Disabled, of which the Prince of Wales was that year's patron. This suggestion would provide Triumph with the opportunity to auction off the No 1 Bonneville Royal in order to generate as much money as possible for the Prince's disabled charity, and achieve excellent public relations exposure once the Limited Edition was launched. The classic Triumph humour brigade had been silent for a while; however, it soon dubbed the sample Bonneville Royal 'Charlie's Triumph'!

Once again the pressure at Meriden was immense. Everyone was involved in one way or another in the final run up to the annual NEC Motorcycle Show. The build up to the new model year changes at Meriden always caused major disruption to normal production, and the greater variation with the 1982 model range would challenge the membership more than ever before. The duration of this challenge, however, depended totally upon how well the new models were received, and the volume of orders that followed. Ever conscious of the extremely stretched financial resources, production of the futuristic NEC show stand was partly undertaken by use of factory carpentry and welding services.

The Sales Director met the UK dealers on 8th April to 'gee them up' in preparation for the new model launch at the show, which also involved various planned promotional events. Those dealers who were able to attend seemed to be enthusiastic regarding Triumph's planned 'higher market profile'. It remained to be seen if this dealer interest would be backed up with orders.

The personal pressure on the Chairman increased somewhat on 9th May, when the Financial Director asked for guidance regarding what could have turned out to be the beginning of the end for the Co-op! The major chromium plating company used by Triumph had started legal proceedings to recover its frozen £10,000 moratorium debt. However, it had indicated it was willing to withhold taking further legal action if arrangements were made to repay one third today, a further third on 31st April, and the final third on 15th May. Rob Murison's note to the Chairman went on to say we could at this moment afford to do what this supplier was asking, but the problem was this would contravene the spirit of the non-binding arrangement we had made with the other creditors. Accordingly, he needed the Chairman's guidance on what action to take. If the frozen Moratorium Creditors' agreement was breached in this way with an isolated £10,000 payment, and it became known, it was not unreasonable to expect that other creditors would demand their frozen debts be settled as well. This we were presently unable to do, which was why it had been agreed to make scheduled repayments to them, over time. We sought the guidance of Fred Tippet, Chairman of the Creditors' Committee, on how we should act in this situation.

Rob Murison was due to meet the creditors' subcommittee later in the month to discuss Triumph's position. I knew Rob was not looking forward to this meeting, at which the Co-op's below operating budget, loss-making performance would be scrutinised and commented upon.

Press day at the vital NEC Motorcycle Show was to be Thursday 16th April. A Co-op membership preview of the 1982 model range would take place in the factory on the afternoon of Tuesday 14th April, with dealers getting their chance at the Manor Hotel Meriden the following morning between 11.00 and 11.30am. All the show models looked impressive except the TS8-1 Triumph flagship model, which was still under construction. Dyson's team had already been working around the clock for nearly a week, and it was looking more and more unlikely that it would be ready for the show. To provide for this eventuality and avoid embarrassment, all Triumph promotional information was prepared without reference to the TS8-1 flagship.

The nine 1982 models to be exhibited were:

T140E	Electro Bonneville US
T140E	Bonneville US
T140E	Electro Bonneville UK
T140E	Electro Executive
TR7T	Tiger Trail
Police AV Special	
TS8-1	AV and 8-valve engine (maybe)
TR65	Thunderbird US
TR65	Thunderbird UK

Triumph's dedicated small engineering design and development team had achieved many technical and evolutionary improvements to the T140E Bonneville model range for 1982:

Headlight – improved to Lucas sealed beam type 60/45 watts.

Headlight – rubber mounting system.

Wet weather disc brake pads (Dunlop).

Twin front disc brakes with Lockheed alloy callipers (option).

Wiring harness now with multi-pin connectors.

New style direction flashing indicators.

Twin seat interior cushion improved, reduced step in top of seat profile.

Overall gear ratio raised – rear wheel sprocket now 45 teeth (was 47).

Gear ratios now: 1st – 11.63:1; 2nd – 8.27:1; 3rd – 6.30:1; 4th – 5.36:1; 5th – 4.50:1.

In addition, the Executive received:

Twin 32mm choke constant vacuum bing carburettors.

New styled side panels.

Optional cockpit or full fairing.

Triumph's dual purpose bike, the Tiger Trail TR7T, remained the same for 1982 as when shown at the Paris Motorcycle Show. Once in production it was to win the 750 class in the gruelling Circuit Des Pyrenees, ridden by British policeman Tony Beaumont.

Triumph's black and white leaflet *The Motorcyclist's Choice* said it all about the totally 'new' 1982 TR65 Thunderbird. Available in UK or US specifications it was a thrifty, economical

650, sacrificing none of the standard Triumph virtues of snappy acceleration, impeccable manners in dense traffic, and a finish that commanded admiration. Ideal for the first time big bike rider; responsive, light and manageable. Easy on fuel and easy on your pocket, it's specification was as follows:

Engine – 650cc twin cylinder four stroke 76mm bore x 71.5mm stroke, single amal carburettor. The engine was basically a reduced stroke version of the 750 model, with the majority of the engine components remaining common to both units. The cylinder barrel height was reduced to suit the new stroke, as were the pushrod tubes. The piston was new to obtain a satisfactory compression ratio. The chain case, timing and gearbox covers were finished in matt black.

Gearbox – The five-speed design as used on other models was retained, with the exception of the gearbox sprocket, which has 19 teeth.

Frame and forks – As T140 Bonneville.

Wheels and brakes – The front wheel was fitted with a single plain 10in diameter cast-iron disc brake and Dunlop wet weather pads. The rear had a 7in diameter drum.

Tyre equipment – Front 3.25 x 19, Avon SM or Dunlop K70; rear 4.00 x 18, Avon SM or Dunlop K70.

Instruments – The speedometer was fitted at the left-hand side of the steering head, and the appearance was balanced with the ignition switch and telltale lamps at the right-hand side.

Petrol tank/handlebars – The new 4-gallon Triumph-style petrol tank was fitted with the traditional 3-gallon style as an alternative. High rise or traditional standard handlebars were also offered as alternatives.

Electrics – A single phase alternator was fitted, with ignition by a 12-volt system and contact breaker.

Centre stand – The usual Triumph easy-lift centre stand was fitted, but a prop stand was not provided. The prop stand lug was retained on the frame, and this part could be fitted by the rider if required.

Exhaust system – Two into one black finish exhaust pipes run into a single silencer, also in black finish, at the left-hand side of the machine.

Finish – The petrol tank and styling side panels were painted in a unique style smoky cherry with mudguards in polished stainless steel.

Press day at the NEC on the 16th April 1981 certainly had the TS8-1 flagship surprise – it wasn't there! However, the press was none the wiser. Pride of place went to the special AV police model, of which a batch of 30 was being hand-built at the factory. As the following day was Good Friday Bank Holiday, no press coverage of the NEC show appeared. Journalists and photographers attending on Good Friday in search of general public reaction were amazed to see the crowds attracted by the new 1982 models on the Triumph stand. Honda also caused a stir, increasing retail prices by 5 per cent across its range, in addition to the forced 10 per cent car tax introduced on 1st April.

Those visiting the Triumph stand the next day, Saturday, were surprised to see an additional exhibit: the TS8-1 had arrived at last! Its futuristic, some said sinister, predominantly black appearance certainly caused debate amongst the Triumph purists. However, its 8-valve engine in the Bernard Hooper designed police AV chassis caught the imagination of high performance enthusiasts.

The motorcycle show could not have been more geographically convenient for Triumph, taking place at the National Exhibition Centre, only 3 miles from the Meriden factory.

**The late arriving TS8-1 certainly caused a stir amongst Triumph purists.
(Promotional picture)**

A majority of the 170 workforce visited during the Easter holiday. Although the financially strapped Co-op could manage to secure only 50 complimentary tickets for the membership, the remainder who visited found ways and means of gaining entry without paying; most in authority seemed to accept that as part owners of the only remaining volume producer of motorcycles in the United Kingdom, they were entitled! Once inside the show and standing on the packed Triumph stand, it was impossible for Co-op members not to be impressed by what they saw on display and heard from the general public. Any Co-op member who claimed they weren't impressed and justifiably proud no longer had Triumph blood running through their veins. Everyone at the factory had played their part in achieving this show success for Triumph. Our growing confidence regarding quality enabled all 1982 models to be sold with the warranty guarantee doubled to 12 months, or 12,000 miles.

I was sure that the pride every Triumph worker felt having attended the show would be needed to fortify them for the new challenges in producing the 1982 model range. The Engineering Department could not have done more with the stretched financial resources available to it. The enthusiasm of the motorcycling fans at the show suggested they liked what they had seen; it was now a matter of whether they liked them enough to place firm orders. Only time would tell.

21

Pay our way
or close

The vital NEC Motorcycle Show achieved a lot by way of re-establishing Triumph as a force to be reckoned with in the UK. Whether the public's enthusiasm was as a result of the tremendous effort being made by the Meriden Co-op to stay in business, or for the new 1982 model range, we would only find out in the weeks to come. Triumph dealers attending the show certainly placed more orders this year than last, when discounts had to be offered to encourage them to commit! However, it was also ongoing steady UK demand that was required from our most profitable home market. Achieving the proportion of home market sales forecast in the annual operating budget was vital, because these sales were more profitable than those to export markets.

As Chairman, I was certainly in no doubt that our show presence could not have been better. Bob Lindsay's high profile, lead from the front approach, meeting and greeting press, dealers and motorcycle buyers on every day of the Easter holiday, was well received by all. Similarly, the Sales Director, Peter Britton, worked tirelessly both in the run-up to the show and during it, and his co-ordination of the various promotional events confirmed Triumph was back with a vengeance. The Sales Department staff were ably supported with technical backup by Chief Engineer Brian Jones and members of his team. This proved to be an impressive show combination.

The workforce returned to the Meriden factory following the Easter holiday with renewed optimism regarding the Co-op's future, a timely boost to morale that would certainly be necessary in order to meet the many challenges in the weeks ahead. Although the Sales Department was now taking orders for the new model range, only the 1982 Bonneville in its various forms was in production, as expected. The remaining 1982 models were still being finalised by the Engineering Department. It was inevitable that UK sales demand would be for the previously unseen new models not yet in production, so it was imperative that design release was achieved as soon as possible.

Messrs Tippetts and McCann of the Moratorium Trade Creditors' subcommittee visited the Meriden factory on 29th April for a progress meeting with Rob Murison, the Financial Director. Rob had the extremely difficult task of reviewing with them Triumph's below operating budget, loss-making performance of the previous six months. This financial situation had been reported to the 6th April Board meeting by Rob Murison in his review of management's performance. The additional summary of performance to date for the first half of the year indicated just how vital it was for all operating budget targets to be achieved.

REVIEW OF MANAGEMENT'S PERFORMANCE

a) General indicators

The trend shown by production and sales figures is encouraging. Orders are well up, allowing a return on 23rd March to 5-day full-time production, although it will take several weeks to 'gear up' to the 80+ motorcycles per week we need.

There are three areas, though, which have given difficulty in the past and are once again showing danger signs:

i) The number of motorcycles 'off track not wrapped' is increasing steadily. This together with 'wrapped stock' must be kept to an absolute minimum as it represents a delay in receiving cash, which we are trying to bring in quickly to keep our overdraft down.

ii) The value of spare parts orders fulfilled weekly has fallen steadily over the month.

While there was a conscious management decision to give priority to building up production of motorcycles at the expense of fulfilling spare parts orders, it must once again be emphasised that taking the year as a whole, meeting the spare parts budget of £19,500 each week is as important a target as producing and selling 79 motorcycles each week.

iii) While the present gradual build-up in production is understandable, we must ensure there is not a similar slow build up after the Easter holiday. This requires good planning and recollection of the problems we encountered after the Christmas break.

b) Cash movements in month

At the end of the reporting period we were once again at the limit of our resources; indeed, were it not for the realisation of a bond which we had given in 1980, our overdraft would have been over £1m, which would have forced us to stop trading.

Cashflow projection:

Once we reach Easter we should have a breathing space. This breathing space we must use to best advantage, as cash will once again become tight when the loss of a week's production works its way through.

Needless to say, there must be no further deterioration of our performance against budget.

First half year performance against budget:

In addition to the normal management performance reports I have included this month a summary of performance against budget for the first half year. This emphasizes just how far we are behind the targets we set ourselves in October 1980.

First half year summary of performance against budget:

	Budget (£000)	Actual (£000)	Variance (£000)	Off budget (%)
Income from sales	2420.7	1534.5	(886.2)	(37)
Cost of materials	(1388.0)	(825.3)	562.7	41
Surplus on sales	1032.7	709.2	(323.5)	(31)
Sundry receipts	–	116.7	116.7	–
	1032.7	**825.9**	**(206.8)**	**(20)**

Expenses				
	Budget (£000)	**Actual (£000)**	**Variance (£000)**	**Off budget (%)**
Wages and salaries	477.9	460.9	17.0	4
Engineering	18.3	11.7	6.63	6
Factory General	25.0	18.0	7.0	28
Establishment	168.8	177.5	(8.7)	(5)
Royalties	17.5	68.2	(50.7)	(289)
Sales	62.5	60.1	2.4	3
Overhead/misc	208.9	141.0	67.9	33
Moratorium 10%	165.0	87.4	77.6	47
	(1143.9)	**(1024.8)**	**119.1**	**10**
Cash outflow in period	(112.2)	(198.9)	(87.7)	

The top section [previous page] *shows receipts from sales of motorcycles and spare parts and expenditure on the materials to make them – it shows that our receipts are almost one third of a million pounds below forecast.*

The only reasons we are still in business are:

i) Various unanticipated receipts such as the sale of machinery (income of £116,700).

ii) Our failure to pay the second instalment due on the Moratorium Trade Creditors' agreement (saving of £77,600).

iii) The effectiveness of our general expenditure control (saving of £41,500) after paying for the Triumph name.

iv) The extension by the bank of an additional £100,000 overdraft.

Clearly the first two cannot be repeated, and it must be equally obvious that savings obtained by trimming expenditure alone will not be sufficient to offset further material shortfalls in production or sales. Finally, the bank has made it very clear it will not increase our overdraft to cover our losses again – if we cannot pay our way we must close down.

The Moratorium Trade Creditors' subcommittee was extremely disappointed to learn that Triumph had not been operating profitably over the winter. As a result, it would require closer communication. A committee representative would attend the factory to study the situation, and it was emphasised that Triumph must turn round to profitability or cut its cloth accordingly.

Bill Beattie's initial agreement to act in the capacity of Spare Parts Manager, followed by his appointment to the position on 1st April, enabled him to produce a hands-on report of his findings and recommendations.

I have believed for some time that to achieve a satisfactory supply of spare parts to stockists you would need a department whose sole function would be the procurement and fulfilment of customer's orders. Since my involvement in the spare parts operation I have seen nothing to make me alter that opinion. On the contrary, what I have seen only confirms to me the absolute necessity of a Spare Parts Department under its own control, which I believe it needs if it is ever to carry out its primary objective. One only has to look at the existing spare parts setup to realise the shortcomings therein, some of which I am afraid to say are self inflicted, even though most of the problems facing the department, as with the rest of the company, are due to the circumstances we find ourselves in. I would like to make it clear that in expressing these opinions I am not suggesting that the company should give any special treatment to spare parts. As a matter of fact I am well aware of the company's position and the problems that confront it. What I am saying, however, is that within whatever strategy is adopted, spare parts liaison with other departments is to be allowed to carry out its prime function – the procurement and selling of those spare parts. Therefore I propose the following.

A separate Spare Parts Department encompassing:

a) Administration, responsible for
– Co-ordination of department
– Raising of orders
– Pricing and extending of invoices
– Credit notes
– Cash from retail sales
– Stock controls and records
– Ordering of parts outstanding from manufacturing and purchasing
– Back ordering system
– Price reviews and catalogue liaising with relevant departments
Personnel required to undertake the above – 2 people.

b) Stores

Spare parts stores to be in line with stockists should be holding no less than one month's current parts stock at any given time, plus of course whatever non-current spare parts that there is a demand for. Obviously our present situation will not allow for the above, therefore I would suggest the process to achieve the desired stock levels should be gradual. Initial stocks for the spare parts stores could be made up from existing non-current plus some of the faster moving current spare parts. The rest would have to be picked as now on availability.

Stores personnel responsible for:
– Maintaining the stores area
– Binning of stock
– The recording of parts on bin location cards
– Picking, packing and checking of orders
– Procurement of parts from the factory

c) Packing

Here I have moved away from the existing system and included packing and checking into the stores personnel's function. I am sure that is the right thing to do.

d) Dispatch and transport

This is an objective the Spare Parts Department must aim for, as it would allow for the control and flexibility required for the planning and processing of orders from start to finish.

It has been my experience that certain stockists prefer to collect their orders from the factory personally. This I feel needs to be discouraged, as I do not believe this to be their sole reason for their visits. It is not uncommon once they are on site to witness the freedom of movement they take upon themselves. A freedom of movement and collection of information that allows them far too much insight into company business, not only on company transactions with other customers, but even more serious, information on future company projects. A medium size van would not only allow

**About to enter production, the new TR65 650cc Thunderbird.
(Courtesy Erum Waheed's archive)**

insistence upon delivery, greatly reducing the need for stockists to visit, but would also provide control over completed spare parts orders.

Summary
It is essential to the future of both the company and the Spare Parts Department that it re-establishes its credibility with both dealers and public, and the only way I know this can be achieved is through customer satisfaction. I believe the proposals put forward in this report would go some way to achieving this. The basic theme of this report is of a department acting as a unit dealing only with the selling procurement and delivery of spare parts orders. A single minded approach if you like, but necessary if it is to carry out its prime function, the supply of spare parts. This is the after-sales service Triumph promises the customer.
    WA Beattie – Spare Parts Manager 6th May 1981

This report provided the Managing Director with positive proposals by which sales and supply of Triumph's highly profitable spare parts could be improved. The reassuring position regarding Bill's recommendations was everyone knew that if his proposals were implemented, he would move heaven and earth to make them work.

For my part, I was now in the thick of it, as expected, as Product Planning and Timing Manager. Inevitably, production of the 1982 models with no component parts to undertake pre-production builds meant initial assembly would be chaotic. On the manufacturing side, the machine shop sections would have to make their own jigs and fixtures once Engineering released the new component designs for production, all of which suggested that my new day job would be more fighting problems as they occurred, rather than planning or timing to avoid them! The TR7T Tiger Trail and TR65 Thunderbird were to achieve engineering design release at the end of May/beginning of June. So the transition from making only the 1982 T140E Bonneville and its variants to production of the new 1982 model range would be the biggest challenge for the membership yet.

In the meantime, however, the successful NEC show had not so far resulted in the desired steady UK demand for the 1982 model range. It was now obvious that once initial production problems were sorted, and 80 motorcycles a week achieved, we would quickly run out of orders. The Directors would discuss this extremely worrying situation at their 17th May meeting after first dealing with matters arising from the previous meeting.

a) The MD felt the ongoing complaints regarding communications could possibly be solved by placing more emphasis on communicating via the leading hands and organiser supervision structure.

b) Electric starter warranty problems continued to be monitored, but did not seem to be widespread.

c) Harry Hughes was elected as Vice Chairman of the Board.

d) Reorganisation of the Meriden Sales Department was delayed for the time being.

e) Finally, the Directors placed on record the Board's deep appreciation for Bill Beattie's efforts on behalf of the company whilst he was Vice Chairman and a Director.

Once again the Managing Director's circulated monthly management report had concentrated on the ongoing problem of motorcycle sales, indicating that the inflow of orders continued to give cause for grave concern:

Orders received in April	313
– UK	166
– Export	147
Motorcycles dispatched	203
Order bank on 1st May	514
Including TR65 Thunderbird	104
Orders received to date	
– UK	660
– ROW	632
– TMA	151
Total	**1443**

The MD indicated that the Spare Parts Manager Bill Beattie had submitted his report recommending the following changes to operating methods in order to create a separate Spare Parts Department from 1st July 1981.

Separate organisation for spare parts:
– Receiving orders.
– Processing orders.
– Delivering orders.
Maintain separate stores comprising:
– 1 months stock of current spare parts.
– Any non-current spare parts available.

– Progressively increasing availability of non-current spare parts.
Spare Parts Department head-count:
– 1 Manager – available.
– 2 in administration – 1 available, recruit 1.
– 3 in stores/packing dispatch/transport – 1 available, recruit 2.
Actions:
a) Necessary to employ 3 individuals.
b) Purchase a delivery van.
c) Create spare parts stores area.

The list of spare parts stockists has been revised, and authorised Triumph dealers will be advised accordingly. New stockists are Roebuck, Reg Allen, Anglo Bike, Abbey Garage, Ben Lloyd and Devine.

The MD's report also indicated the updated position regarding the ECGD disposal agreement.

ECGD disposal agreement
Sales USA

Model	Budget	Actual	Variance
T140D	797	577	-220
T140E	794	863	+ 69
Total	**1591**	**1440**	**-151**

Sales UK*

Model	Budget	Actual	Variance
T140D	596	60	-536

Originally these machines were scheduled to be sold in the UK.

The MD explained that we would be unable to meet the original ECGD agreement deadline of 31st May, and that we were now seeking an extension of the period available for the sale of the motorcycles.

Brenda Price had gone to the United States to obtain an updated report on the ECGD situation, and to gather further intelligence about the prevailing market situation. At the April Board meeting the Directors had expressed their continuing faith in Geoffrey Robinson handling the ECGD position.

The MD then reported that several discussions had taken place with Mr Len Hamilton regarding Australia, and it had been decided to increase our sales efforts in the Australian, New Zealand and Japanese markets, in order to maximise winter-time demand from the Meriden factory. The sale of Triumph's previous distribution facility in Australia as a shell company, with the factory's representative taking orders from his home, would enable the new operation to become a branch of Triumph Meriden, rather than a separate company, thus reducing operating costs.

Financial Director Rob Murison apologised for the lack of a written report and instead gave an oral one, which raised the following points:

In addition to the continuing production problems, he pointed out a disturbing increase in the number of units 'off track not wrapped' and overtime hours worked. Whilst it was acknowledged that our working capital requirements would increase as a result of our higher levels of production, he pointed out that this made it all the more necessary to ensure that dispatches kept pace with production. If this did not happen, we would have a severe and prolonged negative cashflow, which would inevitably result in our exceeding our bank overdraft limit. Rob Murison then updated the Board on the meeting with the trade creditors' subcommittee (covered earlier in this chapter).

The MD expanded on the reasons for concluding a settlement with the five ex-members who won their industrial tribunal claim for unfair dismissal. He explained that any further publicity in this matter was potentially very injurious to Triumph's public image, which we were trying to improve. Ironically, the twenty '90 days late' claims had not been allowed.

In a major effort to try and stimulate sales in our home and most profitable market, Sales Director Peter Britton put together in mid-May a motorcycle sales promotion, about which he wrote to all Triumph's main UK dealers.

Triumph sales promotion
The NEC proved in every respect to be an excellent venue for the Motorcycle Show held over the Easter period, as all who attended will know.

Triumph Motorcycles received excellent exposure in the media, and there is no doubt that the resulting increased public awareness of our new models will produce a healthy number of potential purchasers making their way to showrooms in search of new Triumph motorcycles during the next few weeks.

We want to direct them to the right showrooms, to those dealerships where a range of the latest Triumph models is on display and where they will be well received. Full page Triumph advertisements will therefore appear as follows:

Motor Cycle News 27th May; Motorcycle Weekly 3rd June.
Motorcycle Weekly 17th June; Motor Cycle News 8th July.

The format will be an outline map of the British Isles with the identity and location of the Triumph main dealers superimposed.

To qualify for inclusion in these advertisements dealers will be required to order a minimum of five of the latest motorcycles for delivery as soon as possible, to undertake to replace this stock as sold, and to contribute a small sum to cover the cost of printing their business name and address on each advertisement. Triumph will meet the balance of the total costs of these advertisements.

Additionally, Triumph will arrange for the following special customer benefits to apply to each motorcycle purchased under this scheme:

– Free second year unlimited mileage warranty cover.
– Special low insurance premiums.
– Lower interest rates for HP transactions.

The package, with supporting point of sale material for your showrooms, will attract new Triumph customers to your business. We will keep the programme going for the key months of June, July and August. Be ready to meet the opportunity to increase Triumph sales in your area by returning the enclosed order form without delay – or better still, call us today and we'll make sure your company's name is included in our first list of Triumph main dealers.

Yours faithfully
Triumph Motorcycles (Meriden) Limited
Peter L Britton
Sales Director

The massively ambitious new 1982 model programme, driven by lack of orders for the motorcycles we had been producing, would also, because of the more complex component mix, bring into question if there was still sufficient production capacity within the existing labour

The TR7T Tiger Trail 'Flying Tigers' promotional poster portrayed it in the best possible way. Also very evident were Bob Haines' riding skills.

The TR65 Thunderbird 'Performance with Economy' promotional poster was also made available to the dealer network.

force. Without the guaranteed tremendous effort that we knew could be depended upon from the Co-op membership, we could not have even contemplated what we were trying to do. Due to shortages of components and initial lack of familiarity with the new 1982 model range, by the 8th June meeting we had 150 motorcycles in excess of the accepted norm, off track and awaiting final processing and dispatch.

When the Chairman opened the meeting his first duty was to inform the Directors of the grave financial situation Triumph was now in, as a result of which the Financial Director/Company Secretary had advised that we must consider if it was right to continue to trade. To enable the Directors to make this judgement, Rob Murison quoted the 'William Leach 1932 Precedent'. The Board Beneficiary Directors had faced this difficult decision many times over the years; the Executive Directors were now having to confront it for the first time. It never got any easier, and on each occasion judgement following detailed discussion had to be made on the merits of the facts. Rob Murison also pointed out that the Directors must remember that Triumph's bank was just as much a creditor of the company as the ordinary trade creditors.

Bob Lindsay indicated the numerous production difficulties that had led to our present 150-bike excess inventory, and how he intended we should clear the backlog over the next two and a half weeks. After general Board discussion and consideration of the William Leach 1932 Precedent, the Chairman John Rosamond asked each Director in turn their view of the practicality of reaching the two and a half week target. Whilst acknowledging that there would be considerable problems in achieving this goal, the Board was unanimous in expressing their faith in Triumph's ongoing future. It was further agreed that the precariousness of the company's financial situation should be explained to the Beneficiary owners of the Co-op, and the best vehicle for doing this was a mass meeting. This would take place the following day, Tuesday 9th June at 3.30pm.

As expected the mass meeting was well attended. The seriousness of the Co-op's financial situation was explained, as was the plan to retrieve it over the next two and a half weeks. A forthright question and answer session followed, as was the customary way at the Co-op in 'battle on or close' situations. The Chairman put it to the Beneficiaries that although the Directors had been cautioned regarding continuing to trade, they had decided unanimously to continue, expressing their faith in Triumph's ongoing future. However, the Directors' faith in the future could be justified only if it was backed up by each and every member. Without that sort of commitment we would fail to rectify the serious financial situation. If members agreed that once again the Co-op could rise to the challenge, the Board would monitor the financial situation closely and return with a detailed plan of action for their approval. A unanimous vote in favour of fighting on followed.

Six days later on 15th June, the Board meeting to consider the advisability of continuing to trade agreed that in order to improve the company's chances of survival, the following was to be recommended to the membership:

• The works should forthwith go on to a 44-hour working week, with 9-hour days Monday to Thursday and 8 hours on Friday.

• The premium rates for overtime should be abandoned until the summer holidays.

• The second week of holiday pay, normally paid before the break, to be paid on return from holiday.

• On return from holiday members' pay should be paid one day later each week so that by the third week in August, the members' weekly payroll would be one week in arrears.

It was agreed that the above measures should be put to the members at a mass meeting on 17th June, and the Board meeting was then adjourned until 3.30pm on 17th June.

The mass meeting approved the package of measures proposed to improve Triumph's financial situation and the Co-op's chances of survival. At the reconvened Board meeting afterwards, MD Bob Lindsay proposed a shadow arrangement by key managers, whereby senior management would take a more active part in day-to-day running of the company. The positions involved were as follows:

a) Bob Lindsay – Purchase and Sales
b) Brian Jones/John Rosamond – Assembly and Dispatch
c) Alec Bottrill – Machine Shops
d) Bill Beattie – Asset Disposals
e) Rob Murison – General Cost Savings

Bob Lindsay then outlined the overall position of the company, informing the Board that an intensive sales drive was on the way, concentrating on those Triumph dealers who had not that year taken a reasonable number of motorcycles. He also reported that TMA had increased its sales forecast for the forthcoming year, potentially increasing the Meriden factory dispatches during the winter period.

Finally, the company's weekly target for the next few weeks was reiterated as being 80 motorcycles produced – 120 motorcycles dispatched together with £20,000 worth of spare parts. The Board of Directors agreed that in view of the matters discussed during the meeting, Triumph should continue to trade.

I knew I would not be the only one reflecting on the MD's comments regarding an intensive sales drive being on the way. Communication with the membership so far as this information was concerned would certainly not be a problem. As in the past, the Beneficiaries were already very much of the opinion they had to pay the price of failure to achieve budgeted sales targets. The MD's detailed involvement in the dealer charm offensive and fact finding mission, which resulted in Board acceptance of the recommended rationalisation of the UK dealer network, would certainly now be in question. Geoffrey Robinson MP, whilst continuing to undertake his agreed day-to-day non-executive responsibilities, had not attended a monthly Board meeting for several months. It was likely that the first port of call for concerned Beneficiaries who were also his constituents would be his weekly surgery.

The following day was the management meeting, and a further sales/product surprise was in store for me. The royal wedding commemorative limited edition mock ups, styled by industrial design student Dave Carpenter as part of his six-month industrial placement at the Meriden factory, had now been shown to selected UK dealers, and in view of their comments and the necessity to obtain orders, a marketing plan based upon the original idea was to be drawn up!

• The Royal will be a limited edition.
• Possibly limited to 200 US specification/200 UK specification.
• UK and US samples to be available for photography in 3 days' time.
• Each dealer to be offered one motorcycle.
• No. 1 to be disposed of for Prince Charles' charity, in line with the Chairman's letter.
• Rob Murison to establish the selling price.

The Bonneville Royal Limited Edition idea, first proposed by the Chairman on receipt of the royal couple's response, had been considered a non-starter on both sides of the Atlantic, where it was said there was little interest. Suddenly, due to desperation from lack of orders, the Chairman's 'folly' – proposed in the first week of his new day job as Product Planning and Timing Manager – was given the green light! A 650cc TR65T Tiger Trail utilising the Thunderbird engine was also now being actively considered.

The MD's Senior Management emergency shadowing arrangement to attack the present major cashflow crisis was a good one. Brian Jones and I worked well as a team in the assembly and dispatch areas. Brian's 'what do you want to die of' attitude to problem solving, and hands-on leadership approach to clearing the backlog was infectious, and proved inspirational to the membership. No one worked harder or longer than he did, and in my mind's eye I can still see him climbing the grand, main Triumph building's marble-like staircase three steps at a time. Keeping up with Brian was certainly a challenge, although there was no doubt that everyone played their part. The Meriden Co-op was always at its best in times of great adversity, striving and succeeding to achieve what would have been impossible in 'normal' industry. We all went home physically exhausted at the end of each of these very long days, but the satisfaction everyone felt from a job well done was immense. The weekly operating budget for production of bikes and supply of spare parts was also looking more and more achievable, Bob Lindsay making a major difference to the latter.

At last, on 20th June there was some very good news about the ECGD negotiations, which I was able to convey to the membership via the company notice boards. During the last two months Geoffrey Robinson, Brenda Price, Rob Murison and I (mostly Geoffrey and Brenda) had been involved in negotiations with ECGD to secure an extension of time in which to sell off the remaining stockpiled motorcycles in a positive manner. Agreement had now been reached, and an announcement had been made in the House of Commons, by way of a statement from Conservative Industry Minister Norman Tebbit.

The agreement with Export Credit Guarantee Department was for the sale of motorcycles financed by the Meriden Co-op's bank with ECGD support. These were stockpiled in the USA and Australia. The sale was to be completed by 31st May 1981 and established that £1.95m would be raised for ECGD. In the event the target has not been met although substantial progress has been made and £1.05m has been paid to ECGD by 31st May 1981. A number of factors have adversely affected the plan, the recession has depressed sales of motorcycles in the USA and severe price cutting and the weakness of the yen have made competition with the dominant Japanese manufacturers more difficult. The strength of sterling during most of the period of the sale has affected the return in sterling from the USA sales. The result of the adverse conditions is that there has been a shortfall both in the number of machines sold and in sales revenue per machine. In light of these difficulties the Government has relaxed the requirements of the agreement and has now agreed to write off the company's loan from the Department of Industry, together with accrued interest, if the total of at least £1.3m is raised for ECGD by 30th April 1982. On the target being met, ECGD agree as before, that it will release Meriden from its obligation to repay to ECGD the difference between the sterling amount accrued by the bank and that raised from the sale of the stockpile of motorcycles. This arrangement does not constitute more financial assistance to Meriden from either ECGD or the Department of Industry, nor does it preclude further ECGD revenue if events made this possible.

Geoffrey Robinson and Brenda Price had masterminded an extension to their original Co-op saving debt write-off deal, and with a Conservative Government. There were also signs of possibly increasing 1982 model motorcycle sales in the vitally important American market.

22

CAULDRON OF ACTIVITY

Bob Lindsay's emergency shadow management system was more effective than any other structure previously tried at the Co-op – so much so that near operating budget manufacturing performance was achieved when subcontract supplies of components were available. Vital inroads into the 150 inventory backlog were also made; a fantastic achievement by all concerned.

Alec Bottrill's return to direct supervision of the machine shops (his area of extensive expertise and experience) had a dramatic impact on supply of in-house machined components.

Rob Murison's general cost-saving expertise was equally impressive; no one was immune from his activities. The cost-saving benefits to cashflow were important, as was the clear message that unless operating budgets were met, it would be only a matter of time before Triumph and the Co-op went under. The company's telephone system was the first area tackled. Major cost savings were achieved by removing the 'dial 9 – free for all' that previously existed for external calls, replaced by a strictly controlled number of direct lines for heads of department. Access to the telephone system for the majority would be via the switchboard operator. Monthly budgets for subcontracted design engineering projects (Dyson and Diana) were halved, as was the PR budget until we had fought our way out of the cashflow crisis. The two UK 'on the road' sales reps who had been fighting and losing a costly battle to secure orders were withdrawn to the factory. They would now pursue the long overdue sales approach of applying pressure to underperforming UK dealers to honour their franchise agreements, with failure to comply resulting in termination. Use of all personal vehicles for Triumph business was stopped – in future, only company vehicles would be used. These were only a few of the higher profile cost-cutting actions implemented that made an immediate impact.

Bill Beattie found it extremely difficult to dispose of obsolete stocks, whilst also concentrating on the Spare Parts Department's efforts to achieve its budgeted weekly targets.

Tremendous pressure was now felt by all, not least Engineering Director Brian Jones. Most design changes to create the 1982 model range were modifications by the engineering department of well-proven existing Triumph practice. Accordingly, prototypes could nearly always be depended upon to work first time, prior to brief development testing and production. However, in these desperate times I suppose it was inevitable that relying on this principle would incur a setback. Surprisingly, it was not that a new model component failed – it was that we failed to test thoroughly the 'first off' production motorcycles, instead relying on the long-established practice of rolling road tests and final adjustments prior to dispatch. With hindsight, regardless of the fact that they were very similar to those that had gone before, new models needed extra evaluation. This was an embarrassing mistake, and one discovered by the UK dealers who received the first new models. Surprised, they phoned Harry Woolridge, the Warranty/Service Supervisor, asking this question about the 1982 Bonneville and Tiger Trail: "Don't you test them anymore?" Harry had played a key role working with the dealers and all areas at Triumph to achieve the much improved quality situation before this setback, which to everyone's dismay at the factory had not been corrected before dispatch. He sent the Chief Engineer a memorandum with the subject "Evaluation of first-off production motorcycles," in which he suggested a more thorough two- or three-hour test was required for new production models.

Uncharacteristically, Brian Jones replied in kind to the MD Bob Lindsay, copied to Harry Woolridge and the Chairman. He indicated the severely stretched engineering environment in which he and his team were working, and the calculated risks they were taking to provide instant designs to try and keep the Co-op in business. Harry Woolridge and Brian Jones had both made valid points; however, a 'paper war' was not going to solve the position we were in, and it was up to the Chairman to calm the situation by way of a little old fashioned diplomacy. Needless to say, the embarrassment was sufficient to ensure we were more thorough when the Thunderbird entered production.

The 6th July Board meeting was to be dominated by two major issues: our ability to continue to trade by clearing the motorcycle inventory backlog, and the ongoing lack of motorcycle orders. The MD's circulated monthly management report focused on both.

First Rob Murison updated the Directors on legal proceedings against Triumph brought by Nahib Dajarni, who was claiming unpaid commission of £15,000 to £20,000 relating to a 1979/80 order from Libya for 150 police motorcycles. Whilst the initial legal advice had suggested there was only a slim chance of defending against this legal action, statements since provided by the sales staff involved at the time suggested our chances were 50/50.

The MD now reported that by the end of the week, the backlog of motorcycles between the end of the assembly track and the door would be down to 112 units, the bulk of which would be cleared during the two week summer holiday. John Rosamond commented on the significant improvement in performance following the transfer of Alec Bottrill to the machine shops and Bob Lindsay taking charge of the overall production function. The Chairman was concerned that production might return to below-budget levels if the previous structure was reinstated, and the Board agreed, but stated that this was a matter for management and should be left to it!

Peter Britton, the Sales Director, expressed concern over the timing and quality of police motorcycle production. The first ten 1982 AV police models were scheduled for that week. Peter emphasised that there had already been a considerable delay in supplying forces, and that there was a real danger of losing credibility if we failed to deliver in the near future. As regards build quality, he pointed out that all police motorcycles must be extremely carefully built and a pre-delivery test mileage of approximately 100 miles per bike was desirable to eliminate any possible faults.

The sales/order situation in the MD's report was now reviewed.

Orders received in June	113
– UK	43
– Export	70
Motorcycles dispatched	329
Orders in hand July 1st	394
Motorcycles in hand	200

Orders received year to date 1980/81

UK	885
TMA	151
ROW	739
Total	1775

Sales continued to be disappointing, although it was felt that the effects of the UK advertising campaign had not yet materialised. Also, it was only during June that the Tiger Trails were dispatched to dealers, and it was expected that when seen in showrooms and in use they would help generate further orders.

Production of the Thunderbird commenced week ending 26th June, and as with the Tiger Trail, it was expected that public exposure would generate sales. Whilst the letter of credit for the sixteen police motorcycles for Trinidad had now been received and dispatch could proceed, the twelve cancelled Ugandan police motorcycles had all been reallocated.

Mr Mark Elvide's employment had been terminated as of 31st July; it had become obvious that the only successful agents for Triumph in Europe were those distributors that also retailed. Peter Britton would shortly visit France to review the situation. Our position in Germany could also be improved. We had received our first order from a newly appointed dealer in South Africa and were presently quoting for orders from Israel, Sri Lanka and Peru.

John Rosamond in his Product Planning capacity explained to the Board the sales strategy for the Bonneville Royal Limited Edition models that would commemorate the wedding of His Royal Highness the Prince of Wales to Lady Diana Spencer (as covered in chapter 21). The press and dealer launch was to take place on 9th July. Initial, unofficial indications suggested orders of over 200 could be expected.

Bob Lindsay then informed the Board that, subject to its approval, Geoffrey Robinson was prepared to take total responsibility for Triumph's American operation, TMA, obtaining orders for 1000 motorcycles and $1m worth of spare parts. Geoffrey Robinson would report to the MD in respect of the American market, providing a monthly indication of progress. Whilst some doubts were expressed by the Directors about the reporting arrangements, Geoffrey's bold approach in taking personal responsibility for what was acknowledged to be a difficult area was welcomed.

The final business of the Board meeting was to agree the notice to be displayed thanking the membership for their co-operation in attaining the recently much improved levels of production. Highly experienced production man Bob Lindsay stated that this could only have been achieved in a co-operative!

The meeting over, there was time for reflection on Geoffrey Robinson's new role – total responsibility for TMA. Since Geoffrey's resignation as Chief Executive he had concentrated on his non-executive duties for the Board. With little progress to report in these areas, this had understandably not required his regular monthly attendance at Board meetings, allowing Bob Lindsay to firmly establish himself in the role of MD without the previous Chief Executive scrutinising his every move. However, it now appeared that it wasn't only members of the Co-op who had been talking to their constituency MP; the MD had also been in discussions with his 'mentor' concerning the critical cashflow situation and lack of motorcycle orders.

Clearly, Geoffrey had built on Wayne Moulton's 19th May TMA 1981-82 operational plan, which embodied some of the points the Chairman had discussed with him on the January visit to California (chapter 19) – not least, of course, the American disposal of the 600 ECG T140D models originally scheduled for return and sale in the UK. In addition, based on Brenda Price's recent visit to TMA and her discussions with Wayne Moulton, Geoffrey had established a plan to sell 1000 1981/82 motorcycles and $1,000,000 worth of spare parts – a step in the right direction.

The Meriden factory now had motorcycle orders to build for America. The 'catch 22' question was how this could be done without the quick cashflow money previously provided by the ECGD facility.

In the afternoon, the Board of Directors met the Trustees for the quarterly update on Co-op progress. Unfortunately, only John Tomlinson was able to attend. Discussion took place on the following subjects:

a) Level of production and sales

It was agreed that recent production had been encouraging, but concern was expressed over the continuing poor motorcycle sales performance, particularly in the UK. The Directors pointed out that some improvement should be forthcoming as a result of the imminent Limited Edition Bonneville Royal models and police motorcycle projects, but these were not going to solve Triumph's long-term sales problems.

b) Proposed co-operation with BMW

John Tomlinson expressed an interest in the proposed co-operation with BMW, but it was explained that this was still very much at the first contact stage.

c) Co-operative members' morale

In answer to John Tomlinson's question regarding the membership's morale, he was informed that this was generally very high.

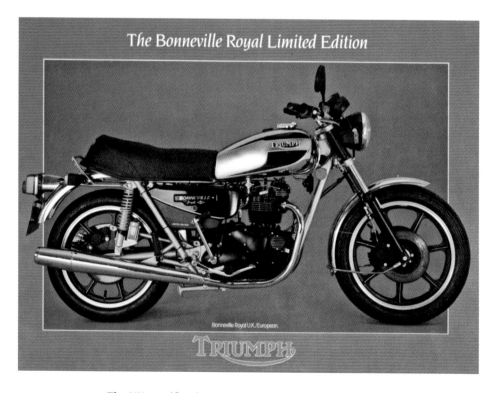

The UK specification Bonneville Royal Limited Edition.
(Brochure picture)

The next Trustees' quarterly meeting was scheduled for 5th October at 4.00pm.

The Bonneville Royal Limited Edition press and dealer launch took place on 9th July and was extremely well received. Both UK and US specification models were based on the standard 1982 T140ES Bonneville, the electric start option being standard on all Royals.

T140LE UK Bonneville Royal (distinguishing features):
Chrome plated petrol tank/gold lined black panels
Silver grey frame/swinging arm
Matt black engine/gearbox unit
2 bing CV carburettors
Marzocchi air shocks
Morris mag alloy wheels
Twin front disc brakes
Royal badged side panels
Extra comfortable dual seat
Retail price including car tax and vat £2245

T140LE US Bonneville Royal (distinguishing features):
Chrome plated petrol tank/gold lined smoked blue panels
Standard black frame and swinging arm
Highly polished engine/gearbox unit
2 bing CV carburettors
Marzocchi air shocks
Wire wheels
Single front disc brake
Polished front forks
Royal badged side panels
Chromium plated headlamp shell
Mini-style 'king and queen' dual seat.
Retail price including car tax and vat £2195

All buyers of the commemorative edition Bonneville Royal models would receive certificates of authenticity. The initial response to the Bonneville Royal models suggested that the Chairman's confidence in the idea had been justified.

The worrying unease regarding Triumph's failure to secure operating budget motorcycle orders, particularly in the UK and Europe, had led to a growing belief that a far more professional sales approach was required. Robin Marlar and Associates Management Consultants' help was enlisted to enable recruitment to take place, and it provided two shortlisted candidates for our consideration. Having witnessed the master salesman Brian Reilly (GEC's seconded Sales Executive responsible for the very successful Silver Jubilee Triumph models in 1977) I had no reservations about asking him to cast his highly experienced eyes over them. Brian rated both as "definitely worth seeing," and felt either individual could do the Triumph job, suggesting it would probably come down to who we felt would best fit in with the existing Triumph team.

The annual two week summer holiday began on Friday 10th July. Under Brian Jones' supervision, a skeleton workforce would continue working on specific tasks for the fortnight. One of these tasks was the clearance and dispatch of the remaining excess motorcycle inventory.

Bonneville Royal American style.

The US specification Bonneville Royal Limited Edition. (Brochure picture)

On Friday 24th July, Geoffrey Robinson and I interviewed Nigel Usher and Alistair Richie (the two shortlisted sales candidates). Both candidates conducted themselves in a highly professional manner, providing an insight into their ability and leaving us spoilt for choice.

On the same day I had to place a notice on the factory boards indicating the Directors' regret that unlike many other local engineering companies, because of the financial state of the Co-op it would not be possible to give members a day's holiday on 29th July, the date of the Royal Wedding. Ironically, all members were desperately needed to produce Bonneville Royals, for which orders were now coming in thick and fast.

Those who did not work during the holiday fortnight returned to the factory on Monday 27th July, suitably refreshed and ready to renew the production battle. Unfortunately, due to lack of component stocks and failure to synchronise Triumph's two-week break with some major suppliers, initial production was restricted. Next year, the factory summer holiday would be two weeks later.

Monday 3rd August was the Directors' monthly meeting, and Geoffrey Robinson was present.

The MD's circulated monthly management report gave the usual operating budget updates, starting with motorcycle sales.

Motorcycle orders received in July	407
– UK	111
– Export	296

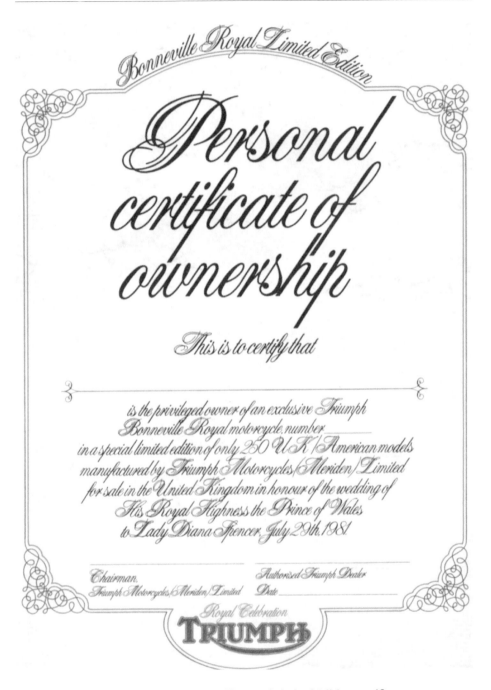

**The commemorative Bonneville Royal Limited Edition certificate.
(Courtesy John Nelson's archive)**

The Bonneville Royal Wedding Limited Edition was presented to the press on Thursday 9th July, and the dealers were advised at the same time.

Royal orders received up to 27th July	189
– UK	105
– TMA	84

An order for ten police motorcycles had also been received from a state in Nigeria.

Having quickly dealt with matters arising from the July meeting, detailed discussion of the Managing Director's report got under way:

MOTORCYCLE SALES

In reply to Geoffrey Robinson's questioning, Peter Britton reported that sales in the UK were down by one half and that export sales were also well down, though not as far below operating budget as the home market. Geoffrey Robinson noted that not only was the volume drop extremely serious, but that the effect of the decline was compounded by the lower financial contribution to overheads provided by export sales. He further observed that special attention was required in France, Germany and Italy, as these were potentially major markets. Geoffrey requested that in future the MD's report gave greater detail of sales performance.

ONGOING MODEL RANGE EXPANSION

Geoffrey Robinson expressed concern over the proposed downmarket extension to the model range, illustrated by the 650cc Tiger Trail and the study of viability of a 125cc motorcycle. He believed that expansion of the model range should be upwards, as it was in the upper price ranges that Triumph would be better able to counter Japanese competition. In view of this, the 8-valve cylinder head needed to be regarded as a corner stone in our development projects, and engineering resources were not to be squandered in other directions if it meant a delay in producing the 8-valve engine. Geoffrey expanded his reasoning, pointing out his belief that to a considerable extent, sales of the Tiger Trail and Thunderbird had been a substitution for sales of Bonnevilles, but they made a lower financial contribution to overheads. In general discussion that followed, it became apparent that whilst the whole Board shared his concern that levels of contribution should not be reduced, there was a strong feeling that sales of the Tiger Trail and Thunderbird had been 'incremental' rather than a 'substitution'. It was agreed that it would be wrong to spend valuable engineering resources on the 125cc project at this time, but that it would be equally wrong to dismiss the project out of hand without establishing whether it had a chance of viability.

PRODUCTION

The Directors noted that production in the first week back from the summer break had been extremely disappointing, with only 30 bikes being built, largely due to component shortages. It was agreed that it was vital this shortfall be pulled back. The MD pointed to the continued production disruption being caused by lack of work in progress, noting that he believed some £60-70,000 of extra work in progress would be necessary to substantially reduce the number of stoppages due to shortages.

TMA

The Board of Directors acknowledged circulation of the TMA operating budget. Geoffrey

Robinson emphasised that attaining the TMA budgeted performance was entirely dependent on the Meriden factory supplying the required motorcycles and spare parts in line with the indicated requirements. In reply to specific questioning regarding profit or loss arising from currency fluctuations of the US dollar from the proposed parity level of $2 to £1, he replied that this would be dealt with through a separate bank account and would not be to the gain or detriment of TMA.

FINANCIAL REPORT
In support of the Financial Directors' circulated review of management performance for July, Rob Murison emphasised the vital importance of the following:
• A rapid return to budgeted production levels for spare parts and motorcycles.
• The revised operating budget of 75 motorcycles (down from 80) and £25,000 worth of spare parts (up from £20,000) each week should not be seen as a soft option; it was vital that both targets were met to enable us to continue in business.

The Financial Director agreed to call an emergency Board meeting if he thought financial circumstances were sufficiently serious to warrant it.

Rob Murison also reported that the representative of the Moratorium Trade Creditors had made his report to the committee, following his visit. The main point was the urgent need of the company to reduce establishment overheads and interest charges. This view exactly corresponded with our own, and whilst the theoretical level of interest charges was being reduced by the proposed settlement with the Government, a real contribution to reduce establishment costs and overdraft interest could only be made by the sale of the 22 acre Meriden factory site. A second sales agent was to be appointed.

With that, the August Board meeting was over. Geoffrey Robinson's decisive re-involvement was certainly welcomed, and whilst the Directors did not agree with all the points he had made, no one could doubt his impact.

There were no longer any communication problems with the membership regarding the necessity of achieving operating budgets, with off-track weekly motorcycle production now exceeding the 75 budgeted level – although with all Bonneville Royals being electric start models, supply problems were starting to be experienced. The need for black frame/swinging arm assemblies for US specification Royals and silver grey for UK Royals, with minimal stocks of finished parts, also caused problems not experienced before. The Mazocchi shock absorbers supply from Italy forced UK Royals to be built with slave dampers; the same bikes had to be fitted with slave wheels when supplies of Morris wheels from America did not materialise on time, both of which caused these bikes to be reworked once supplies arrived.

When the UK supplier of large petrol tanks discontinued production at short notice, we turned to an Italian supplier, taking the opportunity to update the petrol tank style to a more appropriate Triumph shape. The new supplier committed to providing 200 tanks prior to the 1st August, but failed to deliver due to its labour difficulties and some late tooling payment on our part. The first 40 petrol tanks were air freighted on Monday 7th September, with a further 200 leaving Italy by road on Wednesday 9th. The aforementioned production difficulties provide a small snapshot of the factory problems we were experiencing. Triumph's purchasing, manufacturing and financial departments continually had to live with these difficulties, due to insufficient components stock/work in progress. This situation also resulted in additional financial difficulties when it came to dispatching export motorcycle orders, when a container load could not be shipped awaiting specific parts to complete one or two models in the order.

Triumph's presence at Bike 81 at Earls Court was made possible by support from Abbey Garage and the Triumph Owners' Club. (Courtesy London Motorcycle Museum)

A rumour circulated that the MD was considering a more normal factory hierarchy of full-time foremen to supervise manufacturing, replacing the less formal working leading hands system – this certainly did no harm, and seemed to spur the membership on to make the Co-op system work more effectively.

Peter Britton's preparations for the MCN Bike 81 Show at Earls Court were now well advanced. The successful NEC show stand was partly reused, now featuring the Bonneville Royals not exhibited earlier at Birmingham. This sales promotion was only made possible by major help from Abbey Garage and the Triumph Owners' Club.

Bike 81 Show models to be available by the morning of 19th August.

1 TS8-1
1 US TR65 Thunderbird – Red/Black
1 TR7T Tiger Trail – Yellow/Black
1 US T140 LE Royal
1 US T140 K/S – Smokey Blue
1 UK T140 K/S – Smokey Flame
1 UK T140 LE Royal
1 UK T140ES – Twin disc Mag wheels, Black/Gold
1 US T 140ES – Twin disc Mag wheels, Smokey Blue
1 Executive – Full fairing, Smoked Red

America now got involved with the Limited Edition, devising its own Bonneville Royal model specification. (Courtesy Erum Waheed's archive)

The Bonneville Royal Limited Edition had really caught the imagination of Triumph buyers on both sides of the Atlantic, and by the third week of August 325 orders had been received, including 102 TMA-specified 1982 Bonneville Royal models that featured a black European-style petrol tank, side panels and chassis. The tank and side panels had classic Triumph gold pinstriping. The fenders were of the triple chrome plated variety preferred by the US market.

Despite the component supply difficulties during August, production off-track had been good.

Production off-track

Week commencing 3rd August   85

Week commencing 10th August 51

Week commencing 17th August 88

Week commencing 24th August 82

The Spare Parts Department was having great difficulty securing suppliers' immediate reaction to Triumph's spare parts requirements, as these were constantly changing. However, the department was now adequately manned, although there would be a learning period for new members. During the last two weeks of August a marked improvement was achieved; every effort was now being made to achieve the £25,000 a week budget on a regular basis.

Spare parts sales
August 1980   £17,950
August 1981   £66,700
Year to date: 1980   £583,992
Year to date: 1981   £640,115

The value of spare parts picked for TMA during August was £24,500 against a budget requirement of £20,000. September's TMA budget was £17,000.

The circulated MD's monthly management report for the 7th September Board meeting focused upon the disappointing motorcycle sales performance. This could now be judged against Geoffrey Robinson's requested detailed market sales information over the past year.

MOTORCYCLE MARKETS SALES INFORMATION

Sales: UK	1979/80	1980/81
North	608	397
South	833	738
Total end July	1441	1135
Total year	1670	(projected) 1305

Sales: Europe	1979/80	1980/81
Total end July	720	351
Total year	722	(projected) 400

Sales: TMA	1979/80	1980/81
To end July	420	112
Total year	420	703

Sales: ROW	1979/80	1980/81
To end July	1339 (incl 1004 Nigeria)	337
Total year	1339	(projected) 534

MOTORCYCLE ORDERS RECEIVED IN AUGUST 1981
Home   139
Export   142
TMA   326
Total   607

UK MARKET
The home market continued to appear very depressed, and without the Royal Limited Edition motorcycles, sales would have been very poor. The Triumph share of the market continued to deteriorate.

EXPORT MARKETS
Most of Europe was on holiday during August, but the performance of our French and German distributors continued to give cause for concern. It was worth noting the considerable improvement in Switzerland.

Sales	1979/80	1980/81 (end July)
France	263	61
Germany	141	102
Australia	38	202
Switzerland	73	108
Belgium	66	17
Holland	110	18
Sweden	30	10
Japan	114	28

TMA

A big improvement in demand:

Orders in hand   531   Total year to date   703

Motorcycles supplied   172

BONNEVILLE ROYAL MOTORCYCLES – ORDERS UP TO 31ST AUGUST

Model type	Home	Export	TMA spec	Total
UK	99	67	102	268
US	67	28	-	95

TOTAL MOTORCYCLE ORDERS RECEIVED UP TO 31ST AUGUST

UK	1123
ROW	904
TMA	703
Total	2730

SUMMARY

Regarding the overall position of sales, the European and UK markets needed urgent attention. Without the introduction of the Bonneville Royal Limited Edition models, and the dramatic increase in TMA's orders, the company would be in a very serious position with regard to motorcycle orders.

The Board of Directors' meeting on 7th September first concentrated on the below operating budget motorcycle sales position illustrated in the MD's management report. Geoffrey Robinson asked whether in future it would be possible to include market by market comparisons between actual sales and budgeted sales. Extensive discussion then took place, with all the Directors indicating serious concern regarding the immediate requirement to improve the company's sales performance. Bob Haines and Cyril Miller, two of Triumph's fantastic sales/service ambassadors, were back in Nigeria in hot pursuit of the follow-up police and military order.

The Directors noted the generally improving manufacturing performance of the past month, but also recognised that one week's loss of targeted volume had a significant effect on profit.

The MD Bob Lindsay suggested the possibility of an alternative factory hierarchy of full-time foremen replacing the present working leading hands. Following discussion, the Directors felt a return to the pre Co-op factory structure was unlikely to achieve any improvement in performance. However, it was agreed that in future, Alec Bottrill would hold section meetings in an attempt to improve co-ordination. It was also agreed that leading hands were not primarily

**Bob Haines and Cyril Miller are back in Nigeria. Bob demonstrates his practical skills whilst in pursuit of the massive, highly profitable follow-up order.
(Courtesy Bob Haines' archive)**

**Cyril Miller, amongst the many Nigerian friends they made in Lagos, Nigeria.
(Courtesy Bob Haines' archive)**

**Cyril Miller does a little bartering
at a Lagos street market.
(Courtesy Bob Haines' archive)**

**Cyril Miller with one of the many
friends at the Lagos street market.
(Courtesy Bob Haines' archive)**

responsible for section discipline; this was the responsibility of the two organisers, Bill Roberts or Roger Bryant.

Brief discussion of the cause of component supply difficulties determined that the problems had occurred as a result of various unrelated matters, which together had an immediate impact due to restricted work in progress. However, the MD's report provided reassurance that "given adequate materials/work in progress and providing some component outsourcing was undertaken we could meet the production operating budget."

Brian Jones reported that he believed design engineering answers had now been found for the warranty electric starter gear failures and Bing carburettor problems. The improved electric starter design had now completed 3000 road miles and 6000 starts without fault. The modification to the design had been implemented in all new motorcycles being produced. Previously-built motorcycles would be upgraded under the warranty guarantee. Similarly, Bing carburettors would be upgraded to correct the carburation problem.

The Directors were advised that Wayne Moulton's American styling model (inspired by Pennsylvanian Triumph dealer John Monaco) had now arrived at the factory. Wayne had suitably refined the original concept to create a Triumph 'raw street machine' in total contrast to the Japanese competitors. Market introduction was targeted for the spring of 1982. The Design Department was now investigating the TSX production implications.

Geoffrey Robinson introduced the format for TMA reporting, which had been circulated as part of the MD's management report. Brenda Price, TMA's Chairman, had produced for Geoffrey Robinson detailed figures showing how the subsidiary would be monitored.

Richie Horton asked whether Geoffrey Robinson considered that he had sufficient information to monitor TMA's performance. He believed that he had. In his Financial Director's capacity, Rob Murison queried what controls were available to ensure TMA was not now building up slow-moving spare parts stock, as in the past. Geoffrey Robinson believed that this was under regular review, but did not think that it was likely.

The TSX Custom styling project was achieved on a Meriden-size budget by Wayne Moulton's small team in the US and would now be produced. (Promotional picture)

At the end of Rob Murison's review of management performance for the month of August, the Directors moved on to the Financial Director's extremely serious cash movements summary:

"We have only been able to continue trading over the past two weeks because the bank allowed us to use a temporary measure, some bonds derived from our arrangement with ECGD to cover the overrun on the overdraft. This is an extremely short-term concession and I do not believe that we would have been able to have obtained it at all, but for the absence of the Manager on holiday. He returns next week and I believe will insist on an immediate reduction of our overdraft to the £1m limit agreed with the bank. It is important to remember that the £1m limit is itself a concession which the bank has granted and is subject to review in November."

Geoffrey Robinson suggested that in view of the acute cash shortage the meeting should be adjourned for a short while to give him the opportunity to discuss in greater detail the financial situation, and to ascertain what steps might be taken.

The Board meeting was adjourned. When it reconvened, Rob Murison reported that he had made an appointment to meet the National Westminster Bank in London on Wednesday 9th September. The Board agreed that making a final decision as to the factory's working pattern could be postponed until after the meeting with the bank.

Finally in other Board business, Rob Murison indicated that due to lack of progress in the sale of the Meriden factory site, the present agents would be given 3 months' notice and a replacement would be appointed.

The front view of the TSX, Wayne advised, was the vital look revered by so many US buyers. (Promotional picture)

The rear view of the TSX was equally important to US buyers. (Promotional picture)

The Chairman reminded the Board that an Annual General Meeting was almost due. The Financial Director outlined reasons for delays in producing the annual accounts for the year ended 30th September 1980. John Rosamond suggested that in view of this, and the criticism that had been voiced in the past about delays in the annual appointment of Directors, the election of Directors should be performed in the near future, even if the accounts were not then available. The Board of Directors agreed with this approach.

The Chairman also introduced the matter of the annual pay review, making the observation that it would come as no surprise to the Board that in view of the below operating budget performance over the year, funds were unlikely to be available for increasing rates of pay. However, consideration was being given to a productivity scheme whereby bonuses could be earned by the membership for performance in excess of budgeted levels. Detailed plans were being drawn up.

The Board meeting over, the Directors agreed to meet again on Wednesday 9th September when Rob Murison returned from the vital meeting with Triumph's bank in London.

On 9th September, Rob Murison reported to the Board that he had been able to persuade the bank to extend the Co-op's overdraft temporarily, by a further £60,000. This new limit was to be effective until 31st October. On the basis of the cashflow projections he had prepared, the new overdraft limit should be adequate providing the company produced and sold £20,000 worth of spare parts and 80 motorcycles each week.

In response to a question from the MD, the Financial Director agreed that the target of 80 motorcycles could not be met this week, and confirmed that he had not assumed it would.

John Rosamond then called on the Directors to inform the workforce that it was only possible for the Co-op to continue trading without the necessity of short-time working if required targets were met.

Once again these were extremely uncertain times at Triumph. A year had now passed since the original Co-op-saving, HMG debt write-off. This fantastic achievement was supposed to have put the Co-op on the road to viability and long-term security; it hadn't! Below operating budget performance during the year now under review had once again seen Triumph facing closure on several occasions. The Financial Director's final summary of the operating budgets for the year ending 30th September 1981 certainly made sober reading.

	Budget	Actual	Variance
Motorcycle production	3640	2400	-1240
Overtime hours worked	nil	12982	+12982
Motorcycle orders	3640	2537	-1103
Spare parts shipments	£900,000	£700,000	-£200,000
Number Employed	170	200	+30

Everyone at the company, Beneficiaries and Directors alike, was considering what could be done differently in the new financial year, to ensure profitable operation and a future for Triumph and the Co-op.

Towards the end of September, Peter Britton left. The Sales Director would not be replaced. Nigel Usher was appointed Export Sales Manager in October and made an immediate start on improving performance in France. Alastair Ritchie was appointed in November as UK Sales Manager.

The Chairman provided the formal Annual General Meeting notice, having first agreed with the Trustees the Board's proposed course of action: Director elections and then adjourn until Rob Murison was ready to complete the remaining financial AGM business.

The Beneficiary Co-op owners nominated their candidates to become Directors, and the election went ahead at the AGM on 13th November 1981. Of the serving Beneficiary Directors, only the Chairman John Rosamond was re-elected to the Board. The return to the Board of Bill Beattie was welcomed by many, including myself. His forthright contribution had certainly been missed during his absence. George Mackie, a previous Director, also returned. John Birch and Ron Briggs were the other two Beneficiary Directors elected and new to the role, although Ron's son was the Sheet Metal Workers' Director when I returned to Triumph in 1975. The Financial Director/Company Secretary, Rob Murison, and Engineering Director Brian Jones both secured the required AGM Beneficiary votes needed to confirm their continued role as Directors, but Managing Director Bob Lindsay did not! Accordingly, the Beneficiary Committee of eleven, specifically elected to serve for the duration of each AGM, democratically cast their deciding votes. They also confirmed there was no longer sufficient support for the MD to continue his employment at the Co-op.

In view of this happening at the Annual General Meeting – the Beneficiary owners of Triumph dismissing the Managing Director – any lingering doubts that Triumph was still a true worker's co-operative disappeared!

23

MANDATE FOR CHANGE

On reflection, it was not really surprising that the traumatic AGM events occurred. During the month leading up to the meeting, morale at the Co-op had dropped to an absolute all-time low. Yet another cashflow crisis had developed as a result of part-finished motorcycles awaiting bought-out components, completion and dispatch. There for everyone to see by 19th October were 244 motorcycles 'strangling' the Co-op's cashflow – this during a period when the factory had at last been consistently achieving near production targets.

The American supplier of Morris alloy wheels for the UK and TMA variants of the successful Bonneville Royal was partly to blame. A problem at its foundry had stopped supply, and with Triumph's zero factory stock, the impact was immediate. However, with a little of the Co-op ingenuity that we had become so good at, we were at last starting to fight our way out of the problem as the wheel foundry came back on stream. Wayne Moulton at TMA arranged for the American supplier to send shipments of wheels to both the subsidiary in California and the Meriden factory in England. By so doing, the containers of Bonneville Royals now en route across the Atlantic would receive their wheels on arrival at US Triumph dealers. To enable this to happen, the factory sent wheel carriers to TMA for Wayne's staff to complete the alloy wheel assemblies, prior to their shipment to individual dealers.

In the same week that this inter company co-operation was implemented, the workforce at Meriden received an American market bombshell: the cancellation of 142 motorcycle orders for TMA until money committed to earlier shipments had been repaid to the factory, at a time in the very slack winter sales period when the weekly orders averaged at only eight. Devastating news for the workforce, which meant only one thing as far as it was concerned – further short-time working and financial hardship in the run-up to Christmas. Overnight, TMA went from hero to villain. Back came the previously held majority view that the American subsidiary was a millstone round the Co-op's neck whose services should be dispensed with as soon as possible!

It had become generally known that since the debt write-off agreement with HMG, there had been a further £500,000 outflow of cash as a direct result of the Co-op's below operating budget performance. Not surprisingly, the Beneficiary owners of Triumph decided at the AGM to make fundamental changes; it was now a case of determining how those were to be implemented.

Clearly, there was a mandate for change, and the new Directors began immediate discussions regarding the structure of the policy-making Board and management of the company. At the end of a weekend of intensive Board discussion, outline proposals had been drawn up. It was vital that these proposed changes be urgently discussed with the company's bank at its head office in London. Geoffrey Robinson and Rob Murison would undertake this difficult task when our temporary agreed bank overdraft limit had been exceeded by a further £60,000. An early meeting with the bank the next day, Monday, was vital. Past experience suggested that media reporting of the Co-op's traumatic AGM could be expected, and would provide an opportunity for sensational front page stories. If the bank was notified of these developments by a *Financial Times* headline "Anarchy at the Meriden Co-op" or "MD sacked by workers", once the temporary agreed overdraft limit had been breached by a further £60,000 it was likely it would immediately withdraw support.

Whilst Geoffrey and Rob were away at the bank, the Board continued developing the detailed proposals to be placed before the workforce. A formal Board meeting took place on Tuesday 16th November to discuss the bank visit, with a mass meeting of the workforce to take place at 8.30am the following day. If we were going to survive this dramatic event and rectify the excessive motorcycle stock cashflow crisis, there would need to be an immediate return to Co-op normality, albeit within the proposed new Board structure and management policy.

The 17th November mass meeting began at 8.30am. The Chairman indicated that a detailed presentation of the proposed 'new approach' for running the Co-op would take place, with ninety minutes to be allocated at the end for questions. The Co-op would now be based upon open government; every member of the workforce would be involved more than ever before. With this new approach would come a collective responsibility for achieving the desired results. The Board of Directors would meet out of normal working hours on Mondays starting at 4.30pm, and the structure of the new Board would continue for the foreseeable future in the form that had resulted from the departure of the former Managing Director and Sales Director. The Board of Directors would therefore be the five elected Beneficiary Directors, the two Executive Directors (Rob Murison and Brian Jones), and Geoffrey Robinson MP, the Non-Executive Director. In the new circumstances Rob Murison and Brian Jones had agreed to take on a much broader range of responsibilities. Effectively the company had been split into two divisions, Rob Murison becoming the Financial/Commercial Director and Brian Jones the Engineering/Manufacturing Director. For this corporate reorganisation to succeed, the collective responsibility in achieving the Co-op's survival plan, now to be explained, would play a massive part.

Rob Murison outlined to the meeting the vital financial/commercial objectives the Co-op had to achieve if it was to carry on, indicating in detail, department by department, what had to be done to retain the bank's support. Due to the excess motorcycle stocks, the Co-op was presently £60,000 above the agreed absolute maximum temporary overdraft limit. The bank had only agreed to maintain this further extended overdraft level till 9th December, by which time it had to be reduced by £60,000. The financial assumptions put to the bank, based upon which it had agreed to this very temporary concession, were that the excess stock would be cleared by 9th December – to survive we therefore had to achieve this. It would involve continuing the short-time working pattern, and in order to generate the required cash, in the 3-day weeks ending 4th and 9th December we had to manufacture 45 new motorcycles per week, together with the clearance of at least 60 of the excess motorcycle stock. Shipments of spare parts over the three-week period ending 9th December had to average £25,000 per week.

Finally, Rob Murison stated that provided the Co-op was still in business after the 9th December, a start would be made with the planned factory move, regrouping production facilities in the relatively modern structure of the 100,000sq ft Butler Building. Financial calculations that had been completed indicated this move would enable annual operating overhead cost savings of over £100,000. In addition to the move, we would continue efforts to sell the Meriden factory site on two fronts: firstly, the sale of the whole Meriden site, which would involve Triumph relocating elsewhere, and secondly, the sale of the old factory and outbuildings that the move to the Butler Building would free up. The best financial overhead reduction and long-term solution to Triumph's excessive overheads expenditure would be achieved by a move to a smaller, more appropriate factory.

Brain Jones then outlined the engineering/manufacturing approach for the next three weeks until the 9th December survival deadline. This would be along similar lines to his previous manufacturing involvement under the emergency shadow management system, with total mobility of labour needed from everyone. When required, design/development engineering staff would be floated into production areas to meet the vital targets previously mentioned by Rob Murison. Extra days working over and above the standard three days may be required in some areas to achieve the £25,000 per week spare parts quota. His previously adopted, emergency 'what do you want to die of' decision-making process would be applied for the foreseeable future!

At the end of the one hour mass meeting there was a multitude of questions, answered collectively by Executive Management and Beneficiary Directors. Many of the questions concerned the American subsidiary and the 142 cancelled orders. The cashflow difficulties involved in building for the American market were explained, and reassurance given that financing solutions were still being pursued to reinstate those cancelled orders, which helped a little.

As always, the Meriden Co-op Executives and membership rose to the survival challenge, now empowered by a collective responsibility for achieving the desired results. Having successfully implemented the survival plan, a Board meeting was called on 7th December. Brian Jones was able to report the following impressive progress:

SURVIVAL PLAN PRODUCTION
110 new motorcycles manufactured and 195 motorcycles dispatched. However, with the cutback in the motorcycle orders, the track build requirement was now zero. It was therefore not planned to run the track again for the next two weeks.

There were still in excess of 100 unfinished motorcycles between the end of the assembly track and dispatch; labour would now be concentrated in this area to clear the backlog. The restricted availability of rear Morris alloy wheels could affect this clearance programme. The machine shop would continue to concentrate on spare parts, firstly against Bill Beattie's list of current spare parts priorities, followed by production of non-current spare parts. A concentrated effort was also planned to clear the list of customer motorcycles due to return to the factory for various warranty guarantee work that dealers were not able to carry out themselves. With engine assembly not taking place, surplus labour was now available to undertake this work.

PRODUCT
The drawing release of the eight-valve engine was now virtually complete, with installation in the TS8-1 AV frame proceeding. It was originally planned to install the eight-valve engine in Bonneville cycle parts, creating the TSS model for the 1982 NEC Motorcycle Show. In view of lack of orders and the critical cashflow situation, efforts were being made to bring forward the TSS market introduction. The design office was about to start the drawings for the TSX; this was originally intended as job one for July 1982.

Brian Baldwin's purchasing department was examining further cost reductions. However, the vast majority of these involved testing, so the benefits were therefore protracted. A visit to the Meriden factory was planned by Derbi Motorcycles of Spain, for Wednesday 9th December; possibilities of future mutual co-operation were to be discussed.

MILAN MOTORCYCLE EXHIBITION
Brian Baldwin and Brian Jones visited this exhibition with a view to establishing personal contacts with existing Italian motorcycle component suppliers. The possibility of procurement for Triumph was assessed, with a view to improving the product and reducing costs. Only time would tell if the visit was worthwhile, but we were optimistic.

FACTORY RELOCATION TO THE BUTLER BUILDING
Alec Bottrill was now concentrating totally on the factory relocation plan. To enable this with the least amount of interruption, Bill Roberts had taken control of the machine shop. As part of the factory move, consideration was also being given to the provision of a motorcycle service centre and Triumph Social Club.

PERSONNEL
Bill Roberts assumed control of the machine shop (mentioned earlier).

Mr Martyn Roberts was to join Triumph as Chief Development Engineer on 4th January 1982, and as such help ease the increased senior engineering workload.

Unable to attend in person, Rob Murison provided financial figures for the Board. Phil Bragg, Rob's Financial Controller, would play an increasingly important support role.

A Board meeting was called on 18th December, specifically to discuss TMA. TMA's unpaid Chairman, Brenda Price, and Geoffrey Robinson MP, who had assumed responsibility for US sales of 1000 motorcycles and $1m worth of spare parts, were both present. They agreed when possible to attend future meetings.

Bill Beattie stressed the concerns expressed by the workforce regarding the American subsidiary. During initial discussions, Geoffrey Robinson and Rob Murison agreed that at present, TMA was on budget. As of 31st December 1981, TMA would be in line with its agreed cashflow returns. The expected inflow of $200,000 from TMA would enable the Financial Director to pay postdated cheques that were now falling due. Brenda Price was asked to confirm the American TMA motorcycle order situation for the period immediately after Christmas, and the availability of finance to pay for them. Rob Murison felt that in view of the start date of the American spring selling season, further motorcycle builds should be delayed to ease the cashflow situation. However, if we delayed, as in the past the season would be missed. A financial solution needed to be found. Although Geoffrey Robinson was able to confirm his commitment to selling 1000 motorcycles in the US market in line with the agreed budget, the major difficulty would be how builds of motorcycles to sustain factory production were financed. Brian Jones reminded that if further factory builds of motorcycles for America were to go ahead in the New Year, manufacturing would require a detailed breakdown showing each model type and numbers involved. With very little component stock, this would enable the factory to schedule its manufacture. Geoffrey Robinson requested 100 available to sell in America during February, 200 in March, 250 in April, 150 in May and 50 in June: a total of 750 motorcycles. Rob Murison asked if it would be possible to sell direct to American dealers, bypassing the time delays presently involved in the public warehousing procedure. This would secure a significantly quicker return on finance to the factory.

The possibility of free-floor planning using the Borg Warner facility was discussed. There was concern expressed that the projected American sales were optimistic – TMA still owed $200,000 to the Meriden factory on motorcycles already supplied! In these circumstances, floor planning would not continue.

Next we dealt with the supply of TMA spare parts. As the factory was already £36,000 ahead with the required budget, it was agreed that in future only urgent parts would be air freighted. George Mackie, the head of production control, would be provided with a three month programme of future spare parts requirements.

This extremely forthright and candid Board meeting was certainly in keeping with the Co-op's new 'total open government' policy. The majority of the Beneficiary Directors had for the first time been party to the difficult financial reality of tying up the Co-op's very limited cash resources in motorcycles produced for its main market, America. Without the ECGD facility that in the past provided relatively immediate cash returns for motorcycle export sales to America, the Co-op was now confronted with building motorcycles for America and running out of cash, or a factory already on short time running out of motorcycle orders.

The mood of the workforce in the run up to the festive holidays was indeed very sombre as knowledge of the Co-op's financial predicament spread. At least members would be able to forget matters at work for a little while whilst celebrating Christmas and the New Year with their families.

With the enjoyable holidays over, it was obvious that all that could be done in 1982 was to stretch our meagre cash resources and pursue a more long-term solution. An attempt would be made to hang on until the anticipated spring UK sales demand that would accompany the planned early introduction of the two new, more profitable models: the 8-valve TSS and the TSX Lowrider. The UK market also offered the quickest cash return. In the meantime, we would build whatever motorcycle orders we had, including those for America when cashflow allowed.

Rob Murison, Brenda Price and Wayne Moulton considered that 3x28 small containers of T140ES Bonnevilles and 1x56 large container of TMA Bonneville Royals were required during January/early February. Although the Financial Director continually tried to speed up the return of cash committed to motorcycles ordered by TMA, the financial policy born out of necessity inevitably resulted in further financial crisis.

Once again the bank was extremely concerned. The maximum overdraft limit had been considerably exceeded yet again, and the latest cashflow projections indicated further rises would occur during mid-February. Although the President of TMA, Wayne Moulton, felt some cash would be forthcoming, a total sum of $1m still remained outstanding to the Meriden factory. Whilst the Chairman felt the bank was unlikely to foreclose on the Co-op at this time, it was generally accepted by all that a crash programme of cash collection was needed. The Directors agreed that to regain the bank's confidence, it was vital that cash be collected more quickly. There would be no further investment by way of tying up cash in motorcycles for TMA. No factory production of motorcycles would take place in the following week.

By the last week of January, although steps had been taken to improve cash collection, target income had not yet been achieved. Outstanding export debts from Trinidad and Australia were expected to be paid during the week, although inflow of cash from TMA was still causing the Financial Director grave concern. Although Geoffrey Robinson was not present at the Board meeting, he had advised the Chairman that he believed the only solution to the Co-op's cashflow problems was to lay the company off and await the inflow of money from debtors. Having thoroughly discussed the situation, the Board felt that it would be wrong to lay the company off on the eve of the London dealer seminar/TSS press launch. Limited TSS production was to begin in the first week in February, and the crash cash collection process would continue. Brian Jones reported that 50 sets of TSX parts were also being purchased or manufactured, to enable assembly of this new model to begin in March.

The Chairman advised that Rob Murison had indicated he should be in a position in the very near future to provide a timetable for the Directors and Trustees to reschedule the adjourned AGM. A formal notice period of 21 days would be required.

On 29th January an emergency Board meeting had to take place. A disturbing rumour was circulating the Meriden factory: the agreed cashflow crisis budget of £2500 for the London dealer seminar/TSS press launch at the Kensington's Royal Garden Hotel was being exceeded! Rob Murison confirmed that the budget was based on UK Sales Manager Alastair Richie's detailed costing, and he would be expected to stick to it. Alastair was requested to join the Board meeting, and provided an excellent presentation and explanation of exactly what he had planned. Further information regarding this vital promotional event would now be provided to the workforce. The rumours, it seemed, had been without foundation.

At the scheduled 1st February Board meeting, Rob Murison informed us that the latest cashflow projections indicated a peak would be reached the following week. In these circumstances it was extremely important that the Directors' decision to continue to trade on the behalf of the creditors was correct. The Directors recognised that this was certainly the case, based upon the introduction of two new models, the belief that a Nigerian order was imminent, and the new selling season providing a more profitable situation – all of which would better protect the creditors' position.

On the general financial front, Rob Murison indicated that whilst our present achievements were right on target, earlier slippage would ensure the maximum overdraft level would be exceeded in the next two weeks. There was a choice: plan an approach to obtain higher levels of credit, or close the company for a period of three weeks. Bill Beattie suggested that Geoffrey Robinson's offer to personally intervene with the creditors may well achieve a satisfactory result. Rob Murison advised that it was his own intention to contact the major suppliers with a view to agreeing credit arrangements in the very near future.

Rob then reported that he had asked TMA's President Wayne Moulton to research the possibility of factoring the debts resulting from motorcycle sales to American dealers. He then spoke on the telephone to Wayne Moulton regarding this possibility, and in an attempt to gain an up-to-the-minute report on inflow of TMA cash. Following the telephone conversation Rob Murison confided in the Board that he was still extremely concerned regarding the situation at TMA. He doubted due to lack of detailed knowledge of the American subsidiary, his own ability to put together a meaningful cashflow projection. He would discuss the situation further with Brenda Price and Geoffrey Robinson.

Not for the first time, it was the view of the Board that it seemed likely that Rob Murison would have to visit TMA in order to make a first-hand assessment of the financial situation and its implications for the Meriden factory. In addition, the Board suggested that Chairman John Rosamond, who had visited TMA on a number of previous occasions, may well be of assistance if Rob Murison chose to visit.

On 4th February Rob Murison tabled a financial survival plan for the Board's consideration. The plan commencing 8th February would deal with the immediate cashflow crisis over the next two weeks.

Week 1 – Assembly/finishing

The assembly/finishing side of the business would complete as many motorcycles as possible working five days, Monday to Friday.

Week 2 – Assembly/finishing

The whole of the assembly/finishing side of the business would be laid off Monday to Friday, and in receipt of guaranteed week payment where appropriate.

Week 1 – Manufacturing areas

All manufacturing areas of the business would be laid off, and in receipt of guaranteed week payment where appropriate.

Week 2 – Manufacturing areas

All of the manufacturing areas would work five days, Monday to Friday.

Detailed Board discussion then took place, including a possible alternative proposal put forward by the Chairman whereby everyone at Triumph would work five days in each of the two weeks in question, but receive only three days pay. The owed four days pay from these two weeks would be paid in March when the present cashflow crisis was over. Although there were reservations from Brian Jones about the machine shop being underutilised, George Mackie felt he could use this capacity to do work he could never get done under normal circumstances; raw materials were available!

The Chairman's alternative proposal was agreed by the Board and placed before a mass meeting for acceptance.

At the behest of the Board, Rob Murison and John Rosamond visited TMA in California to try and establish a better financial understanding between the factory and its American subsidiary. It was hoped that based upon this new awareness, future cashflow projections would be achieved. If the Co-op's credibility with the bank was ever to be returned to an acceptable level, future inflow of cash from TMA would have to be as forecast.

Whilst we were away in America, Richard and Mopsa English turned up at the Meriden factory. They had previously written to the Chairman indicating their intention to circumnavigate the world by motorcycle, following in the footsteps of Ted Simon. With a surname like English, they had to be aboard a Triumph, and the recently introduced 650cc Thunderbird was chosen. The Chairman's reply to their original letter took the form of an open-ended invitation to the Meriden factory – "come along and we will talk about your plans." Unfortunately, John Rosamond was not there to greet them when they arrived, but George Mackie did an excellent job deputising. He organised the required new Thunderbird at a factory ex-works price – it was all the financially strapped Co-op could do at that time, but by all accounts the pair were happy, as it was the best offer they had received! The Chairman would see them several months later when they returned fully prepared to begin their global adventure.

After a nights sleep, Wayne Moulton collected us from our Los Angeles hotel and transported us to TMA. On arrival we made an immediate start. Some of the American systems were initially difficult to understand, but having visited several times before I was able to help Rob a little, and he very quickly got up to speed. There was no doubt in my mind that the Co-op had always been well blessed with extremely thorough, hard working, competent accountants, and Rob was certainly in that mould. He soon set about gaining an in-depth understanding of the TMA financial operation. Wayne Moulton and his staff could not have been more helpful, and a friendly banter easily developed. At one point shortly after our arrival, a phone rang in an adjacent office and was answered in a loud American voice – "Hi Meriden, what's that, send money? How much would you like?" The scene was set for an interesting visit! Most of the financial opportunities had already been explored by Brenda Price and Wayne Moulton in an effort to improve TMA's profitability and thus its benefits for the Triumph factory, and these were looked at again. There was no doubt in my mind that when Rob Murison returned to Meriden, his understanding of TMA's financial position would be vastly improved. Whether that knowledge would reassure him or make him even more concerned, we would have to see.

The Chairman returned to England three days earlier than Rob Murison, who was to complete the remaining arranged meetings with the various banking institutions. On my return to the Meriden factory on Friday 19th February, an early 7.15am Board meeting was scheduled to provide the Directors with some preliminary information about the TMA visit.

1) Cashflow

On the spot investigation of the cashflow situation at TMA had revealed that it was in fact approximately $25,000 ahead of its projected levels. So far, total net receipts by Triumph Meriden had been $850,000.

Motorcycle stocks held by TMA:

T140D 1979	282
T140E 1982	13
TMA Royals	nil
Executives	nil
Total motorcycle stock	295

During the visit, in an effort to speed up cash inflow to the factory, the possibility of shipping a further sixty 1979 T140D Bonneville Specials back to Europe was investigated. No decision had

Whilst visiting TMA, the author and Rob Murison managed to make a brief visit with Wayne Moulton to Performance Machine, the manufacturer of Morris Wheels. (Author's archive)

yet been taken. A deadline for selling the remaining D-model stock had been set for the end of the month. To enable this deadline to be met, Wayne Moulton had been given the flexibility to offer slightly reduced prices for volume commitment, free delivery and various other sales aids in an effort to generate money more quickly.

Whilst in America, Rob Murison had been trying to reduce the 12-week repayment time cycle between the factory building the motorcycles and TMA paying for them. He would report further if he had succeeded on his return. His efforts to recover all or part of the Borg-Warner floor-planning recourse bond had not proved successful.

2) Spare parts

TMA would fall short of its spare parts budget by at least $300,000. As was becoming clear in the UK and the rest of the world, demand for Triumph spare parts seemed to be decreasing.

A subsidiary and parent company misunderstanding about the definition of current spare parts had been discovered: TMA identified current spare parts as all spare parts for Triumph twins since the 1975 formation of the Co-operative, i.e. the current owners of Triumph, whereas the Triumph factory's definition of current spare parts was those parts that fit the current year's production! The factory's non-supply of TMA 'current' spare parts – those from 1975 to 1982 that the factory defined as non-current – could therefore make up some of TMA's spare parts budget shortfall. It had also been discovered that TMA had managed to accumulate a further slow-moving spare parts stock of $130,000. These were described as slow-moving TMA current spare parts for Triumph twins. A list of these spare parts was being produced for Brian Baldwin, to assess feasibility of use in new motorcycles.

3) TMA operating position

TMA would continue to strive for self-financing on sales of spare parts and interest payments from the $250,000 Borg-Warner and $50,000 Maryland bonds. All finance from sales of the remaining D-models and 1982 motorcycles would be transferred entirely to Triumph Meriden. In these circumstances, where a shortfall on spare parts turnover/profit seemed inevitable, Wayne Moulton was researching other avenues to cover present operating expenditure.

4) Ongoing cashflow situation

Following his in-depth look at TMA and the ongoing cash inflow from that source, Rob Murison felt Triumph Meriden would experience a further financial crisis at the end of March. It would therefore be necessary for the factory to reduce the bank overdraft facility to a maximum of £1.1m by 31st March, and it appeared that the three-day working week would continue for the foreseeable future.

Bill Beattie commented that Rob Murison's cashflow strategy to date had depended on speeding up repayments of outstanding cash from TMA. Following his on-the-spot investigation, it now looked like this would no longer be possible. An early meeting with Rob Murison and Geoffrey Robinson to discuss a new strategy was essential. As a holding position, the Board agreed the three-day working week would continue, the one exception being the move to the Butler Building. The machine tool movement that was gathering momentum also had to be continued.

5) Sale of remaining D-model stock to Mexico

A potential Mexican sales contact made through GEC was showing interest in purchasing the remaining D-model stock. This sales prospect was being followed up by Rob Murison whilst still at TMA.

6) TSX model sales potential

Wayne Moulton believed that TMA could sell 1000 TSX models in America provided the first ones arrived no later than the end of June 1982, ready for the 1983 spring selling season.

The Board meeting closed at 8.15am.

With the long-awaited introduction of the 8-valve TSS model imminent, very limited subcontract supplies of cylinder heads and cylinder barrels from Weslake, plus the new Meriden machined crankshafts, were now starting to flow through to the engine bench for assembly. The whole workforce at the Meriden factory eagerly awaited the UK motorcycle market response. Ever since Jack Wilson's 'Big D of Texas' rider Jon Minonno was clocked at 152mph in practice at Daytona, we knew we had a potential winner. It was common knowledge in the factory that Alastair (Jock) Copland was regularly achieving MIRA standing quarters in below 13 seconds, with terminal speeds of 102/103mph and a best top speed of 126mph on the well worn TSS pre-production prototype. At last, Triumph had a competitive sports model to give the company back its performance image, lacking in recent years with the ever faithful Bonneville. Loyal Triumph enthusiasts had dreamt of this day for a long time.

Alastair Richie's Kensington Royal Gardens Hotel, London dealer seminar/TSS press launch of the 8-valve Triumph TSS on Thursday 25th February went extremely well. Excited dealers and press were suitably impressed. Coinciding with the nearing completion of the Government debt write-off, there was much to celebrate and many positive stories appeared in the specialist press. Firm orders were placed by dealers and there was a clamour for road test bikes from the weekly and monthly motorcycle press. First to appear were the road tests in *Motor Cycle News* and *Motor Cycle Weekly*. Both were impressive, confirming Triumph's own feelings regarding

The high performance Triumph 750cc TSS classic British sports motorcycle.
(Brochure picture)

the performance potential of the 8-valve TSS. Both also mentioned that the new crankshaft had made a major contribution to reducing the inherent parallel twin levels of vibration that previously existed with the Bonneville. The last paragraph of the Terry Snellings *MCN* TSS road test said it all: "It could be argued that it's the best bike to roll out of Meriden. It could certainly be a British classic for nearly half the price of a Hesketh."

The black with gold lines, classic looks of a traditional high performance British sport motorcycle, capable of holding its own in the 1980s, certainly captured the imagination. Triumph's usual fantastic road-handling once again had performance to match. The specification of the TSS was as follows:

Engine type OHV parallel twin, four stroke (4 valves per cylinder)
Bore 76mm (2.992in)
Stroke 82mm (3.228in)
Capacity . . . . 744cc (45cu in)
Gearbox type 5-speed
Carburettors . . . . twin 34mm chokes
Tyre front 410x19
Tyre rear 410x18
Brake front . . . . twin 9.8in (250mm) disc
Brake rear . . . . single 9.8in (250mm) disc
Wheelbase 56in (1422mm)
Seat height 31in (787.4mm)
Dry weight 410lb (186.4kg)
Fuel capacity . . . . 4.0 imp gals (18.2 litres)
Electrics . . . . 12v alternator
Ignition system . . . . electronic
Electric start . . . . standard
Instruments . . . . tachometer and speedometer
Optional extra . . . . cast aluminium wheels

The surge of public optimism created by the TSS launch and the apparent improving future prospects for Triumph, did not in fact reflect the reality of the cash-starved Meriden factory's situation. However, the launch of the TSS had brought firm UK orders for this much more desirable and profitable Triumph model, and we now had to produce them.

We did not make a very good start. A Board meeting was called on 18th March to consider a two-week layoff of all production areas to secure cash, with the exception of those that enabled motorcycles and spare parts to be dispatched. At the meeting, Rob Murison outlined the up to date financial situation. We were £35,000 down on expected cash, although he believed this would be made good by week commencing 29th March. George Mackie asked if five-day working (i.e. the 45-hour week spring/summer practice) would be possible on the factory's return, commenting that if this was not possible, cashflow would continue to be seriously interrupted in future weeks. Rob Murison agreed, and felt that it was feasible to build 28 motorcycles for Australia and forty 8-valve UK TSS models very soon.

Bill Beattie asked for exact details of the parts available for building into finished motorcycles, in view of the present financial situation. Brian Jones and George Mackie conferred, and agreed that 37 sets of materials would be available on Monday 22nd March to build TSS motorcycles. George Mackie indicated that previous discussions with Brian Jones had determined that a further commitment of £10,000 to purchase components would enable a build of 45 motorcycles. In view of the fact that there were presently 98 orders for the 8-valve TSS model,

Bill Beattie suggested that the Sales Department should approach the dealer network for its support in paying cash on delivery during the present difficulties. Rob Murison thought this was a good idea; arrangements would be made for delivery drivers to collect cheques. Commenting on the present three-day week working pattern, George Mackie said that Rob Murison would not presently raise cheques to enable the purchase of components for week commencing 29th March. Rob agreed, stating that he had no alternative but to adopt this stance. Bill Beattie asked Rob Murison for a reassurance that all incoming money would be re-invested in the production of new motorcycles, otherwise Triumph was likely to miss the start of the spring selling season; he felt this was a fundamental point to which he wanted a yes or no answer. Rob Murison replied that he would make money available for the Purchasing Department as soon as possible; $60,000 was expected from TMA that week, with a further $110,000 for week commencing 29th March. In view of this, he felt Triumph would then be able to work a whole week profitably. A mass meeting was to be called to advise the workforce of the cashflow position, and subsequent need for a two-week layoff.

Moving to the position of the Co-op's bank, the National Westminster, Bill Beattie asked Rob Murison where it stood in supporting Triumph's finances to continue building motorcycles. Was it the case, as it appeared, that once the D-models had been completely sold and the money returned from TMA, the bank was likely to cut Triumph's throat? Rob Murison stated that this was certainly not the case, providing we did not exceed the £1,148,000 overdraft limit. In the event that Triumph exceeded this limit, the Bank Manager had categorically stated that he would bounce cheques. The idea was to get the overdraft below that ceiling, and keep it there. If all the D-models at TMA had been sold by now, the money raised would have already been benefiting the Meriden factory's situation.

The Directors unanimously agreed that in future, further short-time working as a short-term expediency to buy time was out of the question.

24

MAKE OR BREAK

The run-up to the annual International Motorcycle Show at the NEC was always hectic. With the majority of the workforce laid off, pressure was even greater for the 1982 event. Full-time working was due to restart on Monday 28th March, leaving just 10 days including the weekend until Thursday 8th April, the press day.

The 1982 NEC show would provide the first opportunity for the general public to see Triumph's 1982/83 model range, the stars of which were the two completely new Super Sports and Custom models: the TSS and TSX. There were no doubts in anyone's mind that Triumph now had an impressive range of models – the best for a very long time. Our future depended on UK motorcycle buyers agreeing.

TRIUMPH'S MODEL RANGE FOR 1982/83

TR65 Thunderbird (UK Spec)	£1875
TR65 Thunderbird (US Spec)	£1899
TR6T Tiger Trail	£1975
T140E Bonneville (UK Spec)	£2025
T140E Bonneville (US Spec)	£2049
T140ES Bonneville (UK Spec)	£2075
T140ES Bonneville (US Spec)	£2099
TSX Custom	*£2249
TSS 8-Valve Sports	£2399
T140ES AV Executive	£2449
TS8-1	£3149

NB Listed UK retail prices include taxes
*TSX available from May 1982

Substantial firm orders had to be placed following the show. This was not an option; it was make or break for Triumph. Potential buyers simply had to react positively by putting their hands in their pockets and placing sustained numbers of orders for the exhibited models, especially the more profitable TSS and TSX. It was only through this that Triumph would be able to secure further time to reduce the excessive, crippling, Meriden factory overheads, and continue pursuing long-term viability.

During the two-week layoff, small teams had conducted the usual cash generation exercises, finishing and dispatching motorcycles and spare parts. Machine tool movements to the Butler Building had also continued. In addition, finishing touches to the in-house work on the NEC show stand had been completed. Deliveries of 8-valve cylinder heads and cylinder barrels from Weslake continued to be poor.

The factory returned to full-time working on Monday 28th March. The majority of TSS orders taken at the February dealer seminar remained outstanding, and everything was now being done to ensure that this year's crucial NEC show was the best ever – that is, everything that did not involve spending more money!

During the layoff, I had honoured my undertaking to the Triumph dealers who attended the London dealer seminar. The dealers had made it crystal clear that Triumph's point of sale showroom presence was nonexistent. If the factory expected dealers to improve their sales performance, then at least a colour brochure and poster showing the 1982/83 model range was required; dealers were prepared to purchase this point of sale promotional literature, but the factory had to provide it first. Whilst their message could not have been clearer, and was heard by all present at the seminar, when discussed back at the factory in the atmosphere of the latest crisis, point of sale material inevitably was not seen as a particularly high priority. However, I had indicated that I would take a personal interest in seeing what could be done, believing that nothing happened in business until we made a sale. As it was UK motorcycle sales in particular that were a major concern, a way had to be found to provide the dealers with this basic retail requirement.

The dealers had given me a clear brief of what they would like from us – a colour brochure and poster, something different from the standard Japanese approach, emphasising the unique and different qualities of Triumph ownership. With this in mind, I set about investigating what could be done on a do-it-yourself, low budget basis, with a little bit of help from Triumph's friends! Soon, excellent and very cost-effective photographs of all the models in the 1982/83 range had been taken, together with the different features of each model. Also, the brief asked for photographic evidence emphasising that it was not only Triumph's motorcycles that were different; the Meriden factory provided that additional unique selling point, and as such would also be featured in the brochure. Now with a *lot* of help from Triumph's friends, I had a clear picture in my mind of how the brochure could look; the poster or posters, however, were a different matter. Armed with my information, several printers were contacted. Their production costs varied wildly, seemingly dependent on just how busy they were at that time. One printer that was extremely quiet was very enthusiastic and helpful, and detailed discussions took place, during which it transpired that the most cost-effective way of producing a colour brochure and poster was by combining the two. The full-size Triumph colour poster would show all the 1982/83 model range, plus an iconic photograph of the new TSS 8-valve engine. On the reverse of the poster, the 8 x A4-size pages of the brochure would be printed, also in colour. As part of the printing/production process, the poster would be folded to create the combined Triumph poster/brochure.

A detailed and fully costed proposal was now prepared. The dealers, as they said, would pay for their point of sale material; however, there was still the question of how those for the general public at the NEC show were to be funded. Always up for a challenge, the Chairman suggested to the Co-op's Purchasing Department that it seek a small contribution from each of Triumph's famous British specialist motorcycle component suppliers; in previous years they had always enjoyed free exposure in our brochures. Apparently the response to our suggestion was astonishment, and "no" – their support was duly reciprocated in the brochure!

Hearing the efforts that had been made to provide the do-it-yourself promotional literature, Rob Murison came up with the required cash to enable production to go ahead. The final detailed layouts for the printers were now produced. Brian Jones and Martyn Roberts provided the technical input for the model specifications, and I produced the remaining text, including the brochure back cover:

TRIUMPH – A SPECIAL FEELING YOU WILL NEVER FORGET
The Triumph factory at Meriden is situated in the heart of the Midlands, looking out over open countryside. The previous Triumph factory in Coventry was completely destroyed in the famous Blitz, forcing a new purpose built motorcycle factory to be erected at Meriden. The 'Bull-dog spirit' which was created amongst the workforce then, has been handed down through the generations and prevails just as strongly today. This is what makes Triumph bikes individually special. Triumph enthusiasts travel many thousands of miles each year to visit their own personal Mecca, the Triumph factory.

As Triumph motorcycles are almost totally hand-built, the workforce's dedication maintains a high level of quality control, as shown in the present model range. Commencing in the frame shop, Triumph's highly skilled craftsmen are very evident, with welding standards higher than achieved on any other production motorcycle.

Our machine shop manufactures all the major motorcycle engine components with highly qualified and experienced machinists, who number in total more than one third of the Triumph workforce. Close tolerances are essential on components such as crankcases, cylinder heads, cylinder barrels, conrods, crankshafts, flywheels, camshafts and many more. Triumph's experience concentrates on engine component production, leaving the more specialised supply of such items as carburettors, electrics, brakes and tyres to the subcontract manufacturers.

Triumph's 'keep it simple' design policy enables engine and motorcycle assembly to be straightforward in practice, the underlying objectives being that if assembly at the factory is kept as simple as possible then those Triumph owners who so wish can undertake their own running maintenance. With this in mind engine and motorcycle assembly is undertaken by Triumph's highly skilled fitters working in small groups. On leaving the track, all motorcycles pass to the rolling road test cells, where assimilated road conditions enable the Triumph high performance engine and all other motorcycle functions to be extensively checked. Following satisfactory completion of these procedures final adjustments are made, seats and petrol tanks fitted prior to dispatch. Having spent a great deal of time on attention to detail Triumph's crowning glory is in its final finish, achieved by highly skilled paint-shop personnel. Over the many years of experience, it has been found that there is no shortcut to quality, it only comes with painstaking attention to detail, all of which is totally worthwhile when one views the finished Triumph motorcycle.

Triumph – A special feeling you will never forget.

The brochure/poster was well received by Triumph dealers, who paid up with a smile. It was hoped that there would be a similar response from potential customers, following what they had seen at the NEC show.

On 30th March the Board of Directors met the Co-op's Trustees for the quarterly update on the Co-op's position. Bill Beattie, Geoffrey Robinson MP and John Haynes were unable to attend.

Rob Murison outlined for the Trustees the company's precarious financial situation, explaining that Triumph's present weekly expenditure was totally dependent on received incoming cash. Whilst trading with UK dealers and overseas distributors affected this situation,

Triumph's "A special feeling you will never forget" 1982/83 model range brochure/poster was well received by all concerned. (Point of sale promotional material)

the major influence on the factory's financial position was receipts from sales of D-model motorcycles in America. The introduction of the higher-priced TSS 8-valve model and the TSX Lowrider motorcycle could make a much larger contribution towards factory overheads. If sold in the expected numbers, a significant positive impact on the Co-op's financial situation would be achieved. Triumph was also on the verge of receiving a £135,000 order for 100 military/police motorcycles from Uganda. The latest information from Geoffrey Robinson regarding the follow up Nigerian order was that he still felt Triumph would receive the order; it was just a matter of time.

Rob apologised to the Trustees regarding the lack of a firm date for the reconvened Annual General Meeting. At the moment there were disagreements with the auditors regarding the Moratorium Trade Creditors' debt, trade balances, and how to introduce the ECGD write-off into the awaited annual accounts. However, the AGM was likely to go ahead by the end of April, and the Trustees would be informed of a definite date in the next nine to ten days.

Rob then reminded the Trustees of the Co-op's seasonal production strategy of 45

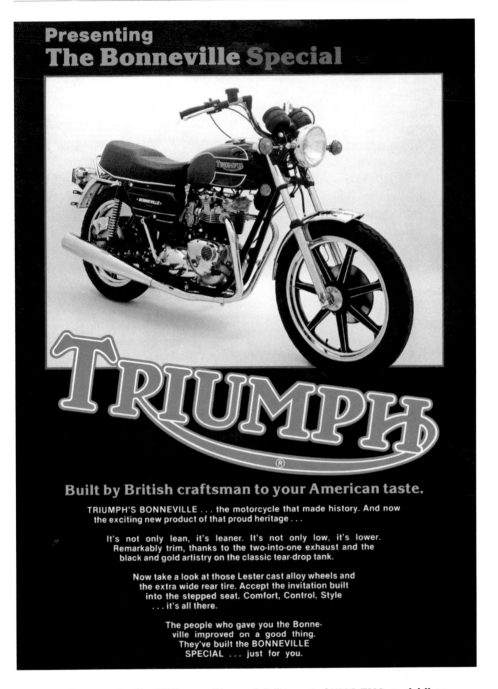

Presenting
The Bonneville Special

TRIUMPH ®

Built by British craftsman to your American taste.

TRIUMPH'S BONNEVILLE . . . the motorcycle that made history. And now the exciting new product of that proud heritage . . .

It's not only lean, it's leaner. It's not only low, it's lower. Remarkably trim, thanks to the two-into-one exhaust and the black and gold artistry on the classic tear-drop tank.

Now take a look at those Lester cast alloy wheels and the extra wide rear tire. Accept the invitation built into the stepped seat. Comfort, Control, Style . . . it's all there.

The people who gave you the Bonneville improved on a good thing. They've built the BONNEVILLE SPECIAL . . . just for you.

The slow-moving T140D Bonneville special discounted HMG, TMA stock bikes. (TMA brochure picture)

motorcycles per week during autumn/winter months, which equated with three-day working, and inevitably incurred substantial losses. These losses had to be made good by corresponding increased hours and production in the spring and summer months, in order to break even. The recent London dealer seminar/launch of the TSS 8-valve motorcycle had generated orders, which we were endeavouring to supply. Whilst we had carried orders for America throughout the winter months, we had not been able to finance the building of many of them, due to the 90 day period it took for Triumph to receive the original production investment. Touching on his and John Rosamond's visit to TMA, Rob explained the lengths to which he had sought alternative finance without success. This finance would have enabled the building of the aforementioned motorcycles for America.

John Tomlinson asked Rob Murison why the D-models had not all been sold yet. It was felt that this was due to the fact these motorcycles were now three years old, and the extremely poor weather conditions in America had led to a late spring.

Ron Marston asked what Triumph's present weekly motorcycle build potential was. A theoretical production capacity of 80 motorcycles per week was confirmed once the membership had hit the restricted short-time target production of 120 motorcycles, set for completion during February.

Information on the sale of the factory site was requested by John Tomlinson. Rob explained that there were two main runners at the moment interested in the purchase of the Meriden site: Espley-Tyas, looking at a potential residential development, and ICFC, who was indicating a purchase and lease back, plus re-equipment of the Meriden plant. Espley-Tyas was talking of an offer in the region of £800,000, and ICFC £700,000. Both offers excluded provision to be made by the purchaser for conversion of the private Triumph sewage system to public mains.

Brian Jones now explained to the Trustees the position regarding the factory reorganisation and move. The regrouping of manufacturing facilities was three fifths complete; over three hundred machine tools had now been repositioned. The long-term strategy was, of course, to attack the prohibitive overhead costs of the Meriden factory on two fronts: the first, the sale of the factory as described by Rob Murison, and the second, the relocation of production into the relatively modern structure of the 100,000sq ft Butler Building, effecting a saving of approximately £100,000 per year in operating overheads, with the move to be completed before the onset of winter. By proceeding with both proposals at the same time, in the event of the site sale not being immediately accomplished, the £100,000 overhead reduction could still be realised.

John Rosamond explained to the Trustees that the new TSS 8-valve Super Sports model and the TSX Custom Lowrider would be shown to the general public for the first time at the 1982 National Exhibition Centre International Motorcycle Show, commencing on 9th April. The Trustees were invited to visit the show and see the response for themselves. It was predicted that the orders following the show would enable the company to return to regular five-day working, and continue full-time production for the foreseeable future. Rob Murison explained that this was the only way Triumph could fight its way out of the ever increasing cashflow problems being experienced.

John Rosamond commented that whilst it was hoped that UK motorcycle market demand for Triumphs would improve significantly with the introduction of the two new models, he felt the long-term viability requirement of 80 motorcycles per week would not be satisfied without unlocking full access to the American market, one way or another. To that end, Triumph intended to re-approach ECGD. Officials had stated to Geoffrey Robinson at the time of the write-off deal that Triumph should not come back until 1983, but Triumph needed to finance motorcycle builds for America much sooner than that. The Meriden factory was scheduled to start building 1983 models for America in June 1982. Therefore, an approach to ECGD was likely to be made then, although the success of such a request was extremely doubtful.

Analysing all that had been said to date, Ron Marston said that it looked as if Triumph's best position could be accomplished by moving to a new site with lower overheads, and manufacturing and selling 80 motorcycles per week – a position with which all the Directors agreed.

John Tomlinson asked Rob Murison how Triumph stood regarding payment of PAYE and National Insurance. Rob Murison advised that we were currently paying off a major debt in line with an agreement we had with the Inspector of Taxes, the debt arising at the time of the Civil Servant's dispute. John Tomlinson asked what would happen if, when the next interest payment on the overdraft fell due, the bank simply debited the overdraft account, which would take Triumph over the overdraft limit? Rob Murison replied that the bank would bounce cheques as they were presented. The only way for Triumph to stay in business was to trade profitably.

John Tomlinson then asked what the situation was regarding orders from the UK police. John Rosamond advised that a development exercise was taking place with the Derbyshire Police authority utilising the new 8-valve engine, and the results at the moment were encouraging. Accordingly, it was hoped that the extremely negative publicity generated by Derbyshire Chief Constable Mr Parrish's comments to the media, that the previous 4-valve engine Triumph police demonstrator was unsafe, would soon be countered by the force placing an order for the new TSS police motorcycle it had helped to develop, thus influencing other UK police forces to do the same.

Ron Marston asked Rob Murison what the situation was regarding the former Managing Director Bob Lindsay who failed to be re-elected at the adjourned Annual General Meeting. It was explained that following discussion with Triumph's solicitor Peter Davis, notice had been given to Bob Lindsay that he had been dismissed. Bob Lindsay was presently in receipt on a monthly basis of his contractual twelve months' notice.

The first week of April was hectic, as the show stand came together at the NEC. The saving grace for Triumph was that help was readily available only 3 miles down the road at the Meriden factory. Once completed, the simple but impressive Triumph show stand, with all the usual features plus a large raised turntable, would enable the two completely new models (the TSS and TSX) to be the centre of attention. The elevated approach had been chosen in anticipation of the large crowds it was felt would pack the Triumph stand.

Further TSS and TSX models plus the rest of the significantly improved 1982/83 range would be available at ground level for Triumph enthusiasts to sit on. The new colour scheme options certainly sparkled under the show stand spotlights. Triumph's brilliant engineering design and development teams on both sides of the Atlantic had created a range of models to be proud of.

TECHNICAL AND EVOLUTIONARY IMPROVEMENTS ACROSS THE MODEL RANGE
Dog leg clutch and brake levers
Lighter clutch operation
Improved seat padding
Updated transistorised ignition
New petrol tank filler-cap seal

The NEC show 'turntable' display allowed visitors to the Triumph stand the best possible view of the new TSS and TSX models. (Author's archive)

Keeping it in the family; my children try the TSS for size. (Author's archive)

Angled grease nipples to swinging arm bearings
New improved tool kit
Twin rear mirrors

Triumph TSS:

The all new TSS specification remained exactly as at the 25th February London dealer seminar and press launch (chapter 23). Unfortunately, due to very poor supplies of 8-valve cylinder heads and matching cylinder barrels, less than half of the original orders placed had been supplied. Brian Baldwin and his Purchasing Department were in the process of trying to improve this situation to cope with the anticipated continuing demand following the NEC show. Alastair Ritchie, Triumph's UK Sales Manager, was already very concerned that the wave of optimism created by the very successful dealer seminar and press TSS road tests would be lost if those already ordered were not delivered in the very near future.

Triumph TSX:

A new concept in styling, but still unmistakably a Triumph. The low slung 'West Coast' look of the TSX was developed specially for the European market by Triumph Motorcycles America Inc. The Street Cruiser image still offered lively 750 performance and flexibility, and was as much at home on winding country roads as on Sunset Boulevard. Practicality and style combined to give the TSX that something extra.

TSX – brief specification:

Engine type ...... OHV parallel twin, four stroke
Bore 76mm (2.992in)
Stroke 82mm (3.228in)
Capacity .... 744cc (45cu in)
Carburettors .... twin CV32mm chokes

```
Tyre front  . . . . . . . . . . . . . . . . . . . . . . MJ90 x 19 rib
Tyre rear  . . . . . . . . . . . . . .  MT90 x 16 low profile
Brake front  . . . . . . . . .  single 9.8in (250mm) disc
Brake rear  . . . . . . . . . .  single 9.8in (250mm) disc
Gearbox type  . . . . . . . . . . . . . . . . . . . . . . . 5-speed
Wheelbase . . . . . . . . . . . . . . . . . . . 56in (1422mm)
Seat height . . . . . . . . . . . . . . . . . . . . . 30in (762mm)
Dry weight . . . . . . . . . . . . . . . . . . . . 415lb (189kg)
Fuel capacity . . 2.3 imperial gallons (10.45 litres)
Electrics . . . . . . . . . . . . . . . . . . . . . . . 12v alternator
Ignition system . . . . . . . . . . . . . . . . . . . . electronic
Electric start . . . . . . . . . . . . . . . . . . . . . . . standard
Instruments . . . . . tachometer and speedometer
Optional extra . . . . . . . . . . .  twin disc front brake
```
Triumph Bonnevilles:

Demand for the T140E Bonneville models in their US and UK-spec forms, with or without electric start, was anticipated to continue as strong as ever. In addition to taking full advantage of all the technical and evolutionary improvements for 1983, both UK and US models now had a quartz halogen headlamp unit, and the UK-spec Bonneville had Marzocchi rear suspension units.

Triumph Thunderbirds:

The popular TR65 Thunderbirds would also continue, significantly upgraded to resemble their larger capacity big brother, the Bonneville. The US-spec model was to have twin exhausts, tachometer, gleaming chrome and special polished alloy features for engine and trim, plus the technical and evolutionary model improvements. The UK-spec Thunderbird was also to receive all the technical and evolutionary improvements, plus twin exhausts and tachometer.

Triumph Tiger Trail:

The Tiger Trail was built for rough riding: a 650 engine, flexible performance with standard features such as tachometer, twin mirrors and pillion footrests. For extra protection, there was the new leg guard on the exhaust. Also featured was an engine in practical black finish, an extended sump guard, modified frame and swinging arm, plus a new silencer. Tiger Trail: at home where the going's roughest.

TR65T Tiger Trail – brief specification:
```
Engine type  . . . . . .  OHV parallel twin, four stroke
Bore  . . . . . . . . . . . . . . . . . . . . . . . .  76mm (2.992in)
Stroke  . . . . . . . . . . . . . . . . . . . .  71.5mm (2.185in)
Capacity  . . . . . . . . . . . . . . . . . .  649cc (39.6cu in)
Carburettor  . . . . . . . . . . . . . . . .  Single R930/108
Tyre front  . . . . . . . . . . . . . . . . . . . . . 3.00 x 21 trial
Tyre rear  . . . . . . . . . . . . . . . . . . . . . . 4.00 x 18 trial
Brake front . . . . . . . . . . . . . . . .  9.8in (250mm) disc
Brake rear . . . . . . . . . . . . . . . . .  7in (178mm) drum
Gearbox type  . . . . . . . . . . . . . . . . . . . . . .  5 speed
Wheelbase . . . . . . . . . . . . . . . . . . . 56in (1422mm)
Seat height . . . . . . . . . . . . . . . . . . .  32.5in (828mm)
Dry weight . . . . . . . . . . . . . . . . . . . .  383lb (174kg)
Fuel capacity . . 2.3 imperial gallons (10.45 litres)
```

The TR65T Tiger Trail, now with the 650cc engine, is exhibited for the first time. (Brochure picture)

Electrics . . . . 12v alternator
Ignition system . . . . electronic
Instruments . . . . . tachometer and speedometer
Triumph TS8-1:

Triumph's most expensive model, the TS8-1, now in limited production, was also featured on the show stand. In its 1983 production form, observant Triumph enthusiasts would spot the two main differences to the late arriving prototype model shown last year. The twin headlights were now rectangular in shape, and the direction indicators were faired into the bodywork.

Triumph Bonneville Executive:

The T140ES Bonneville Executive-Electro also made a show appearance. As with the TS8-1, it utilised the AV frame developed exclusively for British police forces. The Triumph Super Cruiser now offered the ultimate in long distance comfort and smoothness, with quickly detachable roomy executive panniers, top box and twin CV carburettors. The new Bonneville Executive-Electro was the ultimate touring machine for the Triumph connoisseur.

Bonneville T140ES AV Executive Electro:

Engine type ...... OHV parallel twin, four stroke
Bore 76mm .... (2.992in)
Stroke 82mm (3.228in)
Capacity .... 744cc (45cu in)
Carburettors .... twin CV 32mm chokes
Tyre front 4.10x 19
Tyre rear .... 4.10 x 18
Brake front .... 9.8in (250mm) disc
Brake rear .... 9.8in (250mm) disc
Gearbox type 5-speed
Wheelbase 56in (1422mm)
Seat height 31in (787.4mm)
Dry weight 482lb (219kg)
Fuel capacity ... 4.0 imperial gallons (18.2 litres)
Electrics .... 12v alternator
Ignition system .... electronic
Instruments ..... tachometer and speedometer
Optional extras:
Cast aluminium wheels
Twin disc front brake

The final Triumph model on the show stand was the latest prototype TSS AV Police Special that was being developed with the Derbyshire authority.

All was now set for tomorrow, Thursday 8th April 1982, NEC show press day. Wayne Moulton, TMA's President, had flown in from California for the launch of his brilliant TSX Custom model. He had every right to be proud of his £3000 shoestring budget creation and the small team that produced it. The premier 1982 motorcycle show was UK Sales Manager Alastair Ritchie's responsibility. His Sales Department staff had done an excellent job organising Triumph's vital appearance. Alastair and his sales team would man the show stand, with engineering support from Brian Jones and Martyn Roberts, plus the usual participants from the drawing office and experimental. The Chairman would be available as required to answer 'politically motivated' questions regarding the Co-op and its future.

There was no doubt the stars of the 1982 NEC show were the Triumph TSS and TSX models, and they rightfully received most of the media attention. Wayne Moulton's presence was much appreciated by the specialist press, and he was constantly occupied throughout the day, providing in-depth interviews regarding Triumph's new TSX Custom model. Brian Jones and Martyn Roberts continued where they had left off at the London press launch of the TSS – the only difference was that most of the journalists now had firsthand road test experience of Triumph's new 8-valve Super Sports modern day classic. Accordingly, they all remained extremely positive about the potential joy of future ownership. Alastair Ritchie was able to announce two small but important recent Triumph sales successes in the previous week. The Royal Military Police Display Team had switched from Japanese models to purchase seven white TR7T Tiger Trails, and the British Cycle Federation had ordered ten specially adapted 650cc Triumphs for the World Championship 'Motor Paced' events to be held in August 1982, just up the road in Leicester. All in all, press day could not have gone better for Triumph.

The fantastic reception subsequently received from the general public possibly eclipsed press day, but only just! Very enthusiastic crowds packed the Triumph stand and the aisles around it for the whole show, in an effort to get a glimpse of Triumph's 1982/83 models. The majority of the Triumph Sales and Engineering personnel manning the stand could not have been more positive about the likely outcome. Motorcycle order expectations were indeed very high. However, those like the Chairman who had similar thoughts following the previous year's NEC show reserved judgement. The majority were understandably devastated when less than 100 orders came in.

Factory morale was once again rock bottom, although it rose a little when the write-off of all outstanding debts to Her Majesty's Government was finally achieved. With this satisfactory conclusion reached, and growing pressure from other work, Brenda Price, Chairman and Director of TMA, indicated her intention to resign on 12th April 1982. (Whilst Brenda remained a Director of Mercia Sound and continued a watching brief over their finances, she had now joined Geoffrey Robinson's company Trans Tec as full-time Director of Finance, Sales and Administration). Almost simultaneously, Rob Murison, the Financial and Commercial Director, gave 3 months' notice of his intention to leave Triumph on 9th July 1982. Rob had reminded the Chairman that he had accepted a directorship in October 1980 with a view to giving the best possible start to the new organisation that we had just established. He had made it clear then that it was not his long-term plan to stay with Triumph, and he now believed that the time had come for him to also withdraw.

In view of recent developments, the Chairman discussed what looked to be Triumph's bleak future prospects with Geoffrey Robinson MP on 22nd April 1982. Geoffrey agreed that he would consider possible commercial options that still remained open to the Co-op, these to be discussed with the Board of Directors at the scheduled 10th May Board meeting.

Rob Murison's continuing concerns regarding our failure to meet budgeted production targets were partly addressed by the introduction on 3rd May of a bonus/guarantee pay and conditions package. The scheme for factory floor workers provided the opportunity to recover lost production by exceeding operating targets, and with it the lost wages that had resulted from short-time working. Although Rob Murison was concerned on the grounds of additional expense, when introduced it was reasonably successful. It was also recognised at this time that the decision to subject commercial areas of the business to short-time working, on the grounds of fairness to all, had been a mistake.

Prior to the scheduled Board meeting on 10th May, the Executive Directors' commercial and engineering reports had been circulated for consideration. Initially at the meeting, Rob Murison focused on the fact that the overdraft had now reached the limit set by the bank. To mitigate this situation, Rob was proposing the following drastic cash gathering action:
• TMA to immediately transmit all money available.
• Triumph survival fund – £5000.
• Social club funds. Lines of communication were to be opened to gain access to the Triumph survival and Social Club funds.
• Dispatch 12 TSS models as a matter of urgency, raising £24,000 from cash on delivery.

The latest forecast indicated that the overdraft limit would be exceeded by a maximum of £20,000 this week, before returning to below the £1.18m acceptable to the bank.

Geoffrey Robinson indicated to the Board that he would have to leave for other business at 1.00pm, in view of which he requested that the Board move on to discuss the long-term options that remained open to the Co-operative, the Chairman having brought him up to date on 22nd April regarding our present situation. These were his suggested commercial options in order of preference:

1) Financial assistance from the West Midlands Development Authority.
2) A satisfactory conclusion of a Nigerian institutional order.
3) A merger with Hesketh Motorcycles to raise £2m from the public sector.
4) A public appeal associated with a BBC programme featuring receivership.

Touching on option 1, Bill Beattie advised that the accountancy firm Price Waterhouse was looking at the Co-op's financial situation, and in particular short-term cashflow. The West Midlands Development Authority was very much in the picture regarding the need for an early decision, which at this time looked promising.

Moving to option 2, another Nigerian order, Geoffrey Robinson said that he was still certain Triumph would get this, it being just a matter of time.

Summarising what had been said so far, Geoffrey Robinson felt that a combination of options 1 and 2 could well see the Co-op through at least another winter.

Regarding option 3, the merger of Triumph and Hesketh Motorcycles to raise £2m from the public sector; Rob Murison felt there was a basic point of principle that first had to be decided by the Triumph Board of Directors – one of the Co-op being prepared to accept a minority stake in the new venture. Geoffrey Robinson felt this was less of a problem, and there was no need to look at this point until after further investigation, when the Directors would know whether or not a deal was possible. Geoffrey Robinson then had to leave the Board meeting for other commitments, stating that he would return later when these matters could be further discussed.

When the Board reconvened following a half hour lunch, the Commercial and Engineering Directors' reports were discussed in detail, particularly the impact of the NEC show and resultant lack of orders.

The first two pages of the Commercial Director's circulated 6-page Board report focused on sales.

SALES
In general, the international market for motorcycles was extremely poor as a result of reduced demand and very high capacity. The Japanese manufacturers had been forced to revert to extreme measures in terms of discounting and credit terms to keep motorcycles flowing out of their factories.

The Triumph UK order bank precisely reflected orders taken at the NEC Motorcycle Show, and as yet unfulfilled orders for the TSS model. The show was a grave disappointment in terms of sales, with Triumph taking less than 100 orders from the UK market. The real problem, however, was that the sales force was having great difficulty in selling those motorcycles presently in production in proportion to the factory's productive capacity, the bulk of the demand being for TSS and TSX models. The non-availability of the TSS had caused considerable problems in the market, as the euphoria created by its London launch was evaporating. Demand remained high, however, and it was anticipated that the TSS would account for a steady 40 per cent of Triumph's total sales. In view of this, it was vital that the present component supply problems for that model and the proposed resourcing programme were completed with all speed.

Brian Jones' circulated engineering report highlighted the efforts being undertaken to ensure improved supplies of TSS 8-valve cylinder heads and matching cylinder barrels, at the levels agreed when Triumph placed the order with Weslake. However, the reality of the situation was that Weslake was in almost as difficult a cashflow situation as Triumph! If another customer turned up on its doorstep with cash in their hand, it was prepared to interrupt Triumph's production to secure immediate access to ready money. Brian Baldwin, Triumph's Purchasing Manager, went to the Weslake factory in Rye in East Sussex to clear the air, following which he phoned the Meriden factory to advise of the reassurances he had received that supplies would now improve. We asked Brian to go and have some lunch before returning unannounced to the Weslake factory. Sure enough, when Brian returned, Triumph's work had been put to one side and Weslake was now undertaking work for another customer. Further forthright exchanges took place, which resulted in Weslake agreeing to Triumph sourcing the supply of cylinder barrels from another foundry. Triumph would also now machine these cylinder barrels in-house, enabling Weslake to increase production numbers of the more difficult 8-valve cylinder heads. Weslake's cashflow situation was subsequently eased by Triumph Financial Controller Phil Bragg's introduction of weekly payments for supplies received, instead of the original payment at the end of the month. By the end of April, Triumph had received 93 cylinder heads from Weslake against a total order bank of 166. With it promising a further 12 cylinder heads on May 7th, followed by 25 on May 14th, and then deliveries at the rate of 25 a week thereafter, Weslake's performance was now being closely monitored.

The Sales Department was extremely concerned by the continuing poor performance of Triumph in terms of total UK market sales. Penetration appeared to have been dropping steadily over the previous fifteen months, and there had been no indication of an improvement following the employment of the new Sales Manager in November 1981, or the dealer seminar in February 1982. Clearly it was one thing to be suffering from the generally constricted market; it was quite another to have a decreased share of it. The conventional sales argument about Triumphs had always been that market share should improve as the total market contracts, due to the speciality nature of our motorcycles. However, it should be noted that the figures were up to the end of March, and so did not include any significant sales of new models.

The Board were also made aware that a dealer stockist plan in conjunction with FCF was being explored. This would have the dual effect of improving our service to UK dealers and enabling the factory to obtain receipts from UK sales more quickly. We were working towards implementation in June. Speed was crucial, as our finances were heavily reliant on cash on delivery from TSS models, and there was no doubt that we would shortly be coming under considerable dealer pressure to discard that requirement.

Triumph was continuing to experience problems in central/southern England as a result of our proposed introduction of a new volume dealer. Judging by the furore that the proposal was creating, there was no doubt that local dealers believed the proposed new dealer would sell significant numbers of Triumphs. The exclusive areas granted to Triumph dealers in 1981 was causing considerable difficulty, especially with a particular major motorcycle dealer, who had not in the past been a strong supporter of Triumph, and even then did not hold many of our motorcycles in stock. Dependent upon the outcome of discussions (which included an attempt to mitigate the effect of the dealers' 'exclusion zone') we would be in a position to establish the likely consequences for one of Triumph's strong supporters, who already sold in excess of 50 motorcycles a year.

Motorcycle sales volume in Europe remained reasonable, with strong demand in Germany and Switzerland. Demand was also improving in Holland (19 motorcycles now on order) and France (31 units). As regards France, having met the new General Manager of CGCIM, it was believed he was endowed with considerably more commercial acumen than his predecessor, indicated by his rapid decision to open a retail outlet. We were therefore taking no further steps towards termination at that time.

Regarding the foreign institutional markets – it was important to appreciate that the Ugandan order was not a single self-contained order, but the first of a series of Ugandan institutional orders. The next was understood to be 100 police motorcycles, probably fitted with AV frames. In view of this, it was clearly vital that the first shipment be of sufficient quality to encourage re-ordering. We had also been requested to air-freight two demonstrator motorcycles to Jordan at the customer's cost. It was again vital that these motorcycles be of the very highest standard, and dispatched as soon as possible. The longer they were outstanding, the longer our competitors had to sway the customer away from Triumph. At the time, the customer appeared to be leaning in our favour. There was no firm news as regards the Nigerian situation, although it was understood that the moratorium on imports should start to be relaxed within the following month, and that proposed expenditure had not been significantly reduced.

Australia continued to be one of our strongest markets, with high levels of new orders anticipated for the June/July period. Guy Sanders' factory visit enabled us to identify certain problems that had clearly been endemic in the past, notably poor communication procedures between ourselves and Triumph in Australia. This had caused a feeling of isolation to be suffered by our Australian distributors. We had taken steps to correct these deficiencies, but time would tell whether they had been successful. It was disturbing to learn that every single container sent to Australia in the past twelve months had been contaminated by excessive moisture. Therefore, we were once again altering our packing procedures in an attempt to rectify this problem, which was causing unnecessary ill will.

The United States of America was starved of Triumph motorcycles, which would have severe repercussions for the ongoing viability of TMA. A pilot scheme for financing motorcycle shipments to TMA had been agreed in principle with FCF, and we hoped to have the scheme operational within the next month.

Geoffrey Robinson returned to the meeting at 4.00pm, and indicated that he felt the Board should be making provision to replace Rob Murison, whose notice of resignation had been placed on the boardroom table, effective 9th July 1982. Geoffrey Robinson thought the Board should also look at the possible need to restructure the company following Rob Murison's departure.

Geoffrey placed on record his personal appreciation for the tremendous job Rob Murison had accomplished in the successful negotiations with Her Majesty's Government. The Board of Directors concurred with Geoffrey Robinson's previous statement.

Moving to the recruitment of a replacement for Rob Murison, Bill Beattie felt that a possible approach to the West Midlands Authority to secure a Financial Director by way of secondment may well bear fruit. Bill Beattie would pursue this avenue.

Returning now to the commercial options left open to the Co-op, and in particular Geoffrey Robinson's option 3, the merger with Hesketh Motorcycles, the Board felt that a lot more information was required before any firm commitments could be made. Accordingly, the Board agreed the following should be conveyed by the Chairman to Mr 'Bubbles' Horsley, Managing Director of Hesketh Motorcycles:

"The approach from Hesketh Motorcycles to Triumph Motorcycles (Meriden) Ltd was considered by the Triumph Board on 10th May. The Board noted the proposals and on the limited information available at present it would be prepared to consider seriously more detailed proposals. In particular Triumph would need to be satisfied on the new operations proposed location, its share structure, source of finance and proposed management structure. The eventual decision would be subject to a vote of the entire membership of Triumph Motorcycles (Meriden) Ltd."

The Board now moved to the US sales item in Rob Murison's commercial report. The

Board of Directors reluctantly accepted Brenda Price's resignation from the position of Chairman and Director of Triumph Motorcycles America Inc. A vote of thanks was recorded for the tremendous work she had undertaken for the company, which had often been far beyond the call of duty. It was moved, seconded and agreed by the Triumph Meriden Board that John Rosamond should become Chairman of the American Subsidiary's Board of Directors. In these circumstances, Geoffrey Robinson felt John Rosamond should undertake the following regarding TMA: continue weekly returns, make provision for a bi-annual audit, keep the Triumph Meriden Board in the picture regarding TMA developments, and report to the Triumph Meriden Board. Geoffrey Robinson would no longer be responsible for the American company. John Rosamond suggested that in view of the complete handover of responsibility for the American company, matters would be a lot tidier if Geoffrey Robinson did a final written report on any items outstanding.

The Board generally agreed that the introduction of a bonus system for production workers in an effort to address the seasonal demand for motorcycles and resultant loss of earnings through short-time working had so far worked quite well.

By the same token, it was now felt that within the constraints of the Co-op's financial situation non-production workers should be offered a guarantee of 40-hour full-time working throughout the year. A further mass meeting would be required to implement this important change.

The Board meeting was adjourned at 6.15pm, to be reconvened when the detailed Hesketh merger proposals were received.

25

CRISIS MANAGEMENT

It was with a certain amount of trepidation that the Directors considered Geoffrey Robinson's suggested commercial options that remained open to Triumph Meriden and the Co-op.

Getting into bed with the so-called 'landed gentry' certainly inspired no thoughts of optimism, but neither did relying on the local Government support of the West Midlands County Council. We had been the political route before, albeit at national level. It was quite clear that however much Geoffrey Robinson wanted to be involved in these negotiations, because of his increased business workload, it would be difficult for him to do so. The Board's new subcommittee/negotiating team was therefore Messrs Rosamond and Beattie, with vital support when required from the Engineering and Commercial Directors.

The approach from Hesketh Motorcycles PLC, which wanted to merge with Triumph to convince the public sector that a combined new enterprise was worthy of a £2m investment, was certainly a surprise. Most of the Co-op's Directors had little or no knowledge of Lord Hesketh's motorcycle business, although Triumph's Chairman and the Engineering Director had some insight to the initial management of its engine design project ...

For over 12 months, Brian Jones and John Rosamond had been making weekly/fortnightly Diana project progress visits to the subcontract design engineering company Rye Tools. Under Triumph's supervision, Weslake's sister company was making excellent headway on the new engine project. The Chief Engineer and Product Planning Manager had established a regular routine, leaving late on Friday afternoon to make the 340-mile round trip to East Sussex, staying overnight at the Oast House Hotel, Tenterton, spending Saturday with the staff at Rye Tools, and returning to the Midlands on Saturday evening. Inevitably during the detailed discussions with Rye Tools' workers, many of their colourful memories of previous involvement in the design and development of the Hesketh V-twin surfaced – unfortunately, these did not inspire confidence!

The Directors, Trustees and Beneficiary owners of the Co-op had detailed knowledge of exactly what needed to be changed at Triumph to enable long-term viability and future security to be pursued. The worst thing that could happen now was that pursuit of those long-term solutions be prevented by having to sort all the unknown but suspected problems of Hesketh Motorcycles PLC. Brian Jones and John Rosamond were not at all surprised when Triumph's request for merger proposal clarification from Hesketh left fundamental questions unanswered. On 12th May, Rob Murison, who felt a merger of the two motorcycle companies had distinct possibilities, recommended a number crunching exercise as a possible way of achieving clarity.

This got under way, tying up senior financial staff from Triumph and Hesketh for several days. What emerged, though, demonstrated that the agreed brief to "achieve clarity" had not been followed!

On 17th May, Rob Murison was trying to explain to the Triumph Board how this had happened, when the meeting was suddenly interrupted by the arrival from Hesketh Motorcycles PLC of three copies of a document outlining the merger of Hesketh and Triumph. The Directors read what looked like a merger proposal, and concluded a great deal of effort had been put into a funding research exercise, but very little, it would seem, into whether a merged company could actually succeed! The indication that a public statement regarding discussions between the two companies had to be made within the next 2 or 3 days helped the Triumph Board to reject the Hesketh merger approach. The Directors were not prepared to be pressured into any deal. Rob Murison was concerned that this fundamental Board decision had been reached without Geoffrey Robinson's presence, but the Directors decided one vote would not have changed the outcome, so the decision stood.

At the same Board meeting, John Rosamond in his new additional role as Chairman of Triumph Motorcycles (America) Inc outlined Wayne Moulton's proposal to try and raise sufficient capital to purchase the American subsidiary. Wayne believed an independently owned TMA would be able to raise sufficient working capital to purchase 2000 Triumph motorcycles a year from the Meriden factory, where the parent company clearly could not.

Bill Beattie raised fundamental reservations about losing control of Triumph's American subsidiary, and with it the major US motorcycle market. John Rosamond agreed, feeling that such a proposal could only be pursued as a final resort if every other avenue had failed, including restructured support from the West Midlands County Council. In the meantime, Rob Murison suggested a valuation of TMA be undertaken. Triumph's American auditor Coopers and Lybrand would verify the figures.

Geoffrey Robinson attended the reconvened 21st May Board meeting to present a report on his responsibilities as Non-Executive Director.

It was now abundantly clear that Nigerian military orders were not presently being affected by the recently proposed financial restrictions. This had been further confirmed by Mr Tiny Rowland of the Lonhro group of companies.

An approach had been made to the ECGD Minister Mr Peter Rees, but as yet it had not succeeded in extracting a commitment to future availability for Triumph. Rob Murison's pilot FCF scheme to finance motorcycles for America was about to be introduced. This would enable twenty motorcycles presently under manufacture to be shipped to the United States. This limited FCF experience could possibly lead to larger amounts of funding.

Having completed his report on his non-executive responsibilities Geoffrey Robinson commented upon the 18th May Triumph letter rejecting the Hesketh merger proposal.

Geoffrey Robinson agreed with 90 per cent of the rejection letter; however, he had recently met Lord Alexander Hesketh in London, and wished to make the following observations to the Triumph Board of Directors.

Lord Hesketh had not taken out any of his original financial stake in the Hesketh Motorcycle Company.

The document placed before the Triumph Board of Directors was not in fact a merger proposal.

It was clear that Triumph had the whip hand, and accordingly a very good chance of achieving a satisfactory proposal, and any such chance, however remote, should not be ignored. If the Meriden factory site could be sold and leased back, then we had to pursue that opportunity.

The National Water Board Authority was showing an interest in purchasing the site for £2m and then offering a lease-back facility. Hesketh was interested in the merits of the Butler Building. The Water Board was looking more at the site than the activities taking place on it. Potential offers from both ICFC, which had indicated a possible interest in the Triumph site at £6-700,000, and Espley-Tyas, which had suggested £900,000, were insufficient to offset Triumph's overdraft borrowings of £1.18m. Triumph needed to accomplish a sale of the factory site for a minimum of £2m prior to a lease-back arrangement. Rob Murison felt the figure of £2m for the sale and lease-back arrangement could prove to be excessive. George Mackie asked whether Triumph could deal directly with the Water Board. This was not possible; contact had to be made through Hesketh.

Mr Horsley MD of Hesketh Motorcycles had phoned the Chairman the previous evening, indicating that they had some further ideas they were working on that they hoped would be more acceptable to Triumph.

Geoffrey Robinson asked Brian Jones what he thought of the Hesketh Motorcycle. Brian believed the Hesketh fitted into the equivalent of the Aston Martin slot of the motorcycle market, and felt sales of possibly 500 per year could be achieved at the retail price being suggested. To Geoffrey's question "do you think it is worth making?" Brian agreed that it was, provided profitable sales could be achieved.

The Hesketh cost £2800 to manufacture, which equated to a £500 contribution to factory overheads at the ex-works price of £3300; this contribution was down on Triumph models.

George Mackie stated that the Triumph Directors were not against any feasible proposals; however, it was abundantly clear that any pressure applied as with the last Hesketh document was bound to result in a negative reaction.

On reflection, Geoffrey Robinson felt that the Hesketh 15 per cent/£500 contribution, even on a minimum of 500 and a maximum of 1000 units per year, could prove fatal for Hesketh. Even so, Triumph's position in negotiations was so much stronger than Hesketh's. It was therefore felt that we ought to continue exploring the possibilities of putting together a merger plan that reflected the relative positions of the two companies. Triumph's Chairman would contact Mr Horsley, MD of Hesketh, in order to invite the Water Board Authority and Hesketh to Triumph to see what could be done. (The exploratory merger talks were unproductive. Unable to sort its engineering and financial problems on its own, Hesketh Motorcycles PLC was to go into receivership in August 1982, reportedly having produced fewer than 150 motorcycles.)

During the 30 minute break for lunch, the Chairman reflected further on Triumph's approach to the West Midlands County Council. The County Council's Chairman, Councillor Geoff Edge, had introduced its new economic development policy initiative in November 1981 when he wrote as follows:

The need for a new approach
The West Midlands, once the workshop of the world, is facing the worst economic crisis in its history. Unemployment in the county area is currently at an official level of 15.1 per cent and within certain inner city areas we can expect to find levels of 30 per cent or more. Levels of this sort show every sign of remaining permanent, and even increasing further as the recession deepens. What is more, the West Midlands have shown the greatest decline relative to other regions in the UK. The Cambridge economic policy unit has shown that the area has suffered the greatest reversal, and that it is rapidly assuming the same relative status as the North West and Northern Ireland. The unit has also shown that public resources and investment are currently flowing out of the region at the rate of £119 per year for every head of resident population, while the equivalent figure for the prosperous South East which is supposed to be assisting other regions is only £36 per head.

The relative decline of the West Midlands can be considered in a European perspective too. Research on some of the older regions in Western Europe (such as Nord-Rheine Westphalia, Lorraine, Rhône-Alps and Scotland) has shown that the West Midlands had the lowest industrial investment per head during the 1970s and lowest investment per employee when compared to the national average in each country. Relative decline and lack of investment on this scale needs some new and clearly defined policies.

Focus on medium and large firms
Existing policies are inadequate. We need to make a clean brake with traditional local economic planning. There is no reason for concentrating on small firms when we hope to have at least £10m to spend. Research has shown that the greatest job losses occur in large firms and the small firms can only play a very small part in compensating for this. There is no evidence that the decline in the UK economy, or in any region, has been caused by an under representation of small firms. Germany is often quoted as a country with a vibrant small firms sector and a prosperous economy, but the Wilson Committee found that small establishments in Germany have been declining as they have elsewhere, and that by 1976 they accounted for 31 per cent of total manufacturing employment. The equivalent proportion for the UK was 29 per cent, hardly enough to allow for the alleged differences in economic performance. We need instead, to focus our attention on medium-sized and large firms. This is not to say small firms have no long-term role to play, only that their role is residual.

Co-operatives
Some of these arguments also apply to new firms, or start ups. There is a danger in supporting new enterprise where one person is pursuing an idea but where the growth prospects are restricted or where the spin off for jobs and production elsewhere is limited. One exception is in the case of the redeployment of unemployed workers attempting to develop a product where it is important to retain their active skills.

Co-operatives are especially relevant here and should be supported primarily for this reason. The council may have to take a leading role in launching new municipal enterprise to produce what it wants for its own needs, to preserve and use the skills of the unemployed, and to help the most underprivileged.

This extract from Councillor Geoff Edge's 3-page paper was adopted by the West Midlands County Council's Economic Development Committee in November 1981. It provided the framework for the development of the County Council's specific economic policies, and the approval of individual projects.

Terry Pitt was recruited in 1981 as Senior Advisor to the Council on economic development. Although Terry was a Council official, he was also an extremely committed and highly regarded socialist who had served the Labour Party extensively at national level as head of research, where he had played a key role in running Labour Party General Election campaigns and drafting manifestos. Although he had stood for election as an MP, he had so far failed, and in 1978 became the founding Director of the Institute of National Affairs of Papua New Guinea, prior to being recruited by the West Midlands County Council.

At the beginning of February 1982, the West Midland Enterprise Board was formed by the County Council. The Enterprise Board, a limited company, was completely separate from the Council, but its role was to implement the West Midland County Council's investment strategy. Mr Norman Holmes, the former head of the Northern Ireland Development Agency, was appointed as Chief Executive. The Directors of the Enterprise Board would consist of

Councillors and key individuals recruited to ensure economic development policy objectives were achieved.

So far we had received a positive reaction from the County Council regarding our request for help – not being shown the door at the first mention of the fact that we were a workers' co-operative owned by the employees was indeed a welcome change!

After lunch we reconvened (Geoffrey had departed for other pressing business commitments). The review of the two Triumph Executives' monthly Board reports for May continued. Much of the detailed discussion was influenced by the ever increasing financial crisis due to worsening production. The initial success of the bonus scheme had been lost, as any surplus components there that had been in 'work in progress' due to previous underperformance, were used up. This created a disastrous, morale-destroying atmosphere of trying to apportion blame to those who were preventing the bonus being earned. Putting on his accountant's hat, Rob Murison felt the bonus system should be applied on a cumulative basis both forward and backward – previous weekly shortfalls should be made up by way of increased production bonus targets in following weeks, and previous bonuses paid should be taken back when production levels failed to meet minimum targets. Bill Beattie argued strongly that if it was not the production workers' fault that they were unable to hit their targets, bonuses should apply as soon as component parts supply was restored. Rob Murison came back with the point that in a co-op there is no difference between the membership and the company, therefore it's a joint responsibility.

The Chairman intervened as this was an argument going nowhere. A subcommittee of the Board was set up to investigate possible production organisational changes that could be made to improve the situation. It eventually came up with remarkably similar findings to those determined by John Rosamond and Bill Beattie's investigation back in September 1978.

The bonus scheme was suspended indefinitely. The membership had to decide at a series of section meetings addressed by John Rosamond and Bill Beattie whether the Co-op was still worth fighting for, as most of the production shortfall problems were due to the financial position Triumph was in, not individual members. The decision was as expected: "we fight on!"

The final business of the marathon 10th May Board meeting at 5.30pm on 28th May 1982 was receiving an embarrassing report from Commercial Director Rob Murison. An overspend on the agreed £2500 cashflow crisis budget for the London dealer seminar had occurred. This was the budget discussed and confirmed at the specially convened Board of Directors meeting on 29th January 1982, because of a rumoured overspend. Invoices now received indicated that the rumours had in fact been true – the dealer meeting had cost Triumph in the region of £3700!

The Directors felt Mr Murison should take the appropriate action and explain the Board's concern regarding this excess to the individual concerned. Rob Murison undertook to advise the Board in due course regarding the cost of the National Exhibition Centre International Motorcycle Show, relative to the agreed budget.

At long last, Rob Murison had been able to sort out the problems created when Triumph's original audit partner tragically died halfway through the completion of the overdue 1980 annual accounts. The Commercial Director was now able to give notice that the adjourned Annual General Meeting could go ahead on 8th July 1982. Acceptance of the accounts for the financial year ending 30th September 1980 would then take place, following which they would be forwarded to the company's registration office.

On 11th June the Directors met to discuss the continuing cashflow problems. Rob Murison outlined developments since 28th May discussions, and advised that he was now committing finance predominantly to motorcycles, for which we could receive cash on delivery. Accordingly, if Engineering Director Brian Jones did not meet his commitment to produce forty-five TSX and twenty TSS motorcycles during the week ending Friday 18th June, for progressive delivery at the rate of fifteen per day, it would almost certainly bring about the closure of the company. The Commercial Director further said that the bank overdraft interest was due towards the end of the following week, and provided this programme of manufacturing motorcycles for cash on delivery was achieved, Triumph would be in a position to make this payment. Failure to do so would of course take the company over the overdraft limit, and into a position where the bank would bounce cheques.

The Chairman reported that following Price Waterhouse's positive report to the West Midlands County Council, this accountancy firm would help Triumph prepare a 5-year corporate plan, detailing future operations following the restructuring of the business. The corporate plan would be discussed by the Board of Directors in the very near future.

Finally, in view of the critical financial situation and the imperative nature of achieving the previously discussed dispatches of forty-five TSX and twenty TSS motorcycles during the following week, the Directors agreed that John Rosamond and Bill Beattie should conduct further brief section meetings with the membership, it being felt that this form of communication had been very effective in the past times of crisis.

The workforce magnificently rose to the production challenge, beating the dispatch target by seven. The bank overdraft interest was paid and the Co-op struggled on.

On 2nd July Rob Murison was able to report to the Board that he had been successful in arranging a part shipment of 56 motorcycles against the recently received institutional order for Ghana. These had to be dispatched from the Triumph factory by Wednesday 7th July – any slippage on this programme would result in the bank overdraft exceeding the £1.18m limit. Provided the dispatch of the first 56 was on target, Triumph would be in a position to complete the second half of the Ghanaian order prior to the fortnight factory summer holidays. By so doing, the company would be able to meet pressing financial obligations, including the membership's holiday pay. Rob Murison advised that from a cashflow point of view there were two further production options that could be considered to complete the order for Ghana:

• Build the order gradually and ship when completed on 22nd July.
• Effect an immediate workforce layoff including the summer holiday. This would mean a 4-week factory shutdown.

Detailed discussion determined that the plan to build and ship 56 motorcycles for Ghana by Wednesday 7th July was accepted, and we would proceed with the greatest urgency.

As a result of the latest annual audit work for the year ending 30th September 1981, it had been discovered that individual debts to Moratorium Creditors were in a state of imbalance. To correct this situation (in line with the moratorium agreement) payments of approximately £25,000 would need to take place. This would happen as soon as possible.

A visit by the accountancy representative of the Moratorium Creditors' Committee had generated a disturbing follow-up phone call to Rob Murison. During the phone conversation, it had been suggested that Triumph was continuing to trade whilst knowingly being insolvent! Whilst the Commercial Director had countered this statement by stating that the Board of Directors was continuing to trade on behalf of its creditors, the Directors agreed that further legal clarification should once again be sought from the Company Solicitor. Finally, Rob Murison advised that the adjourned Annual General Meeting, scheduled to go ahead on 8th July 1982, was now extremely unlikely to proceed. Difficulties had been experienced regarding what Rob believed to be "trivial" matters in the annual accounts for the financial year ending 30th September 1980, upon which the Audit Manager was now insisting he would place further qualifications. In view of the fact that it seemed the accounts would not be finalised in time for the reconvened AGM, the Chairman agreed to contact the Trustees, explain the situation, and invite them to still attend to meet the Board as arranged on 8th July. A meeting with the Directors would then take place to update them on Triumph and the Co-op's present position.

All three Trustees attended the 8th July meeting. Most concerning, however, was that Rob Murison had not yet arrived when the meeting started, and with his scheduled resignation to take effect tomorrow we all the feared the worst!

The Chairman opened the meeting, explaining to the Trustees that the position communicated to them privately on the telephone regarding support from the West Midlands County Council and Enterprise Board had moved on significantly. The Council had asked Price Waterhouse to undertake a preliminary investigation as to the Meriden Co-op's long-term viability. This had established that in the right circumstances, there could well be a future for Triumph. In view of this, the County Council had asked Price Waterhouse to help the Co-op put forward a five-year corporate plan that demonstrated ongoing viability in a new restructured situation. At this point it was felt that due to Rob Murison's late arrival, it would be best to concentrate on the engineering content of the five year corporate plan, and return to commercial matters once Brian Jones had finished.

Brian Jones explained that the Diana engine, which would power a complete new range of Triumph motorcycles, had been under secret development at consultant engineers for the last fifteen months, and to date a six-figure sum had been spent on it. Whilst subcontract consultant engineers had been used, Triumph's Engineering Director had maintained strict control and was satisfied that the new design utilising a patented double link balance device (which had been proved in principle) plus the very latest technology would see Triumph through into the 1990s. The Co-op membership had been fully apprised of this new engine design project the week before, as it had reached the stage where it was important to bring the prototype engine back into the Meriden factory to start endurance testing and normal development work.

John Rosamond explained to the Trustees that BBC television had been making a documentary programme of the Triumph design and development work for the past nine months, including the mass meeting at which the Diana engine was presented to the membership. The documentary would be screened at the time of the new Triumph models being introduced to the market, providing the Co-op with extremely valuable free advertising.

Rob Murison joined the meeting, offering apologies for his unavoidable 45-minute late arrival.

Returning to the commercial aspects of the five-year corporate plan, Rob explained the fundamental assumptions that had been made, most of which the Trustees would be familiar with, due to their previous involvement. One of the assumptions was the sale of the 22-acre Meriden factory site, not as industrial land, but for a residential housing development. The resulting increase in value would enable substantial inroads to be made into Triumph's present vast debts. Providing a discounted arrangement with Moratorium Creditors could be reached, plus continued support at a lower level from Triumph's bank, the National Westminster, together with support from the West Midlands County Council and West Midlands Enterprise Board, then a viable ongoing situation could be achieved. Rob Murison advised that initial discussions with Triumph's head office Bank Manager had gained his support for pursuing the aforementioned plan.

John Tomlinson mentioned that it may also be possible to secure help from the EDC, to whom he had recently been speaking. He would make further enquiries and report back.

John Haynes expressed severe reservations as to whether the approximate 4 acres of 'green field' that formed part of the total 22-acre factory site could be converted for residential use. Industrial to residential was one thing; green belt to residential, especially in Meriden, was another! Ron Marston and John Tomlinson concurred with John Haynes' view, believing that if progress was to be made in that direction, an urgent planning application should be submitted.

With that the meeting with the Trustees was over. The matter of the further delay on reconvening the adjourned Annual General Meeting had been completely overlooked in light of news of a possible brighter future for the Co-op and its members.

The reader will appreciate that at the heart of the five-year corporate plan being drawn up to secure financial restructuring was the vital, totally new Diana engine design project. One of the biggest previous criticisms levelled at the Co-op and Triumph was that its motorcycles were based on engine designs going back to Edward Turner's 1937 speed twin, and as such they failed to meet the needs and aspirations of present day motorcycle buyers or imminent tighter noise and emission legislation. It was with this stinging criticism in mind that Brian Jones had drawn up the design specification for the ultimate Triumph parallel twin.

In the years since the Meriden Co-operative came into being in 1975, the Beneficiary owners had on several occasions been extremely indebted to the support of very special friends. One such special friend was Paul Morton, seconded by GEC in 1977 to try and come up with a quick solution for the existing Triumph engine's vibration problems, which were deterring UK police forces from buying British. Paul Morton was GEC's highly respected vibration expert, and he and his team quickly got to grips with this and other engineering problems that the Co-op was experiencing at the time. Unfortunately, the vibration solution, although totally effective, involved the production of many extra parts and new tooling, the costs of which were beyond the Co-op's resources.

An alternative simpler single link balancer design was later proved 'in principle' in an experimental Bonneville engine. However, as with the previous contra rotating balancer shafts, a major engine redesign and retooling investment to accommodate it was required. Once again, this prevented this solution going ahead.

Years had passed since GEC withdrew after its brief but satisfactory involvement with Triumph. Out of the blue, John Rosamond received a phone call from Paul Morton just at the time Brian Jones, Triumph's Chief Engineer, was starting with a clean sheet of paper to draw up the detailed specification of the next generation ultimate parallel twin cylinder engine, codenamed Diana. Paul recalled in the telephone conversation how inspirational he and colleagues had found their involvement with the Co-op, particularly the membership's total commitment to do whatever it took to keep Triumph in business. Accordingly, in his own time, he had continued to think about the Triumph twin's vibration problem. As a result of these deliberations he had come up with a simple, unique balancer design that solved the parallel twin's vibration. In recognition of the Triumph membership's dedication, he intended to give the balancer design to the Co-op.

Paul Morton's device was indeed a simple solution to the age-old vibration problem inherent in all parallel twin cylinder engines. When now specified at the heart of the new Diana Triumph engine, it would balance out all primary and most secondary vibration, making the new Triumph twin smoother than a four. Whilst John Rosamond advised Paul Morton that he appreciated his extremely generous offer, it would have been wrong not to point out to our very good friend the precarious financial position Triumph was in, a position that could at any moment result in the Co-op slipping into receivership or liquidation. In view of this, Triumph's Chairman suggested that a simple legal agreement should be drawn up to enable Paul Morton to secure the return of his balancer design in the event the Co-op went into receivership or liquidation. The deal was done. The membership would enjoy the right to use Paul's gift whilst the Co-op remained in business.

**The prototype Bonneville single link balancer, when viewed from the left, shows
the major engine retooling requirement that was beyond the Co-op's means.
(Courtesy James Crosby photography, London Motorcycle Museum)**

The Board of Director's subcommittee investigating possible production reorganisation
also quantified the labour loading imbalances that had arisen from the introduction of the
new 1982/83 model range. Unfortunately, these imbalances had recently increased as a result
of members leaving due to Triumph's uncertain future. As in the past, the majority were from
the machine shop, where eleven new recruits were in the process of settling in. The paint shop,
engine bench and main assembly track also received one new recruit each, as did production
control and goods receiving.

At this time the Chairman had another opportunity to become involved with the UK dealer
network. The distributors of the Paramount film *An Officer and a Gentleman*, starring Richard
Gere and Debra Winger, contacted John Rosamond to see if Triumph was interested in taking
part in a joint promotional opportunity; the third star of what they expected to be a very popular
hit movie was a T140E US-spec Triumph Bonneville.

Viewed from the right, the prototype single link balancer Bonneville engine shows how neatly the design change fits between the P39 frame cradle tubes. (Courtesy James Crosby photography, London Motorcycle Museum)

Richard Gere, a known Triumph enthusiast, had previously purchased a Bonneville whilst on tour in the UK with the stage production of *Grease*. This purchase is said to have been made with his first pay cheque from the musical. (Richard's association with Triumph Motorcycles was to continue in the 1993 film *Mr Jones*.)

John Rosamond was provided with a personal London screening of *An Officer and a Gentleman* and needed no further persuading of what would be a great promotional opportunity for Triumph and its supportive dealers. Occurring at the peak UK sales registration letter change, this exposure could not have been better timed. A plan was hatched whereby cinemas would provide space in their foyers for Triumph dealers to display motorcycles. The Triumph dealers would display *An Officer and a Gentleman* promotional posters in their dealerships, advertising their local cinema. By the time the Chairman had phoned the sixth dealer to assess potential interest, Triumph's switchboard was blocked by incoming calls from dealers all wanting to take part. A list of cinemas showing the film was soon matched with their nearest local Triumph dealership, and what could turn out to be a very successful promotion was organised. The Paramount film was to go on general release on 28th July 1982.

Triumph's UK market profile was already being raised in July by the excellent TSS 'White Cliffs of Dover' advertising campaign. The brilliant art work captured Triumph's classic British high performance sports bike with the White Cliffs of Dover in the background. All dealers supporting the TSS promotion were identified on the advertisement. In addition, a classic piece of Triumph humour appeared: "Triumph TSS – one day you'll be ready." The ironic slogan could not have been more appropriate in view of the major difficulties we were experiencing trying to supply our most popular model! The advertising campaign continued in August.

Several very difficult weeks had passed since the marathon Directors' meeting in May, where we had discussed detailed management reports from the Commercial and Engineering Directors. Rob Murison was still with us, although his notice of resignation had expired. He was about to begin married life and embark on a five-week honeymoon. In preparation for our 13th July meeting, he produced for the Board a detailed review of all his responsibilities. The Engineering Director had done the same, circulating it for the Directors' consideration prior to

The TSS classic high performance sports motorcycle is portrayed here with the famous White Cliffs of Dover in the background. (Advertising campaign)

the meeting taking place. Unfortunately, Rob Murison explained, his marriage preparations had caused matters to overtake him and he had not been able to circulate his report until earlier on the day of the meeting. Accordingly, the Directors agreed that Rob Murison should walk them through the contents of his report; any decisions required would have to wait until they had time to consider what was being proposed. The report certainly outlined the exact position of the Commercial and Sales Departments, and Rob was leaving them with some suggested actions the Board should consider.

Phil Bragg, the Financial Controller, would deputise in Rob Murison's absence and would arrange for the auditors' return in August to finalise the annual accounts for the financial year ending 30th September 1981, the 30th September 1980 annual accounts having now been completed. Rob Murison had been obliged finally to accept that the additional stock valuation qualification placed on the 1980 annual accounts by the new Audit Manager was not worth spending more time and money arguing about, when the stock figures related to a period two years earlier! The new plan was to finalise the 1981 annual accounts as quickly as possible and present both the 1980 and 1981 audited accounts at the reconvened Annual General Meeting.

Brian Jones' circulated monthly engineering report initially focused on production developments over the previous 10 weeks. During this period, he had concluded that the system of individuals taking hours off in lieu of unpaid overtime worked was now out of control, with over 110 members having 'banked' hours. The Engineering Director's view was that the company needed to return as soon as possible to a normal system of strictly controlled, paid-for overtime.

The Commercial/Sales decision to pursue duplicate sand-casting facilities for the TSS 8-valve cylinder head and cylinder barrel at a dual-source foundry, because it was the most economical and time-effective way of achieving volume supply, was about to come on stream. Brian Jones was still of the opinion that a reliable long-term solution was the laying down of gravity dies, which although more expensive should still be pursued. Tooling costs of £4500 to subcontract machining companies to augment the in-house Triumph production of TSS components had taken place, and work was about to start.

Any motorcycle assembly hold-ups continued to be mostly due to component supplies from subcontract companies, that week's 'stopper' being Lucas Electrics.

The first batch of 42 TSX models dispatched to the dealers had suffered an unexpected rear brake problem, and was recalled to the factory to be rectified. The subsequent 48 produced were problem free, and a high level of TSX model customer satisfaction was now being reported by dealers.

However, TSS oil leak problems were a disturbing development. Detailed investigation was being undertaken by the Engineering Department and dealer feedback was being monitored by the Warranty Manager, Harry Woolridge. In the meantime, the rolling-road test duration had been doubled in an effort to try and discover any oil leaks prior to dispatch. Demand for the TSS model was already suffering as a result of this problem. The Sales Department reported reluctance from dealers to take further deliveries, let alone place new orders, until they could be reassured that the oil leak problems were over.

In view of the negotiations with the West Midlands County Council, the factory relocation into the Butler Building had virtually stopped until future plans were clearer. This growing uncertainty regarding Triumph's future was also having a major impact on morale, and several key production workers had already left. UK Sales Manager Alastair Ritchie's notice of resignation was certainly unexpected. Rob Murison felt the reason for his planned departure was because Alastair felt he hadn't received the support he should have from Sales Department staff. The Commercial Director suggested that if the sales force was to be strengthened by way of recruitment, it may well be necessary to restructure the entire sales team! In comparison, Nigel Usher, Triumph's Export Sales Manager, seemed to be happy, coming up from time to time with extremely profitable RoW institutional orders, such as the one for Ghana.

The other managerial change that had taken place resulted from Bill Beattie's negotiating involvement with the Chairman on the Board's subcommittee; this had effectively prevented Bill from continuing as Spare Parts Manager. Harry Woolridge, the Warranty Manager, had taken on the additional role as acting Spare Parts Manager in his absence – a move welcomed by the dealers, who got on very well with Harry Woolridge, but that worried Rob Murison because of warranty parts control.

We were now in the final week before the summer holiday shutdown. Having successfully built and dispatched the first 56 of the institutional order for Ghana the previous week, it was now vital that the second half of the order plus spare parts be completed and dispatched in time to catch the ship, if Triumph was to survive the holiday and return on Monday 2nd August. When that ship sailed, Triumph would get paid £159,000!

Phil Bragg, deputising in Rob Murison's absence, requested a Board meeting on 14th July, the first day of the Commercial Director's honeymoon. He was concerned that the Directors were fully aware of the present cashflow position. The detailed figures Phil presented indicated just how narrow the margins for error on income and expenditure were. Accordingly, we accepted the Financial Controller's recommendation that to provide a little bit of flexibility, one week of the membership's holiday pay should not be given until the company resumed production on 2nd August. A mass meeting would be organised to enable the Chairman to update the membership regarding the circumstances that made this change unavoidable.

For once, John Rosamond now had an enjoyable task: welcoming back Richard and Mopsa English to the Meriden factory. Where else than at Meriden should a young married couple aboard a Triumph begin a circumnavigation of the globe following in Ted Simon's wheel tracks? The 650 Thunderbird, now equipped with leading link front forks and attached to a squire box sidecar, was suitably run-in with over 2000 miles on the clock. The Triumph was given a very thorough factory service, before the sidecar was loaded with the requested list of basic 'global touring' back-up parts. Brian Jones took Richard and Mopsa to one side to point out in his West Country way the rudimentary service requirements of Triumph ownership. If religiously observed, these would guarantee their trusty steed would endure endless punishment and serve them well.

Owner John Callichio and his brother, from JRC Engineering in Calfornia, provide Richard and Mopsa with a very hospitable welcome in November 1985. (Courtesy Richard and Mopsa English archive)

John Rosamond bids Richard and Mopsa English bon voyage at the 1982 start of their circumnavigation of the globe. (Courtesy Richard and Mopsa English archive)

Then it was yours truly's turn to pose for the mandatory press photographs, shaking hands with Richard English (Richard and Mopsa aboard their Triumph) and bidding them farewell. You've guessed it – the photographs were taken on the well-manicured front lawn with the famous Triumph factory in the background, Union Jacks flying.

As I wished them bon voyage on what turned out to be a 90,000-mile journey through sixty countries taking four and a half years to complete, I knew they were excited, but understandably a little apprehensive about what the future held for them. (Of course, they were not aware of just how uncertain and difficult the position was at Triumph!) Their subsequent book *Full Circle* provides an excellent and interesting account of their tremendous journey around the world.

Many of the membership started their well earned summer holiday early, using up some of their banked overtime hours. However, this did not stop everyone having the satisfaction of knowing they had achieved the deadline for completion of the very profitable, Co-op saving, institutional order for Ghana. Packed into export shipping containers, it had left the factory en route for the docks. Most of the Senior Management personnel worked the first week of the holiday; in view of the critical cashflow situation, Phil Bragg was working both. By the end of the

Richard and Mopsa with the pristine-looking Thunderbird outfit in Sydney, Australia, in August 1983, the famous Opera House in the background. (Courtesy Richard and Mopsa English archive)

Richard takes a memorable picture of Mopsa at the Egyptian pyramids on 7th December 1986. (Courtesy Richard and Mopsa English archive)

Back in the UK in February 1987 having conquered 90,000 miles, the 650cc Thunderbird outfit 'Tommy' enjoys front of house billing at the National Motorcycle Museum. (Courtesy Richard and Mopsa English archive)

27 years after they first set off, John Rosamond meets Richard and Mopsa English for a reunion at the National Motorcycle Museum, where Tommy still generated tremendous interest. (Courtesy Richard and Mopsa English archive)

first week of the holiday, we knew the order for Ghana had reached the docks. If all now went to plan, Triumph would get paid when the ship sailed early the following week.

With the order safely at the docks and to provide for all eventualities, a Board of Directors meeting was scheduled at the factory on Sunday 1st August at 10.30am, the day before the factory was due to reopen. I managed a short family holiday in Barmouth, Wales, phoning Phil Bragg for cashflow updates as the second week progressed. Each phone call left me more concerned, as I heard that the sailing of the ship taking the order to Ghana had been cancelled yet again! When Phil Bragg was spoken to at midday on Friday 30th July, he was still unable to provide reassurance that the enormous pressure which had been applied would succeed. However, it finally did. The sense of relief was tremendous; provided we had been able to deposit the £159,000 in the bank before it closed, the factory would be able to reopen on Monday 2nd August.

The Triumph Board meeting at 10.30am on Sunday 1st August was well attended, with apologies from Rob Murison and Geoffrey Robinson. Phil Bragg the Financial Controller deputised for Rob Murison.

John Rosamond explained that payment of £159,000 for the second half of the shipment for Ghana was finally secured half an hour before National Westminster Bank closed on Friday 30th July. This had not occurred without immense pressure caused by several cancelled sailings, and final payment was achieved when the customer paid up whilst the motorcycles were still warehoused on the dockside!

As a result of this, Financial Controller Phil Bragg, who had done a tremendous job to resolve this situation, was able to explain that the cashflow projection discussed at the previous 14th July Board meeting had been slightly bettered. Accordingly, the company was now in a position to recommence production the following day, Monday 2nd August. Providing a minimum of 25 cash on delivery motorcycles were dispatched that week and the money collected, production of 50 cash on delivery motorcycles, plus normal credit terms motorcycles, could be financed during the week commencing Monday 9th August. Phil explained that the money received from the second shipment of the order for Ghana unfortunately did not reach the bank in time to enable Securicor to complete the normal payroll procedure. He would therefore implement a manual pay-out of owed holiday pay when the membership returned tomorrow.

The Board meeting closed at 12.30pm.

26

BUYING TIME

hen Triumph applied to the Economic Development Unit of the West Midlands County Council, it had been initially for export finance to replace the lost HMG/ECGD facility, thus enabling a restart of motorcycle production for the American market. The County Council commissioned the accountancy firm Price Waterhouse to undertake a financial viability report on Triumph. Whilst the report confirmed that there was indeed possible long-term viability, it also concluded that the provision of export finance would be unlikely to solve the underlying problems of the Meriden Co-op, which were much more basic. To give Triumph a chance of sustainable profitability leading to long-term viability, a complete financial reconstruction of the business would be required. It was only by so doing that a firm financial base upon which to operate could be achieved. With the help of Peter Johnson, senior partner at Price Waterhouse, the Triumph Board's internal planning document was turned into the 5-year corporate plan requested by the County Council. The likely need for an equity investment in the financial reconstruction resulted in the involvement of the West Midlands County Council Enterprise Board.

On Monday 1st August, the Meriden factory restarted production following the summer holiday. The question on everyone's lips was "how do we stay in business long enough to effect the financial reconstruction?" Our bank had made it crystal clear that whilst it would not precipitate bankruptcy if the Co-op exceeded the overdraft limit, it would bounce cheques, inevitably bringing about the same result. The Co-op's 5-year plan confirmed that replacement Managing, Executive Financial, Manufacturing, and Sales Directors would be recruited at the time of financial reconstruction. In the meantime, we would have to soldier on, running the business the best we could purely on a cashflow basis, buying time to achieve the reconstruction. Whilst we no longer had a Commercial Director, in Phil Bragg we had a Financial Controller who had already proved he was worth his weight in gold.

The West Midlands Economic Development Unit and Enterprise Board was fully informed of the critical state of Triumph's affairs, and the need for speedy action on the financial reconstruction application.

Terry Pitt, Senior Advisor to the West Midlands County Council on Economic Development, wrote to Triumph's Chairman John Rosamond on 5th August 1982.

Meriden Works

Further to my letter dated 17th June, concerning our discussions about the possible acquisition of the Meriden Works, I can now let you have some indication of the value of the Meriden site. These figures are provided by the County Secretary's Department (Valuation & Estates Division), following their visit to the site and subsequent investigations.

On a forced sale basis, the site is estimated to be worth £750,000, but a change of use of the industrial part of the site (18 acres) to housing increases the valuation to £900,000. This figure takes account of the cost of demolition and clearance and the costs of the sewer connection. An allowance of £250,000 has been made for these costs, which is only an approximate figure. More recently, demolition and clearance costs have been more accurately estimated at £177,000. Your proposal that Triumph Motorcycles could undertake this work might well reduce these costs and raise the market value of the site.

I believe the views of our own and Coventry City Planning Department are that there are unlikely to be any objections to a change of use from industry to housing on the site; indeed the change would probably be welcomed.

On the 4-acre field, which is presently designated as agricultural/open space, there are more fundamental objections to a change of use on planning grounds, and I am advised that a change of use to housing is most unlikely to be approved. This means the field has presently very little commercial value and a figure of only £10,000 has been included in the calculations.

You will appreciate that this letter does not constitute a formal offer to acquire the site, but is rather for your information on the commercial value of the site. I understand you are in discussion with a number of potential purchasers. I must stress again that the County Council's main interest is helping to secure the long-term viability of the business. Perhaps you could let us know whether you wish to begin negotiations with the County Council to sell the site?

I know that you have made an approach to the West Midlands Enterprise Board, which is considering how a financial injection could be made to help the restructuring of the co-operative. The Chairman of the Board is most anxious to be positive.

You will also know that the County Council has launched a range of initiatives designed to encourage the development of co-operative enterprises. In some cases, grant aid has been made available, and I am sure that the Economic Development Committee would be prepared to consider making a substantial grant to Triumph as part of the total financial package required to restructure the business. It is difficult to give you a precise figure at the moment, particularly since the Committee has not had the opportunity to consider the matter. Grant aid would normally be made available to cover a specific cost, but there is some flexibility over what can be considered. In your case, the relocation costs of moving to a new site or interest relief on loans could be two possibilities, but I am sure there are many others. Perhaps we could discuss this at some time in the near future?

I hope this information is helpful.

Yours sincerely

Terry J Pitt

Senior Adviser on Economic Development

Discussions continued in anticipation of an early response to Triumph's 5 year-plan, based upon which financial reconstruction was anticipated. During the latter part of August as the Co-op continued its day-to-day critical cashflow existence, it became apparent that Triumph's 5-year plan was now to be reviewed by the internationally renowned London management consultants Arthur D Little. This further delay ruled out any chance of an Enterprise Board reconstruction decision at their scheduled early September meeting.

The sales promotion in conjunction with the August screening of *An Officer and a Gentleman* was a success for Paramount Pictures and Triumph. Participating sold out cinemas and busy Triumph dealers guaranteed increased sales demand, especially for US-spec Bonnevilles. The film's box office success was later matched with an Academy Award for Louis Gossett JR for his brilliant portrayal of Theo Foley, the tough drill instructor.

Although Rob Murison had now left Triumph, he was still available to us on the telephone. This was vital to Phil Bragg in order to maintain continuity of work, especially with the auditors, who were now pressing ahead with the completion of the 30th September 1981 annual accounts. Unfortunately, Rob Murison's plan to secure acceptance of both the 1980 and 1981 annual accounts at the reconvened Annual General Meeting was scuppered, when the Directors received a letter from the Companies Registration Office warning that failure to provide the overdue 1980 audited accounts would leave them liable to prosecution. This legal action would be discussed at the scheduled monthly Board meeting on 10th September.

The Chairman reported to the Board meeting that the West Midlands Enterprise Board Directors had requested an opportunity to visit the Triumph factory and would be doing so the following Wednesday, 15th September. John Rosamond stressed the need for the factory to be in full production and as clean and tidy as possible for the visit, in order that we may achieve the best lasting impression. Negotiations with the Enterprise Board were progressing, although there could now be a delay until 16th September whilst the management consultants employed to review Triumph's 5-year plan submitted their report to the Chief Executive, Norman Holmes.

Phil Bragg, Triumph's Financial Controller, explained that the tabled cashflow projection up to 24th September indicated just how little scope there was for error or shortfall. Provided 13 TSS, 3 TSX and 12 other motorcycles, plus 3 for Verstegen were shipped during week ending 17th September, we would be in receipt of sufficient cash to enable the purchase of raw materials in week commencing 20th September. Whilst this cashflow projection took account of a payment of £20,000 to the Inland Revenue – which was now pressing extremely hard – two weeks' wages, and one month's salary, no provision had been made for the approximate £45,000 overdraft interest payment owed to the National Westminster Bank. It was therefore inevitable that Triumph would once again exceed the overdraft limit. The Directors agreed that every effort must be made to better the Financial Controller's cashflow projection in order to improve this situation. Only by so doing could we ensure production continued following the imminent week-long September break.

Bill Beattie described for the Board the sudden build up of pressure that had taken place from the following sources:

a) The Companies Registration Office

Most Directors had now received correspondence from the Companies Registration Office regarding the outstanding annual accounts in respect of the financial periods ending 30th September 1980 and 30th September 1981.

Accordingly, it was essential that the adjourned 1980 Annual General Meeting be reconvened in the near future. This would enable audited and signed accounts for the first period ending 30th September 1980 to be delivered to the Companies Registration Office, prior to 30th September 1982. Failure to do so would leave past and present Triumph Directors liable to prosecution. John Rosamond would be arranging for the reconvened AGM to take place as soon as possible. Once it had, the 1980 accounts plus the scheduled date for the 1981 AGM were to be provided to the registrar at the Companies Registration Office. This positive action would hopefully prevent legal proceedings against Triumph's Directors.

b) Inland Revenue

A meeting was being arranged with the Inland Revenue Inspector of Taxes in order to discuss Triumph's current arrears, and its future ability to pay off those arrears following the planned financial reconstruction. Discussion with Rob Murison had suggested a minimum payment of £20,000 would be required to hold the situation in the short-term. However, it was felt this was bound to be extremely difficult.

c) *Coventry Evening Telegraph*

John Rosamond outlined a telephone conversation he'd had with the Coventry Evening Telegraph industrial reporter earlier that day. Various questions had been posed by the journalist regarding the sale of the Meriden factory site, residential planning permission, the 5-year corporate plan, approaches to the West Midlands Enterprise Board and Geoffrey Robinson's "recent Co-op Board resignation."

Bill Beattie felt that the sudden build up of pressure being experienced at the same time as reconstruction negotiations neared decision point was much more than coincidence. It seemed to suggest that a person or persons unknown were deliberately leaking information in order to make difficult decisions even more difficult.

The Directors agreed that there was very little that could be done in the circumstances to determine who had leaked the information. However, in the event of the culprit coming to light positive steps would be taken to deal with the matter.

In view of the subjects discussed, the Chairman felt it was imperative that the members be brought up to date to enable them to play their full part. This would be fundamental in allowing Triumph to buy time in order to reach the financial reconstruction decision point – it was now felt this would be at the end of September or the beginning of October. The Board agreed, and to minimise loss to production, the mass meeting would be called at 4.00pm, 30 minutes before the end of the shift.

An extended visit by most of the West Midlands Enterprise Board Directors and officials took place on 16th September. The neat and tidy Meriden factory was in full production and the Enterprise Board Directors (many of whom were very enthusiastic about the future employment potential offered by co-operatives) took the trouble during their visit to discuss with individual members their experiences so far. The candid replies to their questioning indicated the Co-op members' appetite to fight on until the financial reconstruction took place, and could not have failed to impress. After all, it was the commitment and numerous sacrifices by the membership that had managed to keep the Co-op and Triumph alive for so long.

The expected article in the *Coventry Evening Telegraph* appeared on 20th September, indicating the items mentioned to the Chairman. However, the reference to the "Coventry Labour MP Geoffrey Robinson who until recently was a Triumph Director and is now a Director on the Enterprise Board" was unexpected.

What the Directors had thought was the *Coventry Evening Telegraph* industrial reporter's speculative questioning of the Triumph Chairman, possibly referring to Geoffrey Robinson's resignation from responsibilities for the American subsidiary TMA, was now clarified somewhat in the 20th September article. It was unlikely that this respected journalist would make such a claim about a local Member of Parliament without confirming with the person concerned that the story was factually correct. The Directors felt that if it was Geoffrey Robinson's intention to formally resign from the Co-op Board, he should attend a meeting and provide an update on how he was leaving his previous non-executive responsibilities.

Due to their intensive involvement with Geoffrey Robinson, John Rosamond and Bill

Beattie found it hard to believe that the former Chief Executive and key member of the Co-op's negotiating team was apparently now behaving in this way. We therefore hoped the reported severed connection with Triumph was to enable him to play a full and independent role as a Director of the West Midlands Enterprise Board, supporting the Co-op's financial reconstruction application. After all, this was one of Geoffrey's suggested commercial options in order to secure the future of the Co-op. What was in no doubt from the article was that whoever leaked the politically motivated story, had ensured any Enterprise Board decision to invest ratepayers' money in the Meriden Co-op had just become a lot more difficult!

The reconvened Annual General Meeting took place on 29th September 1982 to accept the annual accounts for the financial period ending 30th September 1980.

The Trustees waived their entitlement to 21 days' clear notice in view of the company's difficulties and the possible prosecution of the Directors. Geoffrey Robinson MP was not present, but former Commercial Director Rob Murison was, attending to answer any financial questions that may arise. Apologies had been received from Ron Marston, who was in America, leaving the other two Trustees, John Haynes and John Tomlinson, to receive instructions from the Beneficiary owners of Triumph. The AGM formalities of accepting the 1980 annual accounts, reappointing the auditor Coopers and Lybrand, and authorising the Directors to fix their remunerations duly completed, these accounts were now to be urgently delivered by hand to the Registrar at the Companies Registration Office. They would be accompanied by a covering letter from the Triumph Chairman, outlining the action being undertaken to quickly provide the audited annual accounts for the period ending 30th September 1981.

The almost daily contact with the West Midlands County Council Economic Development Unit via its Co-operative Development Officer, Tom Fitch, continued during the first days of October, as the downward spiral of Co-op cashflow continued. The monthly Board meeting on 7th October concentrated on the Co-op's financial situation.

Phil Bragg explained that due to a delay in receiving payments from Australia for 28 motorcycles and a consignment of motorcycles for Wust in Germany (the total value of which was in excess of £50,000), once again we were experiencing another crisis. However, Wust had made a telegraphic transfer of £19,000 earlier in the week and TMA was transferring $30,000 today, easing the cash situation slightly. Until the two aforementioned amounts reached Triumph's bank account, the overdraft ceiling had been reached. Therefore there was no alternative but to defer the week's wages payment until funds were available – likely to be the next day, Friday. It was agreed to advise the membership of this at a mass meeting.

The Chairman reminded the Board of Directors that it was extremely important, in the present financial situation, to review the likelihood of successfully concluding the current negotiations to restructure Triumph. It was only in these circumstances that the company could continue to trade on behalf of its creditors. A letter written by Peter Johnson of Price Waterhouse to the West Midlands County Council stated that "in the circumstances of a completely restructured company there should be long-term viability." This initial view, expressed by the accountants Price Waterhouse, had been further supported by a report from management consultants Arthur D Little, commissioned by the West Midlands Enterprise Board. Although the management consultants had a few misgivings, their report was generally supportive of the plan to financially restructure Triumph and thus achieve long-term viability. The Board of Directors voted unanimously to continue to trade.

The motorcycles and spare parts order situation was then discussed.

a) Triumph Motorcycles America (Inc)

TMA had recently launched the new 1982/83 range of motorcycles, and secured 289 orders for immediate delivery in week one, with week two resulting in a further 100 orders being placed. Wayne Moulton, TMA's President, had emphasised the need for speedy delivery of these motorcycles in order to display the latest Triumph models in dealers' showrooms. This situation was not unlike the one that prevailed twelve months earlier when, due to lack of a suitable credit line to replace the lost ECGD facility, the Triumph factory was unable to supply motorcycles to America. It was in these circumstances that the Chairman was again pursuing a line of credit to enable motorcycles to be supplied to the US; progress to date towards this end was encouraging.

b) Australia

Len Hamilton on his recent visit had indicated an Australian requirement for 112 motorcycles, to be supplied during the following month of November. Specific details of each of these motorcycles was to be provided.

c) Japan

The letter of credit for 28 motorcycles destined for Murayama Motors of Japan was expected before the end of the week.

It was a very different-looking Triumph Bonneville for America that secured 389 orders for immediate delivery within two weeks of going on sale. (Brochure picture)

d) Nigerian spare parts order

During the previous week, Triumph had received a spare parts order for the Nigerian army, to the value of £184,000. Nigel Usher, Triumph's Export Sales Manager, was currently pursuing the letter of credit which was expected before the end of October when supply would begin. He had been advised that this initial Nigerian Triumph spare parts order was the first part of the overall order, worth in excess of £1m.

The Directors discussed the improved order situation at some length, noting that there was also a strong likelihood that military motorcycle orders from Saudi Arabia for 60 and Jordan for 500 were likely to be placed during the month of November. In these circumstances, Triumph's potential and firm order books were the strongest they had been for some time.

On 15th October, the Chairman had to call a further meeting to report to the Directors that because of the delay in completing the financial reconstruction negotiations with the West Midlands Enterprise Board, it had agreed to provide Triumph with a 'secret' £150,000 export finance facility, to enable motorcycles to be built for the USA.

Councillor Geoffrey Edge, Chairman of the Enterprise Board, had informed John Rosamond and Bill Beattie that it was accepted the £150,000 loan would be initially unsecured, allowing the purchase of component parts, and payment of factory overhead costs and wages. However, subsequently the Enterprise Board loan would become secured against specific motorcycles as they were built and shipped to America. Whilst difficulty had been experienced in formalising this decision in a practical manner, both John Rosamond and Bill Beattie had received indications from Enterprise Board personnel that an initial sum of at least £30,000 for the purchase of parts and labour/factory overheads would become available later that day or early next week. This export finance loan would make possible a motorcycle build of 125 out of the current TMA order bank of 400. As availability of the Enterprise Board loan facility now seemed imminent, the Directors voted unanimously in favour of committing to the first motorcycle build of 56. One of the most sensitive concerns the Enterprise Board had was that this loan facility must remain completely secret, a condition that the Co-op Directors readily agreed to. In view of the urgency to reach a legal agreement, Ron Briggs proposed and Brian Jones seconded that Bill Beattie and John Rosamond should be authorised to act on behalf of the Triumph Board of Directors in this matter. The following resolution was unanimously agreed by the Board:

The Board of Directors of Triumph Motorcycles (Meriden) Limited hereby accept the terms and conditions laid down by the West Midlands Enterprise Board Limited regarding the provision of a £150,000 loan facility to export motorcycles to the United States of America, as laid down in legal documentation duly signed by Mr J A Rosamond Chairman and Mr W A Beattie Director for and on behalf of Triumph Motorcycles (Meriden) Limited.

Moving now to the delay in achieving the full financial reconstruction of Triumph's affairs, Geoffrey Edge had indicated that Arthur D Little, the management consultants employed to review Triumph's 5-year plan, had flagged up three areas where further detailed answers were required from Triumph:

i) Detailed engineering information regarding the likely successful outcome of the new Diana model range.

ii) Detailed in-house cost information on motorcycle manufacture.

iii) Detailed cost information on purchase and manufacture of the new Diana model range.

Mr Richard O'Dell Poulden, project leader with Arthur D Little, had indicated that to provide the aforementioned detailed information (which the Enterprise Board contended was part of its original brief), would take until the end of December 1982. In these circumstances, Councillor Geoffrey Edge indicated to the negotiating team that he would be asking the Enterprise Board at its scheduled 29th October meeting for a further £500,000 of export finance for Triumph. In so doing, the Enterprise Board would be enabling Triumph to continue production until the ultimate decision on the financial reconstruction at the end of the year.

With this requirement in mind, Triumph's Directors felt management hierarchy changes would have to take place in order to provide the Diana project detailed information required by Arthur D Little. The new Diana models were the cornerstone of Triumph's 5-year plan, so Brian Jones would have to get the opportunity to direct his full attention to them. Recognising the large contribution Brian was making to the manufacturing side of the business, the Directors were conscious of the loss of production engineering co-ordination that would now occur, so the Chairman asked Bill Beattie if he would undertake the production co-ordination role for the foreseeable future. John Rosamond further stated that whilst he would continue in his present commercial role, he would of course also be giving as much support as possible to Brian Jones and Bill Beattie in the new management changes now so vital to securing Triumph's future.

The Directors accepted that if the required Diana project information for Arthur D Little was to be provided, there seemed to be few alternatives. Brian Jones felt Bill Beattie had a good chance of success, being good at the numbers game; however, the difficulties would be in his lack of production engineering experience.

Summarising, the Chairman stated that early the following week, when the Enterprise Board export finance facility was secured, a further mass meeting of the membership would take place. The members would be provided with an update on the financial reconstruction negotiations, and the reasons for the forced management changes that had to be made. They would be expected to play a full part in supporting Bill Beattie in order to achieve the company's survival.

Board Director Ron Briggs was seriously injured in a motorcycle accident on 19th October. His injuries required a lengthy stay in hospital.

Having narrowly avoided court proceedings against them for non-registration of Triumph's annual audited accounts, the Triumph Directors were about to receive a further legal shock. During the £150,000 export loan contractual negotiations with the West Midlands Enterprise Board, Company Solicitor Peter Davis had disclosed that the Nahib Dajani litigation proceedings were about to go to court!

John Rosamond reported this to the Directors the following day. What we had thought to be a dormant litigation claim had in fact been proceeding against Triumph for in excess of two years. Nahib Dajani was claiming £16,000 by way of lost commission for an export order for motorcycles to Libya. Peter Davis had referred the Chairman to Tim Burnhill, a solicitor colleague of his at Ward and Rider, who was currently representing Triumph on this case. Tim Burnhill had met Geoffrey Robinson MP, Brenda Price, and Ian Rush – the three individuals to represent Triumph in the court proceedings – on 16th October. Tim Burnhill had stated that in the event of Nahib Dajani being successful with the litigation claim, his compensation plus legal expenses would be in the region of £25,000. In these circumstances, Tim Burnhill readily accepted the Chairman's request for further information, immediately recognising the position we were in, where the Triumph witnesses no longer worked for the company, and the present Board of Directors and management had no up to date information concerning the case.

The Triumph Directors expressed their astonishment at how such potentially drastic litigation proceedings could continue against the company without their knowledge. It was agreed that a letter should be sent by the Chairman to Mr Geoffrey Robinson MP, inviting him to attend a meeting to update the Directors on all matters for which he had previously held responsibility, following which the Board would formally accept his resignation.

Moving now to the financial situation, Phil Bragg reported that as Triumph had not yet succeeded in drawing on the £150,000 West Midlands Enterprise Board facility, the cashflow crisis was deepening – Triumph's overdraft had been breached to the tune of £22,000. However, provided a minimum of £33,000 could be drawn from the export loan by the next day, Thursday 21st October, plus the expected income from Jordan and Australia on 22nd and 25th respectively, he felt a deferred wages payment could be made to the membership on Monday 25th October at the latest.

The negotiating team reported that the delay in drawing export finance from the West Midlands Enterprise Board facility had occurred as a direct result of the time taken in legal debate whilst it tried to achieve full security for the £150,000 loan. This contravened completely both the spirit of and the decision reached by the Enterprise Board on 1st October, as communicated to Bill Beattie and John Rosamond by Enterprise Chairman Councillor Geoffrey Edge. The formal legal agreement was now due to be signed at the Enterprise Board's solicitors, Wragge and Co, the next day, 21st October, when the first drawing of £33,000 secured against 56 TSX completed engines should take place. In view of what appeared to the negotiating team to be complete reneging on the original offer to Triumph, John Rosamond and Bill Beattie would push for a further upfront payment to redress the disastrous effect this had had on Triumph's cashflow position, leaving the company in a critical financial situation.

The Directors decided that a mass meeting should take place at 8.05am the following morning, at which time the Chairman would update the membership on the continuing financial crisis and consequent deferred payment of wages.

The final business of the Board meeting was to advise the Directors that further detailed management discussion had taken place, and it had been resolved that Brian Jones would relinquish day-to-day control of the manufacturing side of the business, thus enabling him to concentrate on the Diana product engineering information for Arthur D Little. Bill Beattie would assume responsibility for manufacturing, acting as Brian Jones' deputy.

The £150,000 export loan facility agreement for US-bound motorcycles was duly completed with Amersdown Limited, a wholly owned subsidiary of the West Midlands Enterprise Board.

The Chairman had to call yet another Board meeting on 28th October to allow discussion of extremely disturbing news from the West Midlands Enterprise Board. John Rosamond reported that the commitment given by Enterprise Board Chairman Councillor Geoffrey Edge that "the Enterprise Board would agree a further £500,000 worth of export finance at its Board meeting on 29th October," was not now achievable. Reviewing the situation earlier in the week, a meeting of the Economic Development Unit Committee had decided that in view of what it described as Geoffrey Robinson's anticipated opposition to any further financial support for Triumph Meriden, and the influence that this would undoubtedly have on other Enterprise Board Directors, it made the successful achievement of the half million pounds export facility extremely doubtful. (The negotiating team would try and investigate Geoffrey Robinson's alleged opposition.) In these circumstances, it had been decided that an easier and therefore more prudent way of achieving a £500,000 loan injection in Triumph was to apply on 9th November to the Economic Development Unit Committee.

Triumph's Chairman reported that he had had a lengthy telephone conversation prior to this Board meeting with Terry Pitt (head of the Economic Development Unit) who in clarifying the general situation explained that the report now being compiled, whilst politically and socially biased, would also have to show the commercial good sense for an injection of half a million pounds. To be achievable he had to demonstrate that not only would the financial injection be going towards protecting jobs, but also giving the Co-operative a better chance of achieving lasting viability.

John Birch asked what the latest situation was regarding negotiations with the West Midlands Enterprise Board to achieve financial reconstruction. John Rosamond explained that the promised half million pounds of export finance had been to enable Triumph to continue production whilst the questions raised by the Arthur D Little consultancy report were answered. Once answers to those areas of concern had been provided, a decision on the complete financial restructuring of Triumph would take place.

Bill Beattie added that whilst the West Midlands Enterprise Board was no longer going to provide the half million pounds of export finance, indications to date regarding the reconstruction were favourable. The West Midlands County Council Economic Development Unit would now provide the financial injection, enabling us to still meet the aforementioned timetable. It was agreed that switching the provider of the finance had been unavoidable, given the circumstances.

The Directors now had to consider the implications of a further delay of at least eleven days, prior to the availability of the money. Phil Bragg reported that it would be impossible to continue normal manufacture throughout that period. The Chairman commented that he felt it was important to remain within the overdraft ceiling of £1,195,000 if the bank's continued support was to be maintained. Following discussion, the Directors agreed that the only way we could make it through to 9th November was for manufacturing to cease on Friday 5th November, with the company laid off pending securement of the West Midlands Economic Development Unit loan. A mass meeting would be called in one hour, at 4.00pm.

Finally the Directors considered an update from the Chairman on the Nahib Dajani litigation proceedings, based upon a telephone conversation with solicitor Tim Burnhill. John Rosamond would attend a meeting at Ward and Rider's office in Coventry at 9.00am the following morning.

In the brief time that was available prior to what was bound to be an extremely difficult mass meeting of the membership, the Chairman reflected upon why Geoffrey Robinson could be behaving in this alleged unhelpful way towards the Meriden Co-op, when previously his leadership and total commitment had been fundamental to our survival. Could it be that like the Beneficiary Directors back in 1978 (chapter 9), Geoffrey was now also confronted with the "inherent and irreconcilable contradictions" of his dual role? On the one hand of being a socialist Labour MP representing Coventry North West constituents (many of whom worked at Triumph Meriden and had elected him) and on the other, his highly experienced commercial views as a Director of the West Midlands Enterprise Board. Was he really saying, as was being reported from County Hall, that he was "opposed to any further financial help for Triumph Meriden," or perhaps much more likely, that short-term export loans would not solve Triumph's problems, only a complete financial reconstruction of the business?

In the political hotbed of the West Midlands Authority it would have been very easy for anti-Triumph forces, and we already knew there were many, to misrepresent Geoffrey's comments. What was certain was that everyone at Triumph knew – as did the West Midlands Enterprise Board and Economic Development Unit, plus their advisors Price Waterhouse and Arthur D Little – that further export loans from any source would not stem the losses. Only a complete financial reconstruction had a chance of achieving long-term viability for Triumph.

27

POLITICS TAKE OVER

T he mass meeting to discuss a complete factory layoff from 5th November 1982 was, as expected, tough. The membership found it extremely difficult to understand how a supportive West Midlands County Council, with detailed financial knowledge of the Co-op's critical cashflow situation, could now delay for a further eleven days the vital £500,000 loan. Furthermore, once we accommodated members' outstanding guaranteed working week payments, and time off in lieu in return for unpaid overtime, little labour savings would be achieved – only less spent on component parts. This would lead to even more production losses during the 5-day layoff.

On 9th November, Triumph's negotiating team was invited to attend the County Council's Economic Development Unit Committee meeting at County Hall, Birmingham. The first agenda item was the approval of £465,000 worth of loans to Triumph Motorcycles (Meriden) Limited. Immediately after this had been agreed, the Committee Chairman Councillor, Geoffrey Edge, adjourned the meeting for a pre-arranged press conference.

COUNTY COUNCIL SUPPORT TO TRIUMPH MOTORCYCLES (MERIDEN) LTD
The County Council's Economic Development Committee today approved loans of up to £465,000 to Triumph Motorcycles (Meriden) Ltd. The Committee made this decision in the light of substantial investigations made into the company by accountants Price Waterhouse and consultants Arthur D Little. From these and their own appraisal, the County Council believes that Triumph Motorcycles can be made into a viable exporting company in the short-term, and that everything possible should be done to secure the long-term future of the company.

The County Council was informed of a large number of export orders to the United States, Australia and Europe that would not be fulfilled without further assistance to ease the current cashflow position of Triumph. In addition, the company is pursuing orders in the Middle East and Africa which would lead to substantial increases in production.

Working closely with the workforce at Triumph, officers at County Hall believe they have identified a number of areas where substantial savings in production costs can be achieved.

In recommending his Committee approve the loan, Councillor Geoff Edge, Chairman of the Committee said:"I believe that we should support this company on the basis that this represents the sole surviving manufacturer of motorcycles in the country; that the company appears viable for the term over which the loan is made, that the loan is secured against individual machines, and that we have identified ways of reducing production costs. This represents a substantial achievement for the County Council."

> *For further information contact:-*
> *Terry J Pitt*
> *Senior Adviser on Economic Development, County Hall.*

Shocked by what had just taken place at County Hall John Rosamond and Bill Beattie returned rapidly to the Meriden factory, it being vital to explain loan developments to the Board of Directors and membership before they were notified by the media. We explained to the Board that the West Midlands County Council would make available to Triumph Motorcycles (Meriden) Limited, £365,000 worth of financial aid secured against export motorcycles as they were produced, and that the balance of the £465,000, i.e. £100,000, would be loaned for capital investment in machine tools to enable reductions in manufacturing costs.

Phil Bragg, Triumph's Financial Controller, commented that although the loans from the West Midlands County Council were extremely good news, with the bank overdraft at its absolute maximum there was no choice whatsoever but to cease all production until finance from the £365,000 export loan facility could be drawn down. In effect, this meant that the membership would be laid off again as of 4.30pm that day, 9th November, and would have to remain so until further notice. Wage payments due on 11th November would have to be deferred until finance was available from the West Midlands County Council. It was agreed by the Board that the factory would be laid off until further notice, and that the circumstances making this action necessary would be placed before an immediate mass meeting of the membership.

The stunned members received the news of the forced layoff in complete silence. As the demoralised Co-op membership returned to their sections, they left their Directors wondering how many more key production workers would now seek employment elsewhere.

The following day, 10th November, *The Financial Times* reported on the West Midlands County Council loans to the Meriden Co-op. This is reproduced here with its kind permission.

W MIDLANDS TO LEND MERIDEN MOTORCYCLE CO-OP £465,000
BY ARTHUR SMITH, MIDLANDS CORRESPONDENT
West Midlands County Council is lending Meriden Motorcycle Co-operative £465,000 out of ratepayers' money to ease its cashflow problems.

> *The local authority backed Enterprise Board is also considering taking an equity stake in the Co-operative, to help fund a £1m-plus five-year development programme.*
> *Meriden, with a workforce cut to less than a third of its level two years ago, has suffered a series of crises since it was set up with a £4.2m Government loan by Mr Tony Benn, former Industry Secretary, in 1975.*
> *His action followed an extended workers' occupation of the factory in protest at the planned closure by the troubled Norton-Villiers-Triumph Company.*
> *Mr Geoff Edge, Chairman of the Enterprise Board said last night that the £465,000 was merely short-term finance, which would "tide the Co-operative over for a year or two." A financial restructuring was necessary to provide investment in plant machinery and model development. Under consideration is a plan under which the Co-operative could either move to new premises*

or concentrate in one part of the present site, freeing about 17 acres of land for development – probably for housing. The Co-operative now employs only 188 workers with an output of about 80 motorcycles a week compared with a labour force of 720 and a target production of 350 units just over two years ago. The present Conservative Government wrote off the original Government loan advanced to set up the co-operative. The debt totalled nearly £5.9m, with accrued interest. Mr John Rosamond, Chairman of the Co-operative said last night that £365,000 of the money from the County Council would be used to finance the export of bikes, particularly to the US. A further £100,000 was for investment in machine tools to raise efficiency and productivity. The Co-operative had drawn up a five-year corporate plan based on the present lower levels of output, improved productivity and new models, he said. Mr Edge said the Enterprise Board was examining with private sector bodies the funding of the corporate plan. A decision was not likely before the end of the year, and the Board had three or four other "significant investments" in the pipeline.

The negotiating teams' concern regarding the press involvement grew further, when it was discovered that the Enterprise Board accountancy staff who had been involved in the delays with access to the initial "secret" £150,000 export loan had now been seconded to the Economic Development Unit, to ensure security on the County Council loan. It was hoped that any negative feelings they may have had about the secret loan would not slow down our urgent access to the £365,000 County Council facility. We found it absolutely amazing that after all the detailed financial information provided, and the extensive independent investigations that had taken place, the urgent need to stop the losses with a financial reconstruction now seemed to be ignored as one legal delay led to another – it wasn't as though the West Midlands County Council was not aware of Triumph's critical financial situation, which could only get worse as losses continued to accrue. However, the consistently supportive Terry Pitt, Senior Advisor on Economic Development, came to the Co-op's rescue by writing to the Inland Revenue on Triumph's behalf on 11th November 1982.

Dear Mr Beale,
I have been asked by Triumph Motorcycles (Meriden) Limited to write to you in order to clarify the situation regarding financial support agreed by the West Midlands County Council (see press notice dated 9th November 1982, attached).
*   The West Midlands County Council has approved loans subject to contract of £465,000 to Triumph Motorcycles (Meriden) Limited, £365,000 to be secured against specific export motorcycles as they are built, and in addition, a further loan of £100,000 to enable the company to purchase machinery, which will help reduce the unit cost of production. Preparation of the legal documentation to give effect to the loan is presently in hand. This finance has been made available only after examination of the company's prospects by Price Waterhouse, Accountants, and an in depth report by a firm of consultants, Arthur D Little. The aforementioned financial assistance by the West Midlands County Council is based on the belief that Triumph Motorcycles (Meriden) has a future and should be supported.*
*   I hope these comments are satisfactory for your purposes, and help clarify the role of the West Midlands County Council vis-à-vis this company.*
*   Yours sincerely*
*   Terry J Pitt*
*   Senior Adviser on Economic Development*

On 15th November, Triumph's monthly Board meeting took place. Phil Bragg tabled for discussion his latest cashflow projection. Whilst showing an inflow of £40,000 from Canada and France, outgoings of £29,000 left the forecasted overdraft position on Friday 19th November at £1,194,000. Contained within the outgoings for the week was a payment of £20,000 to the Inland Revenue, making good the previous week's short fall. Mr Terry Pitt's 11th November helpful letter to the Inland Revenue was duly noted. In view of the outlined financial report, Phil Bragg stated that the company was not yet in a position to pay the membership's wage arrears.

The Chairman reported that the legal wrangling continued with the West Midlands County Council, as a result of which the first tranche of money from the £365,000 loan was not yet available. However, a London meeting had been called for 17th November by the Assistant General Manager of Triumph's bank, and this would enable all interested parties to discuss the County Council's required loans security, undoubtedly clarifying the present situation.

After discussion, the Directors agreed that whilst the factory layoff had been total to date, with only key personnel working voluntarily, for the company to survive and have a future the following key commitments would have to be honoured, requiring the recall of appropriate members who would be paid to undertake this crucial work:

a) Complete and re-submit Triumph's 5-year corporate plan for the West Midlands Enterprise Board.

b) Complete the internal factory move to reduce overhead costs.

c) Complete the police/military demonstrator motorcycles for the South Yorkshire Police Authority, Derbyshire Police Authority and the Ministry of Defence.

d) Continue to actively pursue orders for motorcycles and spare parts.

e) Continue to strictly administer financial controls within the business.

f) Finalise the legal agreements regarding the West Midlands County Council's £465,000 loan.

Engineering Director Brian Jones reported that on Saturday 13th November he had conducted a review of the Diana project at Weslake/Rye Tools. The undertaking previously given by the consultant engineers to run the first Diana engine by mid-November was not going to be achieved. Whilst a substantial number of engine components were under manufacture, there still remained a large amount of work to be completed. Once complete, at least one further week would be required for engine assembly before the initial dynamometer test run. Having reviewed the remaining project programme with the consultant engineers, completion date was now targeted for the end of November.

In view of the vital importance of the new engine project to the overall financial restructuring of the company, the Directors decided that a much stricter 'policing' role needed to be undertaken. Brian Jones was in agreement, and would revisit the consultants, initially on Wednesday 17th and again on Friday 19th November.

Phil Bragg reported that accrued warranty for the period ending September 1982 had escalated alarmingly to in excess of £50 per motorcycle, double the recognised budget provision. Board discussion identified three main contributory factors:

i) Electric start gear failures.

ii) TSS cylinder head porosity and camshaft design.

iii) General quality (associated with the increase of the warranty guarantee period from 6 months/6000 miles to 12 months/12,000 miles).

Reference was also made by the Directors to possible breaches of trust that had taken place when faulty parts had not been returned for examination by the factory, prior to being replaced under warranty – a practice totally contrary to established Board policy. This policy determined that all substandard parts covered by the warranty guarantee must be returned to the factory, prior to replacement. The Directors agreed that strict adherence to Board warranty policy would be enforced in future.

The temporary arrangement whereby Triumph's Service Manager would also act (in the absence of Bill Beattie) as Spare Parts Manager, in light of the experience outlined in the warranty discussion, was determined to have been too wide a responsibility for any one individual. Accordingly, the Directors decided that the two functions would be separated again.

Recognising the importance of spare parts profitability and its impact on Triumph's overall financial position, the Directors agreed a new approach to spare parts supply. George Mackie would be appointed Spare Parts Manager. The Financial Controller would provide him with a strict spare parts purchasing budget. As spare parts availability improved, Triumph would adopt a more aggressive strategy regarding selling.

The third senior management change agreed by the Board was to increase Brian Baldwin's area of responsibility, now to encompass production control as well as procurement of motorcycle component parts. All three management changes would be made with immediate effect.

The Chairman reported that Mr Tim Burnhill, the solicitor at Ward and Rider representing Triumph in the Nahib Dajani litigation proceedings, had advised that Triumph's counsel was now recommending an out of court settlement, as there was a possibility that the court could find in favour of Nahib Dajani. Whilst this was the case, a date for the court hearing had not yet been set. If required, Tim Burnhill had offered to address the Triumph Board of Directors prior to the settlement decision being taken. The Directors agreed to this course of action.

The Chairman reported that in view of the extremely delicate cashflow situation relating to both TMA and Triumph Meriden, it was felt that the subsidiary's President, Wayne Moulton, should pay a brief visit to the Meriden factory on Tuesday 16th and Wednesday 17th November. Mrs Kate Murray, seconded accountant for the West Midlands Economic Development Unit, had expressed a wish to meet Wayne Moulton during the visit to discuss possible overhead cost reductions associated with Triumph's American subsidiary.

With that, another monthly Board meeting was over.

In the plan to relocate the factory to the Butler Building to effect overhead cost reductions, the move itself was only part of the story. Bill Beattie's meeting with the Coventry City Council Rates Inspector had determined that if roofs were removed from Triumph buildings no longer in use, the buildings would be rate free. Alternatively, 50 per cent rate reductions could be achieved by knocking down one wall of an unused building. It had been calculated that £40,000 per annum could be saved by zero rating all the unused factory buildings.

The helpful Rates Inspector had also observed some of Triumph's subletting of unused factory outbuildings, and advised this practice would incur a higher rates charge! Accordingly, all short-term leases would now be given notice to vacate.

On 17th November, Wayne Moulton visited the factory and was involved in urgent detailed product meetings with Brian Jones.

John Rosamond, Bill Beattie and Phil Bragg were in London at the head office of the National Westminster Bank for a meeting called by Mr Gerry Esam, Assistant General

Manager. Representing the West Midlands County Council were Mr Terry Pitt (Senior Advisor on Economic Development), Mr Tom Fitch (Co-operative Development Officer), Mrs Kate Murray (Accountant), and Mr Peter Johnson (Price Waterhouse). In addition to the Assistant General Manager, the bank's Advances Officer Mr Andy Philpott, with whom the Financial Controller and Triumph's Chairman currently liaised, was also present.

Mr Esam stated that he had requested the meeting of all interested parties in an effort to ascertain information relating to progress on Triumph's immediate and long-term future.

Mr Terry Pitt explained that the West Midlands County Council representatives were taking part in their own right, and therefore could only comment on the immediate future; any long-term plans associated with a complete restructuring of the business with help from the West Midlands Enterprise Board was a separate issue for others to deal with. Although this was the case, Mr Pitt continued, he was aware of the strenuous behind the scenes efforts being undertaken by the Enterprise Board staff, in order to create an atmosphere in which financial restructuring could take place. Mr Esam commented that whilst the bank was exercising a considerable amount of goodwill in an effort to allow sufficient time for financial restructuring, the National Westminster Bank would not and could not allow any further erosion of their financial involvement to take place. The absolute overdraft limit of £1,195,000 would not be exceeded, and any breach, however minor, would result in the immediate returning of cheques.

Mr Pitt explained that the £465,000 loan from the West Midlands County Council could only go ahead if the bank was prepared to agree the process by which that loan would be secured. The County Council accepted that initially it would be unsecured, moving to a position of security against finished motorcycles in the case of the £365,000 export loan facility.

Mr Esam stated, by way of reply, that there would have to be a measure of trust between the West Midlands County Council and the National Westminster Bank over security arrangements. He felt they were feasible and that an agreement would be reached.

Regarding the details of the legal agreements concerning the West Midlands County Council loan facility, Mrs Kate Murray stated she would communicate directly with Mr Andy Philpott in the very near future.

When the meeting was over, the three Triumph representatives at this crucial bank meeting agreed that the tone of the meeting had suggested that the bank was prepared to go along with the security arrangements for the West Midlands County Council's export loan facility. However, in view of the bank's worsening position, whilst it would not precipitate any action as long as Triumph stayed within the £1,195,000 overdraft limit (allowing time for a complete financial restructuring of the business), the first breach of the limit would result in the returning of cheques that would cause the winding up of Triumph.

Having been involved with Wayne Moulton in product meetings the previous day, Brian Jones had to reschedule his visit to Rye Tools/Weslake to Thursday 18th November. During his visit, he was provided with a complete prototype parts list showing the status of each Diana engine part. The longest outstanding lead time was for the crankshaft, which would be completed by Wednesday 24th November. Whilst all Rye Tools and Weslake's machines were now working on Diana engine components, completing and test running the first engine by the end of the month would be very tight. With only eleven days to achieve completion, there was the added financial incentive for them to work Saturdays and Sundays – an additional £7000 Triumph cheque was due once this project milestone of the first engine run on the dynamometer and the rig testing of the gearbox had been achieved.

Whilst Brian was away at Rye Tools, a long day was spent with Wayne Moulton enabling Phil Bragg to undertake detailed financial cashflow planning. Wayne's TMA input for the security requirements on the West Midlands County Council loan was also vital. His comments to Triumph Meriden and TMA Chairman John Rosamond regarding the low morale amongst the few individuals working only confirmed what we already knew.

Triumph's bank was not alone when it came to trying to understand the massive publicity that had announced the West Midlands County Council £465,000 loans. However, it soon became obvious that the politically motivated press announcement had been made in an attempt to buy time for establishing legal security protecting the County Council's loan, before making it available to Triumph. As this legal requirement had already been established in the agreement for the West Midlands Enterprise Board export loan, we had assumed the same security arrangements would apply. No such luck. It soon became clear that there would be no déjà vu comparison between the secret £150,000 West Midlands Enterprise Board loan facility and the highly publicised £465,000 West Midlands County Council loan to Triumph, although they were both supposed to be for exactly the same purpose. Every day that went by, as Triumph's overall financial position became more and more critical, the £465,000 loan the County Council were trying to legally secure became more at risk!

Mrs Kate Murray had a meeting with Wayne Moulton to discuss TMA overhead reduction possibilities. Most had previously been extensively considered by Wayne and Rob Murison (Triumph's former Financial/Commercial Director). However, at least she seemed satisfied every avenue had now been explored.

On Friday 19th November, the Chairman called a further Board meeting to keep the Directors not directly involved in day-to-day developments fully apprised of what was taking place. In addition, the Board also considered the Financial Controller's most up-to-date cashflow information and specifically how this impacted upon the factory layoff of the majority of the Beneficiary owners of Triumph. A mass meeting progress report was now due and would indicate how much longer they and their families would have to survive without wages!

The first business of this Board meeting was to consider developments and matters arising from the previous meeting.

a) Terry Pitt's letter to the Inland Revenue had had the desired effect.

b) Bill Beattie provided an update on the factory overhead 0-50 per cent rates reduction potential by removing roofs or knocking down walls on unused outbuildings.

c) Brian Jones reported good progress on preparation of the South Yorkshire and Derbyshire police demonstrators. Unfortunately, no progress had been made on the two sample Ministry of Defence motorcycles, due to lack of personnel.

d) Brian Jones also updated on the Diana project progress visit to RyeTools/Weslake. George Mackie's assumption that both the companies involved in the Diana project were now working seven-day weeks was correct. Phil Bragg agreed he would make financial provision in the cashflow for the imminent project milestone payment of £7000.

e) Brian Jones further reported that all faulty parts were now being returned to the factory, prior to being replaced under warranty.

f) Bill Beattie and Brian Jones indicated that whilst the senior management changes agreed at the previous meeting had been implemented, department locations and structures were still being formulated.

g) The Chairman reported that the Ward and Rider solicitor Tim Burnhill, representing Triumph in the Nahib Dajani litigation, would address the Board at 3.00pm on Tuesday 23rd November.

With all matters arising from the previous Board meeting dealt with, the Directors then received an update from the Financial Controller.

Phil Bragg advised that the end of week overdraft level would be £1,151,000, and with an unpresented cheque of £20,000 for the Inland Revenue, this inevitably meant the workforce layoff would have to continue. However, it was the Financial Controller's intention to pay the membership's outstanding wage arrears for 3rd, 4th and 5th November following the 10.00am 23rd November mass meeting. It was also intended to make wage payments to the 29 hourly paid members who had been requested to work on 17th, 18th and 19th November; payment would take place on Thursday 25th November. The closing overdraft position for the week ending 26th November would be £1,190,000.

Moving to the repayment of the First Co-operative Finance (FCF) small export loan facility, provided to enable Triumph to ship 20 motorcycles to the USA. There was now an urgent need for a meeting with First Co-operative Finance senior management, to discuss a delay in repayment. Whilst £23,000 was in the FCF repayment account, a tremendous effort was required by all concerned to increase this amount as much as possible.

Phil Bragg now tabled the schedule of motorcycle orders against which tranches of the £365,000 West Midlands County Council export loan would be drawn. It could be seen from the schedule that if Triumph secured motorcycle orders to support this programme, manufactured and then sold them, it would be possible to make it through to the end of February 1983. This would give sufficient time for complete financial restructuring of the business to take place.

Bill Beattie commented that if Triumph did not significantly better the tabled schedule of orders, production and sales, the substantial losses that would have been incurred during the period would mean it was not possible to roll over the £365,000 export loan facility, making it politically impossible for the West Midlands Enterprise Board to support a complete financial restructuring of the business. Phil Bragg agreed; the tabled schedule of orders was an absolute minimum, and without massive efforts by all concerned to supplement further orders, enabling higher production and sales levels, the present Co-op loss-making trends would continue. The Chairman commented that there were opportunities not contained in the tabled schedule that would improve profitability, which were as follows:

a) Securing of the Jordanian institutional order for early delivery.

b) Pushing the sale of genuine Triumph spare parts.

c) The early introduction of 1983 models in the UK for cash on delivery payment.

d) Component cost and general factory overhead reductions.

e) Payment for only one week's holiday pay Christmas/New Year.

The Directors felt it was important to immediately discuss the final listed opportunity, the Christmas/New Year holiday pay, in the context that in the two months prior to Christmas, the company would have made substantial losses. Accordingly, the Board reluctantly agreed that whilst Triumph would close on 23rd December 1982 and was not scheduled to reopen until 10th January 1983, to try and help a turnaround of the Co-op's financial situation only one week of the Christmas/New Year break would be paid, thus saving about £20,000. The membership would be advised of the Board's decision at the mass meeting on 23rd November.

The negotiating team and the Financial Controller then provided a full report on the meeting in London at the head office of the National Westminster (covered earlier in this chapter). The Directors not present at the bank meeting agreed that like Triumph, the bank had also been very concerned at the worsening financial position. However, the West Midlands County Council staff present at the meeting seemed to have reassured the bank that the financial reconstruction would go ahead.

The Board discussion now turned to the financial hardship being suffered by the laid-off members and their families. Ron Atkinson, the Personnel Manager, had investigated the possibility of Triumph qualifying for Temporary Employment Subsidy to ease the financial pain felt by laid-off members. Unfortunately in the present circumstances, Triumph did not qualify.

The Chairman reported that whilst he had not yet contacted all salaried members, he had already received a negative reaction to his suggestion that wages would not be paid in line with contractual obligations during the first week of the layoff. Whilst this was a disappointing response to the Chairman's request, the Directors did not consider it surprising. Following lengthy discussion and the likelihood that there would be other salaried members who would also insist on their contractual obligations being honoured during the first week of the layoff, the Directors decided that salary payments would be made in full. The Directors asked the Financial Controller to make sure salaried members who worked with other volunteers during the first five days of the layoff repay all their travelling expenses.

The Chairman reported that during the TMA President's factory visit, he had expressed concern that Triumph had not yet completed testing of the TSS 8-valve model confirming that we met USA Environmental Protection Agency (EPA) standards. Wayne Moulton had stated that whilst initially it had been thought a short back-to-back test would establish conformity, he was no longer sure this was the case. There may even be a requirement to complete a full 9000-mile test, with the inevitable delay that this would mean. The Chairman asked the Engineering Director for clarification, in view of the fact that there were already 56 TSS motorcycles en route to the United States, financed by the West Midlands Enterprise Board's secret export loan. If EPA certification could not be achieved by the envisaged test route, it could result in these motorcycles being held in US customs with a catastrophic effect on the West Midlands County Council's involvement in reconstruction negotiations.

Brian Jones confirmed that a back-to-back EPA test would be sufficient; there was no doubt in his mind that the Triumph TSS model was of the same family as the T140 range previously EPA-certified. However, immediate steps were being taken to effect the required certification.

With that, yet another Board meeting was over.

With only a skeleton workforce undertaking vital company activities, we were all starting to wonder if the much-publicised West Midlands County Council loans would ever be received. This was certainly the feeling at the mass meeting of the membership at 10.00am on 23rd November. Unfortunately, it was only possible to tell the members that their layoff would have to continue. However, they could rest assured that the West Midlands County Council politicians and officers had been left in no doubt as to exactly how much these delays were risking Triumph's ability to survive until the financial reconstruction. Finally, the Chairman had to inform the membership that as a result of the ongoing delays, major financial losses continued to be incurred and the Board had had to decide that only one week's holiday pay would be available for the two week Christmas/New Year holiday break.

There seemed to be a certain amount of resignation in the way the members received the Chairman's report, almost as if their determination to survive whatever was thrown at the Co-op was finally draining away.

Later that day at 3.00pm, the Board of Directors received the report on the Nahib Dajani litigation proceedings from solicitor Mr Tim Burnhill. These proceedings had been in existence for almost three years. Initially Mr Tim Burnhill had dealt with Mr Ian Rush, Miss Brenda Price and Mr Geoffrey Robinson MP. Following the aforementioned individuals' departure from Triumph, he had dealt with Mr Rob Murison. The litigation proceedings had lain dormant throughout the last year, with Geoffrey Robinson only producing his draft statement when a date for the court hearing was proposed. Ian Rush had also completed a statement regarding the events of the Nahib Dajani claim. In letters written by Ian Rush to Mr Nahib Dajani, Triumph contracted to pay Mr Dajani 10 per cent of the contract value by way of commission, if he successfully influenced the placing of a Libyan order for Triumph. Whilst both Ian Rush and Geoffrey Robinson contended that Nahib Dajani did not positively influence the Libyan Government in placing an order with Triumph, the plaintiff contended that he did. In these circumstances, counsel's advice had been sought. Copies of counsel's advice to Triumph had been provided for the Directors, and suggested that the decision could go either way. In these circumstances, counsel advocated that a settlement offer should be made, which could save Triumph a considerable amount of money. The full settlement figure that Triumph would possibly have to meet would be £16,300 plus legal costs and expenses – a total likely to be in excess of £30,000. In these circumstances, Triumph's solicitor Tim Burnhill recommended to the Triumph Board that they instruct him to make a settlement offer to Nahib Dajani of approximately £5000, to be paid off at the rate of £500 per month. Tim Burnhill further advised that as a date for the court hearing had not yet been fixed, there was no immediate urgency for the aforementioned Board instruction. The Directors agreed that they would instruct the solicitor on this matter in the near future, and thanked him for his attendance.

At the Meriden factory, the almost hour-by-hour existence continued. We clung onto the edge of a financial precipice, on the verge of bankruptcy, the skeleton workforce manning the barricades, with the vast majority of the membership still laid-off.

The politically-inspired press announcement by the West Midlands County Council, declaring its £465,000 loan to Triumph, had created a financial impression the complete opposite to the reality of the desperate, cash-starved situation at the Meriden factory, reported to the last mass meeting. This had even led the battle-hardened Co-op members to doubt what the elected leaders were telling them. So far, the highly publicised 9th November West Midlands County Council loan decision had only led to further legal debate, condemning the Co-op membership and their families to further layoff hardship and uncertainty.

Those manning the Co-op's Purchasing Department were now under similarly enormous pressure from Triumph's component parts suppliers. These previously supportive suppliers, with loss-making factories and laid-off workforces, had also been alienated by the politically-biased loan announcement, and were now starting to believe they were being deceived by Triumph. It was in this extremely difficult and uncertain situation that on 24th November, *Motor Cycle News* published a double-page news feature on Triumph. This is reproduced here with its kind permission.

STEVE CORDAL had taken a look at what this latest ray of hope meant to Meriden ...
Ever since the Meriden Co-operative rose from the ashes of the British bike industry in 1975, it's

faced a series of crises. Always short of cash, life has been a permanent struggle – with bankruptcy just around the corner. Since they lost their export credit guarantee last year the company have been living from hand to mouth, but with the news last week that the West Midlands Enterprise Board are willing to bail them out of their present troubles there now seems to be some light at the end of the long, dark tunnel.

STARSHIP ENTERPRISE
Massive cash boost sets Meriden for an export lift-off
   Most people think Father Christmas lives in Greenland, wears a red cloak and spends his days playing with gnomes. Wrong. The men at Triumph have inside information. They know for a fact that Santa works in Birmingham wears a natty three-piece suit and is known to his friends as Geoff Edge – Chairman of the West Midlands Enterprise Board.
   Saint Nick isn't supposed to arrive until the end of December, but Saint Geoff paid Triumph an early visit last week – and left them the best Christmas present they've had in years.
   The present was a £465,000 cash injection to help fund their export programme – an injection that could make all the difference to Triumph's chances of surviving as Britain's last major motorcycle manufacturer. And he left news of an even bigger helping hand which could be on its way, namely a capital investment of several million pounds to help Triumph produce new models for the late '80s.
   Since the Meriden Co-operative was set up by Tony Benn back in 1975 with £4.2m of Government money, it's had to plough its way through one crisis after another. The most recent came last year when Triumph lost the Government's export credit guarantee. Since then, the company has been living from hand to mouth, exporting bikes, then having to wait for payment before moving on to the next batch.
   At present the workforce stands at just 188 – less than a third of the number employed two years ago. Production is also down to 80 machines a week, compared to the 300 a week being built in 1980. Most of the initial £465,000 will be used to fund the export of bikes, helping to tide the Co-operative over for a year or two. Up to £100,000 will be used to buy in new machine tools in an attempt to improve efficiency and productivity. But the big carrot dangling in front of the management's nose is that possible investment of several million pounds! But it's not going to land in their lap without a lot of work. The Enterprise Board will only make such a massive investment if they can be convinced Triumph has a real future. And by a real future they mean new models which would sell and make the company profitable again. These new models are already in the prototype stage, and although Triumph are keeping tight lipped about their exact specification, it looks almost certain we're looking at 900cc twins with double overhead cams and water cooling – essential if Triumph are to meet the ever-tightening American noise controls.

SCHEDULES
The Enterprises Board will want to see these prototypes, and more importantly, see them costed out – with detailed production schedules. What's more, they're also insisting on certain cost cutting measures – which could mean Triumph moving from its present expensive 22 acre site. Triumph's Chairman John Rosamond won't talk about his negotiations with the Enterprise Board – nor Triumph's plans for the future. According to him, everything is at rather a delicate stage and he's afraid talking about the future could put too much pressure on the Enterprise Board – perhaps even frighten them off. But if John Rosamond isn't willing to talk about the future of Triumph, Geoff Edge certainly is. A former Labour MP, he has a lot of faith in the Co-operative, and sees it as a source of valuable jobs – something the West Midlands is chronically short of at the moment.

"We see the £465,000 as merely short-term finance – something to tide Meriden over for a year or two," he said. "The factory is extremely short of working capital, and we have to provide that if they're to get back on their feet again. At present they have some 700 overseas orders, and by giving them this money we hope they'll be able to fulfil them," he added.

The Enterprise Board hired two consultants to look into Triumph's finances, and their reports showed that the Co-operative had all the hallmarks of a potential success – providing they had the money to work with.

NEW RANGE

By giving Triumph £465,000 now, the Enterprise Board have bought themselves – and Meriden – valuable time. The cash means Triumph now have a breathing space to produce details of their proposed new range – and to convince the Enterprise Board they're worth investing money in. "We've been talking to several banks and pension schemes – and should we eventually decide to take an equity stake in the Co-operative, it could amount to several millions of pounds," said Mr Edge. But there are conditions. "Firstly we must be convinced the new models are viable – and that means spending much time looking at their costing. We won't be able to judge just what sort of future Triumph has until we've done that," he added. "There'll also have to be a measure of cost cutting. We think it's absolutely vital that Triumph control their spares distribution – that's a must. In addition we think they must build more components in house – instead of relying so much on outside suppliers."

Mr Edge thinks a final decision on further investment will not be taken before the end of this year – or possibly not even until the end of January next year. There's no doubt the Enterprise Board are looking to Triumph as an employer. "Certainly we'd like to see the workforce expand again. It's too early to talk in figures at the moment, but I would like to think Triumph will eventually be employing round about 700 people again," said Mr Edge. Although America is Triumph's major market at the moment, Mr Edge is convinced that it should be possible to build up sales on the home market as well. "Yes, I think Triumph has a great future in America, but I also think it has a big part to play in the UK market as well. What it needs is new models – and these I think it has got," he said.

So Triumph's future now lies in its own hands. The promise of a massive investment to boost their five-year plan is definitely light at the end of the tunnel – and it's up to the men from Meriden to prove they are up to the job of leading Britain's motorcycle industry out of the dark ages and into the eighties.

In normal times this *Motor Cycle News* feature article would have been excellent. However, these times were anything but normal, and Geoffrey Edge's unfortunate comments about the Meriden factory "building more components in-house" would not be appreciated by Triumph's suppliers, and was just about the worst thing that could have been said. The *MCN* story portrayed the County Council-created illusion of Triumph's circumstances, not the desperate financial plight we were in, as the legal wrangling to implement the £465,000 support continued into a third week.

The other unfortunate news on this day was that the new Diana engine's first test run at Rye Tools now looked like being delayed until 6th December. Two pieces of better news from Brian Jones helped Directors' sagging morale: the police demonstrators had been completed on time and delivered, and 8-valve engine EPA homologation back-to-back testing would take place at MIRA the following week.

The Financial Controller and Chairman met Mr T O'Malley of First Co-operative Finance

(FCF) in Manchester on the morning of Friday 26th November. Mr O'Malley agreed to extend the deadline for repayment of the American export finance facility by one month, to the end of December 1982. In an effort to reassure FCF, a copy of Triumph's five-year corporate plan was provided, plus the viability review by Price Waterhouse and the in-depth overview by Arthur D Little. Commenting on the long-term, Mr O'Malley indicated that Triumph's was the only co-operative overdraft facility not currently provided by FCF, and in a restructured situation, FCF may well be interested. Regarding FCF taking an equity stake in the new restructured company, Mr O'Malley did not rate the chances very highly in the present economic climate.

Bill Beattie was overseeing the production exercise to establish which of the 4-bar auto machine tools should be purchased with the £100,000 cost-saving element of the West Midlands County Council loan. He had also taken an immediate first step towards rates reduction; the partial removal of a wall in an unused bay of the Butler Building rendered it 'designated open storage', and therefore qualified it for an immediate 50 per cent rates reduction.

Phil Bragg was now pushing ahead establishing individual departmental consumables budgets. Department heads would be expected to make at least a 10 per cent saving on last year's performance. The Financial Controller and Transport Manager had also determined that by purchasing Triumph's own delivery van rather than using hired transport, a reduction of £37,000 in the first year and £52,000 in the second looked possible. Any surpluses on the West Midlands County Council's £100,000 machine tool spend had been earmarked for these savings.

The Chairman called a Board of Directors meeting at 2.00pm on Monday 29th November to provide the financial news that we had all been desperately waiting for; we only hoped it was not too late!

Phil Bragg reported that the overdraft stood at £1,056,000, plus one unpresented cheque for FCF worth £30,000, equalling an end-of-day position of £1,086,000. The West Midlands County Council had finally advanced the first tranche of £105,000, against a letter of intent confirming Triumph would sign the legal documentation as soon as agreement was reached. Procurement of component parts to restart motorcycle production was under way, and the membership would be recalled to work as materials became available.

In view of this, the Directors agreed that the Chairman should report to a mass meeting of the laid off membership on Tuesday 3rd December, advising them of their progressive recall to work. The laid-off members' outstanding wage arrears for 8th and 9th November, and the three guaranteed week payments – 10th, 11th and 12th November – would be paid following the mass meeting.

The twenty days of legal wrangling that delayed receipt of the West Midlands County Council export finance facility would ensure further loss-making, as a result of the reduced number of motorcycles that could now be produced prior to Christmas. To try and redress this financial position and achieve the highest possible production efficiency between now and the Christmas/New Year holiday, the Chairman suggested the previously agreed end-of-year deadline for the membership to take all their time off in lieu overtime and holiday entitlement, should now be extended until September 1983

Brian Jones reported on the proposed increased sales opportunity that would be created by the early introduction of 1983 models. Two new model opportunities existed:

a) The reduction of the 650cc Thunderbird capacity to 600cc.

b) The introduction of the anti-vibration frame on the TSS 8-valve Super Sports model.

Following lengthy discussion by the Board regarding the risk element involved in premature introduction of unproven models, the Directors agreed to accept the aforementioned proposals. Brian Jones would provide detailed engineering specification changes in due course.

The Chairman felt that management meetings should now be reintroduced as a matter of urgency, as motorcycle production was about to recommence. This would achieve a coherent and uniform approach to running the business.

Brian Jones and Bill Beattie had agreed for some time that the factory senior line management, by which manufacturing was controlled, needed improvement. The recently accepted principle of guaranteeing full-time working throughout the year to members who did not have the opportunity to earn production bonus payments would now be applied to these supervisory individuals, in recognition of the key role they played. In return, they would be required to accept a detailed job description, specifying their responsibilities.

Phil Bragg reported that he hoped to have information from the company's auditors in the very near future to enable a date to be set for the reconvened AGM, in order to accept the annual accounts for the financial period ending 30th September 1981.

The Chairman reported that the porosity warranty problems that had led to oil leaks in service on TSS 8-valve models had been traced to cylinder heads supplied by Weslake. This was because the new dual source supplier cast its cylinder heads in such a way that any porosity that occurred was exposed at the time of machining. Accordingly Triumph would be claiming reimbursement from Weslake for the affected cylinder heads.

On Wednesday 8th December, almost a month to the day since the press announcement of the West Midlands County Council £465,000 loan, the legal agreement was finally signed. Far from being the end of the cashflow problems, it would prove to be at best only a continuation, with some County Council staff now attempting to micromanage Triumph from County Hall – this at a time when the priority was surviving until the promised financial reconstruction decision was reached.

As a result of continuous delays, some component suppliers were now serving legal writs on Triumph for non-payment of previous debts. Other suppliers were insisting that half their previous debts be settled prior to them restarting supply. As a result, in the week ending 3rd December, the Purchasing Department's initial spend of £59,639.92 only secured £38,898.19 worth of ordered component parts – an absolute disaster that would merit further detailed investigation by County Council staff. The publicised involvement of the West Midlands County Council had managed to undermine Triumph's previous excellent relations with the component suppliers; an excellent relationship that had already enabled John Rosamond to reach a full and final settlement agreement with Mr Fred Tippets, Chairman of the Moratorium Trade Creditors' Committee, stipulating that as part of the planned financial reconstruction of Triumph's affairs, he would recommend to the creditors that they accept a final payment of fifteen pence in the pound (equivalent to £150,000) in order to release the company from the outstanding moratorium debt of £850,000.

There was not a great deal to celebrate as Triumph managed to struggle through to the festive holidays, with County Council staff continuing to express surprise at the major financial difficulties 'now' being experienced by Triumph. Their concern would continue to grow at the higher-than-expected spend on components, and resulting shortfall on quantities available for production. Further detailed discussions to resolve this situation would be pursued early in the New Year, the membership having decided to return early from the festive break having taken only one week's paid holiday.

It was indeed hard to recognise the original West Midlands County Council offer to provide sufficient export finance for Triumph to continue production through to the financial reconstruction, given the delay-ridden reality that had led to the present predicament. However, without the support of two totally committed County Council staff, Terry Pitt and Tom Fitch, the Meriden Co-op would have already gone out of business. There still remained hope for the financial reconstruction of Triumph's affairs early in 1983.

28

FINANCIAL RECONSTRUCTION

We returned to work focused on the financial reconstruction decision expected during January 1983. Not taking the full Christmas/New Year holiday enabled manufacturing to begin trying to recover the production/financial shortfalls from November and December. Unfortunately, the ongoing torment from delays and growing uncertainty caused four of Brian Jones' twelve key Engineering Department members to leave early in the New Year. The already massive workload of this department got even bigger, leaving those who remained to share the extra burden.

West Midlands accountancy staff continued their detailed investigation into why their export loan facility was not achieving what had been expected. Triumph's obvious and factual explanation – that delays in providing the production finance was a major factor – implicated the County Council staff, which was something they were not prepared to accept. The seriousness of the problems with the export loan caused John Rosamond and Bill Beattie grave concern regarding West Midlands' vital involvement in the financial reconstruction. As Brian Jones had now satisfactorily addressed the Arthur D Little Diana project reservations in the resubmitted 5-year corporate plan, this was indeed a major blow. Discussions with the Meriden Co-op's two greatest County Council supporters, Tom Fitch and Terry Pitt, had so far been unable to determine a strategy that would lessen the impact of the export loan problems.

It was now obvious to the negotiating team and Peter Johnson of Price Waterhouse that the long-term involvement of West Midlands County Council in the day-to-day running of the reconstructed Triumph business should, if at all possible, be kept to an absolute minimum. There was definitely no comparison between the operating cultures that existed in the County Council and our engineering business. Accordingly, Peter Johnson intensified his search for private sector involvement in the financial reconstruction.

On 9th January, John Rosamond received confirmation from Mr Gerry Esam, the Deputy General Manager of National Westminster, that in principle it was prepared to accept a lump sum payment in full and final settlement of the £1,195,000 overdraft facility. This acceptance was conditional on reasonable assurance that the bank's action would at least help the business towards commercial viability, beyond the short-term. The bank's 'agreement in principle' was obviously a major step forward alongside that already reached with the Moratorium Trade Creditors.

For his part, Bill Beattie was making good progress with the sale of the Meriden site and pursuit of a more appropriate alternative. Due to all the recession-forced factory closures in the Coventry area, there were several options.

On 14th January, the first scheduled monthly Board meeting of 1983 took place, enabling all Triumph's Directors to be brought right up to date with the exception of Ron Briggs, who was still on sick leave.

Phil Bragg reported that expenditure during December had been significantly more than expected, as a result of higher than envisaged material purchase costs and shortfalls on motorcycle dispatches. In effect, this was having a negative influence on the West Midlands County Council's loan, the consequence of which was briefly discussed with County Council staff prior to Christmas, with further discussions taking place. The early return to work following the holiday would help a little to redress this imbalance. Efforts during the first week of the New Year to raise £60,000 to cover bank overdraft interest of £25-30,000, a further arrears payment of £10,000 to the Inland Revenue and the outstanding £20,000 balance to First Co-operative Finance, were going reasonably well. These monies were being raised by the completion of pre-Christmas motorcycle stock and the disposal of ex-engineering development motorcycles.

The Chairman reported that Peter Johnson of Price Waterhouse had recently confirmed that the merchant bank Singer-Frieglander would, he believed, be prepared to provide equity and loan capital investment, thus meeting the private sector involvement that West Midlands County Council/Enterprise Board had indicated was a necessary condition of the loan. To enable further negotiations, Peter Johnson had provided Singer-Frieglander with abbreviated information to use as a basis for its involvement. A meeting with Mr Charles Blunt of Singer-Frieglander and Mr George Bloomfield of Herbert-Sigma, who Blunt saw as a possible Managing Director of a new restructured Triumph company, was being pursued. The Chairman further reported that the many potential constituent parts of the reconstruction package reported informally to the Directors before Christmas were being acted upon. Both the National Westminster Bank and the Moratorium Trade Creditors' Committee were adopting a positive position towards the reconstruction proposal, awaiting further information as negotiations progressed.

Bill Beattie reported that the sale of the Triumph Meriden factory site was progressing. A meeting with Espley-Tyas Homes on 12th January had left no doubt in the potential purchaser's mind that to secure the site it would have to pay a seven figure sum, or very close to it! Informally, Bill Beattie had been told by Mr Byrnes of Espley's intention to pay £1,000,000, a written indication of which Triumph would receive in the near future. Bill Beattie further reported that of the many factory relocation sites, one of the most likely at present was the Maudsley Road Massey-Fergusson factory – further information was being sought from the parent company's Board of Directors, in Canada, and preliminary discussions had taken place with Coventry City Council about the appropriate planning permission for the Maudsley Road factory site. Board discussion regarding the progress to date of the financial reconstruction negotiations determined that in view of what had been reported by the negotiating team, it was right and proper to continue to trade on behalf of the creditors.

Bill Beattie outlined to the Directors his proposal to confirm the roles of senior management working in the production and associated areas. This would be done by offering new contracts of employment under which the individuals concerned would be guaranteed a 40-hour week/payment, but relinquish their right to receive overtime pay. This was only one of several changes he wished to introduce, and he undertook to complete a full proposal for the Directors' perusal in due course. On the basis of Bill Beattie's initial recommendation, the Directors agreed to the implementation of the first stage as soon as possible.

Brian Jones reported that the Engineering Department activity was extremely constrained as a result of four of his personnel leaving the company. As a temporary measure whilst he considered a long-term solution, the Directors suggested the lost hours be covered by extra overtime working. Brian Jones agreed to this temporary expediency, and would in due course put forward detailed proposals that, as well as recruitment, would consider all aspects of the engineering operation in a similar way to that being contemplated in manufacturing by Bill Beattie.

The meeting then moved to other business:

i) Diana project (metric measurement)

Bill Beattie reminded the Board of the likely problems that would be experienced with present Triumph factory machining facilities, due to all measurements associated with the Diana project being metric. Brian Jones stated that he was aware of this problem, and conversions would be issued where appropriate. The original metric decision had been taken based on the fact that a large proportion of component machining would be outsourced, and metric measurement was the standard of the day.

ii) Clocking-in clocks

Bill Beattie reported that the clocks used by members to record their presence at work were more trouble than they were worth, because of their regular failure. Consideration should be given to a more enlightened way of recording attendance at work, other than further expenditure on maintaining the worn-out clocks.

iii) Delivery of United Kingdom motorcycles

Phil Bragg and John Birch agreed to provide proposals on the long-term viability of the purchasing/leasing of motorcycle delivery vehicles for use in the UK.

iv) Warranty component parts

George Mackie requested detailed consideration be given to the fact that there was a heavy demand for warranty parts. He felt these replacement parts supplied under the warranty guarantee should be drawn from a separate location, other than the spare parts store. The present practice was having an adverse effect on the company's ability to fulfil spare parts orders. Brian Jones agreed to investigate the problem as a matter of urgency.

v) Outstanding annual accounts for the period 1980/81

Phil Bragg reported that Triumph's auditor, Coopers and Lybrand, had indicated that it was not prepared to complete any further work on the 1980/81 annual accounts until Triumph paid it the £3500 presently outstanding. Phil Bragg agreed to make the £3500 payment as soon as possible to enable completion of the audit work and the reconvening of the overdue Annual General Meeting.

With that the first Board of Directors' meeting of 1983 was over.

West Midlands County Council's growing concern continued during January, as it became more and more apparent how much financial difficulty Triumph and its loan facility were now in.

The first running of Triumph's new prototype Diana engine took place at Rye Tools on 20th January. In view of the significance to the financial reconstruction of Triumph, the West Midlands Enterprise Board and County Council were well represented. Brian Jones, Bill Beattie and John Rosamond represented Triumph. Ron Valentine, the owner of Rye Tools, hosted this historic event and the BBC TV documentary crew filmed the occasion for *The Money Programme*. All present seemed suitably impressed, and given what was happening at the Meriden factory with the County Council's export loan, the occasion could not have been better timed.

However, the excellent impression created at Rye Tools in East Sussex was undermined the following day by the story in *The Guardian* newspaper, from Alex Brummer in Washington.

"A United States move to block imports of Japanese motorcycles could deal a fatal blow to the remnants of Britain's beleaguered moto cycle industry, it emerged yesterday."

When contacted regarding this story I simply stated that 60 per cent of Triumph's sales were achieved in the American market, so anything that made those sales more difficult would have a serious effect.

That day, 21st January, was also memorable for another reason, as it was the day Singer-Frieglander was due to advise on its intention to provide private sector investment in the financial reconstruction package, without which the West Midlands Enterprise Board would not proceed. Unfortunately, the day passed without decision. Peter Johnson and Triumph's negotiating team now pressed for a face-to-face meeting with the merchant bank. Once again, Triumph was experiencing a further financially crippling delay, jeopardising our chances of survival.

Price Waterhouse had been independently auditing the West Midlands loans on its behalf since the end of November 1982, and subsequently the £100,000 cost-saving capital loan element of the £465,000 County Council package was withdrawn.

Just before departing on a three month sabbatical to India, Peter Johnson, who secured Singer-Frieglander's initial interest in the Triumph financial reconstruction, succeeded in arranging a meeting with the merchant bank at Triumph on Friday 28th January. Mr Charles Blunt of Singer-Frieglander and Mr George Bloomfield of Herbert-Sigma met the Triumph representatives. Charles Blunt stated that if George Bloomfield agreed the Triumph financial reconstruction proposals, he would require three to four weeks to raise the necessary private sector funding. George Bloomfield said for him to do this, he needed one or two weeks to satisfy himself on two counts:

i) Could he work with the existing Triumph management team?

ii) Could Triumph, already in 'intensive care', be saved?

The meeting lasted about two hours. George Bloomfield, who was seen as the potential Managing Director of the reconstructed business, stated as he departed, "I believe the chemistry is right and I could indeed work with the existing Triumph management. Two weeks of further investigation will establish exactly where we go from here."

The positive meeting over, Triumph's management team contemplated how we could survive a period of two weeks, during which George Bloomfield satisfied himself that Triumph was saveable, and then a further four weeks whilst Charles Blunt raised the private sector funding. Six weeks in our desperate financial situation was an extremely long time, and could mean only one thing – an immediate layoff of the entire workforce with the exception of a small skeleton team. Phil Bragg, Triumph's Financial Controller, expressed grave concern about the passing of more reconstruction deadlines. The statement in the *MCN* 'Starship Enterprise' story that "a final decision on further investment will not be taken before the end of this year or possibly not even until the end of January next year," had been made in November 1982, and significantly increased the pressure from Triumph's creditors, compounding Triumph's financial problems. A further delay and extended factory layoff would obviously add to the critical financial position. John Rosamond commented that although the West Midlands County Council was aware of exactly what was happening regarding its export loan facility, it was also becoming more and more uncertain about the eventual outcome of the financial reconstruction. Accordingly, in order to guarantee its support, it seemed there was little choice but to pursue the reassurance that private sector involvement would bring. The Triumph Board of Directors would need to be fully updated on the latest financial situation, and the inevitable further delays, in order to secure merchant bank private sector funding.

The Board meeting took place on the evening of Sunday 30th January, and considered in detail over a period of three and a half hours the extremely difficult situation Triumph now faced. Courageously, the Board of Directors decided that we would continue to trade; once secured, a financial reconstruction of Triumph's affairs would be in the best interests of both the creditors and the workforce. This decision inevitably meant a layoff of the majority of the workforce until the reconstruction took place.

At the end of the Board meeting, Brian Jones informed the Directors of a worrying commercial/legal development at Weslake/Rye Tools. Work on the Diana engine project had stopped pending the payment by Triumph of £4500. The amount being claimed was a part payment of the £7500 project milestone cheque, due when the first prototype engine ran and prototype gearbox was rig tested. The consultant engineers were stating that the lack of progress on the gearbox design was because Brian Jones had not finalised it. The Directors decided legal advice should be secured in order to hold Weslake/Rye Tools to the original Diana project agreement. In the meantime, no split payment would be made.

The mass meeting of the Beneficiary owners of Triumph took place early on Monday 31st January 1983. Reluctantly, the membership agreed to the immediate indefinite layoff. A skeleton workforce of 41 individuals would keep vital Triumph services at the factory going whilst the financial reconstruction was pursued.

Skeleton workforce:

Department	Team size
Spare parts	5
Security	2
Sales	2
Carpenter	1
Engineering	8
Tool room	8
Finance	1
Secretaries	1
Salaried staff	13
Total	41

On 1st February Triumph received a bombshell. The merchant bank Singer-Frieglander had turned down involvement in the Triumph financial reconstruction, the major reason apparently being that it would have to become involved in the political arena of West Midlands County Council. If ever there was a classic catch 22 situation, this was it! The politically-inclined West Midlands Enterprise Board would not go ahead unless its decision was confirmed by private sector investment, and the Merchant Bank would not go ahead because of the political involvement of the West Midlands County Council. Singer-Frieglander's withdrawal had a dramatic effect on how the West Midlands County Council was considering the major difficulties with the £365,000 export loan facility.

Having made the Triumph Directors aware informally of Singer-Frieglander's position, all the negotiating team could do was to concentrate totally on securing as many of the other parts of the financial reconstruction package as possible, before trying to rekindle the merchant bank's interest.

Triumph's most loyal supporter at County Hall, Terry Pitt, was now also under almost unbearable pressure because of his known allegiance to the Meriden Co-op.

On Friday 11th February, Triumph's negotiating team and Financial Controller met senior representatives of the National Westminster Bank in London to update them regarding Singer-Frieglander's withdrawal. Triumph was now left with the reconstruction proposal that existed prior to the merchant bank's arrival on the scene in December 1982, with less money available to share with creditors by way of settling outstanding debts. The National Westminster Bank was provided with copies of the Price Waterhouse overview of Triumph's five-year plan, Arthur D Little's review, and Triumph's subsequent answers to the latter's areas of reservation. These documents had been requested by the bank when it agreed in principle to a lump sum settlement of Triumph's outstanding debt.

The major progress recently made in putting together the other parts of the financial reconstruction package were also discussed in detail. Finally, in the new circumstances Triumph requested that the National Westminster Bank consider accepting a full and final settlement of £600,000 to clear the outstanding overdraft facility of £1,195,000. The bank agreed to give Triumph's offer serious consideration and respond in due course. The Triumph representatives felt they had received a fair hearing by the bank, and looked forward to its response.

On return to the Meriden factory, there was a letter waiting addressed to the Triumph Directors. The letter was from Terry Pitt, Senior Advisor on Economic Development at the West Midlands County Council.

Dear Sirs
Triumph Motorcycles (Meriden) Ltd
Following my letter to you yesterday, regarding payments and roll-over potential, I called together my staff and external financial advice, in order to work further through the financial statements provided from time to time in recent weeks by yourselves.

We both know that these are incomplete and not in a form which has often been requested. As a result our analyses and conclusions have to be seen in that light, nevertheless I feel that on the evidence I have available, it is my duty to convey to you my considerable disquiet and fear that you could, as a Director now be trading from a position of insolvency.

I shall therefore unfortunately have to regard this as the actual position you face, unless and until you can provide me with evidence to the contrary, or realistic proposals to resolve your present difficulties and ensure a long-term future, indicating an enterprise able to meet its debts as they fall due.

As it happens, we had already scheduled a meeting with our Chairman and Vice Chairmen for Thursday of next week, to discuss various proposals relating to your organisation. I must therefore ask you to communicate before 3.00pm on Wednesday 16th February your response to the points I have raised in the above paragraph.

Yours sincerely
Terry J Pitt
Senior Advisor on Economic Development

It was now totally clear that whilst the West Midlands Enterprise Board and County Council export loan facilities had been provided to buy time to enable a complete financial reconstruction of Triumph's affairs, this was no longer the situation. The secret £150,000 Enterprise Board export loan had gone reasonably to plan. The £365,000 County Council export facility, announced with a blaze of inappropriate publicity and subsequent delayed availability, certainly had not. Mrs Kate Murray's detailed accountancy reconciliation work regarding the latter confirmed the major shortfalls in the County Council export loan performance that had occurred. Her work did not, of course, tell the whole story of the loan's political publicity, which created an illusion that the Co-op now had money, stimulating legal writs that had to be settled if the Co-op was not to be wound up. Some major component suppliers took advantage of the same illusion, insisting on the reduction of previous debts before being prepared to resume supply.

Over the weekend and following Monday, the Chairman worked on a draft response to Terry Pitt's letter. This was the subject of a Board meeting on Tuesday 15th February.

The Chairman reported to the Board that a very disturbing tabled letter dated 9th February had been received from Terry Pitt at the County Council. The Board could see that it was an extension of the growing concern that had already been indicated to the Directors. Discussions regarding the position of the West Midlands County Council's £365,000 export loan facility had continued in an effort to resolve the situation. Assisted by Triumph's Chairman, Mrs Kate Murray of the County Council had undertaken detailed reconciliation work, producing the charging information for the County Council and Board's perusal. Although not specifically indicated in Terry Pitt's letter, the growing concern would seem to have been brought to a head as a direct result of a negative response from Singer-Frieglander. Whilst the existence of this 9th February letter had been indicated informally to the Directors, it had been felt by the negotiating team that it was important to use the little time available prior to the West Midlands County Council's deadline to try and make significant progress, enabling the Co-op to continue pursuing financial reconstruction. Following the most intense few days of pressure, the Chairman, on behalf of those involved with the negotiating team, was pleased to be able to advise the Directors of the important progress that had now been achieved; the extent of it caused George Bloomfield of Herbert-Sigma to indicate in a telephone conversation with the Chairman that he and and the company were now "reconsidering their position."

This progress features in the Directors' draft reply to Terry Pitt's 9th February letter, prepared by the Chairman and also tabled for discussion.

Dear Mr Pitt

Thank you for your letter dated 9th February 1983, received on 11th February. We have given due consideration to the contents of your letter, including discussion with our legal advisors and would point out that the Triumph Board of Directors continue to trade in the belief that this course of action is in the best interests of our creditors. It is also worth noting that whilst like yourselves we were extremely disappointed at the negative response from merchant bankers Singer-Frieglander, substantial progress was made last week on other vital constituent parts of any financial reconstruction, which therefore gives us encouragement to persevere with our original plan. The basis of which was available before Peter Johnson of Price Waterhouse introduced Singer-Frieglander into the picture in December 1982.

Can I take this opportunity of thanking you and your staff for endeavouring to re-interest Charles Blunt of Singer-Frieglander. We also tried desperately hard to build upon the interest we believed to be there. However, when I re-contacted George Bloomfield in this context he categorically refused to speak to me, stating, and I quote, "if there is anything to say to Triumph it will be coming from Charles Blunt." In these circumstances I then tried to discuss matters with Charles Blunt who stated their reasons for lack of interest were the "value of site stocks at Meriden," about which Phil Bragg Triumph's accountant had been totally honest, and the "inter company debts between Triumph UK and Triumph USA." It is extremely hard to reconcile the amount of interest they had, as reported by Peter Johnson and the final outcome.

However Peter Johnson did convey one 'element of fear' in their minds before departing for India. They seemed deeply concerned about operating in the political environment of the West Midlands County Council and Enterprise Board; perhaps this is nearer the truth of the matter.

Bill Beattie at his meeting with you and Tom Fitch yesterday, I know made you aware of the vitally important progress made last week on the constituent parts of our revamped financial reconstruction plan, which for the record I have detailed as follows:

• Sale of the Triumph factory site to Espley-Tyas (with residential planning passed)

Following lengthy negotiations an acceptable offer of £1,000,000 was made last week by Espley-Tyas for the 16.4 acre non-green belt part of the Triumph factory site. (See copy of offer letter, appendix

1.) You will remember their opening offer was £700,000 for the whole 22 acre site including the green belt field. It now of course remains for detailed planning permission to be secured before their offer can be acted upon, your assistance in this matter will be of great help.

• Purchase of the Dunlop site, Cash's Lane, Coventry

Triumph initially offered Dunlop £225,000 for the Cash's Lane site, which was rejected. Last week Triumph offered £250,000 for the Dunlop site which was originally on the market for sale at £400,000. The £250,000 offer was accepted by Dunlop on a 'quick sale' basis. (See acceptance letter, appendix 2.)

• Detailed factory layout – Dunlop site

A detailed factory layout on the Dunlop site was completed last week. This shows the Triumph operation in the new circumstances. (See copy of the factory layout, appendix 3.)

The overhead savings associated with the move to the Dunlop site have already been indicated to Tom Fitch and are also present in the projected profit and loss forecast which indicates our changed position. (See profit and loss forecast, appendix 4.2.) (Appendix 4 includes full financial projections.)

• Moratorium Creditors' settlement offer

It has been confirmed that Mr Tippets (Chairman of the Moratorium Creditors' Committee) is still in exactly the same position as indicated in his letter dated 6th November 1982, when he stated that an honourable settlement of the outstanding moratorium debt could be effected by the payment of 15p in the £1. (See Mr Tippet's letter to the Triumph Chairman dated 6th November 1982, appendix 5.)

• National Westminster Bank overdraft position

A meeting took place with the National Westminster Bank last Friday 11th February, at which they were advised of the new circumstances relating to the negative response from the merchant bank, this inevitably meaning that there was less money available for all interested parties, including the bank. Having familiarised them with the facts stated above, we have undertaken to provide them with our new financial reconstruction proposal by today Tuesday 15th February. The part we will be asking them to play will be to accept a payment of £600,000 in full and final settlement of the overdraft debt of approximately £1,195,000. They have agreed to give us an early response to our proposal. The bank had requested copies of our five-year plan, the Arthur D Little report and Triumph's subsequent review document. These they were provided with at Friday's meeting.

• Support by the West Midlands County Council.

Our financial reconstruction proposal shows the rolling over of the £140,000 export finance available under the West Midlands County Council export loan cover in return for motorcycles built and shipped to the USA.

• First Co-operative Finance

We propose to pursue an extension of the export finance available from First Co-operative Finance (FCF) up to £100,000, which like yourselves, we believe to be achievable. Indications from FCF would confirm this to be the case.

• West Midlands Enterprise Board

We will be applying to the West Midlands Enterprise Board for an export credit facility of £500,000 which as you are aware is the sort of level required to take advantage of the opportunities that exist in the USA with the exchange rate in the $1.50s to the £1. We believe there to be a measure of support within the Enterprise Board Directors for this facility.

• New bank overdraft facility

A new overdraft facility of £500,000 will be raised against security from land and buildings and book stock, initially of £1,250,000 and moving to security of £1,500,000 against the aforementioned plus book debt, once manufacturing has recommenced. We are in the process of discussing this overdraft facility in principle, with the Co-operative Bank.

The aforementioned information demonstrates the total resolve we still retain. We look forward *to your continued support in our battle to achieve a financial reconstruction of the Triumph Motorcycle business, which has become the vanguard of the co-operative movement in this country.*

Yours sincerely
Triumph Motorcycles (Meriden) Limited
John A Rosamond
Chairman
JAR/HDH
15th February 1983.

PS. Following your meeting with Bill Beattie yesterday, I phoned George Bloomfield to acquaint him with the major progress we have accomplished during the last seven days. He was very impressed, stating that we had "already made good progress in key areas towards cleaning up the business." I asked him if he would be interested in heading up the business in the new circumstances. He stated that he would like to discuss matters further with our accountant Phil Bragg by telephone. He would be in the Coventry area on Friday when he would call in for further discussions and hopefully be in a position to give an indication.

Following a lengthy discussion of Terry Pitt's 9th February letter and the proposed 15th February reply, the Triumph Directors agreed that the substantial progress should be formally conveyed to Mr Pitt at County Hall as a matter of urgency. Terry Pitt's letter, plus the response to it indicating the important areas of progress, would be appended to the minutes of the Board meeting.

Reflecting on the last seven days of intense pressure, the negotiating team were conscious of the tremendous support they had received from members of the Co-op. Amongst many, three individuals in particular played vital roles in the financial reconstruction progress. Phil Bragg's accountancy contribution was fundamental, Alec Bottrill's vast manufacturing experience helped in selection of new factory premises and preparation of the site layout, and Daphne Hornby's tireless secretarial work enabled accurate presentation of the progress to the West Midlands County Council. There was still fight in the Meriden Co-op. The pursuit of the vital financial reconstruction would continue.

Line drawing of the new Triumph factory layout, Cash's Lane Coventry – see rear endpaper for large version. (Author's archive)

29

CLASH OF OPERATING CULTURES

W ith all but 41 Co-op members laid off, the skeleton workforce at the Meriden factory was working harder and longer hours than ever before in a final effort to keep Triumph in business until the financial reconstruction. Whilst the negotiating team's support at the factory was total, unfortunately it was now obvious that this was not the case at County Hall. Having been involved in negotiations with the County Council for nearly a year, we were very conscious of exactly what Singer-Frieglander described as the political environment. The County Hall operating culture was far removed from any engineering business. Persuading Singer-Frieglander to reconsider its position had certainly been a major achievement. We only hoped its further involvement with the County Council and Enterprise Board did not result in a return to the catch 22 impasse that previously existed.

Terry Pitt held a meeting at County Hall on 17th February. Present were the Chairman and two Vice Chairmen of the Economic Development Committee, Norman Holmes – Chief Executive of the West Midlands Enterprise Board – Kate Murray and Tom Fitch. The meeting considered in detail the 9th February County Council correspondence to Triumph, and our response. Phil Bragg, Bill Beattie and John Rosamond were required to attend County Hall for the meeting, 'standing by' should they need to answer any questions! They didn't, and Terry Pitt updated the Triumph representatives when he left the meeting. Whilst no decisions had been made, the politicians were concerned that the Triumph Co-operative would need to be supported "at least past the next General Election," and they wanted to know the funding required to do this. Accordingly, the County Council had employed consultant accounting firm Peat, Marwick, Mitchell to determine this figure. The only note of concern from Terry Pitt at this time was that he and the other officers had been excluded from the final part of the meeting when the politicians went into private session. He was therefore unaware of what had transpired.

Over the next seven to ten days Peat, Marwick, Mitchell's accountants worked with Triumph personnel to establish the funding amount required.

On 18th February, Terry Pitt had a private meeting with Mr Charles Blunt of Singer-Frieglander and Mr George Bloomfield of Herbert-Sigma. Terry Pitt gained a clear indication that they were interested in assisting Triumph, providing a solution could be found to the interim position and there was a strengthening of the management at Triumph. Strengthening of management by recruitment at the time of reconstruction had always been stipulated in Triumph's proposals.

An emergency Board of Directors' meeting was called on 23rd February, the Triumph

Directors having received summonses as a result of non-registration of the audited 1980/81 annual accounts.

We were summonsed to appear at Cardiff Court on 23rd March 1983 as a result of not conforming to statutory obligations to register audited annual accounts for the period October 1980 till September 1981. The Chairman had discussed the situation with the Company Solicitor, Peter Davis. He advised that the best mitigating circumstances to this situation would be to have registered the offending accounts by the date of the court hearing. There was no doubt that the Directors were guilty and should plead guilty by letter, offering the aforementioned mitigating circumstances at the appropriate time.

Following detailed discussion with Phil Bragg regarding the outstanding audit work required by Coopers and Lybrand to finalise these annual accounts, the Directors agreed that the Chairman should advise the Trustees of the present position. The Trustees would be requested to waive their notice entitlement, allowing the reconvened Annual General Meeting to take place on Friday 18th March at 3.00pm. The Chairman would forward the draft annual accounts to the Trustees as soon as possible. The Directors believed it would be helpful if the Trustees attended a pre-AGM briefing meeting with them on Wednesday 16th March at 4.00pm.

The uncertainty regarding ongoing County Council involvement was now massive, and it was decided to utilise the UK International Motorcycle Show at the National Exhibition Centre to showcase the long-term potential of a financially restructured Triumph Motorcycle business. Press day at the NEC was Friday 18th March. As a result of the current long and deep UK recession, Triumph was not the only motorcycle company suffering badly as a result of falling retail sales. Many dealers selling Japanese models had also gone out of business. Therefore, in recent years each UK annual motorcycle show had been significantly smaller and less impressive than the previous one. In view of this trend, Japanese manufacturers now rarely chose to launch their new European models at the UK annual show. Accordingly, a major showcase presentation by Triumph of new models and a potentially bright future would almost certainly capture mass international press coverage – coverage that could lead to further private sector sources of funding. We knew there would be no opposition from the West Midlands County Council and Enterprise Board politicians, always eager to promote their 'potential' involvement in the financial reconstruction. The BBC documentary being produced for *The Money Programme* was also keen to feature Triumph's showcase event.

Triumph's brilliant yet depleted Engineering Department continued to work flat out to complete the new 1983 NEC show models. There was no doubt that the short stroke 600cc Thunderbird and Daytona models, targeted at the lower insurance bracket would be well received. *Motor Cycle News* published show preview photographs of Triumph's two new 600cc models on 2nd March. The TSS Super Sports 8-valve, now to be available with the AV chassis, would be welcomed by the long-distance rider of Triumph's most popular and profitable model. The 8-valve option in the new TSX-8 Custom model was also expected to be in demand on both sides of the Atlantic. All in all, the new model range provided Triumph with a very impressive and profitable product line-up with which to restart production at the new Cash's Lane Triumph factory, once the financial reconstruction was complete. Bill Beattie had already secured access to the new factory, and teams of laid-off Co-op members had voluntarily started to prepare the new factory for Triumph's early occupation. Triumph's show-stopping finale at the NEC – to demonstrate we were also working on new designs for the future, designs that were capable of sustaining profitable operation well into the 1990s – was the first public showing of the top-secret Diana project. Whilst Brian Jones had been overseeing the Rye Tools/Weslake subcontract design work on the engine project, Martyn Roberts had been leading a

Meriden factory team on the design and development of the intended rolling chassis, the two projects had now merged at Meriden. A basic styling mock-up was being prepared by Andrew Charters, and would allow the general public to gain a first impression of what Triumph's all-new 900cc Phoenix model might look like when introduced. Triumph's carpenter, Stan Grundy, who had been assisting with production of the NEC show stand, suitably reinforced the office roof structure to enable the Phoenix styling mock-up to be exhibited in an elevated position, where every show visitor was sure of getting a good view of Triumph's exciting future. To prove that the Triumph styling mock-up was not just another 'string and ceiling wax' affair, continuing the long line of previous British motorcycle industry visions that never reached production, a dynamometer Diana test engine was also to be exhibited on the show stand, allowing press and general public to become intimately acquainted with Triumph's potential future.

On 4th March, Terry Pitt telephoned John Rosamond to advise that at a 4.15pm meeting the previous day the Chairman of the Economic Development Committee, his two Vice Chairmen, and officers of the EDU and Enterprise Board met to consider the commissioned Peat, Marwick, Mitchell Triumph funding report. A copy of the consultant's report was to be delivered by Tom Fitch to Triumph that day.

Norman Holmes, the West Midlands Enterprise Board Chief Executive, was sending a copy of the Enterprise Board's internal working papers on Triumph's 5-year plan, which covered some of the same ground as the consultant's report. Terry Pitt advised that although both of these documents were confidential, they should be discussed with Triumph's lawyers and fellow Directors, as the consultant's report indicated an extremely serious situation – the funding figures were both "high" and "complex"! The committee meeting discussed these for almost three hours, at the end of which the elected members felt they had to have more time to consider their final response. They decided to meet again in five days' time on Wednesday 9th March. Triumph was advised not to read anything into this decision, either positively or negatively, as far as further Council or Enterprise Board assistance was concerned. Meanwhile, if Triumph wanted to make any points about the two documents, it should feel free to contact him.

As Terry Pitt had indicated, Tom Fitch provided a copy of the Peat, Marwick, Mitchell consultant's report on 4th March; three days later, two letters from Terry Pitt arrived at Triumph. One, dated 1st March, confirmed earlier verbal discussions regarding Triumph's 15th February correspondence, and the other, dated 4th March, confirmed the details of the 3rd March meeting with consultants Peat, Marwick, Mitchell. In the same post was a letter from Norman Holmes, also referring to the recent report on Triumph by Peat, Marwick, Mitchell, which, he stated, highlighted the very difficult financial position of the company. As a result, he felt it proper to advise that whilst the Enterprise Board continued to consider Triumph's request for further funding, it should not be assumed that funding would be forthcoming in relation to the ongoing management of Triumph's affairs. There was a brief postscript to Norman's letter indicating that he did not have a spare copy of the Enterprise Board working papers on Triumph's 5-year plan, and that Kate Murray would be providing one! These also arrived in the avalanche of West Midlands County Council/Enterprise Board post on 7th March, just two days before the critical decision-making meeting on Triumph at County Hall.

That the Peat, Marwick, Mitchell consultant's report on Triumph covered some of the same ground as the West Midlands Enterprise Board internal working papers on Triumph's 5-year plan – as suggested by Terry Pitt's comments – seemed to be more than a coincidence. It now appeared that something more sinister than coincidence could be at play.

To have any chance of influencing the discussions on Triumph's immediate future in two days' time, a detailed response pointing out the report's inaccuracies had to be drafted that day, agreed by the Board of Directors the following day, and delivered by hand early the following day in time for the West Midlands County Council meeting.

At the 8th March Board of Directors' meeting, the Chairman reported that the negotiating team was concerned regarding the lack of consistency between the information reported to them by Terry Pitt on the evening of 17th February, and recently received correspondence dated 1st and 4th March. Phil Bragg, Bill Beattie and John Rosamond had been summoned to County Hall on 17th February to be available to the West Midlands Enterprise Board/Economic Development Unit Chairman and his two Vice Chairmen, plus appointed officers, "if required" (and we weren't) to take part in their meeting on Triumph. However, following the meeting Terry Pitt invited the Triumph representatives into his office for an update, where he gave a brief outline of matters discussed.

Whilst he advised there was certainly no agreement reached at the meeting, it was implied that the meeting had decided to utilise the services of a further consultancy group of accountants – Peat, Marwick, Mitchell – to ascertain quickly the overall cost of supporting the Triumph Co-operative, at least past the next General Election. This, the politicians present had felt, was a very necessary and desirable requirement. Terry Pitt, who had consistently supported our efforts during Triumph's involvement with the County Council, did however state that although he was aware of the outcome of the meeting during the officers' presence, the politicians had gone into private session at the end and he was therefore unaware of what transpired. County Council support past the next General Election, whilst not our long-term objective, did offer further time to achieve the financial reconstruction of the business.

As a result of their own involvement with the Peat, Marwick, Mitchell staff, the other Triumph Directors were aware that every assistance had been given to them, as had been the case with the previous consultant's personnel from Price Waterhouse and Arthur D Little. However, on this occasion the recently received letter seemed to confirm that there had been a complete change of emphasis from that indicated by Terry Pitt on the evening of Thursday 17th February.

A brief review of the Peat, Marwick, Mitchell report had been undertaken, and the Chairman felt an immediate response in writing was required. This would be for consideration by the County Council politicians and officials when they met again the following day, 9th March, to consider the Triumph situation. The written response needed to point out that Triumph felt the latest County Council/Enterprise Board correspondence suggested they had adopted a considerable change of emphasis, going from an overview of Triumph's long-term potential to a short-term view.

The tabled draft reply pointed out the shortcomings in both the confidential working papers for the Enterprise Board and in the Peat, Marwick, Mitchell report. Finally the letter listed Triumph's recent substantial achievements in the financial reconstruction negotiations.

Dear Mr Pitt
Thank you for your letter with attached postscript dated 1st March, received on 7th March 1983.
In an effort to make at least an initial response for consideration at your next meeting on Triumph, which we understand to be taking place tomorrow Wednesday 9th March, we have concentrated in the time available to us on the broader aspects raised in your letter. Answered under separate cover to follow, are items 1 and 2 and matters detailed in your attached postscript.
For the record, we also received on 7th March a further letter from yourself dated 4th March, a letter from Norman Holmes of the Enterprise Board dated 4th March and from Mrs Kate Murray a copy of her Enterprise Board working papers on Triumph's 5-year plan. Tom Fitch provided a copy of the Peat, Marwick, Mitchell report on 4th March!

Both the letters dated 4th March seem to reflect a distinct change of emphasis as a result of the Peat, Marwick, Mitchell report, to that of your previous position of taking an overview of the long-term Triumph potential as supported by Price Waterhouse and Arthur D Little. This would now appear to have changed in favour of taking the more short-term view contained in the latest Peat, Marwick, Mitchell report. If this is the case, it is of course a complete misconception. Whilst the funding remains the same, the short-term and long-term potential of Triumph is, as we have been discussing for almost twelve months, at totally opposite ends of the spectrum.

As both the Kate Murray working papers on Triumph's 5-year plan and the Peat, Marwick, Mitchell report were considered by your last meeting, we believe it important for Triumph to have the opportunity to comment on their content.

WEST MIDLANDS ENTERPRISE BOARD – WORKING PAPERS REPORT
As Triumph's copy of this confidential report to the Enterprise Board is not dated, we can only assume that this is the report that was being compiled by Mrs Kate Murray for the last Enterprise Board meeting held on 25th February. In which case, it is totally understandable that the report is considerably out of date. However the report is very useful indeed to outline the considerable amount of progress achieved by Triumph's management, on major issues fundamental to the financial reconstruction of Triumph's affairs and detailed in my letter to you dated 15th February. Recognising the aforementioned, it would seem a fruitless exercise to deal in detail with every individual point and we would suggest if you wish to do so, we would discuss these matters at a future meeting.

PEAT, MARWICK, MITCHELL REPORT TO WEST MIDLANDS COUNTY COUNCIL AND ENTERPRISE BOARD
There are several areas within the report where we feel that the funding requirement has been overstated. Whilst we accept that there are quite a few assumptions incorporated into the projections, it is felt that the report's concluding requirement of £2m is far too conservative.

2.1 ACCOUNTING RECORDS
The report is critical of the accounting records maintained by Triumph and points to the likelihood of a "proper books of account" qualification in the 1980/81 accounts by our auditors, Coopers and Lybrand. The effect of these inadequacies, however, on the funding requirement has not been properly investigated.

a) Cost of sales. The absence of an accurate year-end stock figure will certainly effect the balance sheet and the net assets position of the company. As regards the working capital calculation, it omits two important elements:

i) The material content of each model is costed for every single component which enables the company to accurately calculate the cost of sales content of a projected build programme. The material specification is also analysed by individual supplier, thus facilitating a projected payment schedule based on the payment terms applicable to those suppliers.

ii) A full stock take in the week ending 25th February 1983 identified nearly £200,000 of current stock available for production. Out of this amount, about £105,000 is available for the first 10 weeks of production and therefore effects the peak working capital requirement.

b) Debtor collection. Examination of the company's records would have confirmed that the average collection periods assumed for the various markets are quite reasonable. The comment on page 15 "our experience is that customers generally take in excess of the credit period allowed," ignores several factors:

i) For most of the 1982 season, dealers were paying cash on delivery for motorcycles.

ii) The dealer stocking plan jointly prepared with the First Co-operative Finance Limited will guarantee payment within 7 days of delivery. It is anticipated that at least 25 per cent of the UK market will be covered by this plan.

iii) All police and military sales are covered by irrevocable letters of credit.

No work was carried out to validate the Company's assumptions regarding credit periods. Such work could have been carried out quite easily and would have removed the necessity for the subjective comment quoted above.

2.2 EXPENDITURE

a) Additional stockholding of £200,000 has been included in the report which equates to 5 weeks' stock of bought out components. These suppliers will be scheduled at least 3 months ahead and since the lead times for all of these items is only a few days it is considered that 3 weeks' stockholding is quite adequate.

b) A payment schedule has been proposed to the Inland Revenue. A meeting with the collector of taxes on 4th March suggests that this schedule will be acceptable.

c) The reaction of the trade creditors to an injection of funds has been the subject of much speculation, particularly in view of the experience of the West Midlands County Council loan in December. There are however, several factors to be considered with regard to any new financing:

i) Those suppliers who are less likely to be patient given the company's difficult circumstances were dealt with in December, e.g. Automotive Products, Pulley Bros and Brookhouse Kaye. The overall level of trade creditors had been reduced quite considerably and those remaining have been made well aware of the consequences of legal action to recover their debt. Payment schedules have been proposed to most of the larger suppliers and their reaction has been favourable.

ii) The crucial reason for the patience shown by suppliers is that they appreciate that any restructuring of the company will be a long-term venture as opposed to the short-term 'prop up' loans received before Christmas. Firms will accept 8-week repayment schedules if they can see that the company is in full production way beyond that point.

2.3 RELOCATION

The ability to sell the Meriden site and relocate as quickly as possible is fundamental to the overall funding requirement. The report shows a peak expenditure on the old site of £214,000. Recent information reduces this figure very considerably.

a) The bank's acceptance of £700,000 including roll-up of interest, as full and final settlement means that £112,000 of bank interest can be removed from the estimated old site costs.

b) The District Valuation Officer has indicated that the first 3 months vacant possession of the Meriden site will be rate free or at least the bill will be reduced.

2.4 CONCLUSION

The moratorium has been eliminated since the sale proceeds of the site will cover the anticipated 15 per cent pay-out.

The report continually stressed the possibility of disruption during the initial weeks of production which might jeopardise the projected 70 units per week targeted build. It is interesting to note however, that even if production is reduced by 40 per cent in each of weeks 3-6, there is still no effect on the peak requirement. This is because the market most affected by reduced production is the USA and receipts from this source would not be received until well after the peak has been reached.

We hope the aforementioned comments will be accepted in the comradely spirit in which they are offered, and recognition of Triumph management's recent substantial achievements will be forthcoming. We feel it is useful to list again our recent substantial achievements as they represent the 'mountains' that Triumph has been asked to climb, in pursuance of long-term financial support, from the West Midlands County Council and Enterprise Board.

TRIUMPH'S RECENT SUBSTANTIAL ACHIEVEMENTS
Sale of the 16.8 acre portion of the Meriden factory site, for £940,000 net (subject to planning permission).
    Purchase of the Dunlop site, Cash's Lane, for £250,000.
    Agreement with the National Westminster Bank London, to accept £700,000 in full and final settlement of the present Triumph overdraft facility of £1,195,000.
    Agreement with the Moratorium Creditors' subcommittee, to recommend acceptance of a full and final settlement figure of 15p in the £, equalling £150,000 approximately, to write off the total moratorium debt of £850,000.
    Initial discussions with the Co-operative Bank suggest that, with the help of the West Midlands, a new overdraft facility can be established.
    Mr Alec Kitson, Assistant General Secretary of the Transport and General Workers' Union, has kindly involved Mrs Jeannie Buckham, who is making representation on Triumph's behalf at the EEC Parliament, and is optimistic that grants for purchase of plant and machinery, and research and development on Triumph's new Diana model range, are achievable.
    Discussions on Monday of this week, 7th March 1983, with the Inland Revenue, indicate a new repayment schedule can be agreed with them, in line with Triumph's assumptions.
    Discussions with major current creditors, indicate that they are prepared to readily accept payment schedules in line with Triumph's assumptions, all recognising the significant difference between the situation that prevailed with short-term loan facilities and a long-term solution to Triumph's underlying financial problems.
    Positive indications lead us to believe that Export Credit Guarantee facilities will be restored following the financial reconstruction of Triumph. Accordingly, application has been made towards this end, to ECGD, supported by copies of Triumph's five-year 'warts and all' plan and review document, plus Price Waterhouse indications and Arthur D Little's review. The aforementioned has also been copied for information to the Department of Industry.
    A completely new model range (Diana models) has been designed, and prototype engine development running is now under way.
    Having achieved what were thought to be impossible targets, set by the West Midlands County Council and Enterprise Board, during our twelve months of negotiations, it should come as no surprise that those responsible for achieving the above '10 commandments' feel very much as Moses must have felt having climbed the mountain, and now looking over into the promised land.
    The Meriden Co-operative, recognised by all the financial experts as being doomed to failure from the outset, has only survived as a direct result of the continual sacrifices made by the working class people who have only one thing in common, their total belief in Triumph as a workers' co-operative. Now, for the first time, the Meriden Co-operative has the opportunity to succeed and become the rightful vanguard of the British co-operative movement. It would be a pity if those to whom we look for support in our final hour of need are not forthcoming, and that inherent success there for the taking, is subsequently stolen by private enterprise.
    Yours sincerely,
For and on behalf of the Triumph Board of Directors.
John A Rosamond, Chairman
JAR/HDH
8th March 1983

The Directors discussed at length the Enterprise Board working papers on Triumph's 5-year plan, and the Peat, Marwick, Mitchell accountancy report, following which they agreed with the negotiating team that an immediate response in line with the draft letter discussed should be urgently delivered to Terry Pitt at the West Midlands County Council. This was subsequently done early on 9th March, enabling Terry Pitt to circulate Triumph's comments to all those attending the vital committee meeting later that day.

On 12th March, *The Financial Times* published the following story (reproduced with its kind permission) on the American above 700cc motorcycle market – by Jurek Martin in Tokyo and Terry Byland in New York.

JAPAN MAY BOOST US SUPERBIKE

The Japanese motor cycle industry, which brought Harley-Davidson, the US motorcycle maker, to the brink of extinction, may soon help rescue it at the request of Japan's Ministry of Trade and Industry.

A MITI official in Tokyo said yesterday that such a scheme existed as one of several contingency options being examined in case President Reagan approved a sharp increase in tariffs on motorcycle imports.

Under US law, Mr Reagan has until April 2nd to pass judgement on a US International Trade Commission recommendation that tariffs be raised for five years to provide Harley-Davidson some relief against Japanese competition.

Mr Reagan's reaction to the ITC recommendations is widely regarded as a test of his Administration's frequently voiced commitment to free trade.

On January 25th the ITC upheld a complaint by Harley-Davidson that its 700cc machines had lost market share (they now represent only 14 per cent of the US market for heavy motorcycles) and had been forced to lay off 1600 workers because of the flood of competition from Japan.

The US motorcycle market is in serious difficulty. It has enough stockpiled machines to provide 12-18 months' sales, and they are overwhelmingly Japanese.

The result has been heavy discounting, making competition extremely difficult for Harley-Davidson which has a high-cost base.

The MITI official emphasised that it would be wrong to assume that any rescue plan involving the Japanese makers was being given a higher priority than other options.

These include voluntary export restraint, negotiating with the US over higher tariffs and other, unspecified actions.

But if the version of the possible rescue given yesterday in Nihon Keizei Shimbun, the leading Japanese business newspaper is correct, Suzuki and Yamaha would end up as Harley-Davidson's customers and would buy the equivalent of one year's sales. In the longer term Honda, Japan's biggest manufacturer, would provide Harley-Davidson with technical know-how and possibly engines. Kawasaki, Japan's fourth largest manufacturer, would not be involved because it is particularly heavily burdened with excess stocks in the US.

The MITI official acknowledged that there had already been a "preliminary brain storming session" with the four Japanese manufacturers, but neither he nor the companies wished to be drawn into details.

From Milwaukee, Wisconsin, Harley-Davidson said the idea was a "complete surprise" but declined to comment further pending confirmation.

I recalled that this was not the first occasion that the might of the Japanese motorcycle industry had united to protect its mutual interest. A similar act of self-preservation had occurred in the late 1970s, when legislation to introduce leg protection on motorcycles was being seriously considered in the UK.

At Triumph, we understood that Her Majesty's Government, in the form of the Ministry of Transport, was under increasing pressure from the Treasury to reduce the escalating costs to the National Health Service of motorcycle accidents, particularly those that resulted in leg injuries – it was often said at the time that if you were unfortunate enough to be admitted to a hospital orthopaedic ward, the person in the next bed would almost certainly be a motorcyclist with leg injuries.

Accordingly, it was believed the Transport and Road Research Laboratory (TRRL) had been asked to undertake research to establish how motorcycle injuries could be reduced, especially to the rider's legs. UK Government legislation would then be introduced based upon the findings, and this would ensure that in future manufacturers produced motorcycles with leg protection. Triumph Meriden personnel were invited to the research establishment to observe the practical crash testing. TRRL subsequently ordered a T140E Bonneville modified to incorporate leg protection and a chest restraint based upon its findings. (A 1979 picture of this significantly modified Bonneville appears in Roy Bacon's book *Triumph – T140 Bonnevilles and their derivatives.*)

When the motorcycle manufacturers became aware of the claimed safety improvements achieved by specifying leg protection, based upon which it was proposed to introduce new legislation, it was generally felt that the research findings could be flawed. Although safety issues were of major importance to all motorcycle companies, leg protection legislation based upon suspect research would benefit no-one. I soon realised, however, that there was, of course, the other major commercial consideration. Safety legislation introduced in the UK would inevitably, because of the growing global safety lobby, spread worldwide – especially, it was anticipated, to the USA.

Not surprisingly, with massive motorcycle stocks in the US, this certainly captured the 'big four' Japanese manufacturers' full attention! Legislation that introduced leg protection in the UK was potentially an American product liability nightmare in the making. How could a manufacturer continue to sell stockpiled motorcycles in the US without leg protection, when at the same time producing and selling safer motorcycles with leg protection?

It was not surprising, therefore, that TRRL's research findings would be challenged by the combined hi-tech research resources of the Japanese motorcycle industry. It is believed that this research established that in certain circumstances, the proposed UK leg protection could increase the severity of injuries sustained by motorcycle riders – the opposite of the desired effect! The legislation was not pursued and the industry breathed a sigh of relief.

Preparations for Triumph's showcase appearance at the NEC International Motorcycle Show were now well advanced. Installation of the Triumph show stand was nearing completion, awaiting only the 1983 model range. Just down the road at the Meriden factory, the Engineering Department had been burning the midnight oil to complete the show models, especially the 900cc Phoenix styling mock-up. The placement of the headline-grabbing Phoenix on the roof of the show stand office would be deliberately kept secret until the last possible moment, ideally for the planned press day unveiling. No fancy elaborate poster brochure this year, just A4 colour flyers.

The 18th March would be a special day for Triumph, not just because it was NEC press day. Back at the factory, the Beneficiary Co-op owners of Triumph (75 per cent of whom were still laid off) would be attending the long awaited reconvened Annual General Meeting to accept the overdue 1980/81 audited accounts. Owing to the non-registration of these accounts, Triumph's Directors were due to appear before Cardiff Court in three days' time.

In anticipation of possible private sector investors coming forward following Triumph's showcase appearance at the NEC, Phil Bragg had produced an excellent document outlining the proposed financial restructuring of the business. Peat, Marwick, Mitchell's very conservative funding figures were utilised.

TRIUMPH MOTORCYCLES (MERIDEN) LIMITED – FINANCIAL RESTRUCTURING SCHEME
The proposed restructuring of the financial base of the Co-operative can be divided into two main elements:
    a) Funds generated by Triumph, and
    b) Funds provided by outside interests.
    Triumph has received an offer from Espley-Tyas Limited of £1m net of associated costs for 16.8 acres of the Meriden site, subject to planning approval for change of usage from industrial to residential.
    Payment terms are:
    i) £500,000 on completion.
    ii) £500,000 in the form of a 12 month bill of exchange.
    Discounting the bill of exchange would cost approximately £60,000, leaving net proceeds of £940,000.
    The West Midlands County Council (WMCC) has consistently stated that it could justify supporting Triumph's future funding requirements, but could not contribute to clearing past liabilities. These liabilities consist of:
    a) A bank overdraft of £1.195m secured against premises, plant, stock, book debts and the Triumph name.
    b) A creditor's moratorium established in 1979, which currently stands at about £850,000.
    The objective of the Co-operative has been to eliminate £2.045m of liabilities using £0.940m proceeds from the sale of the site. The proposed scheme is as follows:

	Current debt (£000s)	Amount offered (£000s)	Written off (£000s)
Bank overdraft	*1.195*	*0.700*	*0.495*
Moratorium	*0.850*	*0.150*	*0.700*
Removal costs		**0.050*	
Stamp duty, professional fees, etc		**0.040*	
Total	***2.045***	***0.940***	***1.195***

    * Relates to costs associated with moving to a new site in Coventry.

    National Westminster Bank has accepted an offer of £700,000 in full and final settlement of its debt (see attached letter). The Moratorium Creditors' Committee, which represents about 250 companies, has agreed to recommend to those creditors an offer of 30p in the pound in full and final settlement. Since the moratorium was established, payments totalling 15p in the pound have been made, so the final payment will be 15p to arrive at the settlement figure of 30p (see attached letter).
    It is anticipated that the capital injection will be in the order of £2.0m and will involve the West Midlands County Council, West Midlands Enterprise Board and the private sector. The injection will almost certainly consist of a mix of equity and loans.
    The £2.0m equates to the independent assessment of the funding requirement by Peat, Marwick, Mitchell, which was employed by WMCC to examine Triumph's scheme.
    Enclosed are figures showing the current balance sheet and a projected balance sheet after

restructuring. As the precise form of the capital injection has still to be determined, certain assumptions have been made regarding the new capital structure.

Two days before the 18th March Annual General Meeting, the Triumph Directors met the Trustees for the scheduled pre-AGM briefing. All three Trustees were in attendance.
The Chairman welcomed John Haynes, Ron Marston and John Tomlinson, and explained that the circumstances under which the AGM for the accounting period 1st October 1980 to 30th September 1981 was being held could not be worse. In what had proved to be extremely long and protracted financial reconstruction negotiations, the Directors had received summonses (dated 21st February) to appear at court in Cardiff on 21st March. They were to face the charge of non-registration of company accounts for the aforementioned period.

It was believed that a certain amount of political stirring by creditors complaining to the Companies Registrations Office had resulted in the summonses being issued. They had been issued without further notice, and Peter Davis, Triumph's solicitor, had advised that the Directors plead guilty by letter, offering as mitigating circumstances the fact that the offending audited accounts would be registered by the time of the court hearing. Accordingly, the AGM had been organised as soon as possible, to be held on Friday 18th March at 3.00pm.

Phil Bragg, Triumph's Financial Controller, explained that to date we had only draft accounts, which lacked the final audit report. However, at a meeting with auditor Coopers and Lybrand, the audit partner Mr Peter Court indicated that audited annual accounts for the period in question would be available prior to the scheduled AGM taking place. Qualifications associated with these accounts were likely to be extensive, as the time available had been such that very little work was possible to satisfy the auditors on the queries they had raised. In this situation, it was likely that the auditors would qualify everything including the kitchen sink!

Following discussion, the Trustees agreed to arrive early on Friday 18th March, in order to discuss the audited 1980/81 accounts prior to the AGM taking place. It was therefore a very important day for Triumph. First, we represented the company at press day at the NEC Motorcycle Show. The team arrived early, and the combined efforts of the Sales/Engineering Departments and carpenter, plus additional laid-off volunteers, had achieved a Triumph show stand presentation to be proud of. The 1983 model range was certainly impressive. The elevated Phoenix styling mock-up and dyno 900cc DOHC test engine, both still under wraps, added a little mystery to the Triumph stand that had been lacking in earlier days of the Meriden Co-op.

Due to lack of customer interest, the Tiger Trail, Executive and TS8-1 models were dropped from the 1983 model range, to be produced profitably at the Cash's Lane Triumph factory. Whilst the Executive model had gone in its own right, Executive equipment accessories would still remain available to Triumph buyers. Also gone were non-electric start model options, electric start now being standard across the range.

1983 UK specification models would benefit from 'rear set' gear and brake foot controls, providing a more appropriate riding position. The UK-spec dual seat also had more comfortable padding and a moulded tail. All UK and US models in the range, with the exception of TSS and TSX, now received a 7in drum rear brake. 1983 models also benefited from Triumph new chromed full megaphone shape silencers.

1983 MODEL RANGE TO BE PRODUCED AT THE NEW FACTORY – PROMOTIONAL MATERIAL
TSS
The Triumph TSS for 1983 has many new features. As you would expect all are in line with the finest British motorcycle tradition. The heart of the TSS is Triumph's very latest high performance

Doug Mogano with the new 600cc Daytona development bike. (Courtesy Doug Mogano's archive)

750cc 8-valve engine now installed in the patented 'enforcer frame' developed extensively in conjunction with British police forces. This unique hand-built high performance motorcycle with road handling to match, offers a combination which would be incomplete if it was not for very special 'lean machine' styling introduced for 1983. To ensure that you are at one with your TSS from the moment you take delivery, Triumph have revised the riding position, foot rests and foot controls are now more 'rear set' and as such are in keeping with this truly magnificent Super Sports motorcycle.

TSX4 (Continues with 3 alternative colour options.)

TSX8
In 1983 Triumph introduces the very special TSX8 Custom, with all the merits of the original TSX4 plus the added bonus of the Triumph high performance 8-valve engine. When it comes to turning heads the TSX8 has it all. The low-slung 'west coast' look now with additional performance ensures that every proud owner not only stands out from the crowd but stays ahead of the pack.

T140ES Bonneville UK (Continues with range improvements and colour options.)

T140ES Bonneville US (Continues with a new 16" rear wheel and colour options.)

Thunderbird 600
The brand new Thunderbird 600 was conceived by Triumph engineers for the young and young at heart. Bristling with all the very latest features you would expect and totally in keeping with the finest British motorcycle tradition. The Triumph Thunderbird is a hand-built high performance custom motorcycle with handling to match. A combination which would be incomplete if it was not for the very special 'west coast' look guaranteed to put the opposition in the shade.

The new 750cc TSS Super Sports, now with the enforcer frame, developed with the help of UK police forces. (Promotional picture)

The high performance 8-valve engine was introduced in the TSX-8 Custom model for 1983. (Promotional picture)

Thunderbird 600 – brief technical specification:
Engine type .... *OHV parallel twin four stroke*
Bore .... *2.992in (76mm)*
Stroke .... *2.598in (66mm)*
Capacity .... *599cc (36.5cu in)*
Compression ratio *8.4:1*
Carburettor .... *one 30mm choke*
Tyres front .... *MJ90 x 19 rib*
Tyres rear .... *MT90 x 16 low profile*
Brakes front .... *9.8in (250mm) disc*
Brakes rear .... *7.0in (178mm) drum*
Gearbox type .... *5-speed, top gear 4.95*
Top gear rpm at 10mph *685*
Frame .... *all welded steel cradle type*
Rear shock absorbers .... *hydraulic*
Wheelbase .... *56in (1422mm)*
Seat height .... *30in (762mm)*
Dry weight .... *415lb (189kg)*
Fuel capacity .... *2.8 imp galls (12.7 litres)*
Electrics .... *12v crankshaft alternator*
14 A/H battery
Electronic ignition
Electric start

The new 600cc Thunderbird introduced for 1983. (Promotional picture)

Instruments .... *tachometer and speedometer*
Finish .... *4 colour options*
Optional extra .... *twin disc front brake*

Daytona 600
The brand new Daytona 600 is introduced for the young and young at heart. Embodying all the very latest Triumph specification developments you would expect whilst remaining true to the finest British motorcycle tradition. The Triumph Daytona is a hand-built high performance sports motorcycle with handling to match, a combination enhanced by its very special 'lean machine' styling.
Daytona 600 – brief technical specification:
Engine type .... *OHV parallel twin four stroke*
Bore .... *2.992in (76mm)*
Stroke .... *2.598in (66mm)*
Capacity .... *599cc (36.5cu in)*
Compression ratio *8.4:1*
Carburettors .... *twin 30mm choke*
Tyres front .... *410 x 19*
Tyres rear .... *425 x 18*
Brakes front .... *9.8in (250mm) disc*
Brakes rear .... *7.0in (178mm) drum*
Gearbox type .... *5-speed, top gear 4.95*
Top gear rpm at 10mph *664*
Frame .... *all welded steel cradle type*
Rear shock absorbers .... *hydraulic*
Wheelbase .... *56in (1422mm)*
Seat height .... *31in (787mm)*
Dry weight .... *405lb (184kg)*
Fuel capacity .... *4.0 Imp galls (18.2 litres)*
Electrics .... *12v crankshaft alternator*
14 A/H battery
Electronic ignition
Electric start
Instruments .... *tachometer and speedometer*
Finish .... *stainless steel mudguards, 3 colour options*
Optional extra .... *twin disc front brake*

The show stand now complete, Triumph's 1983 7-model range in the various new colour options, could not have been displayed better. With factory help, the specialist motorcycle press had been building the general public's and motorcycle trade's expectations regarding Triumph's 1983 model range. What the press, trade and general public did not expect and would catch them completely by surprise was the first appearance of Triumph's Super Sports 900cc Phoenix.

But first, Bob Currie's nostalgic *Motor Cycle Weekly* story, "Welcome home Triumph" caught everyone napping! – "Now Triumph are moving back on two wheels instead of four – small world isn't it?" This article, written by a journalist who was Triumph through to the core, referred to a bygone era when Triumph cars were produced at the Cash's Lane Coventry factory site we were to occupy following the financial reconstruction.

The NEC press day impact was exactly as intended, guaranteeing mass media coverage of

The very impressive Triumph show stand, with the high performance Super Sports 900cc dohc Phoenix styling model on the roof. (Author's archive)

Triumph's showcase presentation. Brian Jones and John Rosamond were fully occupied with media interviews from 10.30am till 1.30pm. There was no doubt that journalists were very positive regarding the 1983 model range, the intended financial reconstruction and the 'futuristic' 900cc Phoenix, about which there was the expected clamour for technical details. Brian Jones did an excellent job in whetting their appetite a little. We knew the NEC press day would provide the necessary international coverage to establish if there were any further private sector financial investors interested (no asset strippers).

The Phoenix development engine was removed from the dynamometer to be exhibited at the show. (Author's archive)

TSX-8 in the foreground, and a Doug Cashmore-sectioned engine with moving parts activated by the kickstart mechanism in the background. (Author's archive)

By 1.30pm, the journalists had completed their interviews and departed for a liquid lunch. This allowed Brian Jones and John Rosamond to undertake the 10-minute journey back to the Meriden factory for the Annual General Meeting, leaving a small but enthusiastic sales/engineering team at the show.

The Board of Directors met the three Trustees at 2.30pm to continue the pre-AGM briefing started two days earlier. As with previous AGMs, Company Solicitor Peter Davis was also present, although surprisingly no representative from the auditors. Once again, John Haynes, Ron Marston and John Tomlinson were in attendance.

Continuing from where we had left off, Phil Bragg reported that he had received accounts for the period 1st October 1980 to 30th September 1981 half an hour before the meeting started! They were unfortunately incomplete, and the auditors had dropped a bombshell. They were

The 1983 version of the legendary Bonneville that had been at the heart of Triumph's survival continued to attract massive show attention. (Author's archive)

now uncertain as to whether TMA's accounts had been audited, and were considering a further qualification. Looking at the accounts, the Directors and Trustees were very concerned at the extent of the qualifications, two of which implied that there had been criminal acts committed during the period under review.

The Chairman informed the meeting that Rob Murison, present for the AGM as the Financial Director responsible during the accounting period under consideration, was extremely concerned at the latest developments. He believed that it was merely a question of insufficient time to resolve the queries raised by the auditors, and in this situation the accounts should not be presented in their present form.

The Trustees and Directors agreed with Rob Murison's view, and decided that it should be explained to the now gathering Beneficiaries that it would not be possible for the AGM to

371

Senior design draughtsman Doug Mogano steadies the Phoenix styling model outside the experimental building on its return from the NEC show. (Courtesy Doug Mogano's archive)

go ahead, as the accounts were still incomplete and therefore unavailable for presentation. In view of the aforementioned position, once he had explained to the Beneficiaries that the AGM could not proceed, the Chairman would totally update the membership on the present state of the financial reconstruction negotiations.

The Board meeting was adjourned at 3.45pm, to reconvene following the meeting with the Co-op members.

Having first explained that it was not possible to unable to proceed with the AGM, the Chairman provided a comprehensive report on the financial reconstruction negotiations including the recent vital progress achieved. There then followed a detailed membership question and answer session, responded to by John Rosamond, Bill Beattie and Phil Bragg, after which it was agreed that the AGM would be rescheduled as soon as the audited 1980/81 annual accounts were available.

The one hour Beneficiary meeting concluded, the Directors' Board meeting with the Trustees and Company Solicitor Peter Davis was reconvened. The Chairman advised that Rob Murison had indicated his willingness to help answer the auditor's queries, and believed if this course of action was adopted many of the qualifications would be removed. Rob Murison had further undertaken to draw up a proposed 'course of action' list, which would be forwarded to the Trustees in due course.

Under these circumstances, and following discussion with Peter Davis, it was decided that the Chairman would write to the Cardiff Court requesting an adjournment of the hearing for approximately six weeks, to enable the aforementioned action to be accomplished and a rescheduled AGM to take place. The Trustees asked if it would be possible to have a representative of the auditor Coopers and Lybrand present when the rescheduled 1980/81 Annual General Meeting took place.

Having heard the full report to the Beneficiaries on the financial reconstruction negotiations currently taking place, and being aware that the vast majority of the membership had now been laid off without wages for six weeks, the Trustees offered to bring pressure to bear within the Labour Party movement. This would be accomplished during the policy making weekend at Dudley, due to take place on Saturday 26th and Sunday 27th March 1983.

It was suggested by the Trustees that this decisive action would be in an effort to sit Triumph representatives down with Geoffrey Edge and other senior political leaders of West Midlands County Council.

The negotiating team felt this was an excellent idea, and if the Trustees were successful, they would have achieved the first official meeting with senior West Midlands County Council politicians for many months.

30

MORE SINISTER THAN COINCIDENCE

The last few days could not have turned out more positively for the Co-op and Triumph. The NEC showcase appearance before the media achieved exactly what had been planned. The general public's response since the show opened was also extremely supportive. Even the aborted Annual General Meeting enabled a full and frank exchange of information with all the Beneficiary owners, and gave a massive boost to the sagging morale of those who had been laid off for six weeks. All of this provided Triumph's negotiating team and Board of Directors with renewed enthusiasm to push on for our ultimate goal: the financial reconstruction. However, this was all to change on the morning of Tuesday 22nd March, when the Chief Executive of the West Midlands Enterprise Board contacted Triumph's Chairman with a specific instruction that could mean only one thing: legal steps were being taken by it to appoint a receiver.

Having confirmed this, John Rosamond called a Board of Directors meeting at 3.15pm.

The Chairman reported that earlier that day he had received an extremely disturbing instruction from Norman Holmes, Chief Executive of the West Midlands Enterprise Board. He had instructed the Chairman to send the following telex to Wayne Moulton, President of Triumph Motorcycles (America) Inc:

To Mr Wayne Moulton, President AM Brit STD time
Triumph Motorcycles (America) Inc. 22.3.83.
Reference WMEB/Amersdown Limited agreement
Transfer immediately all monies available, resultant from the sale of WMEB/Amersdown financed motorcycles.

Do not sell, repeat do not sell any more motorcycles financed under the WMEB/Amersdown Limited facility.

a) Withdraw all WMEB/Amersdown financed motorcycles in stock, from their present warehouse location, and re-site in new warehouse location.

b) Make payment for new warehousing of WMEB/Amersdown Limited motorcycles for one month.

Following Norman Holmes' telex instruction, the Chairman contacted Triumph's solicitor, Peter Davis, and confirmed that the contents of the telex indicated that the process

374

of appointing a receiver for the West Midlands Enterprise Board. Before sending the telex, as soon as the British/USA time difference allowed, the Chairman discussed its contents on the telephone with TMA President Wayne Moulton. Wayne was amazed, especially as the Chairman had secured with Mrs Kate Murray (accountant for the Enterprise Board) a one month extension of the loan repayment period, and there were still seven days before this expired. However, Wayne stated, TMA had collected more of the loan monies than had been expected, and was, therefore, in a position to totally repay the outstanding debt earlier than previously thought. Accordingly, it was agreed that TMA would transfer the outstanding monies to Triumph Meriden immediately.

In view of the telephone conversation with Wayne Moulton, the Chairman tried to contact Norman Holmes at the Enterprise Board, but he was not available. In his absence, the Chairman spoke to Mrs Kate Murray, and asked whether the Enterprise Board would prefer the loan repaid or the Holmes receivership telex sent to TMA. Mrs Murray readily accepted the repayment of the debt, agreeing that Triumph's Chairman should not send the telex. By way of explanation, Mrs Murray alleged that Geoffrey Robinson MP, a Director of the Enterprise Board, had "panicked" Norman Holmes into taking action to protect the loan to Triumph. Obviously what had happened could not go unanswered!

The Enterprise Board was due to hold its monthly meeting the following Friday 25th March, providing an ideal opportunity to write to Norman Holmes, copying the correspondence to all the Enterprise Board Directors. This would also enable Triumph to provide copies of the recently received written confirmation from the National Westminster Bank PLC and Moratorium Creditors' Committee that they were prepared to play a fundamental part in the proposed financial reconstruction. This written confirmation had not been available when the 8th March letter to Terry Pitt had been urgently delivered, and as such represented important progress towards Triumph's financial reconstruction.

WRITTEN CONFIRMATION FROM NATIONAL WESTMINSTER BANK PLC

National Westminster Bank PLC
Domestic Banking Division
41 Lothbury
London EC2P 2BP

J A Rosamond Esq.
Chairman
Triumph Motorcycles (Meriden) Ltd
Meriden Works
Allesley
Coventry CV5 9AU
Dear Mr Rosamond
Further to our recent discussions I write to confirm that National Westminster Bank PLC is prepared to accept the sum of £700,000 in full and final settlement of the company's overdraft at Balsall Common and Berkswell Branch, subject to:

a) Satisfactory arrangements being made with all other parties involved in the restructuring proposals, most importantly the Moratorium Creditors and other lenders, including the West Midlands County Council.

b) Payment being received by the bank in full on completion of the sale of the existing factory premises.

c) National Westminster Bank is not prepared to extend increased facilities meanwhile or subsequently, and you should have committed overdraft facilities available from another bank for continued working capital needs as indicated in your funding requirement statement dated 15th February 1983. We understand that there is a possibility of alternative bridging finance and we will consider this on its merits.

d) The company does not enter into a commitment to purchase the Dunlop site until contracts have been exchanged for an unconditional sale of the Meriden site for £1,000,000.

e) There are indemnities entered into by National Westminster Bank on the company's behalf totalling £11,065 (counter indemnified by the company). Given that all other conditions have been fulfilled we will not ask for security but would expect the company to use its best endeavours to clear any liability which arises under these indemnities.

f) National Westminster Bank is prepared to release the whole of its security as soon as repayment in full in accordance with the above is made.

Pending receipt of the above mentioned payment, all the bank's rights are reserved, including the right to repayment on demand and the right to take action under the security held by the bank.

I trust that you will be able to arrive at a satisfactory conclusion with the West Midlands County Council and other parties involved. As you know I shall not be available for the next three weeks, but my colleague, John Melbourn, Chief Advances Manager, has been fully apprised of the position and stands ready to meet you and the other parties in due course. Perhaps you will liaise with Mr Philpott to arrange the meeting.

Yours sincerely
D T Trenbath
Deputy General Manager

CREDITORS' COMMITTEE PROPOSED ACCEPTANCE LETTER TO MORATORIUM CREDITORS

The Wholesale Traders' Association Ltd
72 Middleton Hall Road
Kings Norton
Birmingham B30 1BZ
Dear Sirs
Re: Triumph Motorcycles (Meriden) Limited
Although it was as long ago as the 15th June 1981 when I last wrote to you in connection with the above, when you received a payment of 5p in the £ on your moratorium account, this does not mean that strenuous efforts have not been made by the company and the committee to improve the position.

Not withstanding that the company's order book has been maintained, the very high overheads in maintaining the factory premises with interest rates, insurance etc, have been a very heavy drain on the company's resources resulting in an ever worsening position.

Extensive efforts have been made by the company and the workforce, but it has been patently obvious for some time that the only chance of the company's survival was to consolidate into a smaller factory unit.

Following extensive and protracted negotiations, throughout which the interests of the moratorium creditors have always been paramount, a deal is now being set up whereby the company dispose of the present premises and move to a smaller site in Coventry.

A potential purchaser has been found, subject to local authority permission at a figure

*sufficient to satisfy the secured creditors, pay costs of removal and leave a small surplus sufficient
to pay a further 15p in the £ to moratorium creditors in final settlement.*

*Whilst this falls far short of the company's and committee's original expectations, the
alternative at any stage in the proceedings would have been liquidation with no return whatsoever.
It has to be emphasised that certain secured creditors, and particularly Crown departments, have
also made substantial concessions in order that a viable productive unit can be maintained which
will give some suppliers a continuing customer and maintain a British interest in the motorcycle
industry.*

*The committee are totally satisfied that no better return can be achieved and strongly
recommend acceptance, and it will be a condition of the offer that all creditors participate as the
present financial reconstruction proposals would fail if the parties now prepared to invest in the
company felt that further funds would need to be found to prevent proceedings by moratorium
creditors.*

*The funds should become available on completion of the sale of the Meriden site which will
inevitably take a matter of several weeks, but it would be preferable if the creditors agreement
were available in advance and the distribution could take place immediately the funds became
available without the need for further circularisation.*

*Accordingly, a form of acceptance is enclosed which we recommend that you complete and
return to the company at your earliest convenience.*

Yours faithfully
F Tippetts
(Chairman of the Informal Creditors' Committee)

Triumph Motorcycles (Meriden) Ltd
Moratorium creditors form of acceptance
*I/We .... of .... being a creditor
of Triumph Motorcycles (Meriden) Ltd., hereby agree to accept further dividends against our
claim in the above matter to a total of 30p in the £ and to accept such sums in full and final
settlement.*

** The common seal of .... was hereunto affixed in the presence of
....*

*Or * proprietor/partner in the said firm
....*

(Delete and complete as appropriate)

As the Directors were aware, there had been further important developments at the
NEC show. The styling mock-up of the Phoenix 900cc, the first of the new Diana model range,
plus the test bench engine, had been exhibited for the first time. Press day on the 18th March
was certainly a major triumph! Geoffrey Edge (Chairman of the County Council Economic
Development Committee and Enterprise Board) had undertaken a BBC television interview
for *The Money Programme* documentary. He publicly stated that provided the private sector
was prepared to make one or more investments of £500,000, the West Midlands County
Council and Enterprise Board may provide the balance to complete the proposed financial
reconstruction. Following this interview, Terry O'Reilly, the producer of the programme,
approached Michael Jordan, senior partner in the City of London based accountant Cork Gully.
As part of Triumph's ongoing search for private sector funding, Mr Jordan had been provided
with a copy of Triumph's financial reconstruction proposals, plus the accountants' and

consultants' reports. Terry O'Reilly was able to show Mr Jordan the rushes of the programme on Triumph, including the Geoffrey Edge interview at the Motorcycle Show. Michael Jordan stated that he felt the required private sector investment could be raised in the City allowing the Triumph reconstruction proposals to go ahead, and he would be prepared to undertake an interview for *The Money Programme* saying just that.

In view of all the aforementioned circumstances, the Chairman was now placing before the Triumph Board a draft letter to Mr Norman Holmes, Chief Executive at the Enterprise Board, that contrasted his attempt at receivership with the fundamental progress being made towards achieving the financial reconstruction. This letter would also be copied to all the Enterprise Board Directors for information.

Dear Mr Holmes

Further to your instruction yesterday 22nd March 1983, I believe it is imperative for Triumph to place on record our following comments.

You instructed Triumph Motorcycles (Meriden) Limited to send the following telex to Triumph Motorcycles America Inc:

"To Mr Wayne Moulton, President AM Brit STD time

Triumph Motorcycles (America) Inc. 22.3.83.

Reference WMEB/Amersdown Limited agreement

Transfer immediately all monies available, resultant from the sale of WMEB/Amersdown financed motorcycles.

Do not sell, repeat do not sell anymore motorcycles financed under the WMEB/Amersdown Limited facility.

a) Withdraw all WMEB/Amersdown financed motorcycles in stock, from their present warehouse location, and re-site in new warehouse location.

b) Make payment for new warehousing of WMEB/Amersdown Limited motorcycles for one month."

In view of the contents of this telex, and in order to act in a professional manner before sending the telex, I discussed it with the President of Triumph Motorcycles (America) Inc, Mr Wayne Moulton, as soon as the UK/US time difference allowed. I was immediately able to establish that far from the WMEB loan being at risk, final repayment of the outstanding loan and interest would be achieved one week earlier than we had at first believed possible, and as previously indicated in my correspondence with Mrs Kate Murray dated 7th March 1983. In these circumstances I contacted Mrs Kate Murray in your absence, and established that the WMEB would prefer to receive a cheque for £53,993 which I have enclosed, rather than send the aforementioned telex.

When one considers the foregoing facts and the rumours that are now circulating, it would appear that steps were being taken by you, to appoint a receiver. We find this action very difficult to understand in view of the immense progress in reconstruction negotiations, we have been able to demonstrate to you in the last few weeks (see letter to Terry Pitt dated 8th March 1983 and copied to you again). We are further confused in that we believed that in our recent discussions with you, we had established that the demonstrated progress, plus involvement from the private sector, of £500,000 to £750,000 would be sufficient to secure joint investments from the West Midlands County Council and Enterprise Board of £1,250,000. It therefore came as a body-blow that on the very day we received confirmation from our City backers of their willingness to support the Triumph financial reconstruction, terminal action was being taken by you.

Can I in closing, reassure you that it remains our total belief that a financial reconstruction can be achieved with your help, in the very near future and furthermore that the financial

reconstruction is in the best interests of all associated with Triumph.
    Yours sincerely,
    Triumph Motorcycles (Meriden) Limited
    John A Rosamond
    Chairman
    JAR/HDH
    23rd March 1983
    PS Having recently received from Geoffrey Robinson MP a copy of his correspondence to you dated 16th March 1983 (further copy appended) requesting discussion of the Triumph situation at the next Enterprise Board meeting on Friday 25th March, I have copied this letter and enclosures to all of the Enterprise Board Directors for their urgent consideration.

Geoffrey Robinson's letter to Norman Holmes dated 16th March, copied to Triumph for information, was also tabled for the Board of Directors' consideration.

From: Geoffrey Robinson, MP
House of Commons
London SW1A 0AA
March 16th 1983
Dear Norman
I understand from my discussions with the Directors of Meriden that the private sector has decided not to back a financial reconstruction of the Co-operative. This does not surprise me, and leaves the ball firmly in the court of the Council and Enterprise Board – the only two current backers of the Co-operative!
    In the light of this situation, I have spoken with external Directors, and there is strong feeling that the question of export finance commitment should be discussed. I would be very grateful if you could arrange to put this on the agenda for our next meeting on 25th March.
    With best wishes
    Yours sincerely
    Geoffrey Robinson, MP

A lengthy Board discussion took place, during which the Directors expressed their wish that their major concern be placed on record. It was then unanimously agreed that the draft letter to Norman Holmes, copied to the Enterprise Board Directors, should be delivered as soon as possible.

There then followed a negotiating team report regarding further development as a result of the County Council and Enterprise Board's involvement with accountants Peat, Marwick, Mitchell. During the Triumph Directors' previous discussion on the 8th March, we had concentrated on a change of emphasis that appeared to have taken place, resulting in focus switching from long-term potential to short-term. However, another Peat, Marwick, Mitchell report, dated 18th March, was now available, which further considered Triumph's 5-year plan and review documents, and it was now fair to say that there appeared to have been yet another change of heart!

At the end of the Board meeting, the Directors agreed that the negotiating team should continue to push on as quickly as possible to identify and secure sources of private sector finance, as this would almost certainly commit the West Midlands County Council and Enterprise Board to the Triumph financial reconstruction.

The information regarding the latest involvement of Councillor Geoffrey Edge, Chairman of the Enterprise Board, and Michael Jordan, senior partner at accountancy firm Cork Gully, had been provided in a note from Terry O'Reilly, producer of the BBC's *The Money Programme*. Terry's note had fortuitously arrived in the morning post whilst John Rosamond was anxiously awaiting the time he could have a telephone discussion with Wayne Moulton in the USA, regarding Norman Holmes' receivership telex. Terry O'Reilly's comments on the negotiating team's contribution provided a little light relief in what was obviously yet another extremely stressful period. The note gave an insight into the documentary Terry was making:

THERE'LL ALWAYS BE A TRIUMPH (WE HOPE) BY TERENCE O'REILLY
March 18th was press day at this year's International Motorcycle Show and the unexpected star was the mock-up and working engine of a new model from the Triumph Motorcycles Co-operative. The new model stood in pride of place on the top of the Triumph stand and Chairman John Rosamond didn't bother to hide his pride and pleasure. Triumph had brought off the impossible dream, without money, hounded by creditors, against the advice of the experts they'd fought their way back to where they belonged, back on top. His fellow Director from the shop floor, Bill Beattie shared his pride in the new model but was just as proud about the stand itself. The workforce had cannibalised redundant offices, improvised their own designs, worked through the night and met another deadline. Triumph enjoyed a double distinction at the show. They were the last major British motorcycle manufacturer and their factory had been laid off for the past six weeks.

So, how has this co-operative, which according to John Rosamond "was set up to fail and never stood a chance," survived eight years of continual crises and defied the laws of economic logic to produce a new engine that will (when it's in production) astound their competition? The answer is simple ... the Triumph workforce and the dynamic duo of Rosamond and Beattie. I have been involved with that workforce for over five years and I know that when it comes to bitching and moaning "about what that lot up there think they're doing," they are second to none. And after they've had their moan they meet every deadline that's been asked of them. They have endured short-time, work without pay, layoffs, no holiday money and because they signed away their pensions so that their Triumph could start again, no security. When the company couldn't afford to buy fuel last winter they worked in their overcoats. When it comes to True Grit, they make John Wayne look like Andy Pandy. They have been the secret weapon that Rosamond and Beattie have been able to use in their negotiations. Politicians, accountants, consultants, Civil Servants and Japanese industrialists all agree that meeting the workforce is a revelation. The dynamic duo that leads this workforce is a strange but effective combination. Rosamond is a stolid soft spoken welder from Warwickshire while Beattie is the shrewd but volatile street politician from Belfast. Although they'd been entrusted to secure some kind of future for the Co-op, these two were interested in much more than survival, in fact, they would settle for nothing less than a new model, a new act of faith in the future of their Co-op.

As always Triumph was broke and the creditors were threatening them with closure. Their professional management told them they didn't stand a chance. The first act of faith had to come from Rosamond and Beattie. They began negotiations with the West Midlands Enterprise Board who sent in Peter Johnson from Price Waterhouse "To see if there was anything worth supporting." Johnson met the workforce had a long look at the books and in the Triumph tradition came up with the good and the bad news. Triumph surprisingly was economically viable if the company could be totally restructured and if sufficient capital could be found. The dynamic duo split the chores. Rosamond would deal with the creditors to buy time and negotiate a settlement while Beattie would find a buyer for the Meriden factory, the symbol of their ten-year struggle. And then find Triumph a new home.

I first became involved with Triumph five years ago when I made a film on their struggle for survival which was transmitted in the Man Alive *series. Since then, people ask me why I have stayed involved with them. The truth is I had no choice.*

Whenever Rosamond and Beattie find somebody who can be useful, they turn them every way but loose. They cheerfully admit they'll shamelessly exploit anyone who can "just do us a favour for the workforce." They'd approached me when the new engine was just a mass of undecipherable drawings and graciously declared "We wouldn't want anyone else besides you to make this film about Triumph's comeback."

After hawking it around the BBC to cries of "Good God, are they still going?" The Money Programme *bravely decided to commission a film and Triumph and the BBC resumed its uneven partnership. Since then I've practically lived with Rosamond and Beattie as they've schemed and hustled to keep their factory going, negotiate with the local politicians, woo the creditors and in their spare time push the development of the new model.*

Although by now the West Midlands County Council had agreed to provide a half-million pound loan to finance outstanding orders from America the debate continued interminably as to whether they should invest in the Triumph restructuring programme. Meanwhile, Beattie had found a buyer for the Meriden site at the price needed so that Rosamond could offer a payment that would provide both the preferential and non-preferential creditors with a "full and final payment." Beattie also found a new home for Triumph after haggling down the price pointing out that there was a glut of empty factories in Coventry. While they waited for the politicians to make up their mind, Beattie asked for volunteers from the now laid-off workforce to clean up the factory for no pay. The workforce fell on him. All the frustrations and uncertainties about their future poured out. He stood and took it and gave back as good as he got and at the end told them the address and the time they were expected and left it to them. He'd asked for twenty volunteers, thirty eight showed up. By now, the County Council had asked for yet another report, and the third group of experts swarmed through Triumph. Like their predecessors they agreed that Triumph could be viable but that it would require more capital than was originally called for. Cllr Geoffrey Edge visited the Triumph stand at the Motorcycle Show and announced "that while the West Midlands might be prepared to invest in Triumph they would require a partner from the private sector who would have to provide at least half a million pounds." Fortunately, Triumph through their contacts had made approaches to Michael Jordan, senior partner in Cork Gully, who had ironically handled the receivership of Norton Villiers Triumph, the company that had wanted to close down the Meriden plant ten years ago. Michael Jordan's reaction was "anybody who has survived all that they have for the past eight years and still come up with a new model has earned support."

It is now well over a year since Triumph began negotiations to secure a future and the signs look good that there will be in the best traditions of melodrama a dramatic rescue. But knowing Rosamond and Beattie I am sure that they will insist that the negotiations result in a real future with the Co-operative in charge of their destiny.

I don't know how the workforce will handle success but if anyone has earned it, it is they, the men and women of Triumph.

Having made the final £53,993 repayment of the Enterprise Board's secret £150,000 export loan on 23rd March, we were able to read the excellent *Motor Cycle News* NEC show report in a little more relaxed state of mind:

"Triumph Steal the Show – by Steve Cordall

Wooden model – with a REAL 900 twin motor that could take on the Japs!"

We had achieved the NEC media exposure required; the *Motor Cycle News* coverage was a fair representation. The County Council politicians were certainly impressed with the positive NEC publicity gained for Triumph's 1983 model range. Even more important, though, was the equally positive comment regarding the futuristic Phoenix 900cc model, the first model of the proposed all-new range at the heart of Triumph's planned return to viability.

Unfortunately, this reassurance was short-lived. Councillor Carol Yapp circulated a critical report on Triumph's plans that she had received from a bitter ex-Meriden Engineering Department founder Co-op member. In the covering letter to Councillor Geoff Edge which accompanied the report, she described its author as "an absolute motorbike fanatic" and as such "consideration should be given to what he was saying"! The report titled, "MERIDEN – a few ad hoc observations" was exactly that, the author having no knowledge of Triumph's Diana design project, or the 'modular' model range marketing strategy. However, to inherently insecure politicians always looking for expert third party confirmation and reassurance that they were doing the right thing, this was yet another distraction. At least the massive County Council concern regarding Triumph's vital access to its major export market, the USA, was lifted on 6th April when Alison Preece broke the story in the *Coventry Evening Telegraph*.

The Meriden Co-op was already out of time and money when Councillor Geoff Edge made his spectacular press declaration of West Midlands support for Triumph on 9th November 1982; not surprisingly, therefore, financial losses had continued since that date. When on 28th January 1983 Triumph's management team subsequently contemplated surviving a further six weeks, it was felt this would be almost impossible in the desperate financial situation the Co-op was in. The skeleton workforce had now enabled a further four weeks' survival since that deadline passed. Although major progress in firming up the constituent parts of the financial reconstruction had been achieved during those ten long weeks, inevitably, losses had also continued to accrue. Triumph's creditors were now becoming more and more impatient for the financial reconstruction to happen and production to restart, as they also had laid-off, loss-making production facilities. The longer it went without the all-important private sector funding in place, the more likely all of the Co-op's efforts would turn out to have been in vain!

In hot pursuit of this exclusive end of the Meriden Co-op story was, unsurprisingly, the local *Coventry Evening Telegraph*, whose industrial correspondent, Colin Lewis, was fully aware of the efforts that were being made to achieve the financial reconstruction. On 13th April, Colin Lewis cornered the Co-op's Chairman and asked the obvious question: "How much longer can Triumph survive?" John Rosamond's reply featured in the front page story that followed – "£800,000 or Meriden goes under."

On 14th April, Triumph's Directors scheduled a Board meeting to receive an update from Tim Burnhill, the Ward and Rider solicitor dealing with the Nahib Dajani litigation proceedings. Prior to Tim Burnhill's arrival the Directors reviewed the latest financial report provided by Phil Bragg.

He reported that the majority of creditors were being very patient, awaiting the endeavours of Michael Jordan at Cork Gully, who was directing his efforts to raise £800,000 from the private sector to enable Triumph's financial reconstruction to go ahead. However, with payments to the bailiffs of £3000, £4000 to avoid a creditor from entering a winding-up petition against Triumph, an electricity bill of £2700, a gas bill of £1000, skeleton workforce wages of £5000, and contingencies of £4000, the current week's spend was a good example of the present levels of weekly expenditure. As expenditure at this level would have to be maintained for a short period, Phil Bragg commented, the company must make every effort to control overall losses, the funding of which indirectly came from the West Midlands County

Council's £365,000 loan. Losses to date from this source were approximately £220,000. Following discussions with County Council staff, it was believed that these could be redressed by way of an equivalent 'equity stake' in the new restructured Triumph company.

Responding to Phil Bragg's request to restrict further weekly expenditure, the Directors conducted a total review of the present 29-member skeleton workforce's activity, the majority of the membership still being laid off. Following this exercise it was agreed that the skeleton workforce would be reduced to 21 by week ending 22nd April.

Continuing his financial report, Phil Bragg advised that the Moratorium Creditors' Committee recommendation letter to the creditors stating that they should accept a further 15p in the pound as full and final settlement of the £850,000 moratorium debt (subject to the financial reconstruction proposals going ahead) had now been implemented. Triumph's Company Solicitor, Peter Davis, had advised the negotiating team that unless a 100 per cent positive acceptance of the offer was received from those creditors, it was likely that Triumph would still have to apply to the court for a "legal financially binding reconstruction of its affairs." However, response from the Moratorium Creditors to date was encouraging.

The Chairman reported that a brief discussion with Andy Philpott of the National Westminster Bank PLC, Lothbury, London indicated that it was maintaining its supportive stance and awaiting the next meeting, when Triumph could provide full details of the financial reconstruction proposals for discussion.

Tim Burnhill, the solicitor representing Triumph on the Nahib Dajani case, joined the Board meeting at 4.00pm. He reported that working on the Triumph Directors' brief to settle the Nahib Dajani litigation proceedings at the appropriate time, thereby restricting the drain on available cash, had as a result of three adjournments been successful in avoiding any settlement payment to date. However, recent new and better particulars provided by Nahib Dajani's solicitors had enabled a request for further information, from which it had become clear that Triumph had a good chance of success in the litigation case if supportive evidence could be secured from Libya. To this end, following discussion with the previous Triumph employees involved, Geoffrey Robinson had undertaken to secure the required evidence from Libya. Several weeks passed by, and, unfortunately, the Libyan evidence had not been secured. Also, the court hearing date had been confirmed. Geoffrey Robinson and the other two previous Triumph personnel had been subpoenaed to be sure of their availability as key witnesses during the court case. Due to his belief that evidence could be secured from the Libyans, Geoffrey Robinson had previously totally opposed any settlement offer. Earlier that afternoon he had suggested that Triumph should offer Nahib Dajani £1000 to £2000 to settle. Tim Burnhill advised the Board that he felt he could put it to Nahib Dajani's solicitors that Triumph was in the depths of financial reconstruction negotiations to secure the company's future, and that the only settlement offer that could be realistically made at this time would be one of £5000, to be paid at the rate of £500 per month.

Tim Burnhill was given full authority by the Board of Directors to make the settlement offer of 10 monthly payments of £500, whilst stressing the point that the only payment that Triumph could guarantee was the first payment of £500.

Tim Burnhill further requested that in the event of the case proceeding to court and the hearing going ahead, he would require at least two Triumph Directors to attend the hearing so that he may have full advice and instruction, should it be required.

The Board meeting over, John Rosamond and Bill Beattie, as veterans of previous cliffhanger negotiations to save the Meriden Co-op and Triumph, were very conscious of the fact that it had always appeared darkest just before the dawn of a new era. However, during these negotiations there had already been several false dawns, and whilst politics and brinkmanship had always played a part in previous deals, on this occasion there was to be an ongoing political involvement.

The *Coventry Evening Telegraph*, however, had already made its mind up on the likely outcome when it published its editorial comment "Requiem to a dream" on 14th April.

But of course, the *Coventry Evening Telegraph* had not had the opportunity over more than 12 months to study, with the help of extensive expert independent financial and marketing advice, Triumph's 5-year plan!

31

WORDS ARE NO LONGER ENOUGH

T he 'end of the Meriden Co-op' coverage by the *Coventry Evening Telegraph* was followed by similar stories in the national dailies, stories that focused minds on the need for action before it was too late.

On 15th April, Rob Murison advised the Directors on the areas where he felt further work could be undertaken to address and discharge the auditor's concerns in the 1980/81 annual accounts. The former Triumph Financial Director would now help in a subordinate role to the Financial Controller, Phil Bragg, who indicated that whilst progress was envisaged, it was inevitable that some qualifications would remain. These were likely to be in the areas of Trade Creditors' records, warranty accounts, Moratorium Creditors, and the physical stock audit. Phil Bragg and Rob Murison's agreed objective was therefore to complete the aforementioned workload as quickly as possible, enabling Coopers and Lybrand to finalise the 1980/81 audit by week ending 29th April 1983. Achieving this deadline was vital to enable seven days' notice prior to the scheduled 10th May AGM. The registration of the mitigating audited 1980/81 annual accounts at the time of the 11th May Cardiff Court hearing would then follow.

The *Coventry Evening Telegraph* carried a further front page story on 19th April: "Triumph top men face court ... A spokesman for Companies House said today, the case would not be pursued if Triumph Motorcycles went into liquidation."

Richard O'Dell Poulden, Arthur D Little's Project Manager, was responsible for the independent, in-depth, 5-year plan consultancy work commissioned by West Midlands County Council. His tireless, extensive attention to detail and 'what if' probing played a fundamental part in the substantially refined and strengthened Triumph corporate plan. Although Arthur D Little was no longer involved, and Richard had moved on to become Chief Executive of Merlin Communications Ltd, he had still kept in touch via the media coverage with Triumph's efforts to achieve the required financial reconstruction. Accordingly, when he read that Triumph was trying to secure private sector equity, he provided a personal introduction to De Loete and Bevan Ltd, which suggested Triumph's 5-year plan, accountants and consultant's reports should be sent to Equity for Industry Ltd as a possible source of private sector investment.

With Triumph poised on the brink, it was vitally important to keep all the Co-op Directors fully aware of recent developments. To do this, a Board meeting was called on

26th April. Phil Bragg was unable to attend the initial part as he was involved in a series of meetings, trying to reassure creditors.

The negotiating team reported that a meeting would be taking place with representatives of Chadwick Holmes Ltd (Espley-Tyas), the purchaser of the Meriden site, on Wednesday 27th April at 10.00am. The meeting was to finalise the purchase/sale contract details; few problems were envisaged, as solicitors from both companies would be present. The next step would be to provide the National Westminster Bank PLC with further details of the proposed transaction. The bank retained total control of proceedings, holding title to the Triumph factory site under its 'fixed and floating charge' security for Triumph's £1,195,000 overdraft facility.

Bill Beattie reported that the West Midlands County Council had commenced the acquisition procedure of the Cash's Lane ex-Dunlop site through the various committee stages. Peter Davis had forwarded to the County Council the prepared contract and search enquiries evidence. He had further advised Dunlop that the County Council was proceeding to acquire the Cash's Lane site. The likely outcome, the Chairman stated, was that the County Council would lease back to Triumph the newly purchased factory premises at the time of financial reconstruction. Bill Beattie advised that he had already had meetings with County Council staff regarding preferential leasing terms for the Cash's Lane factory.

The Chairman stated that Terry Pitt had made it clear to the negotiating team that, with the likely investment of equity funding from the private sector, it was almost certain that the West Midlands County Council would provide the remainder of the funding package. Whilst this was the situation, it would be expected that the £365,000 County Council export loan monies presently at risk would be taken account of in the financial reconstruction of the company, possibly as an equity stake.

John Rosamond and Bill Beattie reported that they had attended a meeting in London on 19th April with Michael Jordan of Cork Gully, Terry Pitt of the County Council, and Richard O'Dell Poulden, ex-Arthur D Little consultant. Michael Jordan had pushed Terry Pitt to confirm the West Midlands County Council position. This he did, confirming it to be as previously reported to the Board. Michael Jordan then stated that he believed the most likely private sector equity investor in Triumph would be Electra. The head of this organisation was a Mr Michael Stoddard, who he was presently pursuing. Michael Jordan continued that Mr Stoddard had a vast number of connections with venture capital funds and accordingly could provide a good insight into exactly what was and was not possible. Meetings had been arranged in the very near future, which Michael Jordan hoped would be fruitful. Richard O'Dell Poulden introduced Michael Jordan to the British Linen Bank and Venture Link Ltd; both, he advised, were possible candidates in the search for private sector equity. Representatives of the British Linen Bank had already flown down from Scotland last week for discussions with Triumph representatives, and were considering a full package of information on the financial reconstruction proposals. Finally, Michael Jordan indicated that he felt it would be possible to achieve an equity investment decision, at least in principle, within seven to ten days.

The Chairman reported that George Bloomfield of Herbert-Sigma and Charles Blunt of Singer-Freiglander had been re-introduced to the financial reconstruction negotiations by the County Council. George Bloomfield had contacted John Rosamond the previous day, 25th April, to advise that lengthy discussions had taken place with Terry Pitt over the weekend, and it had been agreed that he would contact Triumph regarding the running of the new company. Accordingly, he was now requesting a meeting with the heads of the Sales, Manufacturing and Finance Departments, plus Messrs Rosamond, Beattie and Bragg. When this meeting took place, George Bloomfield's initial statement was "where negotiations have become protracted amongst the financiers, it was essential that detailed planning was not only completed, but, wherever possible, acted upon"! George Bloomfield further explained that it was also customary, once the financiers finally made up their minds, for them to expect an immediate reaction; we had to be prepared. This initial meeting lasted over three hours, during which time George Bloomfield discussed many of the key management objectives in the aforementioned Triumph departments. At the end, he detailed extensive work which now needed to be undertaken to enable a further meeting on 3rd May.

John Rosamond and Bill Beattie both commented to the Board that during the meeting, George Bloomfield had been extremely enthusiastic for the task in hand, which had given them the distinct impression that the West Midlands County Council had already offered him the Managing Director's mantle!

Following lengthy discussion of the financial reconstruction negotiations' progress report, Brian Jones proposed and John Birch seconded that Triumph continue to trade on behalf of its creditors. The proposal was once again unanimously carried by the Board.

John Birch and George Mackie, the two Directors who supported Mr Burnhill (Triumph's solicitor) and Mr Cole (Triumph's counsel) at the court hearing in Birmingham last week, reported that Triumph had appeared to be fighting a lost cause from very early in the proceedings. The court had found in favour of the plaintiff, Nahib Dajani, and Tim Burnhill was now endeavouring to agree a settlement schedule that was within Triumph's ability to pay. At the same time, Tim would be making it clear that whilst the first payment was guaranteed, until the financial reconstruction had been achieved other payments were not. Triumph's solicitor would also be pointing out that as soon as the financial reconstruction negotiations were completed, full payment of the outstanding debt would be made very quickly.

The Chairman reported that the date of the 1980/81 reconvened Annual General Meeting was now fixed for 3.00pm on 10th May, and the Trustees had been advised accordingly. All members would receive notice by way of the AGM agenda. Laid-off Beneficiaries would receive this in the post on 28th April, giving them at least seven days' notice. Good progress was being maintained finalising the 1980/81 annual accounts for audit in preparation for the AGM.

In view of the problems that Triumph had experienced with financial accounting systems during the year 1980/81, which were drawn to the attention of the Board of Directors by the auditor Coopers and Lybrand, the Chairman had approached audit partner Mr Peter Court to undertake a review of the 1983 financial systems. Whilst Phil Bragg was confident that the present Triumph financial systems were a significant improvement on those employed in 1980/81, both he and the Chairman felt that further advice from the auditors would be welcome. Coopers and Lybrand staff would be undertaking the financial systems review during week commencing 3rd May.

The Chairman advised the Board that Peter Davis would be briefing a local Cardiff solicitor to appear in court on their behalf on 11th May 1983. The Cardiff solicitor would have in his possession the audited Triumph 1980/81 annual accounts, which he would undertake to register, following the court hearing. Peter Davis would be drafting a letter for the Directors regarding their guilty plea, when he next attended Triumph on 28th April.

In other business, Bill Beattie requested clarification from the Company Solicitor on the duties of Directors who were also Triumph Social Club Trustees, if the club was to close. His request was based on a comment made by the Club committee treasurer, who allegedly stated that in the event of the club being closed by the members, who had now been laid off for over 3 months, the committee would automatically resign and the Trustees would be expected to resolve all outstanding issues on behalf of the membership. If this was the case, Bill Beattie felt it was important that the Club Trustees knew in advance.

Bill Beattie asked if payments could commence to discharge Triumph's liability to Mrs Hearnden. Mrs Hearnden's husband had died whilst in service at Triumph when the company had lapsed payment of life insurance premiums; the deceased was therefore not covered by the contractual insurance benefit. However, this had occurred prior to the membership being notified that life insurance cover had ceased, so the company remained liable for the death benefit. In these circumstances, the Directors agreed to commence payments to Mrs Hearnden to reduce the outstanding death benefit liability of £21,840.

The 26th April Board meeting had enabled all of Triumph's Directors to be brought right up to date. Board unity in these extremely difficult times was imperative.

Terry Pitt, the West Midlands County Council's senior official dealing with Triumph, was forced to take leave through ill health during the early part of April. Tom Fitch coped extremely well with the massive burden that the Triumph Co-op now represented in Terry's absence. Inevitably on Terry Pitt's return he was anxious to clarify exactly what had taken place whilst he was away.

A further Board meeting on 2nd May 1983 welcomed back Ron Briggs, now recovering well from his serious motorcycle accident in October 1982.

Phil Bragg reported that the bank overdraft was £5000 below the absolute limit. With an identified spend of £18,000 during the current week ending 6th May, the spare parts operation would need to generate this money. Spare parts sales the previous week had realised £18,900, and accordingly George Mackie felt this was possible, although as each week went by the task became more difficult. Reporting further, Phil Bragg stated that the figures requested by Terry Pitt in his latest West Midlands County Council correspondence demonstrated the size of the task already undertaken in order to secure sufficient time to conclude the financial reconstruction negotiations. Moving to the receipt of writs from creditors, Phil Bragg felt confident that the present situation could be held for a further two weeks, £10,000 worth of writ settlements being earmarked in this week's expenditure. The threatened winding-up petition from Leicester Boiler Engineers had been averted by payment of half the sum, £2000 on account.

The Chairman reported that he had received confirmation of Tim Burnhill's actions regarding payment of the Nahib Dajani settlement. An initial payment of £1000 had been made, following which Nahib Dajani's solicitor had suggested that they could go the route of securing a writ by a County Court action to achieve settlement of the outstanding amount, which, after the inital payment, came to £26,000. However, on being told that the National Westminster Bank PLC had a fixed and floating charge over Triumph's assets, and therefore such action would be the same as a winding up petition, Nahib Dajani's solicitor reconsidered their position. A further payment of £1700 was being negotiated, £1000 being offered immediately and a further £700 in a fortnight's time, and then £1000 per month. Tim Burnhill stressed at all times that due to Triumph's position, only the initial payment could be guaranteed until the financial reconstruction. Further contact between solicitors was anticipated the following day, 3rd May.

Phil Bragg reported that the two remaining items of qualification on which it was believed progress could be made to reassure the auditors, i.e. identification of amounts owing to suppliers and adequate procedures for identifying obsolete stock, were now virtually complete. A lengthy meeting had taken place on Friday evening with Company Solicitor Peter Davis, Rob Murison, John Rosamond and himself regarding drafting the Directors' report for the 1980/81 annual accounts. Rob Murison was going to meet Peter Court at Coopers and Lybrand's offices the next day in order to conclude the final audit qualifications and Directors' report. Peter Davis had advised that in view of a possible taxation problem associated with the Government debt write-off, which Coopers and Lybrand had advised verbally was not likely to happen, it was essential that Triumph secured the auditor's advice in writing. Rob Murison had written to Peter Court to seek this assurance. The Directors would be required for discussion of the finalised 1980/81 accounts, qualifications and Directors' report tomorrow afternoon. This would finally enable completion to take place, so that these annual accounts could be posted on company notice boards and circulated to the Trustees seven days prior to the 10th May reconvened Annual General Meetings.

Terry Pitt was seeking further written confirmation of items previously discussed with the negotiating team regarding the financial reconstruction. The Chairman had confirmed on the Board's behalf that it had always been Triumph's intention, since the major financial problems occurred with the £365,000 export loan facility, to take full account of the outstanding indebtedness to the West Midlands County Council in the overall reconstruction. The Directors agreed with the Chairman's action.

The Chairman then reported that in discussions with Michael Jordan to arrange the next day's meeting, Michael had stated that he had not yet secured the required private sector equity investment. He therefore proposed a meeting at Cork Gully in London with County Council representatives Terry Pitt and Kate Murray, and Bill Beattie and John Rosamond from Triumph. When the Chairman confirmed the availability of the aforementioned representatives for the meeting, Michael Jordan indicated that he felt it would be helpful if George Bloomfield and Charles Blunt of Singer-Freiglander could also be present. In addition, it would be useful if he could contact them via the telephone over the bank holiday weekend, to discuss matters further. John Rosamond had contacted George Bloomfield and asked him to telephone Michael Jordan. The Triumph Board of Directors agreed that they would be in a much better position to assess developments once the negotiating team returned from the Cork Gully meeting.

On the team's return, a 4.00pm Board meeting was called, at which Phil Bragg summarised the George Bloomfield management meeting at Triumph earlier in the day.

Phil Bragg reported that following George Bloomfield's discussion with Terry Pitt last weekend, it had been suggested to him that unless Terry Pitt contacted him further, he should not attend the meeting with Michael Jordan. Accordingly George Bloomfield had felt it worthwhile to proceed with the previously scheduled Meriden factory meeting with those senior managers who were available. It had been a useful meeting, continuing the detailed planning of the running of the new company.

The Chairman reported on the Michael Jordan meeting at Cork Gully in London. He advised that the meeting reviewed at some length all contacts made to date with Merchant Banks and Venture Capital Funds. Michael Jordan stated that as yet he had not received any positive indications of support. Whilst this was the case, he still had one or two contacts from whom he was expecting a response very shortly. Terry Pitt asked Michael Jordan what reasons he had been given for rejection. Michael Jordan commented that the commercial aspect of the reconstruction proposal had not been challenged, and it seemed to be down to Politics, with a capital P. Terry Pitt reaffirmed the County Council's position, stating that whilst the West Midlands County Council would have the largest stake in the new company, he felt they would be more than prepared to have the smallest say. John Rosamond asked Michael Jordan if by politics he meant the Co-op retaining control of the company. Michael Jordan replied that this was certainly not the reason, he had always assumed and indicated during his discussions with all potential equity providers that the Co-op would be prepared to relinquish that position if the company's future was to be secured. It was then agreed that a further meeting would take place on Friday 6th May.

Following Board discussion of the Chairman's report, Bill Beattie asked the Directors where they stood if the Co-op had to relinquish control of its own destiny, and working at Triumph became just a job like any other. The general view expressed by the Directors was that if, at the end of the day, the only deal possible was on that basis, it would have to be put before the Beneficiary owners of Triumph for their consideration and decision. The Chairman stated that whilst he had noted the Directors' response, he had to underline the fact that even on the aforementioned basis there was, as yet, no private sector equity offer!

The Chairman tabled for the Directors' comments the draft 1980/81 annual accounts Directors' report, produced as a result of discussion on 30th April between Phil Bragg, Rob Murison, John Rosamond and Company Solicitor Peter Davis. Rob Murison had gone to some lengths to give explanations regarding the individual areas of qualification indicated in the Coopers and Lybrand audit report. These concerns were as follows:

Creditors – books and records
TMA – review rather than accounts audit
Stocks – value of obsolete stocks

Following detailed Board discussion with Rob Murison, who had been requested to join the Board meeting for this item, the draft Directors' report was adopted for the audited 1980/81 annual accounts.

Rob Murison had attended a meeting earlier that day with audit partner Peter Court. The Chairman asked Rob Murison if the auditors had replied to the Company Solicitor's advised letter dated 2nd May, regarding possible future tax implications as a result of Her Majesty's Government's earlier debt write-offs. Rob Murison stated that the auditors had now decided that the write-offs had taken place in separate years, as he had been suggesting to them and as had been planned from the outset. There was therefore no longer a problem regarding tax liability for Coopers and Lybrand to give written assurance on. Rob Murison was thanked for his help in enabling the satisfactory completion of the audited 1980/81 annual accounts, and the Board meeting ended at 5.30pm.

On the 4th May, *Motor Cycle News* published a story on the Birmingham High Court findings against Triumph in the Nahib Dajani case.

"Meriden blow – The financially ailing Triumph Motorcycle Co-operative at Meriden faces a legal bill of more than £27,000 after losing a case at Birmingham High Court."

The scheduled meeting in London with Michael Jordan on Friday was postponed until the following Monday, 9th May when it took place at the London home of Mr David Wickens, Chairman and Managing Director of British Car Auctions (BCA).

Also present at the meeting were Michael Jordan of Cork Gully and Mr Chris Hughes of Coopers and Lybrand. Representing the West Midlands County Council (WMCC) were Terry Pitt and Kate Murray. Triumph was represented by John Rosamond and Bill Beattie.

Michael Jordan introduced Mr David Wickens, who, he reported, had agreed to head a consortium of companies that would provide the private sector equity stake, indicated by WMCC as being vital to secure the overall investment package. Constituent companies of Mr Wickens' private sector consortium were each prepared to invest £100,000 of equity, as follows:

British Car Auctions (BCA)	£100,000
United Dominion Trust (UDT)	£100,000
Forley Investments	£100,000
Keep Investments	£100,000
GEC/Binatone	£100,000
	£500,000

Following Michael Jordan's initial statement, he commented to Terry Pitt that he had now completed his undertaking to source private sector equity; if it had been clearly indicated originally that private sector equity was the requirement, not export credit, six weeks of the elapsed time could have been saved! Michael Jordan then asked Terry Pitt if the County Council would put up the outstanding £1.7m to reach the Peat, Marwick, Mitchell overall funding requirement of £2.2m. Terry Pitt denied that the County Council had ever stated that they could make available £1.7m for the Triumph financial reconstruction, they would match the private sector £ for £ and could possibly go to £1.2m in total.

In an effort to overcome the £500,000 shortfall, it was suggested by David Wickens that the County Council and private sector should make available, by way of a written undertaking, a £500,000 contingency fund to be drawn on if necessary in alternating £100,000 units. Repayments of the contingency fund would be carried out on a similar basis.

Michael Jordan stated that all loans to the reconstructed company, whilst being on a commercial basis, should be interest free for the first 2.5 years to give the company the best possible chance of success. Michael Jordan and David Wickens both felt that recruitment of management should be by secondment, avoiding the immense cost that would otherwise be involved to secure the best people.

Terry Pitt and Kate Murray both questioned what was in it for the private sector equity consortium. David Wickens replied that the £100,000 investments were on a punt basis in an effort to keep Triumph alive, and accordingly no dividends on the investments were envisaged for at least 2.5 years. Pushed further by Kate Murray about how the private sector would withdraw its stake, David Wickens stated that there was no wish to withdraw; its only interest was to see British motorcycles returned to their rightful place. David Wickens then commented that the amounts of private sector money involved were merely a decimal point on the balance sheets of the companies concerned. He saw an opportunity for a true partnership between capital and labour.

Michael Jordan reported that after having had further meetings with the National Westminster Bank regarding the Triumph £1,195,000 overdraft, he was now of the opinion that it might possibly be prepared to accept £500,000 in full and final settlement. Michael subsequently stated that in view of the urgency involved, it was essential that the financial reconstruction negotiations were brought to a rapid conclusion, as all the constituent parts of the deal were now available! Accordingly, at the end of this positive meeting Michael Jordan indicated that he had instructed Chris Hughes of Coopers and Lybrand to enter into final negotiations with all parties concerned to establish heads of terms agreement by the week commencing 23rd May 1983, when he would return from Australia.

The four scheduled meetings at the Meriden factory the next day would be of vital importance. At 1.00pm on the 10th May the negotiating team would report to the Board of Directors on the important private sector equity investment progress. At 2.30pm the Directors would meet the Trustees to update them on the financial reconstruction progress, and the finalised 1980/81 audited annual accounts were to be discussed at the 3.00pm AGM of the Beneficiary owners of Triumph. At 5.00pm the company AGM of Triumph Motorcycles (Meriden) Limited would take place, the Trustees having been previously instructed by the Beneficiaries on how to vote.

The 10th May 1.00pm Board meeting began with a financial report from Phil Bragg. He advised that the company was presently £2000 below the overdraft limit, and to cover outgoings during the present week we would need to raise £8500 from the sale of spare parts. The previous week's shortfall on spare parts required monies to be used from the sales of motorcycles – money that had been earmarked for repayment to the West Midlands County Council, but had to be used to pay writs and wages. Every effort would be made during the current week to make good this County Council payment shortfall.

Phil Bragg then reported that Mr Beale of the Inland Revenue had given notice that he could no longer take personal responsibility for waiting for a successful outcome of the financial reconstruction negotiations, and had passed the Triumph case file to national level. Triumph would receive a demand for the outstanding Inland Revenue total, which was of the order of £250,000, in the very near future. The proposed repayment schedule agreed with the Inland Revenue could only start on the successful completion of the financial reconstruction negotiations. The Directors agreed that all parties involved would be advised accordingly.

The Chairman provided the Board with a detailed account of the previous day's private sector equity investment meeting (covered earlier in this chapter). However, the Chairman continued, whilst travelling back to the Midlands with Terry Pitt and Kate Murray, they had made it clear that for investment to be secured from the West Midlands County Council, even at the £1.2m level, following reconstruction the new Triumph Company would still have to be seen by its political masters as a Co-operative. Bill Beattie reported that further meetings would take place to try and meet the West Midlands County Council's 'Co-operative structure' precondition.

There then followed lengthy Board discussion, and it was proposed by George Mackie and seconded by Brian Jones that in light of the further real progress reported, Triumph should continue to trade on behalf of its creditors. The proposal was once again unanimously carried.

The Chairman reported that Mr R Brett, a Cardiff solicitor, had been briefed by Company Solicitor Peter Davis. Mr Brett would represent the Directors at the Cardiff

Court hearing on 11th May. Following the Directors' guilty plea, he would be offering the court a prepared statement as mitigating evidence. John Birch would also be present at the hearing should any further information be required from a Triumph Director. The audited Triumph 1980/81 annual accounts were to be registered immediately after the court case.

As the Board meeting ended, the three Trustees arrived for their scheduled 2.30pm pre-AGM briefing. When the Board last met the Trustees seven weeks earlier, the Directors had undertaken to update them further as soon as real progress on the financial reconstruction was achieved. Remarkably, it was only the previous day that "real" progress, with the sourcing of private sector equity investment, had been achieved. Accordingly, the reporting of this major accomplishment was a boost to the morale of both the Trustees and Beneficiaries alike.

Triumph Motorcycles (Meriden) Limited
Annual General Meeting of the Beneficiaries held at 3.00pm Tuesday 10th May 1983
Agenda
• Election of Beneficiaries' Committee
The following have retired from the Committee and are offering themselves for re-election:
Mr A Bottrill
Mr J Flowers
Mr M Bone
Mr B Evans
• Waiving of Notice
Proposal to the Beneficiaries that they agree to waive notice of the calling of the Annual General Meeting of Triumph Motorcycles (Meriden) Limited, the Trustees not having had the required 21 days' notice.
• Approval of Minutes
a) Annual General Meeting: 13th November 1981
b) Meeting held 29th September 1982
• Matters arising from minutes
• Acceptance of accounts for the period 1st October 1980 to 30th September 1981
• Election of Directors
The existing Directors (as under) have resigned and are offering themselves for re-election to complete the present negotiations:
Mr J A Rosamond
Mr R Briggs
Mr W A Beattie
Mr B E Jones
Mr J S Birch
Mr G L Mackie
• Appointment of auditors
• Fixing of auditors' remuneration
• Any Other Business
J A Rosamond JAR/HDH
Chairman 28th April 1983

Following the Annual General Meeting, the Beneficiary owners of Triumph went home a little happier than when they had arrived, now aware that the private sector equity requirement insisted upon by the West Midlands County Council had at long last been secured, and we were now moving towards heads of terms agreement for the financial reconstruction of Triumph's affairs.

The Annual General Meeting of Triumph Motorcycles (Meriden) Limited started at 5.00pm. With all discussion and controversy always being dealt with at the Beneficiaries' AGM, Triumph company AGM's were simple and straightforward affairs, and this one was no different. The three Trustees – John Haynes, Ron Marston and John Tomlinson – having received instructions at the Beneficiaries' AGM, now implemented these at the company AGM. In attendance at both AGMs were Peter Court (audit partner – Coopers and Lybrand) and Peter Davis (Company Solicitor – Ward and Rider). The agenda was exactly the same as at the Beneficiaries AGM, with one exception: the election of a Beneficiaries' Committee. This unique committee was elected at and served purely for the duration of each Beneficiary's AGM. Its sole purpose was to decide in favour or against any Beneficiary AGM resolution that did not receive the required majority vote.

The company AGM business completed, including the re-election of Board Directors Bill Beattie, John Birch, Ron Briggs, Brian Jones, George Mackie and John Rosamond (all having agreed to stand again in order to complete the financial reconstruction negotiations), we were sure everyone concerned would sleep a little easier that night.

The next day the negotiating team would begin discussions to meet the latest West Midlands County Council requirement, namely that to retain the investment support of the politicians, Triumph must remain a Co-operative – not quite what had been indicated to potential private sector equity investors in pursuit of their support! However, the head of the private sector equity consortium, David Wickens, had made a very enlightened statement when he suggested there was "an opportunity for a true partnership between capital and labour." An excellent place to start when drafting a revised constitution for the new Triumph Co-operative.

Time was certainly not on our side. Everyone involved in the financial reconstruction negotiations now knew that with an Inland Revenue demand for £250,000 about to arrive at the Meriden factory, the heads of terms agreement deadline must be met.

Having spent several long days working with Peter Davis, architect of the original Meriden Co-op constitution, the negotiating team was satisfied that it had a framework that met the criteria of a true partnership between capital and labour. The negotiating team left Peter Davis to finalise the initial draft, which would be discussed with Terry Pitt and returned to the Meriden factory on the afternoon of Friday 13th May.

On arrival, we were devastated to learn that the West Midlands County Council which was supposedly in the final stages of acquiring the ex-Dunlop Cash's Lane factory site for the Triumph factory relocation, had in fact, due to lack of progress, lost the deal. Not only had it lost the deal, it had already had a £50,000 increased sealed bid purchase offer (£250,000 up to £300,000) turned down, and was now searching for a suitable alternative Coventry factory premises! The negotiating team knew immediately the traumatic effect that this County Council dithering and lack of faith would have on the Triumph workforce, many of whom were already of the opinion that the West Midlands County Council had become part of the problem, not the solution, to achieving Triumph's financial reconstruction. Collectively, the laid-off Meriden Co-op workforce had invested over 3000 unpaid hours of its own time, refurbishing and making ready the Cash's Lane factory site for Triumph's promised occupation. Dunlop had run out of patience with the

West Midlands County Council, and had found another buyer prepared to pay a higher price for the site, now in pristine condition. Disillusioned and knowing exactly what Triumph's workforce would think when it found out, Triumph Chairman John Rosamond wrote the following letter to Terry Pitt.

Dear Mr Pitt

Our meeting with Michael Jordan in London last Monday, 9th May 1983, succeeded in placing on the table the final elements of the Triumph financial reconstruction package, private sector equity. Michael Jordan, having undertaken to secure the support of the City, introduced Mr David Wickens of British Car Auctions, who had successfully assembled a consortium of five companies willing to invest £100,000 each as an equity stake in Triumph.

Your statement during our return to the Midlands, that to secure support from your political masters, Triumph would have to remain a Co-operative at first seemed a little difficult to marry with West Midlands County Council and Enterprise Board insistence on the fundamental point of private sector equity investment prior to their own support. However, having analysed the noted points made by the private sector at the 9th May meeting, and with the tremendous help of Mr Peter Davis, the architect of the Meriden Co-operative legal structure, we have established that it is possible to meet totally your conditions for investment. This has been accomplished by adopting the stated position of the private sector, in a true partnership between capital and labour. This of course can be achieved on a 50/50 basis, neither party dominating, all working for the common goal, the success of the company. Starting with this premise, providing there is the will from all parties concerned, a way can always be found.

In view of the Triumph immense demonstrable progress to date, the ten commandments, private sector equity, the maintenance of the co-operative ideal, all of which 'with a little help from our friends' Triumph has succeeded in securing, you will understand how disappointed and disillusioned we were to discover that, far from acquiring the Cash's Lane Dunlop factory site, in readiness for the financial reconstruction of Triumph's affairs, the County Council, due to lack of action, had lost the Triumph negotiated £250,000 deal and was now bidding against another purchaser, an offer of £300,000 having already been rejected. You may be interested to note, that laid-off Triumph members on the dole, who had a little more faith in the financial reconstruction of the Meriden Co-operative, have to date invested in excess of 3000 unpaid hours in the refurbishment and redecoration of the Dunlop premises. It therefore seems strange, in view of our very close relationship involving almost daily contact, for you not to have advised Triumph regarding the demise of the negotiations to purchase the Dunlop premises.

There is therefore a limit to which one can believe in a comradely way that the West Midlands County Council and Enterprise Board's support of the financial reconstruction will finally be forthcoming, and without this belief there seems little point in prolonging the agony much longer. With a likely demand from the Inland Revenue for the full settlement of arrears during the course of this week, the second tranche of the product liability insurance premium due in America this week, matters are becoming desperate. I hope you will understand therefore, that the stated Michael Jordan deadline, for heads of terms agreement to be reached during week commencing Monday 23rd May 1983, must be achieved.

In conclusion, if the intention is as once previously stated, to support the Meriden Co-operative at least to the calmer waters of a post General Election period, then we hope you will understand that this is not acceptable or possible. It is therefore with a large amount of foreboding that we must ask for the final time for the West Midlands County Council and Enterprise Board to back up their often stated 'will to support' with action, words however well meaning are no longer enough.

Yours sincerely
Triumph Motorcycles (Meriden) Limited
John A Rosamond
Chairman
JAR/HDH
16th May 1983

32

CAPITAL AND LABOUR PARTNERSHIP

The impact on the Co-op membership caused by the West Midlands County Council's lack of faith in the reconstruction negotiations, demonstrated by the loss of the promised Cash's Lane factory site, cannot be over-emphasised. Whilst the County Council now frantically searched for an alternative Coventry factory, the negotiating team and Peter Davis continued their work on the new Co-operative legal structure. Terry Pitt secured the help of Mike Campbell, previously MD of the Scott Bader Commonwealth and now with the Industrial Common Ownership Movement (ICOM). His advice and assistance, along with that of Tom Fitch (the Co-operative Development Officer at the Council), proved extremely useful in confirming that our thinking on a 'true partnership between capital and labour' was on the right lines. This led to the following 17th May 1983 letter to Terry Pitt written by Triumph's Company Solicitor, Peter Davis.

Dear Terry
Re: Triumph Motorcycles (Meriden) Ltd.
I have been asked by John Rosamond to set out for you the basis of their thinking concerning the preservation of the Co-operative in the new financial structure of the above company. I have had several meetings with them to try and formulate the principles to be adopted, and to convert that into a formal proposal. The details have been discussed with you and subsequently a meeting has taken place with Mr Chris Hughes to explain this, and also with Messrs Tom Fitch and Mike Campbell who is an advisor with ICOM.
  The basis of the approach has been to preserve the Co-operative in its present form as established under the trust document that was set up when the Co-operative first came into existence. It is felt that the pressure of time precludes any variation of this trust document at the present time since this would inevitably raise legal, technical and tax questions which would have to be resolved with the consent of the workforce and the Trustees. Although the trust document will need variation as a result of the experience of its working over the past years, it is felt that its provisions are adequate to enable this to form the basis of the Co-operative for the immediate future until much more detailed consideration can be given concerning the workings of the Co-operative. Any shares that are issued to the Co-operative would therefore be held by the existing Trustees in the trusts already declared in that document.
  The new factor which has been introduced for the first time into the workings of the

Co-operative is that of outside bodies holding an equity stake in the company for which they would in due course expect an income and a reasonable hope of capital appreciation in the future. The best approach therefore appeared to be to create a partnership between the Co-operative and the equity participators within the existing legal framework of the limited company. Various combinations of interest were considered, but we were constantly brought back to the concept of creating a partnership between the two elements and in particular trying to establish a common interest in the company so that speedy decisions could more readily be achieved in the day-to-day management of the company in its commercial transactions.

Due to changes in tax law the previous attitude of the Co-operative to pay benefits by means of bonus on wages can now be abandoned in favour of giving the members of the Co-operative an interest in any dividends paid. It is this aspect of ownership which should give the members of the Co-operative a clear and tangible interest in ownership and the profitability of the company through its trade. This has meant therefore that the previous attitude of totally disregarding dividends has now been changed into one whereby the achievement of dividend will be a positive benefit to the Co-operative and create a common interest. At the present time any distribution of dividend to the Trustees would be expected to be distributed on to the members of the Co-operative directly as an immediate financial benefit when the dividend is declared.

Various proportions of share ownership were considered in order to achieve this partnership. After much discussion it became clear that a division of the share ownership to be held half by the Co-operative and half by the equity participators, be they the private sector or the County Council, was the best method of creating this atmosphere of partnership among the interested parties. The details of the method of creating such a situation will have to be worked out among the partners but the Co-operative's interest would be based upon a revaluation of its interest in the restructured company taking into account the valuation of the name, research and development and reconsidering the valuation of certain other assets in the going concern. If all the parties can agree realistic valuations to achieve this end that will resolve the problem but if that end cannot be reached the creation of founder shares to establish the partnership could be considered and any balance made up in non-voting ordinary shares. If the principle is accepted the details would not appear to present an insuperable problem.

In order to further this ideal of partnership in the new venture it is suggested that the Board representation should be divided in a similar way so that the Co-operative would appoint half of the Board members from among its own members and the remainder of the Board to include management, County Council and private sector representatives, would be appointed by the outside equity participators. It would also be expected that the Chairman would be appointed from among this latter group but although he would have a Director's vote he would not have a Chairman's casting vote so that in the true sense of an equal partnership the parties would have to agree without one side having the ability to impose its will on the other.

It is recognised by the co-operative that there are deficiencies in certain functions in the Company and these have been recognised by the private sector. It is expected that the private sector should be in a position to contribute greatly to the selection and appointment of suitable nominees for positions that should be filled at Board level and it would therefore appear to be entirely within the spirit of the above suggestions that they should nominate persons to fill these positions subject only to a veto by the Co-operative. Having been appointed however the co-operative would not be able to dismiss the appointees without the agreement of its partners and this would no doubt give the nominees greater security than the previous managers of the Co-operative enjoyed and therefore might make the task of identifying suitable candidates rather easier and less costly.

The details of the above package will clearly have to be the subject of further discussion but the members of the Co-operative who have been delegated to produce a satisfactory result for the future feel that an organisation founded on these principles would offer an excellent opportunity for partnership between the parties involved whilst still preserving for the members of the Co-operative a clear interest, not only in the financial success of the undertaking, but also in the decision making on a day-to-day basis.

The equity participators on the other hand would have freedom to deal with their shares as they saw fit without this causing any concern to the members of the Co-operative and they would not be involved in any procedures of the Co-operative in decision making concerning the interests in the Co-operative shares. It is also felt that it leaves a greater scope for the issue of further shares for additional funds in the future which, due to the unique concept of the company, might be issued as non-voting shares if the partnership between the workforce and the equity providers had proved a success.

Yours sincerely
Peter Davis

In view of Triumph's well publicised critical financial position, the negotiating team was well aware of the possibility that 'asset stripping vultures' could be circling for potential easy pickings. Accordingly, when an anonymous approach from a possible investor arrived via a firm of solicitors, efforts were made to establish the identity of the company they represented. As a result of these developments a Board meeting was requested by concerned Directors on 19th May in order to discuss the negotiating team's actions in dealing with the anonymous approach.

Brian Jones expressed concern regarding information he had received from Financial Controller Phil Bragg, relating to the potential investor. Phil Bragg had felt that the company concerned was not receiving our correct consideration.

The Chairman reported that a letter dated 16th May had been received from a firm of London solicitors, Lloyd Denby Neal. The Directors could see from the tabled letter that the firm had an unidentified client interested in possible investment in Triumph, for whom it was requesting confidential financial information. Advice had been sought from the Company Solicitor regarding the divulging of confidential information to an unknown organisation when we were currently deeply involved in delicately balanced financial reconstruction negotiations. Peter Davis had advised that we should try to determine the identity of the company concerned before releasing the requested information. In an effort to do this, Lloyd Denby Neal had been telephoned. Mr Denby had sought further clarification from his client, but having done so, was still unable to divulge their identity.

Bill Beattie commented that it must now be obvious to the Directors that this contact was at a very preliminary stage, and as such, the negotiating team had acted in line with the legal advice received. The Chairman stated that the tabled telex response had been sent referring Lloyd Denby Neal to Triumph's solicitor, Peter Davis, in an effort to establish the identity of those concerned and enter into normal negotiations. John Birch suggested Phil Bragg should be invited to address the Board meeting, as he seemed to believe that to date this investment approach had not been dealt with in a satisfactory manner.

Phil Bragg provided the following explanation. He had received a telephone call from Nigel Usher, the Chairman not being contactable on the evening of Sunday 15th May. Nigel Usher had asked that he speak to a Mr Hassan Bilgrami, a senior manager in a large international trading company with substantial interests comprising over 700 individual companies. Having briefly discussed Bilgrami's interests, Phil Bragg had suggested a letter be written to the Triumph Directors, and this had been done via solicitors Lloyd Denby Neal copying the letter to Phil Bragg and Councillor Geoffrey Edge Chairman of the West Midlands County Council. Subsequently he had received a telephone call from Mr Bilgrami, who was upset with Triumph's telex response to what had been his normal approach when considering investment. Mr Bilgrami continued to insist on anonymity until an investment decision had been made. Phil Bragg believed this anonymous approach was quite normal in the circumstances, and the Directors should agree to provide the requested confidential financial information. To enable this to take place, Mr Bilgrami had stated that provided he received a telephone call in Rotterdam before 4.30pm today, his company would still be prepared to progress matters. Phil Bragg withdrew from the Board meeting to allow the Directors to continue discussion on this anonymous investment approach.

The Board accepted the negotiating team's action to date. George Mackie proposed and John Birch seconded that the Chairman should telephone Mr Bilgrami in Rotterdam in a final effort to ascertain the identity of his company. Without this information, the possible risk of divulging confidential information to an unidentified third party whilst financial reconstruction negotiations were delicately poised, was considered by the Board to be too great.

The telephone conversation took place but no progress was achieved. At a brief reconvened Board meeting the Directors were satisfied that they had done all in their power to pursue a possible investor in Triumph, without running the risk of damaging the almost completed negotiations – exactly the conclusion the negotiating team had reached.

The Chairman received a letter from Chadwick Holmes Limited on 20th May; this indicated the detailed stages through which the Meriden factory site residential planning permission application was passing. It now looked like it would be granted in July 1983, enabling the site sale to go ahead.

In preparation for the crucial financial reconstruction funding meeting on 25th May, Phil Bragg had updated the detailed funding requirement figures he had originally completed at the end of March. The dramatic financial consequences of delay after delay could not have been more apparent!

	£000s
Working capital peak	1528.0
TMA funding requirement	160.0
Accrued Meriden rates	40.0
Removal expenses	50.0
	1778.0
Add: 10 per cent contingency	178.0
Total requirement	**1956.0**

The working capital peak requirement had increased substantially since the last projection was prepared at the end of March for two major reasons. Firstly, increased stockholding to reflect the reservations expressed by Peat, Marwick, Mitchell without adopting its own unrealistic preferred stock levels. Secondly, the prolonged inactivity and stock depletion resulting from a 15-week layoff period meant that it would take ten weeks to produce motorcycles from the date of moving out of the Meriden site. A period of about 3-4 months would have to be funded before receipts were forthcoming in any significant amounts. The 1983 selling season in the USA would have effectively passed by, given the projected restart date. Motorcycles would not be dispatched to the USA until October/November 1983, with the result that the TMA operation would have no source of income other than current receivables and stocks of motorcycles and spares. Assuming all income from these sources was retained, TMA would have to be funded to the tune of at least £160,000 for it to survive, until such time as it could generate income of its own.

CASHFLOW ASSUMPTIONS [Detailed cashflow workings were also provided.]

Payments –UK – weeks 1-24		Pro-forma
	– weeks 25-40	50 per cent pro-forma/50 per cent 45 days credit
– Overseas		Letter of credit
Receipts –UK		4 weeks
– Europe/ROW		6 weeks
– Australia		1 week
– Jordan		2 weeks
– TMA		12 weeks
– Spares		Cash on delivery
PRB/HDH		
20th May 1983		

Present at the 25th May Triumph funding meeting at Coopers and Lybrand's Birmingham offices were representatives from Cork Gully, the Private Sector Consortium, Officers of the County Council and Enterprise Board, three Directors of the Enterprise Board, and Triumph's negotiating team. Lengthy detailed discussions took place regarding the £2.2m funding package proposed by the Chairman of the West Midlands Enterprise Board and Economic Development Committee.

Private sector consortium equity investment	£500,000
WMEB – Equity investment	£500,000
WMEB – Loan (with a 2 year capital moratorium)	£250,000
WMCC – Loan (with an interest/capital 2 year moratorium)	£500,000
Bank – overdraft	£250,000
Export credit finance	£200,000
Total	**£2,200,000**

The above proposed funding package had been established by the Chairman of the WMEB and Economic Development Committee in consultation with his officers, based upon the Peat, Marwick, Mitchell report covering Triumph. Whilst there was still uncertainty regarding the new company start date, (it being impossible to undertake an exact cashflow or set a precise figure of funds required), the three financial projections considered by Geoffrey Edge and his officers had all been within the £2.2m funding estimate now proposed. Further comfort was based upon Peat, Marwick, Mitchell's report on a 'new start company' using Triumph's 5-year plan and the West Midlands Enterprise Board's adjusted figures, which forecast profits of £750,000 plus in years 3, 4 and 5. However, officers had also drawn the attention of Enterprise Board Directors to the fact that whilst negotiations were in hand, there were still seven areas on which agreement was needed in order for an investment package to be finalised. These were:

- County Council to complete the purchase of an alternative factory site.
- Discussions with Triumph's bank regarding a future role.
- Secure export credit facilities.
- Identify and recruit top management.
- Resolve issues relating to the US subsidiary TMA.
- Discuss and agree with the private sector consortium the complex issues of ownership and control, when private equity is invested in a co-operative.
- Discussion with Triumph and the consortium to finalise an agreed opening balance sheet, start date, profit and loss and finally a revised cashflow forecast.

Geoffrey Edge would seek urgent approval of the proposed Triumph investment package at the next Enterprise Board meeting on 27th May, and Economic Development Unit Committee meeting on 1st June.

The negotiating team reported the aforementioned progress to the Triumph Board of Directors the following day, 20th May.

The Chairman reported that whilst the West Midlands County Council had made an increased 'sealed bid' offer of £300,000 for the Dunlop factory site, it had been unsuccessful. The County Council was extremely embarrassed regarding what had happened, but confident about obtaining alternative factory premises for Triumph. A shortlist of three empty factory possibilities had been drawn up: Alfred Herberts, Climax and Brico. The council was now in urgent pursuit to finalise the most appropriate one and make a purchase in the very near future.

The negotiating team reported that a meeting had taken place the previous day, 25th May, at Coopers and Lybrand's Birmingham offices. Present were representatives from all parties concerned:

John Feltham – Deputy Chairman, British Car Auctions for the Consortium
Michael Jordan – Partner, Cork Gully
Chris Hughes – Coopers and Lybrand
Geoffrey Edge – Chairman, Enterprise Board & Economic Development Committee
Gary Titley – Vice Chairman, Enterprise Board & Economic Development Committee
Roger Willis – Vice Chairman, Enterprise Board & Economic Development Committee
Terry Pitt – Senior Advisor on Economic Development
Kate Murray – Accountant
Tom Fitch – Economic Development Officer
John Rosamond – Chairman, Triumph Motorcycles
Bill Beattie – Director, Triumph Motorcycles

Lengthy discussions had taken place regarding the overall Triumph financial reconstruction funding package, which Peat, Marwick, Mitchell had established as being £2.2m. Michael Jordan had indicated that the private sector consortium had been willing for some time to invest £500,000 of equity in the Triumph reconstruction, in line with Geoffrey Edge's request. However, in view of the company's precarious financial situation, it was vital during the course of this meeting that the remainder of the funding package be identified. Whilst the private sector monies were available and on the table, they would not remain there forever.

Geoffrey Edge stated that due to a recent Government legislation change, the absolute maximum available from the West Midlands County Council and Enterprise Board was £1.25m. As a result of this West Midlands funding position, a detailed debate then took place, during which it became apparent that unless funds already committed by the County Council and Enterprise Board to other projects were clawed back (which was considered politically impossible), £1.25m investment in Triumph was indeed the absolute maximum!

In these circumstances and following further discussion, the meeting decided that it may be possible to realise the remaining £500,000 funding shortfall by way of new bank and or export credit facilities. Geoffrey Edge agreed that he would put forward the discussed funding package for Enterprise Board and County Council Economic Development Committee's acceptance at their next meetings on 27th May and 1st June respectively.

Triumph's Board of Directors discussed at length the County Council and Enterprise Board's financial investment position. John Rosamond and Bill Beattie both felt that the indicated financial support would now be forthcoming, enabling the total reconstruction package to be put together. The Board agreed that good progress continued to be made.

As an insight into the proposed new Triumph company structure based upon partnership between capital and labour, the Chairman read to the Directors the 17th May letter to Terry Pitt (reproduced earlier in this chapter). This letter from Peter Davis was a response to Terry Pitt's request that the negotiating team should indicate how socialist politicians could be asked to support Triumph when it was inevitable that the company structure would have to change from the present membership-owned Co-operative. Peter Davis' letter to Terry Pitt had been compiled following the negotiating team's lengthy discussions with Mike Campbell of the Industrial Common Ownership Movement, Tom Fitch, Economic Development Unit Officer with special responsibility for co-ops, and Peter Davis, the Ward and Rider solicitor responsible for the original Meriden Co-operative legal structure, or constitution.

A substantial amount of what was contained in the letter was based on my and Bill Beattie personal experiences at Triumph during its operation as a workers' co-operative. The letter to Terry Pitt had been deliberately sent on Ward and Rider notepaper, penned by Peter Davis, the negotiating team feeling this would carry more weight with the County Council and Enterprise Board. It was further explained to the Triumph Board that whilst this letter and its contents were primarily designed to establish a benchmark in order that a stake in ownership could be achieved for the Co-op, it had also been very important to identify how socialist politicians could back the intended partnership between capital and labour.

The Directors discussed the indicated new company structure at length, unanimously agreeing that if it was possible to achieve a partnership similar to that proposed, it would be a magnificent achievement.

The Chairman reported that as part of the financial reconstruction negotiations, Peat,

Marwick, Mitchell had been requested by the West Midlands County Council to review the operation of Triumph's US subsidiary, TMA. Whilst this work had commenced over two months ago, the report had only just been finalised. Although copies of the TMA report were not yet available, Tom Fitch of the Economic Development Unit had advised that it was likely to contain references to pending product liability claims against Triumph Motorcycles (America) Inc, one of which was for $25,000,000. Telephone discussion with Wayne Moulton, President of TMA, had established that there was indeed a claim of this magnitude against Triumph. It concerned personal injuries that had occurred in connection with a Triumph Trident T150. This motorcycle had been manufactured and sold in 1974 by Norton Villiers Triumph (NVT). Wayne Moulton had advised that similar claims against TMA had been successfully defended on the basis that the company that manufactured and sold the offending motorcycle was no longer in existence. Whilst this information had been indicated to Tom Fitch, it was likely that the West Midlands County Council would request independent legal advice regarding a product liability claim significantly outside TMA's product liability insurance cover.

The Chairman reminded the Directors that the following morning at 11.00am the next mass meeting of the laid-off membership would take place, enabling a detailed update to be provided on financial reconstruction negotiation progress.

Brian Jones raised the matter of outstanding holiday entitlement, in particular with reference to Alistair (Jock) Copland, Triumph's Experimental Department resident motorcycle road racer. In the past, Jock had enjoyed non-standard holidays that suited the company and his motorcycle racing activities. At this time of year, by not taking earlier holidays he would have normally amassed sufficient holiday entitlement to cover his annual racing in the Isle of Man.

Whilst the Chairman recognised the major contribution Jock Copland had made to Triumph, he asked the Directors to initially consider the much wider issue of monies owed to members, for past hours worked as well as outstanding holiday entitlement. A breakdown of this was tabled for discussion.

OUTSTANDING HOLIDAY ENTITLEMENT
Christmas	2 days
Easter	3 days
Spring bank	3 days
May Day	1 day (statutory)
Total	9 days

9 days x £4000/day   £36,000 approx (total membership)

MONEY OWED TO MEMBERS IN LIEU OF HOURS WORKED
30 members = £4362.24

The Chairman continued that whilst there was no doubt that both the holiday entitlement and monies owed to members for unpaid hours was correct. it was very difficult at this stage of financial reconstruction negotiations to pursue payment or the taking of outstanding holiday entitlement.

The Directors agreed that this matter should be raised with the workforce at the mass meeting. The members would be asked to consider giving the 'new' Triumph company a completely fresh start, by wiping the slate clean regarding past holiday entitlement and monies owed to members for unpaid hours worked. It was generally felt by the Directors that the membership would be prepared to agree to this course of action, as within the financial reconstruction proposals was a 10 per cent pay increase, the first Triumph basic rate wage review for 3 years.

Regarding Jock Copland's situation, the Board agreed that he should be allowed to take his road racing holiday as requested. However, his overall holiday entitlement over the year would remain the same as all members.

George Mackie requested an update on the situation regarding the preparation of the annual accounts for the 1981/82 period. In view of the problems that had been experienced in previous years, he felt every effort should be made to avoid a reoccurrence. The Chairman undertook to provide a progress report at the next Board meeting.

With the Board meeting over, the negotiating team's thoughts focused on the next day's mass meeting. This had been scheduled at the end of the Beneficiaries' AGM on 10th May. A very tough meeting was expected, as this would be the first opportunity to discuss with the membership the lost ex-Dunlop factory site. Inevitably, as the negotiating team had requested the membership's help in preparing the new factory for Triumph's early occupation, the Directors would be the focus of their understandable anger and frustration. However, this would not be the first occasion that the Board had experienced such hostility, and it was certainly capable of giving as good as it got. As there would be many other positive reconstruction negotiation developments to discuss, the Directors were confident the mass meeting would end on a more positive note.

Not surprisingly, the 11.00am, 27th May mass meeting was well attended; a public flogging of Messrs Rosamond and Beattie was certainly an event not to be missed! However, by the time the meeting had received a detailed report on the positive progress achieved since the Beneficiary owners' 10th May AGM involvement, the totally wasted 3000 hours of member's unpaid time became merely one more sacrifice in a long list they had already made to ensure a future for Triumph and the Co-op. The real surprise for the membership was when the Chairman read out details of the proposed new company partnership between capital and labour. The members were stunned and listened in complete silence. That such a possibility was even being considered was accepted by the membership as a major achievement. So those – and there were a growing number – that had for some time believed that the negotiating team had been wasting everyone's time, now had to come to terms with the distinct possibility that the Co-op and Triumph were on the verge of achieving financial reconstruction. The laid-off Beneficiary Co-op owners of Triumph certainly went home in a more positive state of mind than when they had arrived, even prepared to consider wiping the slate clean so far as owed monies and holidays were concerned!

On 3rd June, Chairman John Rosamond received a copy of a Geoffrey Edge letter to Michael Jordan at Cork Gully. This as can be seen below, indicating the West Midlands Enterprise Board and Economic Development Committee's progress since the 25th May funding package meeting in Birmingham.

Dear Michael Jordan
Triumph Motorcycles (Meriden) Ltd
Following our constructive meeting in Birmingham on 25th May regarding the financial package required to re-launch the above company, I thought that it would be helpful if I informed you of the progress made so far by ourselves.

First, however, so that there is no misunderstanding, may I set out the financial package which we agreed to seek:

Private Consortium equity investment	*£500,000*
WMEB equity investment	*£500,000*
WMEB loan with two year capital moratorium	*£250,000*
WMCC loan with an interest and capital moratorium for two years	*£500,000*
Bank overdraft	*£250,000*
Export credit finance	*£200,000*
Total	*£2,200,000*

With regard to the £365,000 County Council loan to the company, it was agreed on 25th May that the new accounts would reflect this still outstanding figure.

I shall assume that there is no difference between us on the objective of achieving the above package. From the West Midlands point of view I am now able to tell you that the package as outlined was reported to the Directors of the Enterprise Board on Friday last and the members of the County Council's Economic Development Committee on Wednesday this week. Both meetings were entirely confidential, but it is right for me to tell you that the three sums referred to relating to the WMCC and the WMEB were acceptable to the Board and to the Committee Labour Group provided that the other component parts come together, and provided that rapid progress can be made on outstanding issues especially those relating to new management and the structure and accountability of the company. In view of this I would welcome an early statement in writing from yourself that this is acceptable to the private consortium and an indication of any progress you have made in relation to obtaining the bank overdraft.

The points on which I think we must now make urgent progress – and these were fully endorsed by my fellow Directors and Committee Members – are as follows:

a) The first priority must be to identify which new management skills have to be recruited, and then to approach suitable individuals willing to take on the task. I feel strongly that this is now our top priority, and would be grateful to explore your offer to find a Director of Finance and that of the consortium to provide a Director of Marketing and Sales.

b) A realistic start-up date must then be agreed, and on the basis of this decision I think we need to verify the state of the order book and prepare a new cashflow forecast and profit and loss account.

c) The above will require a further assessment of overseas markets given the new late start-up date.

d) Export credit facilities have then to be established, preferably by access to Government EGCD. I would welcome any approach you can make to Government on this or, alternatively a statement of the present position of Greyhound Securities.

e) The new management will also wish to look at the new site which the County Council is in the process of purchasing for lease to the company. I have in mind here the details of plant layout etc., and the best judgement we can make on how quickly the move can be accomplished.

f) There are still issues relating to the US subsidiary which have to be resolved. Peat, Marwick's Californian Office has prepared a report. (Copy enclosed).

g) Whilst we are making progress on the above subjects, I think we should also begin to put on paper our views on the ownership, control and management structure of the new company in the light of the fact that substantial fresh capital is being injected.

The above check-list is by no means exhaustive and you may wish to add items yourself. If so, I would welcome you doing so on paper so that our respective officers can start to put in hand the necessary legal documentation for the agreements I hope we are about to make. We were expecting at the meeting on 25th May that Chris Hughes would present a preliminary 'heads of agreement' which the meeting at David Wickens' home on 9th May had agreed that he should do. In the event we were able to make substantial progress without it, but I feel now that time is no longer on our side. I look forward to your response to the above, and hope that we can meet at your office on Monday next.

Yours sincerely
Geoff Edge.

In view of the vast amounts of time that had passed since the November 1982 *MCN* 'Starship Enterprise' article, the ironic last paragraph of Geoffrey Edge's letter regarding "time no longer being on our side," seemed like pure politics!

In the same post as the copy letter from Geoffrey Edge was a letter from Rupert Scott, Managing Director of Chadwick Holmes. He was also stressing how essential it was that progress was made regarding his company's interest, namely the acquisition of the Meriden factory site. All the legal contracts had been agreed for some time, and Chadwick Holmes would soon be in a position to exchange. The granting of residential planning permission was imminent, and he had a Board of Directors meeting in five days' time at which he would be required to provide a firm progress report. Triumph's Chairman sent a reassuring reply to Rupert Scott, bringing him right up to date on the recently achieved financial reconstruction progress. Whilst doing this, he was reminded of the 'chicken and egg' situation that Triumph faced with its bank, before the factory site sale could proceed – National Westminster Bank retained total control and first had to be reassured that all the various parts of the financial reconstruction deal were in place, and would create a new Triumph Motorcycle business with a viable ongoing future. It was only then, having provided the bank with this reassurance, that it would agree to the sale of the Meriden factory site.

On 6th June, a further Triumph Board meeting took place to bring all the Directors up to date on the latest developments.

The Chairman tabled a copy of the 2nd June Geoffrey Edge letter to Michael Jordan at Cork Gully. As the Directors could see, this letter confirmed agreement had been reached by the West Midlands Enterprise Board for a £500,000 equity investment and a loan of £250,000 for the Triumph financial reconstruction. The West Midlands County Council Economic Development Committee had also agreed a loan of £500,000. Both bodies' support was on the proviso that rapid progress could now be made with the Triumph funding package discussed at the Cooper and Lybrand Birmingham meeting on 25th May. Geoffrey Edge's letter also went on to detail a number of outstanding items that, subject to their satisfactory resolution, would enable the investment package to go ahead. One of the items to be resolved was the Peat, Marwick, Mitchell report on Triumph's US subsidiary TMA, which was now available for the Directors' perusal. The major area of concern was regarding product liability insurance claims against TMA, as reported at the previous Board meeting.

Following lengthy discussion by the Board of the intended financial funding agreed by the West Midlands Enterprise Board and Economic Development Unit Committee, George Mackie proposed and Brian Jones seconded that in view of the significant progress which this now represented, Triumph should continue to trade in the best interests of its creditors. The proposal was once again carried unanimously.

The Chairman reported that Financial Controller Phil Bragg and his staff were pushing ahead as rapidly as possible with the preparation for audit of the annual 1981/82 financial accounts. Coopers and Lybrand would commence its audit work as soon as the accounts were available. The auditors were fully aware of the delicate position Triumph was in regarding previous years' delayed registration, and would help as much as possible to avoid further problems. However, the Chairman drew the Directors' attention to outstanding monies owed to Coopers and Lybrand by Triumph's US subsidiary, TMA. This debt would have to be cleared before the start of the 1981/82 audit work. With that, the Board meeting came to an end.

The financial reconstruction funding package agreement by the West Midlands County Council Economic Development Unit and Enterprise Board would be discussed with the Beneficiary owners of Triumph at the next mass meeting on 10th June. Also to be discussed were the additional loose ends that still had to be tied up prior to the financial reconstruction going ahead. It was very clear to everyone concerned that the major problem still faced was the continuing passage of time. This was not helped by the politically inspired West Midlands County Council now being totally gripped by General Election fever, which completely stopped any Triumph financial reconstruction progress. Normality at County Hall would not return until after the 9th June polling day, and this at a time when at last, major funding progress had been achieved. But the funding progress did not prevent creditors' writs from being served, any one of which could have brought about the end of Triumph.

The General Election over, the manufacturing industry that still remained in the UK had to face up to more of the same Conservative Government policies that some believed had resulted in factory closures and unemployment at levels not seen since the 1930s.

9TH JUNE 1983 PARLIAMENTARY GENERAL ELECTION

Party	1979			1983		
	Votes	Share	Seats	Votes	Share	Seats
Conservatives	13.69m	43.9%	339	13.01m	42.3%	397
Labour	11.53m	36.9%	269	8.46m	27.6%	209
Liberal	4.31m	13.8%	11	7.78m*	25.4%	23

* SDP/Liberal Alliance Party

Whilst the Conservatives' core vote had stood up remarkably well (due, it could be argued, to the 'Falklands War effect') over 3 million disillusioned Labour party voters seemed to have favoured the policies being offered by the SDP/Liberal Alliance party. The 'first past the post' UK parliamentary electoral system helped the Conservative party to a net gain of 37 seats and a further term in office. Against national trends, Geoffrey Robinson MP retained the Coventry North West seat for Labour.

There still remained the practical concern of restarting a very seasonal motorcycle business following the financial reconstruction. Numerous component parts were now sourced in Italy, and a six-week lead time to supply would be required. The whole of Italy went on holiday for the month of August, compounding these serious problems.

However, any thoughts of these practical problems paled into insignificance when on the 14th June, Terry Pitt telephoned the negotiating team to advise that the private sector consortium had decided not to proceed with its equity investment in the financial reconstruction of Triumph, because of the complexity of the funding package discussed at the 25th May meeting. Triumph's Board of Directors was immediately notified 'informally' of the private sector funding problem. In the time available, the negotiating team then concentrated totally on trying to rekindle private sector interest. Coincidentally, the day after the consortium withdrew, Fred Tippets, Chairman of the Moratorium Creditors' Committee, wrote requesting an update on Triumph's financial reconstruction progress! Those he represented, he said, wanted to know what was happening – there's nothing like rubbing salt in the wounds!

A Board meeting to discuss formally the private sector equity funding problem was called on 20th June.

The Chairman reported that confirmation had now been received from Councillor Geoffrey Edge regarding the private sector consortium's decision not to proceed with its previously agreed £500,000 equity investment in the Triumph financial reconstruction package. There follows a letter from British Car Auctions Ltd, dated 14th June 1983:

Dear Mr Edge
Triumph Motorcycles (Meriden) Ltd
I am writing to advise you that unfortunately the consortium has now decided it is not able to proceed with its investment in this company. Although I was not present myself, I understand from David Wickens that at the original meeting, when the investment was discussed and the format agreed, the make-up was as follows:

Loan from WMEB	*£1,200,000*
Interest bearing loan or equity capital from WMEB	*£500,000*
Equity capital from private sector headed by BCA	*£500,000*
Total cash investment	*£2,200,000*
Share capital from Triumph Co-operative against assets	*£500,000*
Total	*£2,700,000*

When we met at the offices of Coopers and Lybrand in Birmingham on 25th May, it had become necessary for you to make substantial changes which you subsequently set out in your letter to Michael Jordan dated 2nd June. We appreciate that the reasons for having to do this were beyond your control.

The original scheme was attractive to the consortium, because it was financially speaking quite simple. There were basically only two parties involved, namely the WMEB and the consortium. It now seems to the consortium that with the additional involvement of the bank and the ECGD the flexibility and simplicity of the original arrangement has gone.

David Wickens and the other members of the consortium hope and feel sure you will find a replacement source of finance for this project.
Yours sincerely
John Feltham,
Deputy Chairman

Details of the letter were received by telephone on 14th June, and a copy was sent to Triumph's Chairman together with Geoffrey Edge's 16th June reply to David Wickens, Chairman of British Car Auctions:

Dear Mr Wickens
Triumph Motorcycles (Meriden) Ltd
I have received from your deputy, Mr Feltham, today a letter advising me that the consortium headed by you cannot now proceed with an investment in Triumph. I am obviously disappointed, but frankly most surprised at the reasons given. At no time was the package set out in his letter on offer, and both my Vice Chairmen and me (and our officers) have said and written to you and to Michael Jordan to this effect in the past. I believe it will be helpful if I list what our files show as being the progress of negotiations.

On the 30th March, together with Councillor Titley, I met Michael Jordan to discuss a possible funding package. He felt he could obtain up to £400k equity and up to £700k export finance from the private sector to put towards a total funding package of £2.2m. The next day I wrote to Michael and suggested we had identified the need for a higher private sector risk contribution of between £600k and £700k and a lower export finance factor of £400k; the private sector equity being matched £ for £ by ourselves. Michael then undertook to seek such private sector finance whilst County Council officers were also contacting possible sources of finance. At a meeting at Cork Gully on 2nd May progress was reviewed and final contacts agreed upon. It was also agreed that a further meeting would take place in one week's time to review progress.

Michael reported that he had contacted you, and a meeting was arranged for 9th May with you and my officers. Although Michael opened discussions along the lines of Mr Feltham's letter, my officers corrected this misinterpretation and sent their minutes of the discussion to Chris Hughes of Coopers and Lybrand. Discussions also included those outlined in my letter of 31st March. The meeting discussed the need for export finance and Chris Hughes was to draw up a heads of agreement and look at the funding need in detail with Triumph. Our position was again put in a letter to Chris Hughes dated 12th May 1983 which was handed to Chris for you to see.

The meeting at which we expected to discuss the heads of agreement on 25th May 1983 was in fact totally concerned with persuading me to find additional funds on more favourable terms. I offered £500k equity and £250k loan from the WMEB in addition to a loan from the WMCC of £500k on very favourable terms. This still left a 'gap' of £450k, which we suggested could be made up by a £250k bank overdraft and £200k export credit. The meeting agreed that this could be done, and Mr Feltham was specifically asked his view – which was positive.

That meeting, at which all parties were represented, had therefore agreed a £2.2m financial package, leaving each of us to make some further progress – all of which was set out in my letter of 2nd June to Michael Jordan which again was copied to you. I also outlined in that letter the considerable progress made by ourselves in just five working days.

Having moved very much towards meeting all your requirements, I find it difficult to believe that your real reasons for now withdrawing are based on the complications of having a bank involved in a small way in financing the running of Triumph. I doubt that there are many companies at the moment operating without overdraft facilities.

In spite of all this, you may wish to know that the County Council and WMEB are still prepared to leave the West Midlands' package 'on the table' and hope that your certainty of

another source of finance to replace your own promised contribution will be forthcoming.
Yours sincerely
Geoff Edge
Chairman, EDC and WMEB

Both of the aforementioned tabled letters were discussed at length by the Triumph Board.

The Chairman reported that indications to date from Chris Hughes and Michael Jordan regarding the possibility of reinstating the private sector consortium's equity offer were not encouraging. Whilst the full outcome of this initiative had not yet materialised, it was felt that work on an alternative Triumph funding proposal should be started. With this in mind Michael Jordan, Chris Hughes John Rosamond and Bill Beattie had met representatives of the National Westminster Bank on Friday 17th June. Michael Jordan had told the bank that he felt the private sector consortium was reluctant to proceed due to the political climate that involvement with the West Midlands County Council engendered. David Trenbath, the National Westminster Bank Manager responsible for the Triumph account, expressed his disappointment as earlier matters between the County Council and the private sector seemed to have been resolved. Triumph's Chairman indicated to the bank meeting that in view of the situation, with the private sector deciding not to proceed because of the political implications, it was now Triumph's intention to approach the full West Midlands County Council to make good the half a million pounds shortfall of equity funding. Replying for the bank, David Trenbath said that they would still be prepared to consider investment in the new Triumph reconstruction proposal, providing it was forthcoming in the very near future.

Following the negotiating team's meeting with the National Westminster Bank, a meeting took place with Triumph's Company Solicitor, Peter Davis. Peter suggested that an indication of the full West Midlands County Council's attitude towards Triumph's new funding approach was needed before he could offer meaningful advice to the Board. Following further detailed discussion of the private sector consortium's withdrawal, the Directors agreed that the negotiating team should pursue as rapidly as possible the new funding application to the full West Midlands County Council.

The Chairman reported to the Directors that he had today received two letters from Terry Pitt, dated 15th and 16th June respectively. Both the tabled letters, as the Directors could see, indicated a considerable change of heart regarding the £365,000 export loan facility, probably as a direct result of the great uncertainty now created by the private sector consortium's decision not to proceed. John Rosamond proposed to reply to Terry Pitt, pointing out that Triumph would be applying to the full West Midlands County Council to make good the required £500,000 equity investment. Our reassurance would also be offered confirming what had been stated by Geoffrey Edge in his 2nd June letter to Michael Jordan, that "with regard to the £365,000 County Council loan to the company, it was agreed on 25th May that the new accounts would reflect this still outstanding figure," following the financial reconstruction. The Directors agreed that the Chairman should proceed with the aforementioned action.

The Board meeting over, it was now clear that in the brief time available we had to determine if the political will still existed in the full West Midlands County Council to make good the required £500,000 equity shortfall; or had its support for the Co-op and Triumph now gone with the passing of the General Election?

One person from whom support was never in doubt was Tony Benn. His handwritten reply to the Chairman's recent update on the Co-op's situation said it all in the final sentence: "Our work is really just beginning, keep at it. Tony."

33

ON THE BRINK OF RECEIVERSHIP

S adly, Triumph's efforts to establish the basis for a forward-thinking true partnership between capital and labour, meeting the requirements of both the private sector consortium and West Midlands politicians, failed to address what seemed to be a increasing lack of trust. The County Council had serious doubts about the consortium's 'punt' decision to invest in Triumph, and the consortium had serious doubts about the political climate that involvement with West Midlands County Council dictated. Sandwiched between this potential marriage of convenience was Triumph, hardly the basis for a successful union! Following the previous months of financially disastrous delays, the almost inevitable had happened, and the Meriden Co-op was still no closer to implementing the vital financial reconstruction.

On 23rd June a Triumph Board meeting was called to update the Directors.

The negotiating team reported that on 21st June, a formal application had been made to Councillor Gordon Morgan (leader of the full West Midlands County Council) to make good the £500,000 equity funding shortfall left when the British Car Auctions consortium withdrew its proposed private sector investment in the reconstruction of Triumph's affairs.

Geoffrey Edge, Chairman of the Enterprise Board and Economic Development Unit Committee, was advised of Triumph's additional County Council funding application. Confirmation was received from Coopers and Lybrand that the consortium's reason for withdrawal was indeed political. Terry Pitt and Tom Fitch were also reassured that the consortium would not be publicly announcing its reason for rejection. This major setback was discussed fully by Councillors and officers of the Enterprise Board and Economic Development Unit Committee later that afternoon, following which they decided to spend one further, final week attempting to finalise a Triumph deal. Meetings would be arranged with Michael Jordan and National Westminster Bank the following day, Friday 24th, or Monday 27th June, in an effort to make urgent progress.

Triumph's Directors discussed at length the report and agreed that, without a response to the request for additional County Council funding, the next day's mass meeting of the membership should be adjourned for a week.

The Chairman advised that as agreed at the last Board meeting, a reassuring reply had been sent to Terry Pitt's 15th and 16th June letters. Triumph's 22nd June response confirmed that full account would be taken of the £365,000 export loan in the financial reconstruction proposals.

The Chairman reported that Coopers and Lybrand had agreed to schedule the 1981/82 annual accounts audit in its workload for end July/beginning of August. In view of previous late registration problems, the auditor was advising that a letter should be sent by Triumph to the Companies Registration Office in Cardiff outlining the preparatory work now being undertaken with latest annual accounts.

On Monday 27th June, the negotiating team was in London involved in the previously mentioned meetings at Cork Gully and the National Westminster Bank. (The following notes of these meetings were produced by the County Council.)

Meeting at Cork Gully
Present:

Michael Jordan	*Cork Gully*
Chris Hughes	*Coopers and Lybrand*
John Rosamond	*Triumph*
Bill Beattie	*Triumph*
Geo. Bloomfield	*Herbert-Sigma*
Terry Pitt	*EDU*
Tom Fitch	*EDU*
Kate Murray	*WMEB*

Terry Pitt outlined the WMCC's position:

a) Legal constraints dictated that £1.25m was all that was available from WMCC and WMEB in 1983/4.

b) Private sector involvement had been seen not only as a source of funds, but as validation of the WMCC's commercial judgement and also as a potential source of management skills.

c) The WMCC wanted to know if a further trawl had any hope of success.

d) Strategy had now been reviewed and the emphasis put on bringing a management team together, in order to validate the WMCC's decision and perhaps later attract private funds.

e) Look at funding requirement – was £2.2m needed immediately? The peak in week 29 would allow some financing in financial year 1984/5.

f) Meetings were to be less fragmented, and would in future involve new management and Triumph Directors in decision making.

MJ felt £2.2m was needed as per Peats and ADL and below that figure the project was too risky. Private sector finance was probably needed to get the bank's co-operation. MJ did not know of alternative sources of finance.

KM suggested having missed the 1983 selling season the new cashflow associated with a delayed start-up might look considerably different.

Geo Bloomfield said he saw the cashflow decision as a timing issue and he would head a management team who were prepared to develop a plan which they believed was achievable.

It might take the following form:

a) Spares operation immediately

b) Limited production in October

c) Australian sales in the winter financed immediately by Scholfield Goodman and USA bikes after Xmas for shipping in January and February. He advocated a clean sheet basis as an essential prerequisite.

Discussion then centred around the creditors of £570k + £180k = £750k. It was agreed £250k on day one was the minimum needed and £750k on day one was the maximum. The effect of this on £1.25m was such that MJ suggested a liquidation initiated by the Directors and creditors was inevitable. The liquidator would sell the name, patents and plant and machinery.

Who would buy the assets?

The WMCC might lead a consortium. But there was a risk of someone else coming in to run it or break it up. JR said he did not know of interested buyers. Geo B agreed. The ownership of the name was discussed and although it was suggested it was unfettered on the company it was also suggested it must be under the bank's debenture (fixed and floating charge). The latter was assumed to be the position.

£150k (£135k machines and £15k stock) was suggested as a figure upon which to make a bid, before valuing the name.

MJ formally advised JR & BB to call in their creditors prior to liquidation.

GB asked if creditors might convert to equity. MJ advised that a S206 court sanctioned agreement with creditors to accept reduced and delayed payments or equity conversion would be expensive and time consuming.

TP raised the possibility of Cork Gully or Coopers involvement in future management and planning. MJ said his advice was free, but Chris Hughes would be on a consultancy basis. He would try to identify a finance Director from existing lists. Strengthened management was needed to keep the bank in.

The whole meeting adjourned to the National Westminster Bank, Lothbury.

Andy Philpot and Mike Campion for the bank joined the meeting.

John Rosamond opened the meeting by saying that he was leaning towards receivership/ liquidation.

Michael Jordan said that £2.2m was recommended in the Peats and ADL report (actual figure was £1.9m). It was his view that the £1.25m on the table from the WMCC was not sufficient if the creditors had to be paid. In liquidation the value of the assets would be established (probably £250k), leaving £950k for working capital after a £50k cost of moving. This was insufficient. The only risk of liquidation was that somebody else might buy the assets and restart production outside the West Midlands. MJ made the position of Cork Gully quite clear in that he was very sad that BCA had withdrawn and now advised Triumph Directors to call in their creditors together with a view to creditors' liquidation.

JR said that Triumph's Directors would discuss this point.

The finance available to the WMEB/WMCC was outlined. The bank said that the previous consortium proposal had certainty in that they knew how much money they would receive, and felt confident that the consortium would attract strong management.

George Bloomfield asked whether, if strengthened management put a plan together, the bank would look at it as any other plan. MC confirmed the bank had no objection in principle to dealing with a new Triumph.

In liquidation the bank would take all it could get. MC was surprised to hear he could get as much as £800k that is more than £700k agreed to. JR said he would do all he could to smooth planning permission.

TP said if sufficient funds could not be found the WMCC could not go ahead and neither would new management be willing to take on the task.

MJ concluded the meeting by saying that he believed Triumph's Directors should call their creditors together with a view to voluntary liquidation.

After the meeting George Bloomfield asked JR, BB, KM, TF and TP about the workforce putting part of their statutory redundancy money into shares. He asked JR and BB to say what a co-operative was. GB stated that he was not in favour or against worker co-operatives; he supported management buy-outs and looked for strong, effective management.

Worker equity might be worth £50 – £100,000. The Directors agreed to come back on this point.

The following day 28th June, Terry Pitt attended a meeting with Singer and Friedlander, and Peat, Marwick, Mitchell.

Meeting with Singer and Friedlander and Peat, Marwick, Mitchell 28th June 1983
Present:
Charles Blunt – Singer and Freidlander
Alan Adam – Peat, Marwick, Mitchell
Terry Pitt – West Midlands County Council
TP outlined the decisions taken by the County Council in the light of BCA's withdrawal of their proposed equity, and reported broadly on the reaction of Cork Gully and the National Westminster Bank at meetings held the previous day. These meetings, like this one, had been arranged hurriedly, and George B, J Adcock (Peats) and M Noakes (Peats) were absent. Hence Alan Adam was sitting in.
The bleak conclusion of Cork Gully and National Westminster's sympathetic but firm views, were considered. CB said that, contrary to Cork Gully he felt £1.25m plus bank commercial borrowing was adequate, if slightly risky. He felt however, that whilst he was keener now on Triumph than 4 months ago, he would "find better uses for County money." S & F saw no possibility of private sector finance either now or within six months of restart.
Both AA and CB felt that cash available would only be:

County	1250k
Minus cost of plant	35k
Spares	15k
Name and patents	100k
Move to new site	50k
Leaving	£950k for working capital
Plus	£400k bank and export borrowing

Even with the best management (which could now be both costly and difficult to obtain) this was a very risky project indeed.
On the subject of liquidation and receivership AA and CB both said receivership was best, and bankers only wanted liquidation to avoid a role by themselves. Compulsory liquidation would be vastly complicated by high cost, time taken and legal disputes. At the end of day there was no essential difference between voluntary liquidation and receivership except the latter would be cheaper, quicker and a clean sale of the non-land assets. But the company must move quickly to avoid a court petition from any maverick creditor just hoping for publicity.
Directors do not have control over appointment of a liquidator (creditors do that) but with the bank they do control the appointment of a receiver.
TP finally outlined the arithmetic and political problems of the county's search for private investment even at this stage. Apart from validating county's commercial judgement and supplying or supporting new management members, they could obviate the need for WMCC 1984/85 second funding. Without this the county it now seemed, had neither the cash to enter a bid to the receiver nor the chance of attracting top management as a team.
AA and CB said Peat, Marwick, Mitchell's financial controller was far too expensive. Why not have Peats as reporting accountants on a 3 days a month basis to help management and serve the county? The same may apply to a Marketing Director. Then work with G Bloomfield and a General Manager?

The meeting ended by agreeing substantially with the Cork Gully/Nat West conclusions (with the exception of the receivership preference) and a long discussion took place on the options for a slimmed down Triumph, making spares and doing development of Diana, producing Bonnevilles only to cash order. It was agreed that figures for this were needed before the county could consider a bid.

TJP/29th June 1983

On the evening of Wednesday 29th June, the negotiating team attended a County Hall meeting of Councillors and officers to review financial reconstruction developments. A full report was provided to Triumph's Board of Directors the following day.

The Chairman reported that the previous evening, the negotiating team had attended a West Midlands County Council meeting of Councillors and officers chaired by Geoffrey Edge. During the meeting, it was explained that County Council leader Councillor Gordon Morgan, whilst supportive of Triumph, was also insistent upon any investment from the County Council coming from the financial budgets of the West Midlands Economic Development Committee and Enterprise Board. Councillor Morgan's stipulation, Geoffrey Edge advised, was not of choice, but because of legal constraints that prevented any other County Council funds being used for investment. Whilst the West Midlands County Council/West Midlands Enterprise Board £1.25m investment was still on the table (half of the investment possible provided out of this year's budget, and half out of next) it was now looking less concrete. Terry Pitt had provided the County Councillors and officers with a detailed report of the meetings that had taken place with Cork Gully and the National Westminster Bank on 27th June, and his meeting with Singer and Freidlander/Peat, Marwick, Mitchell on 28th June 1983. The County Council notes of these three meetings (already covered in this chapter) were tabled for Triumph's Directors' perusal. Terry Pitt had advised that no alternative investment options had been forthcoming from these meetings, making receivership or liquidation more likely if a replacement for the British Car Auction consortium was not found in the near future. Terry Pitt also raised the possibility that with the County Council's £1.25m funding package still on the table, publicity would enable a final trawl for replacement private sector equity. Chairman Geoffrey Edge felt that with final County Council meetings prior to the summer 'semi-recess' taking place the following week, it would be counterproductive if we had any publicity about Triumph going into receivership before this happened.

The Triumph Directors discussed at length the negotiating team's report. George Mackie asked the reason for the totally differing views between the County Council and the National Westminster Bank on the appointment of a receiver or liquidator. Bill Beattie replied that it would be difficult to find more opposing points of view on what should happen, should Triumph's financial reconstruction proposals turn out to be impossible. As the bank and County Council were so opposed, further discussion with both parties would have to take place before any terminal action.

Finally, the Directors' discussed the rescheduled members' mass meeting taking place the next day. It was agreed that the membership would be provided with an update on the present financial reconstruction negotiations.

The mass meeting at 11.00am on Friday 1st July was a sombre occasion, members already aware due to the hastily adjourned meeting last week that major problems must have developed. Accordingly, they were not totally surprised when the Chairman reported in the strictest confidence the major investment problems that the Co-op now faced. As a result of the private sector consortium withdrawing its agreed £500,000 equity investment offer, there was now a shortfall of that amount. The reason for the consortium's withdrawal was stated as the political climate that involvement with the West Midlands County Council dictated. The members were already aware that the £500,000 private sector element in the £2.2m reconstruction package was the catalyst that the County Council had stipulated in order to confirm its own commercial decision to invest. Accordingly, the whole financial reconstruction proposal was now at risk. As a result of this major funding problem, the mass meeting was told that Michael Jordan (Cork Gully), Terry Pitt (County Council), and Triumph's negotiating team had been trying to rekindle private sector interest, without success. When the consortium withdrew, a meeting with National Westminster Bank in London had determined that it would still accept an alternative investment proposal from Triumph, provided it was in the near future. A further application had been made to the 'full' West Midlands County Council, asking it to make good the £500,000 equity shortfall. During the last week, further meetings had taken place with Cork Gully, National Westminster Bank, Singer and Freidlander, and Peat, Marwick, Mitchell to explore any possible financial reconstruction options that still remained. That day, the meeting was told, we had received the West Midlands County Council response to Triumph's application for a further £500,000 of equity investment. The County Council letter was read to the mass meeting by the Chairman.

Dear John
Triumph Motorcycle Co-operative
Thank you for your letter of the 21st June. I am very disappointed at the news that the private sector consortium has withdrawn from negotiations for the refinancing of the Co-operative. I heard this direct from Geoff Edge, but your letter served to underline the effort which has been devoted to the project and the very weak support we have received from the private sector.

I was interested to read your suggestion that the County Council should now consider funding the entire package. As you would expect I have given this very careful consideration and have spoken to Geoff Edge on the matter. All that has only served to confirm my initial feelings that this is a matter which must be considered by the Economic Development Committee, which is responsible for all economic initiatives, and as such is allocated in full the appropriate economic part of the County Council's budget. I know that Geoff Edge and his officers are in close contact with you and are doing everything possible to explore the scope for an alternative funding arrangement now that the consortium has withdrawn.

I think Geoff will have spoken to you by now on the legal difficulty of the County finding the full £2.2m and will, I am sure, have explained the constraints on his budget given the very wide range of initiatives which we are trying to mount to deal with the serious employment problems of the West Midlands County. Perhaps the most significant constraint we face is the fact that we depend on a very limited range of powers for our Economic Development Programme. Most specifically we are limited in our total expenditure on most such initiatives to the proceeds of a two penny rate. Any further funding for the Triumph Co-operative would have to be mounted against that total, and it is already under severe pressure.

I hope this letter helps to give a little of the background to the problems we face and I hope it reflects continuing support for you and your colleagues in what continues to be a very difficult time for the Co-operative. I am optimistic that together we may find some means to continue the manufacture of Triumph Motorcycles in the West Midlands.
Yours sincerely
Councillor Gordon Morgan
Leader

"In my experience," the Chairman commented to the meeting, "I have never received a 'Dear John' letter that conveyed good news." As the meeting had just heard, the leader of the County Council had advised that it was unable to make good the financial reconstruction equity investment shortfall. Once again, John Rosamond stressed to the mass meeting the vital requirement of complete confidentiality. At the next mass meeting in a week's time on Friday 8th July at 11.00am, Triumph's Directors would have a clearer understanding of their legal responsibilities, and it would be possible to explain exactly what the present situation meant to each individual Co-op member. The mass meeting over, there was no doubt that every member of the Co-op was apprehensive regarding what the future held for Triumph.

David Cowen of Walford, Hardman and Brown, Triumph's patent agent, had recently written to John Rosamond regarding the possibility that Triumph had not paid stamp duty in 1980, when the Co-op's then Chief Executive, Geoffrey Robinson, acquired the Triumph name and associated rights. David only had a photocopy of the agreement, and therefore was unable to ascertain whether or not stamp duty had been paid. Solicitor Peter Davis was in a similar position, so the Chairman pursued the original agreement documentation at the National Westminster Bank. Lengthy enquiries at the local branch at Balsall Common and head office at Lothbury, London determined that the original 1980 name purchase agreement was on file at the National Westminster area office in Coventry. In the course of the search for the original agreement, the Chairman became aware that contrary to the Triumph Board of Directors' belief, National Westminster Bank did not hold a charge over the Triumph name and associated rights under its overdraft debenture. During ongoing discussions with Terry Pitt of the County Council and Peter Davis, they were also made aware of what the Chairman had discovered. Like Triumph's Directors, both the County Council and Triumph legal advisor had assumed that the bank's fixed and floating charge debenture covered all Triumph's assets, including the name and associated rights – this intellectual property had been valued by various individuals as being worth between £100,000 and £400,000! Now aware of this valuable, unencumbered Triumph asset, West Midlands County Council not surprisingly began to exert more and more pressure on Triumph regarding repayment of its outstanding £365,000 export loan facility or the provision of additional security.

On 6th July, the *Coventry Evening Telegraph* carried a front page story on Geoffrey Robinson MP: "MP is fined over Meriden returns."

A Board of Directors meeting was called on Friday 8th July to discuss the latest negotiating developments.

The Chairman stated that the Board was already aware of the leader of West Midlands County Council, Councillor Gordon Morgan's, 1st July negative reply to Triumph's request for additional funding. Since that letter, there had been a significant change regarding the County Council's treatment of the outstanding £365,000 export loan facility. Whilst efforts had been made to reassure the County Council, more and more pressure had been exerted on Triumph to deal immediately with this matter. As the Directors knew, it had been previously agreed that full account of the outstanding £365,000 export loan would be taken at the time of the financial reconstruction. It appeared that, in view of the consortium's withdrawal and the financial reconstruction looking less likely, the County Council was backing away from this agreement; however, the negotiating team now believed that the Triumph name and associated rights were in an unencumbered position not covered by the Bank's mortgage debenture! Written confirmation of this was being sought from National Westminster Bank head office in London. Accordingly, the Chairman advised that, due to the massive pressure being applied by the West Midlands County Council, it had been offered 'a charge' over the Triumph name and associated rights, whilst the £365,000 export loan facility would remain outstanding. Terry Pitt's 6th July reply temporarily accepting Triumph's offer had been received the previous day, and was tabled for the Directors' perusal.

Dear Sirs
Triumph Motorcycles (Meriden) Limited
Thank you for your letter of 5th July.
Whilst I appreciate that further funds may be required by you, I am afraid that you must appreciate in return that the interests of the County Council require to be protected so far as possible. In the light of the present breaches by you of the loan agreement (comprised in the loan offer dated the 8th December 1982 and your acceptance) I am afraid I cannot therefore recommend the County Council make available a further £10,000 as requested.
I am bound to recommend to the County Council that it should now consider steps to safeguard its interests. In the ordinary course of events this would involve enforcing immediate repayment of the outstanding loan, which has already become due and payable pursuant to clause 5(C) of the loan offer document, by reason of your company's default in paying the sum of £365,000 or any of the proceeds of sale of the motor bikes into the special number 3 account or otherwise to the County Council.
However, the interests of preserving employment and your company's business are also of paramount concern to ourselves. I am therefore, prepared to recommend that the County Council temporarily defers from taking steps to enforce immediate repayment whether under any charge it holds or otherwise, and that it postpones repayment of all sums presently outstanding for a period until 30th September 1983, on conditions which will be set out in a further security document to be drafted by solicitors acting for us and which will provide for (among other things):
• A charge on all intellectual property rights on your company.
• Immediate repayment in the event that its security is in jeopardy or the company suffers or is likely to suffer a financial catastrophe (the precise events upon which immediate repayment will arise will be set out in the further security document itself).
At the end of the said period we can review the position again.
Perhaps you would confirm to me that you are agreeable to these in principle and arrange for a form of charge to be prepared so that we can give immediate effect to this proposal.
You must appreciate that the Council is affording you temporary accommodation and is in effect waiving its right to immediate repayment of the sums presently due and payable. It is only fair and reasonable that its commitment in this respect should be matched by further charge. Without the further security, immediate repayment would be required or otherwise enforced.
I await hearing from you as soon as possible.
Yours faithfully
Terry J Pitt
Senior Advisor on Economic Development

However, the Chairman continued, there was still tremendous pressure being applied to enter into the legal requirements to effect the aforementioned charge over the Triumph name and associated rights. A telex from the West Midlands County Council demanding that the £365,000 export loan facility be immediately repaid in full was expected. It arrived at 17.30.

311762 Trusty G Loan Agreement
338815 Wemsol G

8th July 1983 Ref. EDU/TJP
For the attention of John Rosamond Triumph Motorcycles/WMCC
8th July 1983
On behalf of WMCC I must hereby demand immediate repayment of the outstanding principle sum of £340,630 with outstanding interest thereon of £25,630. This demand is made pursuant to clause 5(C) of the loan offer dated the 8th December 1982.
  I confirm meeting, 9.00am Monday, 11th July, County Hall. Please ensure that you are represented by Company Secretary and Director, accompanied by your solicitors.
  Sender: Regards, Terry J Pitt, Senior Advisor in Economic Development, West Midlands County Council.
    338815 Wemsol G
    311762 Trusty G

The Directors discussed the report and tabled correspondence, and it was generally agreed that the County Council's action was a direct result of the private sector consortium's withdrawal. The County Council was now endeavouring to move away from the agreement reached regarding the outstanding £365,000 export loan. It was evident the Directors felt that, with the collapse of the British Car Auction Consortium's equity proposal, and no sign of a replacement, the West Midlands Councillors and Officers were running for cover! The Directors believed they had no choice but to offer the Triumph name and associated rights as security for the outstanding £365,000 export loan. The Directors requested the negotiating team seek clarification on the following two points:
  • The requested written confirmation from the National Westminster Bank should be secured, confirming the bank did not hold a charge over the Triumph name and associated rights.
  • Specialist legal advice should be secured confirming that Triumph was able to enter into the proposed arrangement with West Midlands County Council, enabling it to hold a charge over the Triumph name and associated rights whilst its £365,000 export loan facility was still outstanding.
  The negotiating team agreed to urgently investigate and confirm these points.
  The Board of Directors meeting over, the members were now gathering for the scheduled mass meeting at which, as previously indicated a week earlier, clarification of their exact position would be provided.
  Unfortunately, the Chairman reported to the mass meeting, there had been no financial reconstruction progress, and no replacement had been found for the private sector consortium. Action was being taken by West Midlands County Council regarding its outstanding £365,000 export loan facility as a consequence of the loss of the private sector's involvement. Guaranteeing County Council's investment support without private sector involvement in the £2.2m financial reconstruction proposal would be difficult. Accordingly, a new, less costly proposition was being worked on. The new proposal would involve a slower build-up to production, concentrating Triumph's short-term efforts on spare parts, development of the Diana project, and reduced levels of motorcycle production. However, with legal writs continuing to be received, finances were stretched to breaking point, and any one of these writs could bring about the end of Triumph and the Co-op. The County Council's major concern regarding its outstanding £365,000 export loan, the Chairman reported, suggested that it was no longer convinced that the financial reconstruction of Triumph's affairs would be achieved.
  The poor turnout at this mass meeting (only 108 of the 184 membership) suggested a large

number of the Beneficiary owners of the Co-op, following the private sector's withdrawal, had done the same! Certainly the sombre mood of those present was the worst the Chairman had ever encountered. When it was reported that due to the desperate financial position, holiday pay for the two-week summer break could not be paid, a laid off member pointed out the financial consequences of this action to him and all laid-off members. With the exception of holidays, he had been receiving dole payments for the last six months – therefore, laid-off members who would have at least received holiday pay, would now receive nothing during the summer break. With that, the demoralised membership started to drift away, and the mass meeting was over.

The following day's *Coventry Evening Telegraph* carried a Triumph mass meeting front page exclusive by Colin Lewis, the industrialist correspondent:

"Call It A Day, Say Workers" – "All hope gone despair sets in at Triumph."

Even though the members were in despair regarding the position of the Co-op, following the *Coventry Evening Telegraph*'s Saturday coverage of the mass meeting, there was outrage that a member had spoken to the press suggesting the Co-op should give up. Immediate gross misconduct dismissal action was demanded by the majority of laid-off members who phoned the factory the following Monday.

34

RECEIVERSHIP OR LIQUIDATION?

On Wednesday 13th July a Board meeting took place to consider developments. The negotiating team reported that Tom Fitch of the West Midlands County Council Economic Development Unit had requested that they meet representatives of Birmingham accountants Arthur Young McClelland Moores and Co, which had advised the following on receivership/liquidation in a six-page letter, dated 11th July, copies of which were now provided for the Directors' detailed consideration following the Board meeting.

In the light of the trading position of the company and the breakdown of recent investment negotiations, it would appear that this option is no longer realistic as the Directors would almost certainly have to place the company either into liquidation or receivership within the next 7 days. However, it is important to attempt to secure bank support in line with that currently offered under the terms of this option.

RECEIVERSHIP
Under the receivership option, the position of the bank's willingness to settle for £700,000 and indeed the legal position of the 1979 moratorium, remain of central importance. As you will realise, the outcome of both receivership and liquidation are identical as far as a new company is concerned. The primary differences between the two concern the mechanics of the appointment of the receiver/liquidator, the speed of action and the cost. Under receivership, it will be necessary for a receiver to be appointed by a debenture holder (normally the bank). Further bank facilities are required if there is any extended period of trading-on. Liquidation is normally less costly and more efficient. This assumes that a liquidator charges any necessary time rather than scale liquidation rates. You will realise that in a receivership this will have to be followed by liquidation with attendant costs.

LIQUIDATION
At first sight liquidation appears more attractive given the general circumstances of the company. Some of the points to be born in mind are as follows:
• There is no stigma to the appointment in that the creditors must confirm the suitability of the liquidator, recommended by the members of the company.

• The liquidator will have to report to a committee of inspection and as such, his actions/ compromises can be vetted.

• In liquidation, the creditors can immediately reclaim the VAT element of their debts.

As suggested above, we believe that the cost would be minimised through this course of action.

In considering the future of the company and raising equity from external sources, we would consider the following possible course of action:

• Confirm the legal position of the 1979 moratorium.

• Confirm the position of the bank and its proposed waiver.

• Confirm the position of the West Midlands County Council in relation to the loan of approximately £370,000 – in particular, whether or not this would rank as an unsecured creditor. This may prove to be an important factor in expediting the liquidation process since, if confirmed as a more substantial unsecured creditor, WMCC would then have enhanced voting power.

Conversely, the WMCC may well be able to take any other remaining security, and therefore achieve its commercial objective by another method. In the meantime both options are relevant.

Following the above, it should be possible to establish the levels of dividend payable to creditors. The bank position is critical as a settlement of £700,000 would make funds available to creditors, whereas a full repayment would result in no monies being available for distribution to creditors. The value of tax losses should also be considered as these could be substantial and of benefit to a future investor carrying on the same trade. The course of action would then continue as follows:

• The Directors should be advised to 'hive down' the assets with a view to protecting the company's losses in a new company. This action could make investment in a new company particularly attractive to private investors under the terms of the Business Expansion Scheme recently announced by the Government.

• Department of Employment agreement should be sought to pay (by way of loans) sums due to employees whilst waiting the outcome of the liquidation. It is of course possible that some of the 140 plus people who have been laid-off for some time now, may welcome the opportunity to receive such payments.

• Convene (subject to legal advice) a meeting of the 1979 Moratorium Creditors and gain their agreement to a settlement.

• Prepare notices convening a meeting of creditors under Section 293, such notices to be sent only after the agreement with the 1979 Moratorium Creditors has been agreed.

Under this scheme, we would feel that a minute from the West Midlands County Council on the proposed basis of investment would be of central importance. It should be noted that this should follow the 'hive-down'.

You will see from the above that it appears that liquidation offers a potentially more attractive route to restructuring. In addition, there may be wider considerations which may be addressed by use of a major vote amongst unsecured creditors. This might include improving the WMCC's investment in a successor company, for example, by retaining the support of strategic suppliers. In the meantime, we believe the Directors are preparing a business plan amended for the effect of time delays and we feel that a 'lower level' of trading will be sensible in the early months.

We hope that the above notes will be helpful to the Directors when reaching a conclusion over the next few days. For our part, we will welcome the opportunity of becoming involved with this project on a formal basis and we look forward to meeting you to discuss the matter further.

The Chairman reported that the County Council had accepted the increased security offer extracted from Triumph under extreme duress. Whilst this was the case, pressure continued to be applied to Triumph to sign the intellectual property rights debenture in favour of the West Midlands County Council.

Discussions with Triumph's Company Solicitor had determined that the raising of a debenture at this particular time was a specialist area of company law. Mr David Cooke, solicitor at Pinsent and Co, Birmingham, had been asked to advise the Triumph Board on this matter, and the legal advice was tabled for the Directors. The Directors considered in detail the Chairman's report, and discussion centred on the extreme duress exerted by the County Council on Triumph and the specialist legal advice. George Mackie expressed surprise regarding the unencumbered Triumph name and associated rights. He had believed, as had the other Board Directors, that Geoffrey Robinson MP (Chief Executive at the time) had increased the National Westminster Bank overdraft facility in order to purchase the Triumph name and associated rights. Bill Beattie commented that whilst this was the case, the original bank mortgage debenture had been drawn up in 1977 when Triumph first secured the overdraft facility, and at which time the Triumph name and associated rights would have been rightfully excluded as they were owned by the liquidator of one of the NVT companies. When the Triumph name and associated rights were acquired by the Co-op in 1980, no alteration to the debenture was made by the bank to take account of the acquisition of the intellectual property.

The Chairman then produced to the Board meeting draft minutes that contained the salient points regarding the West Midlands County Council's intellectual property debenture. Authority from the Directors to sign these as a 'minuted record' was now required by the Chairman. A copy of these minutes would be returned to the West Midlands County Council's solicitors. The Chairman also requested authority from the Directors for Bill Beattie and himself to sign the West Midlands County Council intellectual property rights debenture document that would take account of the change. Following brief discussion, the Directors unanimously agreed to this action.

The Chairman reported that Phil Bragg had suggested Nigel Usher was in possession of further information relating to the Hassan Bilgrami interest in investing in Triumph, of which he would like to make the Board aware. In view of previous difficulties, the Directors asked the Chairman to meet Nigel Usher and Phil Bragg in an effort to establish what approach was now being made, and in what way it could be progressed. Following a 30 minute adjournment, the Chairman was able to report to the Board that when the British Car Auctions deal fell through, Nigel Usher had recontacted Mr Bilgrami, who had indicated that he was still interested. In the new circumstances, the Chairman had suggested that due to the earlier difficulties, Mr Bilgrami should be invited to send a brief letter to the Triumph Board of Directors expressing his company's interest. Nigel Usher believed that this was a feasible way to progress matters; however, he added as a note of caution that it was still unlikely that the identity of the company concerned would be divulged. The Chairman stated that it would be for the Directors to consider the contents of the Bilgrami letter when received, now that the Consortium proposal was no longer on the table. The Directors agreed.

The following day, even before the Bilgrami letter had had time to arrive, Triumph's Directors were in for a surprise! There had been developments overnight that now required their further consideration.

The Bilgrami situation generated more frustration for both Nigel Usher and the Board.

Tension and insecurity, natural due to Triumph's difficult circumstances, spilt over into serious misunderstanding, which when relayed to him one evening outside the Triumph Social Club, an irritated Stan Grundy reported to the Board. That he did meant that the Board could clear the air with Nigel Usher in a comprehensive and forthright manner, addressing issues concerning not just potential investment but also his outstanding commission and future role reconstruction, whilst emphasising the extremely delicate commercial situation Meriden found itself in, and the importance of not jumping to conclusions in the meantime.

On 14th July written confirmation was received from the National Westminster Bank that its mortgage debenture specifically excluded the Triumph name and associated rights. On Friday 15th July 1983, a Board meeting with the Co-op's Trustees took place to update them on recent developments. Unfortunately, only John Haynes and Ron Marston were able to attend. Peter Davis was also in attendance to advise on the legal receivership/liquidation procedures now having to be considered.

The Chairman reported to the Trustees that the financial reconstruction proposals involving £1.25m of West Midlands County Council Economic Development Unit and Enterprise Board money, plus £500,000 from the British Car Auctions consortium, had fallen through, the consortium withdrawing because of the political implications it believed involvement with the West Midlands County Council would have. Major efforts to rekindle the private sector consortium's interest had taken place, but without success. An application had then been made to the full West Midlands County Council to make good the investment shortfall. County Council leader Councillor Gordon Morgan had explained that, unfortunately, this was not possible because of legal constraints. It was, therefore, unlikely that the financial reconstruction would be achieved, and, as a consequence, the company would have to be wound up. The Board meeting had been called to advise the Co-op's Trustees of these circumstances, in the presence of Company Solicitor Peter Davis. This would enable the Trustees and Directors to receive legal advice regarding the procedures now to be undertaken to involve the Beneficiary owners of the Co-op, in order to effect receivership/liquidation.

The Trustees asked the Company Solicitor what would happen to Triumph's three £1 shares they held in trust. Peter Davis advised that as the likely action of the bank's receiver on appointment would be to immediately dismiss the membership, the Trustees would then have no Beneficiaries to take instruction from. The Co-op Trust Document allowed for the Trustees to sell the three £1 shares for a nominal sum, say £1, and because of the company's total indebtedness to secured and unsecured creditors there would be very little likelihood of legal action ever being taken against the Trustees.

The Trustees asked the Chairman what Triumph's total indebtedness was. Figures dated 15th July 1983 provided by Triumph's Financial Controller, Phil Bragg, were tabled for perusal and showed this to be £3,199,000:

	Amount owed (£000)
FCF	15.0
West Midlands County Council	365.0
Current creditors	310.0
Inland Revenue	290.0
Death benefit	21.0
Legal and general	15.0
Nahib Dajani	25.0

Moratorium	868.0
Bank overdraft	1270.0
Warranties	20.0
Total	**3199.0**

Following discussion, the Trustees were in total agreement with the Board that the company must cease trading and approach the National Westminster Bank to appoint a receiver. The Chairman thanked the Trustees and Company Solicitor for their attendance; they would be contacted again in the near future.

Unfortunately, the receivership/liquidation die had been cast when the private sector consortium withdrew, and a way of enabling the agreed financial reconstruction of Triumph's affairs to go ahead could not be found. Wayne Moulton, President of TMA, had feared there could be funding problems and subsequently resigned to become head of the American Motorcyclists Association, Competitions Department. The West Midlands County Council had secured an intellectual property debenture over the Triumph name and associated rights as additional security for its outstanding £365,000 export loan. This achievement seemed to become its total focus, the previously agreed £2.2m financial reconstruction of the existing business being too costly. It now believed that when the bank appointed a receiver, its debenture would in effect allow ownership of the Triumph name and associated rights to pass to the West Midlands County Council. This would provide the cornerstone for a plan to continue a motorcycle business in the West Midlands. The County Council plan that George Bloomfield and Triumph's Managers were working on is summarised below.

Triumph Motorcycles (1983) Limited
Summary of 30-page plan
The attached schedules have been prepared by Triumph Motorcycles (Meriden) Limited personnel and Mr George Bloomfield, at the request of the West Midlands County Council.

The guidelines set by the limited funding available, as outlined at a meeting on 29th June 1983, at County Hall.

A 'tick-over' operation, comprising:
a) limited production and sales of motorcycles.
b) active manufacture and sales of spare parts.
c) design development and proving of the new Diana motorcycle was envisaged.

At the time of writing, action had been taken to formally advise the National Westminster Bank of the trading position of Triumph Motorcycles (Meriden) Limited, and it is anticipated that the appointment of a receiver by the bank is imminent.

In the notes on the schedules attached a possible course of action is indicated which would lead to motorcycle manufacture continuing on a 'tick-over' basis in the West Midlands area.

Attention is drawn to the key assumptions made in preparing the schedules and in particular to the estimated cost of materials and components, which of necessity would have to be purchased in small quantities, i.e. 500 to 1000 sets per year.

Immediate direct employment in the business is likely to be in the range 50-70 people, and this must be judged against the estimated funding requirement of about £1,000,000.

Certain key intellectual property has already been secured by the West Midlands County Council under a debenture. If a decision is taken to continue with a motorcycle business, the assets to be acquired from the receiver are therefore limited to stocks, machine tools, jigs, furniture and fittings.

In the nature of things, the receiver can be expected to proceed swiftly in his work. The time interval in which decisions can be made and actions taken is now therefore strictly limited – a few weeks at the very most.

The best laid plans of mice and men (and politicians) don't always go smoothly; this was certainly the case with the County Council's proposal to continue a motorcycle business in the West Midlands. When Triumph approached the National Westminster Bank to appoint a receiver, the bank refused, asking that Triumph's Directors seek further guidance from Michael Jordan at Cork Gully! With the bank and the County Council holding such totally opposed views on how the Triumph business should be wound up, this was not too surprising. There followed detailed discussions, initially with Michael Jordan of Cork Gully who introduced potential liquidator Mr Adkins of Thornton Baker. It appeared that the County Council felt the appointment of a receiver by the bank would enable its purchase of the required Triumph assets to bring about the formation of Triumph Motorcycles (1983) Ltd. However, following expert clarification and discussions with the officers of the County Council, an agreed compromise was reached. Triumph would go into voluntary liquidation proposing Peat, Marwick, Mitchell as the company's nominee for liquidator. The County Council believed that previous in-depth work undertaken by Peat, Marwick, Mitchell for the Enterprise Board and Economic Development Unit qualified this firm well for the job. The National Westminster Bank was happy with this solution, and the Chairman would report on the proposed voluntary liquidation approach to a Board meeting on 26th July 1983.

Present:	Mr J A Rosamond – Chairman
	Mr W A Beattie
	Mr J S Birch
	Mr R H Briggs
	Mr B E Jones
	Mr G L Mackie
In attendance:	Mr J Tomlinson – Trustee
	Mr R Marston – Trustee
	Mr P Davis – Company Solicitor
Apologies:	Mr J Haynes – Trustee (on holiday)

The Chairman reported the events for the benefit of the Board: that when Triumph's Directors approached the National Westminster Bank to appoint a receiver, it had refused, referring us instead to Michael Jordan at Cork Gully. Michael Jordan had in turn referred the Directors to Mr Adkins of Thornton Baker, who had confirmed the voluntary liquidation view held by the bank and Michael Jordan. The services of Thornton Baker to undertake the liquidation had also been offered. Meetings had taken place with the officers of the West Midlands County Council, who were hopeful of making a bid for the Triumph assets. Although the County Council had previously been adamant that in the event of the financial reconstruction negotiations failing a receiver should be appointed, following further detailed discussions, and in view of the bank's stated position, the County Council had now agreed to voluntary liquidation. Part of the reason for this change of heart had been due to the National Westminster Bank agreeing to the company's nominee for liquidator, Peat, Marwick, Mitchell. The County Council felt Peat, Marwick, Mitchell was ideally qualified as a result of its in-depth Triumph work already undertaken for the Enterprise Board and Economic Development Unit, and the bank was happy with this compromise.

Having agreed the voluntary liquidation proposal, the Directors requested the presence of Roger Dickens (Partner) of Peat, Marwick, Mitchell, plus his staff Alan Adam (Manager), and Roger Pearce (Accountant). The Directors and Trustees would now be provided with legal and voluntary liquidation advice regarding the procedures that should be followed.

Peter Davis advised that as the Trustees were to attend an Extraordinary General Meeting of shareholders for the purpose of the company's liquidation, they would first need to take instruction from the Beneficiary owners of the Co-op at an Extraordinary Meeting of the Beneficiaries. Taking into account the required notice for this meeting, it was proposed that it should be held on 5th August 1983, at 9.30am. In addition to the agenda item on voluntary liquidation, the Beneficiaries would also instruct the Trustees on the nomination of liquidators Peat, Marwick, Mitchell. Furthermore, because it was unlikely that the Trustees would have received due notice at the time of the Extraordinary Meeting of shareholders, further authority from the Beneficiaries would be required to enable the Trustees to proceed with the voluntary liquidation of Triumph, once formal notice of the shareholders meeting was received.

Moving to the voluntary liquidation, Peat, Marwick, Mitchell partner Roger Dickens advised the Trustees and Directors that whilst the company was nominating the liquidators, the creditors at the creditors' meeting could overturn this nomination. However, this was unlikely. Once a liquidator had been confirmed at the creditors' meeting, a Creditors' Committee of Inspection, comprising a number of professionals and 'lay' representatives of the creditors, would be appointed to oversee all major disposals undertaken by the liquidator. There was also, Roger Dickens continued, the clear cut statutory duties of the liquidator to sell the assets for the highest possible values. Peat, Marwick, Mitchell would be at pains not only to undertake the job on a highly professional basis, but also – as Triumph was a high profile, nationally known company – to make sure that it was seen to be adopting this approach. Roger Dickens stated that he was very aware the Triumph liquidators would always need to be able to justify their actions as being in the best interests of the creditors. As there was, he continued, a possibility of an offer coming from the County Council to purchase the assets of Triumph, he felt it would be in the interest of all concerned if the West Midlands County Council was not represented on the Creditors' Committee of Inspection. Finally, Roger indicated that it would take a little time to arrange the required details of the Extraordinary General Meeting of the shareholders and meeting of the creditors, following the Beneficiaries' meeting on Friday 5th August 1983 at which Peat, Marwick, Mitchell was to be confirmed as the company's nominee for liquidator. In the circumstances where a high profile company was involved in liquidation, he felt every effort should be made to give due notice of the meetings, thus enabling all who wished to attend to do so. Accordingly, a likely date for these two meetings was set as Friday 26th August 1983.

Roger Dickens then tabled standard Board meeting minutes for the appointment of Roger Dickens and Alastair Jones (joint liquidators) from Peat, Marwick, Mitchell.

Triumph Motorcycles (Meriden) Limited
Minutes of a meeting of Directors held at Meriden Works, Allesley, Coventry, CV5 9AU on Tuesday 26th July 1983 at 2.30pm.

Present: Mr J A Rosamond – Chairman
*   Mr W A Beattie*
*   Mr J S Birch*
*   Mr R W Briggs*

Mr B E Jones
Mr G L Mackie
In attendance: Mr J Tomlinson – Trustee
Mr R Marston – Trustee
Mr P J Davis – Solicitor
It was unanimously RESOLVED:

That the Company, by reason of its liabilities, cannot continue its business and that Messrs Peat, Marwick, Mitchell & Co, 45 Church Street, Birmingham B3 2DL, be instructed to take the necessary steps for the voluntary winding-up of the company, to assist the Secretary in the convening of statutory meetings of members and creditors for that purpose and to assist the Directors in the preparation of the statement of affairs and other information required to be laid before the creditors' meeting.

That the proper charges and disbursements in connection with the above be paid out of the assets of the company, it being clearly understood that services so rendered by Messrs Peat, Marwick, Mitchell & Co are procured and given for the benefit of the creditors of the company.

That an Extraordinary General Meeting of the company be called on Friday 26th August 1983 for the purpose of considering and, if deemed expedient, passing as an EXTRAORDINARY RESOLUTION the under mentioned resolution numbered 1, and (subject to such resolution being duly passed) for the purposes of considering and, if deemed expedient, passing as an ORDINARY RESOLUTION the under mentioned resolution numbered 2, that is to say:

1. "That it has been proved to the satisfaction of this meeting that the company cannot, by reason of its liabilities, continue its business, and it is advisable to wind up the same and, accordingly, that the company be wound up voluntarily."

2. "That Mr Alastair Frances Jones and Roger Joseph Dickens, Chartered Accountants, of 45 Church Street, Birmingham B3 2DL, be and are hereby appointed joint liquidators for the purposes of winding up the company."

3. That Mr John Anthony Rosamond be the Director appointed to preside at the statutory meeting of creditors under the provisions of Section 293(b) of the Companies Act 1948.
J A Rosamond
W A Beattie

Roger Dickens then returned to the matter of the Extraordinary General Meeting of Beneficiaries taking place on 5th August 1983, which he stated he would be prepared to attend with specialist members of his staff in order to answer member's questions and start preparatory work to enable Triumph employees to be paid their full entitlement as soon as possible, following the appointment of the liquidators.

The Trustees expressed their deep regret that the tremendous efforts by the Directors, which looked to have been successful only a few weeks ago with the County Council/British Car Auctions reconstruction proposal, had, it would seem, ended up being rejected because of politics. The Trustees further thanked Peter Davis, Triumph's Company Solicitor, and Roger Dickens of Peat, Marwick, Mitchell for their advice; this was of major help to the Directors and Trustees alike. In line with this advice, the company would now proceed to voluntary liquidation. With that, the Board meeting was over. Roger Dickens followed John Rosamond into the Chairman's office and asked if he would write a brief history of Triumph Motorcycles (Meriden) Ltd, and the reasons for the company's failure. This summary of Triumph Meriden's history 1973-1983 was to be made available to creditors.

The 5th August 9.30am Extraordinary Meeting of the Beneficiary owners of Triumph and the Co-op was a very sad but well attended occasion. In attendance were Triumph's Trustees, the Company Solicitor, representatives from Peat, Marwick, Mitchell, and the six Directors. Triumph's Chairman chaired the meeting, which was addressed by the Directors, Trustees, Company Solicitor and joint liquidator. There was none of the press-predicted bitter outcry, only the reluctant realisation by the vast majority (the final arbitrators in all major Co-op decision making) that the Triumph Meriden way of life was now coming to an end with voluntary liquidation. No right-minded individual could possibly criticise the total commitment and sacrifices made by the Meriden workforce to try and save the Triumph Motorcycle company. Many Beneficiaries commented that whilst the last eight years had been tough, they had also been some of the best in their working life. The Trustees were instructed to appoint Roger Dickens and Alastair Jones of Peat, Marwick, Mitchell as joint liquidators and to proceed to voluntary liquidation. The Extraordinary Meeting of the Triumph shareholders and the creditors' meeting would take place on Friday 26th August 1983. The Beneficiaries who were owed payments for redundancy, holidays, wages, and in lieu of notice were creditors of Triumph, and entitled to attend the creditors' meeting. They were also able to appoint a representative to serve on the Creditors' Committee of Inspection.

With the Triumph voluntary liquidation on 26th August 1983 now receiving publicity, it was vital that if the County Council's proposal to continue a Triumph motorcycle business in the West Midlands was to go ahead, a finalised plan and agreed funding package need to come together a lot quicker than in previous experience. A fairly positive meeting at County Hall on 10th August, taken in Terry Pitt's absence by his deputy Mick Lyons, suggested this was still a possibility. It was agreed a report proposing a Triumph Spare Parts and R&D business requiring about £500,000 of investment would be placed before the next West Midlands Economic Development Committee meeting on 7th September. However, there were reservations raised regarding the fact that the desired new Executive Management had not been recruited, prior to trying to secure further County Council support! So far as the Triumph liquidation was concerned, Mick Lyons advised that the County Council was now receiving enquiries from interested parties who wished to acquire the Triumph name and associated rights. Racing Spares, which manufactured and sold pirate parts for Triumph Motorcycles, had indicated a desire to take over the Triumph business.

We agreed to meet the County Council representatives again on Thursday 18th August at 5.00pm in order to progress outstanding matters on the Triumph Motorcycles (1983) Ltd proposal.

An exclusive *Birmingham Evening Mail* front page story by David Bell was already available by 5.00pm on 18th August when we met the grim-faced County Council representative:

"Meriden probe call over 'lost' £365,000 – Tory leader consults police chief in loan riddle."

In view of the front page coverage in the *Birmingham Evening Mail*, the County Council Triumph Motorcycles (1983) Ltd progress meeting was very sombre in tone. True to their word, however, the Councillors present pledged to press ahead with their plan to try and salvage as many ex-Meriden Co-op jobs as possible. Finalised funding amounts to purchase the required assets from the liquidator and set up the new Triumph business would be applied for at the next Economic Development Committee meeting on 7th September.

Reflecting on the meeting later that evening, Bill Beattie and John Rosamond had severe reservations about Triumph (1983) Ltd ever seeing the light of day. The massive publicity that was about to focus on the Co-op liquidation and the called-for £365,000 loan police probe would certainly test the conviction of any politician. We did not have long to wait for confirmation of our concerns. Early the following week, an anonymous leaked copy of a Councillor's internal confidential note from 19th August, titled "Triumph – Sales and Marketing", arrived in the Chairman's post. It expressed his disappointment at not having had the opportunity to discuss at the 18th August progress meeting the sales position of a Triumph spares operation. "Indeed, whether or not there was evidence that the company would be able to meet its sales targets had always appeared low on our agenda." He went on to raise eight specific negative queries which he felt should be answered before the 7th September application for funding. The final paragraph of the note suggested a possible complete change of policy. "I had intended to raise all these points at yesterday's meeting but time spent on other matters prevented this. Unless I can be reasonably satisfied on these points, I would question our support for the Triumph proposal and would wish to look at the Racing Spares option in more detail." Racing Spares, as previously mentioned, had approached the County Council to take over the Triumph business. As ex-Prime Minister Harold Wilson once said, "a week is a long time in politics."

All was now set for the 26th August 1983 Extraordinary General Meeting of Triumph shareholders and meeting of creditors to enable voluntary liquidation. The shareholders' meeting was, as expected, a simple formality, the Trustees having already been instructed by the Beneficiary owners on 5th August how they should cast their votes on all agenda items. The 26th August 1983 creditors' meeting, when Triumph's estimated statement of affairs as at voluntary liquidation was to be considered, was a lot more difficult to predict!

TRIUMPH MOTORCYCLES (MERIDEN) LIMITED
ESTIMATED STATEMENT OF AFFAIRS AS AT 26TH AUGUST 1983

	Book value (£000)	Estimated to realise (£000)
ASSETS SPECIFICALLY PLEDGED		
Freehold land and Buildings	*976*	*1000*
Investments in subsidiaries	*340*	*–*
Plant and machinery	*90*	*100*
	1406	***1100***
Less amount due to National Westminster		
Bank PLC under its fixed charge		*1100*
		–
ASSETS NOT SPECIFICALLY PLEDGED		
Plant and machinery)		
Motor vehicles		
Office equipment	*22*	*25*
Stock and work in progress	*377*	*60*
		85
PREFERENTIAL CREDITORS		
Customs & Excise – VAT	*20*	
Inland Revenue – PAYE	*79*	
National Insurance	*111*	

	Book value (£000)	Estimated to realise (£000)
Wages and holiday pay	92	
Rates	135	
Bank's claim for wages	30	
		(467)
Estimated deficiency as regards preferential creditors		(382)
Amount due to debenture holders under floating charges –		
National Westminster Bank PLC	134	
West Midlands County Council	349	
		(483)
Estimated deficiency as regards floating charges		**(865)**
LOAN CREDITOR		
First Co-operative Finance Limited	15	
	15	
UNSECURED CREDITORS		
Moratorium balances	853	
Current trade creditors	447	
Redundancy pay	83	
Payment in lieu of notice	115	
Customs & Exercise – VAT	54	
Rates	12	
PAYE	76	
National Insurance	61	
Warranty claims – estimated	15	
		(1731)
Estimated deficiency as regards unsecured creditors		(2596)
Issued share capital (£3)		–
Estimated deficiency as regards members		(2596)

The packed Triumph Creditors' meeting was chaired by John Rosamond. At his side, as he had been throughout the financial reconstruction negotiations, was Bill Beattie. On the Chairman's other side at the top table was Alastair Jones, partner in the company's nominee firm for liquidator Peat, Marwick, Mitchell. Triumph's other Directors Messrs Birch, Briggs, Jones and Mackie were also at the meeting with the Co-op's Trustees and Company Solicitor. Almost all the Beneficiary owners of Triumph were present; many had been involved in the formation of the Co-op, and were determined to see it through to the end.

The Chairman provided the creditors with a brief update on the failed reconstruction negotiations that had unfortunately led to today's sad meeting and the advised 'winding up' decision. The creditors agreed to the company's nominee for liquidator – Peat, Marwick, Mitchell. A Creditors' Committee of Inspection would be selected at the end of the meeting.

Questions were taken from the creditors by John Rosamond and Alastair Jones. In view of the extremely well publicised succession of Triumph financial crises over the years, it would have been difficult for any creditors to claim they had not been aware of the Co-op's difficulties. However, it did not stop some creditors making wild accusations. One Creditor claimed he had been informed by a senior Co-op Manager (unnamed) that £300,000 had been misappropriated by the American Triumph subsidiary, TMA, shortly after the 1979 moratorium had been agreed by trade creditors. All allegations were noted by the liquidators for thorough investigation.

Finally the Creditors' Committee of Inspection was selected and would meet later for the first time.

Creditors' Committee of Inspection

J Laxton	Midland Die & Tool Ltd
G Stone	West Midlands County Council
W J Kelly	Lucas Electrical
B Johnson	IMI Amal Ltd
F Tippets	Various Creditors
M J Wigley	Hare Industries Ltd
J Reason	J & J Reason & Sons
J Edwards	Various creditors
J Dowling	Triumph employees

With the Creditors' meeting over, Triumph Motorcycles (Meriden) Limited, the Workers' Co-operative, was now in the hands of liquidator Peat, Marwick, Mitchell. Its detailed knowledge of Triumph's ongoing business plan led it to believe that with the financial shackles removed by liquidation, there would be considerable interest in the assets that were now for sale. All Beneficiary members who had attended that creditors' meeting were shellshocked; the colossal effort to save the Co-op had previously blocked out any real thoughts of possible failure. It was only now, in the aftermath of the liquidation creditors' meeting, shaking hands with friends and colleagues and wishing them good luck for the future that the reality of what had happened began to sink in.

As the majority began to drift away to the solace of their families, I withdrew to the sanctuary of the ex-Chairman's office to clear my desk for a final time and collect personal possessions. There was a knock on the half-open door – it was joint liquidator Alastair Jones. "What do you intend to do now?" he asked. The answer was simple: "I have no idea!" Not achieving the financial reconstruction had never been an option, so I had made no other plans. Alastair Jones continued, "How about helping the liquidators sell the Triumph business? Although I can't pay you, other than provide you with petrol money for your car so you are not out of pocket, it is obvious from all the work that has been done that you possess an overview of exactly where the future could lie for a new Triumph motorcycle business. This is key knowledge, and with your contacts will help the liquidators achieve a successful sale on behalf of the creditors, and possibly so far as you and other ex-Triumph Meriden employees are concerned, every chance of an opportunity to be part of that new Triumph business." I agreed in a flash – Alastair Jones and Roger Dickens would line up the anticipated potential purchasers, I would meet and greet them at the Meriden factory. If a new Triumph business could emerge phoenix-like from the ashes of the Meriden Workers' Co-operative and provide employment for ex-members and security for their families, eight hard years of commitment and sacrifice trying to establish a true partnership that removed industrial conflict would not have been totally in vain!

However, with the price of crude oil doubling to nearly $100 a barrel during the Co-op's existence (1975-1983), the sterling's value against the US dollar now at an all time low of

£1 to $1.417, the UK bank interest rate hovering around 10 per cent and annual inflation down to 4.6 per cent, they were indeed interesting times. I hoped Alastair Jones' optimism was correct, and that with the financial shackles removed from the Triumph motorcycles business by liquidation, there would be a number of potential purchasers – purchasers who would ideally offer the desperately needed jobs in the West Midlands, at a time when UK unemployment was expected to reach 3,000,000.

35

EPILOGUE

The first Creditors' Committee of Inspection meeting with liquidator Peat, Marwick, Mitchell took place shortly after its appointment, later on 26th August 1983. It was agreed that the recently acquired West Midlands County Council Triumph intellectual property debenture would be challenged. Full investigation of the US subsidiary company, Triumph Motorcycles (America) Inc, was also planned. This would establish its value, and if there were any grounds for the creditors' meeting allegation, namely that £300,000 had been misappropriated at the time of the 1979 Creditors' Moratorium agreement.

The two major Triumph assets expected to raise the most were:

The factory site – about £1,000,000.

The Triumph business as a going concern – about £550,000.

THE FACTORY SITE

Triumph's bank, the National Westminster, had a fixed charge over the Meriden factory site, so Peat, Marwick, Mitchell would become its sales agent, assisted in this task by valuer Grimley and Sons. The sale of the site on behalf of the bank was, therefore, separate from the liquidation.

THE TRIUMPH BUSINESS

To achieve a speedy sale of the Triumph business as a going concern, the recent granting of an intellectual property debenture to the West Midlands County Council would first need to be investigated in order to establish that a 'fraudulent preference' had not occurred. If it had, the County Council would no longer have a claim against the Triumph name and associated rights, and the sale of the business could proceed.

The employees' representative on the Committee of Inspection raised the possibility of completing part-finished machine shop components in order to increase their value by selling them as spare parts. When fully investigated, this would turn out not to be worthwhile.

On 7th September, the County Council's Economic Development Unit Committee approved funding of £340,000 for Triumph Motorcycles (1983) Ltd in order to continue a motorcycle business in the West Midlands. The spare parts element of the new company was to receive £210,000 and the Phoenix R&D project a grant of £130,000. In view of the negative press coverage about Triumph Meriden's liquidation and the export loan loss of £365,000, this was certainly a surprising development. Our surprise did not last long, however, when on 16th September the Policy and Resources Committee overturned this proposed funding until the situation concerning the County Council's intellectual property debenture had been legally clarified.

The following day's *Birmingham Post* newspaper carried a story by its Midlands political correspondent, Alan Travis:

"Rates rescue plan for Triumph halted – Councillor Edge was the only left-wing Chairman to remain in charge of a major committee after moderates tightened their grip on the group."

The sting in the tail of this article suggested that what had previously appeared to Triumph as political prevarication causing delay after delay, was possibly left-wing 'old Labour' being blocked by 'new Labour' moderates. Maybe this was the political climate that caused the private sector consortium to withdraw from the financial reconstruction of Triumph Meriden – we would never know! However, what we did know was that any further County Council financial support for a new Triumph business was now extremely unlikely.

In the first week of October, the liquidator fired off legal warning shots to three pirate spare parts companies that were infringing Triumph's copyright protection. These three companies all received a solicitor's letter, warning that action against them would be pursued if they did not stop this practice. On Triumph's liquidation, each of these companies had employed ex-Meriden senior staff with detailed knowledge of the suppliers from which outsourced component parts were purchased.

Acting as the bank's sales agent, the liquidator succeeded in mid-October in selling the Meriden site to developer Tarmac Homes, virtually clearing the Triumph debt to the National Westminster Bank. The sale was achieved without residential planning permission or vacant possession, a licence to occupy the site until the end of November being negotiated as part of the deal. This achievement increased the effort to resolve the County Council's intellectual property debenture, which would allow the sale of the Triumph business as a going concern.

John Rosamond was now deeply involved with prospective purchasers of the Triumph business. They were:

Mr Castigilone – Cagiva
Mr Teerlink – Harley Davidson
Mr Bloor
Mr Shah
Mr Hall
Indian consortium 1
Indian consortium 2

Although great interest had been shown by all seven, only the two Indian consortiums had bid at least the liquidator's asking price of £550,000. However, neither were able to proceed, one because of the lack of a licence from the Indian Government that would allow the purchased production machine tools to be imported into India, and the other because of difficulty transferring funds to the UK.

Negotiations between the liquidator and County Council's solicitors to arrive at an acceptable figure that would secure the release of the Triumph intellectual property debenture had stalled at £75,000! With time running out, and the need to vacate the Meriden factory site looming ever closer, the liquidator decided it had no choice but to break up the Triumph business into its various parts, as these were now attracting serious interest.

Bernard (Bunny) Hallard, one of the Triumph machine tool fitters who kept the obsolete machinery working, surveys the silent machine shop in readiness for the auction. (Courtesy photographer Suresh Karadia – Times Newspapers Limited)

Bunny Hallard looks at the racks of paint masks that made possible the fantastic finish on Triumph motorcycles. (Courtesy photographer Suresh Karadia – Times Newspapers Limited)

COMPANIES INTERESTED IN PURCHASING THE VARIOUS PARTS OF THE TRIUMPH BUSINESS

Intellectual property rights	Factory/office contents	Spare parts and work in progress
John Bloor	John Law Machinery	Andover Norton
Racing Spares		Racing Spares
2nd Indian Consortium		W E Wassel

John Bloor's proposed purchase of the intellectual property rights would be to allow major investment in a completely new Triumph motorcycle company.

The contents of the Meriden factory plant and machinery, stock and work in progress were sold early in November to John Law Machinery. A 3-day auction comprising 3500 lots was to take place in the factory at the end of November. Unable to vacate the Meriden factory site by the agreed 30th November deadline, the liquidator negotiated a licence to continue occupancy.

There was now no doubt in John Rosamond's mind that of the five companies still showing interest in Triumph, John Bloor's proposal, based on investment in a completely new business following purchase of the intellectual property rights, provided the best possible chance of substantial employment in the West Midlands.

In an effort to solve the legal impasse, John Rosamond and Bill Beattie turned to Terry Pitt at the County Council for advice. John Bloor's proposal to purchase the Triumph intellectual property rights from the liquidator once the Council-held debenture had been resolved was explained in detail. When the intellectual property rights were acquired, it was intended to invest substantially in a new Triumph company in the West Midlands. Amazingly, in view of everything that had previously happened, Terry Pitt was just as supportive now as when Triumph had first approached him for help with the Co-op in 1982. He advised John Rosamond to send a letter to him recommending the aforementioned Bloor proposal, which is exactly what happened. Countersigned by Bill Beattie, it suggested that the proposal offered the best possible opportunity for a new Triumph business and major employment in the West Midlands. To enable this to happen, all the County Council needed to do was to agree a reasonable deal with the liquidator allowing the release of the Triumph intellectual property rights. The intervention advised by Terry Pitt, coming from the two ex-Meriden Co-op negotiators, had the desired political effect and the liquidator's offer was subsequently accepted.

John Bloor's company purchased the intellectual property rights, securing total control of the Triumph motorcycle business. The new company, Triumph Motorcycles (Coventry) Limited, would concentrate on the design and development of a new range of motorcycles. Advised of the need to protect the trademarks and associated rights from being challenged because of lack of use when it was not in the marketplace, and concentrating upon research and development, the new Triumph business would enter into a strict 5-year licence agreement with Racing Spares. Racing Spares proposed to undertake limited production of the classic T140 Triumph models and spare parts. This legal arrangement was made more feasible due to the fact that Meriden's ex-Chief Engineer, Brian Jones, had joined the Newton Abbott concern. Triumph Meriden's engineering design drawings and specifications were provided, and had to be strictly adhered to by Racing Spares! The licence fees paid to Triumph Motorcycles (Coventry) Ltd, John Bloor's new company, during the 5-year agreement would help in a small way to offset some of the major investment in the new business. Existing Triumph owners would also receive genuine spare parts.

John Rosamond was appointed General Manager of Triumph Motorcycles (Coventry) Ltd, and was asked to identify five other ex-Meriden personnel to join the new business. These six individuals would be the first of many employees working in John Bloor's new team to bring the ambitious plans to fruition.

On 13th December, the long awaited West Midlands County Council auditor's report on the £365,000 export loan to Triumph Meriden was privately discussed by a Labour Party subcommittee. Not surprisingly, the report's contents did not remain private for long, and politically motivated facts found their way into the following day's *Birmingham Post* story by Alan Travis – "Auditor's rebuke over £365,000 Triumph loan."

All six of the intended Triumph Motorcycles (Coventry) Ltd employees were now looking forward to their festive holidays and starting employment on the new project in 1984. None intended to return to the Meriden factory – it held so many memories, and would soon be demolished to make way for residential development.

I had honoured my undertaking to joint liquidator Alastair Jones, playing a role in finding

Factory demolition brought many a tear to the eyes of those who chose to visit their Triumph Meriden mecca for one last time. (Courtesy Mick Duckworth's archive)

a purchaser for the Triumph assets. Alastair's prediction that my involvement in this way may lead to a job opportunity for me and other ex-Meriden employees could not have been more accurate. All who previously worked at the Meriden Co-op had now moved on, leaving the liquidators to continue their detailed work on behalf of the creditors – work that, surprisingly, would not be concluded until 1995, the liquidation having taken twelve years; four years longer than the Workers' Co-operative had been in operation!

Triumph Motorcycles (Meriden) Limited (in creditors' voluntary liquidation)
Liquidator's final report to the Committee of Inspection.
I report on the conduct of the liquidation as follows:

Once the demolition was complete, residential development began, Bonneville Close paying homage to the previous occupants. (Author's archive)

1. Realisations
The realisations achieved are significantly greater than those estimated in the statement of affairs.

	Statement of affairs (£000)	*Actual realisations (£000)*
Freehold property	*1000*	*1118*
Book debts		*95*
Property rights		*120*
Plant, machinery and stock	*185*	*280*
Total	***1185***	***1613***

2. Creditors
2.1 The debenture holder has been repaid a total of £1,219,366 under its fixed charge.
2.2 Preferential creditors have received a total of £224,190 which represents a payment of 60 pence in the £ on their preferential claims.
2.3 There are no funds available for unsecured creditors.

3. Liquidation fees
To date I have drawn fees on account totalling £68,898 which have been approved by the committee of inspection. Fees have been drawn on a time cost basis.

4. Receipts and payments
I attach to this report my receipts and payments to date which show a balance in hand of £9488. Subject to the committee's approval I propose to draw the balance as a final fee to cover my outstanding fees and costs in this liquidation.

John Rosamond phoned Companies House and enquired if there had been a problem with the Triumph Motorcycles (Meriden) Limited liquidation that had caused it to take so long? No was the reply, some complicated ones take that long and others take even longer! Accordingly the liquidator's fees of £78,386 when spread over 12 years were certainly not excessive.

On payment of a small fee to Companies House they provided a 'Dissolved Certificate' for Triumph Motorcycles (Meriden) Ltd.

07 – 12 – 95

DISSOLVED

01161960 TRIUMPH MOTORCYCLES (MERIDEN) LIMITED

The liquidators account and return of final meeting having been registered, this company is deemed, pursuant to section 585(5) / 595(6), as applicable, of the Companies Act 1985 to be dissolved on the expiration of 3 months from the registration date shown below

RFM REGISTERED DATE 30/08/95

Mrs S M EDWARDS

For Registrar

RIP – TRIUMPH MOTORCYCLES (MERIDEN) LIMITED

The motorcycle legend created at Meriden will live on forever in the hearts and minds of every enthusiast with Triumph blood running through their veins.

John Nelson, patron of the Triumph Owners' Club, unveils the memorial to the site of the Triumph motorcycle factory, Meriden, on 7th October 2005. (Courtesy Mick Duckworth's archive)

INDEX

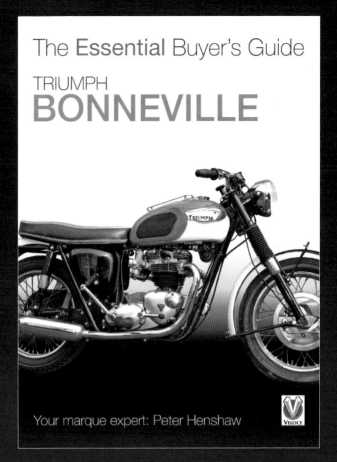

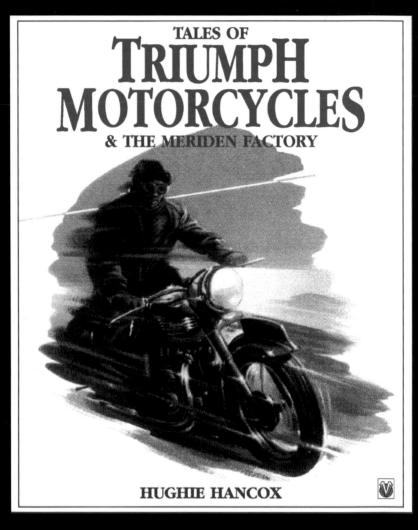